PICKETT'S CHARGE—
THE LAST ATTACK AT
GETTYSBURG

· · · · · · · · · · ·

CIVIL WAR AMERICA

Gary W. Gallagher, editor

PICKETT'S CHARGE— THE LAST ATTACK AT GETTYSBURG

· · · · · · · · · · · · · · · · · ·

EARL J. HESS

The University of North Carolina Press

Chapel Hill and London

© 2001
The University of North Carolina Press
All rights reserved
Manufactured in the United States of America
Set in New Baskerville and Smokler types
by Keystone Typesetting, Inc.
The paper in this book meets the guidelines for
permanence and durability of the Committee on
Production Guidelines for Book Longevity
of the Council on Library Resources.
Library of Congress Cataloging-in-Publication Data
Hess, Earl J.
Pickett's charge — the last attack at Gettysburg /
by Earl J. Hess
p. cm. — (Civil War America)
Includes bibliographical references (p.   ) and index
ISBN 0-8078-2648-0 (cloth: alk. paper)
1. Pickett, George E. (George Edward), 1825–1875.
2. Gettysburg (Pa.), Battle of, 1863. I. Title. II. Series.
E475.53 .H47 2001
973.7'349—dc21   2001027492

05   04   03   02   01   5   4   3   2   1

MAPS

· · · · · · · · · ·

ILLUSTRATIONS

· · · · · · · · · · ·

PREFACE

. . . .

Pickett's Charge is probably the best-known military action of the Civil War. Indeed, along with Bunker Hill, the Little Big Horn, and the Bulge, it is among the most popular military actions of all U.S. history. Schoolchildren and adult history buffs alike have been familiar with the story for many generations, particularly if they happened to live below the Mason-Dixon Line. It has come to symbolize the Confederate war effort itself, representing a valiant effort in a hopeless and somehow romantic cause. Celebrated as the high-water mark of the Confederacy, Pickett's Charge has always seemed to be the pivot point beyond which the United States would either remain united, with slavery eliminated from its borders, or dissolve into separate and eternally antagonistic nations. Even though few modern Americans regret the ultimate outcome of the attack and of the war, they still insist on celebrating the heroism of the men involved. Knowing the outcome, many Americans still love to ponder what might have happened if the assaulting column had broken through the Federal line and swarmed across the stone fence and over the crest of Cemetery Ridge.

Pickett's Charge easily lends itself to anyone who has a taste for the might-have-beens of history. It has assumed legendary proportions, both for its supposed impact on the course of the war and for the bravery of the nearly 12,000 men who swept across open, ascending ground under heavy artillery fire and into the face of massed musketry. When I speak to groups about the Civil War, the most commonly voiced sentiment is "How could those men have attacked in the open and up that slope? What motivated them to do it, and how did they find the courage?" The assault has become the ultimate example of the Civil War soldier's bravery and willingness to sacrifice his life for a cause.

xiii

Yet this very fame has somehow distorted the event in the minds of most Americans. Carol Reardon, in her recently published *Pickett's Charge in History and Memory*, has pointed out that there are many differing perspectives on the attack, accumulated by veterans who had axes to grind or who indulged their highly selective memories. The same is true of postwar generations, who have invested the charge with all manner of ulterior meanings. Reardon suggests that there are so many multiple layers of interpretation, lacunae, and reinventions surrounding the history of the charge that perhaps we may never understand it for what it was. Unlike any of the dozens of other military operations of that war, which are unencumbered by the burden of myth, Pickett's Charge may be too shrouded in legend to easily yield its authenticity.

Of course I disagree with Reardon; otherwise there would be no reason to write this book. Pickett's Charge is more interesting to me as history than as cultural artifact. It was a unique military operation that illustrates much about the nature of Civil War history. Reardon has done an excellent job of examining the attack in memory; I want to examine it to understand its military reality. Enthusiasts and scholars alike are so aware of the charge that they tend to take it for granted. I propose to treat the operation in the same way that military historians treat any other engagement, by writing a "battle book" based on thorough research in primary and secondary sources, published and unpublished. My purpose is not only to write a narrative account of the attack but to offer slightly new interpretations of how it took place, so as to blend storytelling with analysis. Every aspect of the operation will be examined, from the initial conception and planning for the attack to the cleanup of the battlefield. Moreover, the story of the participants is vital in understanding the immense human drama of the charge. The background of their war experiences before July 3 and what happened to them after that fateful day are thus part of the story. This book is a detailed tactical study of the assault with special emphasis on combat morale. I agree with those enthusiasts who see the charge as a case study for understanding how men dealt with combat. The assault is also an excellent case study for understanding many technical aspects of military history, ranging from how artillery supported the infantry to the way in which large infantry units maneuvered under fire, and to the role of terrain and fortifications in battle.

Ironically, despite the enormous public interest in the charge, no one has published a fully satisfying work that incorporates all of these elements. For many decades the undisputed authority on the assault was George R. Stewart, whose *Pickett's Charge: A Microhistory of the Final Attack at Gettysburg, July 3, 1863* has long held a nearly legendary status of its own among Civil War students. But Stewart's study has long been outdated. It was based entirely on published sources that were available in the 1950s, and the Civil War centennial sparked a nationwide interest that resulted in an explosion of new books on the war. Dozens of primary accounts that dealt with the attack were published during the 1960s–90s, and there are hundreds of unpublished papers that have relevant material on the attack, none of which Stewart consulted. Moreover, he failed to analyze the attack as a military event, and he did not evaluate its significance in the course of the war.

The only other study of the attack is much more recent, but it too fails to illuminate, explain, or encompass all relevant aspects of the charge. John Michael Priest's *Into the Fight: Pickett's Charge at Gettysburg* is based on a much wider search of the relevant published material than was Stewart's, and Priest has done good but not thorough research in the unpublished collections. I have found some of Priest's points to be excellent and have incorporated them into my study. But Priest tends to have a decidedly myopic view of the attack, providing little explanation for why it took place, how the assault was organized or planned, or what factors affected its outcome.

Several other books and articles have looked at smaller pieces of the topic than the works of Stewart or Priest. Richard Rollins has authored two books, *Pickett's Charge! Eyewitness Accounts* and *"The Damned Red Flags of the Rebellion."* The former is a collection of primary accounts of the battle from both sides, some of which were never before published or used by historians. The latter is a detailed study of the Confederate battle flags, as symbols and military tools, at Gettysburg. Kathy Georg Harrison and John W. Busey, in *Nothing but Glory: Pickett's Division at Gettysburg*, produced a detailed study of the most famous unit in the charge and offered some good insights. Needless to say, however, Pickett's men constituted only half of the attacking force, and there were nearly 6,000 Federals who were involved in repelling the assault who have no voice in the Harrison and Busey volume.

I admit that my book is a traditional battle study, albeit an attempt to achieve the highest standard set in that genre. I do not address the cultural history of Gettysburg, for Carol Reardon has done that far better

than I could. The political background, the social history of the participants, and the home front environment against which the attack took
place are not covered here, even though I find those subjects interesting.
For an operation as famous as Pickett's Charge it is astonishing that there
does not yet exist a full tactical study, and this book is an attempt to fill
that need. After exploring some aspects of the New Military History in
previous books, I have slowly come to the conclusion that the Old Military
History is just as relevant, valid, and exciting as any new methodologies or
viewpoints that come along in the history profession. No other military
operation in the Civil War was more laced with the human drama that
drives our interest in history; there is no need to apologize for writing an
old-fashioned narrative about Pickett's Charge.

A word or two about the name of this operation is relevant. Of course it
is inaccurate to use Pickett's name to designate the attack, for he commanded less than half of the assaulting force and, furthermore, he was
not responsible for conceptualizing or organizing the operation. History
often plays such tricks on us, for example, by misnaming the battle of
Bunker Hill (Breed's Hill) or the battle of San Juan Hill (Kettle Hill).
We usually bow to the inevitable and go along with those tricks. The
operation is so well known as Pickett's Charge that I would feel like a
salmon swimming against the current if I were to insist on calling it
something else. At any rate, the other names sometimes suggested for
it—Longstreet's Second Assault at Gettysburg or the Pickett, Pettigrew,
Trimble Charge—are just as inaccurate or too cumbersome. By succumb-
ing to the historical fiction that it was Pickett's Charge, I can save a lot of
headaches and communicate more effectively by using language the au-
dience already knows.

I wish to thank the Harrisburg Civil War Round Table, whose award of
a James F. Haas Fellowship partially aided me in conducting research
for this book at the U.S. Army Military History Institute. The North Caro-
liniana Society awarded me an Archie K. Davis Fellowship to conduct
research in that state's archival repositories, for which I am very grateful. I
also wish to thank all the archival staff at each of the institutions listed in
the bibliography for their diligence and attention to me when I visited
them or when I asked for long-distance help.

The following people have richly earned my gratitude for helping me
with research materials: Chandra Miller, Ralph Fierro, Daniel R. Zim, Wil-

liam L. Shea, Michael T. Hunter, Ann Greene, Peter Cozzens, and David Madden. They passed on tips, copies of material, and encouragement.

Finally, my wife, Pratibha, has supported me every inch of the way with her enthusiasm, insightful critiques, love, and devotion. And our daughter Julie, who passed away early this year after a hard-fought battle with leukemia, inspired and amazed me with her undying courage, optimism, and love. This book's dedication is a small expression of how I feel about both of them.

PICKETT'S CHARGE—
THE LAST ATTACK AT
GETTYSBURG

· · · · · · · · · · ·

CHAPTER 1
THE LAST ATTACK AT GETTYSBURG

. . . .

Lt. Frank A. Haskell first became aware that Friday, July 3, had arrived when he felt someone pulling on his foot. It was four o'clock in the morning, nearly a half-hour before the sun would rise, and Haskell had managed to get four hours of sleep. If the sky had not been so cloudy, he could have looked up and seen the moon hovering above the sleeping army. The first sound Haskell detected in the dark was the popping of skirmish fire, off to the right front of the Second Corps line. After two days of terrific fighting at Gettysburg, the generals were still not satisfied. Another day of bloodshed was needed to decide a winner and perhaps to settle the fate of the nation.

The man tugging at Haskell's boot was Brig. Gen. John Gibbon, commander of the Second Division of the Second Corps. The two had fallen asleep in the Bryan peach orchard atop Cemetery Ridge, just behind the division line. Haskell found a cup of hot coffee and hastily drank it while getting ready to mount his horse and ride with Gibbon to discover the progress of the skirmishing. The general and his staff officer rode slowly, for neither of them were fully awake. Haskell noticed that most of the division was still asleep on the ridge, even though the skirmishers were only a few hundred yards away. As he looked to the left front, over the battlefield of July 2, he saw wounded horses limping through the growing light of dawn. The "ravages of the conflict were still fearfully visible," Haskell wrote a few months later, "the scattered arms and the ground thickly dotted with the dead."

There was little to fear from the skirmishers; they were simply firing in place rather than pushing or giving way. The skirmish lines remained stable, and only a few men now and then felt the sting of a round. There was time for Gibbon and Haskell to loll about and observe their men

1

waking up with the sun. Soon the normal sounds and sights of a camp coming to life could be detected. "Then ensued the hum of an army . . . chatting in low tones, and running about and jostling among each other, rolling and packing their blankets and tents," wrote Haskell. "But one could not have told by the appearance of the men, that they were in battle yesterday, and were likely to be again to-day. They packed their knapsacks, boiled their coffee, and munched their hard bread, just as usual, . . . and their talk is far more concerning their present employment, — some joke or drollery, — than concerning what they saw or did yesterday."[1]

These were veteran soldiers who knew that taking care of the inner man was the most important preparation for battle. As they readied for the day, the sun rose higher, but it was often obscured by dark clouds all morning. Old soldiers knew that it usually rained right after a major battle, and the fighting on July 1 and 2 had been among the heaviest of the war. But the moon set at 7:29 A.M., and the clouds continued to break apart. There would be no rain today.[2]

To the right front of Gibbon's division a lone regiment was waking up from its bivouac along Emmitsburg Road. The men of the 8th Ohio had been on skirmish duty since the day before. Most of the regiment had slept along the ditch that bordered the west side of the pike while their regimental comrades manned the skirmish line, which was along a rail fence farther west. The skirmishers were only about sixty yards from the Confederate skirmish line, yet the bulk of the Ohio unit had no trouble waking up with the dawn, undisturbed by the racket taking place a short distance west of their ditch. Despite the heat of this early summer, the night of July 2 had been a bit chilly. The sun warmed everyone; it "sent its rays upon unprotected faces and into blinking eyes," wrote Lt. Thomas F. Galwey. The bluecoated soldiers rose with humped shoulders and out-stretched limbs, "followed by a curious peering forward to see what the enemy, beginning to stir too, might be about."

Back to the rear, along Cemetery Ridge, Galwey could hear "an angry neighing" from the battery horses. They were tired of carrying the har-ness "that for more than two days they had constantly worn." The men on the skirmish lines could hardly afford to protest their fate; they spent the first moments of this day quickly building small fires to heat coffee. Gal-wey looked about and saw "little whiffs of blue smoke" rising into the air from numerous campfires. The sporadic skirmishing that continued on various parts of the line could not prevent these "determined spirits" from restoring their strength and energy with a much-needed dose of caffeine.[3]

Much the same scene was enacted on the opposite side of the field, separated from the Yankees by less than a mile of disputed ground. Col. Edward Porter Alexander was among the first to wake up, despite having spent part of the night tending to the placement of his guns. Alexander commanded an artillery battalion in Lt. Gen. James Longstreet's First Corps and had been given temporary charge of several other battalions in the vicious battle the day before. He had visited Longstreet's bivouac at midnight to receive instructions for the morrow and learned that the attack would be renewed. He was to select an advantageous spot for the Washington Artillery, not an easy task in the darkness. Yet the moon shone brightly at that midnight hour, and Alexander surveyed the battlefield, believing he saw a place for the guns that were to reach him at dawn.

Alexander was satisfied and sought a place to sleep at 1:00 A.M. The Sherfy peach orchard was on some of the highest ground along Emmitsburg Road. It had been the scene of particularly hard fighting the evening before when Longstreet's men crushed the Union Third Corps. Now it was a mess, filled with "deep dust & blood, & filth of all kinds," recalled Alexander. The orchard was "trampled and wrecked." He found two fence rails and carefully placed them under a tree, used his saddle as a pillow, and fell asleep surrounded by human corpses and dead horses. He awoke two hours later after a "good sound & needed sleep," having slept no more than two hours the night before as well.

While Gibbon and Haskell still lay and dreamed in their own peach orchard, Alexander began to putter around in the predawn darkness. He had only a dim knowledge of the Union position, but he could see, as the sun began to peek over the horizon, what he thought was the spot where Maj. Gen. Richard H. Anderson's division had attacked the evening before. He assumed this spot was high ground just in front of the Federal lines and that a Rebel line of battle would appear there once the sun was fully risen. Therefore he directed the Washington Artillery to string out in a line through the Sherfy peach orchard, aiming toward that spot. Only later, when the sun was rising, did he realize his mistake. The high ground was Cemetery Ridge, and it was still held by the Yankees. Alexander scrambled to move his guns, fearing that they would be fatally enfiladed by the Union artillery as soon as the enemy gunners woke up and realized what an advantage Alexander had handed them. "It scared me awfully," he confessed, but Alexander managed to readjust the line before any harm was done.

The entire area around the orchard was "unfavorable ground for us," he reasoned. It was an open bump in the wide valley that separated Cemetery Ridge from Seminary Ridge, and the Yankees could see everything that was happening on it. "I studied the ground carefully for every gun to get the best cover that the gentle slopes, here & there, would permit," Alexander wrote, "but it was generally poor at the best & what there was was often gotten only by scattering commands to some extent." The only thing that saved him was a marked reluctance on the part of the Federals to open fire. Alexander was relieved to see that as the sun rose higher, there were only a few scattered rounds from the Union cannon. One of them wounded some gunners in the Washington Artillery, but Alexander refused to be drawn into a duel. The army had brought limited supplies of artillery ammunition, so he only allowed one or two rounds to be fired in reply, letting the Federals fire the last shot. Thus he could "beguile them into a little artillery truce. It worked excellently, & though, occasionally, during the morning, when we exhibited a particularly tempting mark we would get a few shots we got along very nicely." All of Alexander's arrangements were heartily approved by the army's artillery chief, Brig. Gen. William N. Pendleton, when he visited the Sherfy peach orchard later that morning.[4]

· · · · · · ·

PLANS AND EXPECTATIONS

Longstreet, too, was up before dawn to push forward a favored scheme of his, mounting a flank movement around the Union left. Anchored on Little Round Top and Big Round Top, the Federal left was secure against frontal attack but might be vulnerable to a smartly executed march around the hills. Longstreet had been reluctant to attack the left even on July 2, strongly favoring a less costly tactical plan. His men had fought magnificently in the late evening hours of the second and had come very close to seizing Little Round Top. But the casualties were exhausting, and a partial success was not enough for an invading army in enemy territory with little logistical support from home. Longstreet admitted long after the war that he did not intend for the July 2 assault to be pushed so far. He meant that he regretted so many men were lost for no decisive gain. "The position proving so strong on the 2d, I was less inclined to attack on the 3d, in fact I had no idea of attacking."

With this frame of mind, the corps leader did not even ride to Gen. Robert E. Lee's headquarters on Chambersburg Pike to consult with him on the night of July 2. Instead he sent a report of his assault and received a message from Lee that the attack should be continued the next day. He simply gave Longstreet a broad directive to resume offensive operations as soon as possible. Longstreet wanted to take the offensive but not with a frontal assault. He had dispatched scouts into the countryside to find a way for his command to sidestep the Federal left, then turn and "push it down towards his centre." This, he presumed, could be accomplished with minimal bloodshed if the turning movement was successful. With the first light of dawn, Longstreet rode out to see for himself if a way around the heights could be achieved. His scouts offered encouragement, and Longstreet began to plan how his divisions might execute the maneuver. Lee typically gave the responsibility for planning details of operations to his subordinates, so Longstreet felt there was nothing wrong with choosing a line of attack that he personally favored.

His plan came crashing to a halt when Lee rode up about 4:30 A.M., just after sunrise. He was surprised at Longstreet's proposed line of advance and ordered him to cancel it. The army leader then outlined his own thoughts on the coming offensive. He wanted the entire First Corps to strike the south end of Cemetery Ridge in a frontal assault. Two of Longstreet's divisions, Maj. Gen. John B. Hood's (commanded by Brig. Gen. Evander M. Law) and Maj. Gen. Lafayette McLaws's, were already in line holding the Confederate right. They had conducted the fierce attack the day before and had lost at least a third of their strength. Maj. Gen. George E. Pickett's division, not yet engaged in the battle, was on the field but not yet in position. It would serve as a support to Law and McLaws. Lee wanted to better Longstreet's chances of success by coordinating an attack on the extreme left, to be conducted by Lt. Gen. Richard S. Ewell's Second Corps against the Federal right. He had anticipated an early start, hoping to see the assault begin at dawn, and was disappointed it had not yet begun. This apparently had been his thinking all along, even the night before. It represented a continuation of the general plan of attack on July 2.

Longstreet was stunned. He had assumed that the results of the previous day's action provided ample proof that frontal assaults were too costly and unlikely to produce results. He spelled out his views in clear language, arguing that "the point had been fully tested the day before, by more men, when all were fresh; that the enemy was there looking for us." If Law and McLaws were withdrawn to attack the center, the Union left would be uncovered, allowing the Federals to advance and curl around Lee's right wing. No less than 30,000 men were needed, with the support of the rest of the army, to bring a chance of success to this assault on the center; Law and McLaws and Pickett combined could muster no more than 13,000.

Instead, Longstreet suggested the army conduct a major shift to the right. Ewell should disengage from his position on the left, march laterally behind Lee's rear, and position himself so as to hold the Union left flank in place on the rocky hills. The rest of the army would move to his rear and curve around to threaten the enemy rear, march five or six miles toward Washington, D.C., and find a strong defensive position. Then the Rebels could wait for the Federals to attack, slaughter them, and have the strategic initiative in hand. Longstreet later admitted in his official report that this proposed maneuver "would have been a slow process, probably, but I think not very difficult." It was a plan that would come to assume almost mythic proportions in the decades after Gettysburg as a glittering alternative to what actually happened on July 3. Untested and therefore open to unrealistic expectations of success, this maneuver to the right became the great "might have been" of Gettysburg for those who wanted Lee to avoid the slaughter that was to come.

Longstreet hoped to tempt Lee with its possibilities. "General, I have had scouts out all night," he told the army commander, "and I find that you still have an excellent opportunity to move around to the right of Meade's army and manoeuvre him into attacking us." But Lee did not take the bait. He replied, with "some impatience," that a direct assault on the center was the true course of action. Thrusting his fist toward Cemetery Ridge, he said, "The enemy is there, and I am going to strike him."

Lee based his decision on a considered opinion. He had been impressed by the results of the attack on July 2, when Ewell had hit the extreme right and Longstreet the extreme left of Maj. Gen. George G. Meade's line. While Longstreet viewed these limited achievements as proof that something different should be attempted, Lee saw them as one step along the correct line of approach. The results "induced the belief that, with proper concert of action," in Lee's words, a similar movement could be successful on July 3. He believed that there had been too little coordination of effort and that the attack on the third had to be more minutely planned and closely executed. The capture of the Sherfy peach orchard especially encouraged Lee. It occupied the highest ground close to the Yankee line within Confederate reach, and artillery placed there could more readily support an infantry assault than any artillery post had done on July 2. Alexander had already come to the private conclusion that this was a false hope, but Lee grasped at every indication he could find to support his planned offensive. He counted heavily on the artillery to provide the key factor needed to bring success to this venture — artillery plus a well-coordinated tactical plan. Lee foresaw the guns softening the Union position and then moving forward to provide close support for the infantry when it attacked. He also wanted plenty of supporting troops on both sides of the assaulting column to be ready to rush in and exploit any success achieved. True to his command style, Lee did not intend to arrange this himself. He wanted Longstreet to be his right-hand man, as Stonewall Jackson had done on so many battlefields. Jackson had died less than two months earlier as a result of wounds received at Chancellorsville, and Lee was hoping Longstreet would fill his shoes.

Unlike Stonewall, Longstreet balked at the prospect of offensive action against the Yankees. Two other factors intervened to upset Lee's plan. First, the terrain on the southern part of the battlefield was dominated by Little Round Top and Big Round Top. They had almost fallen to Lee's troops the day before and were now held by Meade's Federals in strong force. They could not be easily taken, and to strike the southern end of Cemetery Ridge just north of Little Round Top would expose the attacking column to flanking artillery fire and a possible counterattack. Longstreet argued that Law and McLaws needed to remain in place, fronting this sector of the Union line to anchor the army's right wing. Lee soon agreed and allowed them to remain. He apparently had not fully appreciated the terrain difficulties on this part of the field, partly because Longstreet chose not to report in person on the results of the fighting the night before.

The second factor that changed Lee's thinking came from the far left. During the long conversation with Longstreet, which had started just after 4:30 A.M., the sound of artillery fire could be heard to the north. Maj. Gen. Edward Johnson's division of Ewell's corps had attacked and captured some ground on the army's left the evening before, at Culp's Hill, which it held in close proximity to the Federal Twelfth Corps. Now, at early light, the Federals opened an artillery barrage, and a sharp fight ensued, leading Ewell's command to attack without coordinating its

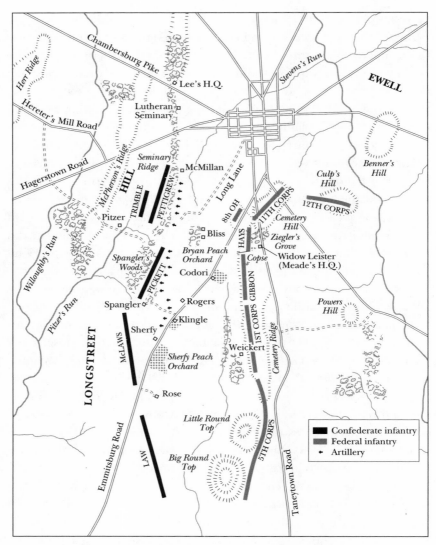

Map 1.1 Gettysburg, July 3, 1863

movements with Longstreet. Historian William Garrett Piston has suggested that Lee might have implemented his plan anyway by promptly ordering Longstreet to throw Pickett, Law, and McLaws into a frontal attack against the southern end of Cemetery Ridge. Although late, this assault might have come off in time to give Ewell support. But Pickett's division was not yet up and in line, averting any possibility that Lee's desire for a cooperative attack on both flanks might take place that day.

With his first plan now impossible, Lee devised his second plan for operations on July 3. Pickett would still be the key; his fresh division would spearhead an assault to take place much later in the day and hit the center of the Union position. Lt. Gen. A. P. Hill's Third Corps, immediately to Longstreet's left, would provide additional troops. When Longstreet asked how many men would be involved, Lee guessed 15,000. The corps commander was stunned. He had earlier suggested that twice this number was the minimum necessary. "General, I have been a soldier all my life," he remonstrated, speaking more bluntly than ever before to Lee. "I have been with soldiers engaged in fights by couples, by squads, companies, regiments, divisions and armies, and should know as well as any one what soldiers can do. It is my opinion that no 15,000 men ever arrayed for battle can take that position." He felt compelled to protest what he felt would be "the sacrifice of my men." After this Lee lost all patience. Longstreet recalled that his chief was tired "of listening, and tired of talking, and nothing was left but to proceed."[5]

Longstreet would brood over the results of this early morning conference for the rest of his life. He was firmly convinced that Lee's plan would fail and cost the lives of irreplaceable men. It was to be one of the most complex and difficult attacks to organize during the entire war, involving elements of two corps, dozens of artillery units, and the thorny problem of coordinating supporting troops. The plan called for one of the most extensive artillery preparations ever to precede an infantry assault. Longstreet had never been given such a tough assignment.

Yet if anyone in the Army of Northern Virginia had the potential to organize it properly, it was Longstreet. Born in South Carolina forty-three years earlier, he had graduated from West Point in 1842. Longstreet was a consummate professional soldier, talented, self-confident, amiable, and almost destined to rise in the army. He had fought bravely in the Mexican War, was badly wounded at the battle of Chapultepec, and had served on the Texas frontier in the 1850s. The Civil War offered him incredible opportunities; he led a brigade at First Manassas that included regiments now serving in Pickett's division and was promoted to division command in October 1861. Personal tragedy intruded on his career the following winter when scarlet fever took the lives of three of his four children.

Emotionally devastated, the general threw himself into the war and took solace in his military responsibilities. Longstreet led his division during the Peninsula campaign, participating in the engagement at Williamsburg and the battle of Seven Pines. He came into his own as a

Lt. Gen. James Longstreet, commander of the First Corps and organizer of Pickett's Charge (LC)

talented subordinate of Lee in the Seven Days, mostly by launching a crushing attack at Frayser's Farm, or Glendale, on June 30, that came close to cutting off a large part of the Army of the Potomac on its retreat to Harrison's Landing on the James River. His division of about 10,000 men advanced alongside A. P. Hill's division in a straight forward line of approach through a matted forest. There was no special artillery preparation here; his men fought their way to a hard-won but very limited tactical victory that yielded few strategic gains.

The following day, at Malvern Hill, Longstreet attempted to organize a large concentration of Rebel guns to soften the strong Union position blocking the way to Harrison's Landing, but he failed. The densely packed and well-placed Union guns pounded the Rebel artillery, denying them a chance to achieve superiority on the field. Then a series of uncoordinated and unwise infantry assaults, launched piecemeal by brigades, took place. The result was a terrible slaughter and a tactical defeat. Yet because the Federals retreated to the James, the Seven Days campaign was a major Confederate triumph.

Longstreet launched a decisive assault that tipped the scales in favor of Lee during the Second Manassas campaign, but he did it in a slow, cautious manner. While Jackson's corps had positioned itself along the unfinished railroad grade near Manassas and received the spirited but piecemeal assaults of Maj. Gen. John Pope's Army of Virginia, Longstreet had quietly positioned his corps to Jackson's right and waited. He arrived early enough on August 29 to attack in the early afternoon with 30,000 men, but disturbing reports of an unknown Yankee force to his right and a desire to know every detail of the terrain and the Union forces in his front led Longstreet to advise postponing the attack. Lee reluctantly agreed, even though the advice ran counter to his own inclinations. The delay did not endanger Confederate chances of success. Pope was myopically concerned with Jackson, and the Federal force on Longstreet's right, Maj. Gen. Fitz John Porter's Fifth Corps, was determined to remain on the defensive. Everything conspired to allow Longstreet the time and opportunity he craved to be fully prepared. When the attack took place on August 30, it was a crushing success. The Federals were driven from the field in a disaster that eclipsed the first battle at Manassas more than a year earlier.

The successful attack on August 30, in which Longstreet was able to influence Lee's decision-making process, allowed him to feel a heady sense of importance within the command structure of the army. But he later came to appreciate deeply how easily the survival of the army could be threatened. The battle of Antietam, fought on September 17, 1862, was one of the most searing days in the history of the army. Heavily outnumbered and fighting on a remarkably open, rolling battlefield, the Confederates were nearly overwhelmed. Longstreet earned the nickname Lee gave him that evening, his old war-horse, by doggedly holding in the center, but the army had barely survived its first invasion of Northern-held territory.

Longstreet later saw the power of the defensive vividly demonstrated at Fredericksburg on December 13, 1862, when little more than two of his brigades were positioned several ranks deep behind a stone retaining wall at the foot of Marye's Heights. The Army of the Potomac foolishly launched repeated assaults up an open, ascending plain into the teeth of massed musketry. The result appalled even the Confederates, for the plain was thickly strewn with dead and dying Yankees by that evening. Longstreet took from Fredericksburg a deep appreciation for the advantages of a strong defensive position, backed by artillery and strengthened by fortifications.

He missed the Chancellorsville campaign, when Lee demonstrated the offensive power of the army by fighting his way out of a trap set by an adroit maneuver of the Army of the Potomac, because he was off on a frustrating campaign against Suffolk, Virginia. The primary purpose of this expedition was to gather much-needed foodstuffs for Lee's army, rather than to regain Union-occupied territory. The place was so heavily fortified that Longstreet could not find a way to pry himself into it. When Longstreet rushed his troops back to Lee immediately after Chancellorsville, Jackson was out of the picture, and he now had to shoulder the responsibility of becoming Lee's right-hand man.[6]

Despite the complexity of the July 3 attack, it was clear that Longstreet had the ability to deal with the situation. He was one of the most able tacticians in the Confederate army, and he had a discerning eye for terrain and a keen appreciation for the role of artillery. He could have dealt with most tactical problems, but the corps leader was severely hampered by a heartfelt conviction that this attack was a dreadful mistake. Longstreet was working out a different relationship with Lee during the Gettysburg campaign. He felt it was necessary to be outspoken on important matters, and often, it was turning out, he did not see eye-to-eye with Lee. The two certainly were not thinking alike about the conception of this campaign on either the strategic or the tactical level. Lee chose to ignore this difference of opinion, losing his patience when Longstreet persisted in arguing for a different approach to the tactical problem. He had grown used to his generals doing the impossible and saw no reason to change his expectations now.

Moreover, Lee had developed extremely high expectations of his enlisted men. Ever since he took command of the Army of Northern Virginia a year earlier, he had seen them conduct juggernaut assaults, stand firm in defensive battles, and display unflappable morale in the face of nearly overwhelming odds. Chancellorsville seemed to epitomize all of this. Outnumbered more than two to one and sandwiched between two powerful Federal forces, they fought the Army of the Potomac to a standstill and then launched a counterattack under Jackson that turned the tables on their opponents. The army's fierce assaults on the morning of May 3, launched through a landscape cluttered with saplings, small trees, and brush and butting against hastily made earthworks, forced the Federal army to retreat from its advantageous position and won the battle for Lee. The Rebel army leader was in awe of his men. While contemplating the reorganization of the corps and assessing the need to promote officers to command them, Lee wrote to Hood that the army would be "invincible if it could be properly organized and officered. There never were such men in an army before. They will go anywhere and do anything if properly led." This was Lee's mindset prior to the Gettysburg campaign.

Lee could have referred to himself when commenting on the common soldier's need to be properly officered, for his command style left something to be desired. It seldom resulted in disaster because his subordinates usually made up for any deficiencies by improvising solutions or by unleashing the fighting spirit of their men. The conception of and planning for what came to be known as Pickett's Charge would become the most controversial episode of Lee's and Longstreet's careers because the attack proved to be a bloody failure. To what extent Longstreet's lack of faith in the attack doomed its chances of success became a matter of bitter debate for many Confederates and their partisans. The two commanders would never again have so much difficulty understanding each other's motives or feelings when discussing plans, for they would form a strong, united team in the 1864–65 campaigns in Virginia. But now, on the morning of July 3, they were like two old friends who suddenly felt they had never really known each other.

Longstreet later confessed that Lee "should have put an officer in charge who had more confidence in his plan." He pointed out that slightly more than half of the attacking force came from a different corps, "and there was no reason for putting the assaulting forces under my charge." There is no evidence that he suggested a change of commanders to Lee. His sense of professionalism held him to discharge his duty, even if he felt it was unwise. "Knowing my want of confidence," Longstreet continued in his memoirs, "he should have given the benefit of his presence and his assistance in getting the troops up, posting them, and arranging the batteries: but he gave no orders or suggestions after his early designation of the point for which the column should march." Lee left everything in Longstreet's unwilling hands. This was true to his instinct and consistent with his history of success.[7]

To his credit Longstreet set about to do the best job he could, considering how severely his lack of faith in Lee's plan hampered his ability to organize the attack. His effort to minimize casualties led Longstreet to limit the number of supporting troops to be engaged. This was a deliberate attempt to limit the size of the attack, but there were other areas in which Longstreet failed to prepare the assault fully. There were examples of shortsightedness, lapses of thinking, or failure to see that directives were properly carried out. Whether deliberately or unintentionally, Longstreet did not give all of his considerable talents to making sure the attack had every chance of success.

Longstreet directed Pickett to place his command "under the best cover that he could get from the enemy's batteries." He designated Pickett as the guide for the attack, in accordance with Lee's instructions, but he did not mean to use Hill's troops as a support, in the strictest meaning of the term. Longstreet instructed those troops to align themselves to the left of Pickett and move forward abreast of his division. They would be equal partners in the attack, extending the line to the left. The unit chosen from Hill's corps was Maj. Gen. Henry Heth's division, now led by Brig. Gen. James Johnston Pettigrew because Heth had suffered a head wound on July 1. The division had fought hard and lost heavily that day and was just as exhausted as Law's and McLaws's men, but it happened to be the rightmost division of Hill's corps and thus was conveniently placed to join the attack.

Encouraging evidence of Longstreet's care in preparing the assault lay in his instructions to division leaders. He asked them to "go to the crest of the ridge and take a careful view of the field, and to have their officers there to tell their men of it, and to prepare them for the sight that was to burst upon them as they mounted the crest." Longstreet took his own division commander, Pickett, to personally show him the field, but he was depressed by Pickett's reaction. The division leader "seemed to appreciate the severity of the contest upon which he was about to enter, but was quite hopeful of success." Longstreet despaired, still convinced of "the desperate and hopeless nature of the charge and the cruel slaughter it would cause. My heart was heavy when I left Pickett."

Pettigrew received instructions to report to Longstreet, and he did so, learning that Heth's division would take part in the attack and that it would advance in line with Pickett's division, not as its support. He also was told that a massive artillery barrage would precede the attack. But there is no evidence that Longstreet or anyone else took Pettigrew to the crest of Seminary Ridge and offered him advice about the lay of the land. Pettigrew passed on the minimal information he was told to his four brigade leaders. One of them, Brig. Gen. Joseph R. Davis, authored the division report after the battle. He indicated that the only instructions were to dress to the right and come into line with Pickett's command. Longstreet failed to see that his enlightened instructions about informing everyone what they could expect to encounter were carried out. He probably led Pickett to the crest of Seminary Ridge because he personally knew the division leader and wanted to gauge his opinion on the prospects of success, only to have his hopes of finding a gloomy ally dashed by Pickett's optimism.[8]

Longstreet's biggest failure was in not properly arranging for support to either side of the attacking column. Contrary to the assertion of a modern writer, there never was a "second wave" planned for Pickett's Charge. That is, no one contemplated a large force following directly behind the attackers to provide additional weight of numbers at a key point in the assault. Second waves were likely only if the attacking force was expected to engage in a prolonged struggle after it made the initial contact with the defenders, as in twentieth-century amphibious landings, where there was little prospect of sending troops in to right or left of the first wave. Whether a second wave was necessary on July 3 is debatable. Lee simply did not have the reserve manpower to form one; he could not afford to pull units out of his long line and position them to follow up Pickett's Charge without leaving a gaping hole somewhere else. Also, there was little likelihood that a second wave would suffer fewer casualties than the first wave while crossing the open valley between the opposing lines, and therefore it would not add significantly more momentum to the forward drive as it reached Pickett's line. After all, Pickett's own men would be in its way, and it was likely that the two waves simply would blend together and lose their momentum due to exhaustion, losses, and the stubborn resistance of the Federals.[9]

Instead the only support contemplated was the advance of units to right and left of the attacking force. This became one of the most bitter controversies to develop after the attack. Several members of Lee's staff who were at the conference that morning insisted that the army leader wanted Longstreet to use large numbers of troops to either side of Pickett and Pettigrew. Col. Walter H. Taylor, Lee's chief of staff, recalled that all or part of Law's or McLaws's commands were to be sent forward. Col. Armistead L. Long, Lee's military secretary, insisted that Lee's instructions to Longstreet on this point were in the form of orders, not suggestions, and that he and at least one other staff officer heard the army commander give them.[10]

Longstreet had a genuinely different impression of Lee's intentions. He stated flatly after the battle that the general had allowed him to keep Law and McLaws in place to secure the right flank, and Lee reported as much in his official report as well. The army leader noted that Longstreet "deemed it necessary to defend his flank and rear with the divisions of Hood and McLaws. He was, therefore, re-enforced by" troops from Hill's corps. It would have been extremely risky to move any part of those two divisions out of line to have them attack behind or in close support of Pickett; such a move would have dangerously exposed the right flank. It could also have endangered Alexander's artillery concentration at the Sherfy peach orchard, as Alexander himself believed. Lee's staff officers were not clear in their language as to exactly how Law and McLaws were to support Pickett and Pettigrew, whether they were to reposition their units farther toward the center or simply to advance straight ahead. The latter maneuver would have continued to secure the flank and possibly could have helped the attackers if it was pressed hard and at just the right time. But the very hard attack of July 2 on this part of the field had failed at high cost, and the Federals were far better prepared for a repetition of it on July 3. It undoubtedly would have failed to capture the Round Tops unless Pickett and Pettigrew broke through the center across Cemetery Ridge in a very dramatic and decisive way.

As a result Longstreet did not include either Law or McLaws in the planning of the attack. He only arranged for two small brigades of Hill's corps to shield Pickett's right flank. These were a Florida brigade led by Col. David Lang and an Alabama brigade commanded by Brig. Gen.

Cadmus M. Wilcox, both of Anderson's division. The two units had been sent to this part of the field the day before and had participated in the battle of July 2, attacking the Union center on Cemetery Ridge nearly in the same area to be hit by Pickett. Lang and Wilcox were instructed to move to the right rear of Pickett's division "to protect it from any force that the enemy might attempt to move against it." In other words, Longstreet did not see Lang and Wilcox as helping Pickett to penetrate the Union line; they were to guard his flank.

McLaws was left completely in the dark, although his division was next in line to Lang and Wilcox. "I was not notified that it was in contemplation even to make any further attacks by either Hood's or my division, nor was I informed that it was the intention to assault the enemy's centre with Pickett's division, with the assistance of troops from other corps." Longstreet stated in his memoir that he instructed Law and McLaws to move forward so they could spring to the attack directly to their front if Pickett and Pettigrew should be successful. But this apparently was not true. McLaws flatly stated, "I was not told to be ready to assist, should the assault be successful, nor instructed what to do should the assault fail and the enemy advance. I contented myself with reconnoitering my ground and vicinity in all the directions necessary for movement in any emergency, and took my position among my troops."

Longstreet did not have an opportunity to use Law and McLaws, for there was little, if anything, they could do to help the attack. The Federals did not transfer troops from the area of the Round Tops to repulse Pickett, and therefore an attack by these two Rebel divisions would not have affected the outcome of the assault. Despite Armistead Long's assertion that Lee bemoaned the fact that the two divisions were not used, there is every reason to assume that Lee knew Law and McLaws were out of the picture. Longstreet was careful to defend himself in this regard. He pointed out that he rode with Lee along the line twice after the early morning conference

to see that everything was arranged according to his wishes. He was told that we had been more particular in giving orders than ever before; that the commanders had been sent for and the point of attack had been carefully designated and that the commanders had been directed to communicate to their subordinates, and through them to every soldier in the command, the work that was before them, so that they should nerve themselves for the attack and fully understand it.

After leaving me he again rode over the field once, if not twice, so that there was really no room for misconceptions or misunderstanding of his wishes. He could not have thought of giving any such orders [to involve Law and McLaws in the attack].

Thus did Longstreet try to prove that Lee had ample opportunity to learn of his dispositions and raised no objection to them.[11]

Longstreet also failed to draw on Hill's corps for support to the left of the attacking column. The only help he derived from that source was recruited by Lee himself. After leaving the conference with Longstreet, Lee rode along the front of Hill's command and stopped in front of Maj. Gen. William D. Pender's division, now led by Brig. Gen. James H. Lane due to the mortal wounding of Pender the previous day. Lane watched as Lee gazed toward the Union position across the valley between the two ridges. Then the army commander said "he needed more troops on the right, but that he did not know where they were to come from." Lane did not volunteer his command, but soon after Lee left, he received orders to leave two of the four brigades in place and move the other two toward the right. Lane was also to report to Longstreet, who instructed him to place the two brigades behind Pettigrew's right wing. One of these brigades was Lane's and the other was Col. Alfred M. Scales's. Both were from North Carolina, and both had been engaged in the fighting on July 1, when Scales was severely wounded. His unit now was led by Col. William L. J. Lowrance. Soon after taking position, Lane was bumped from division command by Maj. Gen. Isaac R. Trimble, and he returned to lead his brigade.

If there was to be a second wave in Pickett's Charge, Trimble's command was it. Positioned only a short distance behind Pettigrew's right, his two brigades were not large enough to cover the entire rear of Pettigrew's division. He had too few men to add much weight to the forward momentum. All Trimble could hope to do was to fill in any holes that might develop in Pettigrew's line or, failing that, simply to push forward and hope to carry the men in his front farther forward if they happened to stall. But his command would have to overcome the same obstacles of exhaustion, terrain obstructions, and enemy fire that Pettigrew's men would have to endure.[12]

Longstreet really stumbled when it came to dealing with Hill. The two generals had nursed a personal feud for a year, ever since the battle of Frayser's Farm during the Seven Days. It started when Richmond newspaper editor John Daniel published inflated stories about Hill's prowess during the battle, which infuriated Longstreet. The two had jointly fought the engagement, side by side, at the head of their respective divisions. Longstreet published a rebuttal in a competing Richmond paper, which infuriated Hill. The quarrel grew worse when Longstreet temporarily placed Hill under arrest for refusing to turn in a routine report. The two managed to patch things up well enough to maintain a coldly formal relationship, but that chill inhibited their ability to cooperate on July 3. They held a private meeting that morning that resulted in Hill's decision to let his two brigade commanders take all their instructions from Longstreet. For his part, the commander of the First Corps may have assumed from their discussions that Hill would do more than this, and the result was a gaping chasm in intercorps communication and cooperation.[13]

Hill's role in the planning and preparation was virtually nonexistent, but a good corps commander should never remain idle while a colleague takes his troops and plans an attack within his area of influence. Hill completely failed to affect what was to happen on July 3. He failed to point out that Pettigrew's division and Trimble's two brigades had been worsted on July 1 and needed time to recuperate. He failed to offer other Third Corps troops that were in better shape, namely Brig. Gen. Carnot Posey's Mississippi brigade and Brig. Gen. William Mahone's Virginia brigade of Anderson's division. Even Brig. Gen. Edward L. Thomas's Georgia brigade of Pender's division was fresh, having seen no action on July 1. Hill exercised no control over the placement of the troops and issued no instructions or advice to any of their commanders. He had a record of success, effectively leading a division in the Seven Days campaign and performing brilliantly at Antietam. But he was now trying to adjust to higher command, which demanded more administrative and planning abilities than he probably possessed. Moreover, he may have felt a bit uneasy about his ability to articulate the strengths and weaknesses of his troops in the face of Longstreet's self-assurance and Lee's legendary persona. However his mind was working, Hill failed to play the role of an effective corps commander on July 3.[14]

Hill left little indication of his attitude toward the attack, and the testimony of other officers on this subject is conflicting. His adjutant, Maj. William H. Palmer, missed the campaign because of a wound received at Chancellorsville, but Hill told him after Gettysburg, "I begged General Lee to let me take in my whole Army corps. He refused, and said what remains of your corps will be my only reserve, and it will be needed if Gen'l Longstreet's attack should fail." Lee confirmed part of this story in his report by writing that Hill "was directed to hold his line with the rest of his command, afford General Longstreet further assistance, if required, and avail himself of any success that might be gained." But one of Pettigrew's brigade commanders, Col. Birkett D. Fry, indicated that Hill was not so sure the attack was wise. Hill asked Fry to go forward and observe the Union position with him. Looking carefully from the crest of Seminary Ridge through a good pair of field glasses, Hill asked Fry what he thought. Fry said simply that it was a strong position, and Hill replied, "emphatically closing the glass; entirely too strong to attack in front."[15]

Thus the elements of Hill's corps taking some part in the assault included Pettigrew's division and two brigades of Trimble's division as part of the assaulting column. In addition Lang and Wilcox would serve as right flank guard for Pickett. The rest of the Third Corps, Anderson's and Trimble's remaining brigades, would be ready to support Pettigrew's left. Longstreet does not seem to have communicated directly with Hill on any of these matters. He only gave instructions to Pettigrew and Lane and would not have had the services of Trimble's two brigades if not for Lee's personal intervention. Longstreet never communicated directly with Anderson or with Trimble during the preparatory phase of the attack.[16]

Despite this neglect from the organizer of the operation, word filtered down the ranks of Trimble's two brigades about what was expected of them. Trimble himself told the troops that the enemy were behind a stone fence on the crest of the ridge opposite and that the Tar Heels were to hold their fire while advancing with bayonets fixed. Company leaders were instructed to "inform their men of the magnitude of the task assigned them, and also to caution the men to keep cool, preserve the alignment, press steadily to the front, and gain the enemy's works." Those were not only detailed instructions, but they served to steel the men for the coming attack.[17]

Even if Longstreet failed to be thorough in his preparations, Lee wasted no opportunity to ride about and see how he could contribute. The army commander did not leave the arrangements for the assault entirely up to Longstreet. Not only did he select two brigades from Hill to reinforce the attacking column, but he rode all over the field to inspect the alignment and placement of the troops. Lee did not leave firm instructions about the employment of supports to either flank of the column, merely letting Longstreet know that he could call on Hill for help if needed. This gave the corps commander the latitude he needed to reduce casualties in what he thought was a hopeless cause. The attack would not extend much farther to the right or left than the fronts of Pickett's and Pettigrew's divisions.

Many soldiers left accounts describing Lee's movements in front of their units, although some of these seem apocryphal. Among the more trustworthy are those by members of Brig. Gen. James J. Archer's brigade, commanded this day by Colonel Fry. It was positioned on the far right of Pettigrew's division and thus would have the responsibility of connecting with Pickett's command after the attack started. John H. Moore of the 7th Tennessee in Fry's brigade recalled seeing Lee, Longstreet, and Pickett riding along the lines "several times — at least three times; if not more — observing our alignment, but principally with field-glasses observing the position and movements of the Federals." Moore interpreted their movements as signs that the high command was not yet sure what should be done on this day.[18]

Fry himself left an even better account. He observed Lee, Longstreet, and Hill riding toward his position, then dismounting and taking their seats on a fallen tree trunk only sixty yards from him. "After an apparently careful examination of a map, and a consultation of some length, they remounted and rode away." Then staff officers began to scurry about, and Pettigrew rode up to inform Fry that an artillery barrage would precede the attack. The Federals would "of course return the fire with all the guns they have; we must shelter the men as best we can, and make them lie down," Pettigrew told him. Fry also was to see Pickett to work out the coordination of their flanks during the attack. The two had served in the Mexican War, and both had participated in the assault on the fortified military academy of Chapultepec, which contributed to the capture of Mexico City nearly sixteen years earlier. Pickett was "in excellent spirits," Fry thought, and both commanders were certain their attack would succeed. Pickett's left brigade was commanded by Brig. Gen. Richard B. Garnett, who now appeared and worked out the arrangements with Fry.[19]

Members of Pickett's division penned some questionable accounts of their army commander's movements over the field. Capt. James R. Hutter of the 11th Virginia recounted an amazing story, if it was true. He was resting under a large apple tree just behind the right wing of his regiment with Pickett and Longstreet when Lee rode up. Longstreet and the army leader engaged in a heated discussion, which Hutter overheard. Longstreet asserted that "his command would do what any body of men on earth dared do but no troops could dislodge the enemy." Pickett, on the other hand, was certain he could do it. Lee then said, "Ask the men if they can dislodge them." Hutter and Capt. Thomas Horton called on several members of Company B, 11th Virginia, for their opinion. The response was not surprising. The soldiers said, as if reading a line in a play, "Boys many a one of us will bite the dust here today but we will say to Gen. Lee if he wants them driven out we will do it." One wonders how much credence to give this report, for it has the ring of a memory manufactured in the wake of the tremendous controversy surrounding Longstreet's lack of enthusiasm for the assault.[20]

Even a member of McLaws's division recalled seeing Lee dangerously exposed on the skirmish line that morning. W. Gart Johnson of the 18th Mississippi claimed that Lee and Longstreet walked past him, "stopping now and then to take observations." Despite the ping of rifle bullets nipping close by, Lee calmly looked at the Union lines through his field glasses. "A few minutes afterward we heard him say to Longstreet, in substance, 'Mass your artillery behind that hill,' pointing to a ridge just in our rear, 'and at the signal bring your guns to the top of the ridge and turn them loose.' " As the two commanders walked toward the rear, Johnson and his comrades felt they had heard enough. They began to dig with bayonets and planks of wood to provide some cover for themselves as soon as the guns opened up. Johnson, like Hutter, remembered a fine story, but there seems little likelihood that Lee and Longstreet went this far forward or that Lee gave such minute instructions for the employment of the artillery. Certainly Longstreet did not deploy the guns or use them in the manner indicated by Lee in Johnson's unreliable story.[21]

Exactly how long the preparations took is difficult to estimate. One modern writer believes Lee and Longstreet consulted off and on from 4:30 until at least 10:00 that morning. The work of positioning troops and artillery went on for the remainder of the forenoon. The guns, in particular, demanded a lot of attention, for they would be the key to giving Pickett, Pettigrew, and Trimble any decisive edge in this action. If the guns could seriously damage the Union artillery and kill at least a few Federal infantry, the assaulting column would have a fighting chance.[22]

Lee and Longstreet were in complete agreement on this point. The artillery needed to, in Lee's words, "silence those of the enemy." Moreover, the Rebel artillerists were to push forward as soon as the infantry made progress over the valley, "protect their flanks, and support their attacks closely." The former objective was possible if the Confederate guns fired accurately. But the latter instruction would be very difficult indeed, and it would be possible only if the first objective was met. Given that both sides used the same kind of ordnance, any batteries that advanced into the open valley to close with the enemy would be subject to a devastating artillery fire by the Federals. There had been very little of this kind of artillery advance thus far in the war, for this very reason. The fact that Lee was ordering his guns to push ahead now was a sure indication of his desire to leave no stone unturned in efforts to give Pickett and the others every chance of success.[23]

Longstreet faithfully passed down these instructions to the artillery officers. No one was put in charge of the barrage that was to come, although it was to be fired by nearly every battery in the army. The logical choice to organize this effort was the army's artillery chief, but the well-meaning Pendleton, who was a minister as well as a military officer, was not capable of the job. He had become a supernumerary since his appointment to this position earlier in the war, for Lee had a number of superb artillery officers in charge of battalions and batteries alike. They could easily carry the burden of positioning the guns and directing their fire.

One artillery officer in particular would play a prominent role. Edward Porter Alexander was singled out by Longstreet for his promise. A Georgian and a West Pointer with experience on the Western frontier, Alexander had shone brilliantly in the Chancellorsville campaign. He was largely responsible for collecting the guns that softened the Union position at Fairview, an open field near the Chancellor House, and prepared the way for the final Rebel attacks that drove the Army of the Potomac back toward their crossing of the Rapidan River. This was the true turning point of the battle, not Stonewall Jackson's flank march, and Alexander deserved great credit for his role in it.

Hardly suspecting what this day would bring, Alexander busied himself all morning with the guns of his battalion. After Pendleton had visited Alexander and approved his dispositions, the young artillery officer went back to find Lee and Longstreet in consultation about 8:00 A.M. He learned from them the details of Lee's projected assault, receiving "more exact ideas of where Pickett was to direct his march."

Alexander was pleased when Longstreet appointed him to take charge of the First Corps artillery for the day's action, and he was careful to record what Longstreet told him to do. "First, to give the enemy the most effective cannonade possible. It was not meant simply to make a noise,

Col. Edward Porter Alexander, who bore much of the responsibility for sending the infantry in after the artillery bombardment (LC)

but to try & cripple him — to tear him limbless, as it were, if possible." After that Longstreet wanted him to "advance such artillery as you can use in aiding the attack." This last phrase hit home to Alexander. He had a total of seventy-five guns available but was convinced he would have to use all of them, firing at the comparatively long range of 1,200 yards, in the bombardment. Moreover, "I had not the ammunition to make it a long business." He estimated a supply of only 200 rounds per gun was on hand, which included a lot of short-range ordnance that would be useful only in repelling an infantry assault. The guns had already expended a large amount of long-range ammunition supporting the attack on July 2, and there were no reserve supplies closer than Staunton, Virginia, in the Shenandoah Valley, about 150 miles away. His guns could fire anywhere from 30 well-aimed rounds to 100 hastily prepared shots per hour. Thus the logistical demands were restricting; Alexander reckoned his barrage should be no longer than one hour. While his reasoning applied to the First Corps artillery, it was quite possible that a similar situation existed with the artillery of the other two corps as well.

For the second part of his mission, providing close support for the advancing infantry, Alexander had a special plan. Since he would have to use all of his available guns in the long-range bombardment, he hoped to obtain a reserve that he could push forward alongside Pickett's men. Fortunately such a reserve force was available. When Pendleton had visited Alexander earlier in the morning, he had told him that Col. R. Lindsay Walker, artillery chief of Hill's Third Corps, had several twelve-pounders to spare. They were smoothbores and thus would be of comparatively little use in the long-range barrage. Walker was willing to loan them to anyone. Alexander jumped at the chance and said, "I had the very place for them." The guns, eight in number, came under the charge of Maj. Charles Richardson, and they were drawn from several different units. Alexander placed them in a small hollow behind Spangler's Woods, near Emanuel Pitzer's house, and told Richardson not to move until he sent for him. Alexander's courier, a soldier named Arthur C. Catlett, was also told to note the position of Richardson's guns in case he should be sent to retrieve them. Alexander intended that his own line of guns should remain in place after they stopped the barrage and prepare to repel a Union counterattack with canister fire while Richardson's guns would roll forward.

Yet even though Alexander was excited by the prospect of actually taking guns into close support of an advancing infantry force, he recognized that the ground was not ideally suited for such a venture. There was no cover for the advancing guns, the Federal artillery had good positions to strike them, and if gunners and horses advanced too far, the Union infantry could also cut them down with rifle fire. Yet he intended to try, if for no other reason than to satisfy a professional curiosity to see if it would work, but he would advance them only until they reached the range of the Union infantry. From there the weapons could cover the infantry's retreat or limber up and continue to advance if Pickett broke through. Just to hedge his options, Alexander also gave instructions for all of his guns, besides Richardson's, "to limber up & follow any success, as promptly as possible."

About 11:00 A.M., when the sky was clearing and the temperature was rising, Alexander felt ready. But then he heard the loud roar of artillery to the left. The guns of Hill's Third Corps went into action to support the Rebel infantry in a sharp little skirmish that amounted to a miniature battle for possession of a large barn on the Bliss farm. It was almost halfway between the lines on Hill's front and had been a bone of contention the previous day as well. Alexander noted disapprovingly that Walker allowed nearly all of his artillery to be drawn into this waste of long-range ammunition. This exchange, which involved a number of Federal guns as well, lasted for about a half-hour, but Alexander refused to let his First Corps artillery participate. The noise was so great that many observers later assumed it was part of the artillery preparation for Pickett's Charge, but fully an hour and a half of silence ensued after it ended and before the true barrage began.

Alexander was prepared and reported to Longstreet sometime between 11:00 and 12:00 A.M., but the corps commander was not yet ready. He told the artillerist that the infantry still had to finish their dispositions — he probably referred to Trimble's command, which was the last to take position. So Longstreet told him he would order the signal guns to be fired, two in quick succession, by the Washington Artillery. Alexander was to take a good position from which he could observe the effects of the barrage, for Longstreet had a special assignment for him. The young gunner was to discern the opportune moment for the infantry to advance. Alexander was not intimidated by this job. He was quite capable of making such a judgment, and he took Catlett and a courier from Pickett's staff with him so as to communicate directly with the infantry. The three men took position just to the left of Lt. James L. Woolfolk's Virginia battery, which was the third battery from the left in Alexander's line, directly in the front and middle of Garnett's infantry command.

During the next few minutes Alexander pondered the best timing for Pickett and the other infantry leaders. He reasoned that the attack should begin twenty to thirty minutes after the start of the barrage. Alexander intended to continue firing even after they started so as to cover their advance as long as possible and allow the foot soldiers to get close to the Federals before the barrage lifted. Alexander was fully confident that all would be well, and his faith in Lee's judgment was the key to his optimism. "But the fact is that like all the rest of the army I believed that it would all come out right, because Gen. Lee had planned it."

Imagine the colonel's shock when, about noon, a message arrived from Longstreet. It demonstrated, for the first time in Alexander's eyes, the corps commander's deep reservation about this assault. "If the artillery fire does not have the effect to drive off the enemy, or greatly demoralize him, so as to make our efforts pretty certain, I would prefer that you should not advise Gen. Pickett to make the charge. I shall rely a great deal on your good judgment to determine the matter & shall expect you to let Gen. Pickett know when the moment offers." Alexander began to worry. "It was no longer Gen. Lee's inspiration that that was the way to whip the battle, but my cold judgment to be founded on what I was going to see." The artillery officer felt a bit unsteady with so much resting on his shoulders. He knew the Federals held a strong position and that the assault would have to be costly. But "while ready to attack anything on Gen. Lee's or Longstreet's judgement, I was by no means ready to go for that place on my own judgement."

Unsure of his role in this unfolding drama, Alexander sought the advice of Brig. Gen. Ambrose R. Wright. Wright was a fellow Georgian who commanded a brigade in Anderson's division, and his men had attacked the Federals the day before almost exactly where Pickett's men were doomed to hit them. He had come tantalizingly close to breaking through and crossing Cemetery Ridge but was repulsed with heavy loss. Now Wright supported Alexander in writing to Longstreet for clarification. "Your letter implies that there is an alternative attack open to us," Alexander wrote. "If so I earnestly advise that it be carefully considered before we open the Arty fire." Alexander assured Longstreet that once cannon smoke filled the valley, he would have little opportunity to do more than observe how much return fire was coming from the Federals, which "may not be safe criterion." If there was any question about the wisdom of this assault, if it was not strongly supported by both Longstreet and Lee, then it would be foolish to waste precious ammunition only to call off the expected infantry advance.

Longstreet responded at 12:15 P.M. by repeating the general instructions. "The intention is to advance the Infy if the Arty. has the desired effect of driving the enemy's off, or having other effect such as to warrant us in making the attack." When Alexander showed this to Wright, the infantry officer accurately noted, "He has put the responsibility back upon you." Alexander was fully aware of that, and he asked Wright's opinion on the prospects of success. Wright succinctly put the problem before him. "Well, Alexander, it is mostly a question of supports. It is not as hard to get there as it looks. I was there yesterday with my brigade. The real difficulty is to stay there after you get there — for the whole infernal Yankee army is up there in a bunch."

At this point a lesser man might have quailed at the responsibility thrust upon him, but Alexander did not. He bolstered his courage and tried to decide what to do. First, the artillerist determined that he could not make a decision about whether the infantry should attack while the barrage was under way; there was no opportunity of gauging the effect on the Union infantry once the smoke obscured everything. He had to make up his mind, before the first gun was fired, that Pickett would either go or stay. To help him make that decision, Alexander rode to Pickett to gauge his spirits. "I did not tell him my object, but just felt his pulse, as it were, about the assault." Just as Longstreet had done before him, Alexander came away from Pickett with the strong impression that he was "in excellent spirits & sanguine of success." But unlike the corps leader, Alexander did not leave him with a heavy heart. Instead he dashed off a short note to Longstreet. "When our artillery fire is at its best I shall order Gen. Pickett to charge."

Thus the die was cast. The infantry assault would take place, and Alexander had handled the most difficult moment of his career. "Gen. Lee had originally planned it," he wrote many years later, and "half the day had been spent in preparation. I determined to cause no loss of time by any indecision on my part. As to the question of supports, that I supposed would be the one to which Gen. Lee himself would have given his own special attention — far more than to any particular features of the ground. And I had heard a sort of camp rumor, that morning, that Gen.

Lee had said he intended to march every man he had upon that cemetery hill that day."

Longstreet had deftly shifted a good deal of the burden of conducting this assault onto Alexander's young shoulders. He later admitted feeling unable to "trust myself with the entire responsibility" for sending the men in. Longstreet hoped to create a situation where the attack would be called off by someone else; thus the lives of the infantry would be saved, and he would avoid the primary blame. This is probably why he communicated with the gunner, who was only a few hundred yards away, by letter rather than consult with him verbally. It enabled Longstreet to create a paper trail of responsibility leading toward Alexander. Also, a face-to-face meeting between the two men would have allowed Alexander to press Longstreet for more detailed instructions, which the corps leader did not want to give. Alexander's resolution aborted Longstreet's plan, for good or ill.

Knowing all this prompted Alexander to rethink his calculations about the proper time to send the infantry forward. "To be too soon, seemed safer than to be too late, so I fixed in my own mind on 20 minutes — with a possibility of even shortening it to 15, if things looked favorably at the time."

Alexander also changed his plans for Richardson's eight guns. He no longer felt comfortable keeping them so far to the rear. A bit of rocky woods through which they had to pass to get onto the battlefield might delay them. So Alexander sent Catlett to fetch the guns, intending to place them closer to the action. In fact, while waiting for Catlett, Alexander even thought of advancing these guns in front, not to the flank, of Pickett. They could deploy just outside Union rifle range and pound the enemy until Pickett's men arrived. After some time had passed, the courier returned with no artillery. Alexander was angry, assuming Catlett had forgotten where he had placed Richardson. "He would not dare to leave there without orders. You go again & find him & don't you come back without him," he warned Catlett. The faithful courier tried again, but the bombardment started before he returned once again with the explanation that the guns were nowhere to be found.

Alexander always regretted losing these pieces. He later admitted that his plan to push them ahead of the infantry probably "would only have resulted in their loss, but it would have been a brilliant opportunity for them, and I always feel like apologizing for their absence." He also regretted not trying his experiment with some of his own guns, as it was "a beautiful chance to handle Arty & to show what it can do." Much later he found out what had happened to Richardson. Pendleton had taken half his guns and repositioned them elsewhere on the field without telling Alexander. Then, during the artillery exchange between Hill's corps and the Federals over the Bliss barn, Richardson's remaining crews were in the way of overshoots. The major decided, without informing Alexander, to move his guns to a safer location. "But, wherever he went, it was where Catlett, who was an excellent & reliable man, could not find him." Alexander was angry enough that he reported the entire incident to Longstreet and even considered preferring charges against Richardson, but he soon dropped the idea.[24]

Longstreet did an effective job of passing down instructions to other artillery officers in his corps, besides Alexander. He sent a message to Col. James B. Walton to see him that morning. Walton had formerly served as the chief of artillery for the corps, but Longstreet had made Alexander acting chief that day, assigning Walton to take charge of the right wing of the corps artillery line. Walton and his adjutant, William Miller Owen, rode to corps headquarters and found Lee and Longstreet conferring with several division leaders. The plans for the assault and the artillery's role in it were spelled out clearly. Owen was told to pass the word to all battalion commanders. He turned to Longstreet when he had finished and was told, "All right; tell Colonel Walton I will send him word when to open."[25]

Exactly how much detail Owen imparted to the battalion officers is unknown. But the battery leaders in Maj. James Dearing's battalion of Longstreet's artillery received remarkably detailed instructions. Dearing told Capt. Joseph G. Blunt and Lt. Joseph L. Thompson of Company D, 38th Battalion of Virginia Artillery, that the guns would fire for fifteen minutes after the opening of the barrage. Then they would be moved forward and fire again in stages, keeping up with the infantry. Dearing told Capt. Robert M. Stribling of Company A, 38th Battalion of Virginia Artillery, that the battalion would advance one battery at a time, starting with his unit on the right of the line. Stribling and Dearing rode forward to examine the ground they would have to cover and found that Emmitsburg Road was a difficult obstacle because it had been cut into the side of a slope in their front. The post-and-rail fences on both sides of the road also hindered movement. They could only take the guns in column through a gate at P. Rogers's house to the right front of the battalion, move several hundred yards down the road, then move through another gate in the fence bordering the east side of the road. It would be a complicated maneuver, exposing the guns to a fearful fire, but Dearing apparently had every intention of trying it.[26]

The instructions also filtered through the layers of artillery command in Hill's corps. Maj. William Thomas Poague, who led a battalion that was positioned in front of Pettigrew's division, was told to wait until the infantry had seized the crest of Cemetery Ridge and then "to proceed as rapidly as possible to the summit with all my guns, and there be governed by circumstances." He was not told to accompany the foot soldiers as they advanced but just to occupy the Federal position once it was taken. While Poague did not identify who issued the order, presumably it came from Walker. Longstreet had virtually no contact with anyone in the Third Corps, and this may account for the difference in the instructions Poague received compared with those given the First Corps artillery. The general sense was the same, but the execution of the artillery support for the infantry was not only different but more realistic as well. The artillery of Hill's corps was not expected to fight its way across the valley but to position itself on captured ground and offer whatever support it could in holding it.[27]

Longstreet probably was right when he told Lee that he had been "more particular in giving orders than ever before" while preparing for this attack. Comparing the preparation with how the Army of Northern Virginia operated in the Seven Days campaign certainly proves his point. That campaign, the first matching Lee with the army that he made famous, was characterized by good strategic and tactical ideas that were seldom put into practice in an efficient way. The army's staff work was poor, and Lee's habit of delegating authority through the issuance of vague instructions was new to the subordinate commanders. The possibility of disaster was averted only because the men were willing to fight hard, as they did at Mechanicsville and Malvern Hill. Only the latter battle resulted in no strategic gain.

Pickett's Charge, while much more minutely planned than these engagements, was less well organized than Lee's last offensive of the war, the attack on Fort Stedman during the latter stages of the Petersburg campaign. Maj. Gen. John B. Gordon was in Longstreet's shoes then, and he planned the operation with an impressive degree of detail and thoroughness. His troops were successful in capturing this Federal strong point in the fortified lines, but the weakened condition of Lee's army meant the

Confederates could not hold it. If Pickett's Charge had been organized with similar attention to every detail, it might have had a better chance of success.[28]

Despite the conclusion of a modern biographer who asserted that Longstreet "had devoted his full talents and energy toward" preparing the assault, there are several weaknesses evident in those preparations. Longstreet failed to follow through on his good intentions to explain the details of the attack to all levels of command in all units. He failed to communicate effectively with anyone outside the First Corps, even though Third Corps troops would make up more than half the attackers. He failed to devise a detailed plan to gauge whether the artillery barrage would damage the Federals enough to justify sending in the infantry, and he neglected to develop and implement detailed plans to push the guns forward in close support of the attackers. He failed to understand, mostly due to his lack of contact with the Third Corps and partly through Hill's reluctance to speak up, the weakened condition of Pettigrew's and Trimble's units. All of these weaknesses fall into the category of lapses of thought, not deliberate attempts to sabotage the assault. For the first time in his career Longstreet was organizing an attack across corps lines and utterly failed to meet the new challenge.[29]

More evidence of lack of thought can be seen in the placement of Pickett. Longstreet simply instructed him to find a spot for his men to ride out the barrage somewhere in the vicinity of the Union center. No one seems to have pinpointed an exact spot for the attack to aim at, a rather odd omission, to be sure. No reliable accounts of the preparation for this assault indicate that anyone pointed out the copse of trees or the angle in the stone fence as key features in the landscape. Pettigrew was given to understand that he was to assault directly ahead, which would bring his extreme right wing toward those two points. Pickett only was instructed to join his left flank with the right flank of Pettigrew. That necessitated a significant and difficult left oblique movement by the Virginians across the valley, under artillery fire. Why Pickett was allowed to start his troops 400 yards from Pettigrew was never explained. No one other than Longstreet could be blamed for this error.[30]

Of course, errors of judgment or lack of forethought were one aspect of the limitations of planning that characterized this assault. Longstreet's deliberate attempts to limit the chances of success and thereby limit the loss of valuable manpower also hamstrung the operation. His decision not to use reserve troops to right and left of the attackers, which Lee

THE LAST ATTACK AT GETTYSBURG

had clearly authorized him to do, was a serious mistake. If he had had his whole heart in the operation, Longstreet should have planned to move Anderson's division forward on both flanks of the attacking column within a few minutes after Pickett, Pettigrew, and Trimble started, so they could have approached the Union line early enough to have taken some pressure off the centrally positioned troops. Instead he chose to use them only if trouble developed or to cover a retreat, a plan that effectively robbed them of any chance to help achieve a breakthrough.

In short, as an example of planning and organizing a complex offensive on the battlefield, Pickett's Charge neatly falls into the middle ground between the haphazard design of the Seven Days and the meticulous preparation of the assault on Fort Stedman. Longstreet's reluctance to push forward the preparations for the attack opened him to a lifetime of charges by Lee's partisans; Lee's old war horse became the scapegoat for the failure of Pickett's Charge.

The preparations on the Confederate side were massive, and they lasted throughout the morning. What was taking place among the Federals during the same time? No one seems to have been certain that a major assault was in the making. Certainly all observers could see that the Rebel artillery was massing in plain view. There obviously was something afoot, but there was no consensus of opinion on the Union side as to what this meant. A heavy bombardment was the prospect, but whether this was meant to cover a general retreat or prepare for an infantry assault was the question. To cover all angles, Meade busied himself with preparing his army for any contingency.

Meade had already signaled his apprehensions regarding Lee's moves by predicting at least two possibilities. The night before, after a lengthy council of his officers, the army commander spoke privately to Gibbon and confided his prediction for the morrow. "Gibbon, if Lee attacks me to-morrow it will be on *your front.*" The division leader was a bit surprised and asked why he believed this. "Because, he has tried my left and failed, and has tried my right and failed; now, if he concludes to try it again, he will try the centre, right on your front." Gibbon was not intimidated. "Well, general, I hope he does, and if he does, we shall whip him."

But Meade also feared that Lee would try to flank his left, which was exactly what Longstreet had vainly argued should be done. In fact, Meade feared this Rebel move the most. A frontal assault could be repulsed, but moving to the rear to catch up with the enemy was a more complex and risky prospect. The Federal commander went about preparing his men with commendable thoroughness. To Maj. Gen. Winfield Scott Hancock, commander of the Second Corps, he explained his plans in case Lee attacked the center. When the Rebels were repulsed, he hoped to counterattack Lee's right flank with the Fifth and Sixth Corps. In case Lee moved around his left, Meade gathered information about the roads and the lay of the land to his rear so he could maneuver more quickly to keep between the Rebels and Washington, D.C. Meade also sent detailed information about the progress of the battle and instructions to Maj. Gen. William B. French at Frederick City, Maryland, and to Maj. Gen. Darius N. Couch at Harrisburg, Pennsylvania. Both men commanded forces that were independent of the Army of the Potomac but that were ordered to cooperate with Meade.

The Army of the Potomac was fully prepared to evacuate its position at Gettysburg and retire to a strong and fortified position along Pipe Creek in Maryland. Located sixteen miles south of the battlefield, Pipe Creek had been Meade's hope for a successful defensive battle against Lee ever since he had taken command of the army on June 28. Meade carefully planned the positioning of his corps here for three days and intended to concentrate the army along the creek even as late as July 1, before it became evident that the fighting at Gettysburg would assume such proportions as to force him to concentrate the army there and fight it out with Lee on Pennsylvania soil. The position along Pipe Creek was strong; artillery chief Brig. Gen. Henry J. Hunt later believed it was stronger than the army's position at Gettysburg. The creek had carved out "a wide, flat valley, bordered on both sides by high sloping wooded hills." Even as late as the afternoon of July 2 Meade reported himself ready to retire to it if the situation demanded a retreat. This was the real reason Meade called a council of war that night to determine if the army should remain at Gettysburg or fall back to this excellent battleground. If Lee had allowed Longstreet to attempt his flank movement, Meade was ready to deal with it effectively.

The army commander also inspected his line from one end to the other. He visited Gibbon's headquarters, at the division commander's urging, for a hastily prepared lunch. Then he started with Brig. Gen. Alexander Hays's division of the Second Corps, positioned just to the right of Gibbon, and rode slowly to the left. He detoured enough to visit Maj. Gen. John Newton, commander of the First Corps, and Maj. Gen. John Sedgewick, leader of the Sixth Corps. While riding on toward Little Round Top, Meade could easily see Alexander's artillery concentration a few hundred yards away. He returned from Little Round Top to his head-quarters at the Widow Leister's house, at the eastern base of Cemetery Ridge just behind Gibbon's division, before 1:00 P.M.[31]

Beyond this the Federals made no special preparations for Pickett's Charge. To be sure, the Army of the Potomac was far more ready for any action, including a massive infantry assault on Cemetery Ridge, on July 3 than it had been on either of the previous days of fighting at Gettysburg. Rebel gunner Alexander thought his opponents had failed to take advantage of an important weakness in the confrontation between the assembled guns of the two armies. He was a bit surprised that the Union gunners allowed his men to lull them into what he liked to call artillery truces. Alexander thought the Yankees should have guessed, from the Confederate reluctance to fire, that they wanted to conserve ammunition. The proper tactic would have been to force the Rebels to use it up "as long as possible before we were ready. For 9 hours — from 4 A.M. to 1 P.M. we lay exposed to their guns, & getting ready at our leisure, & they let us do it. Evidently they had felt the strain of the last two days, but for all that they ought to have forced our hand."[32]

Instead an "ominous silence" descended on the battlefield from a little after 11:00 A.M. until about 1:00 P.M. By eleven the sky had cleared, with only a "few white, fleecy cumulus clouds floating over from the west." There was a slight breeze, and the temperature was quickly climbing into the eighties. The fighting at Culp's Hill was over, the sporadic artillery fire in the center had ended, and skirmishing was reduced to the minimum. The midday lull indicated either exhaustion or preparation for something big, and many Federals had no idea what was to happen next. The Confederates, on the other hand, were all too aware of what was in store.[33]

CHAPTER 2
THE ATTACKERS

. . . .

The Confederates who were about to make this controversial assault were chosen by happenstance, not upon deep reflection. Pickett's command was the only full division that had not yet seen action in the battle, and thus it was a natural choice. Pettigrew's division happened to be in the right place, immediately to Pickett's left, and it at least had a chance to regroup the previous day from its terrible battle on July 1. Lee arbitrarily picked the two brigades of Pender's division. The supporting units to right and left required no reflection; whichever brigades were there had to shoulder the responsibility. Yet all these units were solid and reliable under normal circumstances (except for Col. John M. Brockenbrough's Virginia brigade, whose reputation under fire was soon to be compromised). There was a wide difference in their readiness on July 3 due to their differing experience with battle in the preceding few days.

. . . .

PICKETT'S DIVISION

Pickett's Virginians were the freshest, strongest, and most eager to enter the fray. Not only had they missed the battle of Gettysburg thus far, but the division had never been engaged as a unit since its organization the previous summer. One of its five brigades had taken part in the battle of Fredericksburg on December 13, 1862, and its other component units had seen action in several engagements before the division was put together; but it still was an untested unit. Two of its five brigades were not even at Gettysburg, having been detached in May to guard lines of communication around Richmond.

The three units that were left had commanders with long-term experience. James Lawson Kemper had led his brigade since June 1862, Garnett had commanded his men since November 1862, and Lewis A. Armistead had provided effective leadership for his brigade since before the Seven Days campaign of June 1862. All three were excellent small unit commanders who might have become good division leaders if fate had allowed.[1]

The same cannot be said for their commander. George Pickett was born of a well-to-do Virginia family, but he had spent much of his early manhood living with relatives in Illinois, where his family was marginally acquainted with Abraham Lincoln. John T. Stuart, a former law partner of the future president, arranged for the young Southerner's admission to West Point in 1842. Pickett was an undistinguished cadet and thus entered the regulars as an officer in the 8th U.S. Infantry. He fought valiantly in a number of battles, including Contreras, Churubusco, El Molino del Rey, and Chapultepec, but personal tragedy seemed to hound him in civilian life. Pickett lost his first wife, who died in childbirth in 1851 while living with him at his frontier post in Texas. He met La Salle Corbell the next year while recovering from the loss. The difference in their ages — she was about nine and he was twenty-seven — did not prevent them from developing a lifelong acquaintance, which eventually blossomed into love and a second marriage. Before that, Pickett fathered a son with a Native American woman while on duty in Washington Territory; tragically, his common-law wife died soon after she gave birth. Pickett was involved in a small dispute with British forces over possession of San Juan Island in 1859, which came close to resulting in shots being fired. Two years later he resigned his commission and entered the Confederate army.

Pickett's early war career was undistinguished. He was a close friend of James Longstreet, who shared many a dangerous attack with him in Mexico, but there appears to be no foundation for the rumor that Pickett comforted Longstreet and arranged for the funeral of his three children when they died in February 1862. This was about the time that Pickett took command of a brigade in his friend's division. The brigade, consisting of nearly the same regiments that made up Garnett's brigade at Gettysburg (plus Capt. James Dearing's battery), did modestly well at the battle of Williamsburg on May 5, 1862, losing about 10 percent of its men. He also participated in the battle of Fair Oaks on June 1, 1862. But Pickett's only good day of fighting before Gettysburg was at Gaines's Mill, where he demonstrated the old fire that drove him in Mexico. His brigade played a key role in cracking open the Union position here, the most decisive engagement of the Seven Days campaign. Pickett was shot in the shoulder and suffered what appears to have been a pretty serious wound, despite the charges leveled by his detractors that he inflated the nature of the injury to gain sympathy. Thus Pickett missed Second Manassas and Antietam but gained a new love. La Salle Corbell, now a beautiful young woman, nursed him back to health and started a chain of emotional reaction that would nearly engulf the Confederate officer.

Pickett was promoted to major general and given a division in the late summer of 1862. It had formerly been commanded by Maj. Gen. David R. Jones, who was forced to retire because of serious heart trouble. Pickett now had four Virginia brigades (led by Armistead, Garnett, Kemper, and Brig. Gen. Montgomery D. Corse), a South Carolina brigade (led by Brig. Gen. Micah Jenkins), and an artillery battalion (led by Dearing). He played no role in the battle of Fredericksburg and offered no decisive leadership in the Suffolk campaign the following spring. The relationship between Pickett and Corbell intensified while the division was near Suffolk; she lived with an aunt near her lover's command, and Pickett rode to see her nearly every evening. There was no hint of impropriety associated with these nocturnal visits, except that Pickett's subordinates knew their commander's mind was not fully on his duties. Many of them were disgusted with what they saw as a change in their gallant leader. Col. Eppa Hunton of the 8th Virginia noted that Pickett seemed to have become much more careful of his personal safety when under fire. "Hunton was right," concludes a recent biographer. "George Pickett was losing his stomach for war. His all-consuming love affair with La Salle Corbell had changed him and his relationship with the army."[2]

Yet it was possible that the conjunction of his personal and professional lives might not doom his career forever. There was still enough of the old Mexico spirit left in Pickett for at least one more gallant attack against great odds, which had always seemed to have succeeded against the Mexicans. The working relationship and the personal friendship between Longstreet and his division leader were still strong, and the men were eager for a chance to prove their mettle.

The division's strength is a matter of conjecture, at least concerning the specific figures. Some sources place them at a low strength of 4,300 men on July 3, while others set the estimate as high as 6,260. Both figures include the men of Dearing's artillery battalion. Longstreet's estimate, supported by the memory of Charles Pickett, the general's brother and

THE ATTACKERS

Maj. Gen. George Edward Pickett, whose fresh division of Virginians garnered the lion's share of fame for conducting the attack (LC)

staff member, was 4,500. But recent research more comfortably places the number at 5,830 infantry and 430 artillery.[3]

Lewis A. Armistead led a life before Gettysburg that was similar to that of his division commander. Born in Virginia, he attended West Point but never graduated due to academic and disciplinary problems. Armistead was commissioned directly into the army from civilian life during the Second Seminole War; he served as an aide to his father, Walker Armistead, who commanded U.S. forces in Florida for a time, and held a commission in the 6th U.S. Infantry. Like Pickett, Armistead fought well at Churubusco and Chapultepec and lost two wives in the interwar period. He was commissioned a brigadier general of volunteers in April 1862 and placed in command of the same brigade he would lead for the remainder of his life. Armistead's men did poorly in their first battle, Fair Oaks, where many of them fled. But the Virginians redeemed themselves at Malvern Hill on July 1. The brigade was among the first to fling itself toward the heavy concentration of Union guns, attacking up an open, ascending slope. It failed to crack the Federal position and lost heavily, but no one could fault the men for cowardice. Armistead and his brigade played a small role in Second Manassas, were held in reserve at Antietam, and did not take part in the fighting at Fredericksburg. Armistead also missed Chancellorsville because of his involvement in the Suffolk campaign, which resulted in no serious fighting.[4]

Armistead's reputation among his men was solid but not high. He was a rather gloomy man, a product of his personal tragedies, and a strict disciplinarian. His ideas of proper military conduct often clashed with the feelings of his citizen soldiers. Armistead had worked hard to overcome criticism of his leadership at Malvern Hill, where he allowed part of his brigade to go forward unsupported to fight with Union skirmishers and then sent the rest to conduct a serious assault in piecemeal fashion. The lack of success and heavy losses soured many men in the command. William Henry Cocke of the 9th Virginia wrote home, "We are in a miserable Brigade-reg't & every thing else. Armistead cares nothing at all for the men, he is full enough of saying 'Go on boys' but he has never said 'come on' when we are going into a fight." Armistead had precious little opportunity to prove himself to men like Cocke after Malvern Hill. Perhaps his sterling performance in the coming attack on July 3 was motivated by a desire to show his mettle once and for all.[5]

Of all the men in Pickett's division, Armistead had a unique connection with the enemy. He had been a close friend of Winfield Scott Hancock, who now commanded the Union center on July 3. Little is known of this friendship except that the two met in 1844 while both served in the 6th U.S. Infantry. Neither Armistead or Hancock left any written evidence of their friendship, but Hancock's wife, Almira, remembered it later in life. The two men separated in the midst of an emotional party held in California right after the outbreak of war. Their paths would cross again only at Gettysburg.[6]

Richard Brooke Garnett, born in Virginia, became a close friend of Armistead at West Point. Both men were held back their second year for various reasons, and both wound up getting commissions in the 6th U.S. Infantry. Garnett also served in the Second Seminole War and in the Mexican War. Like Pickett he fathered a son with a Native American woman, a Sioux, in Wyoming. Garnett never tried to contact either his common-law wife or his child after he left the area to serve in the troubled territory of Kansas, which was wracked with a miniature civil war between proslavery and antislavery settlers in 1856. He also attended the sad farewell party at Hancock's house in Los Angeles when the officers of the 6th U.S. Infantry were saying good-bye to each other before shipping off for the East and their respective Civil War careers.

Garnett had a difficult time gaining and keeping a command in the early part of the conflict. He was promoted to brigadier general of volunteers in December 1861 and given command of the Stonewall Brigade, becoming the second of seven men who led that storied unit. The men seemed to have liked him better than Stonewall Jackson, for Garnett was careful of their comfort and welfare. They expressed their preference by refusing to salute Jackson when he happened to ride past, snubbing their illustrious namesake.

This undoubtedly caused ill feeling between the two officers. Jackson lost his temper with Garnett once in January 1862 when the brigade commander halted his men on a march so they could cook food. But the real showdown occurred in Garnett's first Civil War engagement, the battle of Kernstown, on March 23, 1862. It marked the beginning of Jackson's famed Shenandoah Valley campaign and was at best a tactical draw for the Confederates, fought just south of Winchester in the lower valley. Jackson became so angry at Garnett for ordering a retreat under fire without authorization that he preferred charges against his subordinate. The tactical situation actually called for a retreat; Garnett based that decision on his assessment of overwhelming Union strength opposing his brigade, but Jackson refused to see any reason in the affair. He placed Garnett under arrest.

After he was released, Garnett went to Richmond to enlist help. He wrote to Lee, to his family, and to anyone else who would listen to his case. He pressed for an immediate trial so he could clear his name. Jackson's charges "blast my character both as a soldier and a man," he wrote to Sen.

Robert M. T. Hunter of Virginia. "In spite of Gen'l Jackson's course towards me," he assured Hunter, "I can perfectly assure you, I have not lost the confidence of my Brigade, as I am constantly receiving the warmest assurances of regard from the officers, and regrets that I should be separated from them. The men share warmly the feeling of the officers."

The higher authorities hesitated. Adj. Gen. Samuel Cooper noted that all general officers were needed in the field, rather than wasting their time attending a court-martial, but Lee wanted Garnett to have an opportunity to clear his name. To complicate matters Jackson hesitated for months before finally preferring charges, and then only at Lee's urging. The court met in August 1862, and it was an embarrassment for Jackson. Witness after witness testified that Garnett was right to order a retreat. The court adjourned to give Jackson the opportunity to withdraw his charges rather than suffer the humiliation of losing the case. He finally agreed to do so but refused to reinstate Garnett, believing him incompetent to lead a brigade. As a result Garnett was assigned by Lee to command Pickett's old brigade of Virginia troops in the late summer, the same unit Pickett had led in the Seven Days campaign.

Garnett never got over this traumatic assault on his character. When Jackson died of wounds accidentally received at Chancellorsville, Garnett was among the throng that viewed his remains in the parlor of the Executive Mansion in Richmond on May 12, 1863. He told two of Jackson's aides, Sandie Pendleton and Henry Kyd Douglas, who had testified against him at the trial, that he genuinely grieved for Jackson. But he still considered the court-martial an "unfortunate breach" in their relationship, and he could "never forget it, nor cease to regret it." Garnett still brooded, still sought a way to erase the stigma. The fact that his accuser was now gone made his redemption all the harder, for he could never hear from Jackson's lips or read from his pen anything that would erase the shame he felt. Garnett could not hope to ease his pain until his brigade was engaged in another battle, and for that he would have to wait for the last day at Gettysburg.[7]

The men of Garnett's brigade had no involvement in this private war between the generals. Many of them had already seen the hard reality of combat and were under few illusions about how honor and glory grew from its terrible suffering. They had a strong record under fire from Williamsburg to Seven Pines to Gaines's Mill and Second Manassas. Some units had an even longer history. Company A of the 28th Virginia had been organized in response to John Brown's raid on Harpers Ferry in the

THE ATTACKERS

fall of 1859. The men drilled as militia until the war broke out, then offered their services to the Confederacy. Company A, also known as the Blueridge Rifles, exchanged its antiquated muskets for modern Springfield rifle muskets that had been captured at First Manassas. The brigade's greatest day was June 27, 1862, when it played a leading role under Pickett in piercing the Union line at Gaines's Mill. The survivors of the brigade had to battle with the veterans of Hood's Texas brigade for the credit of being the first to break the Federal line and initiating the only tactical victory Lee achieved in the Seven Days campaign. Even though the brigade saw no significant combat for ten months before Gettysburg, ever since Garnett had assumed command, the morale of the men was high. They had received a few substitutes and draftees into the ranks, as did all Rebel units by the midpoint of the war, but mostly the brigade was filled with original volunteers who were just as eager as their commander to see action.[8]

The same spirit infused the men of Kemper's brigade. Led by Virginia-born James Lawson Kemper, this unit also had a good combat record in the spring and summer of 1862 but had not been engaged for many months. Unlike his colleagues Kemper had never attended West Point. He served as a captain of volunteers in the Mexican War and worked as a lawyer in the interwar period. More importantly, Kemper was a successful politician, having served five terms in the Virginia House of Delegates. He was Speaker of that house and chair of the committee on military affairs. Kemper also served as president of the board of visitors for the Virginia Military Institute.

When the war came, he quickly secured an appointment as colonel of the 7th Virginia and fought with his regiment at First Manassas and Williamsburg. He was promoted to brigade command for the Seven Days and temporarily led a division at Second Manassas. Following that bloody conflict Kemper reverted to his brigade command and fought at Antietam. From that point, however, the fortunes of war shunted Pickett's division into the margins; Kemper missed action at Fredericksburg and Chancellorsville. He did not have anything to prove, as did Pickett, Armistead, and Garnett, but Kemper possessed a fiery determination to kill Yankees and win the war. When his command readied itself for action at Fredericksburg, he addressed the men "in that fiery and eloquent language so characteristic of him that if we would do our duty as men and soldiers in the impending battle we would soon be allowed to go home to our wives sweethearts etc." G. W. Sidebottom of the 7th Virginia remarked years later that while Kemper "was a gallant soldier and a great counsellor . . . he drew a very highly colored picture" of war.

The brigade was placed in the center of the Confederate line at Fredericksburg and was not attacked. The men could see and hear the terrific fighting to right and left all that weary day and were transferred to the left after nightfall to relieve Kershaw's South Carolina brigade behind the stone wall at the foot of Marye's Heights, the focal point of the heaviest Union attacks. They strengthened the wall and then listened to the pitiful groans of the wounded who littered the darkened plain in front of their position. When the sun rose on December 14, there were no more attacks, so Kemper's Virginians shot at every Yankee that moved around the houses at the edge of town. They wasted so much ammunition in their eagerness to fight that eventually orders came down for only three men in each company to fire. Sidebottom never forgot the cries of the wounded. He and his comrades thought they were hardened veterans after the Seven Days and Second Manassas, but those cries were the "most horrid experience of our life." They "awakened within us thoughts like these[,] that the glories of war one gained at a dreadful sacrifice." It was an apt lesson to remember as Kemper's men prepared to make their own Fredericksburg-like assault on the last day at Gettysburg.[9]

Pickett and his three Virginia brigades almost were not allowed to take part in the battle at all. His full division had accompanied Longstreet's corps when it was sent to southeastern Virginia and eastern North Carolina in March 1863. As early as April, Secretary of War James A. Seddon began suggesting that Pickett's division might serve the Confederacy's strategic purposes better if it were transferred to the West, either to Gen. Braxton Bragg's Army of Tennessee at Tullahoma or to Gen. John C. Pemberton's Army of Vicksburg in Mississippi. Both Vicksburg and central Tennessee were threatened by superior numbers of Federal troops; if either region fell, it would be a grave blow to Confederate fortunes. But Lee resisted this move. When the Chancellorsville campaign began, he ordered Longstreet to bring his men as fast as possible. Pickett left Corse's Virginia brigade and Jenkins's South Carolina brigade behind and brought Armistead, Garnett, and Kemper along. His men hesitated in the Richmond area for a few days pending the outcome of a threatened Union advance toward the capital from the Yorktown Peninsula. This once again revived discussion about shifting Pickett west. Lee countered with clear arguments. He pointed out how difficult it would be to transfer such a large force so far away and worried that it would simply be

THE ATTACKERS

wasted by either commander out west. "Its removal from this army will be sensibly felt," he informed Seddon. Lee was right. In the days following his brilliant victory at Chancellorsville, he received reports that large reinforcements were being sent to the Army of the Potomac. Seddon should "decide whether the line of Virginia is more in danger than the line of the Mississippi."

The decision was not made until several days later, when Lee went to Richmond for consultation with President Jefferson Davis and his cabinet. Lee lobbied for an offensive into Pennsylvania and needed all the men he could get. The decision to allow him to keep Pickett was finally made in this conference, and the division commander was issued orders to proceed to the Army of Northern Virginia with his three brigades. Just as Pickett started, Maj. Gen. Arnold Elzey, commander of the Richmond garrison, was spooked by Union cavalry raids toward the city from the Yorktown Peninsula and asked that Pickett stay a while. But Lee delayed this request long enough to enable Pickett to get his men away. Pickett would have to go north without Jenkins, whose brigade finally came up from North Carolina only to be diverted to guard rail lines north of Richmond, and without Corse, whose brigade also was directed to guard lines of communication at Taylorsville. The division managed to burst through the administrative roadblocks at the capital to find its fate with Lee's army, but it was being whittled down along the way.[10]

The three Virginia brigades were more than ready for a battle. They took men with illustrious pedigrees to the North. The 53rd Virginia in Armistead's command was led by Col. William R. Aylett, a great-grandson of Patrick Henry. Company K of that regiment also had Pvt. Robert Tyler Jones, a grandson of President John Tyler. Even if they had not seen much action in months, the troops were good campaigners and ready for a hard march northward. "The men were footsore and wearied," later wrote Henry T. Owen of the 18th Virginia, in Garnett's brigade. "The bright uniforms and braided caps of earlier days were gone and had given place to the Slouched hat, the faded threadbare jacket and patched pantaloons. Their faces were tanned by Summers' heat and winter's storms and covered over with unkempt beard. Boys who enlisted in their teens appeared changed now by the weather and hardships & toils of war into men of middle life." Col. John Bowie Magruder of the 57th Virginia, in Armistead's brigade, tried hard to redress this tattered image. While in the Richmond area, he made several trips to town and spent $110 for a uniform coat and $45 for a pair of shoes, and he splurged $10 a day for room and board at a hotel. He enjoyed himself immensely and "spent all the money I could get."[11]

The rank and file were ready for anything. "I think We Will have a good Deal of hard fighting to do up here this Summer," wrote Henry M. Talley of the 14th Virginia, "it is the opinion of Nearly all the Soalgers that old Lee is Going over in Maryland again." It seemed the logical conclusion for Pickett's men; they remembered the excitement of Lee's previous invasion of that border state and were happy to see it repeated. Many of them looked farther north and predicted a thrust into Pennsylvania as well. Henry T. Owen was confident that no matter how far northward the army went, it could handle anything the Army of the Potomac threw at it. Owen thought Lee's army was larger and better disciplined than ever before, which made him "quite willing to advance upon yankeedom. When Lee moves this time I think the yankees will catch fitts." Other soldiers, such as Maj. Robert Taylor Scott, quartermaster on Pickett's staff, admitted to a "shudder at the approaching campaign." But even he was sure that divine intervention would bring success.[12]

When Pickett crossed the line into Pennsylvania, at the tail end of the army, his men marveled at the richness of the countryside. While some of them, such as Edward Payson Reeve of the 1st Virginia, praised Lee's order to restrain the men from pillaging, others wanted nothing more than to eat and burn their way into the heart of enemy country. Lt. William A. Miller of the 18th Virginia called Pennsylvania "one large field of wheat & the best I ever saw. there is no danger of starving out these wretches. we make the country Support the army where ever we go, . . . we are going to do all the injury we can to pay back for what they have done in our country." Miller was in favor of fighting the war to the last. He believed the Federals waged it simply "to make the infernal negro an equal with the white man," and he pledged his undying devotion to stopping the Yankees. "I would rather fight them a hundred years than to be Subjugated by Such a worthless race." In contrast to Miller's virulence William B. Short of the 56th Virginia would have preferred not to fight at all. He was not a coward or a Union loyalist but a kindhearted man who did not want to kill anyone, and he did not want to be shot either. Whether they burned with a bitter desire to face the foe or simply did their duty with quiet conviction, all of Pickett's men seem to have been convinced that Lee's drive northward would decide the war. "I still feel confident," wrote Edward Payson Reeve, "that the present campaign will bring about our independence."[13]

THE ATTACKERS

As if fate was determined to prevent Garnett from participating in the next engagement, he suffered a serious injury that drove him into an ambulance. While crossing the Blue Ridge at Snicker's Gap on June 20, a horse lashed out and kicked him. He was riding his own mount at the time, and the irritable horse was ridden by Maj. Robert Bright of Pickett's staff. The hoof caught Garnett's lower leg and bruised it badly. The general was forced to ride in an ambulance nearly all the way to Gettysburg while Eppa Hunton took charge of the brigade. Garnett refused to let the injury derail his date with battle. Five days later he wrote to a lady friend that the leg was "still quite sore, but is improving slowly. I cannot ride on horseback yet, and fear that I will not be able to do so for a week or more." The crippled brigadier might well have been wary of Hunton, who was an ambitious and rather caustic man with a lot of experience leading the brigade; he had commanded it off and on from Pickett's wounding at Gaines's Mill until Garnett took charge.[14]

Pickett's division reached Chambersburg, Pennsylvania, on June 27 and began to tear up railroad tracks near the town. His men did a thorough job, wrecking installations and equipment as well as tracks. They were still doing this when the fighting at Gettysburg, some twenty-five miles away, began on July 1. They left town at 2:00 A.M. on July 2 and stopped for an hour on top of South Mountain, where they received their first word of the terrific battle that had taken place the day before. The division approached the battlefield just as the assault of July 2 started. Bright reported the arrival of the division to Longstreet, who asked about the condition of the men. Bright told him they were game for an hour or two of heavy fighting, but not much longer than that; the march from Chambersburg had been rushed and the men were tired. Longstreet then told him to encamp the division near Marsh Creek, about five miles from the fighting, and said, "Tell Pickett I will have work for Him tomorrow." Lee agreed with this, and the Virginians bivouacked within sound of the guns. Dearing, however, went forward and volunteered his services to Edward Porter Alexander, who sent him to take charge of two batteries and follow up the Union retreat from the Sherfy peach orchard. The eager young artillerist did well that evening. After the fight ended, Dearing returned to Marsh Creek to his own battalion, which consisted of eighteen guns divided into four Virginia batteries, and brought it forward in the darkness to bivouac just behind the First Corps lines.[15]

Pickett's men were up at 3:00 A.M. on July 3 to eat breakfast and start their march forward. They soon halted for some time so that twenty additional cartridges could be distributed to each soldier. The column was headed by Kemper's brigade, then Garnett and Armistead followed. Leaving Chambersburg Pike, the division made its way by a circuitous route across the rolling countryside. First it moved southward along Knoxlyn Road, then east on Hereter's Mill Road. It crossed Herr's Ridge, the starting point of the first Confederate attacks on July 1, and angled off to the southeast to cross Hagerstown Road, which was the southern boundary of the fighting zone on July 1. Then the Virginians headed east on a small lane leading to Emanuel Pitzer's farm, shielded from Federal view by the low rise of Seminary Ridge, until they reached Spangler's Woods at about 9:00 A.M.[16]

Longstreet assigned Pickett the task of placing his brigades, and he brought them up to Seminary Ridge in a logical spot. The profile of the ground here was a bit steeper than elsewhere, and Spangler's Woods offered additional protection from Union observers. Also, there was a gap in the line here, between Lang and Wilcox on the right and Pettigrew's division on the left, about 1,000 yards wide. The men rested for an hour in column of march, pending the deliberations between Lee and Longstreet about the wisdom, size, and direction of the attack. Then a battle line was formed at the western edge of Spangler's Woods. Pickett seems to have told his three subordinates to choose their own place in it. Since Kemper was the first in column, he took the rightmost position, and Garnett filed into line to his left. Kemper placed the 24th Virginia on his right, then the 11th, 1st, 7th, and 3rd Virginia. A bit later, at noon, Lee issued instructions for all division officers who were under arrest to be released for duty. This returned Maj. Kirkwood Otey to command of the 11th Virginia, relieving Capt. James R. Hutter. All of the other regiments in Kemper's command were under the control of their colonels.[17]

Garnett's brigade, still led by Hunton, deployed with the 8th Virginia on its right, connecting with Kemper, then the 18th, 19th, 28th, and 56th Virginia. Armistead formed about 100 yards behind Garnett with the 14th Virginia on his right, then the 9th, 53rd, 57th, and 38th Virginia on the left.[18]

Dearing's guns had already deployed on advantageous ground atop Seminary Ridge by this time, and Pickett's infantry was about 200 to 300 yards behind them. The men could see the artillery if they peered through the woods. Soon after the battle line was formed, orders came to march forward through the trees; after about fifty yards a halt was called at the eastern edge of the woods. Here a worm fence was dismantled so as

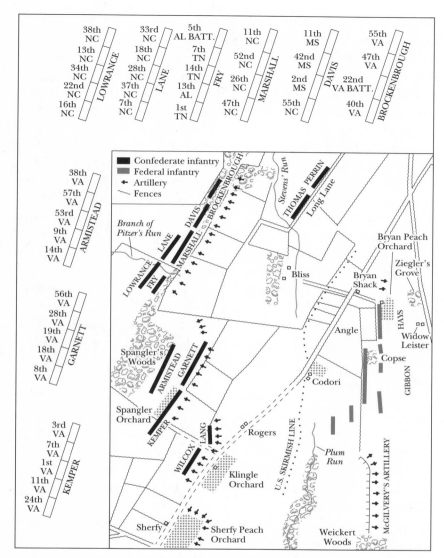

Map 2.1 Confederate Positions, Morning, July 3, 1863

not to serve as an obstacle to the division's orderly advance. Then the men continued forward into the open space just behind Seminary Ridge. They advanced to the foot of the slope and stopped. The color-bearers furled their flags in case the Federals could see them over the ridge top. The line was only about 100 yards or less from Dearing's artillery, and virtually all of the infantrymen were in the open. Only the 38th Virginia,

THE ATTACKERS

49

on Armistead's far left, was in the edge of the woods. Kemper and Garnett sent out skirmishers in front of the guns. It was now about noon and the sun already was "sweltering," according to a man in Armistead's brigade.[19]

The move forward to the foot of Seminary Ridge forced Armistead to protest his position in line. He wanted to be in the front rather than serve as a second line to Garnett, and the brigadier asked Maj. Walter Harrison of Pickett's staff if the division commander wanted him to push out ahead of Pettigrew's right and align with Garnett. Harrison could not find Pickett and was anxious to answer Armistead's question as quickly as possible, so he sought out Longstreet. Harrison found the corps leader in consultation with Lee on the crest of the ridge. Longstreet was irritated to be interrupted with such an issue. He "snorted out, rather sharply, I thought: 'Gen. Pickett will attend to that, sir.'" Harrison respectfully turned and began to ride away when Longstreet, having second thoughts, called out to him, "'Never mind, colonel, you can tell Gen. Armistead to remain where he is for the present, and he can make up his distance when the advance is made.'" Harrison had his answer, but he also had gained his first sight of the ground over which the division was to attack. The view did not encourage him; "truly it was no cheering prospect," he later wrote.[20]

Now that the preparations were completed, Garnett decided to resume command of his brigade. He had no intention of letting this opportunity to redeem his reputation slip away and probably had waited this long to save his strength. Garnett's leg was still not well; he would have to ride across the valley at the head of his troops. Hunton must have been disappointed, but he showed no signs of it. A modern biographer of Garnett suggests that Hunton decided to ride his horse at the head of his 8th Virginia because he was jealous of Garnett. Now the two would be equally prominent in the assault.[21]

The division hospital was set up at Bream's Mill and in the farmhouses of Jeff Myers and John Currens, all of which were in the valley of Marsh Creek about two miles from the battlefield. Asst. Surg. William H. Taylor of the 19th Virginia called it an ideal location, "being in a little dell in a grove conveniently in the rear of the troops." There was a large orchard and an ample supply of apple butter pots. Hospital attendants filled these vessels with water, operating tables were improvised, and everyone lolled about awaiting the wounded.[22]

Pickett's division was ready, but quite a bit later than Lee had anticipated. He had assumed the night before that the Virginians could spearhead an assault by dawn of July 3. It was about 9:00 A.M. before they even reached the vicinity of Seminary Ridge. By then Lee's plan for coordinating an attack on the right with Ewell on the left had long since evaporated. The Federals initiated a renewal of the fighting on the Confederate left at 4:30 A.M. with a noisy artillery barrage by thirty guns that reverberated in the valley fronting Culp's Hill. Before the Union infantry could begin their attack, Brig. Gen. Edward Johnson's division went forward to renew its drive of the evening before. Three separate assaults were made before the Federals counterattacked about midmorning and regained the ground they had lost on the evening of July 2. The infantry and artillery fire petered out by late morning, just before Pickett's men moved up to the foot of Seminary Ridge.[23]

This failure of coordination put increased importance on Pickett's Charge, but the division leader seems not to have realized how onerous was his responsibility. By all accounts he was optimistic, even enthusiastic, about the prospects of success. Both Longstreet and Alexander, as we have already seen, found him to be quite sanguine despite receiving reports indicating how costly the attack would be. Pickett met Lt. Col. George T. Gordon, a former British marine officer whom he had been acquainted with on San Juan Island a few years before and who now commanded the 34th North Carolina in Lowrance's brigade. The two had a nice chat that morning, and Gordon told Pickett that his regiment had been fearfully cut up on July 1. He doubted if his men had the heart to go in again but vowed he would personally "go as far with you as any other man, if only for old acquaintance sake."

A recent biographer of Pickett has speculated whether his optimism was real or an act to inspire his men. He suggests that a rather cynical view of the case would be that Pickett had already decided to direct his division from the rear rather than lead it from the front, and that he did not have to worry much about getting hit. He had decided to be a manager rather than an inspirational leader once the advance began. This was in accord with the demands of the tactical situation, for to supervise the movement of three brigades across an open valley while closing on Pettigrew's division called for Pickett to be close to the rear of his command. Also, his pending marriage to La Salle Corbell was too great a temptation; he wanted to live, and he was happy to find that his personal needs coincided with his professional demands to advance behind rather than in front of his division.[24]

Garnett also received a heavy dose of reality while he waited for the order to go in. Wilcox, who was acquainted with nearly everyone in the army, rode over from his brigade and told him bluntly, " 'Dick, old fellow, you are going against the hardest thing you have struck yet. It is twice as hard as Gaine's Mill. I lost several hundred men there yesterday in fifteen minutes without making an impression.' " Wilcox was not exaggerating, yet Garnett appears to have been unmoved.[25]

The rank and file of Pickett's division were too experienced to be naive about the cost and danger of this attack. But they also were too influenced by stories of the Confederate tactical successes on July 1 and 2, too trusting of Lee's judgment, and too eager to play their role in this great and possibly decisive battle to falter. Many of them assumed success would come their way; others could not dare predict the outcome, while still others heard, saw, and believed ominous signs of disaster. Yet the vast majority were prepared to do all they could regardless of their doubts.

Kemper thought it prudent to inspire his men by giving them the impression they had a particularly important role to play in the assault. He told Col. Joseph Mayo to let his 3rd Virginia know that "the commanding general had assigned our division the post of honor that day." Mayo saw that the news had the desired effect. The men had been "unusually merry and hilarious" before the word was passed around. In fact, some men of the 1st Virginia had been pelting one another with green apples taken from H. Spangler's orchard. Now they "had become as still and thoughtful as Quakers at a love feast." Mayo walked over to Col. Waller Tazewell Patton, commander of the 7th Virginia, and said, "This news has brought about an awful seriousness with our fellows, Taz." "Yes," he replied, "and well they may be serious if they really know what is in store for them. I have been up yonder where Dearing is, and looked across at the Yankees." Patton was not the only Rebel to peek at the field. Lt. William Nathaniel Wood of the 19th Virginia in Garnett's command also walked up the ridge and looked around. He heard Dearing say, "That hill must fall." It impressed him with a strong sense of the seriousness of the mission that lay ahead. Capt. John Holmes Smith of the 11th Virginia in Kemper's brigade walked up the ridge several times that morning. He could see, through his field glasses, that the Federals were strengthening their defenses as much as possible. Dearing also was prominent in Smith's line of view. The artillery officer rode along the line at one point waving a flag to inspire his gunners just before the barrage started.[26]

THE ATTACKERS

The division chaplains held short services consisting of prayers and hymn singing before the show began. Some men shored up their physical stamina by stocking up on water. Cpl. Charles T. Loehr of the 1st Virginia took several canteens to a well near the guns, probably at H. Spangler's house behind Lang's and Wilcox's position. The artillerists pointed out the Union position to him and told him what was to come. When Loehr returned to the ranks, he told comrades that he "would not give twenty-five cents for his life if the charge was made." Over in Armistead's brigade Lt. James F. Crocker of the 9th Virginia remembered his first battle at Malvern Hill while standing with a group of officers gazing toward Cemetery Ridge. He told them it was "to be another Malvern Hill, another costly day to Virginia and to Virginians." Crocker had nearly died in that previous battle, fought one year and two days before. He had thought it was important to stand upright and unafraid that day. "I had a foolish pride to be and to appear fearless—as if it were a shame to seem to do anything to avoid danger." He paid for that foolishness with a serious wound. Now Crocker was much wiser but no less determined to do his duty.[27]

Crocker seems to have spoken for a large number of Pickett's men. They all had a sense of the danger, even if they did not walk to the crest of Seminary Ridge and gaze on the soon-to-be bloody field. Pvt. William H. H. Winston of the 11th Virginia remembered that, when told what they were to do, the men said, "Well it seems impossible, but if Uncle Bob says so, we will make the charge. There was no hesitation or uneasiness. I never saw the division so earnest on the eve of battle. They meant business." The officers of the 11th expressed their views in a similar manner. When told what the ground looked like and how the Federals were positioned, Capt. David Gardiner Houston of Company D "expressed the conviction that it would require a very bloody battle to win the day." Yet everyone quickly expressed their confidence in Lee. This faith became almost a mantra for the men. It was summed up by Capt. Robert McCulloch of the 18th Virginia when he later wrote, "We were flushed with many victories and with a confidence in our leaders that because they ordered us to perform a task we could perform it."[28]

"No men ever went into a charge more thoroughly posted as to what they were up against than Pickett's Div.," recalled Maj. Edmund Berkeley of the 8th Virginia. Yet a number of survivors went to great lengths to argue that Virginians were not faint of heart. There was glory to be had in remembering that Pickett's men attacked with a considered knowledge of what lay ahead, and they did so with enthusiasm. "All appreciated the danger & felt it was probably the last charge to most of them," wrote Eppa Hunton. "All seemed willing to die to achieve a victory there — which it was believed would be the crowning victory and the end of the war." Pvt. Randolph Abbott Shotwell insisted that his comrades went into the assault with higher spirits than before or after. They had no doubt, in his view, "of sweeping everything before them."[29]

So much of this willingness to go in was due to the men's confidence in their leadership on all levels of the chain of command. When Lee, Longstreet, and Pickett rode along the lines that morning to inspect the deployment, the men were already lying down. This was done both to rest and to prepare for the impending barrage. They were told not to cheer, for fear of alerting the Yankees, but they could not resist paying honor to their commander. The men rose and lifted their hats silently in the air.[30]

· · · · · · ·

PETTIGREW'S DIVISION

The other division that would share the major burden of making this assault had a very different past and was in weaker condition to march across the valley to Cemetery Ridge. It was a much newer division as well, having been organized less than two months earlier. Unlike Pickett's three brigades, it was a collection of units from different states with widely varying battle experience. Most importantly, it had been mauled by the vicious fighting of July 1. Pettigrew's was a good division, and it would go on to become a workhorse unit that Lee would rely on repeatedly for the remainder of the war; but it was not up to its future standard on July 3.

The division really was Maj. Gen. Henry Heth's; but since James Johnston Pettigrew led it on this day, the unit deserved to be temporarily named for him. Pettigrew was born in North Carolina, the son of a distinguished and wealthy slaveholding family that owned three plantations in the eastern part of the state. He had no military training but graduated with highest honors from the University of North Carolina at Chapel Hill. In fact, Pettigrew achieved legendary status there, for he scored perfect grades in all his classes for four years. After that he lived a life dedicated to scholarly study, world travel, and heavy involvement in the politics of his era. Pettigrew learned four European languages, plus Hebrew and Arabic, and became proficient in engineering and law. He served in the South Carolina House of Representatives and on two occasions volunteered his services to revolutionary movements, once in Cuba against the Spanish masters and another time in northern Italy against the Austrians. On both occasions he failed to see any fighting; the Cuban revolt never materialized, and he arrived too late to take part in the Italian cause. But the latter trip to Europe, the second of his life, took him to Spain as a consolation. There he became enchanted with Spanish culture and wrote a popular book titled *Notes on Spain and the Spaniards in the Summer of 1859, With a Glance at Sardinia*. It was published in 1861 and favorably compared the culture of the U.S. South with that of Spain.

Pettigrew took an active role in the Civil War from the very beginning. He was an aide to the governor of South Carolina during the Fort Sumter crisis and thus witnessed the bombardment that started the conflict. He later became the colonel of the 22nd North Carolina and commanded a brigade at Seven Pines, his first battle. It nearly was his last as well. Pettigrew was severely wounded only minutes after leading his command into the fight, and later he was captured. Exchanged in early August, he developed a fierce determination to fight the hated Yankees to the last man rather than to submit to their domination. This attitude colored the rest of his short life.

In September 1862 he was given a new brigade consisting of the 11th, 26th, 44th, 47th, and 52nd North Carolina. He operated with it in the backwater of eastern North Carolina during the fall of 1862 and the winter and spring of 1863. He played an important role in only one campaign, Maj. Gen. Daniel Harvey Hill's effort to retake Union-occupied New Bern. In fact he was assigned the key task in Hill's plan. Pettigrew was to capture a small Federal earthwork on the north bank of the Neuse River as a prelude to a general assault by other brigades on the opposite side of the stream, but his poor judgment wrecked the operation. Instead of attacking quickly and overwhelming the small garrison, Pettigrew bombarded for a while and then demanded a surrender. The Federal commander talked him into a truce so he could consider the demand, which gave supporting gunboats the time to steam up and engage Pettigrew's artillery in a duel they could not win. The infantry never attacked, the small fort held out, and New Bern remained in Union hands. Pettigrew's inexperience and softhearted concern for his men (he did not want to lose a single soldier unnecessarily, on either side) caused the whole plan to collapse.

The brigade was transferred to Lee's army in time for the Pennsylvania campaign and was put in Heth's division. Pettigrew played a key role in

Brig. Gen. James Johnston Pettigrew, whose exhausted division made up most of the rest of the Confederate attacking force. He was wounded in the attack. (Pettigrew Papers, SHC-UNC)

the series of events that led to the battle at Gettysburg. He was given orders to push into town from the northwest on June 30 to see what Federal forces were there. The North Carolinian made it to the outskirts but detected signs of a Union cavalry force. Under instructions not to bring on a large fight, he decided to retire rather than develop the

THE ATTACKERS

strength and composition of the enemy force. This compelled corps commander Hill to authorize sending Heth's entire division to do the job the next day. Heth was a far more aggressive leader who willingly brought on the battle of July 1, forcing the commanders of both armies to concentrate their forces at Gettysburg for one of the largest battles of the war.

Pettigrew performed well in directing his brigade that day in a bloody, successful assault on the Iron Brigade, and he quickly was thrust into division command when Heth suffered a modest but debilitating head wound. He also worked assiduously to ready the shattered division for more fighting on July 2. Fortunately for Pettigrew and his men, they were held in reserve that day and had more opportunity to refill the ranks with detached men, walking wounded, cooks, and musicians. They were far readier on July 3 than they would have been the day before, but no unit can suffer what the division endured on the first day and be in top shape for more fighting without several weeks of recuperation. Moreover, Pettigrew himself was still an unknown as a division leader. Despite his performance on July 1, his ability to lead in a sustained battle was not yet fully tested.[31]

The division had probably 4,300 men on July 3, down from its strength of nearly 8,000 at the start of the July 1 battle. That day had been a traumatic introduction to combat for the division, the largest in Lee's army. Its four brigades, each from a different state, grappled with the First Corps of the Union army. Because of the unusually large size of Heth's command and the depletion of the First Corps, the two units were roughly equal in numbers. The first round of fighting took place across Willoughby's Run, between Herr's Ridge and McPherson's Ridge, as Heth made initial contact that morning. He took a lot of time deploying his large force, placing Archer's Tennessee brigade to the south of Chambersburg Pike and Davis's Mississippi brigade to the north. At first they skirmished with cavalrymen of Maj. Gen. John Buford's division, which was positioned on McPherson's Ridge. When the Rebel infantry pushed across Willoughby's Run to drive the troopers back at 9:30 A.M., they were hit by the leading elements of Maj. Gen. John Reynolds's First Corps. Even though Reynolds was killed early in the encounter, the Federals smashed into Archer's brigade, captured Archer and 216 of his men, and sent the survivors reeling back across Willoughby's Run.

Davis initially crushed the Union right wing north of Chambersburg Pike and drove it away when he advanced at the same time as Archer. Then a counterattack by the 6th Wisconsin, supported by two other regiments, aimed obliquely at the Mississippians. There was immense confusion as the Rebel brigade rapidly changed front to meet the counterattack. Davis's men took position in a railroad cut where many of them could not fire over the crest of the slope because it was too deep. As a result the Federals took the position and captured 230 Rebels. The shattered remnants of both Archer's and Davis's brigades retired to rest.

The next phase of the bloody fighting saw the deployment of Pettigrew's large brigade on Herr's Ridge to the south of the pike. One of the Union's best units, the Iron Brigade, deployed opposite it on McPherson's Ridge. When Pettigrew's Tar Heels attacked at 3:00 P.M., they rolled forward like a juggernaut into a sheet of flame. On Pettigrew's left the 26th North Carolina struggled with the 24th Michigan, each unit pouring fire into the other at close range. The Federals slowly retreated up the gentle slope of the ridge through a patch of trees called Herbst's Woods. The center, consisting of the 11th North Carolina, had equally tough fighting to do; but the right wing smashed another Union brigade to the left of the Iron Brigade, and the whole Yankee line was forced to retire to Seminary Ridge, about 400 yards to the rear. Pettigrew had forced his way onto McPherson's Ridge even though he had lost nearly half his men in an hour of fighting. Brockenbrough's Virginia brigade advanced cautiously to Pettigrew's left and followed up his success by pushing the defending Unionists back.[32]

Another division, commanded by Maj. Gen. William Dorsey Pender, now had to relieve Heth's men and capture Seminary Ridge, bringing the fight along Chambersburg Pike to a close by evening. Along with a spectacular Confederate success by Ewell's Second Corps against the Union Eleventh Corps to the north of Gettysburg, this constituted a costly but impressive tactical victory for Lee that encouraged him to concentrate the rest of his army that night and press home with further assaults the next day.

The decision to use Pettigrew's division on July 3 became very controversial. It was chosen simply because it was already in the right position. Yet given the amount of time spent in preparing the assault, it was possible to replace it with another unit. Lee apparently was not fully informed about the losses in Pettigrew's command on July 1 or about its lowered state of readiness on July 3. Maj. Charles S. Venable, one of his staff officers, later admitted that "it suffered more on the first day than was reported and had not recuperated." The loss of officers had been so great that men such as Pettigrew who were not used to higher responsibility were struggling with their new roles. Lee apparently sensed this after the preparations were under way. One member of Davis's brigade recalled that when Lee rode along the lines late in the morning, he noticed a number of slightly wounded men in the ranks. It affected him, according to this soldier, and even brought a few tears from the army commander, who mumbled, "They should not be here." Trimble related a similar story when he described Lee's inspection of Lowrance's brigade just before the bombardment. "Many of these poor boys should go to the rear," Lee said, "they are not able for duty." But nothing was done to shift a different unit into Pettigrew's place.[33]

Both Lee and Longstreet later reported that Pettigrew arrayed his division in two lines, leading a modern historian to assume that half of each brigade's strength was deployed in a second, two-rank line about 100 yards behind the first. But there is no evidence from any survivor of the division's attack to indicate that this rather unorthodox formation was adopted. Moreover, there was no military advantage to deploying a second line. It would have reduced the division front by half and lessened the advantage of spreading the assault along the Union line, one of the few ways it could have succeeded. Lee and Longstreet did have an opportunity to observe the deployment, but they might have been confused by the presence of Trimble's two brigades behind Pettigrew. There is no doubt that Pettigrew formed his men in the traditional manner, one two-rank line. Archer's brigade was on the right, just north of Spangler's Woods and about fifty yards behind the small protective cover of Seminary Ridge. Then Pettigrew's, Davis's, and Brockenbrough's brigades completed the line. The division had been in this position since the late afternoon of July 2.[34]

Archer's brigade was a unique unit consisting mostly of Tennessee troops. It therefore was the only brigade from the Volunteer State in Lee's army, and it had an enviable record of service. Some of its units had fought at First Manassas, but the brigade was not organized until March 1862. Its first commander was Col. Robert H. Hatton of the 7th Tennessee, who was killed at Fair Oaks on May 31. James Jay Archer took over and commanded the brigade through its glory days, turning in stellar performances in the Seven Days, at Cedar Mountain, Second Manassas, Harpers Ferry, Antietam, Fredericksburg, and Chancellorsville. Its losses had been heavy in most of these engagements — 542 men in the Seven Days and 417 at Fredericksburg — but Archer's command always had several weeks to recover after each battle. It suffered 373 casualties, most of whom were captured, on July 1, without the long recuperative period to follow.[35]

With Archer in Union hands, the brigade was led by Col. Birkett Davenport Fry of the 13th Alabama. Fry was born in a part of Virginia that was in the process of becoming the new state of West Virginia. He graduated from the Virginia Military Institute and studied at West Point. Fry was a lawyer, a lieutenant of volunteers in the Mexican War, and a migrant to California during the Gold Rush. Fry's sense of adventure and his commitment to Southern expansionism drove him to volunteer for William Walker's filibustering expedition to Nicaragua. Walker conquered this Central American nation and temporarily governed it before he could realize his attempt either to annex it to the United States or to form a slaveholding empire. Fry then went on to make a living in the cotton business in Alabama. He became colonel of the 13th Alabama early in the war and had lots of combat experience before and after the regiment was attached to Archer's brigade in January 1863. He was wounded three times, at Seven Pines, Antietam, and Chancellorsville.[36]

The men of Fry's command were battered but undaunted. Their spirit was well expressed in the words of Ben W. Coleman of the 14th Tennessee just before the battle of Chancellorsville. Coleman fumed at the Yankees who occupied all of western and central Tennessee by that point of the war, referring to them as "loathsome vandals." He castigated them for insulting elderly men and young, innocent females. "It makes our public rise to fever heat to contemplate some of their daring and vile outrages. How can so many stout and healthy young men of our country remain at home while this state of things are in existence? Are they cowards? Had they rather endure the wounds to their feelings than risk them in their body? If so, let them remain where they are as they would be worthless in the field."[37]

Fry's command was to be the connection with Pickett's division whenever the two units came close in their respective lines of approach to the Union position. A distance of 400 yards now separated them. Fry arranged his units fifty yards behind the crest of Seminary Ridge with the 1st Tennessee on the right, then the 13th Alabama, the 14th Tennessee, the 7th Tennessee, and the 5th Alabama Battalion on the left. He probably had about 400 men left, although it is difficult to pinpoint exact figures because the casualty reports do not differentiate between those lost on July 1 and July 3.[38]

Pettigrew's old brigade was the largest in the division, yet it had attacked the Iron Brigade on July 1 with only four of its five regiments. The 44th North Carolina had been detached to guard the rail lines north of Richmond. The brigade now was led by Col. James K. Marshall of the 52nd North Carolina. Born in Virginia, the grandson of Chief Justice John Marshall and related distantly to the families of George Washington, Thomas Jefferson, Robert E. Lee, and George E. Pickett, Marshall had an impeccable pedigree. His family had been involved in military affairs as far back as the English Civil War and the American Revolution. His father owned thirty-five slaves, according to the census of 1860.

Marshall naturally graduated from the Virginia Military Institute and might have gone on to West Point if the war had not interrupted his life. He served in the 1st North Carolina (six months) after that regiment participated in the first land engagement of the war at Big Bethel on June 10, 1861. He was later elected colonel of the 52nd. The only significant battle in which he led the unit was at Goldsboro, North Carolina, on December 17, 1862. In an effort to stop a Union column from destroying the Weldon Railroad, one of Lee's more important lines of communication from the south, Marshall led the regiment in an assault up an open slope against a battery of Union artillery supported by infantry. The movement had been unwisely ordered by a superior. Marshall's men bravely went forward, but they were mauled and had to retreat. No other units of Pettigrew's brigade were yet on the battlefield, and the regiment was virtually alone in this foolish attack, which led to the loss of sixty-five men.[39]

Besides the 52nd, the only other unit in the brigade to have seen combat before Gettysburg was the 26th. The oldest and biggest regiment in the brigade, it had been engaged at the battle of New Bern on March 14, 1862, where it performed well in a Confederate defeat, and had taken part in the costly attacks at Malvern Hill. Despite, or perhaps because of, their relative inexperience in battle, the men of Marshall's command went into Pennsylvania with great enthusiasm. Lt. William B. Taylor of the 11th North Carolina hoped the army would "devestate the territory and give the enemy a taste of the horrors of war."[40]

Taylor himself got a heavy dose of the horrors of war. The brigade took 2,584 men into its attack on the Iron Brigade and supporting units and lost 1,100 of them in an hour of fighting. The 11th North Carolina suffered 250 casualties of 550 men engaged. The 26th North Carolina lost a staggering number of killed and wounded. Of 843 engaged, 549 were shot down. Thirty-six of the 40 men who fought in Company C were lost. Company F lost all but 1 of its 87 men. There were three sets of twins in Company F, and 5 of the 6 men were killed that day. In addition, 13 color-bearers were shot carrying the regimental flag. It was a devastating day for the Tar Heels.[41]

Although battered and sobered, the North Carolinians quietly stood in the line and waited for the order to go in. Marshall had the 47th North Carolina on his right, connecting with the left of Fry's brigade. Then the 26th was placed to its left while the 52nd and the 11th were positioned on the far left. The Tar Heels were unable to have religious services because their chaplains were tending to the wounded of July 1 in the field hospitals. Marshall's men had to content themselves with catching a glimpse of services held in Pickett's division off to the right.[42]

The next brigade in line to the left had a mixed record, and it was commanded by a neophyte who had gained his position through political connections. Only two of Joe Davis's four regiments had extensive experience under fire. The 2nd Mississippi had fought at First Manassas, in the Seven Days, at Second Manassas, and at Antietam. It had been led by Col. William C. Falkner, great-grandfather of novelist William Faulkner, during the early months of the conflict. The 11th Mississippi also had seen its first combat at First Manassas and had participated in the battles of Gaines's Mill, Malvern Hill, Second Manassas, South Mountain, and Antietam. The 11th was the only regiment in Pettigrew's division that was fresh on July 3; it had guarded division trains on July 1 and thus took more than 400 men into Pickett's Charge. The 42nd Mississippi and the 55th North Carolina both saw their first significant combat on July 1; the Tar Heel unit had not even been added to the brigade before March 1863.[43]

Joseph Robert Davis was the nephew of the Confederate president. He was born in Mississippi but was schooled at Miami University in Oxford, Ohio. He worked as a lawyer and served in the Mississippi senate before the war. He easily gained a commission as colonel of the 10th Mississippi but soon went to Richmond to serve on his uncle's staff. Davis wanted a field command, so the president pulled every string he could to satisfy his nephew's ambition. He had to fight charges of nepotism to get senate approval for his commission as brigadier general, which finally came in September 1862. The younger Davis was given command of a newly organized brigade that missed every important campaign before Gettysburg, although it participated in Longstreet's Suffolk endeavor.

Thus despite the good material and the two veteran regiments, the unit went into battle on July 1 with little experience as a brigade, and Davis was entering his first battle ever. He deserves credit for handling the command well in the initial stage of the fight, but then he lost control of his troops. He allowed the men to pursue the Federals in an unorganized fashion and thus was caught off guard when the 6th Wisconsin, the 84th New York, and the 95th New York counterattacked across the rolling valley between Seminary Ridge and McPherson's Ridge. The result was the disaster at the railroad cut, which led to the loss of 232 men captured from the three regiments Davis had on the field. With the killed and wounded added to the captured, he suffered 54 percent casualties that day. Davis survived without a scratch.[44]

The brigade adjusted its position a bit on the morning of July 3 to align itself next to Marshall's command. The men took shelter behind a thin skirt of trees on Seminary Ridge and dug a crude breastwork, using a few spades left lying around by Pender's men. Davis placed the 11th Mississippi on his left, then the 42nd Mississippi, the 2nd Mississippi, and the 55th North Carolina on his right.[45]

The last of Pettigrew's units had performed solid if unspectacular service in the 1862 campaigns of Lee's army but now was unreliable. Brockenbrough's brigade came into being after the battle of Seven Pines. Commanded by Brig. Gen. Charles W. Field, it was an all-Virginia unit that saw service in Hill's Light Division in the Seven Days campaign. Soon after, the 22nd Virginia Battalion was added to Field's command. Consisting of men who had initially volunteered to serve in heavy artillery units manning the Richmond defenses, the battalion was created when Lee stripped the fortifications to mobilize more infantry for his Second Manassas campaign. These ex-artillerists never reconciled themselves to the change and were sullen, unreliable soldiers. Yet Field managed to get them to toe the line in several grueling campaigns, including Cedar Mountain and Second Manassas, in which he was wounded. Col. John M. Brockenbrough of the 40th Virginia took over the brigade, and the result was a slow decline in its morale and effectiveness. Brockenbrough did not inspire the same loyalty or maintain the discipline that had kept the unit together. When it became apparent that Field would not be able to return to duty for some time, Henry Heth was named the new commander of the brigade. He took charge in early March 1863 and led it in the battle of Chancellorsville, where it participated in Jackson's famed flank attack on the evening of May 2. The men lost heavily and found the tangled jungle of the Wilderness difficult to manage. "I never had such a time in all my life," remarked William J. Hatchett of the 22nd Virginia Battalion, "marching through the woods just as thick as they could be and mud up to my knees in several places and the Battle a rageing at its highest."

Heth moved up to division command soon after, bringing Brockenbrough back to the brigade leadership. His performance was weak, to say the least, on July 1. The Virginians barely supported Pettigrew's brigade in the attack against the Iron Brigade. On the morning of July 3 Brockenbrough aligned his units with the 55th Virginia on the left, then the 47th Virginia, the 22nd Virginia Battalion next, and the 40th Virginia on the right. He also divided the small brigade into two wings, taking charge of the right two regiments and placing Col. Robert M. Mayo in charge of the left units. Why he did this is a mystery. Perhaps Brockenbrough was tired of taking responsibility and hoped to share the blame if anything went wrong. At any rate, the split simply created another likelihood that something would indeed go wrong. Pettigrew appears to have been completely unaware of this odd arrangement.[46]

Many fewer men of Pettigrew's division reported their state of mind and emotion on the eve of the attack than did Pickett's men. Perhaps they had been too sobered by the fighting on July 1 to feel anything but dread. Still, they readied themselves for the attack regardless of their feelings. Sgt. June Kimble of the 14th Tennessee recalled walking forward just before the artillery barrage to carefully examine the field. He plotted the course Fry's brigade would have to take and the point on Cemetery Ridge it would hit. The prospect did not encourage him. "Realizing just what was before me and the brave boys with me, and at one of the most serious moments in life, I asked aloud the question: 'June Kimble, are you going to do your duty to-day?' " He managed to answer yes. Kimble felt a calm after that; "all dread . . . passed away, and from that moment to the close of that disastrous struggle I retained my nerve." When his lieutenant asked him what he had seen, Kimble simply said, "Boys, if we have to go, it will be hot for us, and we will have to do our best." The men of Pettigrew's division were like Kimble; they meant to go in and try their best.[47]

· · · · · · ·

TRIMBLE'S DIVISION

Sixty-one-year-old Isaac R. Trimble must have been the oldest man on the battlefield. Born in Virginia, he was a graduate of West Point and had served in the army for ten years before resigning his commission. Trimble had worked as an engineer in the railroad industry and used his technical skills to supervise the construction of fortifications for the Confederacy early in the war. He received a field command under Stonewall Jackson and played a large role in the Shenandoah Valley campaign of 1862 and the Seven Days campaign. A severe leg wound at Second Manassas put him out of action for many months. The injury healed slowly, with bits of bone working their way out of his leg. Trimble was able to stir about by February 1863, and he began sending unsolicited plans for future campaigns to Lee, carefully lobbying for a return to field duty. He was well enough to take the field in June, but Lee had no command for him. Trimble therefore accompanied the army in its drive northward, waiting for an opportunity.

Lee, who might well have grown tired of his well-meaning presence, suggested that Trimble accompany Ewell's column. Trimble knew the area well, having lived much of his life in Maryland, and understood the lay of the land around Harrisburg, Pennsylvania. In fact, he offered valuable advice to Ewell about the prospects of capturing the state capital. But a message from Lee to concentrate the corps at Gettysburg diverted the Rebels from this prize. Trimble hounded the indecisive Ewell in the march toward that town, eager to come to grips with the Yankees, and mercilessly criticized Ewell for not following up the tactical victory over the Eleventh Corps north of Gettysburg that evening. Trimble, more than anyone, felt Ewell should have gone on to capture Cemetery Hill and Culp's Hill. The corps commander grew tired of his constant meddling (Trimble still held no command in the army) and snapped at him, "When I need advice from a junior officer, I generally ask it." Trimble, who was fourteen years older than Ewell, replied, "I am sorry you don't appreciate my suggestions, you will regret it as long as you live."

Disgusted and burning for a chance to fight, Trimble heard the next day that both Heth and William Dorsey Pender in the Third Corps had been wounded. He asked for one of their divisions, and Lee finally let him take over Pender's command. He arrived just after Lowrance's and Lane's brigades had been detached from the division and ordered to report to Longstreet. In fact, Brig. Gen. James H. Lane, who had led the division since Pender's wounding the evening before, had already received instructions to place the two units behind Pettigrew. He carefully did so, only to be informed that Trimble would take over. Lane returned to lead his brigade without comment. Thus did Trimble assume command of strangers only two or three hours before the attack began. He

Maj. Gen. Isaac Ridgeway Trimble, named to command Pender's division minutes before the artillery bombardment. He led two of its brigades into the attack and was wounded. (LC)

used part of his own staff and part of Pender's, and he felt compelled to say something to the two brigades, "wishing as far as I could to inspire them with confidence." The pugnacious general promised he would "advance with them to the farthest point," a pledge he kept as far as circumstances allowed. Through pestering, tenacity, and brass, Trimble finally had another field command.[48]

These two brigades, consisting of North Carolina regiments, were excellent units. They were the heart of Hill's Light Division. Lowrance's brigade had been Pender's own beginning in June 1862, and he had honed it to a fine fighting edge. Pender fought magnificently during the Seven Days, at Cedar Mountain, at Second Manassas, and at Antietam. Col. Alfred M. Scales's 13th North Carolina, Pender's old regiment, joined the brigade after the latter battle, and Scales rose to command the brigade when Pender was given charge of the Light Division after Chancellorsville.

Lane's brigade had an equally impressive record. It had been organized right after the Confederate disaster at the battle of New Bern in March 1862 and was led by Brig. Gen. Lawrence O'Bryan Branch. The brigade participated in the Seven Days campaign, fought well at Second Manassas, and helped to save Lee's right wing at Antietam by arriving on the battlefield in the nick of time, along with other units of Hill's Light Division. Branch was killed in this engagement and was succeeded by James H. Lane. Lane was born in Virginia and graduated from both the Virginia Military Institute and the University of Virginia. He was a mathematics and tactics professor at the institute and later taught natural philosophy at the North Carolina Military Institute. He served in the 1st North Carolina (six months), saw combat at Big Bethel, and later became colonel of the 28th North Carolina in Branch's command. Lane took the brigade to new heights of combat efficiency and led it during Jackson's flank march at Chancellorsville. Here the brigade gained a sad notoriety as the unit that mistakenly fired on Jackson in the murky darkness on May 2, inflicting the wound that necessitated the amputation of his arm a few days later. Jackson died of complications from that operation. To make the irony complete, Lane had been a student of Jackson's at the Virginia Military Institute; he never quite lived down the reputation gained that dark night in the Wilderness and spent the rest of his life defending "this censured brigade."[49]

The mood of the men in both brigades had been very high while the army drove northward. Scales noted that rumors of a raid into Pennsylvania were flying about as early as April, even before the battle of Chancellorsville. Everyone rejoiced at news that the Northern people were trembling with anxiety after their defeat at Chancellorsville; they wanted to treat the Northern home front to the same level of destruction that Yankee armies were handing out to Southerners, and they were certain that the result of Lee's invasion would determine the fate of the war.[50]

But the fighting on July 1 robbed these men of their optimism. Pender took three of his four brigades into action at about 4:00 P.M., taking up where Heth's exhausted division stopped. The Federals had time between the attacks of these two divisions to establish a strong position on Seminary Ridge, and they mauled Pender's units. Scales's brigade attacked on the left, across the open and gentle swale between McPherson's Ridge and Seminary Ridge, into the point-blank fire of twenty-one Union guns. Scales was severely wounded in the leg, 900 of his 1,400 men were shot down, and the survivors got no closer than seventy-five yards from the Union line. Col. Abner Perrin's South Carolina brigade in the center met almost as much fire but single-handedly exploited a flaw in the Union line and forced the Federals to retire to Gettysburg. Perrin understood that Scales could not make headway to his left, but he was angry that Lane had failed to support him on the right. The North Carolinians had lost contact with Perrin and veered to the southwest, hitting Seminary Ridge a quarter-mile south of the Union line. Lane's only accomplishment was to push back flanking Union cavalrymen with light loss.[51]

While Lane's men suffered little, Scales's brigade was torn apart. Col. William Lee J. Lowrance took charge after Scales was wounded. A twenty-eight-year-old schoolteacher from Rowan County, he had served as a lieutenant in the 34th North Carolina and had been wounded at Gaines's Mill. Lowrance described the brigade's condition as "depressed, dilapidated, and almost disorganized." There were only 500 men left, and Lowrance himself had been slightly wounded as well. The 13th North Carolina lost 150 of its 180 men and had only two officers left on either the regimental or company levels. Yet the division had a small role to play in the attack of July 2. Lane advanced to drive away Federal skirmishers from Emmitsburg Road in preparation for a general attack by the division. Pender rode out to ready his command and was disabled by a shell burst; he had to relinquish command to Lane. The expected attack never materialized due to circumstances beyond Lane's control, and the division avoided any bloodletting that day.[52]

THE ATTACKERS

The combined strength of the two brigades on July 3 was about 1,700 men. Lowrance aligned his regiments with the 16th North Carolina on the right, then the 22nd, 34th, 13th, and 38th North Carolina on the left. Lane's 1,200 men were placed with the 7th North Carolina on the right, then the 37th, 28th, 18th, and 33rd North Carolina on the left. Their placement 150 yards behind Pettigrew became a source of controversy immediately after the battle. Longstreet had instructed that they be located behind Pettigrew's right wing, but Pettigrew apparently understood that they were to be placed to his left rear so he could call them up more easily to support his left. With Brockenbrough's unreliable brigade on that flank, this was especially important. Yet Pettigrew never complained to Longstreet about it, even though he had time and opportunity to do so. Lane also failed to bring this to Longstreet's attention. He seems to have quietly reverted to his role as a brigade leader when Trimble took over the division; he did not even mention it to Trimble, who had little time or opportunity to get his bearings following his last-minute assumption of command.

There certainly was no compelling reason to place Trimble's two brigades behind Pettigrew's right, which was his strongest wing. Lowrance and Lane could have replaced Brockenbrough or at least marched forward directly behind his and Davis's brigades. Alternatively, Trimble could have filled the gap between Pettigrew and Pickett, allowing the Virginia division to advance straight ahead or even more to its right rather than taking the tortuous path of sliding and compressing its ranks to the left — a maneuver that no one apparently planned before the assault began but which the division executed under fire after it started. Again, with hindsight it is clear to see that spreading the attacking column's front as wide as possible, rather than squeezing it into a narrower front, would probably have increased its chances of success. The reasons for this conclusion will become more clear in succeeding chapters. For now, one can conclude only that relatively little forethought went into the deployment of the units on the Confederate left wing of the assaulting column.[53]

One wonders if Pender could have done any better on July 3 than either Trimble or Lane. A West Point graduate who had compiled an impressive record under fire from the Seven Days to Chancellorsville, Pender was new to division command on July 1 and did not perform up to his usual standards. He unnecessarily left one of his brigades behind to guard parked artillery, failed to start his attack early enough to prevent the Federals from establishing a strong position on Seminary Ridge, and did not exert sufficient control over the other three to coordinate their assault. The division's success that day was completely the result of his brigade leaders' efforts to compensate for these deficiencies. The shell that took him out of action on July 2 not only deprived Pender of the opportunity to make up for these failings the next day; it eventually took his life. His leg was later amputated, and on July 18 he died of complications from the operation. Pender was like so many of Lee's subordinates at Gettysburg, new to their increased responsibilities. There is little reason to believe he might have corrected the error in deployment or led his men to greater things than Trimble could have done.[54]

As with the men of Pettigrew's division, the soldiers in Lowrance's and Lane's commands hardly left any indication of their mood just before the artillery bombardment began. E. M. Hays, one of Lowrance's men, later remembered the " 'kicking' in my command as we moved out about the balance of the [division] getting out of it." Hays remembered that the Yankees "were harder to push back" than normal two days earlier, and this colored his perception of the prospects for the assault. He was convinced that even if the attack were successful, the Rebels would never be able to hold the Union line for long. Yet as they were soon to demonstrate, the Tar Heels of both brigades, small in number as they were, had the determination to try.[55]

· · · · · · ·

THE SUPPORTING TROOPS

Of all the units involved in the poorly planned support for this attack, only the brigades of Wilcox and Lang made a significant advance. In fact, their effort was serious enough to make them almost a part of the assaulting column. These two units had a past quite similar to that of Lowrance's and Lane's. They were veteran brigades of Lee's army with lots of experience under fire, and they were led by good commanders. They also had been heavily traumatized by their participation in the July 2 attack and thus were not up to strength for the July 3 operation. Yet the troops manfully did everything they could to make the pending attack a success.

Brig. Gen. Cadmus M. Wilcox had led his Alabama brigade ever since the Seven Days. Born in North Carolina, he graduated from West Point in time to participate in the Mexican War, distinguishing himself in the battle of Chapultepec. He wrote a popular drill manual titled *Rifles and*

Rifle Practice just before the outbreak of the war and served at First Manassas as colonel of the 9th Alabama. Wilcox played a role in every major battle of Lee's army and temporarily led a division at Second Manassas. A garrulous and ambitious man, Wilcox had a wide-ranging reputation in the Confederate army and seems to have known every general officer in Lee's command.

Lang's Florida brigade also had a long history of service in Virginia. Organized by Massachusetts-born Brig. Gen. Edward A. Perry after Antietam, it consisted of the only Florida regiments in Lee's army. Perry led it well until he contracted typhoid fever after the battle of Chancellorsville. He was succeeded by Col. David Lang, who now was leading the brigade for the first time. Lang was born in Georgia and graduated from the Georgia Military Institute in 1857. He rose in rank from captain to colonel of the 8th Florida.[56]

The bloody attack on July 2, in which both Wilcox and Lang played key roles, savaged the ranks and soured the mood of the remaining men. It was a dress rehearsal for the coming offensive on July 3. Lee's plan called for McLaws and Hood to hit the Union left and for Anderson's division of Hill's corps to hit the center in conjunction with these advances. Wilcox went in next to McLaws's left flank, with Lang attacking to his left. The Alabama brigade hit Brig. Gen. Andrew A. Humphreys's division of the Union Third Corps, which was deployed along the east side of Emmitsburg Road from the Sherfy farm to the Rogers house. The latter point was directly in front of Kemper's brigade line on the morning of July 3. Humphreys retired fighting while his troops were roughly handled by the advancing Rebels. Wilcox hit him squarely on his front, Brig. Gen. William Barksdale's Mississippi brigade of McLaws's division hit him on his left, and Lang's Florida regiments struck between the Rogers house and the Codori farm on his right. Humphreys's division was shattered and fled the field.

Then Wilcox and Lang headed for the left flank of Hancock's Second Corps, to their left, taking the fight closer to the battlefield of Pickett's Charge. Hancock played the role of a fire marshal, sending units piecemeal into the path of the Rebel juggernaut. He saw the 1st Minnesota and ordered it to hit the head of Wilcox's brigade and slow it down. The Minnesotans manfully charged, unsupported, and endured a toe-to-toe slugging match with the Alabamans at the bottom of Plum Run, a gentle swale between the lines. The opposing sides traded volleys at point-blank range for a few minutes before Wilcox decided to retire. He realized that he had lost all connection with Barksdale to his right and Lang to his left. The Florida brigade had advanced as far as Wilcox, but Lang pulled back when he realized Wilcox had done so. The Alabamans had exacted a fearful cost for the 1st Minnesota, shooting down 215 of its 262 men, a loss rate of 82 percent.

This was not the last of the assault that day. Brig. Gen. Ambrose R. Wright's Georgia brigade conducted a slashing attack to Lang's left, directly at the point where Pickett's division would aim its attack on July 3, and it actually took brief possession of a part of Cemetery Ridge before it was driven back. Wilcox and Lang could boast of smashing a Union division, but they had suffered terrible casualties. Wilcox lost 577 of about 1,600 men, and four of his five regimental commanders were shot down. Lang's losses were even more debilitating, for he started with fewer men than did Wilcox, but neither Rebel unit achieved a breakthrough.[57]

Wilcox rested his men behind Seminary Ridge that night, and early the next morning he was ordered to move forward and support Alexander's line of artillery on the crest; Alexander delivered the order personally. Even though his men had eaten nothing since the morning of July 2, Wilcox placed them just behind the guns and about 150 yards west of Emmitsburg Road at about 7:00 A.M. His command fronted the orchard at D. Klingle's farm, which lay on the east side of the pike. He was roughly 800 yards from the Union line on Cemetery Ridge, opposite a massive concentration of Federal artillery that was mostly shielded from his view by the undulations of the terrain. Later that morning Pickett's division deployed into line about 100 yards to his rear, at the foot of the ridge. Kemper's brigade extended nearly as far as Wilcox's right flank. Wilcox knew the brigade leaders in Pickett's command quite well and spent a lot of time with them that morning in the yard of H. Spangler's house.[58]

Lang brought his brigade up to Wilcox's left behind the guns, where his men dug a crude trench, throwing down fence rails and using their bayonets to scoop up a bit of dirt onto them. It offered little enough protection against the impending hail of Union artillery fire, but at least one Floridian considered it "quite a formidable breast work." The weather already was excessively hot. Lang had only 700 men fit for duty this morning. With Wilcox's contingent the two small brigades totaled 1,700 men.[59]

Wilcox and Lang were in a peculiar position, thrust far out to protect the artillery in one of the most massive gun battles of the war, and far from their own division commander. Anderson realized the difficulty of this arrangement as well. He sent word to Lang that once the bombardment started, it would be too dangerous for his aides to carry dispatches to both brigade leaders. Orders would go only to Wilcox, and Lang was to watch his movements and conform his own to the Alabama brigade. The two units effectively operated as a demidivision, with Wilcox in charge.

But Wilcox was not his normal pugnacious self this morning. He had already told Garnett that any attack on Cemetery Ridge would be bloody and futile. Now he and Lang engaged in a similar conversation about what would shortly befall their men. Lang frankly told Wilcox that everyone in his brigade was sure Pickett would be repulsed, "as we were confident that what Anderson's division had failed to do on the 2nd. Pickett's could not do 24 hours later when the enemy had reinforced his line." Lang then asked Wilcox what he would do if he was ordered to go as well. "He replied, in substance, that he would not again lead his men into such a deathtrap. But, said I, suppose your orders are imperative and admit of no discretion in the matter? Then, said he, I will do so under protest."[60]

This mood was echoed among the rank and file. George Clark, a private in the 11th Alabama, recalled how his comrades responded when it became obvious that another attack was contemplated. They saw Wilcox surveying the Union position and knew that their advanced post behind the line of guns meant a major push was planned. "There were ominous shakings of the heads among the boys as to the wisdom of the move," and many of them unfairly blamed Wilcox. He had not been "satisfied with having lost half his brigade the day before," they ungenerously concluded, "but was determined to sacrifice the 'whole caboodle' today." Like Wilcox, whom they had unaccountably saddled with the nickname Old Billy Fixin, they had no intention of disobeying orders but would attack under protest.[61]

The Confederate forces to the left of the attacking column were in a position to offer a great deal of help. But things had been going wrong in Anderson's division during the battle. Brig. Gen. Carnot Posey's Mississippi brigade was immediately to Brockenbrough's left, but it had contributed little to the fighting thus far. Posey advanced nearly halfway between Seminary Ridge and Cemetery Ridge on July 2 and had remained there ever since, manning a heavy skirmish line and holding his units in hourly expectation of an attack. He was supposed to go in and support Wright's left flank in the attack later that day, but for some reason he failed to do so. His rightmost regiment, the 48th Mississippi, was stopped by Federal skirmishers at the Bliss farm. Posey lost control of his command, allowed it to advance piecemeal across the open ground, and complained that Brig. Gen. William Mahone's Virginia brigade did not advance to support his own left. As a result, Posey's Mississippians advanced only partway over the ground; none of them reached Emmitsburg Road, and no one ever offered an explanation for Mahone's failure to move. While Wright drove his Georgians in a startling attack that pushed the 82nd New York and 15th Massachusetts from their advanced post at Emmitsburg Road and went on to temporarily take some guns of a Rhode Island battery, the troops to his left wasted their strength in unorganized advances or failed to advance at all. A repetition of this on July 3 could prove even more disastrous, for the attacking column in the center of the Confederate line would be much larger than the forces of Wilcox, Lang, and Wright.

This was a sad tale to tell of Confederate operations in the center of Lee's line on July 2, and the breakdown of coordination would continue on July 3 as well. It was apparent on all levels — brigade, division, and corps. Anderson failed to coordinate the attacks of his brigades on the second, and Hill's actions are a complete mystery. He failed to oversee the proper management of Anderson's division. Anderson had five brigades; Wright, Wilcox, and Lang were in bad shape; Posey's men were tired from skirmishing both days but had done little else that exhausted them; and Mahone was literally not engaged at all. Pender's division had four brigades; Perrin and Scales had been worsted on July 1 and were still not recovered; Lane was in relatively good shape; and Thomas had not been engaged at all. Yet Lee's haste led him to select three of the most depleted of the nine units available. A word to the wise from Anderson and Lane could have placed Thomas and Mahone behind Pettigrew or in a more advantageous position where they could have used their strength to good effect. Posey and Lane could have replaced Wilcox and Lang as supports to the right of Pickett. Also, the uncoordinated attacks by Anderson on July 2 should have been investigated by Hill so that a repetition would not hamper the left flank support for the attacking column on July 3.[62]

None of these things were done, however, and this unevenly prepared attack was scheduled to proceed. Part of Posey's brigade was in line on Seminary Ridge, and the rest was on skirmish duty in the valley. The Mississippians strengthened their earthworks, made of fence rails with dirt piled on them, in the middle of the open ground between the lines

THE ATTACKERS

when word reached them at 10:00 A.M. to prepare for a massive artillery barrage. They ruefully noted that they were just as close to the Federals as to the Confederates and might receive fire from both sides. Few of Posey's men were sanguine about the attack. They "felt that to advance on them double our numbers strongly fortified & their cannons in position to get a fair unobstructed range of us while advancing a mile was a desperate undertaking[,] almost a forlorn hope," wrote Harry Lewis of the 16th Mississippi. So they crouched low and waited for the show to begin.[63]

· · · · · · ·

THE ARTILLERY

The placement of the guns had been an ongoing process since the early morning hours. Decisions were made mainly by individual battalion commanders, who normally put their guns in front of the division to which they were assigned. Corps artillery chiefs often adjusted this placement to ensure that the best available ground was utilized. Lee's army was enjoying the fruits of an important reorganization of this supporting arm, enabling the artillery to be managed at peak efficiency. Lee had stopped allocating batteries to brigades in February 1863 and instead had begun to consolidate them into battalions, usually of four batteries each. One battalion was assigned to each division. This enabled one officer to manage the operations of roughly sixteen cannons in battle, stretching across a division front of several hundred yards. An artillery chief was appointed for each corps with control of three battalions, nearly fifty guns, plus a corps reserve. Since there was no army reserve, the army chief of artillery had no opportunity to manage guns on the battlefield. Pendleton became little more than an administrative liaison between Lee and the corps chiefs. That was well, for Pendleton was not up to the task of managing such an important force.[64]

There were more guns in front of Pickett's division than before Pettigrew's command, but that was due to the availability of better ground before the Virginians. Alexander managed to accumulate seventeen batteries, 67 guns, between the Sherfy peach orchard and the northeastern corner of Spangler's Woods. He kept 12 pieces in reserve and placed the remaining 55 on line. In contrast there were eight batteries, 32 guns, in front of Pettigrew. These 87 cannon would carry the brunt of the artillery preparation that afternoon. They were supported by the fire of 48 additional pieces to Pickett's right and Pettigrew's left, making a total of 135 Confederate guns in action. It was the largest concentration of Rebel artillery on any Civil War battlefield.[65]

Lee paid as much attention to the artillery as he did to the infantry, and he often visited the guns throughout the morning. Once, while stopping with Maj. William T. Poague's battalion of Hill's corps, he saw an artillery officer riding some seventy-five yards in front of the guns, right to left, and called to him, "My friend! this way if you please." Poague soon realized it was James Dearing. The army leader offered a gentle rebuke. "Ah! Major, excuse me; I thought you might be some countryman who had missed his way. Let me say to you and to these young officers, that I am an old reconnoitering officer and have always found it best to go afoot, *and not expose oneself needlessly*." Dearing took the lesson well; he felt embarrassed and rode between the guns to the rear.[66]

The mood of the artillerymen seems to have been as optimistic as that of Pickett's men. W. Greene Raoul, who served in a Louisiana battery of Benjamin F. Eshleman's battalion, went north after Chancellorsville with great confidence. "We had whipped them & why not do it in Penn.," he wrote his father. The long waiting on the morning of July 3 irritated Raoul. "There we lay all day doing nothing, looking at the yankees upon the hills entrenching themselves. Why they were allowed to do this I cannot see. It struck me that we might commence the attack early in the morning But we did nothing."[67]

• • • • • • •

THE TERRAIN

One of the most memorable images of Pickett's Charge in the minds of Civil War enthusiasts is of the open, slightly ascending slope on which it took place. The idea of massed ranks moving over such terrain under a hail of artillery projectiles and into the face of concentrated musketry amazes and inspires most readers. Therefore a detailed examination of the ground is needed both to particularize this general, vague perception of the landscape and to illuminate the experience of marching across it under fire.

The geologic forces that shaped the battlefield placed Gettysburg in the middle of a large wedge of the earth's crust, stretching from northern New Jersey through Pennsylvania and into central Maryland, that had subsided many feet below the level of the surrounding terrain. This occurred as a result of tension that developed as the North American plate split from Africa 180 million years ago. Streams gradually eroded sediments into this depressed wedge, leaving a great deal of flinty shale and brittle sandstone on the surface. Magma also came up from the earth's core and intruded thick channels of solidified igneous rock through the layers of shale and sandstone. The most famous features of the battlefield were formed by this once-molten rock. It reached the surface in two forms. Sills are large columns of diabase and basalt that flowed toward the surface in joints between layers of sediment. Once exposed, the ends of these columns are weathered into rounded ridges. Cemetery Ridge was formed in this way, as was the ground on which the rest of the Federal line was placed, the two Round Tops, Cemetery Hill, and Culp's Hill. Dikes are branches of sills, smaller in size, but they also reach toward the surface by seeping upward along the joints of sedimentary layers. Seminary Ridge was formed in this way, which explains why it is less well formed and smaller than Cemetery Ridge. Thousands of years of erosion had watered and softened this hard, rocky landscape into the bucolic terrain of 1863.

The Confederates had to march across this terrain for a considerable distance. Kemper's right flank was 1,290 yards from the Union line, and Brockenbrough's left flank was almost exactly the same distance. Thus the Confederates had to advance about three-quarters of a mile. The two divisions had a front of one and a half miles, but that includes the gap between them. There would be a lot of compression, oblique marching, and dropping of one brigade on the way, so that the attackers would actually hit a section of the Union line that was only 538 yards long. This was only 20 percent of the length of the original Confederate line.

There is a slight difference in elevation between the opposing positions. Pickett's starting point is about 36 feet lower than the Union line. In fact, all of Cemetery Ridge is slightly higher, on average, than Seminary Ridge. The highest point on Cemetery Ridge is Cemetery Hill, at about 620 feet above sea level. The ridge slopes down as it heads south, averaging between 560 and 600 feet, and becomes very shallow just before reaching Little Round Top, which is 650 feet, and Big Round top, 785 feet. Seminary Ridge has no corresponding peaks at either end and rarely is higher than 560 feet. Moreover, its eastern slope is irregular and very gentle, hardly more than a lip rather than a slope. The western side of Seminary Ridge is a bit more sharply defined and thus was a convenient but not entirely safe place for the infantrymen to find shelter during the bombardment.

The land between the two ridges was described by a Tennesseean as "a little undulating, but nowhere sufficiently abrupt to afford the slightest shelter." That was true in front of Fry's brigade, but the land was more than a little undulating in front of Pickett's division. Its elevation is about 500 feet at its lowest, resulting in a dip about 60 feet deep on average. In open, rolling terrain, this is neither difficult for troops to negotiate nor advantageous in any way to them.

The terrain between the opposing lines is conveniently divided between north and south by a narrow and straight rise of ground. Stretching from the northern edge of Spangler's Woods due east toward the Union line and ending roughly at the famous angle in the stone fence, this narrow and level line of ground naturally separates Pickett's from Pettigrew's areas of operation. A fence ran along this line in 1863, further separating the two divisions.

To the south, in Pickett's front, the ground drains generally to the south, but the runoff takes many directions because the land is uneven. Pickett's men were behind the ridge at a spot where it juts a bit farther toward the Federals than normal, and thus the drain of rainwater angles off toward the southwest, toward Marsh Creek. Emmitsburg Road also angles toward the southwest in front of Pickett's area. It passes over the highest point of land on the southern half of the attack zone at the Sherfy peach orchard. The road constituted a ready line of demarcation, for it was within the effective range of small arms fire for the Union infantry. The road was a well-made pike that cut a couple of feet into the undulating land that it traversed, with ditches and stout fences on both sides. Apparently the fence on the west side of the road was made of posts and rails, with the ends of the rails firmly fixed in holes drilled in the posts. It was the strongest and highest fence commonly used in nineteenth-century America. The fence that bordered the east side of the road, the Union side, apparently was a "slab fence." It consisted of planks or flat boards, rather than rails, affixed to posts.

The effect of these fences along Emmitsburg Road has been exaggerated. They were intact and offered an imposing obstacle in front of Pettigrew's division, but most of them had already been dismantled in front of Pickett's division by the swirling fight that took place there the day before. Many defending Union soldiers tore down sections of the fence

THE ATTACKERS

to build breastworks, and advancing Confederate units often broke down other sections while crossing them in their advance. Many accounts by survivors of Pickett's command do not even mention the fences, testifying to their limited impact on the attacking lines.

Between Emmitsburg Road and the Union line lay the valley of Plum Run, which forced the water to drain southeastward and then south from the eastern slope of Seminary Ridge. The valley began immediately at the level land that ran west to east, separating the two divisions, and thus bordered the entire length of the Union line in Pickett's front. Two shallow swales straddled the Codori farmstead, draining toward the southeast and standing in the way of the Confederate advance toward the angle in the stone fence. Emmitsburg Road also angled across these swales. South of Codori's the valley quickly widened into a large, shallow feature with a line of trees along the small stream that also takes shape here. Wilcox and Lang found this wide valley directly in their front; they had already attacked across it the day before. Plum Run Valley was truly a valley of death; Union artillery placed on Little Round Top could easily fire up its shallow groove as if it were a bowling alley, and Federal infantry could easily counterattack into it. The valley seemed like a wide stage to anyone standing in the Union line near the angle in the stone fence.[68]

Thus Pickett had to contend with a rather rough battlefield; his men first had to climb the western slope of Seminary Ridge to gain their first decent view of the land before them. Then they had to cross Emmitsburg Road and deal with the valley of Plum Run. All the way they would be subject to Union artillery fire, and their commanders would have to decide whether to go straight ahead or angle to the high ground at the angle of the stone fence. They also had to connect with Pettigrew's right flank in transit so the gap between the two divisions could be closed before making contact. Only a division that was fresh and commanded by officers who had been in their positions for a long time, and thus knew their men and were used to exercising command, could accomplish these difficult tasks.

The ground in front of Pettigrew's division was much less complex but also more dangerous to the attacker. The land north of the line of level ground that ran from Spangler's Woods toward the angle formed a wide, shallow swale, the beginning of Stevens's Run. The lowest point in this swale was about fifty feet lower than the top of Cemetery Ridge and about forty feet lower than Seminary Ridge. Stevens's Run ran northward toward town. The swale was almost completely open; troops in the bottom

The "natural glacis" immediately in front of Hays's position, one of several terrain advantages enjoyed by the Federals confronting Pettigrew's division (author's collection)

of it could not easily be seen from the Union position, but that advantage was only temporary. The only man-made feature in this landscape was the William Bliss farm, located just on the Confederate side of the bottom of the swale. A large barn and a farmhouse stood here, and a ten-acre orchard 600 yards from north to south lay just west of the barn. The Bliss farm stood out like a sore thumb between the lines, and thus it became the focus of intense skirmishing on July 2 and the morning of July 3, changing hands several times.

Pettigrew's men would come within the range of small arms fire when they reached Emmitsburg Road. Here the fences were still intact, for the supporting brigade of Posey had failed to cross the road in its disjointed advance the evening before. These fences had a dramatic and catastrophic effect on Pettigrew's attack, far more serious than was the case with Pickett. Pettigrew's staff officer Louis G. Young later wrote that there were a number of other, smaller, fences that crisscrossed the landscape fronting the division — detailed maps of the battlefield indicate their location — but neither he nor any other survivor who mentioned these fences offered any details as to their effect on the advance. Everyone in the division, however, remembered and often vividly described the two fences along the road.

THE ATTACKERS

Moreover, even when they were across the pike, Pettigrew's men had more difficult ground to deal with than did Pickett's. The angle in the stone fence meant that when the Union line continued northward, it would be about eighty feet farther west than the line that fronted Pickett. In fact, this was the highest point of ground along the Federal line that was targeted by the assault; it was about four to six feet higher than the gently sloping land in front of the Virginia division. The shape of the last few yards in front of this Union position north of the angle formed what Young termed "a natural glacis." In short, it naturally sloped at a steeper angle, forcing the attacker to literally walk up and directly into the muzzles of the defending infantrymen. This was a slope that military engineers tried to create in front of fortifications so the attackers would not be able to lie down and take shelter a few yards from the works. The terrain offered several major obstacles to the advance of the Confederate left wing.[69]

CHAPTER 3
THE DEFENDERS

. . . .

Like the Army of Northern Virginia, Meade's Army of the Potomac had reached a new level of experience and ability by the summer of 1863. It was in many ways a magnificent force filled with men hardened by repeated defeats but by no means bowed in spirit. Not even the humiliating disaster at Chancellorsville could break the troops. Frank Haskell assured the folks at home that "the army, the men, and subordinate officers are all right. There never was a better army in the world than this is now, in fine spirits and condition. — The army is capable of doing any thing that reason or duty would require."[1]

Many of the units that were in the path of the coming Rebel attack had long histories stretching back to early 1862, while some were relatively new and untried in battle. Most of them also were greatly reduced in size, for the Federal government had not developed an efficient system of replenishing its field armies with new recruits. The preference for raising entirely new regiments in the summer of 1862 increased the number of units in the Union army but did not increase the size of the old regiments. As a result there were only 5,750 men on the section of the Union line that was to be hit by the Confederate attack. The one brigade there that had never seen combat before Gettysburg was nearly as large as the divisions.[2]

The Second Corps was primarily responsible for the center of the Union line along Cemetery Ridge. It had a sterling history dating back to the Peninsula campaign and was led by one of the most impressive subordinate generals in the Federal army, Maj. Gen. Winfield Scott Hancock. Hancock was born in Pennsylvania near Norristown. He fought in Mexico and served in Kansas and Utah after he graduated from West Point.

Hancock held a commission in the 6th U.S. Infantry with Armistead, Garnett, and Pickett. He and his wife, Almira, hosted the famous farewell party at their home in Los Angeles when the tight circle of friends and acquaintances broke up for the war. Albert Sydney Johnston's wife sang sentimental songs such as "Mary of Argyle" and "Kathleen Mavourneen," and everyone felt deeply the bittersweet nature of this final parting. Armistead was overcome with emotion. He told Hancock, "You can never know what this has cost me, and I hope God will strike me dead if I am ever induced to leave my native soil, should worse come to worst." As parting gifts the Virginian gave Hancock his new uniform as a major of the U.S. Army and presented his prayer book to Almira. It was inscribed with the words, "Trust in God and fear nothing."

Hancock rose quickly during the first half of the war. He commanded a brigade in the Peninsula campaign, and at the battle of Williamsburg he won the sobriquet "Hancock the Superb," given him by Maj. Gen. George B. McClellan for his magnificent performance on that field. He led a division of the Second Corps at Antietam and took over when Maj. Gen. Israel B. Richardson was mortally wounded while attacking the Bloody Lane; he won promotion to major general in November 1862. His men valiantly assaulted the stone wall at Fredericksburg and were engaged in the battle of Chancellorsville. When Maj. Gen. Darius N. Couch gave up command of the corps in utter disgust at the way Maj. Gen. Joseph Hooker had commanded at Chancellorsville, Hancock took his place.

His star rose so fast that Hancock was even considered for the army command. "Give yourself no uneasiness," he assured Almira, "under no conditions would I accept the command. I do not belong to that class of generals whom the Republicans care to bolster up. I should be sacrificed." Almira understood his feelings in this regard. She later wrote that Hancock's "only ambition, was to fight his battles successfully, that he might gain the full confidence of his soldiers, and receive the approbation of the army in which he was serving. That was glory enough." The new army leader, George G. Meade, relied heavily on him at Gettysburg. When Maj. Gen. Daniel Sickles was wounded early in the July 2 attack on the Union left, Meade asked Hancock to take charge of his Third Corps while John Gibbon took over the Second.[3]

Gibbon was as solid and reliable a division leader as any commander could want. Born in Philadelphia, he grew up in Charlotte, North Caro-

Maj. Gen. Winfield Scott Hancock, whose Second Corps was primarily responsible for stopping the Confederate charge. He was wounded in the attack. (Massachusetts Commandery, Military Order of the Loyal Legion and the U.S. Army Military History Institute, USAMHI)

lina, and graduated from West Point to fight in Mexico. Gibbon spent many years after that as an artillery instructor and quartermaster at West Point. Three of his brothers served in the Confederate army, and his wife was from Baltimore, a notoriously Southern city; yet the captain of artillery decided to fight for the Union. He became a brigadier general in May 1862 and later that year led a unit of western regiments in the Army of the Potomac that earned the right to be called the Iron Brigade because of its stubborn performance in the Second Manassas campaign. Gibbon led it at South Mountain and Antietam as well. He was given command of a division in the First Corps in November and was wounded in the hand and wrist by a shell burst at Fredericksburg. Upon his return to duty in March, he was given charge of the Second Division of the Second Corps.

When the officers of the army were gathered for their late-night conference on July 2, it was to Gibbon that Meade made his prediction about Lee attacking the Union center. Gibbon respected his army leader and was solicitous of his health. On the morning of July 3, after he and Haskell had been rudely awakened by the sound of skirmishing, Gibbon asked Meade to lunch with him. His orderly had found "an old and tough rooster" that was already boiling over the campfire. At first the army commander complained that he had too much to do, but Gibbon cajoled him into eating, for "he *must* keep up his physical strength." It was a pleasant meal, as Hancock and Maj. Gen. John Newton, commander of the First Corps, and Maj. Gen. Alfred Pleasanton, commander of the army's cavalry, came by to share the rooster. A mess chest served as a table, and Hancock and Gibbon sat on stools while Meade rested on a cracker box. The other dignitaries sat on the ground. There was much kidding as Newton chided Gibbon about "putting on airs" now that he was temporary commander of the Second Corps. Just how temporary the honor turned out to be was emphasized when Meade told Hancock to resume his old command, as Maj. Gen. David B. Birney was now to lead the Third Corps. Gibbon had to revert to command of the Second Division. Meade also suggested it would be better to return the provost guard to the ranks. Gibbon issued the proper orders, but one of his three brigades, Brig. Gen. Alexander S. Webb's, somehow failed to get the message and kept its provost line intact. The provost detachment stopped stragglers from retreating to the rear, but the shrunken ranks of the Second Corps demanded all available guns on the battle line. Meade immediately rode off after eating, but the rest of the officers remained behind to smoke cigars and loll under the noon sun.[4]

. . . .
GIBBON'S DIVISION

Gibbon's division had only 2,150 men, but it held most of the ground that Pickett's 5,830 men would try to take. Webb's Second Brigade was positioned at the eye of the storm, where the stone fence made its famous angle toward the west. The brigade had a long history, having been formed in Philadelphia during the summer of 1861 by Sen. Edward D. Baker of Oregon. A political crony of Lincoln, Baker had also been a San Francisco lawyer and thus called one of his units, the 71st Pennsylvania, the 1st California Regiment. The brigade also was known for a short time as the California Brigade, but it later became more famous as the Philadelphia Brigade. The 72nd Pennsylvania, known as Baxter's Fire Zouaves because it was recruited from among the city's fire companies, retained its colorful uniforms even through the battle of Gettysburg. The 69th Pennsylvania was a thoroughly Irish unit led by Col. Joshua T. Owen, a native of Wales, while the 106th Pennsylvania was known as the 5th California Regiment.

Baker led the brigade for only a short time. He became involved in the disastrous battle of Ball's Bluff on October 21, 1861, when the brigade was pushed across the Potomac River at Harrison's Island to capture Leesburg on the Virginia side. The operation was poorly planned and executed. The Federals were promptly attacked by waiting Confederate troops who shattered their formations and forced a precipitate retreat down the seventy-foot, nearly vertical river bluff. Baker was killed, and 921 of his men were lost, with 700 of those men captured. His division leader, Brig. Gen. Charles P. Stone, was arrested and tried as a scapegoat for the fiasco, a trial that directly led to the creation of the Joint Congressional Committee on the Conduct of the War. The brigade was then commanded by Owen, and it participated in the battles of Fair Oaks, the Seven Days, Antietam, Fredericksburg, and Chancellorsville.[5]

Owen allowed the readiness of the brigade to deteriorate. A lax disciplinarian, he was arrested by Gibbon at Thoroughfare Gap on the night of May 12, 1863, for allowing civilians to cross his picket line. Webb was now called on to rejuvenate the brigade. Born in New York City and a graduate of the West Point class of 1855, Webb had served against the

THE DEFENDERS

Brig. Gen. John Gibbon, whose division held the line from the angle in the stone fence to the left. He was wounded in the attack. (Massachusetts Commandery, Military Order of the Loyal Legion and the U.S. Army Military History Institute, USAMHI)

Seminoles in Florida the following year but later became a mathematics instructor at West Point. He spent the first half of the war as a staff officer, as assistant to the chief of artillery of the Army of the Potomac and as chief of staff for the Fifth Corps commander during the Maryland campaign. He received his promotion to brigadier general of volunteers on June 23, 1863, and took command of the Philadelphia Brigade five days later, only five days before Pickett's Charge.

"Webb has taken hold of his Brig. with a will," Gibbon informed his wife; he "comes down on them with a heavy hand and will no doubt soon make a great improvement." The twenty-eight-year-old, newly minted brigadier desperately wanted to fulfill Gibbon's expectations. He tried to crack down on discipline but met a lot of resistance. Owen had been quite popular, and the hardened veterans considered the youthful Webb a good joke. He tried to force them to cross the Monocacy River on the way to Gettysburg without removing their shoes. Webb waded boldly into the water to set an example but was chagrined when he found that his tall boots protected his feet even in the deepest part of the ford. This brought howls of laughter. Webb cracked down on officers who deliberately avoided wearing their insignia of rank, so as not to be too conspicuous in battle, telling them sarcastically that he needed to know they were officers when he saw them. Webb also threatened to shoot any stragglers on the line of march to Gettysburg. He did get a thirty-five-mile march in fourteen hours out of his brigade, but the men refused to like or respect him. "Many thought him untempered and fresh," thought a captain in the 71st Pennsylvania.[6]

The brigade was placed from the angle in the stone fence southward on July 2 and played a role in repelling the fierce Confederate attack that evening. Three Confederate brigades of Anderson's division hit the Federal center. Wilcox and Lang attacked Humphreys's division of the Third Corps, shattered it, and advanced to Plum Run. A few minutes later Wright's brigade crossed Emmitsburg Road, scattered some units of the Second Corps arrayed along its east side, and drove for a point just south of the angle on Cemetery Ridge. Gibbon's division had been forced to detach many regiments to help Humphreys, and now it had to repel Wright's frontal attack. Webb primarily was responsible for helping Col. Norman J. Hall's brigade to his left repulse the Confederates. Wright's Georgians struck Hall's front and extended south, where a gap had been created due to the dispatch of troops to help Humphreys. When Wright's line surged up the slope of the ridge, Webb directed the fire of the 69th Pennsylvania to the left oblique and moved the 71st and 106th Pennsylvania to his left to hit the Confederate flank. The latter regiment followed up the Confederate repulse by advancing across the stone fence all the way to Emmitsburg Road, recovering three captured guns of Lt. T. Fred Brown's Battery B, 1st Rhode Island Light Artillery, that had been abandoned by the Rebels. Another of Brown's guns left just in front of the stone fence was recovered by an advance of the 71st Pennsylvania.[7]

That was not all that Webb's men did that evening. A request soon arrived from Hancock to send two regiments to the right, where the Eleventh and Twelfth Corps were desperately holding Cemetery Hill and Culp's Hill. Webb sent the 106th Pennsylvania to the Eleventh Corps minus Companies A and B, which had been sent out on the skirmish line that morning. The remaining eight companies reported to Maj. Gen. Oliver O. Howard but arrived too late to help in the repulse of the Rebel attack on Cemetery Hill, yet Howard kept them for the rest of the battle. Companies A and B, under Capt. James C. Lynch, were later relieved from skirmish duty. When Lynch asked Webb if he should rejoin his regiment on the hill, the brigade leader told him to stay put. Thus were the two companies available to help repulse Pickett the next day.[8]

The 71st Pennsylvania fared much worse when Webb sent it to the Twelfth Corps at Culp's Hill. Col. R. Penn Smith reported to Capt.

THE DEFENDERS

Charles P. Horton, on the staff of Brig. Gen. George S. Greene, whose brigade was bearing the brunt of the Rebel assault. Horton placed it to the right of the 137th New York, at the extreme right of the Twelfth Corps line, and was exasperated by Smith's slowness in taking position. Even so, the Pennsylvanians gave three loud cheers as they entered the earthworks that Greene's men had dug earlier. Smith petulantly complained about the assignment. He later wrote that his men labored under "many disadvantages," and he regretted trusting Horton when the staff officer told him that his right flank would be protected. Soon after arriving in the works, Smith's command was hit by Brig. Gen. George H. Steuart's Confederate brigade. Steuart overlapped Smith's right, and soon the California Regiment was assailed by fierce fire to the front, flank, and rear. "D—n them they had me flanked," Smith related, "it *was not* my fault." He directed his men to retreat without orders from above. Horton was astonished to see the Pennsylvanians stand up and walk to the rear. When he confronted Smith, the colonel told him he "would not have his men murdered." Smith then lied and said he had orders to return to his own corps. Horton's pleadings could not dissuade him. Horton believed Smith's men seemed "plucky enough" to fight and were "much mortified at the conduct of the Colonel." But the retreat continued all the way back to the angle in the stone wall, where Smith reported to Webb about midnight. He had lost about fourteen men in this brief effort. His withdrawal forced the 137th New York to retreat a short distance to a stronger position, where it held, saving the right wing of the Twelfth Corps. Smith's actions were deplorable, for they threatened the collapse of the whole Union position on Culp's Hill. He admitted retiring without orders in his report, but he also pointed out that his decision was "upheld by my Brigade, Division and Corps commanders."[9]

Webb positioned his men as best he could to hold the angle area on the morning of July 3. The 69th Pennsylvania was the only regiment that remained in its initial position along the stone fence with its right flank 155 feet south of the angle. This gap was left to provide a channel of fire for Lt. Alonzo Cushing's Battery A, 4th U.S. Artillery. The guns were placed up the slope about eighty feet from the fence. The 69th itself occupied a linear space of 250 feet along the fence. Another gap existed to the left of the 69th to provide a channel of fire for the guns of Brown's Battery B, 1st Rhode Island Light Artillery.

The rest of Webb's infantry were strung out in a secondary line to the rear. Smith's 71st Pennsylvania was to the right of Cushing's guns. The

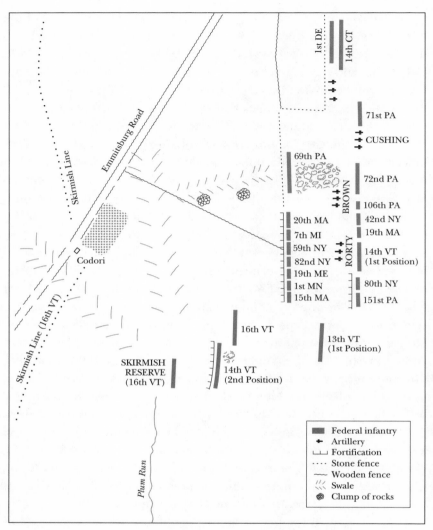

Map 3.1 Gibbon and the First Corps, Morning, July 3, 1863

72nd Pennsylvania was positioned to the left of Cushing and in line with the 71st, but separated from it by a regimental front, and to the rear of Brown's battery. A copse of trees, one of the more prominent features on this part of the ridge, was in front of the 72nd, while the left wing of the 69th Pennsylvania was on the opposite side of the copse. Companies A and B of the 106th Pennsylvania were to the left of the 72nd. The trees in the copse were small, hardly two inches wide, and offered little protection. Also, the area covered by the copse was larger in 1863 than it is

THE DEFENDERS

today, extending nearly to the stone fence behind the left wing of the 69th. No entrenching was done by Webb's command because there were no tools available, and the rocky nature of the ground and its thin soil were not favorable for digging.[10]

Norman J. Hall's Third Brigade was located to Webb's left. Hall was an up-and-coming commander who was born in New York but entered West Point from Michigan. He graduated in 1859 and was present when Fort Sumter was fired on. He served on McClellan's staff during the Peninsula campaign before receiving a commission as colonel of the 7th Michigan in July 1862. Hall was wounded at Antietam and led the Third Brigade at Fredericksburg and Chancellorsville. It consisted of essentially the same regiments from the Seven Days to Gettysburg, where the twenty-six-year-old colonel was to have his best day of the war.

The brigade was divided and pressed hard during the July 2 assault, but it played a leading role in repulsing the Confederate attack. The 19th Massachusetts and 42nd New York were detached to help Humphreys's division, but the rest of the brigade remained in place behind the stone fence. Wright's Georgia brigade hit Hall's front and passed by his left, into the gap left by the transfer of Brig. Gen William Harrow's brigade to help the Third Corps. Wright's leftmost regiment, the 48th Georgia, hit the 59th New York and 7th Michigan frontally while the 3rd and 22nd Georgia knifed into the quarter-mile-wide gap to Hall's left. This gap, about 250 yards south of the copse, allowed the Georgians to climb almost to the crest of Cemetery Ridge before their momentum slowed and Union reinforcements appeared in their front. Many of these men went farther up the ridge than did Pickett's Virginians the next day. Hall's men held firm and blunted the charging Rebels in their front and then turned their fire onto the flank of Wright's right wing in the gap as well. If Wright had been supported to his left by a vigorous advance of Posey's Mississippi brigade, his assault might have fractured the Union center, but Posey failed to advance his men in concert and blamed Mahone's complete lack of forward movement for his failure to approach the Union position. The Federal center held.

Before Wright struck, Hall had sent the 19th Massachusetts and 42nd New York to help the Third Corps, responding to a request by Humphreys himself. The two units were put under the charge of Col. Arthur F. Devereux of the Massachusetts regiment. Devereux had little idea what he was to do; the aide who led his two regiments to the left was poorly informed and could not enlighten him. The Massachusetts colonel was

Col. Norman J. Hall, whose brigade rushed to the right to help seal the breach at the angle (Massachusetts Commandery, Military Order of the Loyal Legion and the U.S. Army Military History Institute, USAMHI)

only told to help Humphreys, which was an absurd notion given that the division was retreating in disorder. He decided to wait until Humphreys's men had passed and then retire fighting. Maj. Edmund Rice of the 19th led the skirmish line as it covered the withdrawal of the two units in the face of Wilcox's and Lang's advance to Plum Run.

When the brigade reassembled on the night of July 2, Hall maintained his position along the stone fence. But the ground here was a bit more suitable for digging, so his men constructed a shallow trench with the one shovel that was available. No one on high ordered this; it was a project initiated by the rank and file. This trench was about 200 yards long, and it connected the stone fence, which petered out just to the left of the 69th Pennsylvania, with a wooden fence to the south. The result was pitiful from the standpoint of military engineering; it was no more than "a large cart rut," in the words of one officer, barely a foot deep. The men obtained some fence rails and lined them in front of the trench, throwing dirt onto them to form a parapet. To get more dirt they scooped out a shallow ditch in front of the parapet, making it a foot tall. The earthwork seemed puny, but it would be a major help in sheltering the men on July 3.[11]

That languid morning was hot enough to inspire the men of Hall's brigade to stretch their shelter tents across sticks or bayonets stuck into the ground to create some shade. It was done so quickly that one veteran was surprised by the "sudden transformation. . . . The green hills all at once became white." The 20th Massachusetts suffered a poignant loss that morning when Capt. Henry Ropes, a beloved officer, was killed by "a bad shell of one of our own batteries in our rear." This occurred about 9:00 A.M., long before the Rebel bombardment preceding Pickett's Charge.[12]

Hall's units were also placed in two lines with artillery intermixed. The 20th Massachusetts was on his right with a gap for Brown's fire between its right and the left flank of Webb's brigade. Then the 7th Michigan was next to the left, followed by the 59th New York. Devereux had brought the 19th Massachusetts and the 42nd New York back to Hall well after dark on the evening of July 2 only to find that their former place had been taken by the right wing of Harrow's brigade. So Devereux asked Hancock's permission to place them to Hall's rear. Col. James E. Mallon's 42nd New York was on the right, about fifty yards to the rear of the 20th Massachusetts, and Devereux's 19th Massachusetts was to its left. The second line had no earthworks.[13]

Gibbon's last unit, William Harrow's First Brigade, held the left of the division line. Harrow was born in Kentucky but grew to adulthood in Illinois, where he was acquainted with Lincoln through his work as a circuit lawyer. He moved to Indiana in 1859 and there became colonel of the 14th Indiana, which saw service in the western Virginia campaigns. The 14th saw its first major battle at Antietam as part of the Second Corps. Harrow was off duty with bronchitis and neuralgia during the winter but received a promotion to brigadier general of volunteers in April 1863; he was leading a brigade for the first time at Gettysburg. The First Brigade had existed since the Peninsula campaign, although about half of its units had been transferred to other commands and new ones had been added by the summer of 1863.[14]

All four of Harrow's regiments were detached and sent to various parts of the field on the evening of July 2. The brigade played a large role in repulsing that attack, but Harrow did not exercise any direction over his command; it was split up and dispersed, creating that infamous gap in the line through which part of Wright's brigade drove up the slope of Cemetery Ridge. The 15th Massachusetts and 82nd New York went forward to Emmitsburg Road before the Rebel attack. There they extended Humphreys's division line along the road and tried to support his right flank. Both units were north of the Codori farm with the 15th on the right. Harrow accompanied the two regiments as they took position. He was a newcomer to the brigade and wanted to impress everyone, so he harangued the men with a bit of histrionics. Drawing his pistol, Harrow said, "The first God Damned man I see running or sneaking, I blow him to Hell in an instant. This God Damned runing is played out, just stand to it and give them Hell." Roland E. Bowen liked this show: "And he called upon all of us by all that was Good & Infernal to kill every son-of-a-bitch that runs without a cause. Said he, if you see me runing I want you to kill me on the spot." The men of the 15th Massachusetts responded well, remembered Bowen: "One says bully for Harrow, another says, he is tight, and a third remarked that he was just the man to lead us. All three of wich I pronounced as correct."

When the Confederate attack was imminent, orders went out for the men of these two regiments to dismantle the fences along Emmitsburg Road. The rails would make good breastworks, and the Federals worked feverishly; but the post-and-rail fence required a lot of labor. The fortifications availed the Federals nothing, for when Wright attacked their front, he did so with irresistible force. The 82nd New York gave way quickly without setting fire to the Codori buildings, as they had been instructed to do. The 15th Massachusetts resisted with a few minutes of frenzied firing, but then it too fell back. "At this point every thing seemed to be in an utter state of confusion," Roland Bowen related. "I won't say that our officers ran away and left, but I *will* say that I could not see any of them." The two regiments had little chance of stopping Wright's brigade in their exposed position and fled to the main line, but they remained intact and suffered moderate casualties.[15]

A few minutes earlier, Hancock had sent another of Harrow's regiments, Col. Francis Heath's 19th Maine, to a forward point just south of the Codori farm to support Lt. Gulian V. Weir's Battery C, 5th U.S. Artillery. The guns were able to fire obliquely at Wilcox and Lang but were in an exposed position. Hancock personally led the regiment forward. When it deployed into line, the corps leader jumped off his horse and excitedly grabbed the nearest man, Pvt. George T. Durgin, pulled him a couple of steps farther forward, and yelled, "Will you stay here?" The surprised Durgin mustered enough courage to reply, "I'll stay here, General, until h—ll freezes over." Hancock, who staged this encounter to inspire the men, told the regimental color guard to align itself with Durgin, then rode away.

Heath had to deal with another general as Humphreys's division retreated in disorder. The 19th Maine was lying on the ground when Humphreys rode up and demanded that it rise, fix bayonets, and stop his men

Brig. Gen. William Harrow, whose brigade also helped seal the breach at the angle and who succeeded Gibbon in temporary command of the division (Massachusetts Commandery, Military Order of the Loyal Legion and the U.S. Army Military History Institute, USAMHI)

from running. Heath protested that the fugitives would break his formation and might cause his regiment to join the stampede. Humphreys refused to listen to reason. He rode along the regimental line ordering the men to stand up. Heath ran behind him countermanding the order. The men listened to their colonel as Humphreys rode off to find some other expedient to stem his division's retreat. The fight did not go well for the Federals. Weir became disoriented when his horse was shot from under him and he was hit by a spent ball; in the frenzied retreat three of his guns were left behind to be taken by Lang's brigade. Heath's 19th Maine held for several minutes in the face of Lang's strong advance but then retreated when the Floridians overlapped both of its flanks. The regiment had done all it could in blunting the Rebel onslaught and retreated without breaking up.[16]

The most famous contribution of Harrow's brigade to the fight of July 2 was made by the 1st Minnesota. Eight companies of the regiment were supporting a battery on Cemetery Ridge when the attack began. Hancock saw them as he rode along the line to the left following his placement of the 19th Maine, and he impulsively ordered the Minnesotans to attack Wilcox's Alabama brigade, which was nearing the bottom of Plum Run Valley. Col. William Colvill Jr. led his 262 men forward at the double-quick. They advanced 150 yards and leveled their bayonets for the last few yards of that distance. Colvill's men reached the bottom of Plum Run Valley just before Wilcox's men; here they stopped and traded fire with the Alabamans at point-blank range. The contest was extremely severe for many minutes until Wilcox retired a few yards. He was unwilling to press forward because Barksdale's brigade to his right and Lang's brigade to his left had fallen away from his flanks. The 1st Minnesota retired, but it had only forty-seven men left. In fifteen minutes of intense fighting, it had lost 82 percent of its manpower. It was the highest loss rate of any Union regiment in a single battle of the war. Colvill's regiment had stopped Wilcox's brigade and helped to save the Union center, but it is quite likely that Wilcox would not have advanced beyond the center of Plum Run Valley anyway because of the absence of flank support.[17]

Harrow was able to reconcentrate what was left of his brigade that night and reassumed his place in line to the left of Hall's command. The 1st Minnesota received its two detached companies, reinfusing much needed manpower into its depleted ranks. Company F had been on skirmish duty, and its men felt "almost stunned" when they heard about the awful casualties suffered in the attack. Company C had been on provost duty with Gibbon's division headquarters and was sent back to the regiment as a result of Meade's lunchtime order to Gibbon on July 3.

The morning of Pickett's Charge began with an order for the 19th Maine to send four companies on skirmish duty along Emmitsburg Road, but the men were exhausted and hungry. They had had no food or fresh water since the morning of July 2. "Our stomachs were getting to be a little shaky," admitted Silas Adams. Harrow aligned his brigade with the 82nd New York on the right, connecting with the left flank of Hall's brigade, then the 19th Maine, the 1st Minnesota, and the 15th Massachusetts. Capt. James McKay Rorty's Battery B, 1st New York Artillery, was placed to Harrow's right and up the ridge slope from the stone fence.[18]

· · · · · · ·

FIRST CORPS UNITS

While Gibbon's division of the Second Corps held the line to be most heavily assaulted by Pickett, elements of the First Corps to his left also played important roles in repulsing the attack. The First Corps had fought its heart out on July 1, losing heavily and shattering its organization but saving the day by mauling Hill's Third Corps. Arguably this had been the decisive fighting of the entire battle, for it kept the Confederates out of Gettysburg and away from Cemetery Ridge and the Round Tops long enough for the rest of Meade's army to come up that evening. There was still a lot of fight left in the First Corps. After Reynolds was killed early in the battle of July 1, Brig. Gen. Abner Doubleday capably led it for the rest of the day. But Meade did not trust Doubleday, whose abilities were limited, and named Maj. Gen. John Newton to command the corps on July 2. Newton was an experienced West Pointer who had led a brigade on the Peninsula and in the Maryland campaign. He later commanded a division of the Sixth Corps at Fredericksburg and Chancellorsville. Newton energetically reshuffled units to put his section of the line in order on the morning of July 3. His Third Division connected with the left of Gibbon's division, but Newton estimated that a gap of over a half-mile existed between his left and the Fifth Corps in the vicinity of the Round Tops. He found an unused division of the Second Corps, a brigade from the Sixth Corps, and additional batteries from the artillery reserve to fill the gap. Birney's Third Corps, resting behind the lines after its trouncing on July 2, provided reserve units. Newton felt quite confident that he had done all he could to strengthen the left center of Meade's line by noon.[19]

Doubleday's Third Division consisted of three brigades; one would play a prominent role in repulsing Pickett, and part of another would contribute to the defense of the center. The latter was the First Brigade, which had been mauled by Pettigrew's North Carolina Brigade on McPherson's Ridge on July 1. Two regiments from that brigade, the 80th New York (also known as the 20th New York State Militia) and the 151st Pennsylvania, had been detached from the brigade on July 2 to help the Second Corps repel Wright. The two regiments were put under the charge of Col. Theodore B. Gates of the 80th New York, but they arrived too late to take part in the repulse. With no further orders, Gates held his units near the copse of trees for the remainder of the battle.

The 80th New York had much experience, having served at Antietam, Fredericksburg, and Chancellorsville, but the 151st Pennsylvania had been organized only in November 1862 as a nine-month regiment. It participated in its first campaign at Chancellorsville but was not under fire. The regiment was severely tested on July 1. Known as the School Teacher's Regiment because more than a hundred of its men were public school educators, it was held in reserve on McPherson's Ridge until the Tar Heels were about to drive away the Iron Brigade. Then its commander, Lt. Col. George M. McFarland, led it in a counterattack against the 26th and 11th North Carolina. The teachers held long enough to give the Iron Brigade and their own brigade time to pull back to Seminary Ridge, then they retired. McFarland was shot in both legs (he later

Col. Theodore Burr Gates of the 80th New York, who led his own regiment and the 151st Pennsylvania in helping to stop Pickett (Massachusetts Commandery, Military Order of the Loyal Legion and the U.S. Army Military History Institute, USAMHI)

lost one to amputation), and his regiment suffered 72 percent casualties during this heroic stand.[20]

The men of Gates's demibrigade felt like orphans separated from their parent unit and seemingly forgotten by Doubleday. They were short of food as well, having had none issued since the morning of July 2. Capt. John D. S. Cook of the 80th New York was content to share a single hardtack with a corporal of his company on July 3. Gates positioned the two regiments — the 151st was led by a captain this day — behind the forward line and about 300 yards to the south of the copse of trees. His men dismantled a rail fence nearby and built a small breastwork for some protection. The 80th New York was on the right of this two-regiment formation.

Gates was in what Captain Cook called a "singular position," without orders from his own commander and ignored by the Second Corps troops to his right. Gates saw that a gap existed between his men, who numbered about 235, and the second-line troops of Gibbon's division. He sent an officer to ask them for support, but they refused; Gates blamed it on intercorps rivalry. He next sent the same officer to report his position to Doubleday, hoping to receive some orders. But the officer returned just

THE DEFENDERS

before the Confederate artillery bombardment with the message to stay put. Doubleday assured Gates "that he knew where we were."[21]

Gates was mixed in with the next First Corps unit to his left, Stannard's Vermont brigade, which was arrayed in an unorthodox formation. The 14th Vermont was to Gates's right, and the 13th Vermont lay to his left and front about twenty-five yards away. Later the 14th Vermont advanced to a breastwork farther to his left and front. There would be more shifting among the Vermont regiments before and during the bombardment, but Gates's little command remained inert until the Confederate infantry attacked.[22]

Stannard's Third Brigade of Doubleday's First Division had a unique history. Raised for nine-month service in response to Lincoln's call for more troops in August 1862, it was properly designated the Second Vermont Brigade and consisted of five regiments. Many of the men, such as artist and postwar frontier photographer William Henry Jackson, enlisted not only out of patriotic motives but also to avoid the coming state draft. They left Vermont in October armed with good Springfield rifle muskets and were sent to Washington to guard its defenses. The Vermonters spent the late fall, winter, and early spring at various posts outside the capital, drilling to perfection but hardly encountering a Rebel. Their commander, Brig. Gen. Edwin Stoughton, was captured by Col. John S. Mosby's Confederate partisans behind Union lines at Fairfax Court House in March 1863. It was a particularly embarrassing episode because Stoughton was taken while asleep for the night.

Brig. Gen. George J. Stannard replaced Stoughton on April 20. Born in Vermont, Stannard had been a schoolteacher, a foundry clerk, a businessman, and a militia officer before the war. He served as lieutenant colonel of the 2nd Vermont and saw service at First Manassas, on the Peninsula, and at Second Manassas. He was colonel of the 9th Vermont when that regiment and many others surrendered at Harpers Ferry to Stonewall Jackson in September 1862 as part of Lee's Maryland campaign. After his exchange Stannard received a commission as brigadier general in March 1863 and took over the Second Vermont Brigade.[23]

The Vermonters were ready to go home by the summer of 1863. Some of them had been mustered in during August 1862, and their nine months were up by late May. But the government could keep them in service until July 4 if the need arose, and the defeat at Chancellorsville and signs of a Rebel drive northward prompted the authorities to exercise that option. Josephus Jackson of the 12th Vermont was philosophical about it: "if we halve to stay untill July that will not bee a long time," but he felt "the days begin to gro longer as the time groes shorter."[24]

The brigade was hastily ordered to join the Army of the Potomac when Lee headed north. It started out from Union Mills, Virginia, on June 25 and began a seven-day, 130-mile march that would take it to Gettysburg. The men moved well until June 29, when fatigue and the circulation of a supply of whiskey caused a great deal of straggling. Stannard was disgusted with their attitude. "They count their time by days," he wrote. "Consequently they do not have any heart in the work. Officers as little as men." On July 1, as he neared Gettysburg, Stannard was instructed to detach two regiments to guard the corps wagon trains. The 12th and 15th were detailed. As a result the Second Vermont Brigade went onto the battlefield that day with three regiments instead of five. The 13th, 14th, and 16th arrived at the scene of action worn out. "Each boy's feet were very badly blistered; and all of us so tired we could hardly stand up," recalled Edwin F. Palmer. They numbered about 1,400 men.[25]

At least one regiment, Col. Francis V. Randall's 13th, took a stirring part in the fight of July 2. Doubleday responded to a plea from Hancock and sent this regiment to help the Second Corps. It arrived just after Weir's battery was partially overrun and the 19th Maine had retreated from the Codori farm. Hancock, who had just before sent the 1st Minnesota on its counterattack against Wilcox, pointed to the three captured guns and asked Randall if his men could retake them. "I can, and damn quick too, if you will let me." The colonel shouted orders, and the Vermonters set out. Fifty yards away a bullet brought Randall's horse down, and his men faltered. The colonel shouted for them to "go on boys I'll be at your head as soon as I get out of this damned saddle." Some of the men helped roll the dead animal off his leg, and soon the intrepid officer was hobbling in front of the regiment. The Vermonters swept across the valley and drove back Lang's Floridians, who had already decided to fall back due to the petering out of the Rebel attack. Randall's men left the guns to be recovered by other regiments from the First Corps, which also had been sent by Doubleday, and continued until they reached Emmitsburg Road. Here they received scattered artillery fire from Alexander's guns at the Sherfy peach orchard and retired to Cemetery Ridge. Losses were light, but the men had demonstrated that they had plenty of heart for the war.[26]

Stannard assembled his units around Gates's demibrigade on the morning of July 3, as earlier described. He also sent out details of ten men from each company to bury the dead of July 2 that lay near his position, or at least to cover them with blankets. Stannard was afraid that "the sight of these bloody corpses might dishearten some of our men." Most of the wounded had already been collected during the previous night. The details also had instructions to gather fence rails and build the breastwork about seventy-five yards in front of the main Union line that Col. William T. Nichols's 14th Vermont moved to. This was necessary because Nichols's men were suffering from the sporadic Confederate artillery fire that came onto the area much of the morning. It fell close enough to Rorty's battery so that several Vermonters were injured when a caisson exploded. Ironically, several other infantry units were just as close or closer than the 14th Vermont. They did not move either because they could not do so or because they were much more experienced and did not consider this danger serious enough to readjust their positions. Nichols's forward post offered the men quite a bit of shelter. It was in the valley of Plum Run where some small trees and bushes helped to shield them. A spring with a gentle trickle of water flowing into the valley lay behind their right wing. The 14th now lay to the front and left of the 13th. The third regiment, the 16th Vermont, was even farther forward. Half of it was detailed on the skirmish line. The men arrayed themselves in picket posts rather than forming a true skirmish line. A reserve for the skirmishers rested about thirty yards in front of the 14th, and the rest of the 16th lay another thirty yards to the right and rear of Nichols's regiment.[27]

Gibbon, Gates, and Stannard constituted what might be termed the left wing of that part of the Union line to be assaulted by the Confederates. Their combined strength of 3,785 soldiers would contend with Pickett's 5,830 men, but they had considerable artillery support.

· · · · · · ·

HAYS'S DIVISION

Another of Hancock's divisions, led by Brig. Gen. Alexander Hays, constituted the right wing, which was the target of Pettigrew's and Trimble's commands. About 2,080 men of this division would bear the weight of repulsing the attack of the combined strength of 6,200 opposing Confederates. The disparity of numbers was far more pronounced than on Gibbon's front. Like Hancock, Hays was born in Pennsylvania, near Franklin, and was educated at Alleghany College. He left that institution in his senior year to accept an appointment to West Point, where he became fast friends with Ulysses S. Grant and graduated in 1844 with Hancock. Hays gained valuable experience in the Mexican War, where he received a leg wound, but resigned his commission in 1848 to enter business in Pennsylvania. He later prospected for gold in California and worked as a civil engineer in his home state. He was living in Pittsburgh when the war began.

Hays became colonel of the 63rd Pennsylvania and served in the Peninsula campaign and the Seven Days. He was severely wounded at Second Manassas and missed Antietam. Hays commanded a brigade of New York troops in the first half of 1863 but saw no combat with them. Promotion to brigadier general of volunteers had come long before, in September 1862, but an important command did not arrive to match it until June 1863, when he was given control of the Third Division of Hancock's Second Corps. Hays was an impressive man and a flamboyant commander. He came into his own as a division leader, and Gettysburg was a marvelous opportunity for him. One of his subordinates fondly recalled the boisterous fellow: "He was a princely soldier; brave as a lion, and was one of those dashing, reckless, enthusiastic Generals, that reminded you of one of the old cavaliers. He seemed happiest when in the thickest of the fight."[28]

Hays's division consisted of three brigades, two of which would bear the brunt of repelling Pettigrew and Trimble. Col. Thomas A. Smyth's Second Brigade held the line from the angle northward. It was a severely depleted unit of tried-and-true regiments. Smyth was new to its command, however, even though he had long experience in the field. Born in County Cork, Ireland, Smyth worked on his family's farm until he migrated to the United States in 1854. He settled in Philadelphia and worked as a wood carver until enticed to join William Walker's quixotic filibustering expedition to Nicaragua. Like Birkett D. Fry on the other side of the valley, Smyth, for some reason, helped Walker try to acquire that Central American country as a venue for the expansion of U.S. slavery. When the expedition collapsed, he returned to the East Coast and settled in Wilmington, Delaware, where he worked as a coachmaker. The war brought him into the army as captain of a company in the 24th Pennsylvania, a three-month regiment. Then he received a commission as major of the 1st Delaware and became its colonel in February 1863. Smyth helped to occupy Suffolk, Virginia, early in the war and then participated in the Maryland campaign, Fredericksburg, and Chancellorsville. He was leading the Second Brigade for the first time at Gettysburg.[29]

*Brig. Gen. Alexander Hays, whose division held the line from the angle to the right
(Massachusetts Commandery, Military Order of the Loyal Legion and the U.S. Army
Military History Institute, USAMHI)*

The brigade started with a solid core of two regiments, the 14th Connecticut and the 108th New York, going back to Antietam. Then the 10th New York Battalion was added before the battle of Fredericksburg. This unit had originated in New York City as an independent Zouave company before the war. When Fort Sumter fell, the men voted to offer themselves for volunteer service, and thus the 10th was born. It saw its first combat at the battle of Big Bethel, where many members of the 11th North Carolina in Pettigrew's brigade had also heard their first sounds of war. The regiment had become much reduced in numbers and now was simply designated as a battalion. It mostly served as a provost guard by the time of Gettysburg. In addition to this demiregiment, the 12th New Jersey was added to the brigade in time for the battle of Chancellorsville. Following that grand disaster, the 1st Delaware was added as well. As senior colonel, Smyth took charge of a brigade that was a stranger to his men less than two months before Gettysburg.[30]

Smyth's brigade, like the rest of Hays's division, retained its position in line during all of July 2 and 3. It was not heavily engaged in the former day's fight except to send skirmishers out to battle with Rebel skirmishers between the lines. This was tiring work. The skirmish line was about 200 yards west of Emmitsburg Road, and the Confederate skirmishers were another 200 yards farther west, on the Bliss farm. The Union reserve was located in the road itself in front of Smyth's brigade. Everyone took shelter so that if a man exposed himself, he became an instant target. "When the reliefs went to their places there was excitement," recalled Chaplain Henry S. Stevens of the 14th Connecticut. "The relieving squad would leave the reserve rendezvous moving in any way possible to avoid the observation of the enemy, but when a place was reached where exposure was unavoidable each would take to running at highest speed, and upon reaching the fence would throw himself at once upon the ground. Then must the relieved ones get back to the reserve in a similar manner; and 'relieving' seemed a misnomer." A "lively" popping of fire erupted whenever this occurred. Even though relatively few men were hit, it was a noisy, stressful experience that seemed to have no end.[31]

The men were fatigued by this constant skirmishing and suffered from the heat and the lack of food. The morning of July 3 was quite uncomfortable. "The sun was dreadfully hot, scarcely a breath of air blowing," recalled Color Sgt. John M. Dunn of the 1st Delaware. Many men created arbors with their shelter tents by stretching them from the low stone fence in front of their position to a stick or inverted gun with bayonet attached. The 14th Connecticut was on Smyth's left. With only 100 men on line, in one rank, the regiment was a shadow of its former strength. Eight companies were armed with Springfield rifle muskets, but Company A and Company B had Sharps breechloaders. Capt. William A. Arnold's Battery A, 1st Rhode Island Light Artillery, was positioned from the angle northward, where the 14th Connecticut would normally have been, so the infantry simply lined up behind the next regiment to its right, the 1st Delaware. The 12th New Jersey was positioned to the right of Smyth's old regiment, and Maj. George F. Hopper's 10th New York Battalion formed a provost line behind Hays's division. Apparently Meade's lunchtime order to Gibbon to put the provost guard into the battle line was not communicated to Hays.[32]

The 108th New York, under Lt. Col. Francis E. Pierce, was detailed to support Lt. George A. Woodruff's Battery I, 1st U.S. Artillery. It was a dangerous assignment, for Woodruff's guns were well to the right of Smyth's brigade in a slightly advanced and exposed position. Hays made it worse by insisting that the New Yorkers be positioned behind the line of guns and in front of the line of limbers. Woodruff told him they would be in the way when his gunners passed ammunition to the cannon, but the stubborn Hays was feeling his oats as a newly minted division leader, and he refused to relent. The infantry would also be terribly exposed to Rebel counterbattery fire and suffer needlessly for it.[33]

The second of Hays's brigades to bear the brunt of the Rebel attack was Col. Eliakim Sherrill's Third Brigade. It had a unique and troubled history. It consisted mostly of regiments raised in the summer of 1862, and its first experience in the field was the disastrous Harpers Ferry campaign of September. Nearly 13,000 Federal troops were trapped by 14,000 Rebels under Stonewall Jackson in a constricted position bounded by high, mountainous ground on all sides. Jackson was to secure Harpers Ferry to open a line of communication through the Shenandoah Valley for Lee's invasion of Maryland. The Federal commander, Col. Dixon S. Miles, foolishly allowed his large force to be outmaneuvered and then refused to fight his way out. The men were humiliated and extremely frustrated by the order to lay down their arms on September 15. Miles surrendered early enough to allow most of Jackson's command to reach Lee in time for the battle of Antietam, two days later, where every man was needed to avert a near disaster in the face of McClellan's ponderous attacks. It was the largest surrender of Union troops during the war.[34]

Every Federal associated with the event was tainted by it, even though

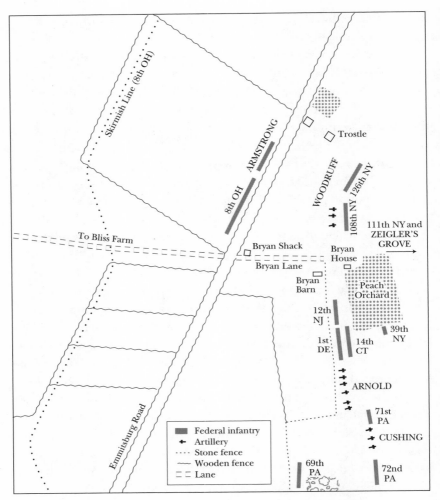

Map 3.2 Hays's Division, Morning, July 3, 1863

most of them had no desire to surrender. The men were given their parole and sent northward to Camp Douglas, Chicago, to await proper exchange. That took place in November, and the regiments were brigaded and sent east to guard the Washington defenses. A New York brigade was organized with the 39th, 111th, 125th, and 126th, under Col. Frederick G. D'Utassy of the 39th. His regiment was a colorful and rowdy unit of men from Alsace-Lorraine, Argentina, Armenia, Austria, Bavaria, Belgium, Bohemia, Canada, Chile, Cuba, Denmark, England, France, Germany, Greece, Holland, Hungary, Ireland, Italy, Nicaragua, Norway,

Malta, Poland, Portugal, Russia, Scotland, Spain, Sweden, Switzerland, and the United States. That admixture had created a divisive, unruly regiment that had the misfortune to be officered by unscrupulous and conniving men.

The Hungarian D'Utassy was largely responsible for allowing the 39th to deteriorate, and he, unfortunately, brought the same conditions on the brigade. An enormously vain and grasping man, he easily was the worst brigade commander in the Union army. He engaged in widespread corruption, from filing false requisitions in order to embezzle supplies and money from the government to forcing soldiers to pay him cash in exchange for official favors. His military ability was nonexistent, and the brigade was fortunate that it never was called on to enter battle under his leadership. D'Utassy was finally relieved of his command in January 1863 and sent to prison.[35]

Alexander Hays replaced him and worked wonders to counteract the bad influence of the Hungarian. He got rid of many bad officers, punished those who failed to obey his orders, and improved camp sanitation. Most of his regiments were filled with good, solid soldiers who were happy to see the hated D'Utassy go. The 39th New York never improved very much, however, because it was still led by men of D'Utassy's ilk, but it was a small unit in a brigade of larger and better regiments. Only four companies of the 39th, under command of the swaggering, boastful Maj. Hugo Hildebrandt, were with the brigade at Gettysburg. The New Yorkers in the other regiments labored under the stigma of being "Harper's Ferry Cowards." They could only erase that opprobrium by fighting well, and Gettysburg gave them the opportunity to do that.

Like Stannard's Vermont brigade in the First Corps, Hays and his men were ordered to join the Army of the Potomac when Lee invaded Pennsylvania. Hays's brigade became part of the Second Corps on June 25, and Hays immediately was given command of the Third Division. Col. George L. Willard of the 125th New York took over the brigade. It was now designated the Third Brigade of that division following the breakup of a previous Third Brigade that had been the former home of Smyth's 1st Delaware. One-third of Hays's division was thus a new brigade "fresh from the defenses of Washington," in the words of Capt. Samuel C. Armstrong of the 125th. "Never before under fire, excepting a little at the miserable affair at Harper's Ferry where we were captured." They had a lot to prove to themselves and to the army.[36]

The brigade had their first opportunity to expunge the ghost of Harpers Ferry on July 2. Willard went into the battle with a long pedigree; his ancestors had fought in the Revolution and the War of 1812. He had also served as an enlisted man in the regulars during the Mexican War and was commissioned soon afterward, rising to the rank of major in the 19th U.S. Infantry. When Meade asked Hancock for a brigade to help the Third Corps, Willard was told to go. The corps commander personally led it to the left, well past the position of the 1st Minnesota, and placed it on the western edge of Plum Run Valley in front of Barksdale's hard-charging Mississippi brigade.

Hancock told Willard to attack. The New Yorkers crossed the valley in two lines, firing and yelling, "Remember Harper's Ferry!" They hit Barksdale's men when the Mississippians had nearly expended their energy, stopped them, and turned them back. Willard's command swept on to Emmitsburg Road, where it recaptured some cannons, but the New Yorkers received a lot of artillery fire from Alexander's guns at the Sherfy peach orchard. One of the rounds killed Willard, and Col. Eliakim Sherrill of the 126th New York took charge of the brigade.

Sherrill felt that he was in a bind. The brigade had done well, but it was exposed and unsupported on either flank. He hesitated about fifteen minutes and then ordered a retreat. Later Sherrill argued that he understood Willard would have done the same if he had lived. Under these conditions the order to retire was prudent. Other units had counterattacked up to Emmitsburg Road and then retreated with no repercussions. But some officers did not agree with Sherrill. Col. Clinton MacDougall of the 111th New York initially refused to retire and did so under protest only when Sherrill insisted.

The brigade made it safely back across Plum Run Valley and was on its way to Hays's position when it encountered Hancock, and he was in a foul mood. The corps commander met Sherrill with "a stream of profanity which one might have expected from a drunken sailor," thought Benjamin W. Thompson of the 111th New York. Hancock "demanded where we were going" and impulsively placed Sherrill under arrest. He ordered the brigade to countermarch to the edge of the valley. Thompson later wrote that this countermarch was "more [for] spleen than for sense as, in a short time, orders came through the proper channels" to rejoin Hays's division.[37]

Sherrill was shocked. His arrest was wholly unjustified, the result of an overcharged temper by a man who had a reputation for feeling the spirit of battle to the utmost when aroused. Sherrill had no military experience before the war. He had been a U.S. congressman and a state senator from Geneva, New York. At age fifty-one he was a bit old to be experiencing his first combat; although severely wounded in the face at Harpers Ferry, he had not commanded in battle there. Only the patient prodding of Hays convinced Hancock to relent that night so that Sherrill was taken out of arrest and put back in charge of his brigade.[38]

The much-abused unit arrayed itself to the right and rear of Smyth's command to act as a reserve. The small contingent of the 39th New York was positioned to the rear of the 1st Delaware. MacDougall's 111th New York was placed at the eastern edge of Ziegler's Grove, about 200 yards from the front line, where the trees, a low stone fence, and the crest of Cemetery Ridge offered some shelter. The men of this regiment were fearfully hungry, having had no rations in many hours. They could only smoke to ease the hunger pangs. The 126th New York was positioned to the right of Woodruff's battery, but the exact placement of the 125th is unknown.[39]

Because they were in reserve, the men of Sherrill's brigade were called on to skirmish on the morning of July 3. Capt. Sebastian D. Holmes of the 111th New York led 100 men on the skirmish line until relieved by a contingent of the 39th New York under Major Hildebrandt. Both officers wanted to assemble their men behind a small building at the intersection of Bryan Lane and Emmitsburg Road. Holmes wanted to take them back to the main line; Hildebrandt, to move them forward under fire. Hildebrandt acted the part of a tyrant, refusing to allow Holmes the shelter of the building and even drawing his pistol on the captain. Fortunately Holmes was quicker on the draw and forced the cowardly German to back down. One gets the impression that the Army of the Potomac would have been better served if the 39th New York had been disbanded.[40]

Capt. Samuel C. Armstrong of the 126th New York had only the Rebels to worry about when he led 100 men of his regiment out to skirmish north of the building where Holmes and Hildebrandt had their confrontation. Armstrong, a college student when the war began, had fought his first battle on July 2. The area between the two armies was "an ugly place," he wrote home. The opposing skirmish lines were, at their closest, only 100 yards apart. The "sharpshooters were butchering each other to no purpose whatever," Armstrong reported. "Both were crouched down flat on their faces behind fences or in the grass, and away they popped all the morning, killing and wounding quite a number." He took cover behind the fence along Emmitsburg Road but often had to rise up to give orders, thus becoming a target.

When orders came for the skirmish line to move forward, Armstrong thought it was a foolish idea, a "fatal" order, as he put it. "I led that charge, if any one did." Three other captains took part in this advance. Two were killed and the other was wounded. His men pushed the Rebel skirmishers back and occupied a rise of ground on the west side of Emmitsburg Road that commanded much of the area between the lines. Yet Armstrong thought this minor fighting within a massive theater of death was a waste of manpower.[41]

Hays also asked for help from Capt. William Plumer, commander of the 1st Company of Massachusetts Sharpshooters, a unit that was assigned to the Second Corps but unattached to any division or brigade. Plumer responded by detailing Lt. Emerson L. Bicknell and twenty men to hold the western edge of Ziegler's Grove, which had come under heavy Rebel skirmish fire. Bicknell's sharpshooters skirmished at long range all morning with the Rebels, finally driving them back.[42]

Hays's last brigade, commanded by Col. Samuel S. Carroll, had only one regiment engaged in repelling the assault of July 3. Lt. Col. Franklin Sawyer's 8th Ohio had been detailed from the brigade, which held a position on Hays's far right, to go out skirmishing on July 2. Rebel skirmishers had pushed up to Emmitsburg Road and were harassing Hancock's artillerymen, even shooting one of his staff members, so the corps commander asked Carroll to do something about it. Sawyer's men moved forward at 4:00 P.M. and drove the Confederates away, occupying a key spot on the battlefield. A "broad, flat knoll" extended about a half-mile to the north and northwest from Ziegler's Grove toward the Confederate lines and some distance to the west of Emmitsburg Road. It was a little lower than the grove but about thirty feet higher than Bliss farm, which was the most prominent feature between the opposing lines. The knoll was the highest ground between the road and Seminary Ridge. Emmitsburg Road cut through it, creating a two-foot-deep passageway that could readily serve as an improvised trench.

Sawyer lost eighteen men while advancing his regiment to a rail fence on the military crest at the end of the knoll. He left a skirmish line there and retired the rest of the 8th to Emmitsburg Road. The fence was about 100 yards from and parallel to the road, with a cornfield between them. Sawyer lost another fourteen men repelling a counterattack that evening and another twenty on the morning of July 3. Since he started with only 218 men, these were significant losses. The 8th would be in this position for the duration of the battle. Normally Sawyer kept two or three companies on the advanced skirmish line along the rail fence while sheltering the rest of his regiment in the road cut. A drainage ditch along the side provided even more cover than the cut itself. The companies at the rail fence were relieved by other companies every two to three hours. The regiment occupied a rather exposed position, but as long as they controlled the end of this elongated knoll, they could hold where they were. The Ohioans were supported on the right flank and rear by Capt. Armstrong's contingent of skirmishers from the 126th New York, who also had advanced across the road onto the high ground.[43]

The skirmishing was constant and deadly, even "murderous" according to Lt. Thomas F. Galwey. The Ohioans went about it with a system. Since the Rebels closely hugged the ground and their butternut clothing blended with the landscape, groups of four or five Yankees naturally formed here and there along the rail fence. They fired as a group at every puff of smoke that emerged from the ground, hoping that at least one bullet among the volley would find its mark. The men called this "Turning a Jack." This fighting continued all morning of July 3 from prone positions, for it was deadly to rise from the ground at all. Fence rails wrenched from the posts and piled in a line, little depressions in the ground, or knapsacks were the only protection for the skirmishers. When Galwey took his company forward at 6:00 A.M. on July 3 after only two hours of sleep in the ditch along Emmitsburg Road, he found that many more men had been killed since dawn. There were so many bodies along the rail fence "that it was difficult for us to find a place to stretch ourselves." The men became deeply involved in this life-and-death struggle. "So destructive, in fact, did [the Rebel] fire become that the wildest imprecations were shouted at" the Confederates, "and threats were made that if taken they would get no quarter."

There were a number of dead and wounded Federals between the two skirmish lines, the result of some attempts to advance the line even farther west. Galwey felt very sorry for these unfortunates. "To be slain on the field of battle for one's country is glorious; to be wounded and left to lie helpless and in pain where the bullets of friends and foes hiss through the air or strike with a wicked thud into the ground near by, and to have a summer's sun burning the already fevered body and adding to the horrible thirst, is pitiful in the extreme."

Position of the 8th Ohio from Hays's line, showing the approximate location of the regiment's reserve post along Emmitsburg Road (author's collection)

Imagine how the men felt, then, when a Confederate skirmisher suddenly arose, his gun slung across his shoulder, and slowly began to walk toward them. He yelled, "Don't fire, Yanks!" and everyone wondered what he was up to. They watched with fascination; when some Federals trained their weapons on him, others restrained them. Suddenly he dropped to the ground, and then it was apparent what he intended to do. The Rebel had a canteen, which he shared freely with a badly wounded Yank between the lines. Everyone cheered, and a number of Federals even stood up to demonstrate their admiration for this unselfish deed. No one was shot on this part of the skirmish line for several minutes. When the Confederate was finished, he quickly walked back to his own line; he yelled, "Down Yanks, we're going to fire," and the killing resumed. The identify and fate of this Good Samaritan was never discovered. He had been taking cover at a shade tree left in the field by local farmers, about thirty yards in front of the Federal line. When the battle was over, "a heap of Confederates was found under that tree."[44]

Sawyer had about 160 men left by noon of July 3. His command had done more intense skirmishing than any other unit in the Union center, and he wanted relief. Capt. James Gregg of Carroll's staff made his way to Emmitsburg Road about noon on July 3 to see how the regiment was

THE DEFENDERS

faring. Sawyer asked him to get Carroll to send a replacement regiment, but the Confederate artillery bombardment started soon after, forcing the 8th to remain where it was. The regiment was to play a role in repelling the attack out of proportion to its small size of only about 160 men.[45]

The total number of Union infantry that met Pickett, Pettigrew, Trimble, Wilcox, and Lang amounted to only 5,750, roughly half the Confederate attacking force. There were ample reserves, however, to right and left and especially to the rear.

· · · · · · ·

THE ARTILLERY

The Federal artillery constituted an important support for the small number of Union infantry. The Yankee guns would play a crucial role in repelling the attack; they were numerous, well served, and in good positions.

Brig. Gen. Henry J. Hunt, the army's artillery chief, was mainly responsible for the Federal advantage in this arm. Hunt was born in Michigan to a family that had deep roots in the regular army. He graduated from West Point in 1839 and served in the artillery during the Mexican War. Hunt served on a board that thoroughly revised the light artillery tactics of the army between the wars; his system was used by both Union and Confederate armies. Hunt had a lot of experience handling the big guns during the first half of the war. He participated in the First Manassas campaign, was chief of artillery in the Washington defenses, deployed a concentration of 100 guns at Malvern Hill that shattered attacking Confederate brigades, and organized a massive barrage by 147 artillery pieces to cover the crossing of the Rappahannock River during the Fredericksburg campaign. He also saw action at Antietam and was promoted to brigadier general of volunteers in September 1862.[46]

Hunt arranged his available guns in three concentrations along Meade's line. All three would participate in the artillery exchange preceding the assault, and two would play key roles in repelling the Rebel infantry. On the left, at the southern end of Cemetery Ridge, Lt. Benjamin Rittenhouse's Battery D, 5th U.S. Artillery, was positioned on Little Round Top. Armed with ten-pounder Parrotts, Rittenhouse could fire all the way to Pickett's waiting division and reach the angle in the stone fence as well. Because of heavy losses the previous day, 40 percent of his gunners were volunteers from various infantry regiments.

A big concentration of thirty-nine guns lay to the north of Little

Round Top, roughly opposite Alexander's guns in the Sherfy peach orchard and the extreme right wing of Pickett's division. It was commanded by Maj. Freeman McGilvery, who led the First Volunteer Brigade of the army's artillery reserve. From left to right there were eight units: Capt. Nelson Ames's Battery G, 1st New York Artillery; Capt. Edwin B. Dow's 6th Maine Battery; Battery B, 2nd New Jersey Artillery; Capt. William D. Rank's section of Battery H, 3rd Pennsylvania Heavy Artillery (acting as light artillerists); the 1st Connecticut Battery; Capt. Patrick Hart's 15th New York Battery; Capt. Charles A. Phillips's 5th Massachusetts Battery; and Capt. James Thompson's Battery C, Pennsylvania Artillery. McGilvery ordered that a small earthwork be constructed to protect the guns. It amounted to little, a parapet made of fence rails with dirt piled on top that stood up to two feet tall and stretched for 380 yards from Weikert's Woods to the right of the artillery line. Small as the earthwork was, everyone agreed that it was a welcome protection. Hancock strengthened McGilvery's line by inserting the 116th Pennsylvania between Dow's and Hart's batteries.

Besides Rittenhouse on Little Round Top, McGilvery had the best ground along the left or center of Meade's line. Hunt later described it as "on a *crest*," but it really was not a prominent rise of land. Rather, the strength lay in McGilvery's line of vision. Rising ground directly to the west shielded his position from the Confederates while open ground to the northwest offered McGilvery a wonderful line of fire. He would be able to enfilade the right flank of Pickett's attacking division and command Plum Run Valley. A recent historian has described his position as "an artilleryman's dream."[47]

The area around the angle in the stone fence would be the center point of the Confederate fury soon to be unleashed. Here was the second of Hunt's concentrations of guns. Capt. John Hazard, artillery chief of the Second Corps, commanded the artillery here, but he was not able to play a major role because both Hunt and Hancock closely supervised the batteries. Cushing's Battery A, 4th U.S. Artillery, was eighty feet from the angle with his guns in a line with the 71st and 72nd Pennsylvania, as previously described. Cushing put his limbers in a second line to the rear and his caissons in a third line behind the limbers.

Brown's Battery B, 1st Rhode Island Light Artillery, was led by Lt. Walter S. Perrin on July 3. Brown and twenty of his gunners had been wounded and two had been killed on the previous day when Wright's Georgia brigade overran their position. The battery was about sixty yards from the stone fence and just to the left of the copse of trees. Its four Napoleons were positioned with the two in the center advanced a few feet to give them a wider arc of fire to right and left. Rorty's Battery B, 1st New York Light Artillery, was posted 150 yards south of Perrin.

From the angle northward, Hays had the firepower of two good batteries to call on. Arnold's Battery A, 1st Rhode Island Light Artillery, was at the northeast corner, where the fence turned north again after returning from the angle. He had an excellent field of fire across the shallow swale of Stevens's Run and the Bliss farm as he occupied the highest rise of ground along the Union line between Cemetery Hill and Little Round Top. Arnold placed his limbers and caissons in the Bryan peach orchard to the rear.

The position of Woodruff's Battery I, 1st U.S. Artillery, has already been mentioned. Woodruff had six Napoleons spotted 420 feet from Emmitsburg Road, exposed in the open. That was why Hays insisted he have the support of the 108th New York between the guns and the limbers. The New Yorkers seem to have done nothing to stop the incessant skirmish fire coming from the Rebels that forced Woodruff to send his gunners back to Ziegler's Grove on the morning of July 3 for shelter. At least one-third of those gunners were volunteers from various units of Sherrill's brigade, as the battery had lost a lot of men on July 2. Woodruff's unit was the anchor of the Second Corps line.

After the artillery bombardment began, two more units were brought up to Hays's line. A section of Lt. Richard Milton's 9th Massachusetts Battery and a section of Lt. John G. Turnbull's consolidated Batteries F and K, 3rd U.S. Artillery, were placed in the Bryan peach orchard. They would add their might to the hail of projectiles crisscrossing the valley during the bombardment but would play little role in repelling the infantry assault. A total of eighty-seven guns were strung out along the nearly two-mile length of the Union line from Little Round Top to Ziegler's Grove.[48]

The last major concentration of Union guns, on the far right, had the best ground. Cemetery Hill and Culp's Hill dominated the area east of Gettysburg. Maj. Thomas Ward Osborn, artillery chief of the Eleventh Corps, commanded thirty-nine guns west of Baltimore Pike on Cemetery Hill, deployed literally among the headstones of the cemetery. He had a commanding view to the south, west, and north; Osborn's guns could reach the Bliss farm, and Seminary Ridge was only one mile from his position. Col. Charles Wainwright, artillery chief of the First Corps, commanded twenty-four guns east of Baltimore Pike outside the cemetery. His position was much more restricted, and his artillery could fire only to the north and a bit to the west. While Wainwright would receive fire during the artillery bombardment, he had no real opportunity to reply. Osborn, on the other hand, would receive fire and return it as well. His guns would play a big role in punishing the Confederate infantry when it attacked.[49]

The morning of July 3 passed quietly for many gunners, but it was fraught with danger for others. Guns near the angle came under Confederate artillery fire as early as 8:00 A.M., probably the result of renewed skirmishing around the Bliss farm or the raging battle at Culp's Hill. Cushing's batterymen were stunned when a shell exploded the No. 2 limber; this touched off the powder in the No. 1 and No. 3 limbers as well and led to a spectacular series of explosions. Hunt, Cushing, and Sgt. Frederick Fuger were standing only a few yards behind the No. 3 limber, but none was hurt. Arnold's battery was close enough so that one of its gunners was knocked down by the explosion, and some of Arnold's draft animals became frightened and bolted toward the Confederate lines. Cushing's gunners quickly returned the fire and soon saw a caisson explode on the Rebel side. By Fuger's account this exchange lasted for a half-hour. Three other exchanges, each lasting about ten minutes, erupted between 8:30 and 11:00 A.M. Then silence descended on the battlefield for the next two hours. The Federal artillerymen fixed their lunches and saw to the replenishment of their ammunition.[50]

During that two-hour lull Arnold noticed that "an occasional shot from different positions" came from the Rebel artillery. He guessed they were repositioning the guns and firing them to fix the range. Osborn could see through his field glasses from the cemetery that Lee was assembling his cannons, stretching for two miles. "It was the longest and finest line of light batteries ever planted on a battlefield," Osborn recalled. "We were fully aware that this line of batteries meant mischief to us and that immediately behind it was a corresponding body of infantry." Hunt was fully aware of this too. He rode along the entire line that morning, beginning about 10:00 A.M., and found that all the batteries were in good shape with plenty of ammunition. He gave detailed instructions to all unit commanders along the way. When the Confederates opened their bombardment, battery leaders were "not to fire at small bodies, nor to allow their fire to be drawn without promise of adequate results." They were "to watch the enemy closely, and when he opened to concentrate the fire of their guns on one battery at a time until it was silenced; under all circumstances to fire deliberately, and to husband their ammunition as much as possible."[51]

Hunt was smart. He knew that the Rebels would attack the left wing somewhere, and he believed they would concentrate their artillery fire on Cemetery Hill. Hunt knew the guns there commanded a good stretch of the Union front and naturally supposed the enemy would want to neutralize them before attacking. Osborn thus prepared for the worst. He knew the mettle of his men; they would not be driven off the hill, but Osborn worried that they would be so decimated as to be unable to do as much damage as he wanted. He could not erect earthworks to protect them, for that would have required "digging up the dead in the Cemetery." His batteries were in plain view of the Confederates and could be taken in a cross fire from west and north. "We made the best target for artillery practice the enemy had during the war," Osborn wrote, yet he knew his men were capable of giving as much as they received.[52]

Meade had about 200 guns altogether at Gettysburg; 126 would play a role in Pickett's Charge. If any battery commanders needed help, and many of them would see their units savaged by the hail of Confederate fire to come, they could call on the army's reserve, which was parked only a half-mile behind Cemetery Ridge. The Confederates employed slightly more guns in the bombardment, 135 of them, but that was not a significant difference. Generally the Union guns were better placed and better served; Rebel artillery still had weaknesses in the areas of faulty ammunition and a tendency to overshoot their targets at this stage of the war. But those weaknesses were disappearing with time. The long arm of each army was close in quality by the summer of 1863, and the coming bombardment would be a terrific match of firepower.[53]

· · · · · · ·

THE TERRAIN

The Federal army occupied the best ground in the area for defense, but there were inequalities and weaknesses in the line. The ends were the strongest. Cemetery Hill, Culp's Hill, and Little Round Top had demonstrated their advantages for the defenders on July 2. The center was weaker, as shown by the near success of Wright on the evening of that day. Rather than the steep profile of the hills, Cemetery Ridge had a very gentle, easy slope that would offer no physical obstacle to a charging unit.

The slope would serve the needs of the defender only when the attacker was very close, for it tended to force the attacker slightly up and into the face of massed musketry. There was no danger of the defender overshooting his opponent, as was common when he was on high ground.

Moreover, the shape of the ridge forced a dogleg configuration in the Union line. The right flank of Hays's division was a bit exposed because the Eleventh Corps line to his right was about 200 yards toward the rear. Woodruff's battery, the 108th New York, and possibly the 126th New York, were thus exposed on the flank as well as on the front. This was partly why so many skirmishers were sent to Hays's right front. If the rest of Anderson's division had been incorporated into the assaulting column, and if it had performed its task with determination, the Confederates might have been able to take advantage of this irregularity. As it was, the Federal skirmishers managed to protect this part of the line without calling on the main line.

Hays's position was strong even though his units were depleted of manpower. In effect he doubled his line by massing two of his brigades on a short section of it. All of Smyth's brigade had the low stone fence to provide some protection. The Bryan farm, owned by a free black man named Abraham Bryan, was at the edge of Ziegler's Grove, which extended farther west in 1863 than it does today. The Bryan barn lay just on the west side of the stone fence, and Bryan Lane connected the house with Emmitsburg Road. As already noted, a small shack or barn stood at the junction of the lane and the road. Hays put his headquarters in the Bryan house. It was empty because the owner had fled with his wife and two sons as soon as word of Lee's raid into Pennsylvania had reached Gettysburg.[54]

The stone fence, which continued south to cover the front of Webb's brigade, became one of the most famous features on the battlefield. It was not a wall, as many people then and now refer to it, but a true fence. That is, it was not tall enough to block the movement of animals but was intended to be a boundary marker. A rail fence could be built on top of it to control animal traffic. Chaplain Henry S. Stevens of the 14th Connecticut was impressed by its construction, calling it "a low, well thrown, stone . . . fence." The angle in the fence, which marked the boundary between Gibbon's and Hays's divisions, was a convenient landmark in the fight to come. It actually was a potential liability for the Federals, constituting what one historian has called "a kind of salient." The fence jutted forward about eighty feet to the west to form the angle before

THE DEFENDERS

continuing south. Attacking Confederates could conceivably outflank the troops along the so-called west wall by moving southward across this eighty-foot extension, thus slicing between Hays and Gibbon. It would be like flood water rushing through a faulty joint in a retaining wall and fracturing it to pieces.[55]

The Confederates often referred to the Union works when recounting Pickett's Charge, and they exaggerated the strength of these so-called fortifications to an unbelievable degree. They were the victims of over-heated imaginations. There were very few, and quite simple, fortifications on the Union line. Hays's men slightly improved the stone fence in their front by piling on a few fence rails taken from someplace in their rear. The result was a protection about two to three feet tall. Color Sgt. John M. Dunn of the 1st Delaware also recalled that some men were about to tear down a rail fence that ran across the field in their front. This fence extended northward from the angle, parallel to Hays's front, and was thus about eighty feet away. An officer on either the brigade or division staff stopped them, "saying that the fence might be of more use in another direction." The officer meant that it might be useful, if intact, as an obstruction to the attacking Confederates.[56]

As already noted, Webb had no earthworks. His men contented themselves with using the stone fence, without improvements, for protection. The only true earthwork involved in the repulse of the Rebel infantry was made by Hall's brigade, and it was a small work that offered no more shelter than the stone fence. Harrow's brigade apparently shared this work with Hall. The First Corps units made some protection for themselves, but they did not dig into the ground. Gates's demibrigade and the 14th Vermont simply piled fence rails on top of the ground, which also offered little more shelter than the stone fence. The Union artillery was hardly more protected than the infantry. McGilvery had an earthwork similar to Hall's and Harrow's. Osborn badly needed protection in his exposed position atop Cemetery Hill but could not make it due to the cemetery itself. Hazard's batteries near the angle also needed protection, but the nature of the ground did not permit it. The topsoil here was but "a few inches deep," according to a modern historian. Hard, loose shale lay beneath the topsoil; it was not easily dug up and could be scattered by artillery projectiles if piled. One artillery commander noted that he tried to fortify near the angle, following the repulse of Pickett's Charge, but "there was not enough soil to make a parapet over a foot high before my guns."[57]

Even though the Confederate survivors exaggerated the Union use of fortifications, the truth was that the Federals did employ earthworks, breastworks, and the available man-made features of the landscape to their advantage. Prewar military manuals encouraged commanders to take advantage of civilian constructions and irregularities in the ground, and they acknowledged that this use made these features "fortifications." The stone fence would play just as important a role in protecting soldiers as any of the military-constructed earthworks or breastworks.

The ground was a bit more complex on the left of that segment of the Union line that would be targeted by the Confederate attack. The land began to slope toward Plum Run Valley to the left in front of Gibbon's division; as already noted, Arnold's battery occupied the highest ground in this area. Also, as noted in Chapter 2, there were two swales in front of Gibbon that drained south to form Plum Run Valley, with the Codori farm buildings between them. The Confederates would have to cross these swales to close with the defending Federals. On the Union side of the swales, between the stone fence and the first swale, there were two clumps of rough ground that formed islands in the surrounding culti-vated land. They were rocky outcroppings about thirty yards wide and several feet tall. The first was located about seventy-five yards in front of Hall's position, and the second was another seventy-five yards west of the first. This last clump was on the shoulder of the second swale that the Confederates would have to cross to reach the Union line. These clumps had already been used by some of Wright's men as cover in the assault of July 2. The trees had been cut down on the morning of July 3 to reduce that possibility if the Rebels attacked again, but the rocks could still offer some shelter. Actually the famous copse of trees just behind the Union line was exactly the same kind of clump as these two, although its tree cover had extended far beyond the confines of the rocky outcropping toward the stone fence.

Also, if one looked closely enough, it became evident that a third and very shallow swale existed between the two clumps in front of the Union line. This swale was little more than five feet deep, and it started near the stone fence in front of the 69th Pennsylvania. It drained southwestward toward the other, bigger swale.[58]

Plum Run Valley widens quickly enough so that the First Corps units had a progressively open and wide landscape in their front. It was wetter and had a few more trees and brush in 1863 than it does today. The tiny rivulet called Plum Run came mostly from the spring that lay to the right rear of the 14th Vermont in its forward position behind the breastwork. When Hancock visited the battlefield in 1885, he noted quite a few trees had already been cut down in the valley during the past twenty-two years. He knew that many of the fences had been destroyed in the battle and surmised that timber had been cut to rebuild them, "and for firewood and other farm purposes." Nevertheless, the upper part of the valley did not offer any cover for an attacker in 1863. The ground was essentially open and excellent from the Union point of view.[59]

The fences were another major factor in the terrain that offered an advantage to the Federals. The broad, open valley between Cemetery Ridge and Seminary Ridge could easily be traversed by experienced troops with little to slow their progress except these fences. As we have already seen, this was much less serious in Gibbon's front, for the heavy fences along Emmitsburg Road had mostly been torn down the day before. Only here and there were sections still intact. The situation was different in Hays's front, where the fences were up and very strong. They were about chest high and not easy to dismantle. Pettigrew's charging men would have to climb them within easy range of canister and small arms fire.[60]

. . . .

THE BLISS FARM

The most prominent feature in the landscape in Hays's front was the Bliss farm. It became the focus of a protracted skirmish that rose to the level of a small fight within the larger battle of Gettysburg. Starting in the late morning of July 2, the fight lasted into the evening of July 3 and drew in elements of Gibbon's, Hays's, Pender's, and Anderson's divisions. The lay of the land here has already been described in Chapter 2. The house was a double log and frame structure sided with weatherboarding. The barn was a veritable citadel, excellent for military defense, with stout logs and a banked entrance to its lower level.

Elements of the 1st Delaware were the first Union troops to occupy the farm buildings on the morning of July 2, having driven off men from Lowrance's and Lane's brigades. Later that day Hays sent in ten companies from Sherrill's brigade, and the Confederates rushed in men from Posey's Mississippi brigade to counterattack. The artillery came into play as Arnold, Woodruff, Cushing, and Poague added their firepower to support either side in the developing fray. The Confederates recaptured the buildings that evening and held them in the face of a counterattack by skirmishers of the 106th Pennsylvania. Sawyer's 8th Ohio advanced west of Emmitsburg Road a bit after 4:00 P.M. to occupy the end of the strategic knoll, positioning the advanced skirmish line behind the rail fence where it was north and east of the buildings. This encouraged the Federal commanders to try to take control of them again. Four companies of the 12th New Jersey attacked at 5:00 P.M. supported by elements of the 1st Delaware and the 106th Pennsylvania. They took the barn, driving out the 16th Mississippi and part of the 12th and 16th Virginia of Mahone's brigade.

But this success was only temporary. Soon after, Wright's brigade conducted its slashing attack that drove all the way to Cemetery Ridge. Posey advanced to his left and recaptured the Bliss buildings; but the right wing of his brigade stopped there, and the left wing was halted by Sawyer's 8th Ohio, which was supported to its right by skirmishers from the Eleventh Corps. Thus Wright's attack was unsupported and failed. Soon after that, about 7:00 P.M., Thomas's and Perrin's brigades of Pender's division advanced to the northwest of the Bliss buildings toward a sunken road called Long Lane. They crossed the road and tried to probe forward, but Sawyer advanced the bulk of his 8th Ohio from Emmitsburg Road up to his advanced skirmish line at the edge of the knoll. This was enough to lead the cautious Confederates to retire to Long Lane and stay there. This convenient shelter would be their position for the remainder of the battle. It was, in the words of a modern historian, "no more than a well-used farm lane" that extended southwest from the town of Gettysburg and crossed Stevens's Run at a diagonal. Two ninety-degree turns then took the lane to the northwestern corner of the Bliss farm.

Aggressive Union activity against the farm kept the Confederates off balance on the morning of July 3. Hays started the ball rolling at 7:00 A.M. when he ordered his men to retake the Bliss buildings. A small detachment from the 1st Delaware and the 12th New Jersey was easily repulsed, to be followed by intense, long-range sharpshooting and artillery fire for much of the morning. Hays ordered a second attempt after Arnold complained of suffering from the sniping. Five companies of the 12th New Jersey ran across the valley and took the building. The retreating Confederates stopped a short distance away, re-formed, and applied pressure on the winded Federals, who held for several minutes before evacuating the buildings and retreating. Again a complaint by Arnold pressured Hays into action. The disgusted Arnold asked Hays to burn the barn, but the division leader tried once again to occupy it. This time four companies of

Site of the Bliss farm and orchard from the Union position. The thin cover of small trees marks the location of the large orchard, but the house and barn were never rebuilt after they were burned during the battle. (author's collection)

the 14th Connecticut advanced at about 10:00 A.M. and were successful in taking the barn. But the rest of the regiment, under Maj. Theodore G. Ellis, had to race across the valley to help them capture the house. They held it only temporarily; the house was not a good fortress, and its weatherboarding allowed small arms fire to come through the walls. The Connecticut men retreated to the barn, leaving a number of Union and Confederate wounded in the house. They held out for nearly an hour before a staff member from Hays arrived with instructions, finally, to burn the barn and retreat. Ellis ordered his men to go back to the house, which had not been occupied by the Rebels, evacuate the wounded, and set the structure afire. Then his men piled hay and straw in the barn and fired it as well. They safely retired to Cemetery Ridge by about noon. During the course of the battle up to this point the Bliss buildings had changed hands ten times. The fight involved 2,160 Federals and 2,310 Confederates. Of those numbers, 16 percent of the Federals and 20 percent of the Rebels had been killed, wounded, or captured while trying to control the farm. What exactly had been gained by either side was difficult to say.[61]

A lull settled over the battlefield from about 11:00 A.M. until 1:00 P.M.

as the Confederates put the finishing touches on their preparations and the Federals welcomed the opportunity to rest. The Yankees were well prepared for Pickett's Charge, probably better prepared to receive it than the Rebels were to attempt it. They certainly were better prepared to receive an attack on July 3 than they had been on July 2. That previous day had seen three Confederate brigades come across the valley like lightning bolts. They were fresh units, eager to punch the Yankees, who could only blunt, deflect, and slow them until the combination of stiffening resistance by the defenders and battle losses and fatigue on the part of the attackers ground them to a halt. The Federal line had not been properly disposed on July 2, with Sickles's unauthorized advance to Emmitsburg Road and Hancock's improvised effort to deploy Second Corps troops piecemeal in all directions to compensate for it. The Unionists had saved their center by gutsy decisions, hard fighting, and a holding tenacity that matched their enemy's offensive power. Ironically, if Anderson's attack on July 2 had been as large and well coordinated as Longstreet's assault of July 3, it probably would have cut through the Union center and might have won the battle. But that did not happen. The Federals had learned valuable lessons about the terrain and what they would encounter if the Confederates tried another attack on the center. They were ready for the assault.[62]

CHAPTER 4
THE BOMBARDMENT
· · · · · · · · · · ·

Col. James B. Walton, commander of the First Corps Artillery Reserve, watched as a courier dashed up to his position. He brought a note apparently written on a sheet torn from a memorandum book. "Let the batteries open," Longstreet told him. "Order great care and precision in firing. If the batteries at the Peach Orchard cannot be used against the point we intend attacking, let them open on the enemy on the rocky hill." Walton passed this message to Maj. Benjamin F. Eshleman, who commanded the Washington Artillery battalion of Louisiana. One gun of Capt. Merrit B. Miller's 3rd Company immediately rang out "upon the still summer air," as one artillerist put it, but the second gun did not detonate as planned. A friction primer failed to work properly, and it took a few seconds to replace it. The second gun then fired, completing the signal, and it was quickly followed by "a roar and a flash."[1]

Professor Michael Jacobs, instructor of mathematics and chemistry at Gettysburg College, was a meticulous recorder of the weather. Not even the occupation of his town by Lee's army prevented the doughty academic from noting that the bombardment erupted at precisely 1:07 P.M. Alexander, who was in charge of the show, recorded the time less precisely as "just one o'clock." Many men remembered where they were and what they were doing when the artillery erupted. Longstreet went to Spangler's Woods "to lie down and study for some new thought that might aid the assaulting column" right after he sent the order to Walton. Lee positioned himself behind Anderson's division just before the barrage began. Walter Harrison, one of Pickett's staff officers, was lounging in Spangler's peach orchard with Garnett and Wilcox, lunching on cold mutton and some whiskey obtained in Chambersburg, when the signal guns fired. The noise broke "the long tedium of the day." Wilcox went off to his command, and

Harrison suggested to Garnett that "we had better be getting back to our line, as the work was about to commence in earnest."[2]

Many Federals also remembered where they were when the guns opened up. Henry Hunt had just finished an inspection tour of the army's batteries and was with Rittenhouse on Little Round Top when Miller's guns boomed. Hunt had mentally prepared for this moment ever since he detected signs of the Confederate artillery concentration. He assumed it meant that the Rebel gunners were preparing to cover a withdrawal of Lee's army or to soften the Union position for an infantry assault, most likely the latter. He had already instructed each battery commander to wait about fifteen to twenty minutes after the Confederates opened up before they replied. This time period would give them the opportunity to gauge where "the most efficient part" of the Rebel artillery line was located and concentrate their fire on it. Hunt wanted them to shoot slowly and deliberately, "making *target practice* of it." He realized that the Federals could bring fewer guns to bear than the Rebels, and they needed to husband their ammunition in case the gray-clad infantry attacked. He hoped to have at least half of his available ammunition left after the bombardment ended. Hunt then watched the incoming Rebel fire for a while before heading for the artillery reserve, where he told everyone to be ready to move forward and reinforce the guns at a moment's notice. Then the artillery chief of Meade's army rode along the line to keep a close watch on developments.[3]

· · · · · · ·

THE FEDERAL INFANTRY

The Union infantrymen, many of whom paid no attention to the Rebel artillery buildup, were startled by the bombardment. The first shell screamed over. "This was followed by two more with pauses of a few seconds between," recalled a member of the 1st Minnesota. A man in Webb's brigade also noticed that the first few rounds were staggered but seemed to bring forth a rapidly accelerating number of explosions. A lot of Yankees were convinced that the signal shots were fired by a Whitworth rifle, a modern, breechloading weapon imported from England. A battery in the Confederate Second Corps had two Whitworths positioned at Oak Hill, but they were too far away to have contributed to the barrage. Lt. Sherman Robinson of Company A, 19th Massachusetts, was one of the first fatalities. He had been eating lunch spread out on a blanket with a group of officers. As he rose and began to wipe his mouth with a handkerchief, a projectile hit his left side below the shoulder, "passing through his body and bearing him to the ground, literally torn to pieces." Other shells knocked down stacks of rifle muskets in front of the 19th. When the Massachusetts boys looked across the valley, they saw Spangler's Woods seemingly "lined with flame and smoke." Looking up, they could even catch fleeting glimpses of shell fragments hissing through the air. It was possible to do this because for the first fifteen minutes or so the air was comparatively clear of smoke — until the Union guns began to reply. Before then, everyone on the Federal side had a wide view of the valley.[4]

Orders quickly went out to take down the shelter tents that had been erected as arbors and to furl the colors as well, for it was believed they served as targets for the Rebel gunners. The teamsters must have thought their buff-topped supply wagons were targets also, for they scrambled to escape the descending hail of shells. Hundreds of these vehicles streamed to the rear, giving the appearance that a defeated and demoralized army was retreating. Cemetery Ridge quickly became bare as the nonessential men fled and the fighting soldiers hunkered down for cover. "A mighty hurricane could not sooner have swept it clean," wrote Hancock's chief of staff. "Ambulances, army wagons, loosed horses, stragglers and sightseers disappeared with a miraculous swiftness." Hancock was dictating an order about meat rations when the shells began to fall. Staff officers and commanders alike sprang forward to grab their horses, for many steeds were frightened by the sudden change from calm to fury.[5]

Some of the more alert Union soldiers had been eying the situation before 1:00 P.M. and were "not particularly surprised when the firing began, for we were expecting almost anything." But they were "astonished at its volume, extent and duration. We were not unfamiliar with artillery fire but this proved to be something far beyond all previous experience, or conception, and the scene was terrific beyond description. It began fiercely, increased rapidly and continued persistently." Some veteran members of the 7th Michigan even wrote their names on scraps of paper so their bodies could be identified if they were killed.[6]

When the Union artillery opened up, the noise and smoke of the bombardment increased rapidly. In fact, it quickly engulfed the Union infantry, located as they were among the guns. The sound was deafening. "Never witnessed anything of the kind that equaled it," declared Maj. Walter A. Van Rensselear of the 80th New York. Soon the two lines of opposing artillery were sending a "constantly moving arch of iron missiles screeching like fiends their defiance while passing each other in mid air." The roar of each gun blended with that of its neighbor, and the witnessing infantry could not distinguish them; they could only hear a continual roar that made many of them deaf for one or two days. The noise severely tried the nerves and the courage of the listening foot soldiers, but it apparently did not bother the artillerists. Thomas Ward Osborn admitted that the sound of the bombardment was deafening, but his gunners paid little attention to it. They were far too busy working the guns. "I have often heard infantry officers speak of it," he wrote after the war, "though I have but a faint recollection of it myself."[7]

Now and then, especially if someone was on the skirmish line in the middle of the valley, it was possible to look up and actually see the projectiles. Members of the 12th New Jersey could catch glimpses of the course of the shells: "We could see a dark line flit across overhead and others cross this towards every point of the compass." It was a bit easier to see them if they were coming directly into one's line of vision, thought a staff member in Stannard's Vermont brigade. They appeared like "black spots in the air" to him.[8]

Most of the infantry could only see smoke. It was so thick at times that they could not see more than twenty yards. While the Union guns seemed to shake the earth with each discharge, the blasts caused "Wild and heated currents" to blow sideways over the reclining troops. What had been "a dull and lazy air was now turned to a dark, wild and sulphurous atmosphere." Color Sgt. John M. Dunn of the 1st Delaware looked back years later and thought it seemed "like some horrible night-mare where one was held spell-bound by the appalling grandeur of the storm." The smoke did not just obscure the vision; it seared the eyes and lungs of the infantrymen. Despite the dense smoke, the Federal gunners continued to fire rapidly. Amazed foot soldiers could not understand how they did this. They also could not understand why they had to endure so much discomfort near the guns. Sgt. Maj. William B. Hincks of the 14th Connecticut was near enough to Arnold's battery so that the concussion of the pieces sprayed gravel onto him with each discharge. He not only was pelted with this annoyance but could taste the harsh powder smoke in his mouth. He and Eddy Hart lay together on the ground and sweated so much that a pool of mud developed below their faces. "No one moved or spoke save the gunners behind us and ever and anon I could hear the ringing voice of the sergeant nearest us giving command to aim, fire, (a tremendous crash) load, to be after a brief interval repeated. Then after a time I judged

THE BOMBARDMENT

that he was wounded, for his voice was silenced, and out of the cloud came another and different voice, repeating the same command."[9]

Several Unionists were fascinated about the rate of fire. Some estimated that 200 explosions per minute took place; others placed it as high as 600. George Grenville Benedict, a staff officer with Stannard, looked at his watch at one point in the bombardment and counted 6 shells in sixty seconds. Thomas Ward Osborn, who knew a great deal about the guns, believed both sides fired 2 to 4 rounds per minute from each piece. "That is about as rapidly as the chief of the gun could take good aim." That made for 1,500 rounds per minute along the line, at least during the heaviest part of the bombardment. Osborn insisted that this was no exaggeration; he knew that a battery had managed to fire 9 well-aimed shots a minute from each gun at Chancellorsville. "The gun, under pressure, can be loaded and fired as fast as one man can bring ammunition from the ammunition chest which is generally about ten steps in rear of the gun." Certainly the artillerists on both sides were doing their utmost to reach that high rate of efficiency.[10]

No infantrymen had a better opportunity to see, hear, and feel the guns in action than those in the 108th New York. Positioned literally in the middle of Woodruff's battery, they were subjected to the worst artillery fire of their experience. It seemed as if a shell screamed overhead every second, often overshooting Woodruff and smashing the oak trees of Ziegler's Grove to the rear. The edge of the grove was close enough to the regiment so that splinters and limbs came flying by or crashing down among the men. Pvt. Chauncey L. Harris of Company F described the scene for his father: "One shell came shrieking and tearing through the trees with the velocity of lightning, striking a caisson, causing it to explode, wounded several." A few New Yorkers were so unnerved by this that they started to their feet, but an alert lieutenant drew his sword and stopped them. "Small trees were cut down and large ones shattered almost to pieces," continued Harris. "Five different cannon balls struck a large oak three feet in diameter which stood not five feet from where I lay, and one of them passed entirely through it. A shell struck right at my feet killing Sergeant Maurice Welch and Private John Fitzner."[11]

Every soldier along the line crouched and scrambled for shelter, and many were lucky enough to find it. The 14th Connecticut took advantage of a "narrow ledge of ironstone" that was exposed and "slightly inclined" just in front of the stone fence. It deflected many projectiles that hit the ground in front of them, causing the shells to ricochet over their heads.

Other men took advantage of every slight undulation of the ground, which meant that they had to lie as flat as possible in the open, burning sunshine. Members of the 1st Minnesota had an undulation in their front; when shells struck it, they ricocheted uncomfortably close over their heads. One man's knapsack, still on his back, was struck by a projectile. Anyone attempting to go to the rear exposed himself to the hail of iron coursing through the air.[12]

Men who had the fortune to crouch behind breastworks, earthworks, or the stone fence were especially pleased. Cyril H. Tyler of the 7th Michigan thought "it did not seem as though a man could get out alive," but the earthwork saved many of his comrades. Even so, the commander of the 7th discounted the value of the slight fortification. Most of the shells simply ricocheted over the work because they bounced off the undulations of the ground in front of it, an opinion seconded by Capt. Henry L. Abbott of the 20th Massachusetts. But Albert Stokes Emmell of the 12th New Jersey derived great comfort from the stone fence topped with rails that protected him. He admitted it was "but a feeble protection against shot and shell. Solid shot would have gone through it as easily as if it had been rotten cheese. Several shells struck it and . . . two or three came through." But he was convinced it offered a major psychological advantage to the crouching troops.[13]

The rookies of Stannard's brigade were nervous about their advanced position. The 14th Vermont had a decent breastwork, but the 13th, just to the left of Gates's demibrigade, was exposed. Randall received permission from Stannard to reposition his command forward, to the right of the 14th. The Vermonters crawled along the ground in a manner "not according to strict military rule," remembered Ralph Orison Sturtivant, but in a "helter skelter zig zag croutching, crawl and run[,] each taking his own way to reach" the spot. They were helped a bit by the odd stone and bush along the way. A few of the men were slightly wounded, and some showed signs of being unnerved; but all made it. Apparently the breastwork occupied by the 14th Vermont extended far enough to the right to shelter at least part of the 13th. Now Randall's men were farther down the slope of Cemetery Ridge with a wider and clearer field of fire to their front. They were also about 100 yards ahead of the main Union line.[14]

Other Union troop repositionings took place during the bombardment. Worried about the intense hail of artillery fire and his thin line, Hays ordered the 111th New York up to the stone fence. This regiment al-

THE BOMBARDMENT

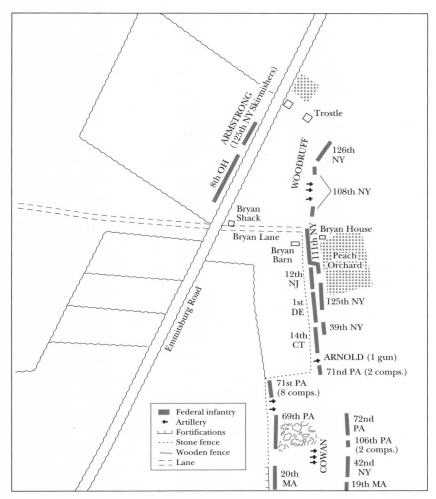

Map 4.1 Federal Unit Positions after Bombardment, 2:00 P.M., July 3, 1863

ready had a good position sheltered behind another stone fence topped with rails on the eastern edge of Ziegler's Grove. The crowned top of the ridge and intervening, open woods of the grove partly shielded them, but the fence offered even more protection. Capt. Benjamin W. Thompson lay next to Col. Clinton D. MacDougall behind the fence, discussing the lack of food and the condition of the men, when the bombardment started. "For a full minute we were terrified," he later admitted. Mac-Dougall was the first to recover. " 'Captain,' he said, 'it won't do for us to lay here; we must get [to] our place in line.' "[15]

When the order to move up arrived, Thompson found it difficult to get his men to leave their comfortable spot. The soldiers had to be herded forward like cattle, as he put it. When they crested the ridge through the trees, the awful danger became even more apparent; the New Yorkers were double-quicking into a hurricane of artillery fire. Most of them made a beeline for the stone fence and its modest shelter, but a few huddled behind the Bryan house, Hays's headquarters. When the division leader noticed this, he told Thompson to get them out and to the fence, and Thompson somehow managed to do it. Just as the harried captain approached the fence behind the Bryan barn, a solid shot crashed through the structure and knocked a board off the wall, which hit him on the nose. Thompson was knocked flat on his back but not badly injured. When the men laughed at this, Thompson had to swallow his pride and laugh along with them. It helped to relieve the tension.[16]

Several men were killed and wounded while advancing through the grove, but the 111th New York had reinforced the line. It took position just to the right of the 12th New Jersey. In fact, in its hasty advance MacDougall's regiment actually overlapped the right wing of the Jersey men. The New Yorkers essentially meshed with the extreme right of the 12th, an easy process since the latter regiment was so thinly spread along the fence that it seemed to be little more than a "heavy skirmish line." The right of the 111th New York extended far enough to cover the Bryan barn and Bryan Lane just to the north of it. The colors were positioned to the left of the barn. Woodruff's battery and the 108th New York were to the right, separated from MacDougall's command by a small gap.[17]

The New Yorkers suffered enormously in this new, advanced position. The barn offered little shelter even though quite a few men sought a place behind it. A shell came through and took off one man's head. "He fell over on me covering me with blood and brains," recalled Sgt. Thomas Geer of Company A. "These circumstances can never be erased from my memory," he laconically reported. A German immigrant named Gustavus Ritter suffered horribly when a shell clipped off the bottom of both his legs. Ritter lay on his back and held up the "poor bleeding stumps by his arms" until someone came to help him. He died that night.[18]

Thompson and his stragglers were among the last of the regiment to reach the fence, and he had to push and shove to find a place behind it. Thompson lay between two men with his head protected by a large rock in the fence. A shell exploded exactly on the opposite side and dislodged the rock, knocking his head. Thompson had no memory of what happened during the next several minutes, although he was told that he staggered to MacDougall, his face covered with blood, and said he was wounded. The colonel sent him to the rear. His company clerk later found Thompson sitting under an apple tree in the Bryan orchard and accompanied him to Meade's headquarters, where he regained consciousness. The shelling forced the pair farther to the rear, to Rock Creek, where Thompson washed his face and discovered that he was not badly hurt. He managed to make it back to the regiment after the fighting was over for the day.[19]

Pvt. N. Eldred was also a wanderer looking for his place in the regiment. He had gone to Rock Creek with sixteen canteens belonging to his comrades before the bombardment began. The walk back to the 111th was awful. "It seemed to me that the heavens were on fire," he later wrote. "Shells striking the ground, dirt, gravel, stones and pieces of shell entirely blocked my way. I cannot tell you how I felt as I was wading through that storm of iron. Trees two feet through would tremble from base to pinnacle." Eldred reached the first position of the regiment only to find his comrades were gone, having left only his rifle musket behind. Walking ahead, the only way he thought to go, Eldred saw a man rushing to the rear with his lower jaw torn off. "That awful spectacle will not be erased from my memory as long as I live," he shuddered. Nevertheless Eldred made it to his regiment under the hissing barrage.[20]

There were a few adjustments in the positions of other Federal units as well. Arnold's battery, its ammunition exhausted and the guns and gunners decimated, withdrew from its position on the high ground at the northeast angle of the fence. When no other battery appeared to take its place, Major Ellis moved his 14th Connecticut to the left to fill the gap. The regiment had been placed behind the 1st Delaware and probably welcomed the opportunity to crouch closer behind the fence. Farther to the left, Company C of the 1st Minnesota was relieved of provost duty at Meade's headquarters and took position on the left of the 19th Massachusetts. The line needed every man Meade could spare.[21]

Meade issued a flurry of orders bringing more troops toward the center, where he was convinced the Rebels would strike. Brig. Gen. John C. Robinson's division from the First Corps was moved forward from behind Cemetery Hill to the right of the Second Corps, shoring up Hays's weak right flank. Brig. Gen. Alexander Shaler's brigade in the Sixth Corps was positioned to the left and rear of Hancock's command to act as a reserve. Two brigades of Brig. Gen. James S. Wadsworth's First Division, including the famed Iron Brigade, were also placed in reserve with Shaler's command. Another Sixth Corps brigade, commanded by Col. Henry L. Eustis, marched from the foot of Little Round Top to a reserve position in rear of the Second Corps.[22]

Many of the reserve troops were placed near Meade's headquarters, and they came under the same hail of Rebel artillery fire that bedeviled the Second Corps troops on the front line. Elisha Hunt Rhodes of the 2nd Rhode Island, in Eustis's brigade, advanced toward this area along Taneytown Road, which was lined with flinty ledges of rock. Overshot rounds meant for the batteries fell here, striking the ledges and fracturing them into dozens of pieces that flew about like shell fragments. "The flying iron and pieces of stone struck men down in every direction," wrote Rhodes. The men tried to take cover as best they could, but Rhodes estimated that his brigade lost thirty men during the barrage.[23]

Meade's headquarters in Lydia Leister's house on Taneytown Road seems to have received the worst of the bombardment. It was located about 400 yards behind the front line on the other side of Cemetery Ridge, and thus many of the overshot rounds fell in its vicinity. Early in the barrage, shells burst in the yard among the assembled horses, most of which belonged to the staff, and devastated them. Sixteen horses were killed before their owners could react. An excited staff officer found his horse so badly wounded that he wanted to put it out of its misery, but he shot an uninjured horse belonging to another staff officer instead. The carnage in the Leister yard dismounted most of Meade's staff for the duration of the battle, much to the "mortification" of the staffers who had to perform their duty on foot until a remount could be found.[24]

The rain of projectiles hammered the little residence. One shell destroyed the step leading into the house, another knocked aside the foundation of the porch on the south side, another crashed through the front door on the west side of the house, another passed through the loft, and a solid shot grazed Meade as he stood in the open doorway. He finally left the building and paced up and down in the small backyard on the east side. Here he noticed his staff members gradually congregating behind the building as well, and he reminded them that it offered little if any shelter. "He joked us about sitting down on the grass in that manner to protect ourselves," recalled staffer Paul A. Oliver, and then he told them an amusing anecdote from his experience in Mexico to calm their nerves. The plight of his large retinue, which as yet had little to do except brave the bombardment, led Meade to move everyone to a barn several hun-

The Leister house, Meade's headquarters. This photograph taken immediately after the battle shows some of the destruction caused by the Confederate artillery bombardment. Note the two horse carcasses in the road. (LC)

dred yards down the road. It was no better, for shells continued to rain on the party. A distant shell burst sent a fragment half as big as a hand toward the group. It bounced off the ground and slapped Meade's chief of staff, Maj. Gen. Daniel Butterfield, in the side. Butterfield "gracefully keeled over" and was transported off the field in an ambulance, even though few members of the staff "were much impressed with the serious character of the wound."

Meade tarried only a short time at the barn. When told that a signal station had been established on Powers Hill, a half-mile to the rear of the Union center near Baltimore Pike, he decided to move there. Meade wanted to keep in touch with his far-flung army and to find a safe haven for himself and staff. He became separated from most of his staff members on the way, for he was still on horse while they were on foot. Only one staffer, Emlen W. Carpenter, rode with him to Powers Hill. When Meade sent a message from the hill to the Leister house, where he had left a signal officer, he found that the house was deserted. Meade immediately decided to return to Leister's. On the way he met several staff members, all of whom were struggling to reach Powers Hill on foot, and he now told them to come back to the original headquarters site. When Meade reached Leister's, he had only a handful of dismounted staff members and a few mounted orderlies. His son, George Meade Jr., who also served on his staff, took a horse from one of the orderlies so he could keep up with his father.[25]

The Leister house was so badly hammered because it was in an area that received some of the worst pounding during the barrage. The main line was partly spared because Rebel gunners tended to overshoot their targets, particularly at longer ranges, and because the infantrymen there took shelter behind the fence and breastworks. The area on the other side of Cemetery Ridge received the brunt of fire; Hunt believed that the majority of Confederate rounds fell here. This benefited the Rebels little. Hunt called it "a mere waste of ammunition, for everything here could seek shelter." Men who did not have to be there left early in the barrage, and those who were forced to remain either moved about, hid behind rocks, or took their punishment. At any rate, the Rebel shells were falling in rear areas instead of softening the front line. Armistead Long, on Lee's staff, had received artillery training from Hunt before the war. The Union officer knew Long was at Gettysburg and, during a long conversation at Appomattox, chided him about his poor gunnery, telling him "he had not done justice to his instruction." Despite the painful duty of surrendering, Long was amused by this bantering and told Hunt, "I remembered my lessons at the time, and when the fire became so scattered, wondered what you would think about it!"[26]

The fire that hit the rear areas was intense and demoralizing, but it did nothing to prepare the way for Pickett's Charge. The men of the small 10th New York Battalion, forming a provost line along Taneytown Road behind Hays's division in their baggy blue pants and Zouave jackets, were hit by it and suffered casualties. Many of the reserve units Meade had rushed up behind the Second Corps were hit. Even the Eleventh and Twelfth Corps off to the right and rear suffered from the fire. Cemetery

Hill endured a hail of artillery rounds that exploded caissons, smashed tombstones and fences, and killed men and horses. Even Culp's Hill, which was 1,000 yards to the rear of Cemetery Ridge, received a faint share of this fire. At such extreme ranges most of the velocity of the rounds had already been spent, but some extralong overshots sailed slowly enough so that Twelfth Corps infantry could plainly see the projectiles arcing toward the earth. They lopped off the tops of trees and caused some casualties. Some men in the 149th New York calculated whether it was better to be on the Union side of the earthworks on Culp's Hill and be subjected to this fire or to move to the enemy side of the works, where they had to contend with Confederate sharpshooters.[27]

Everything east of Cemetery Ridge constituted the outer limits of the area affected by the Confederate barrage, which was intense on the east slope of the ridge but decreased as one moved away. The main area affected by the bombardment was the western slope. John Gibbon wanted to see what his men were enduring. From the outset of the bombardment he had determined to be with them. Gibbon had been lounging in the small draw on the east slope of the ridge where he had hosted the lunch that day when the guns opened. His horse was slow in reaching him; in fact, Gibbon's orderly was killed by a round while riding the horse to the general, and the frightened mount galloped away. The general did not wait for another. He walked hurriedly up the east slope and was joined by Frank Haskell. The two saw a panorama spread before their eyes. It was still early enough in the barrage for the view to be quite open. The hail of projectiles was the first impression; Gibbon, an old artillerist, noted how the rifled rounds sometimes tumbled in their flight, which was the only opportunity one had to catch a glimpse of them in midair. Shells landing on the ground plowed huge furrows, and around the batteries there was already a heavy layer of powder smoke. Gibbon looked beneath the smoke and could see the "rapidly moving legs of the men as they rushed to and fro between the pieces and the line of limbers, carrying forward the ammunition."

He marveled at the scene. The infantrymen were still and quiet behind their shelters or on the open ground; the gunners were frantically busy, but the horses were perfectly still. "Even when a shell, striking in the midst of a team, would knock over one or two of them or hurl one struggling in his death agonies to the ground, the rest would make no effort to struggle or escape but would stand stolidly by as if saying to themselves, '*It is fate*, It is useless to try to avoid it.'" One gunner of

Cushing's battery seemed to have an attitude as practical as the horses'. When a shell clipped off one of his legs, he coolly hopped to the rear on the good one, "the shreds of the other dangling about as he went."

Haskell was just as fascinated with the sights of this bombardment as was Gibbon. The staff officer watched as a shell struck a knapsack on the back of a man who was hurrying refilled canteens toward his comrades. The canteens flew through the air as the soldier spun around, and the knapsack disintegrated "like an egg," its remnants "thrown spitefully against a rock." But the man was not injured. He had a look of surprise and puzzlement, but when he realized all was well, he shrugged his shoulders and calmly walked on. Looking to the sky, Haskell watched the shell explosions.

> Their flash was a bright gleam of lightning radiating from a point, giving place in the thousandth part of a second, to a small, white, puffy cloud, like a fleece of the lightest, whitest wool. These clouds were very numerous. We could not often see the shell before it burst; but some times, as we faced toward the enemy, and looked above our heads, the approach would be heralded by a prolonged hiss, which always seemed to me to be a line of something tangible, terminating in a black globe, distinct to the eye, as the sound had been to the ear. The shell would seem to stop; and hang suspended in the air an instant, and then vanish in fire and smoke and noise. We saw the missels tear and plow the ground.

Gibbon and Haskell walked up to Webb, who was sitting on the ground behind his brigade. "What does this mean?" Gibbon asked the brigadier, and later he remembered that "Webb shook his head. In fact it was a question about which we all felt anxious, but no one could answer it yet. It might mean preparation for retreat; it might signify the prelude to an assault." Then Gibbon suggested to Haskell that they go forward and encourage the men. Later he admitted that a secondary motive was to get away from the worst of the shelling, as he had noticed that it was less intense farther forward. The pair passed by the copse of trees and walked toward the fence. Gibbon waved to the men lying there to make room for them, and the two stepped over the stones and walked to the nearest clump of rocks and trees, about seventy-five yards in front of the line. They tried to peer into the valley but could see only smoke; most of the shells now were passing overhead and exploding on and behind the ridge. An aide came from Hancock with a query: What did Gibbon think

THE BOMBARDMENT

this bombardment meant? He repeated his views, already expressed to Webb, and the aide returned to Hancock.

Gibbon and Haskell now walked back to the fence but remained in front of it; they began to make their way left along the division line. The prone infantrymen noticed their passing and words were exchanged. "What do you think of this?" Gibbon asked them. "O, this is bully," they replied, "We are getting to like it, — O, we don't mind this." The soldiers were inspired by Gibbon's bravado. "See there, see Gen. Gibbons," they said. His actions seemed to tell them, "Boys, this is the way to face danger." As they approached the end of the division line, where Stannard's Vermont troops were positioned forward and covering the little spring in Plum Run Valley, Gibbon and Haskell noticed injured skirmishers coming back to the rear for treatment. They also noticed a man returning from the spring with loaded canteens, hugging the ground and crawling while making his way slowly back to his unit. Gibbon called to him, "Look out, my man, you might get hit!" It was a gentle rebuke. The soldier turned to see the two lone figures standing tall in the hurricane and was ashamed. He quickly "rose to his feet and walked deliberately back to his regiment; no doubt arguing with himself that if two could walk erect there was little danger to a third."[28]

The inspiring effect of such brave acts by officers was well known in the Civil War. Gibbon played the role to the hilt, even though he knew, as an artillerist, that there was comparatively little danger of getting hit while walking in front of the line. Hays also did his share of grandstanding to inspire the men. He rode up and down the line — only he and two of his staff members remained mounted during the barrage — thus exposing himself even more than Gibbon. "Boys, don't let 'em touch these pieces," he told the 108th New York. When Woodruff's guns poured it in, he shouted, "Hurrah, boys, we're giving them h—ll."[29]

Hays knew his own men would hold, but he worried about his flank support. Webb was a young, wet puppy in his view. He sent staff officer David Shields to "go over to Webb and see how he is standing it." The young brigadier had risen from the ground and was smoking a cigar with his staff officers at the copse. Webb, a little irritated, told Shields that he could see the men of the Philadelphia Brigade were in line and that he was doing everything that could be expected of him. When Shields asked if he could hold against an infantry attack, Webb petulantly replied that "he could and would." Hays was not so sure. "We will soon see," he muttered, and then he sent the aide to Hancock and even to Meade, if need be, to complain about his right flank. Shields could not find the corps leader and reached the Leister house just after Meade had evacuated it. The area around the building was horrible. "Nothing could live there," Shields later remembered. "Tons of metal of various kinds seemed to be falling about me and the ground was strewn with dead men and dead and dying horses; some men and many horses dreadfully mangled; some horses on their haunches in the agonies of their death struggles and in other positions that showed too plainly the terror of the occasion. The scene around these headquarters was one of devastation, and my ride was a ride of horror as well as a futile one."[30]

Most officers did not expose themselves deliberately, but very few refused to share the same dangers as their men. Shields found one such man, Lt. Col. Levi Crandell of the 125th New York, when he rode to and from the Leister house. The nineteen-year-old aide took it upon himself to chastise Crandell, who sat on the ground well behind his regiment holding his horse's reins. Crandell claimed to be ill, but Shields did not accept that excuse. He told the lieutenant colonel that the front was safer than the rear, but Crandell still pleaded his case; Shields rode on, leaving him "sitting on the ground a miserable man, sacrificing all, for what he thought was the greater safety of his wretched body."[31]

The fear that gripped Crandell came from the evidence all around him. There was death and maiming everywhere. A shell mortally wounded Col. Paul J. Revere of the 20th Massachusetts, a direct descendent of the Revolutionary War hero; he died two days later. A solid shot hit the ground just in front of a man in the 80th New York and flung his cap off his head and into the air. The soldier "gave a curiously awkward 'flop'" and spun around. His comrades laughed at this strange occurrence until they realized he was dead, even though he had no mark of an injury on his body. Hunt saw another infantryman killed in a similar way. A rifled projectile penetrated the ground just under the prone man and rolled his body over several times. He came to rest several feet away, dead, and a newly plowed ridge of earth was left where he had lain. Hunt was reminded of the old frontier practice of "barking squirrels." Lt. Col. Jacob B. Hardenburgh of the 80th New York recalled that his veterans smoked and joked during the barrage; but the rookies of Stannard's brigade hugged the ground, and "big drops of perspiration stood out on their foreheads and faces." Capt. John Lonergan of Company A, 13th Vermont, suffered the loss of his closest friend, Lt. John Sinnott, during the barrage. An Irish-born schoolteacher, Sinnott was mortally wounded by shell fragments. Lonergan tied a handkerchief around his head and lay beside him under the rain of missiles. "As I gazed on the man — the Soldier — the hero, my comrade pale-wounded-bleeding-dying! He took me by the hand-pressed it — he could not Speak — he was Sensless!"[32]

The infantrymen stolidly endured the bombardment while most of the wounded stayed where they were. It was risking death to make their slow way to the rear, and they did not want to endanger comrades who might feel compelled to help them. Instead they "lay and bled quietly in their places." Many infantrymen grew accustomed to the noise, which started to lull them into somnolence. Several observers remembered the odd occurrence; quite a few Federals actually fell asleep under fire. They were already lying down, and their fatigue, the hot sun, and other factors were conducive to slumber.[33]

· · · · · · ·

THE UNION ARTILLERY

The batteries were the main targets of the Rebel guns. No matter how much the infantry suffered, the gunners got much worse. Those who were fighting around the angle received the most intense concentration of fire, and they suffered appalling casualties. The gunners in McGilvery's large group were barely affected, and Rittenhouse's men atop Little Round Top were untouched. The artillerists serving the guns on Cemetery Hill were hard pressed but holding their own. The Federal gunners earned their pay this day.

Those batteries near the angle — Rorty's, Brown's, Cushing's, and Arnold's — and Woodruff's exposed guns were the center of the storm. They occupied the inner zone of the area affected by the bombardment, where the Confederate fire was felt in the most devastating manner. Two of Rorty's four guns were disabled, and so many of his men went down that he had only three of the original sixty-five left. The captain called on the 13th Vermont for help, and a few men responded. Rorty acted as the No. 1 gunner on one piece for a while, and a lieutenant of the 19th Massachusetts brought water from a spring to swab the tube. Rorty then asked Colonel Devereux for help from the 19th, and the colonel assigned six men to carry ammunition. Later a call for volunteers brought twenty more Massachusetts infantrymen to the gun. One of them said, "Let's go and help. We might as well get killed there as here." Rorty was mortally wounded by the explosion of a limber chest, and Lt. Albert Sheldon took his place.[34]

Brown's Rhode Island battery was likewise worsted, its men decimated, but the survivors grimly carried on. A shell exploded at the muzzle of one piece just after the No. 2 gunner, Alfred G. Gardner, inserted the charge. The No. 1 gunner was decapitated by fragments, and Gardner's left side was shredded, his arm and shoulder torn off. John Deleven, a gunner at the next piece, glanced toward Gardner, and the sight sickened him. Sgt. Albert Straight bent over to see to Gardner, who had only a few minutes to live. Gardner asked him to send his Bible to his wife, then shouted, "*Glory to God, Hallelujah, Amen, Amen!*" and died. The surviving gunners tried to bring the piece back into action, but they found that Gardner's round had somehow been drawn forward by the explosion and was lodged at the muzzle. The metal soon cooled and wrapped around the charge to hold it in place. They tried to ram it home but failed; then an officer ordered them to get an ax and try to drive it down, but that failed as well. The gunners quickly took to other pieces, and the useless cannon later became famous as "The Gettysburg Gun," a curiosity for succeeding generations who fed on unusual and heroic stories of the great war. It had the marks of three artillery rounds and thirty-nine bullets by the time the attack was repulsed.[35]

Cushing's battery was torn apart as the barrage continued. At first it held its own in the rain of projectiles even though the atmosphere soon made targets indistinguishable. Christopher Smith remembered that "the sun through the smoke looked like a great red ball," and the concussion of the cannon sent waves of air and smoke into the valley "like gusts of wind." Unable to see the Rebels, except on occasion, the gunners simply set the proper elevation and "kept on loading and firing as rapidly as possible." Early in the bombardment a shell wrecked the wheel of Cushing's No. 3 gun; its crew panicked and ran to the rear, but Cushing stopped them by drawing his pistol and threatening to shoot everyone. He ordered them to retrieve a spare wheel from a caisson, replace the damaged one, and keep firing. Two other pieces were damaged and fixed in the same way. Twenty-two-year-old Cushing performed magnificently. The brother of William B. Cushing, a Navy officer who would become a hero by blowing up the Confederate ironclad *Albemarle* the next year, he positioned himself between two guns and directed his crews, encouraged their morale, and kept his three-inch Ordnance rifles working despite the accurate Rebel fire. "He was as cool and calm as I ever saw him," recalled Christopher Smith, "talking to the boys between shots with the glass constantly to his eyes, watching the effect of our shots."[36]

As the barrage continued, however, it wore on the battery more and more. A shell struck two draft horses, passing all the way through one and exploding inside the other. A fragment of this shell hit a driver named William Griffin (actually an infantryman from the 7th Michigan who had volunteered to help the gunners), tore apart his abdomen, and left him lying on the ground with his intestines hanging out. Griffin pleaded for someone to put him out of his misery; when no one did so, he drew a revolver out of his belt and shot himself in the head. Fifty soldiers from the 71st Pennsylvania had to help Cushing work his guns as human losses mounted. Cushing himself was dreadfully wounded in the right shoulder and the testicles. The shock and bleeding caused extreme nausea and pain. He vomited but continued to stand and do his duty. When Sgt. Frederick Fuger suggested he go to the rear for help, Cushing replied, "No, I stay right here and fight it out or die in the attempt!"[37]

Near the end of the bombardment only two serviceable Ordnance rifles remained in the battery. Webb came to Cushing and was appalled at his condition, but he told the artilleryman that he thought the Rebels would advance their infantry as soon as the guns fell silent. Cushing replied, "Then I had better run my guns right up to the stone fence and bring up all the canister alongside of each piece." Webb replied, "Do so." Volunteers from the 71st Pennsylvania helped to move the guns by hand down the slope. They were positioned just at the right flank of the 69th Pennsylvania, about ten feet from the fence and about nine feet apart. Fuger and the three remaining gunners manned No. 4 on the left, and the Pennsylvania infantrymen manned No. 3 on the right. The limbers and caissons remained where they were; only the remaining canister was brought up, and Cushing hobbled painfully forward to be with his guns.[38]

Woodruff's battery endured a great deal and, like Cushing's, continued firing. Enough straggling trees from Ziegler's Grove were close to his guns so that large branches occasionally rained down on the pieces from overshot rounds. A shell exploded one of Woodruff's caissons and shredded the nearby draft animals. "The horses rolled in heaps everywhere tangled in their harness with their dying struggles—wheels knocked off, guns capsized and artillerists going to the rear or lying on the ground bleeding in every direction," wrote the assistant surgeon of the 108th New York. Like all the other battery commanders, Woodruff had to ask the infantry for help. Col. Francis E. Pierce sent many of his New York men to fetch ammunition or to handle the guns.[39]

Some reinforcements arrived in the form of Andrew Cowan's New York battery. Cowan, a twenty-one-year-old native of Scotland, served in the Sixth Corps but was told to report to Newton's First Corps that morning. He waited in park near the Union center for a while until he got the nod to go up behind Stannard's brigade, just to the left of Rorty. Here his New York gunners contributed to the bombardment, firing deliberately to the left oblique at the Rebel guns in the Sherfy peach orchard. Then an officer rode up and told him to move to the right. It was Capt. Charles H. Banes, a staff officer Webb had sent to get more guns. Banes had to ride all over the battlefield before he found Hunt, who quickly authorized him to take anything he needed. Banes chose Cowan. The Scotsman did not know if he should listen to Banes's plea, for Webb belonged to the Second Corps; but then he looked toward the copse and saw the young brigadier waving his hat in earnest. Cowan decided to go. Most of his gunners were stripped to the waist because of the heat; they yelled and jumped up onto the limber chests and guns with their accouterments in their hands to get there as quickly as possible. Cowan replaced Brown's decimated Rhode Island battery and opened fire.

His rightmost piece had gone too far, beyond the copse a bit, while the other five were able to fire to the left of the trees. Cowan rode over to see to the gun and discovered it was only a few yards from Cushing's disabled pieces. Cowan arrived just in time to see Cushing advance his two remaining guns to the fence. The Scotsman explained why his lone gun was so close to the regular battery's position, but young Cushing waved it off with "some pleasant reply" and limped forward. Cowan never saw him alive again. His own detached gun was now in no one's way, so he left it in place.[40]

The remaining four guns of Brown's battery were hauled out of the line and to the rear by Hunt's order, but they suffered nearly as much during the withdrawal as when they had been on the front line. While three of the pieces made a beeline across country to Taneytown Road, the fourth took a wrong turn to the north along a cart path to that road. A shell cut a gash on the forehead of the wheel driver, blinding him with blood; he could not manage the horses properly, so the swing driver took his place. But the swing horses were so frightened by the shell that they bolted right and left; they were calmed only when a soldier lying on the ground nearby volunteered to soothe them. Just before reaching Taneytown Road, another shell ripped the bowels of the off-wheel horse, and a fragment broke the leg of one of the swing horses. As the gun and team were swinging into the road cut, which was three feet lower than the surrounding ground, the off-wheel horse stepped onto its own intestines and fell dead in the roadbed, immobilizing the whole gun. It became a stationary target. The wheel was smashed, and the horses either ran away or were killed. There was nothing to do but abandon the piece. Later that night, after the Rebel repulse, the gunners returned but found nothing useful to retrieve. Some enterprising Federals from another battery had taken the gun and all the usable harness, leaving only the carcasses.[41]

Hunt ordered up more reinforcements for the artillery as well. Four more batteries were taken from the reserve and rushed to the area around the copse of trees. Arnold's battery was withdrawn for the same reason as Brown's; but in the confusion no one ordered a replacement for it, and the 14th Connecticut, as mentioned before, filled the gap it left. Also, it is unclear why Cushing was allowed to remain in place. That battery was probably the most savaged, yet no one thought to bring up help for it. Rorty's badly mauled unit also was not replaced, even though it needed relief. The surviving gunners and infantry volunteers were told by Hunt to remain in place and run their remaining two Parrott rifles up to the stone fence between the 19th Maine and the 15th Massachusetts, squeezing among the small 1st Minnesota. Like Cushing, they assembled their remaining canister rounds and waited for the Rebel infantry.[42]

Farther to the left, between Rorty and McGilvery, Lt. Augustin N. Parsons's Battery A, New Jersey Light Artillery, was in the open. Parsons responded to the Confederate fire, but he probably received more than he gave. A German immigrant who served as a driver was smashed with a shell fragment, raised six inches off his saddle, and forced to the ground. The fragment had driven his pocketbook into his bowels, making for a gruesome and bloody injury. He wanted the $20 in the pocketbook, stained with his own blood, distributed to his comrades. Then he died. Another shell burst knocked down five men; none was killed, but one unlucky man lost an eye. He later asked Parsons to verify that he had lost it in action so he could obtain a false eye from the government.[43]

McGilvery's large concentration of guns, most of which were hidden from the view of the Confederates, played little role in the bombardment. This was by design. McGilvery knew that ammunition for some of his eight batteries was short, so he told most of them not to bother replying until the Confederate infantry attacked. The parapet, small as it was, served as a good defense, even though most Rebel rounds that sailed over were grossly overshot. McGilvery described the Confederate fire as "very rapid and inaccurate, most of the projectiles passing from 20 to 100 feet over our lines." The fact that the gray-clad gunners could not see his pieces obviously accounts for this.[44]

Hancock interfered with the management of the artillery, much to the irritation of Hunt and many battery commanders. The Second Corps leader had never been shy on the battlefield, and he eagerly accepted the responsibility of leading the Union center. The bombardment brought out the best and the worst in him. Hancock wanted to make himself visible to everyone, so he rode along the lines on his favorite black horse. He started from the right of the Second Corps line and proceeded slowly to the left, followed by his staff and the corps pennant flying high. Hancock wanted to be seen, but he made such a big show that concerned subordinates worried about his safety. When told that he was too important to risk his life in this way, he replied, "There are times when a corps commander's life does not count." Perhaps realizing the gravity of the risk, Hancock also stopped to converse with some officers whom he had treated harshly in the past and offered them an apology.[45]

The same desire to inspire the troops resulted in a bitter controversy that would fester for many years. Hancock noticed that a large concentration of artillery, McGilvery's, was not firing at all. Despite the fact that these guns belonged to the army's reserve, not to the Second Corps, he sent his corps artillery chief, John Hazard, to order them to join in the bombardment. Hazard returned saying the battery commanders refused, as they had orders from Hunt to remain silent. Hancock then rode up to do the job himself. He was in a foul mood as he approached Capt. Patrick Hart about 1:30 P.M. and demanded to know why his guns were not in action. Hart explained Hunt's instructions, but Hancock reminded him his battery was in the section of line that Hancock commanded and repeated the order. Hart was forced to comply (even though after the war he insisted that he refused and even demanded a written order from the major general), and Hancock went on to do the same with Thompson's and Phillips's batteries. By that time McGilvery had become aware of what was going on and confronted Hancock. The corps leader told him bluntly that Hunt "had no idea of anything like this when he gave his orders" for the guns to remain silent and that his infantry needed to have their spirits boosted by the stimulating effect of Union return fire. He even told them he worried that his men might not stand the bombardment if all the

Federal artillery did not open up. McGilvery reminded him that he "was not under Gen. Hancock's orders, and I could not see why the Second Corps could not stand the fire as well as the other troops, or as well as my gunners." Hancock, frustrated and impatient, rode away. McGilvery ordered the three batteries to cease fire. The artilleryman later recalled that Hancock "seemed un-necessarily excited, was unduly emphatic, and as there was nothing in sight except puffs of smoke 1500 and more yards away his orders would result in a most dangerous and irreparable waste of ammunition."[46]

Hunt did not learn of Hancock's interference until just after the battle, when Meade mentioned to him that one of his generals had complained "that in the cannonade of yesterday an Artillery Captain refused to obey his order to open fire." Hunt was already tired of arguing with infantry officers about who had the right to control the artillery, and with a sigh of patient martyrdom he asked Meade for details. The two then had a serious discussion about the issue, exchanging what Hunt later described as "some warm words." Meade thought that Hancock was right, that any officer of lower rank in any arm of the service must obey a direct order from a general. Hunt argued that the artillery was a specialized, technical service that most infantrymen simply did not understand. The guns had to be commanded by artillery officers if they were to provide the most efficient support for the infantry. Furthermore, McGilvery was not attached to the Second Corps in the order of battle. "A general has no more right to order about the . . . batteries of another corps or division than his own then he has to order about their infantry or cavalry regiment." The two could not agree, so Meade dropped the subject without identifying the general. But Hunt found out who it was when he talked with McGilvery later. Arguments over this incident would heat up again in the 1870s when Hancock published his opinions regarding a reorganization of the artillery in the regular army, claiming that the desire of artillerymen to exercise independent control over their guns on the battlefield was a foolish mistake. This prompted Hunt to issue opinions of his own. The two outspoken officers never reconciled their differences.[47]

The nub of the argument was whether the artillery should be controlled on the tactical level by gunners or by infantrymen. Lee had consolidated his long arm into divisional battalions controlled by trained gunnery officers rather than dispersing them to brigades and allowing the infantry commanders to direct their placement. Meade had more recently done the same thing, but many of his officers had not yet warmed

Brig. Gen. Henry Jackson Hunt, artillery chief of the Army of the Potomac, who skillfully directed the Union guns in the artillery bombardment (Massachusetts Commandery, Military Order of the Loyal Legion and the U.S. Army Military History Institute, USAMHI)

to the new system. Hancock obviously preferred the old organizational scheme and wanted to maximize his control over the resources in the center. Many commentators sided with Hancock. It is not surprising that his staff officer Lt. Col. Charles H. Morgan believed that the morale of the infantry was the most important factor to consider and that canister rather than long-range ammunition was sufficient to repel the Rebel assault. Even Edward P. Alexander agreed with Hancock when he read about the controversy after the war. Alexander believed that with the greater supply of ammunition in the Union army, Hunt should have fired as rapidly and as long as he could to force the Confederates to match the Union assault. "Their policy should have been always to fight us to exhaustion if we would give them the chance. Exhaustion would have come to us first." But it is difficult to see these points. Hunt was right to reserve long-range rounds to punish the Rebel infantry as much as possible even before it came within the range of canister. And there was not an inexhaustible supply of ammunition in Meade's army; wasting it just to help bolster the spirit of the infantry, which obviously did not need bolstering, was foolish.[48]

While McGilvery had little more to contend with than boisterous generals, and Rittenhouse was safely ensconced on Little Round Top, Osborn received the second heaviest punishment of any artillery concentration along the Union line. His guns had an excellent platform on Cemetery Hill, but they were subjected to a cross fire. At first he received fire only from the west for the first twenty minutes or so of the bombardment. He did not suffer extraordinary damage from this, for the Rebels were firing high. The lateral aim was perfect, but most of the projectiles seemed to sail about twenty feet over the heads of the gunners. "The air just above us was full of shells and the fragments of shells," recalled Osborn. "Indeed, if the enemy had been as successful in securing our elevation as they did the range there would not have been a live thing on the hill fifteen minutes after they opened fire." But then another set of Rebel guns, Capt. Charles E. Raine's Virginia battery, opened on Osborn from Benner's Hill to the northeast. Raine's twenty-pounder Parrotts not only had the lateral aim perfect; they also had the right elevation, and they were positioned to hit Osborn in the flank. "It was admirable shooting," he recalled. "They raked the whole line of batteries, killed and wounded the men and horses and blew up the caissons rapidly. I saw one shell go through six horses standing broadside." He wheeled three batteries to face northeast to deal with this, and the result was immediate and decisive. The Federal gunners got the range and elevation quickly and soon reduced the Rebel fire, which in turn became wild. The debris of wrecked equipment that Osborn found on Benner's Hill after the battle attested to the work of his men. Osborn used up so much ammunition that he had to send many caissons back to the army's ordnance train to bring up more. Despite the punishment, his men held and returned the Rebel fire round for round, decimating some of their units.[49]

Soon after silencing the guns on Benner's Hill, Osborn was visited by Hunt, who wanted to gauge how the artillery was faring. The two talked about what was likely to happen after the bombardment ended, and both were convinced that a massive infantry assault must follow. They were joined by Eleventh Corps commander Howard and one of his division leaders, Maj. Gen. Carl Schurz. Osborn suddenly suggested that the artillery cease firing. This would give the Rebels the impression that they had softened the Union position and lure them into starting the infantry assault. Hunt quickly agreed, as did Howard. When Osborn assured Hunt that he could hold his men to their posts if they stopped firing, the plan was sealed. While Osborn walked along the line of batteries on Cemetery Hill, telling the men to cease fire and lie on the ground, Hunt rode to the left doing the same. The artillery chief would later take the credit for this idea away from Osborn, but the latter richly deserved it.[50]

Meade also came up with the idea. The army commander had spent a lot of time thinking, while not dodging artillery rounds, and independently concluded to stop the return fire in order to lure the Rebel infantry into the valley. One of his staff officers passed on the suggestion to Capt. Henry H. Bingham, an aide to Hancock, who in turn brought it to Hunt while the artillery chief was relaying the instructions to his batteries.[51]

As Hunt made his way from Cemetery Hill to McGilvery, he not only commanded the guns to stop but made a hurried examination of their readiness for the next phase of the fight. He ordered some to be replaced by fresh units from the reserve but overlooked others in the hasty inspection. Thus some units around the angle, such as Arnold's, were given orders to withdraw while other badly mangled batteries, such as Cushing's, remained in line. There was no time to sort out these arrangements carefully. Hancock reappeared again to irritate the artillerists. He noticed Hazard's guns in the angle area shutting down and ordered them to resume firing. Poor Hazard "begged him not to insist upon" his order, but the corps leader refused to relent. The guns, or at least those that

THE BOMBARDMENT

were still operable, continued firing. Hancock did not ride to McGilvery, remembering his rebuff there a few minutes earlier. When Hunt realized that Hazard continued to fire, he rode back only to find that the long-range ammunition for these guns was already exhausted; there would be none available when the Rebel infantry started their attack. The artillery at the focal point of the assault would only be able to deliver short-range ordnance at the foe. Hunt summed it up well when he assumed that Hancock did this "on the spur of the moment, without reflection, certainly without forecast, and rushing into the trap set for us, he played the enemy's game by throwing away his own ammunition during the cannonade without taking proper means to replace it for the assault."[52]

Osborn, who deserves much credit for his work in the bombardment, noticed that the lure worked beautifully. "I think it was not more than ten minutes before the enemy's line of battle showed itself coming over Seminary Ridge at the point where we supposed Lee's troops were massed."[53]

. . . .
BETWEEN THE LINES

The area around the angle saw the worst destruction caused by the Rebel barrage; Cemetery Hill was hard hit; the left, where McGilvery was located, was safe; and the rear areas were treated to a frenzied shelling that caused a lot of damage to no effect. Ironically, the skirmish lines in the valley were among the safest on the battlefield. The skirmishing, of course, ended when the bombardment began. No one wanted to add their meager rifle pops to the overwhelming noise to front and rear of the prone skirmishers; the bombardment was far too grand and unique to ignore. Samuel C. Armstrong's skirmishers from the 125th New York huddled along Emmitsburg Road and listened to the shells screeching overhead. Some of them exploded prematurely and rained fragments on the men. Members of the 8th Ohio, also taking cover in the ditch along Emmitsburg Road, lay on their backs and looked at the Union line, catching glimpses of the gunners working their pieces through the billowing smoke. Most of them slept because of the drowsiness produced by the heat and the noise; some were struck by shell fragments while sleeping. A spent fragment hurt Thomas F. Galwey's foot; he laughed at it and recovered quickly from the pain, only to be hit in the thigh by another fragment, but again not badly.[54]

Skirmishers from other Union regiments spent the barrage in much the same way. Members of the 14th Connecticut hid behind piles of rails that offered scant protection. The men counted a half-dozen unexploded shells or solid shot lying within a few feet of them when the bombardment ended. A member of the 19th Maine on picket duty in the Codori barn felt as if "the air was full of Devils . . . shell bursting all around us ploughing up the ground and some times crashing thro the old barn that was rocking as tho there was an earth quake."[55]

Not far from the barn in distance, but on the other side of the war, Confederate skirmishers sent from Pickett's division shared the same experience as their blue-clad opponents. Just before the barrage opened, Capt. John T. James of the 11th Virginia had walked up to the artillery line to view the valley. He was instantly convinced he would die. Later his Company D was sent out as skirmishers in front of the guns. They lay in the tall, thick grass entirely in the open; no wind hit them there, although a slight breeze blew from the south all during the bombardment. Some of his men began to suffer intensely.[56]

· · · · · · ·

THE CONFEDERATE INFANTRY

The foot soldiers in butternut, who waited patiently for the barrage to run its course, also shared the same experience as their Union opponents. Those who were close to trees were showered with limbs and splinters. Those who were lying in the open, and that included most of the men, endured the hot sun and excessive heat. Several of these men became overheated and suffered the effects of sunstroke. The heavy pall of cannon smoke made the heat worse. "The earth seemed to leap from its foundation," wrote one survivor, "the atmosphere seemed to quiver, the smoke rose in balloon-shape and gently drifted to the left. The sun's heat was forgotten and mother-earth embraced with a soldier's ardour."[57]

In Wilcox's brigade, about fifty yards behind the line of artillery, the effect of the firing was enormous. One man "could distinguish no particular sound, it was one continuous and awful roar. The ground seemed to rock." The soldiers had to scream to their neighbors to be heard. They could see gunners now and then when the breeze cleared a temporary breech in the smoke screen. The artillerists "seemed like weird spectres of the dammed in the place of departed spirits plying the hellish work of destruction," in the words of Hilary A. Herbert. The gunners could be found "bleeding at both ears from the effect of concussion."[58]

Most of the Confederate infantrymen had to survive this bombardment without the aid of breastworks and little in the form of any other kind of shelter. Isaac Trimble noted that most of the return Union fire damaged Pettigrew's division, 150 yards in front of his two brigades; thus his men were spared too much damage. A soldier of the 1st Virginia, in Kemper's brigade, was stunned by the hail of projectiles falling about his regiment: "I know I felt almost paralyzed, and would have dug a hole in the ground to escape if it had been possible." Erasmus Williams of the 14th Virginia, in Armistead's brigade, did just that. He dug a shallow pit using a pen knife and his bayonet. One of his lieutenants stood behind the hole and chided him, "Why Williams, you are a coward." Williams replied, "You may call me what you please, but when the time comes I will show up all right." The lieutenant refused to give in to such temptations. He proudly proclaimed his willingness to stand and take whatever came along. Early in the barrage he was smashed by a cannonball; his blood "sprinkled all over me," recorded Williams.[59]

Troops belonging to supporting units to the left also suffered under the Union counterfire. Posey's Mississippi brigade, behind a modest trench and parapet along Seminary Ridge to Pettigrew's left, received many rounds. A solid shot struck the bottom of the parapet and shoveled a large amount of dirt and rails onto several men huddled in the trench. Their comrades had to work feverishly to dig them out before suffocation could claim them. The victims were so stunned and dry that it was difficult for their rescuers to squeeze enough water out of their canteens to refresh them. Not long after that harrowing incident a wounded artillery horse stumbled toward the line and fell into the trench, lodging lengthwise and upside down in it. The poor animal's legs waved pitifully in the air. Several men had to pry it out of the trench with rails and drag it away to make room for the soldiers. After that, orders went out to shoot every wandering horse that came close to the earthwork.[60]

Losses mounted at an alarming rate. The psychological impact of artillery casualties was great, for the big guns not only killed but mangled bodies, tore them apart, or disintegrated them. The memories of this horror lasted a long time and filled the accounts of Confederate soldiers.

Col. Joseph Mayo of the 3rd Virginia, Kemper's brigade, noted that the first few rounds sailed harmlessly overhead. Then they lowered and began to find their targets. One of the first hits produced "a piercing shriek," and Col. Waller Tazewell Patton of the 7th Virginia raced to the scene. Two men were killed and three badly wounded. A few seconds later came another explosion and another scream. A lieutenant's legs were shattered below the knees; two brothers were hit (one killed, the other badly wounded); the orderly sergeant was mortally injured; one private was killed; and three others were wounded—all from one shell. And there was still nearly an hour of bombardment left.[61]

Patton noticed that James Dearing was constantly riding his horse among the guns, encouraging the artillerymen but seemingly immune to danger. He suggested to Mayo that it would be safer to move the infantry closer to the guns too, but Mayo told him it would be unwise to do so without orders. Then another shell exploded very nearby. "A handful of earth mixed with blood and brains struck my shoulder," reported Mayo, and he soon realized that two men were decapitated and three others were wounded. One of the injured was David E. Johnston. He had raised his head just seconds before the explosion to catch a breath of fresh air. Lt. Charles B. Brown told him, "You had better put your head down or you may get it knocked off." Johnston shot back, "A man had about as well die that way as to suffocate for want of air." His ribs were broken by the explosion and his lung was badly bruised. Johnston found that his left side seemed paralyzed. "The marvel is that I escaped the explosion of that shell without being torn to shreds." Brown was wounded as well.[62]

While Dearing rode among his guns waving a flag and cheering his gunners, the infantry a few yards behind him were hammered without mercy. The Union fire "pelted them and ploughed through them," recalled Kemper, "and sometimes the fragments of a dozen mangled men were thrown in and about the trench left by a single missile." A litter carrier was grazed by a ball that smashed his pocketbook and "blended together two half-dollar silver pieces." A single shell killed or wounded eight men in Kemper's brigade; a solid shot lifted a soldier three feet into the air and killed him without touching his body. "In any direction might be seen guns, swords, haversacks, heads, limbs, flesh and bones in confusion or dangling in the air or bounding on the earth," wrote a member of the 7th Virginia. "The ground shook as if in the throes of an earthquake."[63]

To the men of Kemper's brigade it seemed "as if we were placed where we were for target practice for the Union batteries." Kemper decided to ask Longstreet about this when he saw the corps commander riding through the hail of projectiles. Longstreet had risen from his resting place in Spangler's Woods to show himself and inspire the troops, just as Hancock was doing on the other side of the valley. Kemper was greatly impressed. Riding alone, Longstreet sat on his horse with "a magnificent grace and composure I never before beheld." Kemper found his calm courage "the grandest moral spectacle of the war," combining "confidence, composure, self-possession and repressed power, in every movement and look, that fascinated me." The brigadier found his voice as he walked up to the mounted figure. "General, this is a terrible place," he told Longstreet. "What! is your command suffering?" Kemper answered yes, "a man is cut to pieces, here every second while we are talking." Longstreet wanted to know if they could be moved to a safer place, but Kemper pointed out there were none available. "I am greatly distressed at this," Longstreet replied, "greatly distressed at this; but let us hold our ground a while longer; we are hurting the enemy badly, and will charge him presently."[64]

Garnett's brigade received similar treatment, although it might not have suffered quite as much as Kemper's. Capt. Henry T. Owen of the 18th Virginia vividly remembered how the "shrill shot overhead or bounding madly across the field would alike dip through a line of prostrate men and rush on with a wail to the rear leaving a wide track of blood behind." A ricocheting solid shot, apparently from Rittenhouse's battery on Little Round Top, came toward the 19th Virginia. Someone yelled "Look out!" and Lt. Col. John T. Ellis looked up to see what was happening. The shot smashed into his face and killed him. Pvt. Albert J. Morris of Company D, 8th Virginia, was decapitated; his brains were "plaistered" over Maj. Edmund Berkeley's hat and scattered over the faces of nearby men "like rain." The same projectile killed Pvt. Benjamin E. Jackson as well.[65]

Randolph Abbott Shotwell felt the pressure of a shell that flew over his head and landed just a few feet to his rear. When he turned and saw the horrified look on the face of a man to his right, he glanced back to see that the projectile had "ploughed through the bodies of two men of my company, . . . cutting their bodies literally in two!" Lt. Charles G. Dawson unwittingly saved himself when he jumped up to move their remains out of the way, for another shell exploded exactly where he had lain.[66]

Major Berkeley of the 8th Virginia, Shotwell's outfit, felt guilty about the pack of playing cards in his pocket. Victorian society still held doubts about such things as card playing, enjoying the theater, and other innocent pleasures, and under the pressure of the bombardment, when life seemed so easily lost, Berkeley suddenly felt he would prefer not to have his body disgraced by a pack of cards. So he buried it in a small hole and put a stone over it. The deck had given him and Colonel Hunton a great deal of pleasure around the campfire, so Berkeley shed a quiet tear for it as he patted the earth and adjusted the rock. The pressure of war could lead men to do some odd things.[67]

Behind Garnett, in the ranks of Armistead's brigade, the slaughter was much lighter. Col. William R. Aylett of the 53rd Virginia was wounded early in the bombardment, forcing Lt. Col. Rawley W. Martin to take charge of the regiment. The trees at the edge of Spangler's Woods, near the left wing of the brigade, were riddled and cut with shell.[68]

On the other side of the battlefield, in the ranks of Fry's brigade of Pettigrew's division, a shell fragment inflicted a slight but painful wound on Fry's shoulder. Another shell explosion killed one lieutenant but only slightly injured another who was lying beside him with his arm over the victim. Despite his own injury, Fry was so tired of the tension and distress of lying under the hail of projectiles that the order to stand up and attack came as a relief.[69]

Davis's brigade received its share of the punishment. Lt. William Peel watched in horror as a projectile hit the ground in front of Lt. Daniel A. Featherston of the 11th Mississippi, angled up enough to catch him in the chest, and exploded the instant it touched him. The impact lifted his body ten feet into the air and killed him. The wounded of Davis's brigade made their way to the rear where a hospital had been erected near a barn by Dr. Joseph Holt. For the rest of his life the surgeon remembered one particular soldier, Sgt. Jeremiah Gage of the 11th Mississippi. His left arm and a third of his torso had been torn away by a shell. When told he had only a short time to live, Gage dictated a farewell letter to his mother that Holt transcribed for him. "This is the last you may ever hear from me. I have time to tell you that I died like a man. Bear my loss as best you can. Remember that I am true to my country and my greatest regret at dying is that she is not free and that you and my sisters are robbed of my worth whatever that may be. I hope this will reach you and you must not regret that my body can not be obtained. It is a mere matter of form anyhow. . . . This letter is stained with my blood." Gage had been a student of law at the University of Mississippi when the University Greys had been organized on campus. He was badly wounded at Gaines's Mill, and one of his comrades remembered him as a man who "did not know what fear was."[70]

Many Confederate officers took it upon themselves to set an example for their men, just as many Union officers had done. Garnett rode back and forth along the brigade line for a time until someone persuaded him that he had done his duty, at least until the barrage was over. Armistead walked about, refusing to lie down. After some time Robert Tyler Jones, grandson of President John Tyler, decided to stand up too. Armistead ordered him down again. Jones remembered that "when I had justified myself by his own example, he replied: 'Yes, but never mind me; we want men with guns in their hands.' "[71]

Pickett did not put on any such public display. He and staff officer Harrison took cover behind a large oak tree at the edge of Spangler's Woods. Asst. Surg. Clayton G. Coleman of the 24th Virginia saw the two at the height of the bombardment. When a shell exploded against a nearby tree, they mounted and rode away to a safer location.[72]

The rank and file of Garnett's and Armistead's brigades had no such opportunity to escape. So many of them were hit that the number of stretcher bearers had to be doubled. Wilcox rode up to Armistead at one point and asked him what he thought would happen when the artillery stopped firing. "To charge and carry the enemy's position in front of us, he supposed," recorded Capt. Benjamin L. Farinholt of the 53rd Virginia. Wilcox explained that there "had already been heavy fighting over the fields in front of us, that our forces had been ordered to retire from the advanced positions they had taken, and that the enemy having had nearly twenty-four hours in which to strengthen the stone wall behind which their infantry was massed, it would be at great sacrifice of life and very difficult to dislodge them." Armistead still believed Pickett could take the position if he were properly supported. Just as Wilcox departed, a shell glanced off a large tree nearby, barely missed Armistead, and injured a private. The group of officers naturally became restless, but Armistead calmed them by saying, "Lie still boys, there is no safe place here."[73]

· · · · · · · ·

THE CONFEDERATE ARTILLERY

The Rebel gunners were under heavy fire, but it did not do as much damage as they were able to hand out to at least a few Union batteries. Federal guns around the angle received by far the worst punishment of any batteries on either side of the valley. The heavy smoke obscured the Rebel guns enough so that much Union counterbattery fire was imprecise; the Yankees did not need to see the prone ranks of Pickett's, Pettigrew's, or Trimble's men to damage them, only fire in the general area that they occupied.

Felix R. Galloway, who worked his gun in the Sherfy peach orchard, saw the Union artillery open up. "All at once the entire front of Cemetery Ridge seemed to light up in a blaze. I well knew what was coming and bowed my head to the inevitable. It came like a fierce hailstorm. The tops of the trees near us were cut off, the limbs broken, and the leaves fairly covered us. The noise was like the blast of a trumpet on a mountain side. I was completely dazed, but still held to the sponge staff." Galloway became more tired with each round and reached a point of exhaustion, "covered with wet powder, standing half bent to dodge the balls." The return fire came closer and closer to the sweating gunners. He could "plainly feel the wind of the shells as they passed over our heads."[74]

Latham's battery in the peach orchard suffered five gunners killed and "quite a number wounded," according to Lt. Joseph L. Thompson. When a horse was hit by a round, the poor animal disintegrated, and its brains slammed into a gunner. He cried, "Oh I am killed Lieut, look my brains are all knocked out!" Another man was severely wounded in the thigh. "I'm killed Lt. he said to me." Thompson replied, "I cant do anything for you," but the doomed artillerist asked plaintively, "Cant you send me off[?]" He died before he could be moved. When a shell exploded against the wheel of one piece in the Richmond Howitzers, it killed one gunner and wounded another man. Part of the wheel bruised the leg of James Peter Williams "but didn't disable me." The battery suffered two killed and ten wounded in the barrage.[75]

On Pettigrew's front Maj. William Thomas Poague lost his favorite mount, a sorrel mare, when a shell nearly cut off her hindquarters right after he dismounted to tend to one of his guns. He lost his saddle, "a genuine McClellan picked up on field of Port Republic," and his overcoat, which had been made for Stonewall Jackson but sold to Poague because it was too small for Jackson. "It was one of the best material and the best one I owned during the war."[76]

· · · · · · ·

LONGSTREET, PICKETT, AND ALEXANDER

The Rebel artillerymen did their solid best to prepare the way for the infantry, enduring the return fire and sweating through the blistering heat, the searing powder smoke, and the deafening noise. Longstreet continued his ride to demonstrate coolness under fire and inspire the infantry for their work. He rode slowly between the prone ranks and the belching guns, "as quiet as an old farmer riding over his plantation on a Sunday morning, and looked neither to the right or left." His stoicism was interrupted only when shell explosions startled his horse, but Longstreet regained control and rode on. The men watched his slow progress and expected him to fall. They yelled and told him to go to the rear: "You'll get your old fool head knocked off, we'll fight without your leading us." Longstreet ignored or failed to hear these well-meaning comments.[77]

Edward P. Alexander endured the worst few minutes of his career after the bombardment began. He was saddled with the responsibility of gauging the effect of the fire and deciding when the infantry should start. The young artillerist had the experience and the mettle to do this, but his plans for starting the foot soldiers after only about ten or fifteen minutes fell through as soon as he realized how "perfectly terrific" was the Union return fire. "I did not believe any Infantry could traverse half the necessary distance under it," he wrote after the war. "I could not bring myself to do it." The only course of action was to wait, allow the Rebel guns to suppress the return fire, and then give the word.

So Alexander waited for a full twenty-five minutes after the barrage opened at 1:00 P.M. Still there was no reduction in Union fire. Alexander worried that ammunition would be so reduced as to hinder his ability to support the infantry advance. Catlett had already brought word, only about ten minutes after the barrage opened, that the eight howitzers under Richardson that Alexander had held in reserve with a fresh supply of ammunition could no longer be found. This increased his worry about having the resources to support the foot soldiers when they attacked. Alexander was also concerned about the condition of Pickett's men, who had marched from Chambersburg the day before and broiled under the oppressive sun and the storm of missiles. He did not want to wait so long as to exhaust them before the attack began. There was also uncertainty as to how long it would take for the infantry to get ready once he gave the signal. "I could not be sure that Pickett's column might not waste ten minutes or more in dressing ranks, alignments, guides, or some little tactical niceties, & every minute now seemed an hour," Alexander later wrote.

Alexander decided to act, but he did not want simply to say "charge." He "thought it due to Longstreet and to Pickett to let the exact situation be understood." At 1:25 P.M. he wrote a short note to Pickett: "If you are able to advance at all, you must come at once, or we will not be able to support you as we ought. But the enemy's fire has not slackened materially, & there are still 18 guns firing from the cemetery." Alexander actually meant the area around the angle, rather than the cemetery, where sixteen Federal guns belonging to Arnold's, Cushing's, Brown's, and Rorty's batteries were blazing away. He later admitted being a bit confused about the name of this spot, but Alexander clearly understood it to be the focal point of the attack because it lay where Pickett's left was to connect with Pettigrew's right. He knew that Fry's brigade was to make a direct line of march toward this point.

Pickett needed no more encouragement. He mounted his horse when the note arrived and said to his staff, "Boys let us give them a trial." Aides went off to the three brigades to get the men up and in line. It would take a little time to ready the division, but the process had begun.

A few minutes after he sent off the first note, Alexander was surprised and encouraged by a sudden development. It appeared as if the fire of the guns around the angle was quickly decreasing; in fact, it appeared to Alexander as if the gunners were leaving their positions. He also noted that the fire along other parts of the Union line seemed to be decreasing as well. This was an unexpected turn of events. Alexander's experience had told him that the Federals rarely gave in during an artillery contest; they usually had so much ammunition that they never had to reserve ordnance for a follow-up infantry attack. This lavishness with fire now seemed to be breaking down. "I knew that they must have felt the punishment a good deal, and I was a good deal elated by the sight." Alexander wanted to be sure, however; he waited another five minutes, carefully scanning the Union position with his field glasses, desperate to catch a glimpse of some telltale sign through the smoke. Finally he became convinced that this window of opportunity, slight though it might be, was Pickett's best chance. He wrote another note to Pickett at 1:40 P.M. "The 18 guns have been driven off. For God's sake come on quick, or we cannot support you. Ammunition nearly out." Alexander then walked to the nearest gun and sent a lieutenant and a sergeant each with a copy of the note. To make the point more emphatically, he also sent a third messenger with a verbal reiteration of the note. Alexander wanted to impress upon Pickett the need for haste, for he still worried that the division might waste several minutes in dressing its ranks before starting across the valley.

What exactly had Alexander seen to make him so excited about the prospect of success? He certainly detected a slackening of fire coming from the Union guns at the angle. This was a genuine example of the

Rebel guns gaining a superiority over Union artillery, for the batteries at the angle were devastated by the concentrated Confederate fire. Alexander accurately gauged this, although he erroneously believed eighteen guns had pulled out from the angle area. He probably caught a glimpse or two of the withdrawal of Brown's or Arnold's guns and assumed that more were pulling out as well, but that they were hidden by the smoke that still engulfed the field. The slackening he detected along other parts of the line was the result of Osborn's and Hunt's orders to cease firing. Their plan to lure the Rebel infantry into the open worked beautifully.[78]

Pickett went straight to Longstreet after receiving the 1:25 P.M. note. He found the corps leader sitting on the top of the rail fence that stretched eastward from Spangler's Woods toward the Union line, having finished his demonstration of coolness under fire. Pickett showed him the note and asked, "General, shall I advance?" Longstreet found himself at the decisive moment of an unwanted duty. He had already done all he could to abort the operation, and now he was to give the final word that would send nearly 12,000 men into one of the most deadly and difficult assaults of the war. His nerve failed him. "My feelings had so overcome me that I would not speak for fear of betraying my want of confidence to him," he later explained. He simply nodded his head as an affirmative gesture. Both Pickett and his wife later insisted that he bowed rather than nodded his head and even held his hand in the air as if to ward off any more questions. The Virginian said, "I shall lead my division forward, sir." After watching Pickett ride confidently, even happily away, Longstreet quickly mounted and rode up to the artillery for one last report from Alexander.[79]

This occasioned the last effort by Longstreet to abort the attack. When he reached the artillery line about 1:45 P.M., Longstreet found Alexander and Maj. John C. Haskell, a First Corps artillery officer. "His first question was what we thought we had done," remembered Haskell. Alexander thought, and Haskell agreed, that they had "silenced the guns of the enemy." That was well, but when Alexander explained the disappearance of Richardson's guns and the nearly exhausted ammunition supply, Longstreet rose out of his lethargy. He ordered Alexander to stop Pickett (again refusing to do it himself) until more ammunition could be brought forward. But Alexander pointed out that the delay would give the Federals an opportunity to resupply as well. Furthermore, the Rebels did not have enough ammunition in Pennsylvania to fire for more than fifteen minutes anyway.

Alexander's message was clear. Whatever artillery preparation had been done would have to suffice; delay would waste the effort already expended. "Our only chance is to follow it up now," Alexander told Longstreet, "to strike while the iron is hot." But Longstreet admitted his doubts. "I don't want to make this attack," he frankly told the artillery-man. "I believe it will fail — I do not see how it can succeed — I would not make it even now, but that Gen. Lee has ordered & expects it." Alexander remembered this moment in detail. Longstreet spoke these words "with slight pauses in between, while he was looking at the enemy's position through his field glasses. I had the feeling that he was upon the verge of stopping the charge, & that with even slight encouragement he would do it. But that very feeling kept me from saying a word, either of assent or dissent. I would not willingly take any responsibility in so grave a matter, & I had almost a morbid fear of personally causing any loss of time. So I stood by, & looked on, in silence almost embarrassing." Then, sometime between 1:50 and 2:00 P.M., Pickett's division approached the artillery line with a steady tread. Any opportunity for Longstreet to stop the attack was finally ended. "The order was imperative," he later wrote. "The Confederate commander had fixed his heart upon the work." Longstreet admitted in his official report that he would have canceled the assault at that moment if Lee had allowed him.[80]

Alexander's estimate of the remaining artillery ammunition was right. It was fast disappearing in the extended bombardment. Alexander noticed that some of his batteries were already slowing their rate of fire, even stopping altogether, after he wrote his 1:40 P.M. note and before Pickett's battle line appeared. This happened because battery commanders took it upon themselves, contrary to Alexander's orders to keep up the fire, to husband their few remaining rounds. The Washington Artillery battalion of the First Corps and the Crenshaw Virginia Battery of the Third Corps, for example, stopped firing before they ran out of ammunition. But Dearing's battalion, in front of Pickett, exhausted its rounds. With Richardson nowhere to be found and only a few batteries on line with enough rounds left to support the infantry assault, the prospect for Alexander to play a strong role in the rest of the operation was very dim.[81]

The bombardment essentially ended about 2:00 P.M. Many observers reported that it lasted much longer — up to two hours — but no one had synchronized their watches, and there was difficulty even in agreeing on what constituted the end of the bombardment. Many batteries on both sides never stopped firing when the Rebel infantry began the assault, and thus the booming served as a bridge between one phase of the operation and another, causing many Federals in particular to lose their sense of chronology.[82]

What had been accomplished by this tremendous bombardment? The Prussian military observer, Capt. Justus Scheibert, who was traveling with Lee's headquarters, dismissed the barrage as a *"Pulververschwindung,"* which can be loosely translated as "a waste of powder." This description was only partially accurate. The truth was that in a limited but significant way the Rebel bombardment was stunningly successful and did give Pickett's division, if not the entire attacking force, a better chance of success. But in other ways it certainly was a waste of effort.[83]

What did the Confederates need to accomplish in the barrage? First and most important, they needed to reduce Union artillery power significantly so the infantry would not be punished so severely when it attacked. The Rebel guns succeeded in doing this to the Union batteries around the angle, the focal point of the assault. All of the units there, from Rorty's to Woodruff's, were mauled. Cushing's battery was almost completely disabled. Those guns in these batteries that remained operable could not fire on the infantry at long range because their shells had been expended, and there were not enough of them left to stop the infantry at close range with canister. This gave Pickett's Virginians a better chance of making a lodgement on this part of the line, an opportunity they made the most of when the momentum of the assault took them to the high-water mark.

It is obvious, however, that the Rebel guns failed to achieve any significant reduction of Union artillery power on any other part of the line. Rittenhouse and McGilvery were in full force and waiting with plenty of long-range ammunition. Osborn was hurt but still powerful and eager to deal a major blow to the charging infantry. And there were many more batteries in reserve, ready to go into action on Hunt's order.

A second Confederate objective was to demoralize, kill, and wound as many Union infantrymen as possible. The Rebel guns put great stress on the Yankees; they frightened many of them and killed and wounded quite a few. The rookies of Stannard's brigade were more severely tested emotionally than other men. But the Confederates achieved no significant advantage in this respect, for the vast majority of Union foot soldiers survived and were eager to fight when their butternut counterparts showed themselves.

Reports of Union infantry losses in the bombardment are sketchy. Webb reported losing about 50 men in his brigade, while the 72nd Pennsylvania lost roughly a dozen of that number. The 20th Massachusetts suffered 5 casualties. Losses in Stannard's brigade seem to have been higher, probably because the men were in an advanced position and the units were larger as well. The 14th Vermont reportedly suffered 60 casualties. Most observers would have agreed with the commander of the 7th Michigan, who reported that the light losses of his regiment were "little short of miraculous." The casualties in Hays's division were just as modest. One company of the 14th Connecticut lost only 2 men, and the 8th Ohio, along Emmitsburg Road, lost 2 men killed by the barrage. If Webb's brigade was typical, then it might be said that about 350 Federal infantrymen were lost to the Rebel bombardment. That would be only 6 percent of the Union force holding the line to be assaulted.[84]

What did the Union artillery need to accomplish in the bombardment? Very little, it seems. The primary objective of the Yankee gunners was to stand their ground, answer the fire with enough force and persistence to deny the Rebels a firepower advantage, and save enough ammunition to support their own infantry when the Confederates attacked. With the exception of Hazard's guns around the angle, the Federals accomplished their objectives. They only had to survive the first phase of the operation and be serviceable for the second phase. Any Rebel guns and infantrymen they could put out of action would be a bonus. But the losses among the Confederate artillery units appear to have been light, mainly due to the fact that the Federal gunners had not accurately sighted them before the barrage and could not do so after smoke obscured the battlefield. The Federal guns mostly laid down a curtain of fire on and about the Rebel guns and infantry, which did more damage to the foot soldiers than to the pieces.

Arriving at an accurate count of infantry casualties among the Rebels is just as difficult as for the Yankees. David Johnston, who was wounded in the barrage, believed that at least 300 men were lost in Pickett's division alone. Randolph Abbott Shotwell put the number at 800. Most estimates of losses in the regiments ranged from 5 to 10, but some put them much higher. Wilcox's brigade lost about a dozen men. The casualties among Pettigrew's and Trimble's units appear to have been quite a bit lighter than among Pickett's, but it is difficult to tell because of the paucity of reports. Davis's brigade lost 2 killed and 21 wounded. Overall it appears that Pickett suffered the most. The least that can be said is that the

Confederate infantry lost as many men as the Union infantry, and probably more.[85]

Alexander and his compatriots in the artillery had done all they could, but it was far from enough. The infantry stood up and prepared to go into an assault with few more advantages than they had an hour earlier. It was all up to them now.

CHAPTER 5
TO EMMITSBURG ROAD

• • • • • • • • • • •

Alexander need not have worried that Pickett would waste time with "tactical niceties" such as dressing his lines perfectly before starting the infantry across the valley. Garnett's adjutant general had gone along the lines of his brigade telling the men that when the barrage lifted, they were expected to get in line quickly with a minimum of wasted effort.[1]

• • • • • • •
PICKETT'S DIVISION

Pickett rode quickly to his command after getting Longstreet's silent approval for the attack. He stopped at Garnett's position, where the brigade leader asked him if he had any last-minute instructions. "No, Dick, I don't recollect anything else, unless it be to advise you to make the best kind of time in crossing the valley; its a *h—l of an ugly looking place over yonder*." To the rank and file Pickett uttered more inspiring words: "Up, men, and to your posts! Don't forget today that you are from old Virginia!" David E. Johnston of Kemper's brigade recalled that the effect of this exhortation was "electrical"; the men quickly rose up and sorted themselves into line, stepping over the maimed bodies of their comrades hurt in the bombardment. They were ordered to put their blankets and knapsacks in company piles, to load their rifle muskets and fix bayonets, but not to fire until they had reached the Union line. Benjamin L. Farinholt was struck by this efficient preparation for battle; it was "the greatest and most imposing sight I ever witnessed."[2]

As the ranks formed, the officers took their places. Armistead walked twenty paces in front of his brigade while Pickett and his staff moved into position just behind the center of the division. Pickett told one of his couriers, Thomas R. Friend, to ride down the line and tell commanders that the division should close to the left. He was concerned about closing the gap between his Virginians and Pettigrew's division; this was the primary objective in determining the direction of advance.[3]

There were only a few short minutes before the order to start was given, a short time for the men to make their final peace. Many of them said good-bye to one another, to those wounded and still lying on the ground, and to those whose shoulders still rubbed against each other in the line. Friends and comrades who realized there was little chance of surviving the attack wanted to make their final farewell to one another. If they happened to be several files apart, their shouted good-byes could be heard by others.[4]

What were these men feeling in those few minutes before the order to advance? The emotions were varied. Some men were quite confident of success and of their chances of survival. Capt. John Holmes Smith of the 11th Virginia remembered the men as having nothing but confidence in the planned assault, while David Johnston knew they were aware of its dangers but showed no signs of fear. Johnston also knew that all young soldiers assume they will not die — that death will only come for someone else. He also wisely pointed out that the barrage had been a very stressful experience and that most of Pickett's men were eager for it to end and to have a chance to do something. They were not motivated by a love of fighting but by a desire to get the job over with as quickly as possible, whatever the outcome; "realizing if it must be done, 'it were well it were done quickly.'" Johnston also remembered that overconfidence was a common element among Lee's soldiers by this point in the war, "from the commanding general down to the shakiest private in the ranks. Too much over-confidence was the bane of our battle." Yet it also helped to bolster the men's willingness to stand up and make this attack.[5]

Several other survivors of the battle remembered the agonized feelings of the rank and file just before they crossed the valley. John Dooley of Kemper's brigade argued that no one really had the sangfroid to go into this attack without doubts. "I tell you the enthusiasm of ardent breasts in many cases *ain't there*, and instead of burning to avenge the insults of our country, families and altars and firesides, the thought is most frequently, *Oh*, if I could just come out of this charge safely how thankful *would I be!*" Sam Paulett of the 18th Virginia had earlier walked up to the artillery line before the bombardment to survey the field. What he had seen did not encourage him. Now that the men were standing up and dressing their line, he told several comrades, "This is going to be a heller! Prepare for the worst!"[6]

It is clear that a considerable amount of demoralization and shaken nerves existed among Pickett's men. The bombardment itself had caused a lot of this. Seeing their comrades mangled while lying on the hot ground without an opportunity to avoid it or retaliate against the Yankee guns was one of the most trying experiences of the war. Artilleryman W. Greene Raoul of the Washington Artillery believed it was a mistake to have placed the infantry so close behind the guns. "That is the most awful thing in the world, to be under a heavy fire & be compelled to lay down & do nothing." Officers were aware of the dangers. Capt. Richard Logan Jr. of Company H, 14th Virginia, identified three or four men as "habitual 'play-outs' " who always managed to find a way to avoid hazardous duty. He told the file closers "to 'take them into that fight or kill them,' " according to Sgt. Drewry B. Easley; "he didn't care which, and if we killed them he would be responsible."[7]

Not everyone stood up. Of course the injured remained on the ground, to be collected later by stretcher bearers. Others were overcome with the heat and could not stand. The temperature was eighty-seven degrees at 2:00 P.M., and it would rise at least three degrees during the course of the attack. There was only a slight breeze from the south, enough to help clear the cannon smoke but not enough to cool the men. Even some of the soldiers who stood up and formed ranks felt the effects of heat prostration; the exertion brought the symptoms to a boiling point. "All along the line men were falling from seeming sunstroke," recalled Lt. William Nathaniel Wood of the 19th Virginia, "with dreadful contortions of the body, foaming at the mouth, and almost lifeless. Some were possibly shamming but much, real, downright suffering from the sun's hot rays was experienced." Capt. James R. Hutter of the 11th Virginia urged these men on regardless of their suffering, appealing to them "in the name of Virginia to go if possible." Capt. John Holmes Smith became irritated with Hutter when he berated one of his men in this way, telling Hutter, "When he Says he is sick, he is sick." Nevertheless, other men also thought a small proportion of those suffering from heat prostration might have been able to make the charge if they had wanted to.[8]

No one could blame the brigade leaders for failing to inspire the men. Armistead put on a grand show. He walked up to Leander C. Blackburn, color sergeant of the 53rd Virginia, pointed to the Federal line, and said, "Sergeant, I want you and your men to plant your colors on those works.

Do you think you can do it?" Blackburn answered, "Yes, sir, if God is willing." Then the brigadier shared a drink with Blackburn from his flask. This scene was played out in full view of the regiment. Armistead drew his sword "in a manner peculiar to himself" and shouted, "Men, remember what you are fighting for! Your homes, your firesides, and your sweethearts! Follow me!" He then, by some accounts, loosened his collar and threw aside his cravat, a logical course of action in that heat. Whether Armistead put his black slouch hat on the tip of his sword now or later is unclear, but the impact of his show on the brigade was undisputed. "His men saw him," wrote John H. Lewis of the 9th Virginia. "They saw his example. They caught his fire and determination, and then and there they resolved to follow that heroic leader until the enemy's bullets stopped them. It was his example, his coolness, his courage that led that brigade over that field of blood."[9]

Garnett was dressed in his finest, a uniform coat with general's stars and wreath, nearly new trousers, and spurs on his boots. He took post in front of the brigade, mounted a magnificent horse, waved his hat, and cheered his men.[10]

Kemper put on no such show for the troops. When a staff officer rode up from Pickett with the order to dress the ranks, he looked to the left and saw that both Armistead and Garnett were already in line. They had been given the order before it reached his position on the far right. But his men readied quickly and were able to start with the other two brigades.[11]

A final passing of instructions took place along the line: "Go slow, do not cheer, and do not stop to fire" was repeated from man to man down the line of at least some units. The order to bring attention was shouted, followed by "forward — quick time, march." Kemper's brigade was under instructions to dress on the left, as all units were, but Kemper quickly found that he had to move nearly the length of a regiment to close with Garnett's right. It was the beginning of a long march to the left that this rightmost unit of Pickett's division would have to make over the next half-hour. Kemper's men moved out "as if on dress parade, slowly and calmly." When the Virginians passed through the artillery line, many gunners uncovered their heads and raised a cheer. It was both an encouragement and a farewell.[12]

Longstreet was still at the artillery line, having just tried to order Alexander to stop the attack. The approach of the infantry up the slope killed the last chance he had of aborting the assault. Longstreet therefore watched the parade with a heavy heart. "I foresaw what my men would meet and would gladly have given up my position rather than share in the responsibilities of that day." He thought Pickett presented the appearance more of a "holiday soldier than a general at the head of a column" about to make a desperate attack, with his cap worn rakishly over one ear and his auburn locks dangling behind his head. Armistead and Garnett "seemed absorbed in the men behind." Kemper's brigade was Longstreet's old command, before First Manassas, and he had fond memories of drilling the green recruits of those regiments. It was not a happy moment for the old war horse.[13]

A number of men rode into the assault, sixteen altogether in Pickett's division. Most were couriers and staff members, but commanders such as Pickett, Garnett, and Kemper were among the number. Capt. Robert A. Bright of Pickett's staff was sent to Kemper's brigade to order all officers to "go in on foot," but Kemper refused to do that himself. Garnett's leg injury forced him to ride, and Col. Lewis Williams of the 1st Virginia asked for permission to ride, as he "was not well" either. Eppa Hunton claimed that a "physical disability" he had acquired at First Manassas forced him to ride as well. All of these mounted men would be particularly exposed.[14]

Past the artillery line Pickett's men next encountered Wilcox's and Lang's brigades. The Alabama and Florida troops were crouching in their shallow trenches; the Virginians of Kemper's brigade, at least, had to jump across the obstruction and walk between any of Wilcox's and Lang's troops who had stood up to watch the show. They pitied Pickett's unfortunates, saying, "Boys, that's a hot place. We were there yesterday." At least one of the Virginians could not go on. He dropped into the shallow trench occupied by members of the 5th Florida. J. B. Johnson asked the man if he was injured, and he answered quite frankly, "No sir, but I can't go forward. I know I am disgracing my family, but I can't go." Johnson nudged him with his sword and told him to go to the rear if he could not go forward. The man did not hesitate. He left his musket and cartridge belt in the trench and made for the rear. "I thought it would take a pretty swift bullet to overtake him," remarked Johnson.[15]

The morale of other men failed them as well. Drewry B. Easley of the 14th Virginia noticed an old friend from school drop out of the line and lay down, claiming to be unable to move on. When Easley demanded he prove it, the man sprang up and ran. He raced along the line of the 57th Virginia, and Easley saw Sgt. Calvin Garner of his own company cock his gun and run in the same direction. Easley never saw if Garner actually tried to shoot the fugitive. Very few men ran or dropped out of the ranks, but many more had private thoughts about the attack. Lt. Edward Payson Reeve of the 1st Virginia heard several remarks in the ranks while Kemper's brigade was moving forward: "that Pickett's Division had been condemned to be shot and was marching up to execution, not in any spirit of timidity, but showing that all could see that a fatal error had been committed."[16]

The vast majority of soldiers in the ranks, however, were willing to go on and try. Garnett rode along shouting, "Steady, men! Close up! A little faster; not too fast! Save your strength!" His men shouted their distinctive Rebel yell early in the assault. Usually the yell inspired the troops to pick up the pace and close with the enemy. Now they started it too soon because of the tension and excitement of this particularly deadly attack. They could not pick up the pace so far out and could not sustain the shout, so they fell into a grim silence.[17]

The alignment was easy enough to keep in this early phase of the advance. The three brigades maintained their pace and their relationship to one another even though they crossed a rail fence soon after passing the artillery. Armistead was about 100 paces behind Garnett; his right wing overlapped Garnett's right and Kemper's left. Armistead walked about forty paces in front of his men by now, his sword (perhaps with his hat on the tip) raised high over his head. In Garnett's command Company C of the 28th Virginia was inching forward ahead of the other companies. Col. Robert C. Allen had to order Capt. Michael P. Spessard to keep it in line with the rest.[18]

This early phase, during which the division marched about 100 yards past the artillery line, was like a parade ground maneuver because there was little Union cannon fire. It seemed to one Rebel that the Federal gunners were too amazed at the spectacle to open fire. When they had collected their wits, in this man's view, they opened up. The result was "a most terrific artillery fire," according to Maj. Joseph R. Cabell of Armistead's brigade. Virtually all of it came from the right, for Hazard's artillery in the Union center had no long-range ordnance left. Rittenhouse fired from Little Round Top, and McGilvery poured in shell, too. Because McGilvery's concentration was partially obscured by the lay of the land, most Confederates assumed that all of the deadly rounds came sailing over from Little Round Top. From their perspective the two Union gun positions were roughly on the same line anyway.[19]

The losses began to mount quickly. One shell exploded in the ranks of Company H, 14th Virginia, killing Capt. Richard Logan Jr. and knocking down nine of his men. Another shell took out ten men from the 8th Virginia, killing four of them and forcing the rest to limp away or lie bleeding on the ground. Maj. Kirkwood Otey of the 11th Virginia was injured in the shoulder by a fragment. A single shell explosion played havoc with Company C, 56th Virginia, knocking out sixteen men, and a later shell killed two and wounded three men of the same regiment.[20]

Capt. Benjamin Lyons Farinholt of the 53rd Virginia, Armistead's brigade, noted that these rounds fell infrequently, but when they found their mark, they did great execution. He saw and felt one such round sail over his head and explode in the company to his left; it knocked down thirteen soldiers "in a perfect mangled mass of flesh and blood indistinguishable one from the other." Leander Blackburn, the color-bearer of the 53rd, was hit by a fragment of another shell that snapped off the end of the flagstaff and plowed through his body. Another member of the color guard grabbed the flag and kept going. Sgt. William B. Robertson of the 14th Virginia wrote, "They poured in the . . . shells to us like hail. . . . Now & then a man's hand or arm or leg would fly like feathers before the wind." Robertson's waist belt was snipped by a passing fragment that also "tore my jacket and frazzled the skin in my hip." Another shell explosion stunned the sergeant and took him out of action for the rest of the day.[21]

As so often happened, the color-bearers seemed doomed. Not only did Blackburn fall, but the color guard of the 11th Virginia in Kemper's brigade suffered a great deal. The flag went down three times when its carrier was hit, until Adj. H. Valentine Harris stepped up to seize it. He carried it all the way to the Federal line.[22]

Pickett's skirmishers were busy during this first half of the advance across the valley. Positioned about 300 yards ahead of the division, they were in a good spot to see its advance. The perspective produced some doubts among a few of the skirmishers. When Charles T. Loehr of the 1st Virginia looked back and surveyed the field, he came to the conclusion that "we are going to be whipped." Most skirmishers, however, were too busy to think about impending doom. They had to pull down the remaining sections of fence along Emmitsburg Road and managed to accomplish the task at least along some stretches of the roadway. The Rebel skirmishers received fire from the Union skirmishers on the other side of the road and around the Codori buildings. Randolph Abbott Shotwell told his fellow skirmishers of the 8th Virginia to use the remains of the fence to build breastworks and return the fire. This led one Federal skirmisher of the 19th Maine, positioned at the Codori farm, to conclude the Confederates had sent out "pioneers" for some combat engineering. The Union skirmishers held stubbornly and completely stopped the Confederate skirmishers. This came as a surprise to John Holmes Smith of the 11th Virginia, for he was not used to seeing this on other battlefields. Pickett's skirmishers stayed at the road until the battle line approached; only then did the Federal skirmishers retire.[23]

The blue-clad skirmishers of the 16th Vermont, in Kemper's front, and those of the 19th Maine around the Codori buildings poured in a destructive fire as the Rebel battle line came within range. Col. Lewis B. Williams of the 1st Virginia was an early casualty; sitting atop his horse, he made a conspicuous target. Williams accentuated the danger. He had become unpopular with the men because of his strict attention to discipline and wanted to prove his courage. John Dooley wrote that "foolishly and insanely he rode coolly and deliberately in front of the regiment." A rumor spread that he died when he fell on his sword, but the truth was that Williams was mortally wounded by the skirmish fire. Pvt. Thomas H. Oakes of the 14th Virginia was felled by a bullet in the side. He had already been hit by two shell fragments that bruised but did not disable him. The bullet laid him on the ground, unconscious, but he later discovered that another shell explosion had injured his ankle, ripped his shoe off, and frazzled his pants leg. A spent bullet later hit his other ankle after he had regained consciousness. It was all too much for him; he lay there the rest of the day and that night, until he was taken in by the Federals.[24]

Long before Pickett reached Emmitsburg Road, his men had been grappling with problems of alignment and direction of advance, for this was a complicated attack. The governing motif was the need to close the gap between the Virginians and Pettigrew's division. In other words, the copse of trees was not the focal point of the attack from its inception; Pickett did not direct his division there because it was the weakest point of the Union line or because the Rebels had thoroughly scouted the Federal position and wanted to burst through there. Pettigrew was to attack straight ahead, and thus his right flank would end at the copse and the angle. Pickett had been allowed to deploy his division early on the morning of July 3 in such a way as to leave a substantial gap of 400 yards between the two commands, and he now had to close that breach or attack with his left flank in the air. The copse was the convenient landmark that linked the two divisions.

The copse was not identified as a target at the start of the attack. The orders were to use the top of the Codori barn as the initial aiming point, for it could be seen as soon as the troops ascended the rear slope of Seminary Ridge and reached the artillery line. One can also see the top half of the trees at the copse from this spot, but the ground on which the Federals were deployed is not visible. Emmitsburg Road is not visible either, except to the right where it climbs the high ground and passes by the Sherfy peach orchard. One also cannot yet see the ground where Pettigrew was attacking from here, but the top halves of both the Round Tops are visible to the right.[25]

Despite the officers' efforts to be as clear as possible, there was some confusion about how the division should align itself. Members of Pickett's staff later indicated that it was to dress to the left, on Garnett's brigade, but even members of Garnett's command understood they were to dress on Kemper's brigade. The difference is significant. The former meant that a slide, or oblique movement, to the left to close the gap with Pettigrew would be in order; the latter would mean that the division was going to drive straight ahead or even to the right. It is possible that both options were discussed before the attack. The division could have advanced straight ahead and still closed the gap with Pettigrew, by allowing Garnett to oblique left, Kemper to march forward, and Armistead to bring his brigade up between them. That would have widened the division front and maintained connection with Wilcox and Lang to the right, broadening the front of the attacking force even more. Ironically, Kemper wrote in a letter twenty-three years after the event that this actually was done. He obviously was mistaken. But if this possibility had been thoroughly discussed before the attack, Kemper might have confused the discussion and the reality.[26]

Would Kemper's scenario have been a better way to conduct the attack? Walter Harrison, a member of Pickett's staff, believed that a straightforward march would have been more successful than the extreme left oblique that actually took place. There is every reason to believe Harrison was right. Stannard's large, fresh brigade would have been directly in front of Pickett's right wing; but it consisted largely of green troops, and Stannard occupied what was essentially a bulge in the Union line. As such,

TO EMMITSBURG ROAD

he would have been vulnerable to a smashing assault by fresh, veteran troops who equaled or outnumbered his command.[27]

But a straightforward advance was not to take place. A short time into the attack, a mounted orderly came, presumably from Pickett, with instructions for Garnett's brigade to guide on Pettigrew's right flank. When the word reached Eppa Hunton in the 8th Virginia, one of his orderlies, Pvt. George W. F. Hummer, volunteered to take the instructions to Kemper, as he felt the order had not been distributed down the line. Hunton told him to ride to the right and do it. Kemper told Hummer that this was news to him; he had no inkling of it before, but he would obey.[28]

As a result Pickett's division began a movement that probably was intended simply to be a gradual sliding, or dressing, to the left until the command smoothly wound up connecting with Pettigrew's right flank somewhere before the whole reached the Federal line. It did not work quite that way. The men were moving forward too fast, and there were too many of them to maneuver in such a casual way. From a point fairly early in the advance, probably before the Union artillery opened fire and until the right wing under Kemper reached Emmitsburg Road, the division simply dressed left while advancing straight ahead. This brought it slightly more to the left. By the time the men neared Emmitsburg Road, however, it became obvious that a much more drastic maneuver was needed if the command was to connect with Pettigrew. A sharp left oblique was begun about that point. The movement was conducted so sharply that it appeared to the Union observers as a pronounced turn to avoid Stannard's forward position (or to shield themselves from the heavy enfilade fire from Rittenhouse and McGilvery) and aim directly at the angle in the stone fence. Pickett's Virginians accomplished their tactical mission; they managed to connect with Pettigrew in time, and they did so by maintaining the configuration of brigades that they started with — that is, with Garnett and Kemper in the first line and Armistead in the second line. But it was not easy, and it undoubtedly delayed the crossing of the valley and threw the regiments into more confusion than necessary.[29]

Until the division neared Emmitsburg Road, "there was no distinct change of front," remembered John Holmes Smith of Kemper's brigade, only commands to "close, — and dress to the left." The men often huddled a bit as the ranks bunched up during this dressing. Observers often referred to this as evidence of pauses in the advance, but they were mistaken. Pickett's men performed a complex maneuver under trying circumstances without hesitating.[30]

Pickett and his staff had difficulty estimating how much dressing to the left was needed at this point. In fact, Robert A. Bright remembered that Kemper and Garnett seemed to be drifting too much to the left because the Codori barn, the initial target, was too much to Kemper's left. "General Pickett would have altered the direction," Bright recalled, but he thought that more troops would be needed on his left, near the connection with Pettigrew, than on the right; so he allowed the drifting to continue.[31]

The continual dressing to the left snowballed with each step forward. James R. Hutter remembered that "the pressure from our right was so heavy that it almost amounted to a left oblique," as indeed it would soon become. This forced Hutter's 11th Virginia to encroach on the 1st Virginia to its left. Before he was shot by Union skirmishers, Colonel Williams of the latter regiment rode to Hutter and asked, "Can you do nothing with your men they are crowding me out of line[?]" Hutter was miffed; his men were resisting the undue pressure as hard as possible, and he resented being accused of causing the 1st to suffer. He shot back at Williams, "If you will go & attend to that damned little squad of yours . . . and let my Regiment alone we will get along better." Hutter also suggested Williams talk to Colonel Patton of the 7th and Colonel Mayo of the 3rd about the matter. The problem was serious. Lt. John E. Dooley, in charge of Company C, 1st Virginia, was being pressed out of place by Company D to his right, commanded by his old acquaintance Capt. George F. Norton. "I ask him to give way a little . . . , and scarcely has he done so than he leaps into the air, falling prostrate." Norton was wounded but survived.[32]

The pressing became so pronounced that it caused the right flank of Kemper's brigade to curl forward, skewing its line of advance so it was at a diagonal compared with the Union position. Lt. Edward Payson Reeve noticed this and brought it to Colonel Williams's attention that this would expose the right flank even more to the enfilade artillery fire. He asked Williams to change the direction of advance. Williams replied, "I see the situation as well as you do, but have my orders to obey, close your Company to the left." Just then Williams fell, mortally wounded. Captain Norton of Company D took charge of the regiment but was shot right after Hutter spoke to him. Reeve noted with accuracy that "so great was the slaughter, that the opportunity to rectify the alignment was lost." It would have made no difference anyway, for company and regimental officers could not have reversed the slide to the left even if they had wanted to.[33]

As the men of Pickett's division made their way over the valley under a hail of enfilade shell fire and into the determined musketry of the Union skirmishers, they reached a point about halfway between the lines where the ground rose slightly, especially on the left before Garnett, and sloped gradually to the right, or south. For the first time they could see the stone fence and the angle, the copse of trees, and all of the Codori barn. But the landscape to the left, where Pettigrew was advancing, was still only partly visible. The last few hundred yards that Pettigrew would have to traverse before reaching the Union line is visible from here. The Codori barn now loomed ever larger as the major obstacle to be encountered in the advance. The copse of trees is behind and to the left of it when viewed from Kemper's angle of approach.[34]

Pickett did a good job of handling his division in the advance. He and his staff rode between Garnett and Armistead during the first few minutes of the attack. At one point his exuberance got the better of him, and Pickett told the men to double-quick and "give them a cheer." But this request was ignored, and the men continued at their steady pace. Then Pickett and his staff rode to the right to Kemper's rear and beyond to the Sherfy peach orchard, where the higher ground offered an excellent view of the field. The general then rode to the left, leaving most of his staff behind and taking only his courier, Thomas R. Friend. Pickett stopped at one point and dismounted, probably to see the progress of Pettigrew on the left. After walking forward a short time, he remounted and rode toward the division, but he turned right unexpectedly to race back to the orchard and the waiting staff members. At some point, after the Union artillery fire rained fragments around the assembled party, Pickett said to Bright, "Captain, you have lost your spurs to-day instead of gaining them." Bright looked and noticed that a fragment had twisted the shank of his spur on the left boot and pointed the rowel forward instead of to the rear. Pickett would later move up at least as far as the Codori buildings after his division passed that point. When addressing the question of where Pickett was during the attack, long after the war had ended, Thomas R. Friend wrote that "he went as far as any Major General, Commanding a division, ought to have gone, and farther."[35]

When Pickett and Friend returned to the Sherfy peach orchard from their solitary ride to the left, the Virginia division was nearing Emmitsburg Road. Pickett was very worried about Pettigrew. There were increasing signs that his division was not doing well. Several members of Pickett's command caught glimpses of turmoil after they reached positions from which they could get a wider view of the northern half of the battle area. The men on Garnett's and Armistead's left flanks, in particular, had a view of it when they ascended the rise of ground midway between the lines but still well short of the road. "I saw troops on our left in wild disorder rushing by to the rear," wrote Lt. James F. Crocker of the 9th Virginia. These were men of Brockenbrough's Virginia brigade, on Pettigrew's far left, who broke partway across the valley and retreated. Unfortunately many members of Pickett's division made no such fine distinctions. They caught glimpses of men running on the left and generally attributed it to Pettigrew's entire division. The truth was that Brockenbrough did indeed perform badly, but there was no general retreat by the division at this point.[36]

Pickett sent two staff members, William Stuart Symington and Edward Baird, to attempt to rally these men. Symington left behind a fanciful description of his heroic but futile efforts, claiming to have stripped the flag of the 11th North Carolina from the hands of a retreating Tar Heel. It was not true. Marshall's North Carolina brigade and Fry's Tennessee and Alabama brigade were just then grimly moving forward and in fact were about to join flanks with Pickett. Davis's Mississippi brigade was still moving forward as well. The Virginians here began a long campaign that would extend well into the twentieth century, designed to discredit Pettigrew's division and give the impression that it let Pickett down.[37]

Pickett also sent to Longstreet for help. Bright was instructed to tell the corps leader that the division could take the Union position but needed support to hold it. He found Longstreet once again sitting on the rail fence that ran west to east directly toward the angle, observing the attack from a distance. When given Pickett's message, he replied, "Where are the troops that were placed on your flank?" Bright told him to look over his shoulder to the north, where remnants of Brockenbrough were seen scattering to the rear. Just then Col. Arthur J. L. Fremantle, a British army observer accompanying Lee's army, rode up. He gleefully told Longstreet that Lee had suggested he attach himself to the corps commander to get the best view of the event. Fremantle blurted, "General, I would not have missed this for anything in the world." Longstreet could not agree with him. "*The devil you wouldn't! I would like to have missed it very much; we've attacked and been repulsed: look there!*" He was convinced that the battle was lost even before it had reached its climax. "Bright, ride to

General Pickett and tell him what you have heard me say to Colonel Fremantle." The staff officer dutifully started off to do just that, giving Longstreet enough time to recover himself and yell out to him, "Tell General Pickett that Wilcox's Brigade is in that peach orchard, and he can order him to his assistance."[38]

Longstreet worried about the lack of flank support, forgetting that his own inadequate preparation had been partly to blame for the failure to coordinate help on the flanks. In his postwar writings Longstreet tried to give the impression that he had done all he could to ensure flank support for the attackers. He claimed to have ordered Law's and McLaws's divisions to advance closer to the Federals, "to spring to the charge as soon as the breach at the centre could be made." But we have already seen in Chapter 1 that McLaws admitted to having been issued no such instructions. Longstreet blamed Hill for not sending in Third Corps units to support Pettigrew's left, and he also attached blame to Lee for this, since the army commander was in that area during the assault. He seemed to have assumed that Hill would do whatever was necessary to help the attack, and he failed to take personal charge of coordinating efforts across corps lines. Now his men were going to pay a high price for that laxness. Longstreet tried to make up for it by sending a staff member, Col. Osmun Latrobe, to instruct Trimble to move his men forward and replace the broken brigade. Latrobe managed to deliver that message, but his horse was shot from under him. Longstreet also sent his chief of staff, Maj. G. Moxley Sorrel, to see to Pickett's right flank support. Sorrel's horse was killed by a shell burst after he was able to do no more than reach Garnett's and Armistead's commands.[39]

The men in Pickett's ranks could not fully know it yet, but their attack was already running into trouble. They continued to do their duty, suffering heavy casualties and straining to dress to the left as instructed. Pickett quickly acted on Longstreet's suggestion that he call on Wilcox and Lang for support. The Virginian was on his horse about 100 yards behind the division. He sent Baird to Wilcox, then dispatched Symington with the same message, and finally told Bright to follow up, too. Pickett worried that the heavy artillery fire might prevent one or all of his officers from reaching the right. All three of them made it. When Bright rode up to Wilcox, he "was standing with both hands raised waving and saying to me: 'I know; I know.' " Bright delivered the message anyway and rode back to Pickett. The division leader had also decided to send another message to Longstreet for assistance. His brother Charles was given that assignment.

As Charles rode off, he turned back to see George riding slowly behind the lines; he thought it might be the last time he would see his brother. Charles was unable to find Longstreet and never delivered the message.[40]

· · · · · · ·

THE CONFEDERATE ARTILLERY

The Confederate artillerymen might have been able to play a larger role in supporting the charge if they had had more ammunition and more time to prepare. Since the attack came immediately at the end of a massive barrage, the gunners were tired, and they needed several minutes of frenzied effort to reposition their pieces. Precious little time was available. Dearing exemplified this problem. He was quite eager to push his guns forward with the infantry; in fact he had expected to do so, but the foot soldiers rushed forward so steadily that he had no opportunity to follow through. As the 8th Virginia marched by, Dearing yelled to Eppa Hunton, "For God's Sake wait till I get Some ammunition and I will drive every Yankee from the heights." Of course the infantry could not possibly wait and lose whatever softening effect the bombardment had created in the Union line.[41]

Alexander worked hard to bring some guns forward, but the result was meager at best. When Pickett's line came up the rear slope of Seminary Ridge and passed the artillery, Alexander spent a few moments admiring the appearance of the troops. Then he left Longstreet, passed by Garnett to wish him good luck (the two had known each other in the prewar army), and rapidly inspected each gun in his line from left to right. The gunners of any piece with about fifteen rounds of long-range ammunition were told to get spare horses, if needed, and move forward. The others were to wait until the infantrymen were well across the valley, then to fire the remaining long-range ammunition over their heads and at any operable Union batteries. These guns were also supposed to use canister if the attack were repulsed and the Federals attempted a counterstroke. Alexander was able to get only about two guns from each battery for his forward support scheme, totaling about eighteen pieces.[42]

Next Alexander quickly had to determine how best to use this force. He brought the guns forward a few hundred yards, pausing to knock holes in the fence along Emmitsburg Road. Here the road angled away from the Union position so that he was still in moderate range of the enemy. While the gunners were working on the fences, Alexander noticed a badly wounded member of Kemper's brigade "whose entire mouth & chin was carried away" by an enfilading shot from Little Round Top. The infantryman looked up at Alexander, who sat on his horse nearby, and the artillerist could even see powder burns on his cheeks.

After Alexander got his guns into position, he looked south and got a good view of Pickett's advancing men. They were nearing the road. He could also see Stannard's Vermont regiments extended toward the Rebel approach like a knife. Soon the scene would be engulfed in rifle smoke as the Union infantry opened their first major fire on Pickett. Exactly what happened next is unclear. Alexander glossed over the actions of the next few minutes, and only a few clear accounts exist. It is apparent that Alexander was never able to coordinate the fire of his eighteen guns. Events were proceeding at a rapid pace with the infantry, and many Union guns were still firing.[43]

A handful of Rebel guns tried to take on McGilvery, who was shooting at the infantry. A section of the Washington Artillery under Lt. C. H. C. Brown took post northeast of the Sherfy barn and fired at the right wing of this Union line. Hart's New York Battery returned the fire and quickly blew up two caissons, silencing the pieces and badly wounding Brown. Then Lt. William Alexander McQueen led a piece from Capt. Hugh Garden's Palmetto Battery forward to help the Washington Artillery. He placed it ahead of the worsted guns to draw Union fire from them. McQueen received the concentrated firepower of twenty cannon. A shell fragment gouged a hole in the back of one gunner, and another fragment severed the leg of another man. The horses fell at an alarming rate. McQueen was hit in the head and, later, in the thigh. His crew was immobilized, unable to work the gun and without the means to withdraw it. The survivors made their way back to the main artillery line. Later that evening Garden organized a group of volunteers who ran out to retrieve the gun. McQueen would later be nominated for the new Confederate Medal of Honor, and he survived his wounds only to be killed in a minor skirmish in South Carolina on the day Lee surrendered.[44]

Maj. John C. Haskell also had little luck supporting the infantry advance. "Having no special orders beyond that I was to help where I could," he advanced halfway to the Union line and fired a few rounds at Stannard's Vermont troops. Then he received the fire of up to eight Union batteries, Hunt told him after the war. Two of his guns were disabled and the rest retired, out of ammunition.[45]

The Confederate artillery completely failed to support Pickett's attack.

It was exhausted, low on ammunition, overpowered by superior Union gun positions, and lacked a well-conceived tactical plan for helping the infantry. Whatever the guns had accomplished in the bombardment was all they could claim in terms of furthering Confederate aims.

· · · · · · ·

PETTIGREW AND TRIMBLE

On the Confederate left wing Pettigrew's and Trimble's commands experienced much the same emotions as did Pickett's. Their men had an easier time in the advance because their way was straightforward. But the heat was just as oppressive, the artillery fire was possibly worse, and the Union position was probably stronger in their front.

Pettigrew was not privy to the drama that unfolded around the final decision to start the attack. He remained with his division and knew it was time to go only when it became apparent that Pickett's men had stood up and were forming ranks — no one sent him a message. He quickly gave the signal to his brigade leaders. When Fry told his Tennessee and Alabama troops to stand up, they did so "with cheerful alacrity," according to Fry. Davis's Mississippians did the same. The order was shouted, "*Attention*," and they dressed the line. As in Pickett's division, several men were overcome by the heat and the exertion of rising. They were "fainting all along the line before started on the charge," according to a lieutenant in the 11th North Carolina.[46]

Soon the order to start was shouted. Pettigrew could not resist saying something to his old brigade, positioned second to the right in his division line. He reined up in front of it and said to Marshall, "Now Colonel, for the honor of the good Old North State. Forward." Fry and Marshall moved out with dressed lines and steady tread, "in as magnificent style as I ever saw," remembered John T. Jones, commander of the 26th North Carolina. Many of the men shouted the Rebel yell but did not sustain it for long; it was too hot, and the distance to march was too great. There was still a lot of cannon smoke covering the field, which undoubtedly helped to shield Pettigrew's advance for a few moments.[47]

As the men passed through the artillery line on the crest of Seminary Ridge and stepped over the low stone fence, some of them displayed the same doubts that Pickett's men harbored. Joseph Graham, a gunner in the Charlotte Artillery, noted that they advanced steadily, "but I fear with *too feeble determination*." Graham heard some of the foot soldiers say "that

[it] is worse than Malvern Hill," when they caught their first glimpse of the valley and the Union line. "I don't hardly think that position can be carried." It weakened his own faith in the attack. After Pettigrew passed the artillery, at least a few of the Confederate guns continued to fire over the heads of his men, "as if to let us know we had friends in the rear," thought Thomas J. Cureton of the 26th North Carolina.[48]

There were significant problems of alignment from the outset. To begin with, only two of Pettigrew's brigades started in concert. Davis's Mississippians missed the signal to begin the advance and started a few minutes later than Fry and Marshall. Exactly why this happened was never explained. Pettigrew had taken great pains before the assault to see that the division moved out properly; he expressed his concerns to Davis so often that the Mississippian became irritated. Despite this, neither his or Brockenbrough's Virginia brigade emerged from the tree line atop Seminary Ridge. Davis later explained that he had mistaken other troops for Marshall's and therefore did not know the attack was under way. He never pointed out which troops he did see (there do not appear to have been any separating his view from Marshall's brigade). To his credit, when he realized his mistake, Davis got his men up and going quickly. Pettigrew had sent his chief of staff, Louis G. Young, back to the ridge crest after marching a few yards into the valley to fetch Davis. But Young did not have to go far before the Mississippi brigade came rushing out of the tree line.

When Young returned to Pettigrew and asked him if he should try to fetch Brockenbrough, Pettigrew said no. The brigade "might follow, and if it failed to do so it would not matter." Young explained after the battle that Brockenbrough's was a small unit "that had suffered from frequent change of commanders, and had been so badly handled that it was in a chronic state of demoralization, and was not to be relied upon; it was virtually of no value in a fight." Thus there developed the odd occurrence of a division leader dismissing one of his four brigades in a risky attack where every man counted. Brockenbrough's command would start a few minutes later, but it had given up the possibility of connecting with Davis and essentially conducted its own, poorly coordinated and lightly pressed attack. Davis also found it hard to make a firm connection with Marshall due to his late start, and his brigade conducted a vigorous attack that was only loosely coordinated to the movements of the rest of the division. Pettigrew therefore had only two of his four brigades well in hand.[49]

Pettigrew not only failed to have his entire division conduct the attack in a coordinated fashion; he had to scramble to connect with Pickett. Again the gap created when Pickett deployed his men that morning haunted the Rebels. To make matters worse, there is no evidence that Pickett bothered to inform his colleague that he was readying for the assault. He "was not the man to trouble himself about the action of any other division," opined Randolph Abbott Shotwell, "especially if there appeared an opening to win heavy laurels through individuality of movement." Shotwell, who was on Garnett's skirmish line and therefore in a good position to see the northern half of the battlefield, thought Pettigrew did not get started until the Virginia division was some 300 or 400 yards across the valley—in other words, when Pickett's men had already crossed about a third of the distance to the Union line. Only because Pickett was delayed by dressing to the left and the subsequent left oblique did Pettigrew have a chance to catch up with him by the time both commands were crossing Emmitsburg Road. Trimble even went so far as to suggest that Pettigrew and he should have started fifteen minutes before Pickett to ensure better coordination.[50]

No one in Pickett's division was impressed with Pettigrew's performance. Shotwell suggested that his inexperience at division command probably accounted for the fact that he could not compensate for the difficulties encountered in the attack. Walter H. Taylor, Lee's chief of staff, described the advance of Pettigrew's division as "in *echelon*, or with the alignment so imperfect and so drooping on the left as to appear in *echelon*." Pettigrew offered inadequate support for the Virginia division, in his view.[51]

Trimble had no such difficulties. His two brigades stepped off steadily; "there was no hesitation in my command at the start." He received no artillery fire for some time because it all seemed to be directed at Fry's and Marshall's brigades, some 150 yards to his front. Lane commented that his Tar Heels "never moved forward more handsomely."[52]

Just as Trimble's men were crossing the crest of Seminary Ridge, passing through the artillery line, a staff officer from Pettigrew rode back to caution them "not to fire into, nor pass the front line unless it wavered and he added with an apparent feeling of pride, 'the men in front never waver.'" Trimble's veterans hardly needed such advice; they had already seen much more combat than Marshall's brigade. Trimble rode with his staff between the two brigades, "near the line of file-closers." In addition to these men, Pettigrew, Marshall, and Lane were mounted. Of course various staff members also were mounted.[53]

The entire attacking force soon came under the hail of Union artillery fire, mostly from Osborn's guns on Cemetery Ridge. Davis's men received it soon after they crossed through the thin line of trees on Seminary Ridge. Shells "burst & tore the timber behind us in a frightful manner," commented William Peel of the 11th Mississippi. Five men in that regiment were later knocked out by one shell explosion. Artillery rounds punished Marshall's brigade as well. Pettigrew, who rode just behind his old command, was an early casualty. Shell fragments broke some bones in his left hand, causing a painful but not disabling wound. His horse was wounded, too, and the division leader was forced to wander about on foot.[54]

Fry's brigade received a great deal of artillery fire. There was no color guard in the 1st Tennessee, so the flag bearer, Wiley Woods, recruited several comrades to watch him and take the colors if he fell. All three of them, however, were hit during the advance while Woods made it all the way to the Union line. Lt. James M. Simpson of the 13th Alabama was stunned by a shell burst early in the advance. "I think I was providentially save[d] by the wound," he later wrote, "for had [I gone] across the field there would have been little probability of my escape."[55]

When Trimble's command came under artillery fire partway across the valley, a shell explosion killed two men, wounded three others, and knocked down the lieutenant colonel of the 28th North Carolina of Lane's brigade. Trimble also received enfilade fire from the right; McGilvery and Rittenhouse had an effect on the Confederate left as well as on Pickett's division. In fact, a member of Fry's brigade, which also was subject to these rounds, believed that this right flank fire was just as deadly as any that reached his command. In Marshall's brigade a shell burst from somewhere stunned Capt. John W. Brown of Company I, 47th North Carolina. He lay on the ground with enough wits about him to lift his sword and encourage the men as they passed.[56]

There were still Union skirmishers on the Bliss farm, and Marshall came under their harassing fire as he approached the midpoint of the advance. The damage done the attacking column was light, but Lt. James D. Newsom of Company H, 47th North Carolina, was slightly wounded in the shoulder by a skirmisher. He became excited by this and ran to his captain, Sidney Wilford Mitchell. "Captain, they have wounded me, but I want to lead Company H." Of course Mitchell did not give up command of the company, and Newsom had to return to his place in line.[57]

Even though the right wing of his division was advancing well, Pettigrew had to adjust its alignment partway across the valley. This was done for one or both of two reasons. Louis G. Young argued that the men had a tendency to press from right to left, possibly due to the enfilade fire coming from McGilvery and Rittenhouse, which caused bunching in the middle of the division line. Capt. Albert S. Haynes of Company I, 11th North Carolina, argued that Marshall's brigade had advanced a bit farther than the rest of the line and thus was causing the misalignment. For whatever reason, Pettigrew paused briefly to redress the line just east of the Bliss farmstead. Haynes, in fact, believed they stopped a second time farther on to redress again. These pauses were mistaken for wavering on the part of observers, including Trimble, who watched from his position to Pettigrew's rear. Pettigrew told Young to see to Marshall's brigade and try to stop the pressure from the right. Young had great difficulty sorting out the overcrowding there and later reported that the problem was eased "by the thinning of the ranks, done by shot and shell." It was also eased later when the division neared Emmitsburg Road and saw Garnett's left flank approaching. Then the men naturally dressed to the right to connect with Pickett.[58]

Davis's brigade had far worse trouble with alignment than did Marshall's or Fry's. Davis had started his men hastily, a few minutes later than the right wing of the division, and never fully got control of them. They literally ran over the crest of Seminary Ridge, passing through the ranks of Posey's brigade just behind the artillery, and rushed into the open field. They soon caught up with Marshall, but the brigade line was at a right oblique by that time. Even though they slowed down, Davis was forced to pause while Marshall continued his steady pace onward in order to adjust his left flank to align with the rest of the division. Then he had to rush the Mississippians ahead again to catch up. All of this caused "a huddling of the men together," thought Young, "which exposed them to greater loss than should have been." To Thomas, whose Georgia brigade was positioned to the left, it appeared as if Davis "pushed forward, *in advance* of the general line, with too much impetuosity." Davis tried to cover this by noting in his official report that his advance was interrupted by fences, causing the brigade alignment to become disordered. But the truth was that this neophyte commander had not yet learned how to handle his powerful brigade whose men were eager to participate in the assault. Lt. William Peel heard a constant admonition from other officers during the advance: "Steady boys — & slow — Don't break your selves down by running." As a result, Davis's brigade lurched across the swale of

Brig. Gen. Joseph Robert Davis, nephew of President Jefferson Davis, who led his Mississippi and North Carolina brigade for the first time in battle but poorly coordinated its movements in the attack (LC)

Stevens's Run more or less in a jagged line with the rest of Pettigrew's division.[59]

Brockenbrough had far worse problems to deal with than did Davis. His brigade began the attack fractured by a breakdown of communication among its regimental commanders and weakened by the unwillingness of many men in the 22nd Virginia Battalion, his weakest unit, to even attempt the attack. Most of this trouble was Brockenbrough's own fault. Young was right in pinpointing his lack of leadership as the prime cause of the brigade's inefficiency. Brockenbrough was a nonentity who did not know how to control his recalcitrant rank and file; nor did he have the presence to impress his subordinate officers and encourage them to do his bidding.

Brockenbrough made an effort to conduct the attack efficiently, although his plan completely backfired. Before the bombardment, he spread the word that an attack was planned, trying to tell the men and officers what to expect. He then informed Col. William S. Christian of the 55th Virginia that he intended to divide the brigade into two wings. The 55th and the 47th would constitute the left wing under Col. Robert J. Mayo, and Brockenbrough would take charge of the 40th and the 22nd Battalion on the right wing. Why he did this was never made clear. The brigade already was tiny—no more than 500 men were available that day—and it could easily have been handled by one competent officer.

To make matters worse, Mayo was nowhere to be found when the rest of Pettigrew's division began to advance. While Brockenbrough moved out with his wing, Christian and Lt. Col. John Lyle of the 47th Virginia wondered what to do. They had been told not to move out unless Mayo gave the order. After a few minutes Lyle suggested that Mayo might have been hit in the bombardment, so the two commanders ordered their regiments forward without him. "We were a long ways behind," reported Christian, "and had to run to catch up with the rest of the Brigade." The left wing finally caught up with the right wing just before both encountered any resistance. Mayo's whereabouts were never disclosed, even though he wrote a report following the battle. All was still not well. Brockenbrough later admitted to Henry Heth that "he did not believe that 20 men of the 22nd Va Batt. went into the charge made by the brigade; that they shamefully ran away under the shelling prior to the charge."[60]

Brockenbrough was also forced to pause on the Bliss farm to readjust his line, skewed as it was by the hasty joining of the two wings while advancing. Brockenbrough never made a connection with Davis's wildly lurching brigade to his right. Also, he never made a connection with any units to his left, as those commanders had no orders to participate in the attack. The members of Posey's brigade who were still out on the skirmish line partway across the valley expected to join the assault when the Virginians came up to their line, but they were disappointed to be told to stay put by their officers. Even members of Brig. Gen. Stephen D. Ramseur's North Carolina brigade, farther to the left, assumed the attack would extend to include them. They were surprised when it did not go farther to the left than Brockenbrough's little command.[61]

Meanwhile the Virginians were pelted with severe artillery fire from Osborn on Cemetery Ridge. It punished them greatly and further eroded morale in the shaky brigade. Brockenbrough was exposed to this fire more than any other unit on the battlefield. An observer saw it coming and noticed the impact. The open, sloping ground gave the impression that the shells were flying down a bowling alley: "All the way down the inclined plane they throw shells into their lines with as much precision as if in 100 yards."[62]

Despite the difficulties, Brockenbrough managed to make it past the position of Thomas's brigade in Long Lane and plow ahead. At least the left wing under Mayo, the 47th and 55th, did so. It is possible that the right wing, the 40th and what few men of the 22nd Battalion chose to advance, might have simply stopped at Long Lane without going farther.

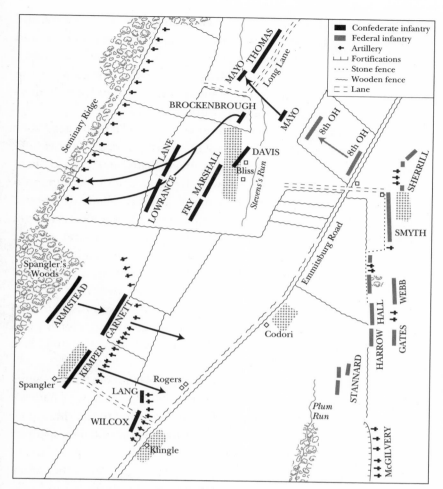

Map 5.1 The Confederate Advance to Emmitsburg Road

The roadway offered some shelter, and the temptation might have been too great for these harried men. The skirmish line of the 8th Ohio was just ahead. The Federals opened fire, but they were too weak to hold back two, possibly three regiments. The Ohio skirmishers fell back, "loading at trail arms, then facing about and firing," in the words of T. S. Potter.[63]

Sawyer was keenly aware that Rebel troops were approaching his position even before the Union skirmishers fought their way back toward his regiment, which was still taking shelter in the ditch along Emmitsburg Road. The view was quite open, although the sight of Pettigrew's division was somewhat obscured by cannon smoke and the trees of the Bliss orchard. Nevertheless it was clear that a heavy force—Fry's, Marshall's, and Davis's brigades—was approaching to the left of Sawyer's position and that a much smaller, detached force was approaching his front. Sawyer acted decisively. He ordered his men up and forward to reinforce the skirmishers. The men deployed in a single line to widen their front as much as possible without diluting their firepower.

It was a magnificent advance, pitting about 150 Federals against at least twice the number of Rebels. The Ohioans ran across the cornfield separating them from the rail fence that their skirmishers had just abandoned. Meeting the skirmishers partway and reincorporating them into the line, Sawyer's men continued forward to the fence. There they found Brockenbrough's command only 100 yards away. It was close enough, thought Capt. Thomas F. Galwey, for him to "readily distinguish the features of their men." The regiment quickly opened fire, and the impact was immediately felt. "We so galled them with our fire," commented Galwey, "that a panic soon took hold of them and they fled." Sawyer noted that the Rebels broke and "fled in the wildest confusion." This ended Brockenbrough's contribution to the assault. His command had not been able to reach Emmitsburg Road, much less cross it and close with the Union line.[64]

The right wing, under Brockenbrough, fled all the way back to Seminary Ridge. As already mentioned, it is possible that this wing had not advanced beyond Long Lane at all. The men returned to the ridge at an angle toward the southwest in order to avoid the hail of Union artillery fire from Cemetery Hill as much as possible. They therefore ran through the lines of Trimble's two brigades in a near panic. The other wing, however, retired to Long Lane and stayed there. Lyle's 47th and Christian's 55th extended their fronts as much as possible in the lane until they deployed only one rank and in effect reinforced Thomas's skirmishers there. They remained for the duration of the attack.[65]

The fugitives of Brockenbrough's brigade interfered with Trimble's advance, forcing Lowrance and Lane to contend with their running retreat. The former reported that these men "came tearing through our ranks, which caused many of our men to break." Capt. J. McLeod Turner, commander of the 7th North Carolina in Lane's brigade, ordered his men to fix bayonets and force the stragglers to go around his flanks instead of disrupting the ranks. Pettigrew was alarmed at Brockenbrough's failure and sent a staff member, Lt. W. B. Shepard, to rally them. Shepard tried but had no success. Brockenbrough's retreating soldiers also alarmed Lee, who clearly saw them from his observation post with Anderson's division. Lee told staff member Charles S. Venable to take him to the spot where Pettigrew's attack began so he could get a closer view of affairs on the Confederate left.[66]

The retreat was visible for all to see. Even many of Pickett's men saw it from their positions on the right. Pickett himself became alarmed at this first sign of a weakening on the left and, as already indicated, sent staff officers to help rally the retiring troops. Despite this, many members of Brockenbrough's brigade tried to whitewash the affair. Mayo applied the widest brush, reporting that the brigade was "managed with remarkable skill, coolness and Gallantry." Since his mismanagement largely contributed to the fiasco, Mayo had a strong incentive to lie. Capt. Wayland F. Dunaway of the 40th Virginia claimed his regiment got so close to the Federals that "I emptied my revolver upon them." This lends support to the notion that Brockenbrough's right wing managed to advance beyond Long Lane and engage the 8th Ohio. But Dunaway also claimed the brigade was still attacking when the fight came to an end, an obvious mistake. Other members of the brigade argued the same insupportable point. Then there were those who glossed over the whole attack with generalizations such as "our infantry then charged them incessantly until night but failed to carry the works[;] the position was too strong." Few of Brockenbrough's Virginians wanted to detail exactly what happened to their unfortunate brigade.[67]

The rest of the division continued across the valley, enduring the artillery fire from both flanks and the interference of retreating friends. Trimble's command developed an alignment problem as Pettigrew's men began to dress right to connect with Pickett. As Fry and Marshall tended toward the right, Lane's left wing was uncovered. With no one in front of them anymore, the men here began to advance faster than the rest of Trimble's command, and Lane's left slowly curved ahead. This caused the 7th North Carolina, on Lane's far right, to overlap Lowrance's left wing. In other words, the 7th began to fall behind Lowrance and sidle behind his brigade. Both Lane and Trimble shouted orders to rectify this, causing Lane's brigade to guide left for a while. It did not exactly work; as a result of these orders, at least the left wing of Lane drifted to the left, and a small gap opened between the two brigades. It is quite possible, and perhaps more accurate, to say that the gap appeared between the 7th North Carolina and the next regiment to its left, the 37th North Carolina, or even within the ranks of the latter regiment itself. At any rate,

Lane's Tar Heels were having a difficult time keeping themselves straight during the advance. All of this took place when Trimble was about two-thirds across the valley.[68]

The right wing of Pettigrew's division advanced with the most steady step, unhampered by misalignment problems after it redressed its ranks on the Bliss farm. Fry did an excellent job of keeping his small, veteran brigade on a straight line. Just as he passed Spangler's Woods, Fry looked south and could see the left flank of Garnett's brigade angling toward him. Garnett rode near his own left, and Fry stayed near his own right. The two kept track of each other as their respective commands advanced. The rail fence that ran straight from the northwest corner of the woods toward the angle in the stone fence provided a guide for Fry's march.[69]

Soon, the two brigadiers were close enough so that Fry saw Garnett give a command to his men, but he could not hear it over the din of battle. "Seeing my look or gesture of inquiry, he called out, 'I am dressing on you!'" The two brigades veered steadily toward each other with every step, but the Union artillery and skirmish fire began to take a heavier toll on the Tennessee-Alabama brigade. Col. Newton J. George of the 1st

Tennessee fell wounded, and thirty steps later Fry was shot in the thigh. "I was so confident of victory that to some of my men who ran up to carry me off I shouted, 'Go on; it will not last five minutes longer!' " Fry also told Capt. Jacob B. Turney to take charge of the 1st Tennessee. "Proceed with the charge," Turney recalled his words, "but don't stop to fire a gun." As his men drove on through the smoke, Fry could hear Pettigrew behind him tell someone to rally Brockenbrough's troops on the left.[70]

The flanks of Pettigrew and Pickett finally joined some time before both commands reached Emmitsburg Road. The gap had finally closed. Even though Pettigrew had lost the use of one brigade and could not rely on the steadiness of another, the rest of his men were solid and moving forward.[71]

· · · · · · ·

GIBBON AND THE FIRST CORPS

"Here they come! Here they come! Here comes the infantry!" The cry rippled through the ranks of Gibbon's division and forced everyone to peer through the cannon smoke that covered the valley. Gibbon and Haskell were still on foot, wondering if an attack actually was contemplated by Lee, when Capt. Francis Wessels, the division judge advocate, came up with a group of orderlies leading horses. Wessels, out of breath with the excitement, said, "General, they say the enemy's Infantry is advancing."[72]

As the smoke lifted, the Rebels became visible advancing beyond their artillery line. It was a sight that impressed everyone who saw it. "The perfect order and steady but rapid advance of the enemy called forth praise from our troops," wrote Norman Hall, "but gave their line an appearance of being fearfully irresistible." To other men the Confederates looked like "an unrolling wave of the sea" or a "rising tide of armed men rolling towards us in steel crested billows." Such nautical similes seemed appropriate for those who felt like the rocks upon which the surf would wash. Other similes utilized the rushing power of snow in a mountainous region. James A. Wright of the 1st Minnesota referred to Pickett's division as an "avalanche of bayonets that was being projected against us." Whatever metaphors the Federals chose, they could not help but admire their enemy. Henry S. Willey of the 16th Vermont had always called them "rebels" before this day; afterward he referred to them as "confederates, . . . a less odious name."[73]

The most famous description of the gray advance was penned by Haskell.

> Every eye could see his legions, an overwhelming, resistless tide of an ocean of armed men, sweeping upon us! Regiment after Regiment, and Brigade after Brigade, move from the woods, and rapidly take their places in the lines forming the assault. . . . More than half a mile their front extends; — more than a thousand yards the dull gray masses deploy, man touching man, rank pressing rank, and line supporting line. Their red flags wave; their horsemen gallop up and down; the arms of eighteen thousand men, barrel and bayonet, gleam in the sun, a sloping forrest of flashing steel. Right on they move, as with one soul, in perfect order, without impediment of ditch, or wall, or stream, over ridge and slope, through orchard, and meadow, and cornfield, magnificent, grim, irresistable.[74]

When the Confederates became visible, the color-bearer of the 80th New York in Gates's demibrigade rose up, waved his flag, and "shouted to them to come on." The few men remaining in the 1st Minnesota prepared for the contest by advancing a few feet to snuggle close behind the stone fence with its additional layer of rails on top. They knelt behind it and laid out extra cartridges on the ground for faster loading, resting the barrels of their rifle muskets on the rails. "Never in my life have I felt so strong as I did at that minute as I looked along our lines and saw that the whole fence was bristling with guns," recalled Pvt. Daniel Bond. He saw on the faces of his Minnesota comrades "nothing but a determination to do or to die." Company officers spread the reminder to aim at the Rebels' feet so as not to overshoot their targets.[75]

In the 15th Massachusetts the only command given by the officers was "Up, boys, they are coming!" It was shouted by an aide to some general, probably Gibbon. "There were practically no general orders," recalled Lt. Col. George C. Joslin. "It was an affair of regiments, or even of individuals, all moved, however, by the same spontaneous impulse to meet and hurl back the foe."[76]

The work of repelling this assault would have to be done primarily by the rank and file, with instructions from company and regimental officers such as Col. Dennis O'Kane of the 69th Pennsylvania. Holding the key position near the angle, O'Kane's men would soon be at the storm center of the assault. The colonel told them to hold their fire until the enemy were very close, "and let your work this day be for victory or to the death." He also reminded them they were defending Pennsylvania soil and encouraged each man to shoot any comrade who flinched in the moment of danger. O'Kane "went along the line speaking encouragement to all the companies." Webb also gave a pep talk, telling the Pennsylvanians to hold their fire until the Rebels reached Emmitsburg Road; "if you do as well to-day as you did yesterday, I will be satisfied," he told them. Anthony McDermott did not think the 69th needed such encouragement. "I do not believe there was a soldier in the regiment, that did not feel that he had more courage to meet the enemy at Gettysburg, than upon any field of battle in which we had as yet been engaged. The stimulus being the fact that we were on the soil of our own state."[77]

Just in case the shock of the attack was too great, a provost guard was already in place to the rear. Webb had ignored Gibbon's instructions about placing every man in the line. Ten soldiers from each regiment of his brigade, led by a captain, formed an extended line 150 yards behind the stone fence to turn back anyone who was not wounded. Hays already had a provost line consisting of the 10th New York Battalion in place.[78]

Gibbon hurriedly rode along his line to encourage the men while they waited for the Rebel infantry. After sending off Haskell to Meade to inform him that the attack was under way, Gibbon told the men to hold their fire until the Confederates at least reached Emmitsburg Road. "Do not hurry, men, and fire too fast; — let them come up close before you fire, and then aim low, and steadily." He even wandered off as far as the 14th Connecticut of Hays's division, telling them, "The fate of the whole army now rests with you. Don't fire until you get the word; then fire low and sure! We must hold this line *to the last man!*"[79]

Haskell and a messenger from Hays both informed Meade of the Rebel advance, which led the army commander to send two staff members of his own with instructions to hurry up reinforcements for the center. Then Meade "rode among the batteries and troops encouraging the men by his voice and presence," according to his son.[80]

The Federal skirmishers fought hard with their gray counterparts until the main Rebel force reached the vicinity of Emmitsburg Road. On the right of Gibbon's division Capt. James Lynch of the 106th Pennsylvania led a group of skirmishers from his own regiment, the 69th Pennsylvania, and the 72nd Pennsylvania that screened Webb's front. Lynch fired at Garnett's approaching brigade and then retired to the main line. The skirmishers from the 19th Maine, clustered around the Codori buildings, saw the Confederate skirmishers approach, followed by the battle line. They came out of the buildings and fired as they retreated.[81]

The Federal artillery went into action as quickly as possible. Most of its execution was performed by Rittenhouse and McGilvery, as Hazard had shot away his long-range ammunition. Rittenhouse had a clear shot from the beginning, but McGilvery could use only his rightmost three batteries at first due to the undulations of the ground in his front. The other six batteries came into play as Pickett progressed across the valley. McGilvery's twenty-eight guns fired a variety of ordnance at ranges of 400 to 800 yards. Hunt rode to McGilvery to personally observe the gunners at work.

The Yankee artillerymen proudly reported the effect of their fire. Capt. Edwin Dow wrote, "I tell you the gaps we made were simply terrible. But they closed up their lines, and closed up and closed them up." McGilvery reported achieving a "raking fire" on the Rebels; he tended to overstate the effect, claiming they were quickly thrown into "broken and confused masses," but the damage was severe enough without any exaggeration. "I never saw artillery so ably handled, or productive of such decisive results," recorded Capt. Charles A. Phillips. "It was far superior even to Malvern Hill. For half an hour our line was one continuous roar of artillery, and the shot ploughed through the rebel ranks most terrifically." Phillips later wrote, "We could not help hitting them at every shot." The results were clearly evident to the waiting Union infantry. Capt. Henry L. Abbott of the 20th Massachusetts saw the rounds "tumble over squads in the rebel lines."[82]

In the center Hazard was forced to wait, his hands effectively tied, until the Rebels closed within canister range. He apparently had a paltry few shells left and waited until Pickett was at least halfway across the valley before firing them, but it had no effect on the surging mass. Hunt was astonished to discover that no long-range firing was coming from the angle, and he rode from McGilvery in that direction. Meanwhile Webb had sent an aid, Capt. Charles H. Banes, to fetch two fresh batteries to replace Cushing and Brown. Banes would quickly find one for Brown, but it has never been explained why a second battery did not come up to replace Cushing's decimated unit.[83]

Instead of retiring for rest, Cushing pushed his two remaining guns forward to the stone fence, as described in Chapter 4. Webb ordered the 71st Pennsylvania forward to the fence to support the guns. Penn Smith dutifully brought his regiment up but found there was not enough room between Cushing's two guns and the northwest angle for all of his men. Only eight companies could fit in this space, and Penn Smith did not want to extend the other two into the open field to the north, where they had no protection and their flank would be fearfully in the air. So he took it upon himself to leave the two right companies at the northeast angle. There was plenty of room there, for Arnold's guns had already evacuated the spot, and the thin line of the 14th Connecticut could easily accommodate the two Pennsylvania companies.

Penn Smith left Lt. Col. Charles Kochersperger in charge of the eight companies at the forward fence and remained with the two companies to the rear. He instructed Kochersperger to fire when the Rebels reached Emmitsburg Road, to load and fire at will, and then to retire if they pressed too closely to his front. He also cautioned the lieutenant colonel to look out for an enfilading fire to his right, which was protected only by the short return fence. The two companies at the northeast angle were to use a pile of discarded muskets picked up from the battlefield of July 2 and all loaded and capped for instant use, so they could maximize their own firepower. But he cautioned them to wait until the eight companies had retired so as not to endanger their comrades. He estimated that each member of these two companies (which were never designated with letters in the accounts) had from three to twelve muskets available in this pile.[84]

Pvt. William J. Burns was among those men who were placed forward; "we went down to the fence and saw the rebs advancing, it was a grand sight and worth a man's while to see it." The infantrymen manning Cushing's gun happily filled it with stones, shell fragments, and even a bayonet, while a gunner from the other piece sighted it toward the road. Despite the improvised nature of the defense at the angle, everything was readied as much as possible for the storm to come.[85]

. . . .

HAYS'S DIVISION

On the Union right wing the first sight of the approaching lines of Pettigrew and Trimble inspired feelings of awe, dread, and excitement. William Arnold, whose Rhode Island battery was out of action, bent low to peer under the slowly lifting cloud of cannon smoke and saw the gray-clad infantry. "It was somewhat quiet & all stood gazing at the sight," he remembered. Farther to the right, on Cemetery Hill, the gunners of

Lt. James Stewart's Battery B, 4th U.S. Artillery, could clearly see the Rebels emerge from the thin tree line atop Seminary Ridge and cross the open space onto the Bliss farm. Stewart gazed at them for a while then turned to his orderly sergeant and said, "They mean business. You notice how few of their offices are mounted. They are going to try to break our center. I think it is their last effort."[86]

The infantrymen of Hays's division also found the sight impressive. Most of them felt some sense of relief. Their nerves had been severely tested during the barrage, when they had no opportunity to reply to the enemy; now they had something to do. "Was scared and that badly during the cannonading," remarked George D. Bowen of the 12th New Jersey, "but as soon as [I] saw them come out to charge us it all faded away." Another Jersey man recalled the shouts that erupted from the regiment when the Rebels appeared: "Thank God! There comes the infantry!" Richard S. Thompson, a captain in the 12th, expressed everyone's feelings when he wrote, "Anything that promised action was better than inaction under the horrors of that cannonade."[87]

The division buzzed with activity. Hays told the men not to fire until the enemy reached the road. This order was repeated by regimental officers several times to ensure that the instructions were carried out. The men were to "take careful aim & fire low." A few minutes of hurried preparation followed. "We were ready," wrote David Shields, one of Hays's staff members. "The ordinary preparation of battle had been made. The men had slid their cartridge boxes in front of the body. Now and then some examined the capped nipples. An occasional click of the trigger told this and the nervous tension under which the men were laboring. There was nothing to do but await the crash that would soon come."[88]

Hays's men were just as ready emotionally. The division leader rode in front of the line yelling, "They are coming, boys; we must whip them, and you men with buck and ball, don't fire until they get to that fence." He was addressing the 12th New Jersey, which was armed with smoothbore sixty-nine caliber muskets. The Jersey men were inspired by this show of confidence; it "caused every man to determine to do his part." The Rebel yell, when it erupted, seemed to Albert S. Emmell as "unnatural shrieks and yells" designed to "strike terror into Yankee hearts." But it did not work. Emmell was "not to be frightened by a little noise coming from Rebel throats." Gibbon added his note of encouragement to the 14th Connecticut during this time, and many members of the regiment noted it. They were sunk in their own thoughts — of their homes, of their families, and of death — as they laid out their cartridges for easy loading. "We must hold this Line to the Last Man," Gibbon intoned, intruding upon their private musings. "The Fate of the whole Army now rests with you. Don't Fire until you get the order, and then fire Low and Sure."[89]

Sherrill's brigade was ordered forward to reinforce the thin front line. MacDougall's 111th New York had already been brought up during the barrage and occupied a position behind the stone fence from the 12th New Jersey to the north of the Bryan barn. Now the 39th and 125th New York were brought up to the rear of the 14th Connecticut, 1st Delaware, and 12th New Jersey. The men were told to crouch down like their comrades in front. "Here we waited in almost breathless suspense for the enemy who was coming on toward us like a vast avalanche," wrote Charles W. Belknap of the 125th New York. In places the men were crowded four ranks deep. Farther to the right Woodruff asked Col. Francis E. Pierce to move the 108th New York from between the guns and limbers, which Hays had earlier refused to allow. Pierce took it upon himself to move the left wing to the left of the battery and the right wing to the right. The men were told to kneel until given the word to fire.[90]

Prepared and in position, everyone had several minutes to watch the advancing host. "Their march was as steady as if impelled by machinery, unbroken by our artillery, which played upon them a storm of missiles," reported Hays. Loren Goodrich of the 14th Connecticut thought the lines and the fluttering red flags were beautiful: "It was a splendid sight to see." Many Federals admired their opponents, the style of the advance, and their courage. They gave the appearance of rigid military precision. "Their lines were unbroken," remarked Chauncey L. Harris of the 108th New York, "and they looked in the distance like statues. On they came, steady . . . moving like so many automatons." Winfield Scott of the 126th New York also noted the machine-like impression. "The men carried their guns, with bayonets fixed, at right shoulder. The regimental flags and guidons were plainly visible along the whole line. The guns and bayonets in the sunlight shone like silver. The whole line of battle looked like a stream or river of silver moving towards us." But some among the Federals reminded themselves that this moving spectacle was a powerful and dangerous enemy. "It was a terrible sight to us," admitted a member of the 126th New York, "fine as it was, for we did not suppose we could repulse them, and we expected to have to fight terribly and suffer heavy losses."[91]

The skirmishers in front of Hays's two brigades also retired fighting, slowly and stubbornly, in the face of this onslaught. They took their wounded and weapons along. The skirmishers rejoined the main line in plenty of time to avoid being caught in a cross fire of hostile and friendly musketry.[92]

Osborn's guns on Cemetery Hill had a perfect opportunity to punish Pettigrew and Trimble without mercy. Osborn could easily see the effect on the Rebel ranks. The artillery fired solid shot at first then switched to shells. The former were aimed to strike directly at the packed lines, and the latter were aimed to explode directly in front of them. "This method was effective to a large degree," Osborn remembered, "as we would see the ranks thinned at many points and here and there a wide gap made as from two to a dozen men were taken out by the men being shot down." Still the Confederates moved forward "as if on dress parade." They suffered most when they paused to redress their ranks on the Bliss farm. Osborn was amazed that they continued marching despite all that he threw at them, and the hail of shell grew fiercer as they neared Emmitsburg Road. By the time they were about two-thirds of the way across the valley, the Rebels moved out of Osborn's view; a projection of Cemetery Hill obscured his ability to see them, so he redirected his guns to the Confederate artillery near Seminary Ridge. Altogether forty-one guns had fired at the gray infantry from and around Cemetery Hill up to that time, and they had done a lot to decrease Pettigrew's and Trimble's chances of success.[93]

In many ways the easiest part of the infantry assault was over by the time the Confederates reached Emmitsburg Road. Now they were to come under the concentrated fire of the Union foot soldiers, a far deadlier enemy than the guns. The road became a bloody dividing line between victory and defeat.

CHAPTER 6
TO THE STONE FENCE
. . . .

The Confederates came to Emmitsburg Road about fifteen or twenty minutes after the start of the attack, and the two wings, Pettigrew's and Pickett's, arrived at roughly the same time. They presented a formidable front when they connected their flanks in front of the angle, but the two wings had very different experiences when they crossed the road. It was almost as if they were fighting two different but related battles that ended the same way.

. . . .
PETTIGREW'S DIVISION

There is some evidence that Marshall's brigade of Pettigrew's division, at least, may have opened fire about 100 yards before it reached the road, but there is no indication that any other unit in either wing violated instructions to hold fire. The post-and-rail fences along the road loomed higher and stronger with each passing step until the Confederates were forced to confront them. The Federals opposite, the 14th Connecticut, opened fire just as they began to climb the fence. Fry's Tennessee and Alabama troops flung themselves over the first one with a desperate energy, a "speed as if in stampeded retreat," recalled John H. Moore of the 7th Tennessee. "The time it took to climb to the top of the fence seemed to me an age of suspense. It was not a leaping over; it was rather an insensible tumbling to the ground in the nervous hope of escaping the thickening missiles that buried themselves in falling victims, in the ground, and in the fence, against which they rattled with the distinctness of large rain-drops pattering on a roof."[1]

After they crossed the first fence, it seemed as if nearly everyone in

Fry's brigade dropped to the ground in the roadbed, which offered some shelter from the rain of bullets. But a shout of encouragement from the officers brought most of them up again. A considerable number of Fry's men stayed put, either wounded or afraid to stand up. The rest clambered over the second fence as they had done the first, the rattle of bullets on planks and posts still ringing in their ears. They paused momentarily after negotiating the second fence, confused and fearful, but then these veterans hastily re-formed their line and pushed on.[2]

The men of Marshall's brigade had much the same experience. They received the same hail of fire from the 14th Connecticut, at least on the right wing of the brigade, and many Tar Heels were shot as they tried to cross the fences. Lt. James D. Newsom of the 47th North Carolina, who had earlier been hit on the shoulder by a shell fragment, had just placed his foot on the bottom rail of the first fence when a bullet slammed into his leg. He fell off the fence and lay stunned on the ground for a few moments. Then Newsom realized the wound was not disabling; he stood up and climbed over the fence.[3]

About this time Col. James K. Marshall became the second brigade commander to fall in the attack. Riding just behind his command, he turned and said to Capt. Stockton Heth, the former division leader's son and aide, "We do not know which of us will be the next to fall." Marshall then cheered on his men until he was shot in the forehead with two bullets and died instantly. Maj. John Thomas Jones of the 26th North Carolina took charge of the brigade.[4]

Marshall's men flung themselves across the two fences as desperately as Fry's had done, and they suffered terribly for their efforts. Trimble, riding 150 yards behind them, was amazed at their bravery and their suffering. They "seemed to sink into the earth under the tempest of fire poured into them," he later wrote. His two brigades passed over many of Marshall's men who had been hit by artillery fire before reaching the road. Trimble heard one of these soldiers call out, "Three cheers for the Old North State," and the Tar Heels of Lowrance's and Lane's brigades responded with a "hearty shout." Trimble turned to his aide, Charley Grogan, and said, "Charley, I believe those fine fellows are going into the enemy's line."[5]

For all their bravery, a large number of Fry's and Marshall's troops did not make it past the road. Many of the men failed because of wounds, but a significant number remained in the shelter of the roadbed rather than risk their lives in further exposure. The remaining 175 yards or so of

Col. James Keith Marshall, leader of Pettigrew's North Carolina brigade since the battle of July 1, was killed when his men neared Emmitsburg Road. Marshall is on the far left and rear in this photograph of cadets at Virginia Military Institute. (Preston Library, VMI)

ground to be covered was completely open, another rail fence was in the way stretching from the angle of the stone fence northward, and there was a stout line of blue-coated infantrymen waiting at the top of the gentle rise.

Randolph Abbott Shotwell in Pickett's division happened to glance to his left about this time, just as Garnett's brigade was crossing the road and closing with the angle. He estimated that 1,000 to 1,200 men of Fry's and Marshall's commands crossed the road. This may well be an accurate estimate, for 1,800 men served in the two brigades. Col. John Fite believed that no more than half of his men in the 7th Tennessee made it beyond the first fence and no more than fifty of the rest managed to cross the second fence and advance toward the angle. If that was typical of the brigade, then only 250 of 400 men of Fry's command crossed the road. Using the same proportion for Marshall's brigade, only 700 Tar Heels crossed the road. The total, 950, is very close to Shotwell's estimate. The roadbed, about two feet deep along Fry's and Marshall's front, was too tempting to pass by. John H. Moore of the 7th Tennessee estimated that as many as two-thirds of the brigade crossed the second fence, a much higher estimate than any other observer made, yet he was still astonished at the sight of so many Rebels lying in the roadbed. Pausing briefly on top of the second fence to glance back, Moore thought "there seemed to remain a line of battle in the road." Moore was convinced that the presence of the road and its fences killed any chance that the attack might have succeeded.[6]

The men who remained in the roadbed claimed it was impossible to push on. They were "compelled to stop at the road, by reason of the heavy loss inflicted," in the words of some members of the 11th and 26th North Carolina. Their claim ignored the example of those Carolinians who did manage to move across the last fence and advance toward the enemy.[7]

Fry's brigade, or what was left of it, marched briskly on after crossing the road. The 1st Tennessee opened a scattering fire as it closed on the angle, but the return fire from the Union side dropped many men as they moved forward. Color-bearers seemed to take the brunt of this fire. The man who carried the flag of the 5th Alabama Battalion was shot down, the private who replaced him was hit, and the third color-bearer was killed as well. The fourth man managed to live at least until he reached the high-water mark. The 14th Tennessee suffered a similar loss of flag bearers. Two of them had fallen before the regiment reached Emmitsburg Road, the third fell just after crossing the road, and the fourth took the flag all the way to the regiment's high-water mark.[8]

The men of Fry's brigade who braved the hail of musketry and moved beyond the road crowded together for emotional support. About 100 feet from the rail fence, Theo Hartman of Company A, 14th Tennessee, came up to touch shoulders with June Kimble. He suggested that they stay together, and the "compact," as Kimble put it, was readily sealed. Twenty-five steps farther, William H. McCulloch stepped up to Kimble's other side and said, "I am with you." The three moved steadily on for a short while before a bullet penetrated McCulloch's head and killed him instantly. Kimble and Hartman had no time to mourn their brave comrade but pushed on into the smoke and fire.[9]

Fry and Garnett hit the angle about the same time. Considerably more of Garnett's brigade made it this far than did Fry's, so much so that the Virginians never mentioned their Tennessee comrades in recounting what happened next. Only a small portion of Fry's brigade, the 1st Tennessee on the far right of the brigade line, actually hit the angle of the stone fence. It was possible that only fifty men of the brigade mingled with Garnett's command at the angle. By this time the 71st Pennsylvania had retired from its position inside the angle, leaving only a few men who were either too slow to retreat with the rest or too brave to run. Wiley Woods of the 1st Tennessee recalled that some of these Yankees "hollered out we surender and no [Confederate] officer said anything. I said crawl over to our side & you shant be hurt." They did so, and thus Fry's brigade took its first and only prisoners in the assault.[10]

The rest of the brigade fronted the rail fence that stretched northward from the angle. This fence essentially marked the farthest advance of Fry's men; no significant body of them appears to have crossed it. The color-bearer of the 14th Tennessee, Pvt. Boney Smith of Company F, made it to this fence and stopped. He propped the flagstaff against the rails and "drew himself up to his full hight," according to a Federal soldier in the 14th Connecticut, "looking us calmly in the face. There he stood for several awful moments, when the sharp crack of two or three rifles fired simultaneously sent his brave soul to its Maker."[11]

Most of this terrible damage was done to Fry's brigade by the 14th Connecticut, small as it was, which poured an incredible volume of fire into the Tennessee and Alabama command. The 1st Delaware and 12th New Jersey to the right opened fire later, after Marshall's brigade crossed the road, but they, too, poured in a destructive and heavy fire. Those men of Marshall's command who managed to tear themselves away from the safety of the road, and who had avoided getting hit, could not re-form their units. They acted as individuals or in small groups. Many of them halted a few yards beyond the second fence to fire while others continued to advance. The 26th North Carolina was "reduced to a skirmish line by the constant falling of the men at every step," recalled Capt. Thomas J. Cureton, "but still they kept closing to the colors," for the flag bearer had managed to cross the two fences.[12]

Davis's Mississippi brigade fared less well than either Fry's or Marshall's. There is some reason to believe that it actually reached Emmitsburg Road before the other two commands, as an observer noted later that it "pushed forward *in advance* of the general line, with too much impetuosity and was driven back." The 11th Mississippi advanced even farther than the rest of Davis's brigade. It had missed the terrible fighting of July 1 and was therefore the only fresh regiment in the division. Several

The fence extending northward from the angle, the high-water mark for many fragments of Pettigrew's and Trimble's commands (author's collection)

officers had already fallen, and Capt. John V. Moore "seemed to be in command" of the regiment, in the words of Lt. Andrew J. Baker. When the 11th was within 100 yards of the first fence, Baker noticed that Moore was in front of Company D, attempting to slow the regiment so it could regain alignment with the troops to the right. This was too much for Baker, who called out, "John, for heaven's sake give the command to charge." Moore replied that he did not feel he had the responsibility to do that, so Baker gave the command himself. It was taken up by other company officers and soon spread along the regimental line. The Mississippians ran for the fence and clambered over it.[13]

How many members of the 11th actually made it across the road is unclear. Baker was hit between the two fences and fell. Only small groups of the regiment and of the 55th North Carolina managed to advance toward the Union line. Lt. William Peel found himself in one such group clustered around the flag of the 11th Mississippi. It was now borne by the fifth color-bearer, George Kidd, who had to deal with a broken staff and a flag that was "dangling in graceless confusion, from one corner." Thirteen men gathered around Kidd to form an improvised color guard, with Peel and Lt. R. A. McDowell as the only officers. Without knowing it the group moved quite a distance ahead of the rest of the regiment until they

TO THE STONE FENCE

The Bryan barn and house from Emmitsburg Road. The barn offered some shelter for approaching Confederate groups, such as Lt. William Peel's contingent from the 11th Mississippi. (author's collection)

reached the Bryan barn, only a few yards from the Union line. Here they took shelter and fired around the corner at the Federals.

These men now had time to catch their breath and look to the rear, but what they saw was disheartening. Peel realized that they were essentially alone, that most of the regiment and the brigade had not advanced beyond the road, and that their closest supports had already retreated when only about 150 yards away. He and McDowell consulted and decided not to waste the lives of their men in an attempt to retreat. They found some white cloth and waved it around the corner to signal a surrender. Sgt. Thomas Geer of Company A, 111th New York, saw it and came forward. Geer told the Mississippians to go through a gate on the north side of the barn, where the lane passed through. They dropped their guns and moved quickly, but a Federal soldier nearby raised his musket and might have fired if not for Geer. He lunged and knocked the musket away and "with a word of reproach, asked the soldier if he did not see that these men had surrendered." As soon as the Mississippians crossed into Union lines, they were met by several Federals who were eager to escort them to the rear.[14]

It appears that far fewer men of Davis's brigade attempted to advance

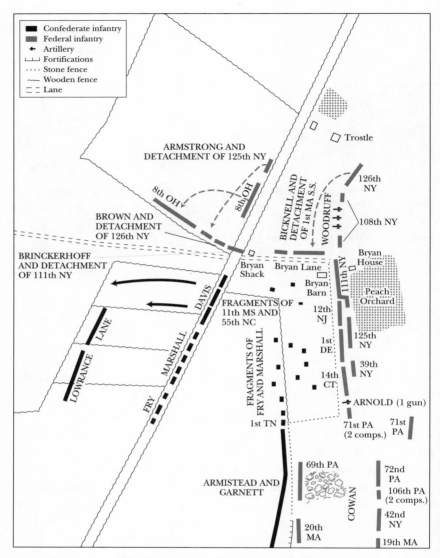

Map 6.1 Pettigrew Crosses Emmitsburg Road

past the road than was the case in either Fry's or Marshall's brigade. W. P. Heflin of the 11th Mississippi noted after the war that "our line was so cut down and demoralized by the enemy's batteries before we got in gun shot distance that we could not carry the works." The scattered groups that surged up the last 200 yards or so of deadly ground to the stone fence had no hope of capturing the Union position; they were either shot down or taken prisoner. The bulk of Davis's command stopped at the road. It had no support to the left, as Brockenbrough's brigade had not provided any help, and it had received the same enfilading artillery fire from Cemetery Ridge that had damaged the small Virginia unit while it crossed the valley. Now an even more deadly threat came from the left, as the 8th Ohio and other Union regiments flanked its position and poured in volumes of musketry. The pressure was simply too much for the Rebels. The brigade suddenly broke and retreated from the road.[15]

When staff officer Louis G. Young reported to Pettigrew about the retreat of Davis's brigade, the Tar Heel general could only send him to Trimble for help. Young was now on foot; his favorite horse had already been hit three times, and he had sent it back to the rear with a wounded man on board. Young later admitted that he worried more for the safety of the horse, which he loved dearly, than for the wounded soldier. He then ran toward Trimble to ask him to shore up Pettigrew's left. Young had a sinking feeling that it was already too late, but Trimble agreed to do what he could.[16]

Pettigrew's left wing was having a terrible time. First Brockenbrough's brigade failed to advance more than about halfway across the valley, as noted in the preceding chapter. Then Davis's brigade careened to a halt at the road and suddenly broke for the rear. Only Fry's and Marshall's commands were reasonably in hand and doing all that was humanly feasible in this situation. It is possible that only 250 of Fry's men, 700 of Marshall's command, 50 of Davis's brigade, and certainly none of Brockenbrough's Virginians crossed Emmitsburg Road. Of 4,500 men, Pettigrew's division threw at least 1,000 into the deadly ground between the pike and the Union position. That number was far too low for the Rebels to have a real chance of taking the stone fence. If the two left brigades had been commanded by more competent commanders, if they had some support from Anderson's division, and if the whole of Pettigrew's division could have moved across the road intact, Hays's Federals would have had a very difficult time maintaining their position. But the failure of coordination on Longstreet's part, the destructive hail of artillery fire from Osborn's guns on Cemetery Hill, the physical obstruction of the intact fences, and the lay of the ground all came together to doom this part of the assault. A few brave men sacrificed themselves between the road and the stone fence during the remaining few minutes of the attack, but the rest of the division was either retreating or saving itself by lying in Emmitsburg Road.

· · · · · · ·
HAYS'S DIVISION

The Federals opposing Pettigrew and Trimble could deliver such a heavy volume of fire because they had amassed a stockpile of weapons. Hays had told the men before and during the cannonade to collect abandoned muskets on the field. They were piled along the line, loaded, and readied for immediate use. Many men had their individual stockpiles of as many as four guns each. They laid out cartridges in a row for easy accessibility, and some soldiers even volunteered to load for those who were quicker or better shots. As Lt. John L. Brady of the 1st Delaware put it, Hays's men had "an embryo arsenal" at their beck and call.[17]

The 14th Connecticut opened fire first, just as Fry's and Marshall's men began to climb the first fence bordering Emmitsburg Road. The distance was no more than about 200 yards, a bit longer than normal for this war but well within the range of the regiment's Springfield rifle muskets. The Connecticut men were gripped with excitement. They sprang to their feet and poured in the fire, shouting, "Now we've got em! Sock it to the rebels! Fredericksburg on the other leg! Hurrah! Never mind who is hit, give it to them! Lay 'em out, boys!" The effect was astonishing and clearly evident to the Yankees. Pettigrew's men "dropped from the fence as if swept by a gigantic sickle swung by some powerful force of nature." Two companies of the 14th Connecticut were armed with breechloading Sharps rifles, and the execution was particularly fearful in their front. Observers thought they could discern "a clean cut through . . . the rebel lines opposite" the two companies. As the hail of bullets continued, the Sharps rifles became overheated. Many Yankees had to pause briefly to pour water from their canteens on the barrels before they could continue firing.[18]

The 12th New Jersey waited a few minutes before opening fire because it was the only regiment in Hays's division armed with sixty-nine caliber smoothbore muskets. Hays had already told the regiment to stay low until the enemy were forty yards away, then to rise and pour it in. Apparently the 1st Delaware, to the left of the 12th and the right of the 14th Connecticut, waited without orders to begin firing with the Jersey men. Many soldiers in the 12th made their weapons even more deadly. They all had been issued buck and ball cartridges, each charge having one bullet and three buckshots. Many of them had opened their cartridges, taken out the bullet, and put in ten to twenty-five buckshots. This turned their

210 TO THE STONE FENCE

muskets into something like a shotgun. At short range they would be able to spray a ragged pattern of lead into the face of an advancing foe.[19]

Facing the rest of Marshall's and Davis's brigades, the 12th and 1st waited until the Rebels had crossed the two fences before opening fire. They even waited, according to some reports, until the Confederates were up to or even beyond the rail fence that stretched northward from the angle. The range was as little as fifty yards, according to some eyewitnesses, before the first shot was fired. Hays rode up and down the line yelling, "Show them your colors and give them hell boys." The Federals rose and began to pour it in; "their first line was annihilated," remembered William Arnold, who continued to watch the proceedings even though his battery no longer played a role in the fight. The first fire seemed to sweep the Confederates "like a tornado." Rebels dropped so quickly it seemed as if the entire attacking force went down. "From the moment we poured the first volley into them," remarked John M. Dunn of the 1st Delaware, "they ceased to exist as a compact military organization. They never got fairly formed after they crossed the Emmetsburg Pike."[20]

While most of the 12th New Jersey rose to its feet to fire into the surging Rebels, part of the regimental line on the right remained prone. These men probably did not fire at all, or at the very least their shots were not rapid or accurate. The extreme left of the 111th New York, which was behind the extreme right of the Jersey regiment, compensated for this by rising up and firing over them.[21]

The rest of the 12th did their duty with a grim determination. George D. Bowen was a file closer that day. He fired thirty of his forty cartridges during the attack, throwing away his musket when it became so fouled with powder he "could not get a load down" it. As he was behind the battle line, Bowen had "to set on one knee and one foot, extending my gun as far to the front as I could reach." Still, the muzzle was next to the ears of those men in the front rank, and they did not appreciate it. "Each time I fired they looked back and told me I would shoot them, swearing about it, I told them they need not fear. Really think there was little danger as I was as cool as I ever was in my life."

When members of Davis's brigade made it to the shelter of the Bryan barn, Bowen noticed that one of them was annoying the Federals by firing around the corner. Perhaps it was a member of William Peel's group from the 11th Mississippi. The Rebel pointed his musket directly at Bowen at one point, but the file closer had just fired his own weapon.

Bowen asked one of his lieutenants to help him, and the Rebel was shot in the forehead, saving Bowen's life.[22]

The 111th New York probably opened fire at the same time as the 12th New Jersey and the 1st Delaware, and when they started, the New Yorkers poured it in as heavily as any other regiment. They held the part of the line that was most heavily pressed along Hays's front, for many observers noted that quite a few Rebels made it to the shelter of the Bryan barn. The structure itself offered some slight protection for anyone advancing directly toward it. Thus Hays and two of his staff members placed themselves at the barn to oversee its defense. Likewise there was a slight crowding of the Union soldiers from left to right as they sensed the Rebel pressure on the barn. Several members of the 111th New York "could not be restrained" and broke ranks to run to the north side of the barn and fire down Bryan Lane, where they had a clear shot past the structure all the way down to Emmitsburg Road.[23]

There was no regimental advance by the Rebels beyond the road; only clumps of individuals came forward to test the Union position. Many Rebels stayed near the road and returned the fire while others tentatively made their way forward, often firing as they advanced. The result was that a considerable volume of bullets reached Hays's infantrymen, and men dropped from the ranks. The color-bearer of the 1st Delaware fell, and the flag dropped to the ground. Lt. John L. Brady picked it up and gave it to Sgt. Thomas Seymour and told him to kneel so he could be better protected and keep the flag waving. Brady turned his attention to another part of the line, and two minutes later noticed that Seymour also had fallen. Brady took the flag and kept it for the duration of the attack. The 111th New York also lost four color-bearers to the deadly musketry Pettigrew's men managed to return to their tormentors.[24]

Charles W. Belknap was worried that his regiment, the 125th New York, might "give way" under the twin pressures of the Rebel advance and their return fire, for he had noticed "the uneasiness of some of the men." But then someone started to cheer, and "the spirit was soon spread along the line and cheer on cheer rent the air and we all fought with increased vigor."[25]

Several officers fell during this phase of the assault. Col. Eliakim Sherrill was shot in the abdomen while riding his white horse behind the 111th New York on his way to see to the right wing of his brigade at the Bryan barn. Two or three men of the 39th New York saw what happened and left the ranks to help him off the field, thus having a good excuse to

Col. Eliakim Sherrill, whose brigade held the far right of the Union position under attack. He was killed at the height of the assault. (Massachusetts Commandery, Military Order of the Loyal Legion and the U.S. Army Military History Institute, USAMHI)

get out of harm's way. Sherrill had little opportunity to redeem the disgrace of his hasty arrest by Hancock on the evening of July 2, cut down as he was at the height of the attack. He was taken to the Eleventh Corps hospital, where he died the next day.[26]

Col. Clinton D. MacDougall also was hit about the same time, shot in the left forearm with a bullet that broke the bone. He was near the center of his regiment, the 111th New York, about 100 feet to the left of the Bryan barn when it happened. MacDougall had been wounded earlier in the war at Pensacola, Florida, when he was fired on accidentally by his own men while serving as a captain in the 75th New York. This second wound of the war was a legitimate battle injury. Bleeding badly, he asked Hays's staff officer David Shields if he thought he should go to the rear for treatment. Shields advised him to wait until the attack was repulsed, as the wound was not life threatening and he needed to command the brigade now that Sherrill was out of action. MacDougall stayed on the field for the duration of the assault.[27]

Hays's other brigade leader, Col. Thomas A. Smyth, also was injured. A

shell burst sprayed fragments into his face, lacerating his head and nose. The wounds were quite painful and produced a lot of bleeding; his face quickly swelled and was disfigured, but Smyth refused to leave the field. Hays saw him and ordered the stubborn Irishman to the rear, "telling him that any man who was bleeding as he was, was a fitter subject for the Hospital than for the field." Smyth made his way to the rear and was treated. When someone told him his profile was damaged by the wound, he stoutly replied that "he was perfectly willing to sacrifice his nose for the sake of his country." Lt. Col. Francis E. Pierce of the 108th New York took command of the brigade.[28]

Most of the artillery support provided Hays's infantrymen came from Woodruff's regular battery. It fired only a few rounds of long-range ammunition at the charging Reels early in the attack, then switched to canister. As the Confederates closed with and then crossed Emmitsburg Road, the canister charges came rapidly and cut great holes in the disintegrating formations. Tully McCrea, an officer in the battery, wrote that "everybody worked with a will and two rounds of canister per minute were delivered from each gun. The slaughter was fearful." McCrea thought Woodruff had an excellent position from which to do this: "Never was there such a splendid target for light artillery."[29]

Woodruff decided to advance one of his pieces and assigned Lt. John

Egan the task of dealing with it. He ordered three rounds of canister placed in the limber of his left piece and told Egan to take the gun forward beyond the stone fence so he could get the clearest shot at the Rebels; the limber would follow with the ammunition. Just after giving Egan his instructions, Woodruff was hit in the side and had to dismount. Egan placed him beside a tree, but Woodruff castigated the lieutenant for wasting valuable time; he sternly ordered him to take the gun forward and savage the enemy.

Egan rushed off and urged his drivers on. They jumped the stone fence, which had already been partly knocked down anyway, and positioned the gun to fire down Bryan Lane north of the barn, far enough forward to get a clear shot to the south and southwest as well. Fortunately Lt. Emerson Bicknell's twenty-man contingent of the 1st Massachusetts Sharpshooters saw what was happening. Bicknell already had his men placed in Bryan Lane about thirty yards from Emmitsburg Road and quickly refused his left wing to clear a field of fire for the gun. Egan had little to fire at, for by this time the men of Pettigrew's division had reached their high tide and were receding. Woodruff did not survive his injury. Shot in the intestines, he suffered immensely and died at 4:00 P.M. on July 4. His body was buried under a tree that had a large mark on it made by a Rebel solid shot during the bombardment. Tully McCrea took over command of the battery.[30]

Everything was happening very quickly at this stage of the attack. The wounding of Sherrill, MacDougall, Smyth, and Woodruff, and the turning of the tide in the Confederate attack, all took place within minutes. Stretching throughout the course of these events was one of the most famous episodes of the charge, the flanking of the Confederate left and the pouring of yet another stream of musketry into the battered Rebels. This flanking maneuver was performed mostly by the 8th Ohio, but elements of several other regiments participated in it as well. It played a large role in stopping Pettigrew's charge and turning back his men.

Exactly when the forward momentum of the Rebels ended is difficult to assess. Union observers offered several views on this point. Lt. Charles E. Troutman of the 12th New Jersey believed the momentum of Pettigrew's command was broken "about five yards on our side of the Emmitsburg road," although fragments of the Rebel line made it to within twenty feet of the Union position. In fact, some Rebels were close enough to be pelted by rocks pried from the stone fence by members of the 12th New Jersey. These were men "who either had no time to reload their pieces or were out of ammunition." They also came close enough so that some Yankees could actually hear the Rebel officers encouraging their men to "close up, guide center, give way to the right or left." Yet the farther they went, the worse their situation. "They had got themselves as it were, into a box canon," accurately remarked John M. Dunn of the 1st Delaware.[31]

The 8th Ohio had already stopped Brockenbrough's brigade a few minutes earlier and now took up the challenge of helping to stop the rest of Pettigrew's division. The regiment returned to its former position in the ditch along the west side of Emmitsburg Road after repulsing Brockenbrough. When he saw Davis's brigade advancing to the left, Col. Franklin Sawyer gave the order for his regiment to move out and wheel left. Orders were shouted and the cry "Come on, boys!" rang along the line. Everyone jumped out of the ditch and clambered over the embankment. Some sixty yards to the south was a board fence that ran west from Emmitsburg Road, with a surging mass of Mississippi and North Carolina Rebels on the other side, heading for Cemetery Ridge. While wheeling toward this fence, T. S. Potter of the 8th Ohio could see the fearful effect of shell bursts on the Rebels. They were already "getting badly demoralized," he thought. "I saw shells burst among them and men were thrown twenty feet into the air by the explosion."[32]

The fence was ideally positioned to allow Sawyer's men to fire into Davis's flank. It started at the north end of a gate that was just south of the cut that had been the position of the 8th Ohio since the evening before. There was some confusion and irregularities in the formation of the regiment as it made its rush toward the fence, but that did not hamper the Ohio fire. They opened up a raging musketry at close range. Sawyer later remembered that "our blood was up, and the men loaded and fired and yelled and howled at the passing column." Some of them lay prone to fire, and others kneeled while still others stood and rested their muskets on the fence. They fired nearly all the rounds left in the cartridge boxes "into this moving almost solid mass."[33]

Sawyer's men opened fire just as Davis's command reached Emmitsburg Road, a few minutes before Hays's battle line opened fire. They did a great deal to slow the forward momentum of the Mississippi and North Carolina brigade. Then when the rest of Hays's division began firing, Sawyer noted the effect was even more immediate and devastating. "The distinct, graceful lines of the rebels underwent an instantaneous transformation. They were at once enveloped in a dense cloud of smoke and dust." The 8th Ohioans could no longer see details, "for the mass appeared more like a cloud of moving smoke and dust than a column of troops." They had to fire blindly into this indistinct vision, but at such close range it probably did not diminish the effectiveness of the fire. The Ohio regiment received little return fire, for Davis's men soon broke and fled, but a few scattered shots came from the west, from Brockenbrough's remaining troops in Long Lane. One such bullet mortally wounded Horace Judson's brother, who rested the barrel of his musket on Judson's shoulder to fire over the fence. The bullet penetrated his chest through his right shoulder.[34]

Sawyer's men were joined by several other units. Capt. Samuel Chapman Armstrong, who led about 100 skirmishers of the 125th New York, instinctively followed the 8th Ohio. Chapman had been greatly impressed by the sight of Pettigrew's division; it "was grand to see those masses coming up, and I trembled for our cause." He took seventy-five men who were in his reserve post along Emmitsburg Road (the other twenty-five were on the skirmish line) and moved south along the road in concert with Sawyer's command. They ran nearly 300 yards, picking up a few scattered soldiers from other commands, then took position west of the road. Chapman was to the left of the 8th Ohio along the fence; his men rested their gun barrels on the top rail and opened fire. He later described how his New Yorkers "gave them fits. Then it was grand." The Rebels "fell literally in heaps." Many of them dropped to the ground or in the roadbed for shelter.[35]

Armstrong had the support of parts of other units to his left. Capt. Morris Brown of Company A, 126th New York, led a detachment of skirmishers who assembled at the Bryan shack on Emmitsburg Road. He accompanied Armstrong to the fence and later captured a Rebel flag that had the inscription "Harper's Ferry" on it, signifying it had been part of Stonewall Jackson's force that had captured Sherrill's brigade the previous September. Lt. John I. Brinkerhoff commanded a small detachment of skirmishers from the 111th New York that also was assembled at the Bryan shack. Brinkerhoff went along with Brown and Armstrong and added the fire of his men to the flanking maneuver.[36]

The whole force consisted of about 260 men. The 8th Ohio was the largest part of this, with about 160 men. It extended well into the field west of Emmitsburg Road and did the most damage to the Rebels. The combined strength of Armstrong, Brown, and Brinkerhoff amounted to about 100 men, and they extended the line across the road. In a postwar letter Armstrong made a cryptic remark about "considerable shirking" among the Federals, but most of the skirmishers and Ohioans stood behind the fence and did their duty. They "closed in upon that ill fated left flank at close range," Armstrong wrote, "and helped to cut it to pieces. I could not but admire the pluck of the enemy."[37]

The 260 or so Federals on the Rebel left flank were aided by still more contingents. From the top of Cemetery Ridge the entire 126th New York added its weight to the flanking maneuver. Hays, who had hovered around the Bryan barn during most of the attack, saw an opportunity to support Sawyer's and Armstrong's efforts. He ordered the 126th, his rightmost regiment, to swing forward and wheel to Bryan Lane. Here it could fire obliquely into the mass of Confederates who were stalled in Emmitsburg Road and at all of the scattered clusters of Rebels between the road and the stone fence. Lt. Emerson Bicknell noticed this maneuver and repositioned his twenty Massachusetts sharpshooters to align with the New York right along the lane.[38]

This nearly completed a thin line of flankers from the top of Cemetery Ridge to a point west of Emmitsburg Road, although there was no connection between Bicknell's little command and the concentration of Armstrong, Brown, and Brinkerhoff at the road. Bicknell and the 126th New York amounted to roughly 320 men, making a grand total of about 580 participants in the flanking maneuver that did so much to stop and repel Pettigrew. The 8th Ohio took its flanking position just as the Rebels reached Emmitsburg Road; the 126th New York and Bicknell's men took their position several minutes later, probably after the high tide had been reached.[39]

Unknown to these 580 men who were flanking the Confederate left, a similar but much larger flanking force was doing the same to the Confederate right. These two efforts helped tremendously to weaken both Pettigrew's and Pickett's advances, but they probably did not play a decisive role in stopping the Rebels. The flanking force was just another in a long list of obstacles Pettigrew could not overcome. Other than Hays's order to the 126th New York, all units involved in this flanking maneuver went into it on the initiative of regimental and company commanders. They followed the lead of Franklin Sawyer and acted in remarkably smooth concert with him, even though none of this was planned or arranged beforehand. It was an impressive display of quick thinking and effective action.

PICKETT'S DIVISION

While Pettigrew's men struggled to make any progress east of Emmitsburg Road, Pickett's brigade commanders were launching his division
like a juggernaut across the pike and on to the stone fence. With fresher
troops, a full complement of regimental and company officers, and a
great deal of unbroken momentum, the Virginians were able to bring
many more men closer to the Union position than Pettigrew could. They
would not be so readily repulsed.

As Pickett's men closed on the road, orders went out to conduct a
sharp left oblique. It is unclear who issued these orders. The maneuver
was done quickly and in concert, so perhaps Pickett himself sent the word
down. It had become obvious by this stage of the advance that merely
dressing to the left, no matter how vigorously it was done by the rank and
file, would not be enough to bring the division in touch with Pettigrew's
right before the Union line was reached. More drastic action had to be
taken. This oblique maneuver, which involved a change of direction of
about forty-five degrees, further exposed Kemper's right flank to the rain
of artillery fire from Rittenhouse and McGilvery, causing even more damage to the brigade. It also offered the men of Garnett's command a better
opportunity to view the field of Pettigrew's advance. Henry T. Owen of
the 18th Virginia therefore was able to see large numbers of troops —
Brockenbrough's and Davis's men — retreating from that part of the
field.[40]

It was a difficult maneuver under fire, and William W. Bentley of the
24th Virginia of Kemper's brigade noted afterward that only "three or
four company officers & a few men" of his regiment failed to stand up to
the increasingly heavy artillery fire. Bentley never explained what he
meant by that, but apparently there was a little wavering in the ranks
under the combined pressures of intricate maneuver and enemy fire.[41]

The maneuver was made more difficult by the lay of the land. Kemper's men would have the most trouble making the oblique, for they
would be closer to the Federals than any other part of the division; they
also had the longest distance to travel, exposing their right flank not just
to the Union guns but even to the fire of Stannard's Vermont brigade in
its forward position. All three brigades would have to negotiate the swales
around the Codori farm as well. As they approached the buildings that
were such a prominent landmark on the battlefield, they would reach the

first swale about 400 yards short of the barn. It drained from left to right, crossed Emmitsburg Road, and separated the approaching troops from the barn. The swale was about ten to twenty feet deep, so a man was mostly protected from the view of anyone at the stone fence while he was in it. The Rebels would have a good view of the angle, about 500 yards away, when they reached the other side of the first swale and passed the barn.

If Kemper had had the opportunity to pass the barn to the left, he could have aimed directly toward the copse of trees, but that was not possible. The positioning and alignment of the division forced Kemper to pass to the right of the barn, aiming well toward the south of the copse. After passing, he could veer more sharply to the left and head for the copse and the angle area, but that would expose his right flank to the dangerous fire of Stannard and other Federal troops on the line even more.

The second swale lay just on the other side of the barn. It was as deep as the first, with a gentle slope leading up to the Union position. This second swale formed a natural bowling alley for the projectiles fired by Rittenhouse and McGilvery; in a sense, the worst artillery fire to be endured would likely be the last for any Rebels who made it all to the way to the stone fence.[42]

As the Virginians could see the Union position more clearly than ever, a stronger sense of purpose came into view. Officers could visualize where they had to go and what they were to do with more clarity. Kemper decided to ride briefly from his command and consult with Armistead to the rear, so as to better coordinate their movements. He trotted his "handsome bay horse" toward Armistead's brigade, which was advancing as "compact and solid as a wedge." Kemper told Armistead, "General, I am going to storm those works, and I want you to support me." Kemper's comments could easily have seemed superfluous, but Armistead had no time to muse. He quickly said yes and then added proudly, gesturing toward his men, "Did you ever see a more perfect line than that on dress parade?" Kemper simply shouted, "I never did," and sped back to his own proud brigade. This little encounter, short as it was, forced Armistead to pause long enough so that he was now behind his brigade line. He ran to get back in front. According to many accounts, this was when Armistead placed his hat on the tip of his sword to better inspire the men. He waved it and shouted, "Forward, double quick!" The hat soon slipped all the way down to the hilt, but Armistead continued to wave it all the way to the stone fence.[43]

TO THE STONE FENCE

All of Kemper's men had to cross Emmitsburg Road and negotiate the obstacle of the Codori buildings before they could start their sharp left oblique. But the extreme right wing of Kemper's brigade had to negotiate a smaller set of buildings as well. The P. Rogers house and outbuildings were located on the west side of Emmitsburg Road about 600 yards south of Codori's. As the 11th Virginia neared this place, described by Capt. James R. Hutter as "a white weather-boarded house with a paling enclosing a small yard," he was told by the regimental adjutant that Maj. Kirkwood Otey wanted Hutter to maneuver the right wing around it. Hutter thought the whole regiment should go to the right, as the house and yard were too big to allow him to order just one company out of line to maneuver around it. He had to split his wing, ordering one company to the left, behind the left wing, and another company to the right, behind the right wing, a more complicated maneuver.

Soon after he passed the Rogers house, Hutter was trying to re-form his wing when the adjutant brought word that Otey was wounded and Hutter was to take charge of the 11th. Hutter asked the adjutant to fetch Capt. Andrew J. Jones to take charge of the right wing, but Jones was wounded. Hutter next asked for Capt. David G. Houston, but Houston was already dead. He then asked for his brother, Capt. Andrew Houston, but he was reportedly killed as well. Hutter could find no one before the compelling need to move on forced him to give up and try to direct the complicated movements of the entire regiment himself.[44]

Once the Rogers house was out of the way, the Codori buildings were next. Kemper's entire brigade passed to the south of them, only about 400 yards from the Union position and much closer than that to the skirmishers deployed by the 16th Vermont. Not only did the blue-coated skirmishers fire on Kemper, but many units on the main Federal line did so at this point as well. At least the 14th and 13th Vermont and the men of Gates's demibrigade did so. The firing was picked up progressively by Second Corps units to their right as the Rebels continued their oblique marching. The extreme right of Garnett's brigade, the 8th Virginia, crossed the farmstead, the right wing passing south of the Codori house while the left wing passed north of it. This regiment contained the four Berkeley brothers, all of whom served as officers. Lt. Col. Norbonne Berkeley was with the left wing but glanced to the right just in time to see Capt. William Berkeley hit by a shell fragment. Blood spurted "in a stream from his thigh, and he hobbled around the end of the house." Shortly after, Norbonne was hit by a bullet in the thigh. His adjutant recovered quickly enough from a shell burst to help him to the rear of the house and stop the bleeding, but Norbonne was surprised to find his brother had already made his way to the rear.[45]

Immediately after moving around the Codori buildings, Kemper started his sharp left oblique. This maneuver took his skirmishers by surprise. They continued to advance forward against the Vermont skirmishers, stepping over the swollen corpses of Union and Confederate dead of the previous day's fight. When Lt. John Thomas James of the 11th Virginia noted that Kemper's battle line was obliquing, he tried to move his skirmishers to the left to regain contact with it. But only a few skirmishers heard and followed him; the rest continued inching forward. By now the 14th Vermont had opened fire on Kemper at a range of about 300 yards, nearly the extreme range for the Vermonters' rifle muskets but still close enough to do significant damage. Kemper's complicated maneuver fascinated observant Union soldiers. David Shields of Hays's staff was able to see it from his position on the Union right, and it appeared to him as if Pickett's entire division was redirecting its line of advance to aim at Ziegler's Grove. This later gave rise to a widespread belief among Hays's officers that their position was the true target of the Confederate attack.[46]

While most of Kemper's skirmishers became, in a sense, attached to their rival skirmishers of the 16th Vermont and continued to move directly forward against them, Garnett's skirmishers remained firmly in touch with their parent units. As the brigade reached Emmitsburg Road, the skirmishers slowed to merge with the battle line. Even so, they took several casualties. Pvt. James W. Clay of the 18th Virginia had the index finger of his right hand nearly shot off by a bullet: "It hung from the stump. I tied it up and marched on, firing 20 or more rounds, pulling the trigger with my second finger." Armistead had no need to worry about skirmishers, for he never deployed any during the advance.[47]

Garnett hit Emmitsburg Road at an angle. The right wing had less difficulty than the left, for the fences around and just to the north of the Codori farm had already been torn down in the fighting of July 2. Some sections that were still standing, however, disrupted parts of his line, which "caused some confusion in getting over." Some of Garnett's men simply pushed down these remnants rather than trying to climb over them. The left wing was delayed a few moments longer by the more intact stretches of fencing on its front. As the Union skirmishers rushed back to their parent units, the way was cleared for more and more Federal regiments to open their musketry. In addition to the intensified artillery fire,

Emmitsburg Road, ca. 1876–77, taken by local photographer W. H. Tipton, showing the area traversed by Pickett's division with the Codori farm in the distance (Adams County Historical Society, Gettysburg, Pa.)

Pickett's men had to face a growing volume of bullets. To William P. Jesse of the 28th Virginia, "it seemed as if we should all be killed." Yet Garnett's command steadily overcame these obstacles and endured the fire of artillery and infantry alike. At some point in this process it also closed with the right flank of Fry's brigade, finally making connection with Pettigrew's division.[48]

Most of Armistead's men found the fences to be a major impediment — "very great obstacles" in the words of Maj. John C. Timberlake of the 53rd Virginia. Another member of Timberlake's regiment, Lt. James Irving Sale, got his head stuck between two rails as he tried to crawl through a fence. The sound of bullets slamming into the rails intensified his anxiety, and Sale was convinced he would die in this embarrassing position. But then he managed to pry himself loose and jumped the fence instead of trying to bore through it. Other men, such as Lt. John H. Lewis of the 9th Virginia, dismissed the fences, recalling that their troops easily climbed over them and re-formed.[49]

Armistead received a lot of fire as he crossed the road, for by this time many Union regiments had opened up on the approaching mass of Rebels. Lt. Col. Rawley W. Martin of the 53rd Virginia wrote that "large numbers were shot down on account of the crowding at the openings where the fences had been thrown down, and on account of the halt in order to climb the fences." One such gap was only twenty yards wide. Right after a part of the 53rd Virginia passed through it and re-formed its line, a shell exploded in the ranks and killed many men. A short time later a solid shot raked the line of Company H of the same regiment and killed twelve men, cutting one of them literally in two.[50]

About this time it became evident to many of Pickett's men that the Federals were up to something on their right flank. Sgt. Francis W. Dalton of the 18th Virginia caught Henry T. Owen's attention and asked, "What troops are those on our right, are they our men or yankees?" Owen looked hard for a while and privately concluded they were Federals. He told Dalton, "March straight ahead and say nothing," but Owen could not hide the truth from himself.

> There off on our right was the grandest sight I have ever seen — A body of yankees 800 or 1000 yards away coming at a double quick "right shoulder shift" Uniforms looking black in the distance muskets glittering in the sunlight and battle flags fluttering in the breeze created by their quickened motion. . . . Their line was perpendicular to our own and they were hastening to strike us before we reached the stone wall. I saw it was to be a race and as Genl Garnett came along saying several times "faster, faster men" I put my men to the double quick and each line was ordered on quick time.

Owen was uniquely aware of this threat to the flank, for he rightly concluded that "not one soldier in a hundred would see this flanking party while advancing upon an enemy in full view in their front."[51]

This mass of Federals was indeed trying to flank the advancing division. It was most of Stannard's Vermont brigade maneuvering to fire into Kemper's right. But Garnett and Owen were absolutely right to keep their focus on the front, for there was little they could do about it. As the division was now moving, Garnett's brigade was the point of a wedge and therefore was the guiding light of the division. Kemper's brigade was "behind and to the right," as Maj. Charles S. Peyton was to put it later, and Armistead was to the rear. Kemper was, in fact, overlapping Garnett's right with his left at this point, due to the sharp left oblique. Either Garnett or the brigade staff thought it would be a good idea to have Kemper "incline to the right" to eliminate this overlapping and to begin confronting Stannard's men. A staff member rode to Kemper's command but could not find the general. He told Capt. William T. Fry of Kemper's staff about the plan; Fry tried to redirect the line but found it difficult because of "the eagerness of the men in pressing forward."[52]

At this point the sharp left oblique began to end, starting with the extreme right wing of Kemper's brigade, and the division began to redirect its line of advance toward the east, directly toward the stone fence. Fry and Col. William R. Terry of the 24th Virginia managed to get most of the 24th and the 11th Virginia, Kemper's two rightmost regiments, to turn and prepare to deal with Stannard. These men eventually wound up facing almost due south while the mass of Pickett's division headed east. The 1st Virginia, next in line to the left of the 11th, failed to refuse its line and face south as the other two regiments had done. Kemper, who was now aware of what was happening, personally ordered the 1st to "move by the right flank," but Lt. Edward P. Reeve, who led the regiment, found it impossible to execute the order. He later explained that "the few men left were shot down as fast as I placed them in position and turning to the adjutant, I told him it was too late and there was no 1st Regiment left to execute the movement." Just then a bullet slammed into Reeve's right arm, disabling him and relieving him of the responsibility.[53]

A fence that ran from near the Codori orchard on Emmitsburg Road eastward to the Union line now divided Kemper from Garnett. All of Kemper's brigade turned east and advanced toward the Federals south of the fence. The 8th Virginia, the rightmost regiment of Garnett's brigade, found that the same fence interfered with its line. By now Stannard's brigade had opened up a hot and close-range fire into Pickett's right. Owen believed that Stannard's men were only seventy yards south of this fence. "In a few minutes all was confusion," he later remembered. Parts of Companies A, B, C, and E, on the right wing of the 8th, were forced to refuse and face south because of the fence and the fire that was being poured in by the Vermonters. "I saw men turn deliberately and coolly commence upon this new enemy while others shot to the front. At one time I saw two men cross their muskets one fired to our right the other to our left." Owen managed to maintain control of only six men in his Company C and face them east toward the stone fence while the rest

TO THE STONE FENCE

225

faced south. He and the other company commanders on the left wing of the 8th Virginia had only about 150 men facing the stone fence, and they never got closer to it than thirty yards.[54]

Owen believed that at least "a few hundred men" turned south to meet Stannard's brigade head on, while Capt. Fry of Kemper's staff later told another staff officer that two dozen men of the 24th and 11th "held at bay and kept from flanking us a full brigade of the enemy." Of course Fry exaggerated on both counts; there obviously were more than twenty-four Rebels in the refused line. Moreover, Stannard never intended to envelope Pickett's line, only to position his Vermonters so they could fire into the flank. Yet the movement to refuse the line was big enough to draw the attention of Yankee observers. William Lochren of the 1st Minnesota estimated that a quarter of Pickett's men turned to face Stannard.[55]

Pickett also saw the Federal flanking maneuver and responded quickly to it. Stannard's move took the Confederates by surprise, probably because they did not know of the forward position of the Vermont brigade. This forward position was the main reason Stannard could so easily position troops to fire into the advancing Confederates. It has also been suggested that Pickett and his brigade leaders assumed that Wilcox and Lang, their right flank supports, would cover their flank. But that was not to happen. Neither Wilcox or Lang had been warned to expect a left oblique by the Virginians. In fact no one in Pickett's division appears to have been warned of that eventuality either. As a result both Wilcox and Lang were just as surprised when Pickett turned left as Kemper's skirmishers had been. Although Pickett had sent messengers to Wilcox with pleas for help, the Alabaman could not start his advance quickly enough to keep Stannard occupied. In fact when Wilcox and Lang did attack, they went straight ahead, to the south of Stannard's position, not directly toward him. Kemper uncovered the front of Stannard's advanced position when he began his sharp left oblique.[56]

Capt. Robert A. Bright had been the third member of Pickett's staff to take the earlier message for help to Wilcox. He had observed the Alabama brigade earlier that day and had already come to the conclusion that it was too small, even with the Florida brigade acting in concert, to help Pickett very much. When Bright returned to Pickett, he saw Stannard's flanking movement and was so impressed by it that he estimated the number of Yankees at 7,000. The division leader sent Bright to Dearing with instructions to use whatever artillery power was left on the Vermonters. Bright could not find the major, so he gave the instructions to

Lt. William C. Marshall of Battery A, 38th Virginia Battalion, who told the staff officer that he had only three rounds of solid shot left. The caissons had been sent back more than a half-hour before in search of the reserve ammunition but had not yet returned, so Marshall fired off his three rounds. Bright believed he saw one of the balls hit the Federal formation, but it had no effect on the Yankees. He reported back to Pickett, who sat on his horse on Emmitsburg Road 200 yards behind his division, with a recommendation to "get the Division out, before the flanking Column shot us up."[57]

The Confederate artillery could not help, and Wilcox and Lang were too late, too small, and not aimed in the right direction to stop Stannard. Pickett's men were on their own as they turned east and crossed the last 200 yards of open ground to the stone fence. These were the most deadly yards of all. The Union artillery fire had been damaging on the other side of the valley, but now the Rebels had to contend with the infantry at close range. They were still more or less in company and regimental formations, but that would soon give way to confusion and admixture of units as each brigade ended the left oblique and redirected its advance. Nearly the whole of Gibbon's division line and the two concentrations of troops from the First Corps were firing at them by now. The devastating artillery rounds from Rittenhouse and McGilvery continued to sail gracefully into the trough created by the swale nearest the angle and tear the Virginians apart.

The men of Garnett's brigade turned east and crowded together as they advanced. They did not yell; the fatigue of the march thus far and the awesome danger they were thrusting themselves into took their voices away. It was a grim spectacle made worse by another shell from the right that took out ten men. This artillery fire and the thickening volume of bullets from the Union infantrymen directly in their front filled the air as if it were a "sleet storm, and made one gasp for breath," recalled Randolph Abbott Shotwell. "I noticed that many of the men bent in a half stoop as they marched up the slope, as if to protect their faces, and dodge the balls."[58]

Many of them were killed and wounded as the pace of the fighting quickened. The 28th Virginia had already lost several color-bearers, and now its Col. Robert C. Allen took the flag. He was killed with the staff in his hands. About this time Eppa Hunton saw Capt. Michael P. Spessard of Company C, 28th Virginia, in a bitter moment. Spessard's son had been hit, and the captain dropped from his duties to cradle his head in his lap.

"Look at my poor boy, Colonel," he cried to Hunton. Spessard could spare precious little time for this. He left a canteen, kissed his son, and went forward.[59]

Partway to the angle Garnett's men began to yell for permission to open fire. They had faithfully obeyed Pickett's order not to shoot during the advance, but now that they were closing with the enemy and receiving a vicious hail of lead, they wanted to protect themselves as much as possible. When they were about seventy-five yards from the stone fence, it became evident through the smoke that many Federals had retired from the angle. The 71st Pennsylvania had already evacuated its position there, and the Rebels in Garnett's left wing sensed an opening in which they could make a lodgement. The Confederates opened fire; no orders to do so came from on high, according to George W. Finley of the 56th Virginia on the far left, only from company commanders. They fired one or two rounds as they closed on the fence. The men appear to have performed well at this stage of the attack. Lt. William N. Wood of the 19th Virginia recalled that with only "one single exception I witnessed no cowardice," but he declined to explain what that exception had been.[60]

Henry T. Owen estimated that Garnett's brigade had piled up on itself, because of the complex maneuvering of the last few minutes, so that it was the equivalent of fifteen to thirty ranks deep as it approached the angle. The men received the worst fire only twenty yards from the fence. The two remaining guns of Cushing's battery fired their last charges of canister directly into the face of the Rebels: "A blaze fifty feet long went through the charging, surging host with a gaping rent to the rear," as Owen eloquently described it. The 69th Pennsylvania now stood up and opened a deadlier musketry fire at short range. Garnett's command "recoiled under the terrific fire that poured into our ranks," reported Maj. Charles S. Peyton of the 19th Virginia. Many men went down in the face of this "tremendous volley"; nearly every member of the brigade who was mounted had his horse shot from under him as well. Only Garnett and Pvt. Robert H. Irvine, Garnett's courier, remained on horse after this hot blast. The brigade hesitated only a moment, and then it resumed its forward momentum and crossed the last few yards.[61]

Several Federals appeared and offered themselves as prisoners. They were either skirmishers who had not yet been able to cross the fence or stragglers from the 71st Pennsylvania who had remained in the angle. They now found themselves caught between two fires and decided to give themselves up rather than risk death from two directions at the same time. The Yankees ran into the advancing ranks of Garnett's brigade yelling, "Don't shoot! We surrender! Where shall we go?" Several Rebels shouted to tell them to head for the rear, but no guards could be spared for them. They were on their own and glad to get away from the fighting.[62]

Kemper's brigade approached the Union position less well organized because of the need to divert significant numbers of men to meet Stannard's brigade. The fence running from the Codori orchard to the stone fence also disrupted its connection with Garnett's command. Kemper received stiff musketry fire even before Garnett, not only from Stannard's waiting Vermonters but from the main Union line as well, for the right wing of Pickett's division came within easy musket range of the Federals before the left wing. A wide range of Yankee units, from the Vermont brigade to the 80th New York and 151st Pennsylvania of Gates's command to Harrow's and at least a part of Hall's brigades, fired at Kemper. The artillery continued to play on him as he closed in on the fence as well. As with Garnett, Kemper's neat battle lines began to merge into a mass of men as regimental and company organization was reduced with each step taken toward the deadly fence.[63]

Yet the men continued to surge forward. Kemper gave them a magnificent example. Still mounted, he rose in his stirrups, pointed with his sword, and shouted, "There are the guns, boys, go for them!" The men opened fire about 100 yards from the Union position, cheered, and quickened their pace. They paid dearly for their bravery. The whole color guard of the 1st Virginia was shot down before the brigade reached its high tide, and the flag was left on the ground unattended. James R. Hutter was hit while leading the 11th Virginia forward. He did not believe his injury was serious until his adjutant put his finger in the exit wound in his back. Then Hutter "saw where it came out and said 'I am a dead man.'" A shell burst over their heads just then and knocked Hutter down, disorienting him. Capt. John C. Ward of Company E offered Hutter a drink of either whiskey or water from his "double barrell canteen." The lieutenant colonel chose water.[64]

Capt. John Holmes Smith of Company G, 11th Virginia, saw his Cpl. James R. Kent go sprawling forward as they neared the Union position. "How are you hurt, Kent?" he called out. Kent replied, "Shot through the leg!" In fact the leg was badly fractured and the injury immobilized him. Pvt. J. M. Williams of Smith's company called the captain's attention and showed him where a bullet had grazed his back and cut a groove as deep as the bullet in his flesh. Just then Smith also was hit in the left thigh. The bullet passed completely through; he did not fall but felt weak and about to faint. Then Smith steadied his nerves with the realization that no bone was broken, and he continued to lead his company forward.

A section of Kemper's brigade found a hole in the Union line. Smith discovered it in front of the 11th Virginia, which had by now become infused with members of the 24th and 3rd Virginia who had not joined their regimental comrades in the refused line facing Stannard. Less than 100 yards from the Federals, Smith could barely see "a good line of battle thick and substantial firing upon us" from right and left. But directly in front he "could see first a few and then more and more and more — and presently to my surprise and delight the whole line break away in flight." This was the 59th New York of Hall's brigade, many members of which retreated without orders. Kemper could not take advantage of this small hole as Garnett was soon to do with the hole left by the retreat of the 71st Pennsylvania, for the troops on either side of it remained in place, firing their weapons. Also, Kemper's brigade had lost a lot of cohesion and its momentum was fast disappearing. Smith noted that the 11th Virginia was "a mass, or ball, — all joined together — without Company organization."[65]

Kemper also had to deal with a small number of Federals who wanted to surrender. Skirmishers and perhaps stray members of the 59th New York who were caught between the lines now ran into the comparative safety of Kemper's formation. Some were shot by the Rebels before their desire to surrender was known. The rest ran to the rear and took cover in every little depression they could find in the valley.[66]

Kemper's command did not go as close to the Union position as Garnett's brigade, nor was it as well in hand when it reached high tide. Despite the withdrawal of many members of the 59th New York, the rest of the Union line held firm and fought hard. The undulations in the ground, and especially the two clumps of rocks and brush, offered some shelter that the advancing Rebels could not refuse. Many of Kemper's men took cover short of the Union position while others inched forward as far as their nerves would allow. The brigade did not close to the stone fence as a unit, although many clusters of men probably came very close to it.

Armistead's brigade was rapidly closing on both Garnett's brigade to its front and the stone fence. Protected from the hail of enemy fire by the wall of Garnett's men, the brigade nevertheless took a number of

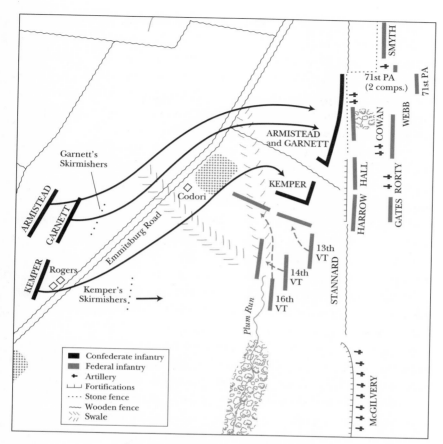

Map 6.2 Pickett Closes on the Stone Fence

casualties. Color Sgt. Leander C. Blackburn of the 53rd Virginia was hit and replaced by Pvt. James T. Carter. But another member of the color guard, Cpl. John B. Scott, wrenched the flag from Carter's hands. He moved about fifteen feet ahead of the regiment, waving the colors, until he fell. Then Pvt. Robert Tyler Jones took over. Armistead yelled to him, "Run ahead, Bob, and cheer them up!" Jones did just that, advancing and shaking the flag over his head.[67]

Armistead did his part to inspire the men as well. He remained about twenty paces in front of the brigade, "cheering all the time and calling his men to follow." Many observers believe that he placed his hat on the tip of his sword at this time, just before he led the men in a rush for the stone fence. When they were about 100 yards from the Union position, Armistead and Maj. John C. Timberlake of the 53rd Virginia went to the rear through the same file. Armistead then gave the order to fire, although what they hoped to hit with Garnett in their way is unclear. The Federal prisoners coming through Garnett's ranks to the rear also interfered with the brigade's fire, but the men sensed the possibility of success when it became apparent that the 71st Pennsylvania had evacuated the angle. "*They are ours! they are ours,*" yelled a member of the 57th Virginia just before he was hit.[68]

The neat alignment that Armistead so proudly pointed out to Kemper when the two had briefly talked a few minutes earlier was now beginning to unravel. As the brigade crowded closer toward the angle, the rightmost company of the 9th Virginia lapped behind the leftmost company of the 14th Virginia, cutting off Sgt. Drewry B. Easley, who was acting as a file closer, from his comrades of the 14th. He looked frantically along the surging brigade line, saw a gap to the left, and hurried through it to regain the front. Here he ran into a group of Yankee skirmishers trying to make their way to the rear. "I brought down my bayonet, but soon saw that every man had his arms above his head; so I crowded through them with no other idea than to locate my company."[69]

By the time Easley made his way through the brigade formation, Armistead had reached the crowd of Garnett's men at the stone fence. Most of Armistead's brigade came up to the rear of Garnett's; his left certainly extended as far as Garnett's, and his right probably went to the fence that stretched from the Codori orchard to the Union line. The extreme right flank of Armistead's command may have participated in confronting Stannard, although there is no clear evidence of this. All three brigades were now massed in an irregular formation, stronger on the left and more irregular on the right.[70]

It is difficult to gauge how many men Pickett managed to bring to the Union position. Estimates place the number relatively low. A modern historian has argued that more than a third of the division made it, which means that more than 1,400 Virginians were crowded before the Federals. Maj. Charles S. Peyton, who wrote the report for Garnett's brigade, believed that less than half the men in that unit reached high tide. Other survivors of the attack estimated the number to be from 1,000 to 1,500 men, while Capt. Robert W. Douthat of the 11th Virginia insisted that each regiment should be credited with "having sent *some men inside* the enemy's works," if for no other reason than to honor the bravery of everyone who tried to make it across the valley in one piece.[71]

There is an argument to be made for an estimate higher than 1,500.

Many of Pickett's men had been felled by the artillery fire west of the pike, but very few of them deliberately remained in the roadbed, in contrast to what was happening among Pettigrew's men. The roadbed offered less of a shelter here, and Pickett's brigades were handled better by their officers, who made sure unit cohesion was maintained longer than was the case on the Confederate left wing. Pickett started with about 5,830 men. If 350 had been lost in the bombardment and another 300 had been felled by the continued Union artillery fire from the start of the advance to Emmitsburg Road, if few men chose to stay in the roadbed, and if 600 might have been hit by artillery or shot by musketry after crossing the pike, then Pickett may have been able to bring about 4,530 men to this point, having suffered nearly 1,300 casualties. It is important to keep in mind that the 4,530 men, if the figure is accurate, were not equally close to the Union troops or equally well organized by this time or firing equally well at the enemy. The strongest and best-organized concentration was opposite the angle, while the strength of the formation steadily declined as one surveyed the division from left to right.

Added to the number of Pettigrew's men who made substantial progress west of Emmitsburg Road, the total now came to a maximum of 5,530 Rebels closing on the Union position. Trimble's two brigades would add to that total within a few minutes. The Federal troops defending the line amounted to about 5,750, minus some 350 who had fallen in the bombardment. It had taken a remarkably short time to bring the opposing sides together for their final confrontation. Just as Pickett's division crunched to a halt, Pvt. William G. Monte of Company G, 9th Virginia, pulled out his watch from a pocket and said, "We have been just nineteen minutes coming."[72]

· · · · · · ·

GIBBON'S DIVISION AND THE FIRST CORPS TROOPS

The first Federal response to Pickett's crossing of Emmitsburg Road was the retirement of the skirmish line. Silas Adams and four companies of the 19th Maine were stretched along the pike from the Codori buildings northward. They waited until the Rebels were very close before picking themselves up and moving back, having lain here since dawn. "I found I had no use of my legs," complained Adams, "having lain so long that they had become numb or paralyzed, but in a few moments they got into working order so I could trudge slowly to the rear." The skirmishers fired two rounds at the advancing mass of Southerners. Soon their own officers behind the stone fence and the earthwork called out to them to hurry so the battle line could open fire. The skirmishers then ran, their pace quickened when a few Yankees opened fire on them believing they were Confederate skirmishers. Most of Adams's comrades made it back to the 19th Maine, but a few got lost and went into the lines of Stannard's brigade or whichever other unit was handy.[73]

The Union line erupted in flame beginning on the left, where Stannard's men were closest to the enemy. Stannard ordered the skirmishers of the 16th Vermont back to their parent unit, reuniting the regiment once again at the reserve skirmish post. Just before this the 14th Vermont had moved forward in anticipation of meeting the Rebel advance. Col. William T. Nichols advanced his men on the ground, on their hands and knees, to the front and right of the 16th Vermont's reserve position. This brought all three regiments out of direct contact with one another, for the 16th was now assembling to the left rear of the 14th, and the 13th was still to the right rear of the 14th, with space between large enough to be filled by another regiment. The three Vermont units now formed an even more pronounced bulge extending toward the advancing Confederates. The progressive creeping forward that brought these units to this spot helped to alter the course of the assault, for it moved Stannard's men into a position from which they could easily deliver fire into Pickett's flank. When the 14th and 16th stood up in "close and steady" lines, they were clearly visible to Henry T. Owen and any other of Pickett's men who had the presence of mind to look in the right direction.[74]

It seemed to all the Vermonters as if Pickett's entire division was aiming directly for them. As Kemper's command advanced steadily toward the 14th, Stannard told Nichols to hold his fire until the Rebels were in short range and to be ready to use the bayonet. He meant to sell his command dearly and defend the forward position to the last man. But the left oblique began before Nichols judged the enemy were close enough to open fire. Some estimates place the Confederates anywhere from 220 to 330 yards away when Kemper sharply turned left. Nichols shouted the order to start firing; his regiment did so "by battalion, and continued it by file." Stannard was convinced the Rebels conducted their left oblique in response to the presence of his brigade, that they had intended to continue advancing straight until they noticed the solid obstruction posed by his doughty Vermonters.[75]

Col. Francis V. Randall's 13th Vermont also took up the fire as Kemper's left oblique brought the Confederates directly across his front. "The men had a short range and deadly aim," Albert Clarke remembered. The regiment had been cautioned beforehand to hold fire "until each one was sure of his man; to aim low and steady." But those instructions were given by officers who had never been under fire. When the order to open was given, this advice was ignored. The range was not as close as Clarke allowed; in fact 300 yards was unusually far compared with the distance in other battles of the Civil War. The 13th simply loaded and fired as fast as it could, unable to pick out individual targets and wisely forgetting the injunction to fire slowly. The men started to shoot while still lying prone on the ground behind their improvised breastwork, another sign of their inexperience. They quickly learned that it was nearly impossible to do much execution this way, and everyone rose up within two or three minutes, "without command and unmindful of danger." Colonel Randall overestimated the effect of his regiment's fire on Pickett's men. It "seemed to level their front rank and all mounted officers." Randall was convinced that his regiment staggered Kemper's brigade, forced it to halt briefly, and led the Confederates into starting their left oblique.[76]

John Newton, commander of the First Corps, readily supported his officers' contention that Stannard's fire forced the Rebels into moving to their left. He was further pleased that more First Corps troops, Gates's two regiments, contributed to this supposed effect. Of course Gates assumed the credit for forcing Kemper to the left as well. All of this was a natural but erroneous assumption on the part of these First Corps officers. Some of the more excitable men of Gates's demibrigade opened fire just before the Rebels began their left oblique, and Gates had to tell them to wait. But when the enemy "suddenly and rapidly obliqued to the left," the order was shouted for everyone to open fire soon after Stannard's men opened. The 80th New York and 151st Pennsylvania stood up behind their breastwork and poured it in at a range of more than 300 yards.[77]

Harrow's brigade took up the fire as the Rebels continued their left oblique. One man in the 1st Minnesota shot his musket when the enemy were still well over 300 yards away, and Lt. Ball cautioned everyone to wait before wasting their ammunition. "They are not close enough," he warned them. But Pvt. Daniel Bond could not wait. "We can throw our balls through their ranks every shot from here," he remonstrated. Ball hesitated only a moment before yelling, "Fire away then," and the whole

line blazed. The effect of the fire at this long range was minimal. "I could see them fall and the ranks close right up as though nothing had happened," remarked Wilbur M. Clifford of the 19th Maine. The Rebels were "moving forward as steadily as before."[78]

While a few inexperienced or nervous men wanted to fire when the enemy was far away, most of the veterans in Harrow's and Hall's brigades (except Daniel Bond) preferred to wait until they were in close range. Hall grew impatient and ordered at least the 7th Michigan and 20th Massachusetts to open fire as the Rebels were conducting their left oblique. The range was a little more than 200 yards by his estimation. Members of the 20th Massachusetts also believed the Confederate oblique maneuver was a direct response to their fire, again mixing up cause and effect. The two regiments tended to fire to the right to keep pace with the advancing front, Garnett's brigade, of the Confederate formation.[79]

Events were moving very swiftly at this point. Even as the Rebels continued their left oblique, drawing the fire of successive Union brigades, they were beginning to slow their pace and redirect their line of advance toward the east again. This started, as we have seen, as soon as a few officers noticed the position of Stannard's Vermonters. It seems that, contrary to many Yankees' viewpoint, the Confederates paid no attention to Stannard when they began their left oblique. That maneuver was undertaken not in response to the roadblock presented to Kemper by the Vermonters but as a result of the overriding need to move the Virginia division to the left and connect with Pettigrew. But soon after the oblique movement started, many Virginians noticed the Vermonters and realized how advantageous their position could be. Thus began efforts to slow and redirect portions of Kemper's brigade to deal with this threat, and eventually the whole Virginia formation began to turn right and head straight for the stone fence.

As soon as he perceived that the Rebels were heading for the Union line somewhere to his right, Stannard got the idea that he could reposition his units and fire into their right flank. The plan was quickly formulated. The 14th Vermont would remain where it was, firing to its front. When Kemper's brigade cleared that front, the 14th could still keep its position and fire at the Confederate skirmishers who had continued to advance straight ahead instead of accompanying the brigade to the left. The flanking fire would have to be delivered by the other two regiments. Stannard ordered the 13th "to change front forward and form again on the flank," in other words to wheel to the right and face mostly north. The 16th would move as quickly as possible by the right flank behind the 14th and fill the space between that unit and the 13th, aligning itself with the latter regiment so it could add the weight of its fire to the flanking effort. Stannard wanted to reposition the 14th as well, but in addition to the Rebel skirmishers, he noticed Wilcox's and Lang's brigades across the valley and worried that they might attack. Nichols's regiment would have to, in effect, act as his reserve.[80]

At least this was Stannard's version of how the flanking movement originated. Norman Hall later recalled that he sent a staff member, Lt. William E. Barrow, to the left to find as many units as possible to throw on Pickett's flank. Hall authorized Barrow to use Meade's name if he met with resistance from unit commanders. Barrow was young and completely green. He later admitted that he did not fully understand what was wanted of these troops except that Hall needed help. He ran on foot to Stannard, who refused to help him and told the young man that he needed an order from First Corps commander Newton before he could do anything, so Barrow ran to find Newton. Fortunately he stumbled across an old school roommate who was serving on Newton's staff. Barrow quickly got verbal permission from the corps leader to use Stannard's regiments; but by then the flanking movement was well under way, and Barrow's hurried mission proved to be a waste of time.[81]

It is not surprising that Winfield Scott Hancock also claimed credit for the flanking maneuver that was to damage Pickett's division. Stannard vehemently denied this. In fact he later claimed that at least six officers of the Second Corps claimed credit for this maneuver. Stannard even related that Hancock had ridden to his position while the maneuver was taking place and asked for an explanation. When Stannard told him what he was doing, Hancock "remarked that I was gone to Hell. My answer was 'that to hell it was then,' as it was the only thing that could possibly save the day." Stannard met Hancock in the fall of 1863 and "dispersed all such ideas from his mind" as to who really initiated the movement. "In fact General," Stannard wrote to Doubleday, "I think he hardly knew what he said or did at that time, a usual occurrance for him in fights." Hancock, in a cooler moment, admitted that his recollection of the incident was confused and that the movement had already begun when he rode up to Stannard and asked him what was going on. Yet he continued to insist that he had the notion to use Stannard's men to fire into Pickett's flank and never publicly or officially withdrew his claim to initiating the maneuver. Stannard, the victim of intercorps rivalry, deserved better treatment.[82]

Hancock was not the only one who remembered the incident differently from Stannard. Col. Randall claimed to have begun maneuvering his 13th Vermont to fire into Pickett's flank even before he received any instructions from his brigade commander. Randall ordered the unit to "change front, forward on first company." Capt. John Lonergan's Company A, the rightmost in the regiment, began to swing around to face north, with each succeeding company to the left duplicating the movement. Randall even claimed, as did Stannard with Hancock, that when the brigade leader noticed what he was doing, he sent a staff officer to stop it, but Randall continued anyway.

Sgt. George H. Scott of Company G recalled the aide's order differently, claiming the staff officer was drunk and abusive: "He wanted to know of Randall what in Hell he was forming a new line for. Randall replied if he had any orders from Gen. Stannard he hoped he would give them to him as Colonel of the regiment, and not interfere with the command; but the line was soon and handsomely formed and advanced a few rods." The conflicting versions resulted from a misunderstanding of the aide's purpose. Stannard had observed Randall's movement and feared "that his order had been misunderstood," that Randall was moving Company A too far toward the Rebels. In effect Stannard worried that Randall was planning to attack Pickett's flank instead of merely firing into it. The aide expressed himself too vehemently without properly explaining his purpose. But whether the regimental commander or the brigade leader deserves credit for initiating the flanking maneuver is unclear. Randall insisted on more than one occasion that Abner Doubleday rode up at a critical point in the confrontation with the aide and supported Randall's actions, even offering to stop the fire of regiments to his right so he could wheel in perfect safety. But Doubleday pointedly denied ever doing it.[83]

Randall had to work hard to get the rest of the 13th into line. He could not make himself heard properly above the din, so he ran along the line, left to right, yelling, "By the right flank, follow me." The left wing had to scurry 200 yards to align itself with Lonergan's Company A, reloading their rifle muskets on the way. The green Vermonters found it difficult to execute this maneuver, given the extreme circumstances; they were literally thrusting themselves ever closer to the moving mass of Pickett's division as they went, exposing their left flank to scattered shots from Kemper's skirmishers. Some companies on the far left of the 13th began to falter as they advanced. The wavering could have spread down the line and endangered the entire regiment, but a staff officer managed to get the hesitating men back into line so they could complete the maneuver.[84]

Once in line, the 13th opened up a raging fire at close range. Most estimates place the opposing forces only eighty yards apart. A broadside of fire tore into Kemper's brigade, which was advancing eastward across the front of Randall's regiment and deploying a short refused line. The Vermonters deliberately fired about ten to fifteen rounds, inflicting fearful punishment, before the stubborn Virginians began to show signs of disorganization. In the meanwhile, Kemper's men returned the fire. Many of them took shelter behind the clump of rocks and brush near the second swale that lay between the Codori buildings and the stone fence. They hit many men in the 13th Vermont. Sgt. Maj. Smith ran up to Sgt. George H. Scott, "spatted his hands, and exclaimed, 'Scott, aren't we giving them Hell?'" Just then he fell dead. "Our men were dropping all along our lines," Scott admitted, but the regiment kept firing.[85]

Stannard relayed the command for the 16th Vermont to move after he ordered Randall's regiment to reposition itself. Thus Col. Wheelock G. Veazey's 16th had a lot of moving to do in a short time. The regiment had been massed several ranks deep to serve as a reserve for the skirmishers

Looking toward the angle from approximately the position of Stannard's brigade. Note the uneven lay of the land in front of and to the left of the copse of trees. (author's collection)

all day. After retrieving his skirmishers, Veazey quickly re-formed the regiment into a battle line of two ranks, and very soon after that he received Stannard's order to move "by flank to the right and forward towards the right and [to the] left of the 13th."

Veazey had to march his men nearly 300 yards, and they performed the maneuver without hesitation. It was easy enough to take the regiment by the right flank behind the 14th, sheltered by the heavy fire of that regiment delivered westward toward the skirmishers and northwestward toward the obliquing main body of Kemper's brigade. But when the right of the 16th neared the left of the 13th, which was just moving into position, Veazey had to wheel his regiment into alignment with Randall. This exposed his left flank to Rebel skirmish fire from the west. Veazey managed to clear the right flank of the 14th well enough, but Nichols's regiment had to cease firing to the northwest so as not to hit any of Veazey's men as they came into position. The 13th and 16th were facing more or less to the north, probably a bit toward the northwest at this point. Veazey believed the two regiments formed about a forty-five-degree angle with the position of the 14th Vermont. The 13th and 16th were in a shallow depression draining toward the swale. The extreme left wing of the 16th extended into the Codori orchard. The two regiments amounted to more

TO THE STONE FENCE

View toward Pickett's right flank from Stannard's flanking position, showing the excellent position the Vermonters had on Pickett's Virginians (author's collection)

than 900 men, twice the number of Federals who were flanking Petti-grew's left wing about the same time.[86]

Veazey found the Confederates to be "in great masses, without much order" when his regiment finished the difficult flanking maneuver. They were "rushing rapidly upon the lines to our right, and regardless of the exposure of their right flank." His own battle line extended far enough to face their rear, if not for the small refused line Kemper had managed to place there. Coming into position after the 13th, Veazey's men fired about half as many rounds as Randall's command before the Confederates began to show signs of confusion and a willingness to break.[87]

Unmindful of Stannard's Vermonters, most of Pickett's men turned eastward and began to close on the stone fence. Battery commander Andrew Cowan had a good view of them, for the artillery on Gibbon's front had not yet opened because of the absence of long-range ordnance. The Scotsman began firing canister when the enemy were about 200 yards distant, each round opening gaps in the mass that quickly closed again. The Rebels were on the run as they neared his position, but the brushy clumps directly in Cowan's front deflected many of them. These Confederates took shelter behind the rocks and opened fire on the Federals while their comrades continued to inch forward.[88]

Henry J. Hunt happened to be with Cowan's guns, and he became overly excited by the near approach of the enemy. Hunt yelled, "See 'em! See 'em!" as he emptied his pistol at the surging mass. "The display of Secesh Battle flags was splendid and *scary*," Hunt later wrote to his wife. Within the space of two minutes his horse was hit five times; the last bullet penetrated its skull and brought the animal to the ground. Hunt managed to escape injury, but he had no mount. Sgt. O. R. Van Etten of Cowan's battery loaned him a big bay as a replacement. Hunt then rode away, turning in the saddle to call out, "Look out or you will kill our men." Cowan was a bit miffed at this unnecessary advice, for he had no intention of firing canister at such a close range and endangering the Federals whose heads he was firing over. Hunt was delighted about his brush with the Rebels. "I have escaped as by a miracle, when it appeared as if there could be no escape," he happily informed his wife.[89]

At this pressing stage of the advance a good number of the 59th New York gave way. Exactly why it happened was never explained; indeed, no one in the regiment even admitted it ever happened. The regiment was placed directly in front of Cowan, who reported that it "turned and broke." There is some indication that those who retreated were in the right wing. This forced the 7th Michigan to slightly refuse its left flank. Members of the 59th put the best face possible on this incident. Capt. William McFadden, who wrote the official report for the regiment, made no mention of any problems. "The behavior of both men and officers during the [attack] was excellent, ably sustaining the past reputation of the Third Brigade." Lt. Henry N. Hamilton went so far as to make the entirely fictitious claim that the 82nd New York and 7th Michigan, to left and right of the 59th, gave way under the pressure, "leaving our regiment to contend with them alone."[90]

Cowan reloaded his five pieces, which were positioned just to the left of the copse, and waited for the advancing Rebels to close on the fence. The gap in the line that allowed him a field of fire now encouraged a number of Confederates who had been sheltering behind the clumps to come forward and try a lodgement. Cowan had double canister in his tubes, which were depressed as low as possible. He waited until several Rebels began to step over the stone fence. One Confederate officer waved his sword and yelled to his subordinates, "Take that gun," referring to Cowan's five pieces. Cowan gave the order to fire, and the close-range blast devastated the advancing enemy. This final round of fire caught the

Rebels at a range of less than twenty yards, and it occurred just as Garnett's brigade reached the stone fence at the angle.

Cowan did not wait to see the effect of this blast. He ordered his men to drag the guns by hand about fifty yards up the gentle slope of Cemetery Ridge to get them out of enemy reach. Here he paused a moment to survey the scene. The Rebel advance toward his front had been decisively stopped. Cowan noticed, however, that many men were running to the rear in Webb's brigade, either members of the 71st Pennsylvania or gunners of Cushing's battery. Some of them ran close enough to his own battery to receive the ire of more stalwart gunners. James Plunkett, a member of Stannard's brigade temporarily attached to Cowan's battery, smashed a coffee pot over the head of one fugitive in disgust. "The bottom burst in and I shall never forget seeing the fellow running away with the pot, down over his head and face." After laughing a bit at this ludicrous sight, Cowan realized his rightmost gun had not kept pace with the other five. Its corporal misunderstood orders and retired it from its position to the right of the copse all the way back to the caissons behind Newton's headquarters, rather than just fifty yards up the slope. Cowan also noted that he had several bullet holes through his clothes.[91]

To Cowan's left, Rorty's battery continued to fire at the oncoming Rebels. Two pieces were near the stone fence between the 19th Maine and the 15th Massachusetts; one was manned almost entirely by volunteers from the Massachusetts regiment. They loaded it improperly and caused the gun to flip off the carriage, crushing a man. Lt. Robert Rogers kept the other gun firing with double and triple loads of canister. Farther to Rogers's left, Capt. William Wheeler's 13th New York Battery came up from the reserve when the Rebels were still some 400 yards away. He fired at least two rounds of canister over the heads of the Union infantry to contribute to the punishment Pickett's men suffered as a necessary price for their advance.[92]

As the Rebels closed in on the Union position, members of the 1st Minnesota could see little more than the lower part of their legs. The cannon and musket smoke produced by the Federals, and by now the Rebels too, was beginning to obscure their view of the advance. Each of the Minnesotans "fired as rapidly as he could handle cartridges and adjust caps." When a mounted officer appeared in front of the 19th Maine, several Yankees yelled, "Shoot that man on a horse." It was soon done.[93]

While Norman Hall had ordered his 7th Michigan and 20th Massachusetts to open fire when the Confederates began their left oblique, the rest of his brigade waited until the enemy were much closer. "Steady men! Steady! Don't fire," shouted regimental and company officers. Edmund Rice, who stood on a rock to get a better view, could not see the Rebels for a moment when they were crossing the last swale. Then they rose "out of the earth and so near that the expression on their faces is distinctly seen." Hall's men opened fire and aimed low; the Confederates returned the fire and disappeared in a cloud of powder smoke.[94]

The 7th Michigan redoubled its efforts when the Rebels were thirty yards away. The men "burned it to them like the dickens," as Cyril H. Tyler expressed it, pouring in a "withering volley" in the words of another member of the regiment. Henry L. Abbott estimated his 20th Massachusetts redoubled its efforts when the enemy were only twenty yards away. The regiment fired two or three volleys at this close range. "We were feeling all the enthusiasm of victory, the men shouting out, 'Fredericksburg.'" They picked out the color-bearers and bowled over the rest "like nine pins," cheering wildly all the while. "I wish you could have been with us," Abbott wrote to fellow officer Oliver Wendell Holmes Jr., who was on sick leave. "By jove, it was worth all our defeats." Abbott noted that he felt "for almost the first time, real elation in battle; our blood tingled with excitement." One of his enlisted men named Daniel McAdams more prosaically wrote, "Well We Just chucked it into them."[95]

The men of Hall's and Harrow's brigades were under less intense pressure than their comrades in Webb's brigade were soon to experience, for the Rebels were not pushing close to the fence on their front. This would later allow both brigades to shift to the right and decisively help Webb hold the angle when Armistead caught up with Garnett and crossed the fence. For the moment Hall's and Harrow's men could fire steadily without worrying too much about an imminent Rebel breakthrough.

The press of Confederates against the angle, however, was greater than on any other part of the line. Here they "looked more than any thing else like an advance of an acre of men." Cushing worked the two guns that had been run down to the stone fence with a grim determination, fighting the painful injury to his groin. Anthony W. McDermott of the 69th Pennsylvania watched him at work. "He would shout back to his men to elevate or depress their pieces so many degrees, his last command, that we heard was, 'that's excellent, keep that range!'" McDermott could not agree with Cushing's opinion about the firing, for the guns were close enough to blow stones at the infantrymen with each blast. They also killed a couple of men in Company I on the far right of the 69th. Cushing's fire also drew more Confederate artillery rounds, which sailed in just before the Rebel infantrymen closed in on the fence.[96]

Soon after, some members of the regiment remarked, "That artillery officer has his legs knocked from under him." When Garnett's men were still about 100 yards away, Cushing was shot in the mouth. The bullet penetrated all the way to the base of his brain, killing him instantly. Sgt. Frederick Fuger, only four feet away, was able to catch Cushing in his arms. Lieutenant Milne, an infantry officer serving the battery as a volunteer, announced that he was in charge but was killed almost immediately. Fuger took over and prepared the two guns for a final blast at the rapidly approaching Rebels.[97]

The 71st Pennsylvania reacted to the Confederate approach by retreating from the angle. At first only one of the eight companies there broke and fled, but then Lieutenant Colonel Kochersperger ordered the remaining seven companies to retire. Colonel Penn Smith had given instructions to Kochersperger to retreat when the enemy came close, so no blame could be attached to the lieutenant colonel. The retirement was prompted by the advance of Pettigrew's men. It was abundantly clear to the Pennsylvanians that if Fry and Marshall continued to advance, they could easily outflank their position. Penn Smith exerted a lot of energy to explain, cover up, and excuse this retirement. He ignored it altogether in his official report, contended in a postwar letter that his regiment "was forced back," and argued in a newspaper interview that his men did not retreat until the Rebels were crossing the stone fence. His superior supported him. Webb praised Penn Smith for placing his men in the angle, ignored the retreat, and noted that he "showed true military intelligence on the field." Hancock echoed this line in his report, noting that most of the retreating regiment rallied and held near the crest of Cemetery Ridge.[98]

Only a few members of the 71st Pennsylvania remained at the stone fence, including Sgt. Maj. William S. Stockton and six of his men. Stockton later remarked of his comrades who retreated, "I must say that, at the time, I thought it was rather cowardly," but most of them re-formed near the other two companies at the northeast angle. Lt. Frank Haskell of Gibbon's staff later took credit for coercing the regiment into line as it retreated, drawing his sword while riding among them and even striking some of the more reluctant infantrymen with the flat of his blade. Webb helped to rally them, too, according to Haskell. "The men that had fallen back facing the enemy soon regained confidence in themselves, and became steady," Haskell wrote. The 72nd Pennsylvania would soon move up in front of Penn Smith's regiment, just to the left of the northeast angle, inadvertently masking it. Even though the 71st re-formed, it played no role from that point in repulsing Pickett's charge.[99]

Fuger and his subordinate Christopher Smith planned a gory reception for Garnett's men when they neared the stone fence. The two gunners loaded their pieces with a final round of canister and lay behind the fence, lanyards in hand. Smith watched the Rebels through a crevice. He noticed that they pulled down their caps over their eyes and bowed their heads "as if meeting a hail storm." He motioned to Fuger to fire, but the sergeant refused, telling Smith to wait a few moments. When the Confederates were about twenty yards away, Fuger yelled, "Let 'em have it!" The guns recoiled, and Smith could see what seemed to be two fifty-foot-wide swaths open in the mass of Rebels. They staggered but closed the gaps and inched forward. The four remaining gunners bolted for the rear; one of them, a man named Hurley, was instantly hit by musket fire. He yelled, "For God's sake don't leave me here," so the other three stopped briefly to take him away. Cushing's battery was finally out of action, its two serviceable guns within easy reach of the enemy.[100]

It was now up to the infantry, and the 69th Pennsylvania was the only regiment nearby to hold the angle. Capt. William Davis remembered that the Confederates were coming so steadily "it would seem as if no power could hold them in check." The regiment held its fire until the Rebels were twenty yards away, about the same time that Smith and Fuger let loose their final blast. The Pennsylvanians "fired with deliberation and simultaneously, and threw their front line into confusion, from which they quickly rallied and opened their fire upon us." The Federals were helped greatly by their own stockpile of weapons. Just as Hays's men had gathered abandoned guns and prepared them for rapid firing, so did these stalwarts of Gibbon's division. Each Pennsylvanian had six to eight guns by his side, according to some accounts, loaded and leaning against the fence for ready use. Some of the weapons were smoothbores with buck and ball ammunition, loaded so that they had up to a dozen pellets in them. With such an arsenal and at such close range, the effect was tremendous. In no other way could one regiment hope to hold off such a mass of the enemy in point-blank fire.[101]

Pickett's division came to a grinding halt at the stone fence, faced with a cascade of musketry along the line from the 69th Pennsylvania down to the flanking fire of Stannard's Vermont brigade. A small group of Confederates would soon make a brief lodgement inside the angle, crossing the stone fence to capture Cushing's two guns and win immortal fame, but most of the division had already reached its high tide. They would confront the Federals face-to-face along the fence and the earthwork that extended south of it. The mass of Confederates stopped where they did mostly because of the fierce fire being poured into their faces, but also because the low fence served as a natural line of demarcation between the two forces. Webb later told artillery officer Charles S. Wainwright that his brigade line seemed to "shake, and for a moment he thought they were gone," as the Rebels came up to his position. But then most of the enemy stopped at the fence. This steadied the Federals and gave them an opportunity to stand firm. "That halt at the wall was the ruin of the enemy," Webb told Wainwright, "as such halts almost always are; yet so natural is it for men to seek cover that it is almost impossible to get them to pass it under such circumstances." The long, steady momentum that Pickett's division had maintained all the way across the valley under the punishing artillery fire and through the storm of musketry had decisively broken.[102]

CHAPTER 7
HIGH TIDE

· · · · · · · · · · ·

While Pickett's division had a firm line—the stone fence and the earthwork—to crowd up to, Rebel forces on the left had only an indistinct demarcation for their high tide. The stone fence receded in their front, back to higher and even more dangerous ground than that which confronted Pickett. Pettigrew's and Trimble's men were less well organized and less numerous than Pickett's command by this stage of the attack. Their high tide therefore came in driblets, scattered all over the deadly ground that lay between Emmitsburg Road and the Union line. For many the high tide mark was the pike itself; for others it was marked only by the blood where wounded and killed had fallen. Every man with Pettigrew and Trimble had his personal high-water mark somewhere on this sunbaked ground.

· · · · · · ·

PETTIGREW'S AND TRIMBLE'S MEN

As Pettigrew's harried men struggled to find their way beyond Emmitsburg Road, Trimble's command came up to help. Louis G. Young had already asked Trimble to support the division by shoring up the left, where Davis's brigade had just broken and fled. Trimble shouted to Lane to move his Tar Heels to the left and forward. Lane gave the command, but Trimble suddenly ordered a bayonet charge before he could repeat it. The division leader was riding between the 7th and the 37th North Carolina, the two rightmost units of Lane's brigade. As a result all of the 7th and the right wing of the 37th listened to Trimble rather than to Lane. The brigade split, with the left wing of the 37th and all of the 18th, the 33rd, and the 28th sliding off to the left under Lane's command; the rest continued forward in connection with Lowrance's brigade.[1]

Lowrance and the regiment and a half from Lane's brigade bore down on Emmitsburg Road with single-minded determination. They had been punished by the enfilade fire from Cemetery Hill all the way across the valley, but that lessened as they approached the pike. Maj. J. McLeod Turner of the 7th North Carolina decided at the last minute to "rush against and push down" the first post-and-rail fence rather than take time to crawl over it. His men did the job with spirit; only by coordinating their effort could they have knocked this stout fence down. But they had no momentum to do the same to the second fence. They were winded by the exertion and, of course, could not pick up speed while crossing the road due to the many men from Pettigrew's division who littered the roadbed. Like their colleagues before them, the soldiers of Lowrance's brigade and Lane's contingent had to climb the second fence under a hail of gunfire. Lt. Thomas P. Molloy of the 7th North Carolina recalled that his regiment reached the pike "as an organized body," but only half of it managed to cross the road.[2]

The 38th North Carolina in Lowrance's brigade hit the first fence at a diagonal and crawled across it, which "deranged our line very much." The regiment managed to negotiate all the obstacles that cluttered the road—fences and reluctant comrades alike—and re-formed what one officer called "a tolerably good line as we had rearranged it the best we could." Then the Tar Heels slowly advanced, stepping over the thickly strewn bodies of Pettigrew's men. Quite a few members of that forward division decided to retreat from their own high tide and broke through the regiment's line, further slowing the advance.[3]

Lane successfully brought the remainder of his brigade to the left and replaced Davis's command. It was not easy to move his men laterally and forward into the teeth of the gunfire, then across the fence. Pvt. Wilbur F. Van Swaringen of the 28th North Carolina was hit by a bullet, "where the shoulder and neck unite," just as he was climbing the fence. He fell on the west side of it, and his rifle musket fell on the east side. Van Swaringen's story exemplified the difficulty Lane experienced while trying to take his command across the road. Regimental and company commanders managed to advance beyond it, but there were too many obstacles for an orderly continuation of the assault. In addition to the ever present fences, there were hundreds of uninjured, wounded, and dead men littering the roadbed. And Lane now had to contend with more than 500 Federals who had assumed their flanking positions to his left. The same hail of small arms fire that they delivered into Davis's brigade, causing it to break and retreat, now was directed on Lane's brigade. Unlike the Mississippians, the Tar Heels at least stood their ground and refused to run, even if most of them failed to continue advancing. But no one could count much on the extreme left wing of the Confederate force; it had gone about as far as it could go.[4]

Much the same was true of the rest of Pettigrew's and Trimble's commands. Fry's brigade was stopped at the rail fence that extended northward from the angle, while the 1st Tennessee crowded just outside the angle itself. The regiment was opposite the spot recently vacated by the 71st Pennsylvania, between the angle and the two abandoned cannon of Cushing's battery. Pvt. Wiley Woods looked to his right and saw Armistead cross the stone fence, followed by a number of his men, just on the other side of the two guns. Inspired by this movement, Capt. Jacob Turney also jumped across the fence and advanced a short distance into the angle, but apparently few if any of his 1st Tennesseeans followed him. Turney soon came back and told his men that as soon as Trimble's command came up in support, he wanted them to cross the fence and fire left oblique at Hays's division. This would help the rest of Fry's brigade to advance to the Union line. Turney watched fitfully as Lowrance's brigade stumbled across Emmitsburg Road, and at least parts of it scrambled forward. He then gave the word, and Woods carried the regimental colors across the fence. The Tennesseeans did not stay inside the angle very long. It soon became apparent that a rain of rifle fire was coming from Webb's brigade and relatively few reinforcements were coming forward. The momentum was gone, so Turney ordered Woods to recross the stone fence. Fry's brigade could not go any farther.[5]

Marshall's battered brigade, or rather parts of it, went farther than the Tennesseeans. Quite a few Tar Heels were shot down forty yards short of the stone fence, well in advance of the rail fence that extended northward from the angle. The regimental flag of the 26th North Carolina made it that far. About 150 members of the 11th North Carolina surged to within fifty yards of the Unionists before they stopped. Capt. Benjamin F. Little of the 52nd North Carolina was severely wounded within fifty yards of the fence. He was surrounded by the fallen bodies of many comrades. Little remained conscious, although later he lost an arm. In response to accusations that the Tar Heels retreated and failed to support Pickett, he wrote, the "only 'giving way' that I could see on the part of Pettigrew's Brigade was the 'giving way' by falling to the earth, killed or wounded."[6]

Their Unionist opponents were keenly aware of the high-water mark of Marshall's brigade. The bravest came within twelve to fifteen yards of the stone fence, according to Capt. Richard S. Thompson of the 12th New Jersey. Another officer of that regiment, Lt. William E. Potter, recalled that one young Rebel ran ahead of his comrades and fell twenty feet from the fence. Another Confederate came nearly as close. "These two men," Potter remarked, "like spray driven from a wave, marked the farthest limit of the enemy's advance in our front." David Shields remembered the lone Rebel who had run ahead of the rest and fallen only twenty feet from the Federals. Many Yankees examined his body after the attack. The Rebel lay flat on his back, his feet pointing toward the fence and his head pierced by a bullet. "He was unconscious but alive the next day, as could be seen from the blubbers on his lips," Shields remembered. Brigade leader Thomas Smyth was very impressed by the bravery this anonymous man displayed. He told a wounded Confederate officer that the Rebels "fought with a fiery determination that he had never seen equaled." This admiration was felt by many men in Hays's division. John M. Dunn of the 1st Delaware praised his opponents. "I never saw dead and wounded men lay so thick," he recalled after the war. "From a space about seventy-feet back to the opposite side of the pike you could walk over the dead bodies of men."[7]

The plight of those Rebels who ventured far into the open ground between the pike and the fence was poignant. The Federals had a clear view of them, except when powder smoke temporarily obscured the scene. Then the light wind coming from the south would clear the air around a particular group, and it could be seen slowly inching closer. "Officers became separated from their men," wrote the historian of Arnold's Rhode Island battery, "and, with uplifted swords, rushed madly up and down, calling to their men to follow. One after another they fell."[8]

Each officer commanding these small groups of men had to decide for himself whether going any farther was worth the cost. Maj. John T. Jones stopped a moment with one such group somewhere in no-man's-land. He saw the Yankees flanking the left of the division. "I asked myself what we should do. I had only about sixty men left in my regiment, and that small number diminishing every moment. The others had suffered as badly." Jones waited until most of the others were retreating before he ordered his pitiful handful of the 26th North Carolina to do the same.[9]

Another small group of about 150 men in Marshall's brigade was led by Lt. Col. John R. Graves of the 47th North Carolina. Graves coaxed them to a spot within forty yards of the stone fence, where they flopped to the ground. He refused to allow them to retreat under any circumstances and ordered them to wait for Trimble's men to come up. But help never arrived, and Graves's stubborn determination eventually caused them all to be taken prisoner. Another officer of the same regiment, Capt. Joseph J. Davis of Company G, led a group that failed to keep pace with Graves's contingent. Davis made it to within 100 yards of the Yankees before his men stumbled to a halt. Sgt. Jesse M. Gilliam of Company K pointed out the weakened left wing of the division and told Davis that all the officers of his company were down. He was left in charge but did not know what to do. Davis reminded him that Trimble was directly behind them. "Our supports are coming and we can whip them yet," he enthusiastically told the sergeant. But the situation soon changed. The supports did not come up in enough force to overcome the deadly hail of fire from the Yankees, so Davis ordered a retreat.[10]

One group of men in the 26th North Carolina had a dramatic high tide. They inched slowly to within about twenty yards of the stone fence before they were met by a cannon blast. One gun of Arnold's Rhode Island battery had been left at the northeast angle. It was double shotted with canister, and Pvt. William C. Barker held the lanyard, unaccountably waiting. Sgt. Amos M. C. Olney yelled, "Barker, why the d—l don't you fire that gun! pull! pull!" Barker jerked the lanyard and plowed open a gap in the Tar Heel group. Capt. Samuel P. Wagg of Company A was among those who fell, "shot through with grape."[11]

Even though most of Davis's brigade had already retreated, the few who had ventured beyond Emmitsburg Road remained. Virtually all of them were members of the 11th Mississippi. According to one historian, at least eight members of that regiment got close to the stone fence, not including the small group led by Lt. William Peel. Several survivors later claimed that members of the regiment actually jumped the stone fence and charged ahead to the crest of Cemetery Ridge, but there is no reason to believe these outlandish claims. The only members of Davis's brigade who crossed the fence did so as prisoners. In addition to the handful of soldiers from the 11th Mississippi, a small number of men from the 55th North Carolina made it to within a few yards of the fence. There is no indication that any members of the 2nd or 42nd Mississippi advanced beyond Emmitsburg Road.[12]

Trimble's two brigades essentially came up and reinforced Pettigrew's division but failed to give it added momentum to go farther. As a result their high tides simply conformed to the marks already established by their predecessor. This occurred through no fault of their own. The Tar Heels that Trimble commanded faced difficult obstacles. They had to worm their way through the remains of Pettigrew's division that barred their path and contend not only with the same deadly hail of rifle fire to the front but with the equally deadly flank fire from the left.

Lowrance's brigade went beyond Emmitsburg Road, but it is unclear how many members of it tagged along. Lowrance reported that his brigade line approached the Union position somewhat skewed, with the right wing about thirty to sixty yards forward of the left wing. This occurred because of the natural tendency of the men to crowd forward on the right, toward the projecting angle in the stone fence. Quite a few members of the 16th North Carolina made it up to the position of the 1st Tennessee just outside the angle, but none of them appear to have crossed the fence. Lowrance himself was wounded before he reached the angle.[13]

The 38th North Carolina, Lowrance's leftmost regiment, might have been a few yards behind the right wing, but it managed to reach the rail fence that extended northward from the angle. The fence forced the men to stop momentarily and "confused" them, throwing whatever cohesion they had managed to maintain into disarray. The Tar Heels fired back at the Yankees for a few minutes here, then, urged on by their officers, many of them crossed the fence and tried to continue. They made it only partway to the stone fence before giving up the effort.[14]

The men from Lane's brigade that had advanced forward with Lowrance gave a good account of themselves. Half of the 7th North Carolina remained at Emmitsburg Road, but the rest tried to move on. Capt. J. McLeod Turner led one group at least ten yards east of the pike before he was shot a glancing blow to his foot and fell. Realizing that only parts of each regiment were advancing beyond the road, Turner decided to order his men back to the pike. They readily obeyed and took shelter in the ditch and behind the fences. His instep was badly bruised, but Turner managed to crawl back to the road, where another bullet slammed into his waist, temporarily paralyzing his lower body. Several other members of the 7th North Carolina and the right wing of the 37th North Carolina ventured into the disputed ground beyond the rail fence. Lt. P. C. Carlton of the 7th got to within forty yards of the Union position before retiring, and Lt. Thomas L. Norwood made it to within twenty yards before he was shot.[15]

Survivors of Lowrance's brigade and the regiment and a half from Lane's brigade tended to overstate their accomplishments after the war. They issued claims that a "large portion" of the command reached the Union line and even held it for fifteen minutes. The only possible justification for such claims is that part of the 16th North Carolina took position with the 1st Tennessee outside the angle for approximately that length of time. Of course neither regiment "held" the angle, which had already been abandoned by the Federals before they got there. Several members of the 16th were so close to the enemy that they could not safely retreat when the tide turned, and they had to surrender. No one in Trimble's command made a lodgement in the line held by Hays's division. Members of Fry's and Marshall's brigades vehemently denied Trimble's troops any credit. They argued that no one in the supporting line advanced beyond Emmitsburg Road, a patently false accusation.[16]

The rest of Lane's brigade had its own difficulties and barely made a presence beyond Emmitsburg Road. The Union flanking force had been seen early by Longstreet, perched as he was on the fence dividing the northern and southern sectors of the Confederate attack. He had sent Maj. Osmun Latrobe of his staff with a message to Trimble and Pettigrew warning them of the danger. Longstreet soon after sent a second messenger to ensure the word got through. It was a wise decision, for Latrobe's horse was shot on the way. The second courier could not find either of the division commanders but delivered his message to Lane instead, just as his brigade was nearing the pike. Lane had already noticed that this flanking force was firing into his left wing as he came up to fill Davis's position.[17]

Just then a bullet felled Lane's horse. Capt. John H. Thorp of the 47th North Carolina, in Marshall's brigade, saw what happened. Lane was riding just behind his men "in the attitude of urging them forward with his hand; a moment later a large spurt of blood leaped from the horse as he rode up, and rider and horse went down in the smoke and uproar." Lane managed to leap from his "wounded and plunging horse" in time to avoid injury. Without hesitation he ordered Col. Clark M. Avery to move his 33rd North Carolina, on the far left of the brigade, to refuse the line and confront the flanking force. Avery shot back, "My God! General, do you intend rushing your men into such a place *unsupported, when the troops on the right are falling back*[?]" Lane looked to the south and saw that many members of Fry's and Marshall's brigades were making their way to the rear; most of the rest were still idle in the roadbed, and the rest were being mauled in their futile attempts to advance to the stone fence. He realized it was useless to confront the flanking force and ordered a retreat.[18]

Before the order was heard and obeyed, Maj. Joseph H. Saunders managed to take a part of the 33rd North Carolina at least a short distance beyond the road. He was trying to straighten the regimental line and maintain control over the men when he was hit by a bullet that penetrated his cheek and "passed out of the Back of his head." Saunders, unable to speak, was left on the field when the retreat commenced. He survived his wound and his imprisonment on Johnson's Island to go home at the end of the war.[19]

While at least 1,000 members of Pettigrew's division crossed Emmitsburg Road and made significant progress toward the Union line, probably at least half of Lowrance's brigade did likewise. They essentially merged their commands with Fry's and Marshall's, duplicating their performance on the field. Also, at least half of the 7th North Carolina and the right wing of the 37th North Carolina that accompanied Lowrance's brigade made it across the pike. It appears that very few of the rest of Lane's brigade did the same, despite Lane's contention that his command surged to within "a few yards of the stone wall." Lane went on to fantasize about his Tar Heels driving Woodruff's gunners from their battery and breaking the Union infantry line. But there is no supporting evidence for any of these far-fetched claims. Saunders took at least a small group a short distance beyond the road, but there is no reason to believe that any other men belonging to the 18th, 28th, 33rd, or the left wing of the 37th went into the no-man's-land that separated the road and the stone fence. Thus a total of at least 1,400 men in Pettigrew's and Trimble's commands ventured beyond the pike.[20]

The attack was essentially over on the Confederate left. Fry's men pulled back from the rail fence, leaving many of their regimental flags on the ground; even Fry himself was left behind severely wounded in the leg, and he fell into Federal hands. The Yankees continued to fire for "some minutes" after the Rebels began to recede. The powder smoke had accumulated to a frightful degree, and the slight breeze from the south could not always disperse it quickly. Many Federals did not even know their opponents were pulling away, so they kept firing. John Thomas Jones and his group of 26th North Carolinians also pulled back to

Emmitsburg Road, but John Graves and his 150 soldiers from the 47th North Carolina stayed where they were, only to be swallowed up by the Federals a few minutes later. The color-bearer of the 26th, Pvt. Daniel Thomas, was wounded but kept the flag flying. He found himself stranded at high tide, either unable to move back or unwilling to risk his life further by trying to escape. Sympathetic Yankees noticed his plight and called out to him, "Come over on this side of the Lord." Thomas trusted them, walked toward the fence, and was taken prisoner. Sgt. James M. Brooks of the 26th saw what was happening and accompanied Thomas to save himself. Another member of the 26th North Carolina, Thomas J. Cureton, retired to Emmitsburg Road with several other officers and tried to re-form the men. They worked only a few moments before noticing the flanking force to the left, which by now was advancing up the roadbed. "We called the men's attention to it and left in a hurry," Cureton wrote after the war. "Despite the warning, many remained and were captured."[21]

Isaac Trimble was badly wounded at this stage of the fight. He had kept close behind, even inside, his line throughout the attack, until he reached Emmitsburg Road. Then the general remained mounted just on the west side of the pike, watching the progress of his two brigades. Trimble estimated that fragments of Lowrance's brigade were at the angle and the rail fence about ten minutes, firing away, before they fell back to the road. Then a bullet penetrated his left leg and entered his horse. He was just then in front of the 1st Delaware. The injury later resulted in the amputation of his leg and the death of his horse, but at the time it was not so painful as to force Trimble to the rear. He stubbornly remained mounted and even conversed with his aide, Charles Grogan. "General the men are beginning to fall back," Grogan told him. "Shall I rally them[?]" Trimble surveyed the battlefield and replied, "No Charley the best these brave fellows can do, is to get out of this." General and aide slowly followed the retreating men back toward Seminary Ridge, where Trimble turned over the division command to Lane. Grogan rode over to Lane to give him the news, telling him, "General Trimble sends his compliments to General Lane, and wishes him to take charge of the division, as he has been wounded. He also directs me to say that if the troops he had the honor to command to-day for the first time, couldn't take that position, all hell can't take it."[22]

The men of Pettigrew's and Trimble's commands now became even more intermixed than before. Crowding in the roadbed of the pike, faced with an undiminished fire to the front and ever encroaching Federals on the left, they had to make a choice. To retreat would expose them to great danger of being hit; to stay would mean a trip to a Northern prison, but it might save their lives. Many of the men chose the latter alternative. Pvt. A. J. Dula of the 22nd North Carolina in Lowrance's brigade did not take part in the attack, having been wounded two days before, but he heard from survivors that a "great many" of his comrades "surrendered and did not try to return to the war again." Federal soldiers clearly saw this take place. "Hundreds of the charging line prostrated themselves on their back on the Emmettsburg road, and waved their hats and handkerchiefs in token of surrender." William Groves Morris managed to retain control of a small group of men from the 37th North Carolina and confronted the Federal flanking party that was advancing up the pike. But Morris had no hope of slowing, much less stopping, it. His men made a futile stand for a few moments and then fled for their lives. Many survivors of the attack later claimed they were outflanked on the right as well, although it is difficult to understand how this happened; no Federal troops swept down on Pettigrew or Trimble from that direction. The confusion that reigned along Emmitsburg Road was intense during the few minutes it took for the attackers to decide whether to flee or surrender.[23]

The time was somewhere between 2:30 and 2:45 P.M. The survivors of Fry's, Marshall's, Lowrance's, and Lane's brigades were either retreating or waiting to be taken by the enemy. Brockenbrough's two remaining regiments, the 47th and 55th Virginia, were still in Long Lane to the far left. They formed a thin line but felt relatively safe. A staff officer came from somewhere and begged them to remain where they were, even though it was obvious that a retreat had begun. "We stood there to be shot at," recalled Col. William S. Christian, "and that was about all that we did, and did not retire until after the retreat had become general." Christian then ordered his men "to scatter" and make their way back to Seminary Ridge. He walked slowly because of a severe wound suffered in the battle of Frayser's Farm during the Seven Days. The color-bearer of the 55th was hit by shell fragments, but he managed to carry the flag all the way back to the ridge. The 47th was less fortunate. Its color-bearer was killed, and the flag was abandoned on the field.[24]

· · · · · · ·

HAYS'S DIVISION

Through the smoke it became increasingly obvious that the attack had reached its crest and that the attackers were pulling back. Members of the 8th Ohio could not tell the dead Rebels from those who still lived, for the roadbed of the pike was layered with people. Only when the live ones waved coats, hats, or handkerchiefs in token of surrender could they locate the prisoners.[25]

All along the line of Hays's division the Federals felt an extra surge of adrenaline when it became obvious they had repulsed the attack. Hays had sent Capt. George A. Dewey to Meade for reinforcements as soon as the Rebels had started their advance. Now Dewey, his division provost marshal, appeared to tell him that help was on the way. Hays "pointed to the disordered masses of the column and said in his blunt way, 'Damn the reinforcements. Look there.' " The color-bearer of the 125th New York was overcome with excitement and raced all the way down to Emmitsburg Road waving his flag, even though the regiment remained in its place near the Bryan barn. Capt. Aaron P. Seeley, who now commanded the 111th New York, advanced some men across the fence to clear out a few Rebels who were sheltering behind the barn.[26]

Smyth's brigade went wild with jubilation when the Rebels turned and retreated. The 1st Delaware conducted an impromptu countercharge over the stone fence to claim no-man's-land, which was littered with bodies and abandoned flags. Color Sgt. John M. Dunn led this attack, which actually resulted in scattered hand-to-hand fighting with a few remaining and very stubborn Rebels. Lt. William Smith, commander of the regiment, was killed in this advance, and Lt. John T. Dent took charge of the 1st. The men were so excited they were described as "crazy," and Dent found it difficult to get them to stop firing "as long as the Rebels were in range."[27]

The 14th Connecticut also fired steadily at the retreating Rebels. Many Confederates simply dropped behind rocks and undulations in the ground, only to raise white cloth. Then the Connecticut men stopped firing and advanced, to be met with willing prisoners who rose from behind their meager shelter. While some Federals rounded up prisoners and looked for trophies left lying on the field, others were ordered by their officers to continue firing left oblique at the remaining men of Pickett's division who were still in range. The 14th Connecticut and 1st Delaware added their fire to the contest that was just ending near the angle.[28]

Hays received additional artillery support near the end of the attack, although he did not need it. Lt. Gulian V. Weir's Battery C, 5th U.S. Artillery, was dispatched by one of Hunt's staff officers to replace Arnold's Rhode Island battery at the northeast angle. Weir's unit had been severely handled by Lang's Florida brigade on July 2, but it raced across the crest of Cemetery Ridge toward its post, arriving just as the Rebel attack peaked and began to recede. Weir's horse was hit, and he fell to the ground just as the guns were deployed. Although groggy, the lieutenant retained command and directed his pieces to open immediately at what he later termed "a dense body of the enemy, (a great big black mass)."

His gunners loaded the tubes with double canister and began firing. "I never saw such a battlefield," wrote Lt. Homer Baldwin, one of Weir's officers, "every recoil of our guns would send them over the dead and wounded, and flashes of our pieces would scorch and set fire to the clothing of those that lay in front of us." This last-minute addition to Union firepower played no role in repelling the attack, which already had broken, and it probably did not kill or injure many Rebels. It did, however, kill one man and wound several others in the 14th Connecticut. The guns were deployed just to the rear of the regiment before it advanced

The angle in the stone fence from Smyth's position. Smyth's brigade could fire easily at Pickett's Virginians in and around the angle. The 69th Pennsylvania monument is in the angle, and the Codori farm is on the left. (author's collection)

on the countercharge into no-man's-land. These unfortunate victims of friendly fire could not get out of Weir's way fast enough to save themselves. Pvt. Henry Hasler of Company K was one of those who saw the battery deploy and was able to jump out of its line of fire. He yelled to inform Weir of what he was doing, and eventually the guns fell silent.[29]

Although a regular, Weir was no lover of battle. He recalled that several Rebel prisoners came into Union lines through his battery after the firing stopped. By then the Confederate artillery had opened up to cover the retreat, and the angle area was once again subjected to a deadly rain of missiles. "Where can I go to get out of this Hellish fire?" one Confederate prisoner asked Weir. The lieutenant pointed to the rear and thought, "I wish I could go with you."[30]

• • • • • • •

PICKETT'S DIVISION

While everyone among Pettigrew's and Trimble's commands argued that they broke and retreated when, or even before, Pickett retired, few survivors among the Virginians agreed with that claim. It is possible that the

Confederates on the right wing stayed longer at their high tide and began to retreat a few moments later than those on the left. Or it might be more accurate to say that the high tide and retreat of Pettigrew and Trimble was much more extended, that the men here left at many different points in time and that Pickett's soldiers retreated more in one group near the end of this extended period. The only thing certain is that neither wing ran out on the other or caused the failure of their comrades' attack.

There were anywhere from 1,000 to 4,300 Confederates pressing against the stone fence, depending on which estimate one chooses. The heaviest concentration was Garnett's and Armistead's massed brigades opposite the angle. They also were the closest to the fence, for most of Kemper's brigade and even the right wings of Garnett's and Armistead's were several yards from it. If any part of Pickett's division had a good chance to penetrate the Union position, it was this concentration at the angle. Not only did the left wing of Garnett and Armistead have strength; both brigade commanders were still alive and active. And the angle was weakened by the withdrawal of the 71st Pennsylvania and the abandonment of Cushing's two guns. There was a gap, in other words, between the right flank of the 69th Pennsylvania and the angle itself — a gap of about fifty yards into which the Rebels could push if they had the courage.

Armistead stepped forward to provide the inspiration for that courage. His men had meshed with Garnett's and then halted for several moments, unable to step through the crowd or to jump across the low fence. Armistead broke the pause by turning to Lt. Col. Rawley E. Martin of the 53rd Virginia and saying, "Colonel, we can't stay here." Martin took up the challenge and replied, "Then we'll go forward!" Turning to the men, Armistead yelled, "Come forward, Virginians! Come on, Boys, we must give them the cold steel; who will follow me?" The effect was electric, at least for a small group of men within hearing of Armistead. As the general stepped across the fence, Martin and about 100 men followed him. One of them carried the flag of the 53rd Virginia. As he crossed the fence, Armistead bumped the right elbow of Lt. Henry Clay Michie. This slightly deflected Armistead toward the right, and he aimed directly for the two abandoned guns left by Cushing's cannoneers.[31]

Maj. John C. Timberlake of the 53rd Virginia caught the enthusiasm. He also placed his hat on the tip of his sword and turned it so it would spin. Timberlake jumped onto the fence and shouted, "Look at your General! follow him!" He further yelled, "Come on my men come over the fence."[32]

The force that piled over the fence was small. Most sources agree that it was no more than 100 men, of whom at least 17 were recorded by name. But it was a determined group of men led by a fiery figure. The group mostly crossed the fence to Armistead's right, it seems, for the men composing the right wing of the 69th Pennsylvania, positioned to the left of Cushing's guns, suddenly saw a small and compact mass of veterans rise over the fence in their front. Armistead's group pushed forward with enough determination to cause the three right companies of the Pennsylvania unit to pull back and refuse the regimental line. Companies I, A, and F, from right to left, were given orders to redirect their front with the enemy literally only feet away, blazing away with their rifle muskets. The first two companies quickly refused their line, but Company F did not. Either the men did not hear the order quickly enough or they felt safer staying put; either way, a crack developed in the line of the 69th. Armistead's group quickly tried to exploit it, nearly engulfing Company F as it advanced and capturing most of the company and rushing the prisoners to the rear through the tightly packed mass of Rebels. Capt. George Thompson, commander of Company F, was killed on the spot.[33]

In what proved to be the turning point in repulsing Armistead's penetration of the angle, the 69th refused to give way any further. Companies I and A stood firm to the right of this crack in the line, and Company D stood firm to the left. This regiment put up a magnificent fight that saved the angle and killed any chance that Pickett's division might push the Federals off Cemetery Ridge. If Armistead's voice had carried farther to his right and inspired many more men to cross the fence at the same time as the 100 did, the Pennsylvania regiment probably would have been crushed, and at least the first line of Union defense would have been swept away.[34]

Armistead's penetration of the angle was short lived, despite its heroic energy. For a few moments there was a sense of supreme exaltation as the Rebels swarmed over the fence, forced back two Federal companies, and swallowed up a third. Armistead was the first to reach Cushing's two guns, placing a hand on one of them and yelling, "The day is ours men, come turn this artillery upon them." He instantly became the target of many Federal soldiers. The two companies of the 69th Pennsylvania that had refused the line undoubtedly loosed a few rounds at him, but the heaviest volume of fire came from the 72nd Pennsylvania, which had just been brought forward from its reserve position to a spot only eighty yards east of the angle. This regiment effectively blocked the further advance of

Armistead's men and helped to prevent them from passing the refused right flank of the 69th. The 72nd poured a heavy fire into the Rebels. Pvt. James Wilson of Company F was among those who deliberately aimed at Armistead. He was encouraged by Maj. Samuel B. Roberts, who told him and others to "shoot that man," for Armistead was very conspicuous. Wilson fired, but Armistead still stood.[35]

Soon after, however, the inevitable happened. Three bullets slammed into Armistead, badly wounding him. The rounds came from the 72nd Pennsylvania. Sgt. Drewry B. Easley, who was near Armistead, saw these Federals grouped around their regimental color just to the left of Cushing's guns and knew it was their fire that felled his general. Armistead was struck in the abdomen, arm, and leg. He winced and bent over, "like a person with cramp," recalled Anthony W. McDermott, who watched the drama from the ranks of Company I, 69th Pennsylvania, only about ten yards away. Armistead "pressed his left hand on his stomach, his sword and hat . . . fell to the ground. He then made two or three staggering steps, reached out his hands trying to grasp at the muzzle of what was then the 1st piece of Cushing's battery, and fell." It appeared as if Armistead tried to break his fall by grabbing the muzzle of the cannon but had not the strength to reach it. He fell within a few feet of the spot where Cushing had been killed only a few minutes earlier, about ten feet inside the angle. The modern monument marking his fall is misplaced.[36]

Armistead was attended by several of his men during the few minutes between his wounding and the Confederate evacuation of the angle. Milton Harding of the 9th Virginia spoke with him when he was conscious and asked if he could help him. Armistead simply wanted a drink from the flask he carried and then advised Harding to save himself. Lt. George W. Finley of the 56th Virginia looked at the general when he was unconscious. Finley believed he was already dead and later regretted not trying to take him off the field when he later heard that Armistead was still alive. Sgt. Drewry B. Easley of the 14th Virginia had little time to tend to wounded generals. He energetically fired away at the group of Yankees that had shot Armistead, aiming over the prone body of the general, until a volley of return fire kicked up so much gravel and pelted him with it that he thought he was wounded. Then he found that the end of his ramrod had been shot off. Easley was forced to look for another gun, but he refused to give up his advanced position inside the angle.[37]

The men who had followed Armistead into the angle, like Easley, were loath to go back. In fact Lt. Thomas C. Holland of the 28th Virginia tried

to push farther. He advanced about ten paces beyond Armistead, waved his hat above his head, and yelled, "Come on, boys." Holland was hit instantly; a bullet entered his cheek and exited through the back of his head. He survived this horrible wound but was later made a prisoner.[38]

There was to be no further penetration of the angle. In fact the 100 men had difficulty figuring out how they could even stay where they were. Some of them had taken Armistead's instructions literally; they turned one of Cushing's cannons toward the foe, but no one seemed to know how to work it. Pvt. Erasmus Williams urged Lt. Col. Rawley W. Martin to order a retreat, as the small group obviously was surrounded on two sides. Martin refused and urged the men to rally and hold instead. But the harsh reality of their situation eventually forced the group to yield. Maj. John C. Timberlake passed the word to pull back to the slight shelter of the stone fence, and even Martin complied with this wise order. Another Federal volley, unleashed by the 72nd Pennsylvania, cut down Martin and many others when they were barely five yards short of the fence.[39]

Drewry B. Easley went down fighting. He frantically searched for a musket to replace the one whose ramrod had been shot off. An apparently wounded man lying near the stone fence offered his weapon, but

Easley found that it was already loaded when he tried to ram a charge down the barrel. Something snapped in the combative sergeant, and he turned his anger and adrenaline on the Rebel. "Where are you wounded any how; I don't see anything the matter with you." The man simply turned over and groaned. Easley raised the gun to strike him but fortunately thought better of his intentions and managed to deflect the blow just enough to annoy the man by whacking him on the head, which led to another groan. He quickly found a different weapon, but its bayonet had been bent and twisted like a corkscrew by a bullet, preventing Easley from loading it.[40]

The fierce determination to stay and fight that Easley exhibited was not felt by all who followed Armistead over the fence. The Confederates had managed to penetrate no more than about twenty yards into the angle. They held there perhaps ten minutes, and 42 of the 100 men fell by the time the penetration was sealed shut by Federal forces. This small but valiant blip on the map of the battlefield marked the true high-water mark of Pickett's division.[41]

About the same time that Armistead was winning renown for himself and his 100 followers, Garnett was unceremoniously killed only a few yards away. He had managed to make it all the way to the stone fence atop his horse unharmed, but his luck would not hold out. His courier, Pvt. Robert H. Irvine of the 19th Virginia, saw the general fall. Garnett was just turning his horse to ride to the left of the brigade, within twenty yards of the fence, when a bullet crashed into his head, killing him instantly. The round probably came from the 72nd Pennsylvania. Nearly at the same time, Irvine's horse was also killed, and it fell over Garnett's body. Irvine managed to escape injury, and he quickly pulled Garnett from under the animal. He took the general's watch and gave it to Capt. Charles F. Linthicum, assistant adjutant general of the brigade. Linthicum told Irvine, "We had better get away quickly, or we will be killed or captured." The retreat had begun by now, and the two made good on their intentions. Garnett's horse was seen racing to the rear with a severe wound in its shoulder. Despite the fact that he was wearing a new uniform, Garnett's body was never identified by the Federals, and he was later buried anonymously with his men. Lt. Elliott Johnston, a member of Garnett's staff who was serving as a volunteer aide for Ewell during the battle, received permission to use a flag of truce to retrieve the general's body, but he could not find the time to attempt it before the Confederates retreated from Gettysburg. Johnston was certain Garnett deliber-

Brig. Gen. Richard Brooke Garnett, or at least a person long identified as Garnett. A raging controversy among his descendants has raised the possibility that this is actually his cousin, Brig. Gen. Robert Selden Garnett, and that no photograph of Brooke Garnett exists. If so, it would be poetic irony, for Garnett was buried anonymously with his men after he was killed in the attack. (LC)

ately exposed himself because of Stonewall Jackson's charges relating to the battle of Kernstown. Garnett's death "was but a question of time," in his view.[42]

Pickett's third brigade commander also went down about this time, but much farther to the right of the division. Kemper had remained on the far right of his command after helping to organize a response to Stannard's flanking maneuver, hovering around the Codori buildings to oversee the safety of that flank. He exchanged a few words with the wounded lieutenant colonel of the 8th Virginia, Norbonne Berkeley, who was lying near the farmhouse. Then the brigade leader rode to the south side of the barn. At the same time, Eppa Hunton, commander of the 8th, was riding to the north of the barn. A bullet passed through Hunton's right leg, "just below the Knee-No bones were broken — but the wound bled profusely," he later recorded. It continued into his horse's body. A soldier volunteered to lead the wounded animal with Hunton still mounted to the rear. The horse died as soon as it delivered him to safety.[43]

Kemper was shot less than 100 yards from Stannard's brigade, probably by the 14th Vermont, which had never stopped firing to the west from its advanced position. He later wrote that he was close enough "to observe the features and the expressions of the faces of the men in front of me, and I thought I observed and could identify the individual soldier who shot me." The bullet penetrated the inside of his left thigh "near the femoral artery—the ball glancing up the thigh bone, passing through the cavity of the body and lodging near the base of the spine." It caused temporary paralysis of the lower half of his body. Immobilized, Kemper lay on the ground until someone found the time to help him. He had a narrow escape from capture. When the retreat began, several Federal soldiers ventured near the Codori barn and found him. They placed him on a blanket and started for their own lines, then a squad of Rebels led by a sergeant of Company D, 1st Virginia, counterattacked and chased the Yankees away. They fired across Kemper's body at the retreating Federals and then swiftly carried the brigadier to Seminary Ridge on the same blanket.[44]

For several minutes surrounding the death and wounding of these three brigadiers, the Confederates fought stubbornly to hold their position outside the stone fence. Adrenaline mixed with fear and desperate hope made those few minutes "a wild kaleidoscopic whirl" for many survivors. Even some officers were caught up in the mood of the moment and searched for muskets they could use on the enemy, who were within very close range. There was a veritable rain of rifle fire exchanged between both sides, and the hail of bullets cut down many men of all ranks. Col. Waller Tazewell Patton of the 7th Virginia was hit in the lower jaw; most of it was literally torn away by the impact of the bullet, and his tongue was badly cut. Blood gushed out of his mouth, making it impossible for him to talk. He was captured and died in Northern hands soon after. Col. James G. Hodges of the 14th Virginia fell near the stone fence, the victim of fire from Gates's demibrigade. His body was surrounded by "a pile of his dead officers."[45]

Cpl. Benjamin R. Lunceford of the 8th Virginia crouched behind some shelter and fired while his brother Evans loaded muskets for him. Another set of brothers in the 8th, Pvt. John L. Bailey and Pvt. Edwin S. Bailey, fought together as well. Both were shot, with Edwin falling dead on top of his brother. John lived and survived captivity. Another member of the regiment, Pvt. William H. Adams, was struck in the leg. Then a shell ricocheted so close to his head that it covered him with a thin layer of dirt. Adams raised himself on one knee and his elbows to crawl to a safer place, but he was hit a second time, in the crazy bone of an elbow, while doing so. The poor private had to flop around to make any progress

Brig. Gen. James Lawson Kemper, the only brigade commander in Pickett's division who survived the attack. He was seriously wounded and never saw battle again. (LC)

to a shallow depression in the ground, where he fainted in the overwhelming heat. A short time later he reawakened just in time to hail a passing Rebel, who helped him to Seminary Ridge. Pvt. Robert W. Morgan of the 11th Virginia had a similar experience. He was hit by a bullet in the instep of his right foot. Morgan was carefully examining the injury, "to see if I was hurt bad enough to go to the rear," when a second bullet tore into his left foot. This one entered at his toes, traversed the foot, and came to rest in his heel. There was now no hesitation; Morgan grabbed two muskets and used them as crutches to hobble all the way to Seminary Ridge.[46]

During this fighting there was no major effort to push across the fence. The Confederates were conducting a desperate holding action with uncertain prospects of success. A regimental color-bearer in Armistead's brigade bravely carried his flag across the fence and into the angle and advanced a few yards into Union territory. But only a handful of men followed him, and he walked calmly back to the Confederate side. Capt. Waller M. Boyd of the 19th Virginia performed the same act. He leaped across the fence and called for the men to follow him. Boyd was immediately wounded in the thigh, and no one answered his summons. The Rebels stayed where they were, too weak to push on and too proud to

HIGH TIDE

retreat until the odds were overwhelming. Their holding action was designed not only to maintain the position they had gained at such fearful loss of life but to sustain their pride as well.[47]

Yet a struggle such as this could not last forever. There would soon come a time when the men realized that no support was on its way to relieve or reinforce them. Joseph Mayo often heard "the despairing exclamation, 'why dont they come!'" Word circulated that help was on the way, only to be countered by other rumors that nothing could be expected from the rear and retreat was the only sensible course of action. The more optimistic among them, such as Capt. John Holmes Smith of the 11th Virginia, "thought our work was done & that the day was over." Holmes "expected to see Gen. Lee's army marching up to take possession of the field." But when he looked to the rear, he "could see nothing but dead and wounded men and horses on the field behind us; and my heart never in my life sank as it did then. It was a grievous disappointment."[48]

When the awful realization began to sink in, the men turned anxiously to one another for answers as to what they should do. To retreat risked death, for the Union artillery continued to traverse the valley with shells. To stay would mean almost certain death or capture, as it was obvious that the remnants of Pickett's division had no strength left to withstand a determined counterattack. Smith sent a courier appropriately nicknamed George T. "Big Foot" Walker to the rear for reinforcements, and later he sent a second man on the same mission. Both made it safely across the field but did not return with help. Then Smith decided to order a retreat, telling the men to scatter into small groups to lessen their chance of injury.[49]

The same process took place among many other groups along the outside of the stone fence. First there was fierce defiance, then there was doubt about the prospects of help arriving, then there was the grim realization that a decision between flight and capture had to be made. Lt. Charles Berkeley of the 8th Virginia gave his handkerchief to Cpl. Benjamin R. Lunceford and told him to put it on a ramrod and wave it as a token of surrender. But Lunceford was so intent on firing, having been supplied with a steady source of loaded and capped muskets by his brother, that he exclaimed, "Hold on awhile Lieut. I am getting two at a crack." His comrades later argued that no one in the division killed more Yankees during these few minutes than Lunceford. John C. Timberlake held his men at the angle for as long as possible. Only when he saw Pettigrew's people withdrawing to the left and noticed the Federals slowly inching

The copse from the Confederate position just outside the angle. Hundreds of Pickett's Virginians were stalled in this position, unable to cross the stone fence because of the ring of Federal troops around the copse. (author's collection)

forward in a countermovement did he give the word to retreat. Some of his men refused and stood their ground, firing to the last minute.[50]

No orders to retreat came from the rear, from either Pickett, Longstreet, or Lee. At least one member of the division blamed Pickett for this, believing he should have resolved the agonizing doubts among his subordinates as to the proper course of action. Many more men might have been saved if an earlier and general withdrawal had been ordered from on high, but there was also an overwhelming need to hang on as long as humanly possible in case some prospect of further success presented itself. The best estimate is that Pickett's division held on at its high tide for at least fifteen and perhaps as many as twenty minutes. It was therefore about 2:40 P.M. when most of his survivors began their retrograde movement across the valley.[51]

Kemper later wrote that the division "found itself in the *cul-de-sac* of death into which it had been hurled, where it met an overpowering fire in front, and raking fires both from the right and left." He also believed that the remnants of the three brigades began to retreat simultaneously, that no part of the division broke and retired before the rest. That was unlikely; after the war Kemper was simply trying to be generous about the

HIGH TIDE

memory of the brave men who made the assault. The sketchy evidence seems to indicate that the right wing broke and retired first, while the far left, the men of Garnett's and Armistead's brigades who were opposite the angle, retired last.[52]

Maj. Joseph R. Cabell of the 38th Virginia, Armistead's leftmost regiment, believed his unit lost two-thirds of its strength while it was within thirty yards of the stone fence. Near the end of its stay there, most of Pettigrew's and Trimble's commands had retired, and the Union flanking party on the left was advancing south along Emmitsburg Road. Col. Edward C. Edmonds was told of this danger. He tried to refuse his left flank to meet it but was shot in the head and died almost instantly. Lt. Col. Powhatan B. Whittle was already out of action with thigh, shoulder, and arm injuries, leaving Cabell in charge of the regiment. He also tried to refuse the left but found it impossible to do so. He then ordered the men to retire to Emmitsburg Road, to the west side of the fences, and they held there for a few moments. Some Confederates from another unit raised a white flag of surrender. Cabell told his own men to take it down, but another was raised again. When the Confederates to his right had all retreated, Cabell finally ordered the small group that remained with him to do the same. They left their regimental flag on the ground to be picked up by the 8th Ohio, elements of which advanced all the way to the angle. It was the only flag from Pickett's division claimed by units of Hays's command.[53]

The artillery was unable to help the retiring infantry very much. After an hour of bombardment and nearly another hour of scattered covering fire, the gun crews were exhausted. W. Greene Raoul of the Washington Artillery reported that he and his comrades "had worked our selves completely down. We were so exhausted that we could not run the piece to the front, but had to fire & let her run back. The excitement kept us up in a great degree but when the battle was over we were so exhausted we could scarcely walk."[54]

· · · · · · ·

GIBBON'S DIVISION AND THE FIRST CORPS TROOPS

Gibbon's division did the most magnificent fighting of its career during the twenty minutes or so that Pickett's Virginians confronted it face-to-face on that hot afternoon. Their stand at the angle prevented the Confederates from breaking through and swarming over the crest of Cemetery Ridge. It was a closely fought contest requiring quick thinking and some difficult maneuvering to reposition troops, but mostly it demanded stamina and a stubborn refusal to move out of the way. The Union defense of the angle was solidly based on the impressive stand of the 69th Pennsylvania and the movement of the 72nd Pennsylvania up to the northeast angle of the stone fence, where it stood directly in the path of Armistead's penetration. This thin line, which sealed the gap made by the earlier withdrawal of the 71st Pennsylvania from the angle, was heavily reinforced by the shifting of Hall's and Harrow's brigades to their right, bringing a lot of eager Federals to shore up the left shoulder of the line. These movements took place very quickly, nearly simultaneously, making for a crowded battlefield on the Union side of the stone fence.

The men of the 69th Pennsylvania were struck with awe when they saw Armistead a few feet to their right, followed by 100 Rebels who swarmed into the face of their right wing like a billowing sail. "We thought that we were all gone," remembered one of them. Companies I and A managed to refuse the line quickly enough, loading and firing as they went and "looking and praying for help," but Company F was unable to do the same. Most of its members were engulfed by Armistead's group and hurried across the fence. Company D fell back a few feet and refused its line in time to stem the tide, sealing the rupture in the regimental line. Many members of Company D were so close to the Rebels that they used their muskets as clubs. "It was D company that had the hand to hand tussle and saved the remainder of the regiment from being enveloped," as Anthony McDermott later put it.[55]

The rest of the 69th Pennsylvania staggered a bit but held. Company C, the color company, retired a few feet, as did two other companies. McDermott believed "the fear of capture had made them cautious about sticking close to the wall." But their rearward movement was stopped, in part, by a clutter of felled trees to the rear. The copse extended nearly to the stone fence; the edge of it had been cut down to make room for troop movements, and the small tree trunks had been scattered on the ground. Cpl. Robert Whittick reported that "there was more danger tramping over the trees in the position we had there than if we stood still." So the left and center of the regiment stayed and fought. Members of Company K, one of the three leftmost companies that remained firmly at the fence, claimed that some Rebels came over it and passed through their line because they were kneeling on one knee, "somewhat crouched," but these intrepid Confederates were soon killed or taken prisoner.[56]

Armistead's penetration affected not only the 69th Pennsylvania but some members of Cushing's battery and the 71st Pennsylvania who remained in the angle. Gunner Thomas Jefferson Moon was caught "between two fires" as the Rebels entered the angle. "I threw up my hands and fell among the dead men & dead horses." It was a wise move, for the enemy assumed he was dead too. "One man stepped on the back of my neck but I layed still." Sgt. Maj. William S. Stockton of the 71st Pennsylvania had remained at the stone fence with five other men when Kochersperger ordered the eight companies of that regiment to evacuate the angle. Armistead's Rebels came over the fence so quickly that they engulfed this little group and pushed them across the fence to the Confederate side. They were ordered by the harried Rebels to go to the rear, but Stockton refused to do so. A Rebel noncommissioned officer charged with the task of taking them back refused to do so as well. So the Yankees took shelter behind the fence, on the Confederate side. They tried to keep alive while plotting among themselves how to get back to Union lines, which were only a few yards away but separated from them by a chasm of fire.[57]

Just before Armistead and his men crossed the fence, the 72nd Pennsylvania moved into position to cover the angle area. Webb ordered it up to fill the space left vacant by the decimation of Cushing's battery. Staff officer Charles H. Banes rode to its post just to the left and rear of the copse to give the word. The troops could see Webb motioning with his sword, and they started moving by the right flank, literally turning to the right in their places and sliding the regimental line to the right and a bit forward as well, making for a slightly oblique movement. The motion brought them toward the northeast angle, where two companies of the 71st Pennsylvania were still holding. The remnants of the other eight companies of Penn Smith's regiment were trying to reassemble to the left rear of the angle.[58]

Lt. Col. Theodore Hesser took charge of the left wing of the 72nd, and Maj. Samuel Roberts saw to the right wing. As Roberts closed on the northeast angle, he passed Webb, who had grabbed a retreating gunner from Cushing's battery. Holding him by the collar, the brigade leader demanded to know where he was going and received the answer that "all the men have left the battery." The 72nd began to receive musketry from the massed Rebels only eighty yards away when Company I, its right flank company, was still forty feet from the northeast angle. The loss was heavy; Roberts estimated it amounted to eighty men. The fire was so severe it prompted the men of Company I to stop twenty feet short of the angle. They turned in place and began to fire in self-defense.[59]

This was not exactly what Webb had wanted. By now Armistead was moving into the angle, and Webb wanted the 72nd to advance down to the west fence and seal the gap properly. He energetically motioned his sword westward, but his shouted commands could not be heard above the noise and confusion. Roberts had assumed all along that Webb wanted him to stop at the northeast angle; in fact he claimed that an order to do so was passed down from someone higher than his own rank. Thus he confidently assumed the regiment was where it was supposed to be, even though the twenty-foot gap between Company I and the angle still existed. In fact Roberts was forced to widen that gap a bit because the next company to the left stopped early and created a space between the two units. He dressed Company I to the left to close the opening. Company A, on the regiment's left flank, also had to dress toward the center. Lt. Henry Russell noticed that its front was partly covered by the northern edge of the copse, and he worried about firing into the refused flank of the 69th Pennsylvania. He held his men's fire until they crushed the files farther to the right. His shouted order to do this was not heard; the good lieutenant "had to go and force the men" to the right. In this compact battle line the regiment did not fire in volleys; the immediacy of the danger compelled the men to load and fire at will.[60]

Tagging along behind the 72nd were Companies A and B of the 106th Pennsylvania. These two units had been orphaned from their regiment since the evening before. No order to move came to Capt. James Lynch of Company B, "but it was one of those actions in which every soldier felt that his duty was to be in the fight," as he later put it. Capt. John J. Sperry, who had assumed command of the contingent, brought his men forward and to the left of the 72nd. Sperry was hit immediately, and Lynch took over.[61]

All of this activity at the angle attracted the attention of other commanders farther to the left. The initial sign that something was afoot certainly was the withdrawal of the 71st Pennsylvania. The subsequent movement of the 72nd Pennsylvania and the emergence of Armistead and his followers confirmed to observant officers in Hall's brigade that help was urgently needed to the right. They began a tumultuous movement of troops to help shore up the endangered sector around the angle. The fact that many of the Rebels in Hall's and Harrow's front did not crowd up to the stone fence gave the Federals the impression that they

HIGH TIDE

had been "repulsed," and therefore it was safe to shift regiments to the right. It was a hasty, poorly coordinated slide that brought maximum force to the spot most seriously threatened by the strongest portion of Pickett's massed line outside the stone fence.[62]

Col. Arthur F. Devereux was the first to see and act. His own regiment, the 19th Massachusetts, and Col. James E. Mallon's 42nd New York were positioned about 100 yards behind Hall's brigade. Devereux noticed the 72nd Pennsylvania move up, but the copse hid his view of the 69th, leading Devereux to assume that a gap existed between the 72nd and the right flank of Hall's brigade. Just then Hancock rode up from the rear. The Second Corps commander had been very active since the end of the bombardment, having gone to Meade's headquarters to get more help for his right flank. Hancock found no one at the Leister house, so he rode directly toward the line of battle, crossing the top of Cemetery Ridge just behind Devereux's command. Armistead's men were streaming over the fence, and Devereux cried out to Hancock, "See, General, they have broken through; the colors are coming over the stone wall; let me go in there." The corps commander did not hesitate or mince words, telling Devereux, "Go in there pretty God damned quick." He then rode off to the left.

Devereux turned to his compatriot and said, "Mallon, we must move." The New York regiment, on the right of the 19th Massachusetts, began a sharp right oblique on the double-quick to connect with the two companies of the 106th Pennsylvania. Devereux followed with the 19th, in echelon to the 42nd. As Hancock rode behind the left wing of the 19th, he yelled, "Forward men! Forward! Now is your chance!" Maj. Edmund Rice, who was in charge of the left wing, picked up Hancock's enthusiasm and yelled, "To our right and front," pointing toward the copse. The left wing took off running for the trees and thus were a few paces ahead of the right wing, essentially executing a right half-wheel on its own, and waited a few seconds for the right wing to catch up. Rice noticed that his extreme left flank brushed within a few yards of Hall's right, and at nearly a right angle to it. Thus it received some enfilade fire from the massed Rebels on the other side of the fence.[63]

The two regiments continued the line of the 72nd Pennsylvania and the two companies of the 106th Pennsylvania, although a few paces to their rear. They were fronted by the copse itself. Curiously, no one in either regiment mentioned the presence of the 69th Pennsylvania on the other side of the copse. The rocks probably shielded their view of the

Federals, while Rebel battle flags were visible through the cluster of small trees. The Massachusetts and New York soldiers assumed they were plugging a gaping hole in the line. Their forward movement had been done with much haste, and there was no time to sort out a neatly dressed line at the copse. The 19th Massachusetts clustered around the regimental colors, "thus, in a measure, holding its identity." The 42nd New York's right flank wrapped around the circular copse. The 72nd Pennsylvania was clearly visible to the men. "The opposing lines were standing as if rooted, dealing death into each other. There they stood and would not move," wrote the historian of the 19th.[64]

Webb felt mortified at the withdrawal of the 71st from the angle and was having the toughest time trying to convince the 72nd to advance to the west wall. He noted and deeply appreciated the arrival of reinforcements. "When my men fell back I almost wished to get killed," he later wrote to his wife. "I was almost disgraced." But Devereux's and Mallon's presence reassured him, although he gave all the credit to their brigade leader Hall. For his part Devereux felt "a reverential awe of the responsibility resting on these two regiments in this conflict." He later came to believe that his little movement to the copse was the key to repelling Pickett's division, for it shored up the ring of fire then encircling Armistead's attempted breakthrough. He greatly exaggerated the significance of his movement, which played a secondary role in the unfolding drama.[65]

Before the movement to the right affected any more of Hall's brigade, Hancock had continued riding to the left. He was not on his favorite horse because the sorrel that had taken him through so many previous battles had lost its nerve during the severe bombardment. The horse "seemed to be utterly powerless, and refused to move notwithstanding I spurred it severely." So Hancock had to borrow "a very tall *light* bay with a white snip on its face or nostril," from a staff officer. On this memorable steed the corps commander had ridden up to Devereux, had given him authority to move up, and then had ridden to the left. Two regiments, probably Gates's 80th New York and 151st Pennsylvania, cheered him as he shouted words of encouragement. Nearing Stannard's brigade, Hancock received word from one of Gibbon's staff officers that the division commander was hit.[66]

Gibbon had also been quite active during this phase of the Confederate assault. He was behind the line of the 19th Maine when the crisis at the angle began to unfold. Gibbon directed his staff officer Capt. Edward Moale to ask an officer of the 13th Vermont to bring his regiment for-

　　　　　　　HIGH TIDE

ward and fire into the Rebel flank. Since the Vermonters were already doing this, the confusion around Gibbon must have been great. Moale reported that the Vermont officer simply refused to listen, telling him he was not subject to Gibbon's orders. Then the division commander sent Moale to get reinforcements for Webb from anyplace he could find them. He then urged the 19th Maine to swing out in front and forward on the right company to "take the enemy's line in flank." But he could not get the troops to understand his intention, and they did not budge. Excited and eager to take advantage of this golden opportunity, Gibbon went out in front of the regiment to cajole the troops, only to be surprised when they opened fire to the front. "I got to the rear as soon as possible," he wrote.[67]

With the Maine boys so uncooperative, Gibbon went to the left where he saw a couple of companies of the 13th Vermont waver and begin to fall back. He hurried forward and helped a Vermont officer to rally them and bring the men back into line. There was no need, Gibbon thought, for these troops to be so unsteady, yet they responded quickly to encouragement and easily rallied. Gibbon hurried back to his own division and once again tried to urge the 19th Maine forward, but he soon felt "a stinging blow apparently behind the left shoulder." A bullet penetrated his left arm and traversed the outside of his left shoulder blade, creating an ugly and painful wound. He turned over command of the division to Harrow. Staff officer Francis Wessels, who had come to tell Gibbon of the trouble in Webb's brigade, took him to the rear, "the sounds of the conflict on the hill still ringing in my ears," as the division commander recalled.[68]

Brigade leader Norman Hall became aware of the need to rally support at the angle when Gibbon's staff officer Frank Haskell rode up to him. "How is it going?" Hall asked the mounted man. "Well, but Webb is hotly pressed, and must have support, or he will be overpowered. — Can you assist him?" When Hall replied in the affirmative, Haskell told him, "You cannot be too quick." Hall later claimed he had an inkling of the need to move to the right just before Haskell rode up, and now he threw himself into the task with energy. After the war Webb showered Hall with well-deserved praise for his actions.[69]

Hall first tried to encourage Gates's two regiments to move to Webb's aid, knowing that the Rebels who were still massed several yards from the stone fence might pose a threat to his part of the line. Gates's men, protected behind their breastwork some 100 yards behind the main line, could easily be spared, Hall reasoned. But these First Corps men refused to listen to a Second Corps brigade officer and simply stayed where they were. There was little friendly cooperation at the intersection of the two corps that day. Hall was forced to use his own troops. He ordered them away from the fence and toward the copse by the right flank, under fire.[70]

Hall's 19th Massachusetts and 42nd New York were already in the new position, taken there by Devereux's initiative. The 20th Massachusetts was next to go. Lt. Col. George N. Macy remembered the order, as brought to him by an aide: "Col. Hall directs that you move the 20th in rear of the line and attack the flank of enemy as they come in, at once." Macy understood that he could not do this easily or cleanly. There was precious little room to maneuver, and the Rebels were already inside the angle. So he ordered Capt. Henry L. Abbott, who was in charge of the right wing, to move the rightmost company "in a mass on the enemy." Macy fully expected a hand-to-hand struggle, and it might as well be quick and messy.[71]

Abbott had difficulty getting the men to respond to his instructions. They continued to fire to the front and right oblique, shouting "Fredericksburg" all the while. When he finally got their attention, they misunderstood his order. Abbott tried to move the company in an orderly fashion, disregarding Macy's instructions, and wanted his men to face and then file right, thus making a new line perpendicular to the old one. But they assumed he simply wanted them to fall back, and they retired about fifteen yards before Abbott could respond. He quickly gave up any attempt to be orderly. Instead Abbott, Macy, and other officers rushed about in full view of the men to demonstrate what they wanted them to do. The noise was too great for shouted orders, and only this pantomime could work. Abbott simply crowded the men helter-skelter toward the right and rear to connect with the left wing of the 19th Massachusetts. Macy described it well when he wrote that the company moved "without regard to order; but as a small compact body with guns charged and bayonets fixed." Abbott's company moved about eighty yards, forming roughly a right angle to their former position.[72]

Macy followed with the other companies, but he was soon hit. A shell fragment knocked him down, flung his sword from his hand, and severely bruised his shoulder. After he got up, a bullet seriously injured his left hand, which later was amputated. Abbott had to take charge of the regiment. The 20th crowded into a small space to Devereux's left and was soon joined by a crunch of men from the rest of the brigade. Regimental

HIGH TIDE

organization melded into a great mass of blue-coated soldiers eager to seal the breach that had opened in the angle.[73]

When Lt. Col. Amos E. Steele Jr. received the word to move his 7th Michigan to the right, he could not make himself understood. Only a few men heard him and obeyed. The other officers thought the movement was an unplanned retreat and tried to rally the troops. "A part of them came back," recalled one observer, "the remainder kept on with Colonel Steele," who was instantly killed when he reached the assigned position next to the 20th Massachusetts. The actions of the 59th New York are unclear. Many members of the regiment had earlier fled their post at the fence. If any remnants still remaining moved to the right, they attracted no one's attention or contributed little to the repulse of Armistead.[74]

Thus Hall was able to pile at least one and a half regiments beside Devereux's two sturdy units, cramming them between the 19th Massachusetts and the stone fence. There was no connection with the left wing of the 69th Pennsylvania. The men of Devereux's contingent were mightily encouraged to see these reinforcements come alongside their formation. Edmund Rice had endured an agony of waiting, even though it took only a few minutes for the 20th Massachusetts to come up. "This is one of those periods in action which are measureable by seconds," he wrote after the war. "The men near seem to fire so slowly, those in rear, though coming up at a run seem to drag their feet." When Hall's boys came up, the 19th Massachusetts and 42nd New York shouted, "Hurrah for the white trefoil!" in admiration of their comrades and the Second Corps badge. "Clubs are trumps! Forward the white trefoil!" they yelled.[75]

Haskell continued to the left to get Harrow's help as well as Hall's. He could not find Harrow, who probably was busy taking charge of the division about this time, so the staff officer took it upon himself to urge the regimental commanders on. It was not difficult to do this, for the movement of Hall's men had alerted them to the danger to the right. There is no description of the movement of the 82nd New York, but presumably it participated in this maneuver. Col. Francis E. Heath quickly set his 19th Maine in motion, but not in any order. "Everyone wanted to be first there and we went up more like a mob than a disciplined force," he wrote. The Maine men took position just to the left of the copse, crowding into the loose formation that already was there.[76]

The 1st Minnesota, small but firing away to the front, needed no generals to tell it what to do. The men responded readily to the signs of trouble. Daniel Bond wrote, "We would now have achieved the victory had we been left without an officer for we could see every movement of the enemy and know how to defend our hills." They ran, cheering all the way, in what one of their number termed "a grand rush to 'get there' in the quickest time, without much regard to the manner of it, and we knew well what we were there for and proceeded to business without ceremony." One company of the 1st squeezed in between the 19th Massachusetts and the remainder of Hall's brigade. The rest pressed forward wherever they could find room.[77]

The 15th Massachusetts, the leftmost regiment of Harrow's brigade, followed the other units and completed the rapid shifting of two brigades toward the copse. This shifting played a significant role in stopping the break made by Armistead's men at the angle, even though it was completed after Armistead fell and perhaps even after his followers were shot down or retreated back to their comrades on the west side of the fence. If nothing else, the arrival of these Federals greatly strengthened the morale of Webb's men. In fact Anthony McDermott of the 69th Pennsylvania wondered if the arrival of Hall's brigade might have emboldened the 72nd Pennsylvania finally to advance toward the west wall, as it soon was to do. Some of Hall's and Harrow's men dropped out of the surging mass of their regiments on the way to the copse to fire at the Confederates. They likely rejoined their comrades later. Still, it is quite possible that about 1,200 men altogether in the two brigades crowded in the 300 yards of open space between the 106th Pennsylvania and the stone fence. If evened out, they would have been about four ranks deep. This was a solid, fiery arc in the ring of iron around the angle. With the 72nd Pennsylvania suffering heavy casualties but firing all it could and the two companies of the 71st Pennsylvania holding firm and firing at the northeast angle, there was little hope of a Confederate breakthrough.[78]

Theodore B. Gates had no intention of being left out of the momentous climax of Pickett's Charge. He had been carefully watching the flow of events ever since the Rebels had come into view. His men delivered what fire they could from their breastwork, 100 yards behind the main Union line, but that could not have been very effective at such long range. With the movement of Hall and Harrow a good stretch of the line was now vacant. Some Confederates moved forward and crossed the fence, penetrating the slashing at the edge of the copse. When Maj. Walter A. Van Rensselear brought word that help was needed near the angle, Gates gave the order to move forward. He pushed the 80th New York and 151st

Pennsylvania to the right front, aiming for a spot near the left of Hall's and Harrow's concentration. The distance to be moved was little more than the front of his demibrigade, so the troops covered it quickly, firing as they went. They came up to the stone fence, only recently vacated by Hall, and began to pour a very short-range fire into the Confederates. Many Rebels took shelter behind the fence and returned the fire just as heavily; apparently the 14th Virginia of Armistead's brigade mostly confronted Gates. The demibrigade shored up the vulnerable left flank of Hall's and Harrow's concentration, fighting magnificently.[79]

Stannard was already maneuvering his two regiments to deliver a blasting fire into Pickett's flank when Hancock rode up and was perplexed by the movement. He asked Stannard what was going on and, not entirely grasping it, exclaimed that Stannard was "gone to Hell," as already described in Chapter 6. Hancock could easily understand the need for a flanking fire, but he probably was confused by the way Stannard was organizing it, for the Vermont general was moving the 16th Vermont by a rather circuitous route to join the 13th Vermont. The Second Corps commander was accompanied by only one aide while Stannard had two staff officers, Lt. George W. Hooker and Lt. George Grenville Benedict, at his side. Benedict admired Hancock's figure during his short conversation with Stannard. "I thought him the most splendid looking man I ever saw on horseback, and magnificent in the flush and excitement of battle."[80]

Then Hancock "uttered an exclamation" and swayed in the saddle. A bullet had hit him in the groin. Hooker and Benedict leaped forward and caught the general as he fell, then carefully laid him on the ground. For a moment Hancock could not speak; he simply motioned toward the wound. Stannard opened his clothing enough to expose an ugly, jagged hole at least an inch in diameter on the upper part of the inside of his thigh. "Don't let me bleed to death," Hancock exclaimed, "Get something around it quick." With Benedict's help, Stannard began to tie his handkerchief around the thigh above the wound. But Benedict knew enough of medicine to tell that an artery had not been severed; the blood was too dark, and it did not spurt out in jets. "This is not arterial blood, General," he told Hancock, "you will not bleed to death." Hancock assumed he was a doctor and thanked him for the diagnosis. Stannard and Benedict used a pistol barrel to twist the handkerchief into a tourniquet.[81]

Maj. William G. Mitchell, one of Hancock's staff members, rode up and uttered "an exclamation of pain" when he saw his chief on the ground. He quickly turned away and raced for a surgeon. Dr. Alexander N. Dougherty arrived fifteen minutes later. He removed the tourniquet and stuck his forefinger all the way to the knuckle into the hole. Dougherty found a "ten penny weight iron nail, bent double," inside the wound, a curious object to be sure. "This is what hit you, General," Dougherty said, "and you are not so badly hurt as you think." Dougherty could not have known from such a cursory examination, but the wound was far worse than he thought. A bullet was still inside Hancock; it had slightly splintered the socket of the thigh bone and was still lodged near that spot. There was no immediate danger of death, but a long, painful recovery awaited the fighting commander of the Second Corps. Buoyed by adrenaline, he had not lost interest in the fight. While waiting for an ambulance, Hancock propped himself on one elbow to observe the battle, with Stannard giving him verbal descriptions of what he could not see.[82]

After the war a monument marking the spot where Hancock fell was placed atop a little rise of ground about 75 yards in front of the Union line and about 200 yards to the rear of the location of the 13th and 16th Vermont. But Hancock believed it was a mistake. He was struck somewhere to the north or northwest of that spot, where there were no rocky outcroppings and where, lying on his back "and looking through the remains of a very low, disintegrating stone wall, I could observe the operations of the enemy and give directions accordingly." A modern historian suggests the bullet might have accidentally come from a Union musket and was an example of the friendly fire that often plagued the battlefield. There is no reason to believe this, for all the firing done by the three Vermont regiments was away from Hancock's position. The bullet undoubtedly came from one of Pickett's men on the refused line or near the angle where that line joined the rest of the Confederate concentration outside the stone fence. Thus one of Kemper's or Garnett's men probably fired the shot that brought Hancock down.[83]

By the time Hancock was shot, all of the Union troops were repositioned to deal with the last phase of Pickett's Charge. The greatest strain was on Webb's embattled brigade, and the young brigade leader fully felt it. He later unburdened himself to his father. "The assault was nobly made," he graciously admitted. "It was a magnificent & terrible military manoeuvre and for a while they fairly overwhelmed me." Yet his men were bravely supported by many others. Webb gave credit to Hall, who "helped me at the right time[.] He sent few men but a good many col-

*Brig. Gen. Alexander Stewart Webb,
whose Philadelphia Brigade held the angle
(Massachusetts Commandery, Military
Order of the Loyal Legion and the U.S.
Army Military History Institute,
USAMHI)*

ors[.] It looked like strong reinforcements." Webb was convinced he could not have held but for the support Hall brought up. He felt the repulse was due to several factors operating in connection with one another: the hesitation of the Confederates to pour over the stone fence, the stubborn stand of the 69th and 72nd Pennsylvania, and the surging forward of Hall and Harrow, all of which caused a stalemate at the angle. For several minutes, which must have seemed like hours, the two opposing forces stood at close range (Devereux carefully measured it to be as little as fifteen yards in some places), pouring fire into each other's faces.[84]

Webb deserves great credit for holding his brigade together under this stress. He tried his mightiest to get the 72nd to advance toward the west wall but with scant success. He placed himself in front of the firing regiment, endangering himself in the face of both Rebel and Union fire, and shouted as loudly as he could. No one seemed to hear or understand him. Webb approached the color-bearer, Sgt. William Finecy, and urged him to advance with the flag, but Finecy refused. He moved about in place but did not go forward, even after Webb grabbed at the flag in an attempt to carry it forward himself. Nothing Webb could do brought the regiment out of its place. Capt. Charles H. Banes, who had come from the regiment to serve on Webb's staff, rode his horse just behind his old comrades, also urging them to do their best. It is unclear if he understood that Webb wanted them to advance.

There were several reasons why the Pennsylvanians did not go forward. First, they were in an exposed position and under heavy fire. Their first instinct was to return it and not expose themselves further by advancing; because they were veterans, they also refused to shame themselves by retreating. Thus they naturally remained where they were for the time being. Webb's entreaties did not inspire them forward partly because few members of the brigade liked or respected the upstart brigadier. He had not yet endeared himself to the rank and file, and everyone in the regiment ignored him, even if they could hear his orders. Finally, Webb is partly to blame, for he failed to deliver his instructions through the proper channels. He did not tell Lieutenant Colonel Hesser or Major Roberts what to do. Instead he tried to cut through the chain of command and talk to the rank and file. It did not work. Frustrated and angry, Webb gave up and walked over to the refused right wing of the 69th Pennsylvania to steady the men there, passing within a few yards of where Armistead and his men were valiantly trying to hold at Cushing's guns.[85]

Perhaps it was during this short walk across the cramped battlefield that a bullet grazed Webb's thigh. It was his only injury during the fight. He later recalled that he was only thirty-nine paces from the Rebels and could see that "their officer pointed me out, but God preserved me." Although the 72nd refused to go forward under Webb's direction, the regiment stood and fought very well. It lost a lot of men. Captain Banes carefully examined its position after the fight and was astonished at the neat rows of bodies. "If they had been laid there by their comrades they could not have been laid more on a line." The two unnamed companies of the 71st that Penn Smith had earlier left at the northeast angle also poured fire into the Rebels. They had a stash of abandoned muskets at their disposal and used them freely. The other eight companies of the 71st were reassembling to the rear of the 72nd and seem to have contributed nothing to the fight.[86]

The same cannot be said of the 69th Pennsylvania. Anthony W. McDermott admitted after the war that "I was afraid we were going to get whipped," but his comrades quickly became energized by the crisis. Capt. William Davis noted that "new ardor seemed to inspire our men to greater exertions." Webb found them eager to fight when he reached the right wing after his futile effort to advance the 72nd. "I went to them & told them to fire to front . . . and to a man they replied that I could count on them."[87]

The regiment put up a heroic fight. Col. Dennis O'Kane inspired them to their best. He was shot and "fell like a soldier in great glee because his men could not be driven from their position," remembered McDermott. O'Kane "was not an educated man, and was gruff in his speech, but with all he had a heart as tender as a woman's and above all things he despised a coward." Lt. Col. Martin Tschudy also was killed, and Maj. James Duffy was wounded, leaving the regiment in the hands of its senior company commander, Capt. William Davis.[88]

While the right wing barely held under the Confederate pressure, the center and left fought stoutly to hold their place. A few Rebels managed to cross the fence to the left of the regiment but were soon repulsed. Other Confederates repeatedly called out over the din for the Pennsylvanians to surrender, but McDermott believed they managed to grab only two men of the regiment, other than those members of Company F who were gobbled up wholesale when Armistead's 100 men crossed the fence. There was some fierce hand-to-hand fighting at and near the position of Company F. The ranks were so tightly cramped that some men were able to strike the Rebels with their musket barrels but could not swing them enough to hurt the enemy. Other Pennsylvanians did have room to swing, and they laid their muskets onto the Rebels with a savage intensity. Pvt. Hugh Bradley of Company D "wielded his piece, striking right and left, and was killed in the melee by having his skull crushed by a musket in the hands of a rebel." Another member of Company D, Pvt. Thomas Donnelly, was called on to surrender. He "replied tauntingly, 'I surrender' at the same time striking his would be captor to the ground."[89]

The 69th Pennsylvania was caught between the opposing lines. Hall's brigade came up to its rear, on the other side of the copse. It fired a lot of rounds toward the enemy, but McDermott was careful to point out after the war that this fire could not have helped his comrades. In fact it more likely hurt them. Many members of Hall's brigade argued that the Rebels were literally in the copse of trees, that they could see their butternut clothing and their red regimental flags, but it was an optical illusion. The only Confederates in the copse were to the left of the 69th Pennsylvania and were dealt with mostly by Harrow's brigade and Gates's demibrigade, and even they had penetrated only the southwestern edge of the copse. No one knows how many victims of friendly fire might have fallen in the

69th Pennsylvania. The regiment truly was contending with fire from front and rear at the same time.[90]

Hall's men could not advance to the stone fence to reinforce the 69th because the copse was in the way; the rocky outcropping was a more effective barrier to troop movement than the small trees. One must remember that Hall's brigade was very jumbled. Unit organization was mostly gone. Hancock later attributed the confusion not only to the haste with which the movement to the right had taken place but also to the "ambition of individual commanders to promptly cover the point penetrated by the enemy, the smoke of battle, and the intensity of the close engagement." Everything was happening so fast that memory could be unreliable. Thus it was easy enough for many Federals to assume the copse was filled with butternut uniforms.[91]

The men on Hall's left near the slashing that fringed the southwestern corner of the copse had real Rebels to contend with. In places they were quite close to them, receiving wounds and having their clothes torn and blackened by the blast of muskets. A rumor circulated at the height of the fight that Maj. Gen. George B. McClellan was on his way to Gettysburg with 50,000 militia troops to save the day. For the men who still idolized the former commander of the Army of the Potomac, this news came as a boost to their morale. A few Rebels, unable to handle the close combat, gave themselves up by crawling on their hands and knees "under the sheet of fire" into Union lines. One enterprising Yankee, Cpl. Joseph H. De Castro of the 19th Massachusetts, captured the flag of the 14th Virginia by knocking down the Rebel color-bearer with the staff of his Massachusetts state flag. He then grabbed the Confederate color and raced to the rear, thrusting it into Arthur Devereux's hands to prove his claim to it, and then raced back into the fight.[92]

With rank-and-file arrangements gone, the men of Hall's command, and Harrow's intermixed with them, fought as individuals. They were "jammed in, five and six deep," recalled the historian of the 19th Massachusetts. The mass swayed as men fired and then stepped back to find room to reload their pieces. More men eagerly crowded forward to take their place. Those in the rear were "dodging around, firing through openings made by the changing crowd, no matter how small." Many soldiers were inadvertently hit by their own comrades in this fluid, disorderly environment. "Muskets are exploding all around," recalled Edmund Rice, "flashing their fire almost in one's face and so close to the head as to make the ears ring." Rice saw one of his sergeants hit in the

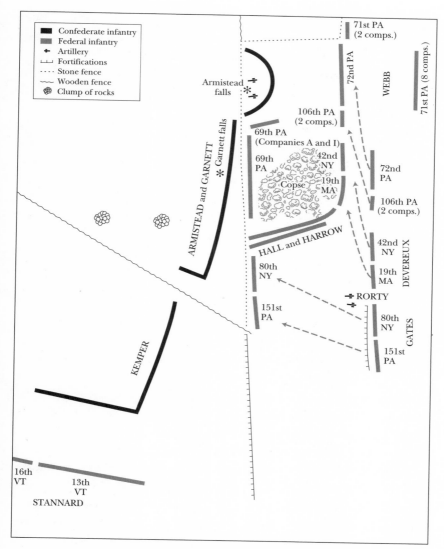

Legend:
- ▪ Confederate infantry
- ▪ Federal infantry
- ← Artillery
- ⊔ Fortifications
- ---- Stone fence
- ～ Wooden fence
- ⊛ Clump of rocks

71st PA (2 comps.)

72nd PA

WEBB

71st PA (8 comps.)

Armistead falls

106th PA (2 comps.)

69th PA (Companies A and I)

69th PA

42nd NY

72nd PA

19th MA

106th PA (2 comps.)

Copse

42nd NY

ARMISTEAD and GARNETT

Garnett falls

19th MA

DEVEREUX

HALL and HARROW

RORTY

80th NY

80th NY

GATES

151st PA

151st PA

KEMPER

16th VT

13th VT

STANNARD

Map 7.1 Pickett at High Tide

back of the neck by a friendly bullet. Whether their rounds fell among the Rebels or unintentionally among their own comrades, the Federals fought with desperate intensity. "I did not see any man of my command who appeared disposed to run away," recalled Norman Hall.[93]

Not only did their own comrades injure the bluecoats, but Rebel musketry cut them down. Edmund Rice felt as if he was a special target for Pickett's men, for bullets knocked the sword out of his hand and tore his cap off. He also was nicked at several places below the knees. Rice saw a few Confederate artillery rounds strike with awesome effect. One projectile shrieked in, tearing "a horrible passage through the dense crowd of men in blue, who are gathering outside the trees and spends its strength on bone and muscle. Instantly another shot follows and fairly cuts a road through the mass."[94]

Harrow's brigade was massed to the left and rear of Hall, close to the Rebels who had penetrated the slashing at the southwest corner of the copse. Some units were closer than others. The 1st Minnesota was about twenty-five yards from the enemy, while others were close enough to engage in hand-to-hand combat. The men formed "a strong though confused line" as they poured fire into the enemy. A. C. Plaisted of the 15th Massachusetts believed they did the Rebels comparatively little damage, as the Confederates were sheltered by the fence, but the presence of Harrow's men prevented them from advancing any farther. The last units to move up to this position fought at high tide for about five minutes; others that preceded them fought at least twice as long.[95]

"We took revenge for what they had done to our poor fellows the day before," wrote Pvt. John W. Plummer of the 1st Minnesota, "and we never had had such a chance before. Most of us fired over twenty rounds." Lt. William Harmon noted that his Minnesota comrades "were crazy with the excitement of the fight. We just rushed in like wild beasts." The 19th Maine fought as hard as the Minnesotans. "We were all loading and firing and yelling and pushing," remembered John P. Lancaster. The Maine men loaded, squeezed through the milling crowd, and even jumped into the air to get off another shot. Color-bearers "would toss their colors up and down to show the enemy that we were not going to give it up, and to encourage us." In the excitement Lancaster put a cartridge in his barrel the wrong way, rendering his musket useless. Another Maine man shot off his ramrod after forgetting to withdraw it. Both of them easily found abandoned weapons on the ground and continued to fire. Other excited Yankees threw stones at the Rebels.[96]

The men of Harrow's brigade took casualties as well. Col. Francis Heath of the 19th Maine was wounded during this phase of the attack. Capt. Nathan S. Messick, commanding the 1st Minnesota, was killed. The color-bearers of the 1st Minnesota were struck down in rapid succession as well. A bullet splintered the staff and passed through Cpl. John Dehn's hand. Cpl. Henry D. O'Brien took the flag and waved it high above the crowd, only to have the staff severed and to receive wounds in his hand and head.

Cpl. W. N. Irvine took the colors and carried them to the end of the fight. After the battle the resourceful Minnesotans took part of the staff from a captured Rebel flag and spliced it to their own mutilated standard with the strap from a knapsack. They took it home to Minnesota with them.[97]

Gates's two regiments also fought hard to the left of Harrow's men. They faced west against the Rebels of Garnett and Armistead who constituted the Confederate right-center. The range was close, and the Rebels had a considerable amount of cover behind the fence and in the slashed timber of the copse. Remembering the hard and losing battle of July 1, some soldiers found it "comparative fun to fight them" this day "when we had some chance." Lt. Col. Jacob B. Hardenburgh of the 80th worried about the swaying mass of Harrow's brigade to his right and tried to encourage the men to steady their irregular formation, but it was no use. His own regiment and the 151st Pennsylvania maintained the normal rank-and-file formation because they had an easy time moving forward to their advanced position. Hardenburgh mistook the swaying for unsteadiness. "It struck me as being to say the least very ridiculous," he ungraciously remembered after the war.[98]

Members of Gates's demibrigade who were close enough for hand-to-hand combat with the Rebels did not use their bayonets, recalled Capt. John D. S. Cook. Instead they used their muskets as clubs, just as the 69th Pennsylvanians were doing. The rest of them loaded and fired at will. Cpl. Nathan Cook of the 151st Pennsylvania fired a total of fifty rounds during the attack, writing home that "I never leveled a gun more deliberately on a squirrel than I did on them." In the 80th New York one man literally "rested the muzzle of his gun" on Cook's left shoulder and fired. It startled the captain, and he turned to chew out the soldier but "was overwhelmed by the laughter of the men at the start it had given me. It was more funny for them than for myself."[99]

This period of fighting in static positions around the angle lasted for no more than ten or fifteen minutes. The stalemate broke when Armistead's leaderless men began to retire from the angle back to the stone fence. This inspired a renewed effort on Webb's part to get the 72nd Pennsylvania to advance toward the west wall. If that regiment could be induced to move, it would naturally draw the other eager men around the angle into a counterattack as well. Even though Frank Haskell later took full and undeserved credit for inducing the 72nd to attack, the honor really belongs to Webb.[100]

A little of that distinction belongs to Anthony W. McDermott as well.

He was a keen observer of events from the ranks of Company I, 69th Pennsylvania, and alerted Webb to the fact that Armistead was down and the Rebels were retreating from the angle. McDermott ran to the brigadier yelling "that their leader had fallen and the enemy was running." Webb turned around to survey the scene, thought a second, and "repeated, almost, my words . . . saying yes boys, the enemy is running, come up, come up!" Webb would completely forget McDermott's little role in initiating the forward movement, but the corporal never forgot it. Webb waved his sword and continued to shout, "Boys, the enemy is ours." The two companies of the 106th Pennsylvania heard him and were ready to respond. The left wing of the 72nd Pennsylvania reacted as well. Lt. Henry Russell, commanding Company A on the far left, heard Webb and passed the order to his men to fix bayonets. The rest of the regiment took up the call from left to right, inspired by the actions of their comrades. Lieutenant Colonel Hesser, on the left wing, also caught up the order and passed it on, adding credibility to it. For the first time since they came under fire, other members of the regiment finally noticed Webb motioning for a forward movement, and they responded.[101]

The 72nd moved forward in a very irregular line, firing as it went. It was not a rapid advance but a slow walk, with parts of the regiment outpacing others. In the words of Capt. Robert McBride, "We fought down to the wall." The advance was irregular because some Confederate prisoners ran through the regiment for the Union rear, and apparently the 71st Pennsylvania was firing wildly and hit a few men in the 72nd. In fact when Webb's staff officer Capt. Charles H. Banes was later asked if he would describe the advance as an attack, he answered no. "It would depend altogether upon what technical terms you were using." Banes had a very good view of the regiment from his horse, just to the unit's rear, and he described it as "more of a melee than a line of battle." The regiment's losses had been severe by this time. Major Roberts remarked that his right wing "looked like a skirmish line" as it advanced toward the west wall. The 72nd split as it approached Cushing's two guns to pass on both sides of them; the ground around the pieces was littered with dead and wounded Rebels and Yankees alike.[102]

The color-bearer put on a bold display, but it was not the same man who had earlier refused to move forward under Webb's direction. Sergeant Finecy had been hit by six to thirteen bullets soon after Webb left him. Sgt. Thomas Murphy then took the flag. Murphy waved his cap high in the air as he carried the flag forward. All but one of the eight-man color guard were killed or wounded; one was shot six times. In his enthusiasm Murphy even jumped across the fence when the regiment reached the end of its advance, and he carried the flag at least 100 feet farther, chasing the retiring Rebels. His comrades had to go out and bring him back. Company E and K followed Murphy a short distance but returned because other Federal units were still firing into the area west of the fence. Murphy was shot the following May at Spotsylvania and died six months later.[103]

The regiment's advance freed several members of the 71st Pennsylvania from captivity. Sgt. Maj. William S. Stockton and four other men had earlier been taken when Armistead's followers flowed over the stone fence. They had refused to go to the Rebel rear and instead took shelter with their captors behind the fence. The steady approach of the 72nd gave them their opportunity to escape. The Confederates were far too busy to tend to prisoners, so the five waited quietly until Stockton judged their comrades were close enough to risk a move. Then they jumped across the fence and raced into the regiment before friendly fire could cut them down. Col. Richard Penn Smith later insisted that his 71st Pennsylvania followed the 72nd in this forward movement to the fence. It might well have done so, but Penn Smith was not a reliable or unbiased witness, and no other sources support his contention.[104]

This forward movement by the 72nd Pennsylvania later became a point of controversy resulting in a major court case to determine where the regiment's monument should be placed on the battlefield. Members of the 69th Pennsylvania argued that their comrades never made it to the west wall early enough to repel the Rebels. The exact timing is difficult to determine. The regiment was the first to begin the counterattack, but its slow advance allowed other regiments to the left—Hall's and Harrow's brigades—to strike faster. By the time the 72nd reached the west wall, most of the Confederates were probably on their way back to Emmitsburg Road. There were still quite a few Rebels stubbornly hanging on at the angle, so the regiment had some real but isolated fighting to do; but the tide probably had turned by then. Even though the 72nd ended the fight by mopping up, its stubborn stand at the northeast angle and its slow advance to the west wall were important factors in the Union victory. Pvt. James Wilson noted that his comrades were "strewed all the way from the crest to the stone wall." He could easily tell them apart from members of other regiments, for many of them still wore their Zouave pants and jackets. The rest wore the regulation blue uniform but retained their white leggings.[105]

Hall's brigade quickly took up the call and went forward. It started with a decision by Hall, who walked up to Arthur Devereux's side and commented, "We are steady now." Devereux agreed but thought something more needed to be done. "Sure," he said, "but we must move." Hall thought a moment, noted that the 72nd was moving forward, and quickly decided to go. He passed the word to as many officers as possible and ordered the colors of all regiments advanced. The men went forward almost spontaneously; many observers described it as a leaping forward. Knowing he would not be heard in the din, Maj. Edmund Rice did not bother to issue orders to his men. He simply raised his sword "to attract their attention and motion them to advance." Instantly a shell fragment knocked the sword from his hand and stunned him. "As I go down our men rush forward past me."[106]

The 19th Massachusetts and 42nd New York advanced around the copse, now that the 72nd Pennsylvania and the two companies of the 106th Pennsylvania were moving forward and the way was clear to the right of the trees. As the two regiments approached the stone fence, they found the Rebels breaking. Some of them were running back to Emmitsburg Road while others were lying down, firing at the Yankees, and still others were rising to surrender. Those who resisted were swamped by the Federal tide. The 19th Massachusetts, or at least a portion of it, continued across the stone fence for a short distance into the field. It had to return soon for Confederate artillery fire began to play on that area. The Massachusetts men took shelter behind the fence, crowding in with the 69th and 72nd Pennsylvania, to take pot shots at the retiring Rebels.[107]

The rest of Hall's brigade advanced too, but to the left of the copse. The 20th Massachusetts rushed forward and took several casualties on the way. Lt. Sumner Paine, a Harvard student who had joined the regiment two months earlier, encouraged his men and shouted "Isn't this glorious" to a brother officer just before he was knocked down by a shell burst fifteen feet short of the fence. His ankle was broken, but Paine continued to shout encouragement and wave his sword until a bullet slammed into his chest, killing him instantly. He was only eighteen years old. Lt. L. E. Hibbard apologized to Paine's father for not stopping to tend to his son. "I will tell you, *unnatural* as it may seem, a Soldier and an Officer *especially* can not stop during an engagement even if his *own brother* should fall by his side, his *whole* duty is to cheer on the men—for if an Officer is seen to *falter*, it *encourages* the *men* to *do the same*."[108]

Harrow's brigade followed right behind Hall's. "Whether the command 'Charge!' was given by any general officer I do not know," recalled William Lochren of the 1st Minnesota, "it seemed to me to come in a spontaneous yell from the men, and instantly our line precipitated itself on the enemy." Lochren was right; Harrow, his brigade commander, appears not to have been involved in what was happening at the copse. His tough brigade did not need direction, however; the men saw Hall's actions and conformed their own to his. Harrow's men advanced to the left of the copse as well. The brigade was in "a mixed and disordered mass, but it was an aggressive, fighting quantity, of tremendous energy, and expended its force on the enemy like an explosion." Color-bearer O'Brien of the 1st Minnesota pushed ahead of the mass and helped to set the pace.[109]

The excitement of the attack was accompanied by losses. Pvt. Joe Richardson of the 1st Minnesota ran beside James A. Wright, stuttering excitedly. "By the l-l-lovely l-l-little angels a-and th-the g-gr-great h-ho-horn s-sp-spoon, we we'l sh-sh-show 'em th-th-there is a God in Is-Is-Israel. We-we are g-get-getting s-s-some s-s-sa-satisfaction now; ain't we, sa-sargent?" Just then Wright was stunned. A bullet hit his gunstock and splintered it, shredding his clothes with pieces of wood and metal and even driving some slivers of both into his face and neck. It was not a disabling wound, so Wright kept running to finish the charge.[110]

As the 1st Minnesota made its way through the slashing, hand-to-hand combat took place with the scattered Rebels who remained. The regiment approached the stone fence ready to take on any Confederates. Daniel Bond reached the fence, and suddenly twenty Rebels stood up on the other side and offered to surrender. Bond told them to go to the rear and turned his attention to two Confederate flags still flying to his right, but he was too late to take them. They were snatched up by his comrades, and thus Bond "did not get a rag."[111]

The 15th Massachusetts started on the counterattack when Pvt. George H. Cunningham of Company B shouted, "*For God's sake let us charge, they'll kill us all if we stand here.*" The regiment sprang forward "all in a mass," according to A. C. Plaisted. The regiment had only a short distance to go through the slashing before it reached the stone fence, where it met many Rebels willing to lay down their arms. They "cried out to us to stop firing and let them come in." The Massachusetts men at first ceased firing, but some Confederates then started to run back to Emmitsburg Road while others came across the fence. The 15th resumed firing until all Confederates who were running were out of range. "We were obliged to fire through those who were ready to come," reported Plaisted, "and many was killed coming tords us; but nearly all lay down untill we ceased firing." When the men of Hall's and Harrow's brigades were down at the fence, a mighty cheer rose from their throats as they "ceased firing and realized the situation."[112]

Gates's demibrigade started its advance in much the same way as the 15th Massachusetts. Capt. Walter L. Owens, who led the 151st Pennsylvania, was tired of the casualties his little regiment was suffering while standing toe-to-toe with the Rebels. At times his men wavered as if they would break. "Seeing that to fight in that position we would not be able to hold out I started the cry that the rebels were running, and ordered a charge." The men obeyed with alacrity. Gates took up the movement to the front with his 80th New York, and the two regiments pushed on through the slashing. They cheered and fired at the same time, causing the Confederates to retreat. Maj. Walter A. Van Rensselear of the 80th had a tussle with a Confederate officer who was holding a flag at the fence. Van Rensselear demanded he surrender himself and the color, but the Virginian refused; "not by a d—d sight!" he yelled. After the Rebel fired his pistol, inflicting a flesh wound, Van Rensselear lunged at him with his sword. A second pistol shot hit Van Rensselear's scabbard. Half a dozen New York privates came to their major's aid, and the Rebel was subdued. Col. James C. Hodges of the 14th Virginia also was killed at this stage of the fight. He was standing only fifty feet from Gates when he went down.[113]

Farther to the left, Stannard's Vermonters were finishing their work on Pickett's flank. The 13th Vermont fired up to fifteen rounds before the Confederates broke and fled; the 16th Vermont, which came into the flanking position later, fired about half that number. When the Rebels gave way, they did so very quickly, lending the appearance of a rout to their retreat, but the green Vermonters could not be restrained. Many of them continued to fire even after the enemy began to leave the field. Colonel Randall had to step in front of his 13th, show his back to the foe, and wave his hat and sword to get the men's attention. He repeated the cease-fire order until the regiment was silent. Then they broke up into squads to collect prisoners. Much the same took place in Colonel Veazey's 16th Vermont. Jittery and resistant to instructions as they were, the Ver-

HIGH TIDE

mont soldiers had performed a valuable service for the Union cause that afternoon. Their fire had blunted the advance of Pickett's right wing and littered the ground in front with the dead and wounded.[114]

Most of the firing died down across the battlefield after the tide decisively turned for Pickett's, Pettigrew's, and Trimble's mangled regiments. The litter of men on the ground was sickening. But before the victorious Federals could fully comprehend their success or begin to clean up the battlefield, there was another forlorn attack to be repelled.

CHAPTER 8
THE REPULSE
· · · · · · · · · · ·

Wilcox and Lang had waited patiently since Pickett's men had passed through their commands early in the attack. Ready for orders but uncertain what they could accomplish, the two brigade leaders had an excellent view of the doomed assault for at least several minutes. In that early phase of the attack, while Pickett was still moving east toward Emmitsburg Road, Wilcox and Lang assumed the direction of march would always be straight ahead. They had not been informed about and did not surmise the need for Pickett to go left and connect with Pettigrew. Little did they know that they would soon be told to participate in the advance, playing out the final act of this tragic drama.

Before the word arrived, no one among their officers or enlisted men had an idea that they were to go in with Pickett. The Alabamans and Floridians gawked at the Virginia division that disappeared into the developing cloud of cannon smoke across the valley. J. B. Johnson, Lang's adjutant, saw one of Pickett's lieutenants come back from the smoke with his left arm shattered around the elbow; "the bone was protruding, and the blood spurting from the arteries." Johnson gave him emergency aid, tying a tourniquet around his arm with a handkerchief and a bayonet. This saved the lieutenant's life, but the Virginian seemed completely disinterested. He was "so much absorbed in listening to the charge in front, that he paid no attention to the arm."[1]

· · · · · · ·
WILCOX AND LANG ATTACK

Some fifteen minutes after the start of the attack, after Pickett's men had gone about 400 yards past Wilcox's brigade, three staff officers brought a request for help. Baird, Symington, and Bright had been sent by Pickett when the Virginian realized his division would need reinforcements. Bright had brought this request to Longstreet first, and the corps commander had hastily told him to draw on Wilcox and Lang. Sending three men was Pickett's idea, for he had been afraid that one or more of them might not survive the hail of artillery fire. Wilcox was exasperated by the attention, but he dutifully readied his command for a quick advance.[2]

No one in either Wilcox's or Lang's brigades felt confident about going, especially since the order simply instructed them to support Pickett and provided no further details. Everyone in the two brigades knew intimately how strong the Union position was and how costly had been their own attack on July 2. "At a glance of the eye from the brow of the hill, . . . every private at once saw the madness of the attempt," remembered Col. Hilary A. Herbert of the 8th Alabama. For the rest of their lives, survivors of what was to follow remained puzzled as to its purpose. "The whole affair is involved in mystery even until today," commented George Clark of the 11th Alabama in 1914. Clark frequently heard his comrades ask, "What in the devil does this mean?" as they dressed ranks and prepared to move out. Lang's Floridians knew they and Wilcox were going in alone, that no support could be expected. The order to advance was "not obeyed with the same alacrity as was the case yesterday," wrote William Penn Pigman of the 8th Florida. Colonel Herbert and his fellow officers could only assume they were being sent forward to prevent a Federal counterattack in case Pickett was repulsed. Nothing could be further from the truth. Wilcox and Lang were being sent out to help the Virginians exploit whatever success they gained. Watching the advance of this little band from the artillery, Edward Porter Alexander pitied the two brigades. He knew they should have been sent much earlier if they hoped to aid the Virginians. "For such an attack as Pickett had to make the supporting lines should follow quick & fast," he wrote.[3]

Wilcox gave the order to advance. Numbering about 1,000 men, his command was arrayed with the 9th Alabama on the right and then the 10th, 11th, 8th, and 14th Alabama on the left. Wilcox moved his command quickly to draw some Federal attention away from Pickett. Lang was under orders to conform his movements to Wilcox's. This arrangement had been made much earlier because division leader Anderson felt it was more efficient to issue orders to only one of his two brigades, isolated as they were from the rest of the division. The arrangement worked only because Lang was an observant and conscientious officer.

Wilcox haughtily ignored the Florida brigade, not even mentioning it in his report or postwar writings.[4]

When Lang heard the shouted commands "Attention" and "Forward" in Wilcox's ranks, he repeated them in his own brigade. Advancing to Wilcox's left and arranged with the 2nd Florida on the left, the 8th Florida in the center, and the 5th Florida on the right, the brigade numbered only 400 men. Like their comrades in Pickett's, Pettigrew's, and Trimble's divisions, many members of both brigades were already exhausted from the heat. They "could hardly go" because they had been lying under the artillery bombardment so long, and heat prostration took several men out of the ranks.[5]

The course of the advance was harried by doubts. Wilcox suddenly realized he did not know exactly where Pickett's men were, for the increasing smoke and the division's left oblique had already taken them from his view. He tried to veer his advance to the left "so as to cover in part the ground over which" Pickett had advanced. The two brigades reached Emmitsburg Road and still could not see the Virginians, but they did receive a storm of artillery fire. Wilcox was convinced the situation was worse than what he had endured the day before. Nevertheless the men pushed on straight ahead, assuming Pickett was in that direction. They encountered some of Kemper's skirmishers who had continued advancing due east while the rest of Pickett's division obliqued to the left. They also stepped across Pickett's dead and wounded men.[6]

While there had been few if any casualties before they reached Emmitsburg Road, now the two brigades began to suffer as the Federal gunners saw them, got their range, and created painful gaps in the ranks. Lang's men were treated to a "terrible fire" that took dramatic effect. Lt. James Wentworth of the 8th Florida thought this was "the hottest work I ever saw. My men falling all around me with brains blown out, arms off and wounded in every description."[7]

Lang began to seek help from the rear when he noticed Union troop movements that were designed to take advantage of his unsupported left flank. These movements were being conducted by Stannard's brigade, for the Vermonters were still in their advanced position. Wilcox and Lang happened to be aiming at a point of the Union line that was south of Stannard's men, in effect placing their brigades exactly opposite Pickett's men in relation to the Vermonters. Stannard was in an excellent place to fire into their left flank as he had been to fire into Pickett's right, and he

quickly made the most of this opportune moment. Lang sent staff officer J. B. Johnson to the artillery line to ask for fire support.[8]

Johnson could not drum up any help for the Floridians. The gunners were willing, but they had no more long-range ammunition. When Lang heard Johnson's report, he decided to abort the attack, without consulting Wilcox. He sent word to his regimental commanders "to move by the right flank as soon as they reached the woods in front." Lang hoped to find some shelter there from the artillery and to prepare his men either to resist the Union infantry or to retreat. He ignored his orders to conform the movements of his command to Wilcox's, and the two brigades effectively were on their own. The Floridians, sensing the opportunity for some kind of shelter in the trees, raced across the widening valley of Plum Run. The terrain was open here, but the belt of trees straddling the run itself and known as the Codori-Trostle Thicket was just ahead and to the right.[9]

The artillery fire that so punished the Rebels was coordinated by Henry J. Hunt. He saw the column approach Emmitsburg Road and first ordered McGilvery to fire and then rode to several batteries to the right, newly arrived from the artillery reserve, to tell them to open up, too. Rittenhouse delivered an enfilade fire on Wilcox and Lang from his perch on Little Round Top. Fifty-nine guns were firing on the two brigades by the time they neared the high point of their advance, and there were essentially no Rebel guns supporting them. The Federals used case shot and shell at longer ranges; then McGilvery switched to canister as the Confederates neared the bottom of the valley. Capt. Patrick Hart thought they were aiming directly for his 15th New York Battery in McGilvery's line. He loaded his tubes with double canister when the Rebels were still 300 yards away and kept it up until the end of the attack.[10]

Stannard's movements offered just as much of a threat to Wilcox and Lang as did the artillery. The Vermonters reacted to the Rebel advance with alacrity and decision. Col. Wheelock G. Veazey had already ordered his 16th Vermont to reform after it broke ranks to round up prisoners from among Pickett's remaining men. He then saw the approach of Wilcox and Lang to the south and, without orders, put his regiment in motion to meet them. Veazey ordered his men about-face and to march to the rear for about eighty yards. A staff officer came from Stannard with instructions to maneuver to his original position so as to fire on the new Rebel force. Veazey told him he already was responding to achieve that end, even though he would not resume his original position. Continuing his plan, Veazey then instructed the men to file right so they could move across the front of the 14th Vermont, which still faced due west. After clearing that regiment's front, he ordered his men to file left. This brought the 16th into line facing generally south and to the left rear of the 14th. The left flank of Lang's Florida brigade would soon be about 200 yards in front of the 16th, which had deployed at an oblique, or diagonal, to Lang's line of advance, rather than parallel to it.[11]

Col. Francis V. Randall naturally tried to move his 13th Vermont with Veazey, for the two had just a few minutes before so effectively joined forces to deliver fire into Pickett's flank. But Stannard noticed this and quickly sent an order for Randall to stop and resume his former position, facing west. Instead Stannard intended to move part of the 14th Vermont, which no longer was threatened to its front, to help Veazey. Four companies of Col. William T. Nichols's 14th were detached and moved forward to help the 16th.[12]

While the Federals maneuvered, Wilcox's Alabama brigade neared its high tide. The men reached the woods, which George Clark called "a scrubby-timbered drain just under the enemy's position." The two brigades had marched about 500 yards to reach this spot. Wilcox wanted to hold in the trees despite the relatively close-range artillery fire from McGilvery. He quickly rode back to the Rebel guns to arrange for support but, like Johnson before him, had no success. He asked the commanders

The upper part of Plum Run Valley, scene of the Wilcox-Lang attack; note how today, as in 1863, the landscape is open. This is also the area where Stannard's brigade was positioned. The Codori farm is on the right, and something of the Codori-Trostle Thicket remains on the far left. (author's collection)

of four different batteries to open on the Vermonters only to be told they had no ammunition left. With no reinforcements, no artillery support, and no sign of Pickett's men, "and knowing that my small force could do nothing save to make a useless sacrifice of themselves," Wilcox gave the order to retreat. The sight of Union troops approaching the left of Lang's brigade also hastened Wilcox's decision.[13]

The 16th Vermont started its forward advance toward Lang just before the Florida brigade entered the skirt of trees, but Lang found it impossible to offer much resistance to the Federals. As soon as his men entered the woods, they scattered to take shelter behind rocks and trees. McGilvery's guns were still firing into the skirt with canister at about 200 yards, and the Floridians had no intention of becoming useless casualties. The noise was so great that Lang had difficulty communicating with his officers. He was convinced that to remain in the woods would result in "certain annihilation." He decided to end an assault that one Union observer described as "a ridiculous demonstration." Lang tried to spread the word, but with the noise and the scattered condition of the men he could not pass it around quickly enough. Most men either heard

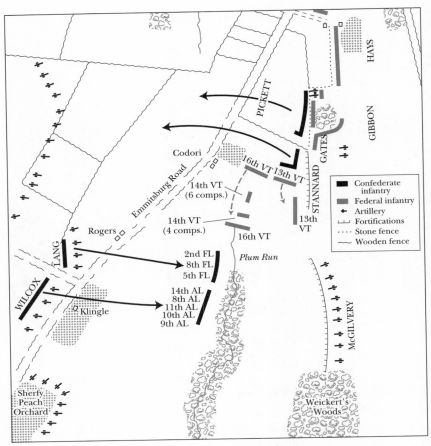

Map 8.1 Wilcox and Lang Attack

the orders or responded to the movements of those who did; others, hidden behind their shelter, failed to hear or see anything. The 2nd Florida, on the extreme left, had particular difficulty responding to Lang's instructions.[14]

As he did with the flanking maneuver against Pickett, Stannard took full credit for ordering the flanking maneuver against Wilcox and Lang. In truth, Veazey deserved at least as much credit, for the two men came to the same decision independently, although they disagreed on whether the 16th should advance toward the Rebels. Veazey suggested this course of action, but Stannard doubted its expediency. He thought the force was too small and the risk too great. "Why, you can't make your men go there, no men can do it," Veazey later recalled the conversation. "I tell you,

General, my men will do what I want them to." Veazey or some other officer asked the 16th if it would charge. "One terrific yell from our men was the response," recalled Lt. Col. Charles Cummings. Stannard thought a second and said to Veazey, "If you won't do as I want you to do, do as you are a mind to."[15]

Whether the conversation played out exactly this way, Stannard quickly gave in to Veazey's urging, and the 16th was off. The ground was open and descending, and the enemy offered virtually no resistance. The Vermonters plowed into the skirt of woods, cheering loudly, and easily gobbled up numerous prisoners, mostly from the 2nd Florida, which had not yet had time to organize a retreat. Veazey's men took the colors of that regiment, a "beautiful silk flag," and the colors of the 8th Florida as well. Veazey reported the taking of a third flag that was lost when the Federal who picked it up was hit by artillery fire. The 16th advanced nearly the full length of the position occupied by the two Rebel brigades, snapping up the remaining soldiers. Because Wilcox's brigade had already retreated before this time, there appears to have been no contact between the Union infantry and the Alabamans. Veazey was immensely proud of his men. "They made the changes of front first to the right and then to the left with almost the precision of a parade," he later gloated. The four companies of the 14th Vermont sent to help him showed up just as the advance stopped in the woods; thus the 16th was solely responsible for clearing the Rebels from high tide. Veazey had many prisoners, but he could not spare men to take them to the rear. They were, in his words, docile and cooperative, and when told where to go, they eagerly sought safety behind Cemetery Ridge.[16]

Stannard was hit by shrapnel just as Veazey began his advance. This presaged the resumption of Confederate artillery fire, finally, but it was several minutes too late and far too little to help Wilcox and Lang. A shrapnel ball inflicted a painful but not disabling injury by striking Stannard's right leg and passing three inches down into his thigh muscle. The stubborn general refused to leave the field until the last shot was fired.[17]

Both Wilcox and Lang lost heavily and accomplished little. Two of the three regiments of the Florida brigade lost their flags. The 2nd Florida color was indeed a beautiful and special banner. Governor John Milton of that state had gathered the best silk, and the women of Tallahassee had sewn it. D. M. Pogue carried the flag into the attack but soon had his left foot torn off by a shell. Then another man named Cob carried it into the trees; but he was also wounded, and the flag was left lying on the ground to be picked up by Veazey's men. The flag of the 5th Florida also made it into the woods despite the falling of several color-bearers. Afraid the flag might be captured, Capt. Junius Taylor tore it from the staff and hid it under his shirt. Thus it was saved. Members of the 16th Vermont found the staff stripped of its flag and turned it over to Veazey.[18]

Among the prisoners taken were James Wentworth, a lieutenant in the 8th Florida. He had been stunned and knocked to the ground by a shell explosion just before the Vermonters struck. When he regained consciousness, everything around him seemed confused. Wentworth jumped up, waved his sword, and tried to rally the men, only to realize that the dead and wounded were all that remained. A Vermont private approached him with an invitation to surrender, but Wentworth haughtily refused to give himself up to anyone of lesser rank than his own. The Yankee uttered an oath and brought forward a lieutenant, and Wentworth officially became a prisoner.[19]

Those men of both brigades who escaped the woods — most of Wilcox's and probably more than half of Lang's — had to endure Federal artillery fire all the way. Lang's men retreated by their right flank up a shallow ravine or depression that connected Emmitsburg Road with Plum Run Valley; it offered some little shelter from the rain of shells. Capt. William E. McCaslin of the 2nd Florida was killed by the artillery just after he remarked to Capt. C. Seton Fleming "that no matter how one escaped the dangers of any particular battle, he was exposed to the same in the next, and it seemed impossible to pass in safety through them all." The survivors of both brigades made it back to the breastwork that marked their starting point and counted themselves lucky to have passed through yet another ordeal.[20]

Just before he reached the breastwork, Lang happened on Wilcox drinking from a spring. He stopped, and the two talked for several minutes. This was the only direct contact they had before or during the attack. Despite Wilcox's indifference to his colleague, the two commanders had coordinated their movements well. Lang was always perplexed and a bit hurt that Wilcox never mentioned his brigade in this action, as if the Alabamans conducted the attack alone. He could only assume that Wilcox had been reluctant to make the advance at all and preferred not to detail its conduct.[21]

Stannard's men were jubilant about their double victory over two Rebel columns. Members of the 14th Vermont who had been sent to support the 16th were desperate to get their licks in and opened fire,

Col. David Lang, whose Florida brigade attacked in line with Wilcox's brigade in the doomed advance (Cook Collection, Valentine Museum, Richmond, Va.)

even though there was really no need for it. Company officers tried to stop the shooting. "One or two men, in their excitement, paid no heed to the order and kept on firing till fairly collared by Major Hall." Stannard then sent all of his units back to the positions they had held before the approach of Pickett's division. This was a more dangerous maneuver than expected, for Confederate artillery fire had begun to pick up alarmingly. When the 13th Vermont moved in column to its former position, staff officer George Benedict heard a "*thud* and cry of horror close behind" him. He turned around to see "a cruel gap" in the ranks. Five men, including the lieutenant colonel, had been hit, and three of them had been killed instantly. One man's body was dismembered; his leg, shorn of all clothing save the shoe and sock, was thrown several feet away. The gory scene repulsed the men marching behind these unfortunate soldiers in the column. They instinctively halted and drew back, but then recovered quickly and stepped over the mangled bodies.[22]

The Wilcox-Lang attack was ordered too late, and it was too poorly coordinated with Pickett's attack, to do much good. By the time the two understrength brigades closed with the Unionists, the tide had turned against Pickett. The Federal artillery had little difficulty blunting the advance and probably would have compelled the retreat without any involvement by the Union infantry. Cadmus Wilcox told Hunt after the war that the guns alone stopped his assault. For his part, Hunt correctly noted that his artillery fire would have been divided and less effective if the two attacks had occurred simultaneously. As it was, the guns could concentrate their maximum fire on each column, Pickett and Wilcox-Lang, in turn. Had the Alabamans and Floridians accomplished anything to justify their losses? Randolph Abbott Shotwell of Garnett's brigade thought so. He noted that their attack "diverted the attention of the enemy from the stragglers of Pickett's division, and enabled a considerable number of them to escape." There is every reason to accept Shotwell's opinion, for he was retreating when the assault swept by.[23]

Despite that meager accomplishment, there is ample room for criticizing the attack. Wilcox and Lang had no opportunity to help Pickett break through the Union line, and Confederate units farther to their right were not used to help them in their own attack. Longstreet never sent orders to either Law's or McLaws's division to advance or demonstrate in their favor. This came as a surprise to members of Lee's staff, who were under the distinct impression that Lee had authorized their use in the early morning conference. McLaws categorically denied there was ever any intention of using these two divisions.[24]

Longstreet had no such reluctance to use troops to the left of the assaulting column. Fairly early in the advance, when it became apparent that Pettigrew's left wing was in trouble, he sent orders to Anderson to go forward and support it. Anderson instructed Wright's Georgia and Posey's Mississippi brigades to advance. As with Wilcox and Lang, the timing of this advance was too late. The Rebels gamely went forward. One Union artilleryman claimed they made it to within 200 yards of the Federal line, while Col. Samuel E. Baker reported that five companies of his 16th Mississippi advanced only fifty yards—the rest were on skirmish duty. However far they went availed them little, for the attack had already been repulsed. Longstreet noted this and sent orders for Anderson to withdraw. Harry Lewis of the 16th Mississippi was glad to receive this order; "it saved many lives, and while we were willing to go to the last man, we were thankful for it." The retreat was rather more enthusiastic than the advance, for corps commander Hill had little luck when he tried to rally the men in a forward position in the valley. They continued to retreat all the way to Seminary Ridge.[25]

THE REPULSE

The attack was finally over about 3:00 P.M., having lasted one hour, but the artillery fire never really ended. The Rebel gunners were gaining a second wind by this time and scrounged up enough long-range ammunition to lay down a spotty but, in places, deadly covering fire to support the Confederate retreat. One round grazed the hand of Lt. William O. Blodgett of the 151st Pennsylvania, tore the skin off two fingers, and bruised his thumb and tore the thumbnail off. The Federal guns were forced to continue firing in self-defense. Andrew Cowan stripped off his coat and directed the fire of one of his guns in this duel, while staff officer Banes brought up a section of the 13th New York Battery to replace Rorty's damaged unit. More guns from the Sixth Corps came up to bolster the line from the angle northward. Additional infantry came up after the repulse as well, the result of well-meaning efforts by several corps leaders to lend support to their comrades. Sent early in the assault, they arrived after their services were no longer needed. Brig. Gen. John C. Robinson's division of the First Corps deployed to Hays's right to fill out more firmly the space between the Second Corps and the Eleventh Corps on Cemetery Hill. Newton positioned other units of the First Corps on his right to take any Confederate force that broke through Hancock's line in flank. Two brigades from the Twelfth Corps at Culp's Hill came up at least as far as the Leister house to offer their help as well. Plenty of extra men were available to deal with anything that could develop in the latter stages of the attack.[26]

·······

THE RETREAT

Already repulsed by the men who made up the main Union line, the Confederates could do nothing but try to save themselves. Retreating was an ordeal that many of them preferred not to attempt, for going back to Seminary Ridge was an extremely hazardous undertaking. They had to fall back over open country with an excited and victorious enemy firing at them within musket range for at least a third of the way and within artillery range the entire distance. It would be just as deadly, even more so, than advancing into the teeth of the Union defenses.

Therefore it is not surprising that many surviving Confederates at high tide debated whether they should even try to retreat. "To remain was life in prison," reasoned Lt. William Nathaniel Wood of the 19th Virginia. "To retreat was probably death in crossing the field, but possible safety within our lines." Wood quickly made his decision; "I turned my back to the fence and started across." He had been bruised on the leg during the advance but fortunately received only a scratch on the torso on the way back.[27]

Capt. John Holmes Smith and Capt. Robert W. Douthat, both of the 11th Virginia, had a more difficult time disengaging from the enemy. Smith tarried to the last to bandage his wounded thigh, cutting a towel into strips. Douthat remained with him, firing an abandoned musket to cover him. Then Smith noticed the Federals approaching and struggled to his feet. "It's time to get away from here," Douthat said. Both men made their way as fast as possible and were not bothered for about 100 yards. Then the musketry began to search them out. "We ran out of range," Smith remembered, "shot after shot falling around us until we go over the Emmittsburg road toward our lines." As soon as the men made it across the pike, the infantry fire ceased to threaten them, and the pair had a lonely walk across the body-strewn field back to Spangler's Woods.[28]

Randolph Abbott Shotwell retired fighting. He picked up an abandoned musket but did not realize it already had three or four rounds improperly loaded in the barrel. When he tried to fire, it "kicked so violently as to nearly cause me to turn a summersault." Finding another gun, Shotwell joined about a dozen men just on the north side of Emmitsburg Road, where the group held and shot at the Yankees for a time. The approach of Federal troops sent them scurrying to the rear, but no one except Shotwell made it back to safety. He believed that one or two of the group deliberately dropped to the ground to save themselves while the rest were hit. Exhausted and depressed, Shotwell came across Capt. Charles F. Linthicum, former chaplain of his regiment and now assistant adjutant general on Garnett's staff. The captain stood on the ground, leaning against his horse and sobbing as he instructed the retreating men where to go. "There are none left," Linthicum said when asked about the attack; "the brigade is gone, the division is gone, and our Noble General too."[29]

To observers who saw the men come back across the valley, there seemed to be order, even bravery in their retirement. Lt. William Alexander Gordon, an engineer officer temporarily attached to Pickett's division, was "particularly impressed by the appearance the men made in coming back, so slowly and so deliberately that at first I thought they were wounded men or prisoners." They probably maintained their composure because of their proximity to the enemy; brave and disciplined men under fire, they did not want to present the appearance of running from danger. As they neared Seminary Ridge, however, Pickett met them and gave orders to retreat past the ridge all the way to their bivouac ground of the night before or, according to some reports, all the way to the division trains parked along Chambersburg Pike. This seems to have broken down their inhibitions. Now well out of danger and with the enormity of their defeat sinking in, the survivors of Pickett's division soon turned into a sullen mob intent on getting as far as possible from the bloody battlefield. They had lost their spirit and discipline as they crowded down Pitzer Lane and tried to cross Willoughby's Run. Here bluffs on one side and a swamp on the other formed a bottleneck. Exhausted men threw away their guns, haversacks, and blankets as they tried to push their way through and tempers flared.[30]

Capt. Henry T. Owen of the 18th Virginia tried to impose some order on this mob. Owen had earlier tried to reform the retreating Rebels at the artillery line but had no luck. Now he managed to recruit about thirty men from different regiments and place them across the road to stop the retiring soldiers and force them to reform ranks and files. He had collected nearly 300 men when Pickett came riding up with tears in his eyes. The division leader told Owen not to detain his men but to let them go farther to the rear. Hearing this, every one of the detainees claimed to belong to Pickett's division, and soon the floodgates were open again. Soon after Pickett left, Owen reestablished his picket line and collected a couple hundred more men. Maj. Charles Marshall of Lee's staff then rode up and told Owen that many stragglers were flanking his pickets. Marshall advised him to reestablish his line farther to the rear. Owen's dedication to duty was impressive, but his efforts were like throwing a stone into a raging mountain stream. The division could not be reorganized until the men had retreated all the way to where their commander had told them to go. Owen was forever ashamed that his comrades had "commenced a rout that soon increased to a stampede and almost demoralization of all the survivors of this noted charge without distinction of regiments or commands." Capt. Jedediah Hotchkiss, an engineer on the Second Corps staff, encountered Pickett's retreating men, "scattered all along the road — no officers and all protesting that they had been completely cut up."[31]

Ironically, there was enough organization left in some units to secure the few prisoners taken as the division neared the stone fence. The 14th Virginia claimed about thirty Federal prisoners brought out by the survivors of the regiment on their return.[32]

James Kemper, Pickett's only brigade commander to come back from the assault, was nearly killed while being transported in an ambulance along Pitzer Lane to the rear for treatment. A Federal shell grazed the top of the ambulance, tipping it over and throwing the badly wounded general into an agonized tumble. The ambulance driver recruited a passing soldier to help him carry Kemper in the same blanket that had been his stretcher since he was picked up on the battlefield. The pair struggled with the wounded man all the way to the division field hospital.[33]

Kemper was not the only Rebel to be harassed by long-range Union fire. Pvt. James W. Clay of the 18th Virginia was horrified to see a wounded lieutenant badly mangled by a shell. It hit him in the head, "leaving only the lower part of his face, with mustache and goatee."[34]

The survivors in Pettigrew's division had equally difficult passages to the rear. John H. Moore of the 7th Tennessee fell back to Emmitsburg Road, where he found the roadbed littered with dead, wounded, and frightened but unhurt comrades. The roar of musketry and artillery added to the groans of the injured to intensify the "horrid confusion in the lane." Moore and many of his fellow soldiers who had been close to the Union position hesitated only a few moments at the road. They were impressed by the rain of bullets and shells, noting that the slab fence on the east side of the road "was splintered and riddled, and the very grass was scorched and withered by the heat" of shell bursts. They decided to run for it. Maj. A. S. Van de Graaff, commander of the 5th Alabama Battalion, had retreated back to the road and lay down to rest a few minutes in its shelter before running back to Seminary Ridge, unhurt but "overheated and broken down."[35]

Sgt. June Kimble of the 14th Tennessee retreated to the road and picked up a Mississippi rifle, with which he took aim at a Federal artilleryman who, with one foot on the stone fence at the angle, was firing his pistol at the retreating Rebels. Kimble thought he was a pretty good shot, but every round failed to take effect. Finally he turned to a young soldier of Armistead's brigade who was nearby and said, "Shoot that fellow in the red shirt to the left." The young man exclaimed, "Why dam him, I have shot at him four times. I am going out of here." The Virginian no sooner got up than he was hit in the back of the head and died instantly. The sight impressed Kimble, who now debated about his own course of action. At first he thought it safer to surrender. No sooner did he lay down his gun and unbuckle his accouterments than "prison bars loomed up before me." He quickly grabbed his equipment and ran for his life. He raced about 100 yards until the bullets zipping past reminded him how disgraceful it would be to receive a wound in the back. Then Kimble gained control of his nerves, faced the enemy, and walked backward toward Seminary Ridge until he was well out of range. He seemed to live a charmed life. Kimble was not scratched either going in or coming out, and he preserved his dignity.[36]

Seminary Ridge was not entirely safe, as Capt. F. S. Harris of the 7th Tennessee discovered. He had made it that far when he witnessed another example of how artillery fire could destroy its victims. A man nicknamed Black Ram was helping Capt. Robert Miller to the field hospital when a shell came screaming toward them. Ram dropped his captain and lurched several feet to the left to avoid it but unwittingly jumped directly into its path. The shell hit his shoulder and exploded at the same instant; it "literally tore him into a thousand pieces and dug a great hole into the ground."[37]

As with all other units in the Confederate attacking column, Marshall's brigade never received a general order to retreat. Capt. Benjamin F. Little, who lay severely wounded a few yards in front of Smyth's brigade, wrote after the war that "Officers and men were about that time mowed down so rapidly, and the fighting so hot, that orders could not be heard if given." Pettigrew's men simply retreated on their own initiative or on orders from their company officers. Capt. Thomas J. Cureton of the 26th North Carolina retired from the road and came across "a solitary man on foot." He soon saw that it was Pettigrew nursing his injured hand. When Cureton asked if he could be of assistance, Pettigrew thanked him and "offered me his unwounded arm, and I assisted him up the steep hill to the artillery." Pettigrew instructed Cureton to form a line and rally the division just to the rear of the artillery. The men responded quickly, and soon the remnants of the division were in hand. Cureton noted that the few men from Pickett's division who straggled this far north refused to stop but continued to the rear, where their own units were ordered to assemble.[38]

Colonel Lowrance reported that his men in Trimble's division were "reduced to mere squads" and that they therefore could not act as a brigade. Groups and individuals took it upon themselves to retire when they wanted to, "leaving many on the field unable to get off, and some, I fear, unwilling to undertake the hazardous retreat." Augustus Evander Floyd of the 18th North Carolina in Lane's brigade was hit by a bullet in the thigh, yet he did not allow this injury to prevent him from running to the rear. He rested near the artillery before making his way to a field hospital, where the surgeon discovered that his pants had not been torn by the ball, just driven into the large hole made through the flesh.[39]

The men who remained on Emmitsburg Road or near the stone fence on Pickett's front were quickly taken prisoner by the Yankees, who advanced in the first flush of enthusiasm following their triumph over the Rebels. John C. Timberlake of Armistead's brigade, one of the small band that had followed the brigade leader into the angle, was captured while tending to a wounded comrade. He was cutting clothes into strips for bandages when he suddenly looked up to see several musket barrels pointing at him. A Federal captain demanded his surrender. "I said to him if you cant wait until I finish this job shoot on." The Yankee allowed him to finish his merciful task, then Timberlake handed over his sword. "Your a Damn Brave set of fellows," said the Yankee captain, "but you couldent come it this time." Timberlake pointed to more Rebel troops off in the distance and replied, "if they had come[,] would . . . we have come it[?] he replyed by Saying I think you would."[40]

Near this scene Capt. James R. Hutter of the 11th Virginia lay near the stone fence nursing a wound. Capt. John Ward was giving him water when a Federal sergeant came up and said, "Gentlemen you are prisoners of war." Ward blurted, "By God sir that remains to be seen." The sergeant failed to take this warning seriously and allowed Ward to help Hutter. The captain could find no wound in his back, only scrapes where Hutter had been struck by a spent bullet. When the Federal sergeant's attention was turned elsewhere, the pair sprang up and ran for their lives. They made it partway back to Emmitsburg Road before they were intercepted by other Federal troops and taken in.[41]

The members of Fry's brigade who remained at Emmitsburg Road were taken prisoner as soon as the Federals stopped firing and advanced to the road. Col. Newton J. George of the 1st Tennessee, too badly wounded to escape, was approached by a Federal private who rudely demanded his surrender. When George told him he preferred to deal with an officer, the Yankee cursed him and threatened to run him through with a bayonet. Another private approached Col. John A. Fite of the 7th Tennessee and said, "I'll take you up and let you surrender to my officer." The polite private introduced Fite to Major Ellis of the 14th Connecticut, who not only accepted the Rebel's sword but demanded his scabbard, too. Fite and George were put under the charge of a guard, but the two refused to move until they had drunk a toast from Fite's flask to "them boys down yonder." Confederate artillery began to play on the area, causing the guard to shout, "Come on they'll kill you," and run. Fite and George made their way slowly to the Bryan barn, where they took shelter for a time before continuing to the rear.[42]

These men were fortunately spared the agony suffered by W. H. Winchester, a lieutenant in the 13th North Carolina. Winchester was badly wounded in the right foot, which was "shot off at the ankle, except the heel-string." He refused to stay put and began to crawl back toward Seminary Ridge. A soldier of his company saw him on the way, and Winchester begged him to cut his heel string. The man refused to do it but was willing to hold the mangled limb while Winchester performed the emergency operation on himself. The gutsy lieutenant could not crawl fast enough to escape; he was taken prisoner and died a month later in Federal hands.[43]

Lt. George W. Finley of the 56th Virginia stayed near the angle because he thought it was his duty to wait until support troops arrived, even if that seemed impossible. After a time it became apparent that to retreat was almost certain death. Finley remembered that he came to this conclusion because when he glanced rearward every few minutes, he noticed how the ground was increasingly dotted with bodies. Then when the Yankees pressed forward and came over the fence, he had no choice but to surrender. Other men were simply too badly injured to even think about retiring. Maj. J. McLeod Turner of the 7th North Carolina found the lower part of his body paralyzed. His men wanted to carry him back to Seminary Ridge, but he thought the stress would kill him and he refused to risk their lives in the process. He told them to go back without him. Turner waited patiently in the roadside ditch for the Federals to come forward and help him.[44]

Lt. Stephen F. Brown of the 13th Vermont gained a kind of fame by engaging in what can only be described as a bizarre act of bravado mixed with greed. When an officer of Pickett's division was being led into the Union lines as a prisoner, Brown waved a camp hatchet in his face and demanded the Rebel give up his sword and scabbard. Brown had lost his own sword several days earlier when Stannard placed him under arrest for allowing his men to obtain water from a well without authorization. He was released from arrest before the battle, but the sword was never returned to him. Brown, buoyed by adrenaline and feeling his oats, desperately wanted a sword and saw his chance to steal one from a prisoner. For some reason this incident became famous after the war and even led to the erection of his likeness atop the regimental monument on the battlefield.[45]

While some Rebels, like the officer who gave his sword to Brown, meekly came into Union lines, many others were well enough to run but undecided if it was the wise course of action. They were caught in a kind of limbo and lacked the decisive spirit to take charge of their fate. As a result many of them wavered between freedom, with its enormous chance for personal injury, and captivity, with its dreary future. The Federals encouraged these wavering souls to give up. The prisoners crouched low to avoid the Confederate artillery fire. When Capt. John D. S. Cook of the 80th New York saw a white rag appear behind a bush, he yelled encouragement, and a dozen Rebels emerged from behind it to give themselves up. Col. Theodore Gates reported that many Rebels who ran toward Seminary Ridge had second thoughts, stopped, turned around, and came in to surrender. Their initial determination to escape often conflicted with the blunt realization that it could not pay. A group of 7th Tennesseeans debated the choice as they lay at Emmitsburg Road. "Let's never surrender," said one, but then a bullet hit him in the head and killed him instantly. Another said, "They've got to get more blood out of me than they have before I ever surrender." He began to run and was badly wounded before he made more than twenty steps. No wonder so many Rebels decided to save themselves by giving up.[46]

Lt. Richard Ferguson of the 18th Virginia was in a similar quandary. He lay on the ground and fired incessantly at the approaching Yankees because he believed it was "certain death" to run. But soon he also realized that fighting was worse than useless; the many wounded men around him begged the feisty lieutenant to stop, as the return fire endangered them. Ferguson then tried to disguise himself as a wounded man, but the advancing Federals saw through his ploy and took him in.[47]

W. P. Heflin of the 11th Mississippi was badly wounded in the foot and ankle and thus could not run. Yet Heflin tried to get his retreating comrades to carry him to the rear, to no avail. He then had to treat with the approaching Yankees. One of them helped him struggle to the Bryan shack at the junction of Bryan Lane and Emmitsburg Road, where he took shelter from the Confederate artillery fire. When a shell came tearing through the house, Heflin cajoled a Yankee into supporting him as he hobbled all the way across Cemetery Ridge to join the other prisoners.[48]

J. A. Bush Sr. of the 26th North Carolina endured a terrible ordeal while wandering in the no-man's-land between the lines. He was hit by five bullets "in less than five minutes" near the height of the attack. Bush almost bled to death and then was nearly hit a sixth time by Yankees who were shooting at a wounded officer. This officer was crawling near Bush at the time, trying to make it back to his own lines, which drew an oath from the badly wounded enlisted man. The officer finally turned around and crawled toward the Union line to give himself up. Bush suffered horribly from thirst and called out for water. Sgt. Alexander Dunlap of his regiment heard him and yelled that he had a canteen but could not bring it to him, as his leg was broken. Bush tried to rise and walk to the sergeant, but he was too weak. Falling down, he rolled a short distance down the grassy slope and ended up near a dead man who had a half-full canteen. Bush nursed this precious supply all afternoon until the Federals finally ventured far enough afield to take charge of him.[49]

· · · · · · ·

PRISONERS AND TROPHIES

As the prisoners were gathered on the battlefield, there was ample time for the exchange of words between captor and captive. In these first few minutes of their detainment several Rebels interacted, probably for the first time, with their enemy. A Virginia officer saw Col. Arthur Devereux holding several Confederate flags and said, "You Yanks think you've done a great thing now." Devereux, full of the flush of victory, responded, "It's our turn, . . . remember Fredericksburg." Many others echoed this Rebel's sentiment with comments such as "You have done it this time" to their captors. On Hays's front the stunned survivors of Pettigrew and Trimble were astonished to see so few Yankees manning the stone fence when they were brought into Union lines. "Where are your men?" asked one of them, "I mean those you had here who gave us such volleys as we advanced?" When told the thin line was all that stood in his way, the Rebel exclaimed, "We could have *gone through* if we had another line of men!" He then thought a moment and added, "My God! we could have gone through as it was if we'd known how few you were! . . . I'd like to try it again!" No one seems to have explained to this observant Confederate that the lack of manpower was compensated for by the stockpile of weapons each man had on this part of the line.[50]

Birkett D. Fry was brought in wounded after the repulse and was surprised to see a Federal soldier "with an ugly wound in his shoulder, which he told me he received from the spear on the end of one of my regimental colors." Fry actually knew what the man was talking about. He recalled laughing at the color-bearer of the 13th Alabama who had found a lance head before the battle and attached it to the end of the flagstaff. Little did he know that it would indeed be used as a weapon.[51]

The Confederate prisoners had to leave the battlefield under a hail of their own artillery fire, the final danger imposed on them during the attack. Most ran quickly, bending and crouching to lessen the chance of getting hit. William Peel was delighted to see the Yankees scurry about as well. A lot of blue-coated stragglers hid behind trees and rocks on the opposite slope of Cemetery Ridge as he passed by. Many of the prisoners were put in charge of the 10th New York Battalion, which had been doing provost duty along Taneytown Road. At some point in the attack Meade noticed them in position and ordered the battalion forward to help fight, probably irritated that his earlier order to bring forward all provost troops to reinforce the line had not been fully implemented. Dressed in their Zouave jackets and baggy blue pants, the eighty-two men of the battalion were led forward by Maj. George F. Hopper. They met a crowd of hurrying prisoners coming over the crest of Cemetery Ridge, hounded by Rebel shells. Hopper began to organize as many captives as he could, assembling several hundred of them before the day was over. The prisoners were exposed to their own fire for nearly a half-mile, finding relief from it only when they reached Baltimore Pike well to the rear.[52]

Franklin Sawyer's 8th Ohio was in a unique position to gather prisoners. It had advanced far along Emmitsburg Road during the repulse and extended its men in a single file as far as possible to nab retreating Rebels. Later when a staff officer brought word to bring the regiment back to Cemetery Ridge, Sawyer placed half of his men in front, the prisoners in the middle, and the rest in the rear with bayonets fixed. It was an impressive sight, a little more than 100 Federals bringing in about 200 prisoners. As the 8th crossed the Union line, brigade leader Col. Samuel S. Carroll jumped onto one of Woodruff's guns and shouted, "Look, you fellows! — there comes my old 8th with the balance of Lee's army!"[53]

The 8th Ohio was not the only regiment to take in more prisoners than it had men on duty. Lt. William Hawley of the 14th Connecticut wrote that "hundreds of Rebs true down their arms & rushed right into our line & surrendered," burdening the 14th with about 200 captives. The 12th New Jersey claimed 500 Confederate prisoners, and the 111th New York reportedly gathered more than 400 Rebels. Webb reported taking in about 1,000 of Pickett's defeated troops. Hays's division claimed between 1,500 and 2,000 captives. The total number of Confederates taken prisoner was estimated at 3,750.[54]

This total meant that Pickett's Charge yielded one of the largest number of Rebel prisoners taken by the Army of the Potomac. Lee lost 7,700 captives, the largest suffered by his command, at the battles along Sailor's Creek on April 6, 1865. Pickett's Charge saw the second costliest loss of prisoners, to be followed by the Federal assault on the Mule Shoe Salient at Spotsylvania on May 12, 1864, where 3,000 Confederates were taken. It is possible that Grant's forces captured about the same number of prisoners on April 2, 1865, when they broke Lee's line at Petersburg, as Meade did on July 3. Confederate casualties amounted to 4,852 on April 2, most of whom were taken prisoner.[55]

The triumphant Federals not only gathered large numbers of prisoners, but they also garnered a rich lode of battlefield trophies. The capture of enemy flags was considered a great achievement by Civil War armies. The Army of the Potomac had usually taken one or two in previous engagements. Now it claimed more Rebel flags than on any other day of battle during the entire war. Thirty-eight banners were taken this day, while a total of forty-one were taken by Meade's army during the Gettysburg campaign. The second highest number of Rebel flags lost on the battlefield occurred during the Nashville campaign of December 1864 when the Army of Tennessee collapsed and fled in disorder. It has been estimated that eleven Rebel flags crossed the stone fence, and all were either captured from the bearer when the Federals counterattacked or simply picked up by trophy hunters. In many cases the capture of enemy flags was considered worthy of further reward. Twenty-four Medals of Honor were awarded to Federal soldiers for repelling the attack, including Webb, Wheelock G. Veazey, Edmund Rice, and Frederick Fuger. Fifteen of those medals were awarded for the capture of enemy flags.[56]

In some cases the award was earned. A few of these medal winners actually took a flag from the Rebel color-bearer. But in many other cases those men credited with "taking" a color had simply picked one up from the ground. The colors of the 53rd Virginia were essentially abandoned when the color guard was decimated. Eight of the ten men composing the guard were killed, and two bearers were severely wounded. Pvt. Anthony McDermott of the 69th Pennsylvania found little honor in claiming an abandoned color. "It was just like picking up muskets that had been thrown down," he later commented. McDermott was too busy gathering prisoners to make an effort to take a flag he clearly saw, its staff leaning against the stone fence. By the time he neared it, a soldier of the 42nd New York dashed past, grabbed it, and ran back to his unit. McDermott yelled that he "did not see anything very brave in that" as the New Yorker ran past. "I could have had that flag without any trouble," he later wrote, "and if I thought acts like that would have brought a medal, its more than likely I would have preferred the flag to the gathering up of prisoners." Altogether, Webb's brigade claimed six flags. The 19th Massachusetts alone, in Hall's brigade, claimed four flags.[57]

Hays's division took a lot of flags, although the exact number is difficult to ascertain due to conflicting evidence. The 14th Connecticut claimed at least five flags, although many members believed that a sixth color was taken but never turned in to the officers. It apparently was sent home by someone. The first flag taken by the 14th Connecticut was that of the 14th Tennessee. Just after the repulse and before the Yankees swept across the fence, the Rebel color was seen leaning, unattended, against the rail fence that extended northward from the angle. "You ought to have heard the boys beg the Major to let them go out & capture the Reb. flag," wrote William Hawley. Permission was finally given, and Sgt. Maj. Will Hincks and two officers leaped across the fence and raced for it. Hincks was the first there. Later another member of the 14th Connecticut grabbed the flag of the 1st Tennessee just when the Rebels grouped around it raised a handkerchief in token of surrender. Flag bearer Wiley Woods recalled that the Yankee said "he reckon I would give him this, I told I reckon he would let me go with him." Both crossed the stone fence together, and the Federal left Wood to consult with someone. While he was gone, two more Unionists approached Wood and demanded the flag, but Wood refused. Only when the first man returned did Wood give up his precious charge. A Federal officer added insult by telling Wood that he did not know how to handle the color; he thought it should be trailed in the dust instead of held proudly in the air.[58]

The 1st Delaware took five flags, but one was stolen by an unidentified soldier. Lt. William Smith seized a color and brought it back to show Hays and Lt. John L. Brady, thus verifying his claim to it. But then Smith started with it toward brigade headquarters and was nearly cut in two by a Rebel shell. When his body was later found, not only had it been stripped of personal belongings, including his insignia of rank, but the flag had been taken as well. Brady later hinted that he suspected a member of the 39th New York, that unit of miscreants, but the flag and the belongings were never recovered. The 8th Ohio also had a flag taken from its "captor." The regiment claimed three colors, but a fourth one was picked up by Sergeant Miller of Company B, who later lost it to an unidentified officer.[59]

Hays was ecstatic following the repulse. When a staff officer came up to pass on Meade's compliments for the work accomplished, some soldiers nearby called out "hard-tack" to signify that congratulations were all well and good, but they were hungry. Hays told the officer, "Never mind me, the honor and credit is all due to these gallant boys. They are hungry, send them up some rations." Then the division leader turned to his own staff members and asked for a captured Rebel flag and insisted that Capt. George P. Corts and Lt. David Shields do the same and follow him. Hays and his subordinates dropped their captured colors on the ground and rode on, trailing them in the "dust and blood of the battlefield." With Rebel artillery fire coming in and prisoners still trickling by, the three men rode behind the division line to the right and then traversed the front as well. They had to "weave in and out" to avoid the wounded. The soldiers of Hays's division cheered this ride as a sort of triumphal procession. They threw their caps in the air and hugged one another. Hays meant to show his "utter disdain" for these symbols of rebellion, and his two young staff officers thoroughly enjoyed the little display.[60]

David Shields later offered a detailed and unflattering description of the flags his division accumulated. They were "mostly home-made affairs like a bed spread, of pieces of muslin sewed together, and even flannel, calico and muslin together. Torn by battle, dirty, and cheap looking, no wonder our boys designated them 'rebel rags.' The inscriptions were made by sewing on the letters. Some were more pretentious; when new, no doubt more agreeable to view. Some had a regimental description only. Seven had the names of battles inscribed on them."[61]

The scramble for trophies produced some fighting among the Federals. Norman Hall reported that several flags were stolen from enlisted men of his brigade by officers. "Death is too light a punishment for such a dastardly offense," he rather sternly commented. Pvt. William Deming of the 7th Michigan was thus accosted by an unidentified officer and threatened with the point of a sword until he gave up his flag. Farther to the left of the line, battery commander Patrick Hart sent men into the skirt of woods in Plum Run Valley to retrieve flags dropped by Lang's brigade. He believed McGilvery's artillery was primarily responsible for stopping the Floridians, and thus, he said, "Those flags ware mine by every honorable right." But the infantrymen of Stannard's brigade claimed them before the gunners could arrive. Hart reported this to Hunt, but the artillery chief cautioned him that he could not force the infantry to give them up.[62]

The Vermonters also ran afoul of Gates's demibrigade. Several of them paraded by Gates "with great ceremony," carrying a gilt eagle they had picked up on the battlefield, assuming it belonged to a Rebel color. But the eagle had actually been shot off the staff of the 80th New York flag. Gates and Capt. John D. S. Cook instantly recognized it and confronted the Vermonters. They had to take their case all the way to Meade's chief of staff but eventually retrieved the eagle. A member of the 80th also claimed that some men of Stannard's brigade had taken a flag he had picked up. The New Yorkers were not so lucky this time. Army headquarters told them not to press the issue, "saying there was glory enough for all of us anyway."[63]

The biggest confrontation occurred between Hays and Webb, and it started with a report by Richard Penn Smith that his 71st Pennsylvania had captured a Rebel flag that members of Hays's division later took. Webb sent a staff officer to inquire. Hays was just then relaxing at his headquarters with Clinton MacDougall, who recalled a pile of twenty-one flags lying on the ground. When Webb's officer explained the complaint, Hays retorted, "How in h—l did I get them if he captured them?" But the division leader decided to be magnanimous and sarcastic all in the same gesture. He called for David Shields and told him to pick out a half-dozen flags for Webb, "as a present, with my compliments; we have so many here we don't know what to do with them and Webb needs them." The insult was not wasted on Webb. He later confided to his wife that Hays "is not capable of commanding a Brigade. He is a real specimen of a weak ignorant political appointment. He is nothing but a personally brave man. No head no education & vulgar beyond measure." Refusing to be associated with him through their West Point connection, Webb decided Hays was "what we call a bogus Regular."[64]

THE REPULSE

THE FEDERALS REGROUP

While the Federals were still grabbing flags, collecting prisoners, and congratulating themselves on their victory, the Rebel artillery intensified its fire on the angle area. It quickly became apparent that no new assaults were under way. It was time to regroup, both physically and psychologically. The "intense feelings" engendered by the attack were subsiding among James Wright's comrades in the 1st Minnesota, to be followed by what he called "the usual relaxation." After two days of tense fighting and heavy losses, the Minnesotans realized that "they were bordering upon a condition of collapse." Many Federals in other units were blackened by the powder smoke, and everyone was drenched with sweat and covered with grime. The burning sun beat down at midafternoon, and there was precious little drinking water available.[65]

Andrew Cowan remembered a poignant moment that occurred at this point. Into his battery position wandered Samuel Wilkeson, correspondent for the *New York Times*. The two had met during the Peninsula campaign more than a year before, when Cowan had detained the journalist overnight, suspecting he might be a spy. Now the two exchanged pleasantries even as the gunners collected harness, stockpiled more ammunition, and generally prepared the battery for further action. Wilkeson and Cowan walked up to the stone fence and surveyed the horrible scene. Dead and wounded Rebels littered the ground, and wisps of smoke still drifted northward. Wilkeson told the gunner that his nineteen-year-old son, Bayard, an artillery lieutenant with the Eleventh Corps, had been mortally wounded two days before north of Gettysburg. Yet he dutifully made the rounds to collect material for a moving account of the battle for his paper. Cowan, noting his sad demeanor, admired the journalist but never found time to read the newspaper and discover what he had written.[66]

Among the infantry at the angle there was an understandable amount of huddling and confused movement. Hall's and Harrow's brigades had lunged to the right during the attack and now were a mélange of units. The Wilcox-Lang attack had alerted officers to the need for a quick reorganization, and Colonel Devereux of the 19th Massachusetts was put in charge of re-forming the division line. He spread the word for the troops to get into line quickly without trying to dress ranks neatly. Capt.

Henry L. Abbott, commanding the 20th Massachusetts, was pleased with the speedy way his men re-formed. Only about 100 of them were left, yet they finished re-forming even before many other regiments had begun the process.[67]

Devereux joined Webb, Hall, and Mallon huddling in a group near the copse after giving instructions for the reorganization. He found that Webb was very angry with the 72nd Pennsylvania; it "should have behaved a little better," in Devereux's words. The brigade leader promised the group that his report "would produce a severe scolding on account of the conduct of the regiment," which "had not fulfilled his expectations." Webb, of course, referred to the refusal of the Pennsylvanians to move forward immediately after they reached the northeast angle. He also told staff officer Banes to initiate court-martial proceedings for those responsible for the retreat of the eight companies of Penn Smith's 71st Pennsylvania from the angle. But neither of these efforts were followed through. Banes was shortly told to forget the court-martial plans. "I suppose it was dropped because we were successful," Banes later thought. And Webb praised rather than scorned the 72nd in his report. The regiment had "fought steadily and persistently," and indeed the whole of the Philadelphia Brigade received accolades from Webb's pen when he wrote, "The conduct of this brigade was most satisfactory. Officers and men did their whole duty."[68]

· · · · · · ·

UNION AND CONFEDERATE COMMANDERS

While Gibbon's division was sorting itself out, Hancock was being treated for his wound. The corps leader received emergency aid from Surg. Alexander N. Dougherty and then sent Maj. William G. Mitchell of his staff with a verbal message to Meade announcing the Rebel repulse. An ambulance arrived a few minutes later. Dougherty rode in it with Hancock a short distance to a less exposed spot, where the general ordered the driver to stop so he could dictate to Dougherty a message to Meade. He urged Meade to bring up the Fifth and Sixth Corps for a counterattack that would crush Lee, reported his wounding, and announced that Brig. Gen. John C. Caldwell was now in charge of the corps. Hancock was transported to the rear and later managed to telegraph his wife, who was visiting her mother in St. Louis, that he was very badly injured but would live. She immediately set out for Philadelphia to meet him.[69]

THE REPULSE

Gibbon, his division now under the command of Harrow, also was transported to the rear by ambulance. Along the way someone offered him whiskey, and he discovered that "however good it might at other times seem, never tasted so delicious as on that occasion." He wound up at the Second Corps hospital near Rock Run just before Hancock arrived there. When staff officer Haskell finally had time to look for Gibbon, he found the division leader sitting in a chair while an attendant bathed his injured shoulder. Hancock remained in his ambulance some time. Haskell himself was not wounded, even though his horse had taken three bullets and a shell fragment. He was so wet with sweat that he "felt like a boiled man," yet the staff officer recounted the Confederate repulse in full for Gibbon, who eagerly absorbed it all. Haskell later accompanied Gibbon to Westminster, Maryland, stayed with him long enough to put him on a train for Baltimore, and returned to help Harrow run the division.[70]

Hays, the other Second Corps division commander heavily involved in the fight, was unhurt but feeling very proud of himself. After his bizarre ride with the captured Rebel flags, he continued to gloat over the victory. "My defenses were stone walls," he later wrote to a friend, "and since Jackson is dead I think I have a claim to his title." Hays could not resist snubbing Webb at every opportunity. The two spoke briefly after the repulse, and Webb admitted that the Rebels had essentially broken his line. Hays "replied briefly," according to his staff officer Shields, "but with curt emphasis, that they did not get to his, and there was nothing more said about breaks."[71]

The Federal commander had played a relatively small role in repelling Pickett's Charge, but he anxiously rode about on the battlefield keeping a close eye on developments. Just when the repulse took place, Meade was all alone and riding over the crest of Cemetery Ridge. Then his son, aide, and namesake appeared through the smoke. "Hello George," said the army commander, "is that you[?] I am glad you are here, you must stick by me now, you are the only officer left." The two rode toward the battle line trying to find someone they recognized who might update them on the progress of the conflict. The younger Meade saw Lieutenant Egan of Woodruff's battery and hailed him. Thus Meade received his first news about the Rebel repulse. He asked the lieutenant "if they had turned." Yes, he answered and pointed to Hays, who had just begun to ride along with his captured flags. Meade retorted ("and mighty cross too old boy," as Egan later wrote the son), "I don't care for their flag." Egan reiterated that the attack was over, and Meade rode on behind the battle line and toward the left. Near the angle he was engulfed by a great swarm of Rebel prisoners who, recognizing his rank, asked him where they should go. Meade found it rather amusing and pointed to the rear, assuring them that if they should "go along that way you will be well taken care of." With the screeching of a few Confederate shells, the prisoners remarked, "Why its hotter here than it was in front," and they scattered in record time.

As Meade continued his ride, first Haskell, then Mitchell came riding up to inform him that the attack had been repulsed, a self-evident fact by now. Mitchell also filled him in on Hancock's condition. "Say to General Hancock that I regret exceedingly that he is wounded and that I thank him for the Country and for myself for the service he has rendered today," the army commander said while rising in his stirrups and uncovering his head. He continued his ride to the left but was cheered so much by the troops that he rode in front of the line of battle so they could see their commander in his hour of triumph.[72]

Meade continued all the way to Little Round Top to see about advancing the left of his army as a follow-up to the repulse. He quickly gave orders for the skirmishers to advance and feel out the weak spots of Law's and McLaws's divisions, but it took a long time to prepare the battle line for a full-scale attack. All troops on the left had been heavily engaged in the previous day's battle, and there was too much to do in too little time. It soon became apparent that an advance was not feasible. Many observers agreed that an immediate counterattack was not only impossible to launch but would likely have failed if attempted. They cited the army's exhaustion after three days of heavy fighting and the fact that the Rebel divisions to the left and right of the attacking column were intact and ready for action. "Genl Meade did not commit the blunder of getting excited and hurling his forces across a mile of open space to be pounded by artillery and flanked by infantry," reasoned battery commander James A. Hall. It seemed as if nothing could be done to follow up the repulse.[73]

Meade had to be content with a defensive victory at Gettysburg. He continued to wander about, tending to his army, for the rest of the day. Other men remembered encountering Meade. Capt. John D. S. Cook found him near the Leister house as he helped a wounded Rebel officer to the rear. The two conversed briefly because Cook overheard Meade discussing the rumor that Longstreet had personally led the attack and had been wounded in the angle. "Any army must be in a desperate condition when a corps commander led a charge like that," Meade correctly concluded.[74]

On the other side of the valley, James Longstreet fully expected "to see Meade ride to the front and lead his forces to a tremendous counter-charge." He sent staff officers to help reorganize Pickett's men and rode to the artillery line. Longstreet felt desperate. He knew the guns were the only line of defense, and he was resolved to inspire the gunners to their utmost, even if it meant his own death. On the way he briefly passed Lee, who already was trying to console the survivors of Pickett's Charge. Federal shells screeched overhead and plowed up the earth near his horse, but Longstreet made it to the guns to find them already in operation with the few remaining rounds of long-range ammunition that were left. After surveying the Federal lines for a few minutes, Longstreet concluded that the Yankees were not coming. He felt more at ease than he had at any time that day, even though the heavy losses among the infantry units were still to be reckoned. It was well that he could not hear the soft criticisms creeping through the broken ranks directed at the man in charge of the failed assault. Among the survivors of Brockenbrough's Virginia brigade, Wayland Fuller Dunaway heard someone say, "If Old Jack had been here, it wouldn't have been like this."[75]

Longstreet maintained his composure, partly because he had great responsibilities as commander of the First Corps and as Lee's effectual second-in-command, but also because he had fully expected the awful results of the attack. Pickett, on the other hand, completely broke down in the aftermath of the failed charge. He had buoyed his optimism to unrealistic heights before the attack and now allowed himself to plummet to the depths of despair. He could not blame himself for the failure, for he had done all a division leader could do. But Pickett felt an overpowering sense of helplessness as he observed the high tide from Emmitsburg Road and the subsequent retreat of his shattered division. It was too much for the mercurial romantic to absorb.

Charles Pickett found his brother George near Spangler's Woods trying to rally the survivors with tears in his eyes. "He was as tender as he was brave," Charles explained much later. To others he just seemed at the end of his rope. "Great God, where, oh! where is my division," some gunners heard him cry. Later he gave up any hope of re-forming at the woods and rode down Pitzer Lane, where he met Henry T. Owen and instructed him to let the division go back and re-form at the trains.

Mingling with a group of men, Pickett overheard a "tall mountaineer" of the 24th Virginia who, unaccountably, wanted more fight. "General, let us go at them again!" he shouted. The plea fell on deaf ears — of Pickett and of everyone else within hearing. The color-bearer of the 1st Virginia also tried to inspire his comrades in the midst of their defeat. He vigorously waved the flag of the Holcombe Legion, a South Carolina unit that had abandoned its flag at Second Manassas only to have it picked up and retained by the Virginia regiment. Charles T. Loehr remembered that "the boys, not seeing any fun in the movement, told him they declined to play color guard, and induced him to cease his demonstrations." There was no more heart for glorious combat that day.[76]

One of the most memorable moments of the day occurred when Lee encountered Pickett and instructed him to position his men behind Seminary Ridge and prepare to meet the Yankees if they counterattacked. The distraught officer replied, "General Lee, I have no division now. Armistead is down, Garnett is down, and Kemper is mortally wounded." Lee refused to give in to despair. "Come, General Pickett, this has been my fight, and upon my shoulders rests the blame. The men and officers of your command have written the name of Virginia as high to-day as it has ever been written before." Robert Bright, who kept Pickett's image uppermost in his mind, insisted that the division commander uttered these famous words with his head bowed. It is quite possible that this was so, but one can easily believe a hint of resentment tinged the comment as well.[77]

It was Pickett's worst day as well as the day of his greatest glory, yet he was not emotionally up to the challenge it presented. Lt. William Alexander Gordon had traveled with Pickett's division as an engineer officer long enough to gauge the man. He was "greatly affected and to some extent unnerved" by the repulse. "I never considered him a great or strong man," Gordon wrote, "but he was a good brave soldier and at Gettysburg did his full duty as I believe."[78]

Soon after Pickett exchanged words with Lee, the army commander noticed Kemper being transported to the rear. "I must speak to him," he said. The attendant soldiers stopped, and Kemper opened his eyes. "General Kemper, I hope you are not very seriously wounded." He had to reply with the worst news: "I am struck in the groin, and the ball has ranged upward; they tell me it is mortal." Lee hoped it was not so and asked if he could do anything for the wounded brigade leader. "Yes, General Lee; do full justice to this division for its work to-day." Lee assured him he would, and the two parted. Kemper was taken by ambulance on the perilous ride to the field hospital, where surgeons continued to tell him he would die. Three of his staff officers sat up all night with him. Kemper was conscious and fully aware of his condition, as he had already demonstrated while conversing with Lee. Although suffering intense pain, he wanted to know all the particulars of the fight, the fate of friends and subordinates, and the kind of bullet found in him, and he assured everyone of his great admiration for the brigade. Kemper, according to Edward Cook Barnes, "made his peace . . . and would die as a christian."[79]

A. P. Hill had played a limited role in the planning and execution of the attack even though half of the men belonged to his corps. He eagerly watched the charge from Seminary Ridge and was stunned when it was turned back. Artilleryman George L. Christian recalled that Hill "looked to me as if he were dazed, if not confounded at the scene before him." He felt a sense of helplessness similar to Pickett's but managed to keep his composure.[80]

While Longstreet and Hill kept their feelings to themselves and Pickett lay his bare for all the world to see, Lee alone rose above the emotions of the moment to present a towering figure to everyone near the scene of the attack. He alone envisioned the assault that morning and pushed it through over the objections of his most important subordinate, asking many exhausted or naively optimistic soldiers to try something that was next to impossible. Now he manfully assumed full responsibility. Lee's partisans tended to see this as magnanimous, the assumption of a responsibility that could easily have been shifted to others. But in reality it was only right for Lee to take the blame for the outcome of the attack — it was his brainchild. Lee was simply stating the truth when he told everyone that it was all his fault. He deserves enormous praise for doing so in a war that saw many commanders try to save their careers by sacrificing others. But in view of the tremendous suffering of his men, it was the least he could do.

Lee had been in Spangler's Woods after the attack started but quickly moved to the left when it became apparent that Pettigrew's left was in trouble. When the division leader came back to the ridge, he met Lee and tried to cover himself by pleading newness to command. Pettigrew told Lee "with much earnestness and feeling" that he was "responsible for his own Brigade, but not for the Division." Lee ignored this attempt to shift the blame for the division's checkered performance, offering words of encouragement. "General, I am sorry to see you wounded; go to the rear." He repeated what he had already been saying to others, that the responsibility for the entire operation was his alone.[81]

Lee moved toward the right, sending staff officer Charles Marshall to rally the troops and telling everyone he met not only that it was his fault but that they should reorganize as quickly as possible behind the artillery and prepare for a counterattack. A badly wounded survivor of the assault passed near him, helped by a comrade. He yelled, "General, I am done for, I am a dying man. I want to shake you by the hand." Lee tarried long enough to do so and rode on. "Take care of that old man, for Heaven's sake," the wounded soldier told those near him.[82]

Lee also stopped long enough at William Thomas Poague's guns to inquire of their state of readiness. Poague assured him he had enough ammunition to repel a counterattack, and Lee seemed much more at ease than when Poague had seen him in the morning. The army commander tarried much longer with Alexander in front of Longstreet's corps. Alexander was convinced he came up to have a personal hand in repelling the expected Yankee thrust and was disappointed not to have had an opportunity to see him do it. Colonel Fremantle rode up to join the pair and asked a lot of questions of Alexander. A cheer could be heard from the Federal lines, and everyone assumed it was the prelude to a counterattack; but it was only the soldiers' response to Hays's ride trailing the captured Rebel flags. Alexander always regretted that Lee did not formally introduce him to Fremantle, even though the gunner and the Englishman had a long conversation about the attack in his presence. Lee perhaps was embarrassed by Alexander's tattered uniform, at least that was Alexander's thought. But he also criticized Alexander's acting aide, Lt. Frederick M. Colston, for spurring his horse when ordered off on an errand: "Oh don't do that. Use gentle measures. I had a foolish horse once, & gentle measures always had the best result."[83]

Fremantle was responsible for presenting the world one of the first pictures of Lee in defeat, for the memoir of his travels in the Confederacy were published soon after Gettysburg. He wrote glowingly of Lee's nobility and the private soldiers' admiration for their chief. "This has been a sad day for us, Colonel—a sad day," Fremantle remembered, "but we can't expect always to gain victories." The English officer found many men who reassured him, "We've not lost confidence in the old man: this day's work won't do him no harm. 'Uncle Robert' will get us into Washington yet; you bet he will!"[84]

Cadmus Wilcox found Lee with Fremantle and, like Pickett, let his emotions show. "General Lee," he said with tears staining his face, "I came into Pennsylvania with one of the finest brigades in the army of Northern Virginia and now my people are all gone. They have all been killed." Lee shook his hand and said sadly, "Never mind, General, *all this has been MY fault*— it is *I* that have lost this fight, and you must help me out of it in the best way you can." Fremantle was very impressed by Lee's demeanor. "It was impossible to look at him or to listen to him without feeling the strongest admiration."[85]

· · · · · · ·

THE DEAD AND WOUNDED

Lee could afford to be noble, for his reputation was such that it could survive almost anything. But the soldiers who tried his experiment and suffered for it littered the battlefield. There were hundreds of dead and wounded men covering a relatively small space of ground. They were thickest between Emmitsburg Road and the stone fence. Wilbur Clifford of the 19th Maine wrote of their "groaning crying for water praying swearing all at once in every direction." On the other wing of the Federal position the litter of bodies and suffering men was just as thick. David Shields found that "the dead lay in appalling numbers" and the wounded had crawled around the shack at the intersection of Bryan Lane and Emmitsburg Road for shelter. Federal efforts to collect the Rebel wounded were hampered by the Confederate artillery fire, which almost killed Abner Doubleday and did kill and injure a small number of Federal soldiers.[86]

The Union dead and wounded were far less numerous, but they offered a painful sight to their comrades. Thomas F. Galwey noted the number of 8th Ohio infantrymen who lay in the ditch alongside Emmitsburg Road after the attack was repulsed. "It was full of pools of blood and the grass for some distance in front was saturated with blood." Many of the wounded died before attendants could transport them to the ridge. Two sergeants had been hit by artillery fire, and the lower parts of their legs were dangling by a small piece of flesh.[87]

On the other side of the valley, overworked Confederate surgeons tried to deal with the flood of wounded who made their way to the field hospitals. Pickett's division hospital at Bream's Mill was "soon filled to overflowing" with the wounded and a certain number of men who were only shocked and bruised. Most of the wounded had to wait some time for treatment; the majority of injuries were slight, and the surgeons had to give primary attention to the more serious cases. "The doctors dont examine unless amputation is necessary or it is extraordinarily dangerous," reported a hospital attendant with the 11th North Carolina. In fact some members of that regiment who had been wounded on July 1 still had not been examined by 8:00 P.M. of July 3. Lt. Edward Payson Reeve of the 1st Virginia grew so tired of waiting for a surgeon that he scavenged a dirty cloth off the battlefield, made a sling for his arm, and traveled to a different hospital at Cashtown to have the ball removed from his shoulder.[88]

In addition to taking care of their own wounded, the Federals had to manage a large lot of captured Confederates. William Peel found himself in a crowd of 1,800 prisoners assembling in a field near Baltimore Pike. Many of them were wounded; Peel himself had a flesh wound in the thigh that a Federal surgeon looked at briefly and pronounced insignificant. Then Brig. Gen. Marsena Patrick, the army's provost marshal, showed up. A Rebel shouted, "What's the news Genl." Patrick decided to pass on the battlefield rumor that Longstreet had been mortally wounded and captured. His prisoners did not believe it. Patrick then welcomed and threatened the Rebels at the same time. "Prisoners, you are here now in my charge; quite a large number of you: I guarantee to you the kindest treatment the nature of the case will permit, so long as you conduct yourselves in a becoming manner. If, however, there should be any attempt, upon your part, to escape me, woe be unto you. My splendid cavalry is at hand armed & ready for action, & in numbers almost equal to your own, & in case of any disturbance among you, they shall be ordered to charge you, cutting & slashing right & left, indiscriminately."[89]

Patrick noticed John C. Timberlake's rank and singled him out for a conversation. The two discussed the rumor that Pickett had been killed in the attack, and Patrick admitted to Timberlake that the assault, in his view, nearly succeeded. A "few more men Maj. and you would have won your independence Right here," as Timberlake remembered the discussion; "and I said to him we have lost it Right here. he said that is just my opinion."[90]

Officers of lesser rank had no such civil conversations with their captors. James Wentworth of Lang's brigade was interrogated by a Federal officer at army headquarters but refused to reveal any information. "Just as I expected," the Yankee officer retorted, "won't tell anything if you knew eve[n]."[91]

THE REPULSE

Later in the evening the large crowd of prisoners along Baltimore Pike was allowed to move 100 yards to Rock Run to get water. They found a group of Federal cavalrymen already there, washing the sweaty backs of their horses in the stream. But it was a hot day, and there was no other water around, so the prisoners drank their fill. When a Federal officer threatened to cut the prisoners down if they tried to escape, some of the Rebels yelled, "Three cheers for Jeff Davis." The Confederates were issued cornbread and meat that evening before marching out toward Winchester, Maryland, where they would be boarded on railroad cars for shipment to various prisons.[92]

Lewis Armistead, the highest-ranking prisoner in Union hands, was badly injured. Webb and his staff carefully measured the spot where he fell and concluded it was about forty to fifty feet in front of the center of the 72nd Pennsylvania and thirty-three feet from Webb. Apparently Armistead called attention to himself after the repulse by giving a common Mason distress signal. He yelled that his mother was a widow. An unidentified captain of the 72nd detailed three men to carry him to the rear. Gibbon's judge advocate, Francis Wessels, saw the group and tried to tell the enlisted men to return to duty, but they identified the wounded Rebel as Longstreet. The Confederate officer "begged me to let them take him off," remembered Wessels, and the Federal officer agreed. Capt. Henry H. Bingham of Hancock's staff encountered the group shortly after Wessels left, and the Federal privates again reported that they had Longstreet. Bingham instantly dismounted and took charge of the important prisoner, only to hear from the wounded man that he was "General Armistead of the Confederate Army." Bingham introduced himself and offered to safeguard any of his personal effects. Armistead told him that Hancock was "an old and valued friend of his" and asked Bingham to send a message. "Tell General Hancock for me," as Bingham recalled later, "that I have done him and done you all an injury which I shall *regret* or *repent* (I forgot the exact word) the longest day I live." Armistead also gave Bingham his spurs, watch, and pocketbook before the men continued to carry him to a surgeon. The Virginian's pistol had already been taken by Capt. Charles Banes of Webb's staff even before the litter bearers took him from the angle. Banes found that it had not been fired. He later gave it to someone for safekeeping and never saw it again. For his part, Wessels always felt embarrassed about telling Meade that Longstreet was wounded and in Union hands, and he seldom told anyone that he had played a big role in spreading this false report.

Bingham later delivered Armistead's personal effects to Hancock at the field hospital, but his report of the Rebel's apparent expression of regret that he had taken the Southern side and fought against his old friend would become controversial. It was never fully explained and would rankle Confederate partisans even as they praised Armistead's bravery in the angle. Yet there can be no doubt that Armistead said it, as Bingham was a completely reliable source. The Virginian probably meant to express his regret at fighting his old friend, nothing more, but Federal partisans twisted the comment into a general rejection of the Confederate cause. As Abner Doubleday would later write in his book on the battle, Armistead supposedly said, "Tell Hancock I have wronged him and have wronged my country." Armistead would not have an opportunity to correct misrepresentations such as this.[93]

Armistead was taken to the Eleventh Corps hospital at the George Spangler house, suffering intense pain all the way. He was placed on a cot under the trees. The physical suffering caused enormous emotional stress. When attendants and surgeons crowded close by he said, "Please don't step so close to me." He was later moved into the summer kitchen of the homestead to spend the night of July 3.[94]

John Dooley of the 1st Virginia was taken wounded to a Union field hospital where the accommodations were spare. He noticed that the Federal wounded received treatment from the surgeons similar to that provided the Rebel prisoners, but their regimental mates often brought extra food or clothing to aid their recovery. The injured Confederates sweltered through the heat with very little to increase their comfort.[95]

By no means were all the Rebel wounded taken off the field by either friend or foe that day. Many of them were stuck in the mid-ground, too far west for the Federals to safely venture forth and too far east for their comrades to rescue them. There was as yet no opportunity for either side to bury the dead, and this allowed the Unionists much time to observe the littered battlefield. Capt. Samuel C. Armstrong of the 126th New York saw the bodies that marked Pettigrew's high tide near the stone fence, "mostly North Carolinians, lean lank fellows in rusty old suits, but heroes." The litter of corpses outside the angle was horrid. Artillery officer Charles S. Wainwright described the scene: "There was about an acre or so of ground here where you could not walk without stepping over the bodies, and I saw perhaps a dozen cases where they were *heaped* one on top of the other." A Pennsylvania soldier, who was not involved in the repulse but who saw the angle area twenty minutes after the Rebels retreated, agreed with Wainwright. "It appeared to me that I could have walked on the bodies of dead and wounded men to the fence and down to the Emmitsburg Pike." An officer of the 126th New York counted sixteen bodies in an area that was only six by six yards square, while Albert Stokes Emmell of the 12th New Jersey likened the appearance of the dead to wheat sheaves laid out in lines across the field. The enormous number of bodies drenched the ground with gore. "I never saw as much human blood before," wrote Richard Penn Smith of the angle area. Later, when it began to rain, red pools pockmarked the landscape.[96]

While the Federals had the best opportunity to see these terrible sights, a few defeated Rebels also gazed on them from a longer distance. "I hope to God that noe of my friends will Ever Look on such a sight as that field was," shuddered Lt. William A. Tuttle of the 22nd North Carolina. "I will Stop about it. I hope I will git home and Desmember it all."[97]

· · · · · · ·

LOSSES

Pickett's division suffered 498 killed, 643 wounded, 833 wounded and captured, and 681 captured. The total, 2,655, amounted to 42.4 percent of those engaged. Garnett's brigade lost the heaviest proportion, 65 percent, with Armistead's brigade a close second and Kemper's brigade suffering 43 percent casualties. Regimental losses ranged from the low of 38 percent suffered by the 3rd Virginia to the 92 percent suffered by the 8th Virginia. Losses among First Corps artillery units ranged from 3 percent suffered by Stribling's Virginia battery to 50 percent suffered by Gilbert's South Carolina battery.[98]

Anecdotal evidence produced by the survivors of Pickett's division tends to support the estimates of modern historians. According to contemporary accounts Company I, 1st Virginia, lost nineteen of its twenty-six men. One of the killed was a forty-six-year-old substitute who had joined the regiment only six weeks before Gettysburg. Capt. Edmund R. Cocke claimed that his Company E, 18th Virginia, literally lost every one of its twenty-three officers and men in the attack. Nine of them were killed and the rest were wounded or captured.[99]

Pettigrew's losses can only be estimated because tabular results were made only of the entire battle, not just July 3, and losses in his artillery units are not included. It appears the infantry of his division lost 470 killed and 1,893 wounded in the attack, with an additional 337 unwounded prisoners taken on the battlefield. (A goodly proportion of the wounded in this estimate also were taken prisoner.) The total of 2,700 represented 62 percent of the number engaged. Estimates of the division's losses for both days of fighting indicate that Marshall's brigade (67 percent) and Fry's brigade (57 percent) suffered the highest proportionate losses. Davis suffered 44 percent losses and Brockenbrough lost 17 percent of his men on both days of fighting.[100]

The University Greys, a company of the 11th Mississippi, lost all of its 32 men in the attack; Company E lost all but one of its 37 men; and Company D had only 9 of 55 soldiers left. The losses affected Davis, who had just finished his first and worst battle as brigade commander. David Holt of the 16th Mississippi in Posey's brigade was acquainted with Davis and talked with him just after the attack. "General Davis, where is your brigade?" he asked. Davis "pointed his sword up to the skies, but did not say a word, and stood there for a moment knocking pebbles out of the path with the point of his sword. He could not talk, and neither could I. He walked on and I went back to my place."[101]

In Fry's brigade the loss of color-bearers was astonishing. The 1st Tennessee lost three carriers and its flag, the 13th Alabama also lost three carriers, the 14th Tennessee lost four bearers, and the 7th Tennessee lost three flag bearers.[102]

Maj. John T. Jones was the only field officer left in Marshall's brigade after the attack, and very few of the company officers were still on their feet. "Our brigade is in a bad fix," Jones informed his father. The 26th North Carolina had about 800 men on the morning of July 1; right after the attack on July 3 it could gather only about 70 able-bodied soldiers, enough to form "a very good skirmish line." Company F of that regiment had lost every man except one on July 1. The sole survivor, Sgt. Robert Hudspeth, managed to scrounge up four or five more members of the company who were on ambulance and pioneer duty and led them into the charge on July 3. All of them, including Hudspeth, were killed or wounded. Company C of the 11th North Carolina, the Bethel Regiment, lost thirty of its thirty-eight men. Its commander, Capt. Francis Bird, was one of the few survivors. Bird saved the regimental flag after eight color-bearers were killed or wounded. He grabbed it and held on, even though bullets cut the staff twice, and he brought it back to Seminary Ridge. The 11th was the only regiment in Marshall's brigade to retain possession of its colors. Truly, each regiment in that hard-hit brigade could repeat what the historian of the 47th North Carolina later wrote: "The skeleton of its former self" was all that was left of the regiment after the attack.[103]

Trimble's two brigades suffered 155 killed, 650 wounded, and 80 unwounded prisoners, for a total of 885 losses, or 52 percent of those infantrymen engaged. Lowrance's brigade had suffered terrible losses on July 1 and now was forced to suffer more heavy casualties. Company A of the 38th North Carolina lost every man, and the entire regiment could muster only forty able-bodied soldiers at the end of the attack. Lt. Col. William H. A. Speer of the 28th North Carolina, in Lane's brigade, put it well when he wrote to his family, "If all others were as we are we would hardly have any army."[104]

Cadmus Wilcox reported losing 200 infantrymen of the 1,000 engaged in the assault, amounting to 20 percent. Lang took about 400 infantrymen into the attack and lost roughly 115, amounting to 28 percent. Both brigades suffered heavier casualties on July 2. Lang lost 455 of 742 men at Gettysburg, 61 percent casualties, according to a modern estimate.[105]

Total Confederate casualties in the attack of July 3 can be summed up as 6,555, or 55.4 percent of the 11,830 men engaged. Not counting the losses in Wilcox's or Lang's brigade, which were not enumerated according to category, at least 1,123 Confederates were killed on the battlefield. Another 4,019 Rebels were wounded, and a good number of the injured were also captured. The total number of Confederates taken prisoner was at least 1,931. Because we do not know exactly how many men were also wounded and captured in Pettigrew's or Trimble's command, the number of prisoners, both wounded and unhurt, was higher than 1,931. As indicated earlier, Union reports fixed the number at 3,750 captives, and that seems to be a fair accounting.

Casualties among the Rebel officers were striking. Of the 3 division leaders, 2 were wounded — Trimble severely and Pettigrew slightly. Pickett was unscratched. Three of the 11 brigade leaders were killed — Armistead, Garnett, and Marshall — and 3 of them were wounded. The Virginia Military Institute produced 11 of the 15 regimental commanders in Pickett's division, and all 11 were lost; 6 were killed and 5 were wounded.[106]

Because all Federal units involved in repelling the attack had seen action on July 1 or 2, it is difficult to estimate how many men were lost solely on July 3. Gates's two regiments of the First Corps lost very heavily at Gettysburg, suffering 59 percent casualties in the 80th New York and 72 percent casualties in the 151st Pennsylvania. Undoubtedly the great proportion of these losses occurred on July 1. Stannard's Vermont brigade lost 18 percent of its men on July 2 and 3 combined.[107]

Gibbon's division suffered heavy casualties, and a good proportion of them, perhaps more than half in some cases, were lost on July 3. Hall's brigade lost 40 percent of its members, and Harrow's brigade lost 56 percent casualties. Maj. Sylvanus W. Curtis alone differentiated the losses on the two days of fighting for his 7th Michigan. The regiment lost 9 killed and 10 wounded on July 2 and an additional 12 killed and 34 wounded on July 3. Webb reported losses of 524 of 974 men engaged during the fighting on both days. He listed 47 of them as missing, most of whom undoubtedly were lost from Company F, 69th Pennsylvania, when Armistead's band crossed into the angle. A recent tabulation indicates that Webb's brigade lost 418 of 862 men engaged on July 3, or 48.4 percent. The 69th Pennsylvania lost 121 men that day, while the 71st Pennsylvania suffered 100 casualties and the 72nd Pennsylvania lost 197 men. Estimated percentage losses among Gibbon's hard-fighting regiments hovered mostly in the 40 to 60 percent range.[108]

Losses in the Federal batteries near the angle were enormous. All of Cushing's guns were rendered unserviceable or needed repairs to their carriages before they could be fired. Sixty-five of the 115 horses of the battery were killed or injured, and 40 battery personnel were lost. Sgt. Frederick Fuger led the tiny remnant that had survived. Arnold's Rhode Island battery lost 36 men and 56 horses. He was given permission to scavenge equipment, men, and horses from Brown's Rhode Island battery and Cushing's Regular battery to rebuild his unit. Eight infantrymen from the 12th New Jersey, 42nd New York, 15th Massachusetts, and other units had helped Arnold work his guns; all of them were lost in the furious bombardment of July 3. The percentages of loss in Second Corps batteries, counting the entire battle of Gettysburg, amounted to anywhere from 24 to 30 percent.[109]

The casualties among Hays's units were similar to those of Gibbon's command. According to modern estimates of total casualties on both days of fighting, the 8th Ohio lost 48 percent of its men; Smyth's brigade lost 32 percent (ranging from the 12th New Jersey's 25 percent to the 108th New York's 51 percent); and Sherrill's brigade suffered a loss rate of 47 percent (ranging from the 125th New York's 35 percent to the 126th New York's 50 percent). Hays's division lost 35 percent of its men in the two days of fighting. Woodruff's battery lost 25 of its 112 men and many horses. Three days after the attack, Frank Haskell rode over the battlefield and counted 71 dead horses in a space only fifty yards square where Woodruff's guns were positioned.[110]

George Stewart has estimated total Federal casualties during the repulse of the Confederate attack at about 1,500; that would be 26 percent of the total number of Yankees involved. About 150 of them were taken prisoner by the Rebels. Clearly the Federals expended less force to repel the attack than the Confederates used to make it, and they suffered less for it. Less than half as many Union infantrymen and roughly an equal amount of Union artillery power were involved, compared with their opponents, yet the Federals suffered less than half the casualty rate they inflicted on the Rebels.[111]

. . . .

EVENING AND NIGHT, JULY 3

The sky had been clear all afternoon, the sun had warmed the temperatures up to above ninety degrees, and a slight breeze had blown from the south during the charge. A brief rain shower came over the battlefield late in the afternoon, some time well after the repulse, and another, "pelting rain" rampaged across the field just at dusk. The sun set at 7:32 P.M., according to Professor Jacobs's precise measurement; this was four and a half hours after the attack ended. The moon shone for some time in the early night; but clouds soon thickened, and a fog settled into low-lying areas, making the night darker and more gloomy.[112]

The Federals were busy that evening. Many soldiers near the angle strengthened their breastworks in case Lee decided to try another attack the next morning. Only one spade was available in the 7th Michigan, but the men had a much improved fortification ready in short order. At 7:00 P.M., just before dusk, the 1st Delaware was sent out to evict a few remaining Confederate skirmishers taking refuge near the ruined Bliss buildings. The regiment did this easily and returned to the line, harassed by Rebel artillery fire. Ironically, the day was ending as it had begun, with skirmishers popping away and cannon barking. Lang's brigade posted a picket line on its front just after dark. J. B. Johnson, who led the men forward, found that "dead and wounded literally covered the ground." Johnson ran into a group of Federals, probably skirmishers probing into the no-man's-land between the lines, but they retired rather than contest the ground. Quiet settled over that part of the battlefield, broken only by what Johnson called "the pitiful appeals from the wounded for water, water."[113]

Many survivors on both sides had an opportunity to rest, to scrounge for food, or to wander over the battlefield during the night. Capt. Benjamin W. Thompson of the 111th New York had recovered sufficiently from the disorienting effects of a shell burst during the bombardment to survey the field.

> The track of the great charge was marked by bodies of men in all possible positions, wounded, bleeding, dying and dead. Near the line where the final struggle occurred, the men lay in heaps, the wounded wriggling and groaning under the weight of the dead among whom they were entangled. In my weak and exhausted condition I could not long endure the gory, ghastly spectacle. I found my head reeling, the tears flowing and my stomach sick, at the sight. For months the spectre haunted my dreams, and even after forty seven years it comes back as the most horrible vision I have ever conceived.[114]

Most of the Federals had not been able to eat much, if anything, all day, and they were desperately hungry. Rations had run out on the night of July 2, and the fierce bombardment the next day had driven the trains farther to the rear. It would take some time for food to be brought forward, so many Unionists looked for something to eat among the dead. Rebel haversacks seemed to be filled with biscuits and unsalted meat foraged from the Pennsylvania countryside. John P. Lancaster of the 19th Maine at least waited until one wounded Confederate died before he took his food. Loren Goodrich of the 14th Connecticut found nearly every haversack stuffed, and several wounded Rebels stared at him with "the stamp of death" on their faces. One Confederate, whose head was "covered with blood," implored Goodrich for water, and the Yankee carefully gave him all he could, three pints, even though the wounded man was desperate for more. All night long Goodrich heard the groans of the wounded, but hunger drove many Federals to eat their fill despite the gory scene before them. Benjamin Thompson indulged too freely of the unsalted meat and "was not on friendly terms with my digestive organs for twenty four hours afterward."[115]

When proper rations finally were brought forward for the troops, it was discovered that there was far too much food. Hancock had arranged for the issue just before the start of the bombardment, and thus it was calculated on the strength of the units before the attack. Now there were significantly fewer men alive to eat it. "As a consequence," wrote the historian of the 19th Massachusetts, "a great deal of fresh beef was thrown away."[116]

On the other side of the contested valley, a Confederate artilleryman named Felix R. Galloway went to the field hospital to see to his comrades, three of whom had been wounded that day. Dr. William H. Green took time from his duty to respond to Galloway's questions. "You see that pile of hands, feet, arms, fingers, ears, noses, and legs, about four bushels, over there?" he asked. "John Tyson's leg and Dupont Gary's arm are in it. We did the best we could for them and sent them farther to the rear for safety." Both men died later that night as Dr. Green continued his gruesome and often futile work.[117]

At the Bream farm along Willoughby's Run, where Kemper was spending a terrible night of pain, David E. Johnston of the 7th Virginia was also trying to deal with his own battlefield injury. While Kemper lay in the farmhouse, Johnston stayed in the barn, but he could hear Kemper's groans nevertheless. The barn was filled with wounded men. "I spoke to no one," Johnston recalled, "and no one to me, never closed my eyes in sleep; the surgeons close by being engaged in removing the limbs of those necessary to be amputated." There was no rest for Johnston or his compatriots.[118]

Some angelic souls tried to do everything possible for the sufferers who remained on the battlefield, caught between the lines. Sgt. George D. Bowen filled his canteen and slowly made his way as far into the field as he dared, giving water to everyone who was alive. He soon ran out of water and refilled the canteen in the ditch beside Emmitsburg Road, not thinking in the darkness that it might be unclean even though the ditch was clogged with bodies. When he ministered to another Rebel, the wounded man gently asked him for "some clear cool water[;] that is so full of blood I cannot drink it." This was the first time Bowen had been among the dead and wounded after a fight, and the ordeal was enough to last him a lifetime. Later he wrote, "the sight and sound were terrible, no one can give an idea of what it is like, the pain and misery of those poor fellows whom we shot down only a few hours ago — it is [a] heart breaking sight."[119]

The rain that fell that night drenched the wounded, increasing their discomfort and in many cases contributing to their deaths. Even the wounded who were in field hospitals suffered, for there was very little shelter for the hundreds of injured men lying about. Wounded Rebels at the Second Corps hospital were in danger of drowning when the rains caused Rock Creek to flood. They had to be quickly moved to higher ground, but hospital attendants did not bother to move the bodies of those who had already died. "It's no use moving him, look out for those yet alive," they said. Hancock's staff officer Charles H. Morgan came across one wounded Rebel prisoner who refused to let the rain dampen his mood. Birkett Fry was a strong, noticeable character, and many Federals remembered encountering him in captivity. Despite being wounded for the fourth time since the start of the war, he spent the night of July 3 calmly smoking "a little old pipe" in the rain. When Morgan inquired about his injury, Fry readily showed him the damage, which resulted in a compound fracture of the thigh bone. "I was very certain that a man who could, with such a desperate wound, lie out all night in a rain so heavy as to cover the ground where he lay some inches under water, and then smoke his pipe with apparently so serene a satisfaction . . . , was not going to give up the ghost yet, and was not surprised afterwards to hear of the Colonel's recovery."[120]

At 2:00 A.M., after the rain had stopped falling, Alexander Hays rode over the battlefield to see what it looked like. Gone was the excited bombast that had characterized the division leader's attitude following the repulse. His gaudy ride dragging the captured Confederate flags and his silly insults to Webb had given way to a tender realization of the enormity of death that his division had created in front of the line. Hays found it difficult to guide his horse across the battlefield without treading on bodies, and the "shrieks of anguish and prayers for relief were heartrending." Hays believed that only someone "trained to the 'butcher trade'" could see and hear this without being overwhelmed. He reminded himself, in a letter to his mother, why he fought this battle: "I was fighting for my native state, and before I went in thought of those at home I so dearly love. If Gettysburg was lost all was lost for them, and I only interposed a life that would be otherwise worthless. But if we suffered the poor Rebels suffered terribly tenfold." Hays commented in his official report that the "angel of death alone can produce such a field as was presented" to him during his early morning ride. Only under cover of darkness, it seems, could the gruff general dwell in his own thoughts and emotions about the "butcher trade" and its human cost.[121]

CHAPTER 9
GLORY ENOUGH

· · · · · · · · · · ·

It had rained off and on throughout the night of July 3, and the pattern continued on July 4. A shower at 4:00 A.M. gave way to clear skies that were darkened by another shower at 6:00 A.M. A much heavier storm came over the area during the middle of the day and drenched the battlefield for two hours. Altogether nearly an inch and a half of rain fell on Independence Day, increasing the misery of the wounded, and it barely lessened at dusk.[1]

There were still a lot of Rebel wounded lying between the lines and suffering in makeshift field hospitals. Samuel Chapman Armstrong was moved by their plight and recalled their groans and prayers. "The usual expression is 'Oh, Lord!' — it can be heard on every side, and when one approaches they cry for water most piteously. Oh, how they beg to be carried away to a doctor." Armstrong decided to make his preparation for death, should it be his lot to fall like these men. He kept a book of Psalms and assured his mother that "I feel simply resolved to do my best, to lead my men, and to accept my fate like a man."[2]

Lt. Abner R. Small of the 16th Maine had not participated in repelling the assault but wandered among the Confederate wounded on the morning of July 4. He found many men who were in the process of dying. Sgt. William S. Jinkins of Company G, 7th North Carolina, pleaded for "Only a drink of water," then he told Small, "I'm cold; so cold. Won't you cover me up?" Jinkins asked Small to write to his home in Chatham County "and say how he loved them, and how he died." Small also found a soldier of Kemper's brigade who was fearfully wounded in the breast but appeared unafraid of dying. He told Small that he was "going home" and said good-bye, even though Small was a complete stranger. The

Maine officer watched as he slipped away and recalled, "I did weep; I couldn't help it."[3]

Even those Confederate wounded who made it back to their own lines on July 3 had a great deal of suffering to endure. Many of them could not be tended for many hours due to the heavy load imposed on the surgeons. James W. Clay of the 18th Virginia stood in line for four hours on July 4, soaked to the skin, while waiting to see a doctor. He saw men collapse due to exhaustion, and a few even died while waiting. Clay was not lightly wounded. A bone in his forehead had been fractured by a shell fragment, and a finger had nearly been cut off by a bullet. When he finally reached the head of the line, a surgeon reset the bone and cut off the dangling finger without anesthetic.[4]

Eli Setser of the 26th North Carolina had been severely wounded on July 3. Three bullets plunged into his arm, and a third shattered his thigh bone. His cousin Thomas W. Setser of the same regiment put him into an ambulance to be sent to the rear on the morning of July 4. "I hate to tell you what he Said," Thomas wrote home, "but he requistted mee to tell you all how it was. . . . he Said that he was a going to die and he node it. and Said he was willing to die and he wanted mee to tell you how it was." Thomas tried to communicate the reality to the hometown folks, but he could not soften the fact that Eli died of his wounds later that day.[5]

· · · · · · ·

GOOD-BYE TO GETTYSBURG

While the privates were trying to survive, the generals had already made up their minds to get away from Gettysburg. The decision was easy enough. Lee held a council the night before at Hill's headquarters on Chambersburg Pike, where the decision was communicated to all concerned. "Owing to the strength of the enemy's position, and the reduction of our ammunition," Lee later reported to Richmond, "a renewal of the engagement could not be hazarded, and the difficulty of securing supplies rendered it impossible to continue longer where we were." He sent for Brig. Gen. John D. Imboden, whose cavalry brigade was still relatively fresh, and gave him instructions to guard the wagon train of wounded he planned to start for the Potomac River on July 4. Imboden organized the train under a drenching rain that afternoon and left the battlefield with it at 4:00 P.M. on July 4.[6]

The surgeons were busy all morning deciding who should be loaded onto the wagons for the hazardous trip home and who were too badly wounded to risk the journey. Dr. Charles Edward Lippitt of the 57th Virginia sent off all of his slightly injured patients, leaving 109 severely wounded men at Pickett's division hospital at Bream's Mill. While Lippitt assumed the responsibility of deciding who should go, other doctors simply encouraged those who could move to get into the wagons. In Pettigrew's division hospitals Dr. H. H. Hubbard of the 2nd Mississippi decided to detail his assistant surgeon, Dr. Wilson, to remain behind with the badly wounded. He did so with the best of intentions, knowing that Wilson had worked exceedingly hard and that the trip home would be dangerous. But Wilson refused to stay. "Doctor, I will obey orders," he said, "but if you have any duty more dangerous or more arduous, let me have it. I don't want to fall into the hands of the enemy although I know they will treat me right. I am real cranky on this subject. Please give me something else." Moved by the intensity of his feelings, Hubbard gave in and asked Wilson if he could be ready to go in a half-hour. "I am ready now," Wilson replied, "just as soon as I can get my blankets and pocket case of instruments, bandages and a bottle of morphine, and I thank you to boot."[7]

The two highest-ranking wounded of the July 3 attack were left behind by Lee's retreating army. The lower third of Trimble's left leg was amputated on the morning of July 4 at the Cobean farmhouse by Dr. Hunter McGuire, who had treated him for his Second Manassas wound, which also was in the left leg. McGuire told him that the stump would likely become inflamed if he made the rough journey to Virginia. "I decided to fall a prisoner," he later recounted. Trimble was taken by his Federal captors to the Robert McCurdy house in Gettysburg, where he stayed for two weeks before removal to the Lutheran Seminary. He was transported to Baltimore on August 20 and held at Fort McHenry, where Union surgeons later fitted him with an artificial leg. Trimble was joined by Kemper while he stayed at the seminary. Pickett's brigade commander was too badly injured to risk the trip to Virginia and was transported from Bream's Mill to the seminary by his Union hosts. Kemper's staff officers somehow received word from him as late as July 6, but there seemed to be little hope for his recovery. Indeed, the entire South assumed Kemper was dead for several weeks before word that he had been shipped to Baltimore with Trimble reached his family in late August. Unlike Trimble, who was not exchanged until February 1865, Kemper was sent home on September 22, 1864, in exchange for Brig. Gen. Charles K. Graham. This Federal officer had commanded a brigade in the Third Corps and had been wounded and captured during the bloody fighting in the Sherfy peach orchard on July 2.[8]

Less famous men who were left behind suffered enormously, the physical pains of their wounds compounded by the emotional trauma of being surrounded by the enemy. Many of them did not survive their captivity. Capt. William W. Goss of the 19th Virginia had been badly wounded in the left lung on July 3 and was in Federal hands. "He suffered considerable pain, but bore it with a fortitude and patience I've never seen equaled," wrote a friend. Goss wanted the folks at home to remember him as dying bravely, even patriotically. He could hardly speak but did manage to tell E. W. Rowe that he " 'was not afraid to die' and 'hoped to meet you in Heaven.' " Goss was buried in the yard of the school building in Gettysburg where he died.[9]

The Army of Northern Virginia slipped away from the battlefield on the night of July 4 with hardly anyone on the Union side realizing it. The wagon train loaded with wounded had the lead, charting the straightest possible course to the Potomac while the fighting men brought up the rear. The various divisions began pulling out of their positions at 2:00 A.M. of July 5, and all were gone by dawn. The rain continued to fall nearly all night, but the worst of it was over when the new day arrived, although the battlefield was very muddy. Only now and then did the sun shine on July 5. Meade began to move his own units out of their battlefield positions that afternoon, sending them in a cautious follow-up to the Rebel retreat.[10]

The Second Corps remained behind long enough to clean up at least part of the field in its front. The men were astonished to see quite a few wounded Confederates in the valley that separated the two lines. Loren Goodrich of the 14th Connecticut looked "down on to the field in front of us[.] there you could see the poor fellows that we thought were dead draging themselves out of the mud holes[;] the fields were covered with the dead and wounded." Hays advanced his line at 10:00 A.M. that day to collect the remaining wounded and to bury the dead. It had been nearly forty-eight hours since the dead had fallen, and they had become what John P. Lancaster of the 19th Maine called "disgusting, and at the same time heart-rending sights." The corpses were "Piled several deep in places and thickly scattered over the whole ground."[11]

The situation called for the utmost efficiency. Squads gathered the dead and placed them in rows to be counted, separating the Rebels from

.

the Federals. Then they dug a trench eight feet wide and three feet deep and quickly placed the corpses, described by Thomas Francis Galwey as "black as ink and bloated from exposure to the sun," in the bottom. As many as eighty dead were put in each trench, and then the ground was heaped up on top to cover them. Wherever possible the squads tried to place crude markers indicating the unit to which the Federal dead belonged, but much more often than not they simply wrote "that distressing word, 'Unknown.' "[12]

There was no time for ceremony, sympathy, or compassion. The dead were disposed of as if it were a dismal chore. The burial trenches were placed so that few corpses needed to be dragged more than about twenty-five feet, and with the nature of the soil, the heat, the rain, and the fatigue of the soldiers, the trenches were often as little as eighteen inches deep. George Bowen of the 12th New Jersey recalled that the burial squads often treated the dead irreverently. When the arm of one corpse, rigid with rigor mortis, stuck out of the trench, one Federal soldier broke it off with a shovel rather than go through the trouble of heaping extra dirt over it. Bowen criticized his action, but the Federal said "the man was dead, and [it] would make no difference to him." When the corpses were laid in layers, their feet and heads positioned alternately, some soldiers joked that it was "head and points." Bowen also remembered one Rebel who was shot through the head and, miraculously, still lived. It was so obvious that he could not last much longer that the Yankees dug a grave nearby rather than try to take him to a field hospital. He remained unconscious and now and then would "gradually stretch out his hand, feel around till he got something between his fingers, whether grass or dirt it did not matter, then he would gradually raise his hand to his head and try to poke the stuff into the wound." Bowen and his comrades were ordered away before the man finally died.[13]

While many Federals busied themselves with the unpleasant task of burying the dead, others collected the many abandoned muskets and other equipment left on the battlefield. Thomas M. Aldrich of Arnold's Rhode Island battery noticed a loaded and cocked gun lying on the ground. He called out to the busy infantrymen to be careful and stick its attached bayonet in the earth. It was a natural way to handle such a problem, for many other soldiers were already doing it. Soon the field of Pickett's Charge was littered with these guns, "standing as thick as trees in a nursery." Webb reported collecting 1,400 muskets, and Hays's division gathered 2,500. One of Hays's officers estimated the division left 1,000 more muskets on the field for lack of time to gather them. While the other units did not report how many weapons they collected, it is clear that at least 3,900 guns were abandoned by the Rebel attacking force of nearly 12,000 men. It is interesting to note that the number of muskets picked up by the Federals roughly corresponds with the number of prisoners they captured.[14]

The Yankees not only buried the dead and gathered weapons; they also took personal items from the battlefield. A Pennsylvania soldier named Hawkins picked up a morning report listing those men present for duty on July 2 in Company E, 14th Virginia, and later gave it to a lady friend. It finally made its way back to Virginia to be deposited in the Museum of the Confederacy. Sgt. Russell Glenn of the 14th Connecticut came across a dead Confederate who was clutching the daguerreotype of his sweetheart close to his breast. He had obviously died while holding the picture and looking at her face. Glenn carefully wiped the blood off the image and took it, hoping to return the photograph to the man's family after the war, but he was unsuccessful.[15]

Many of the Federals were hardened, cruel men who did not hesitate to plunder the Rebel dead. Staff officer Charles H. Morgan noticed some corpses whose pockets were turned inside out, and he happened upon a Yankee who was desperately trying to pull the ring off a dead man's finger. As Morgan rode by, he heard another Yankee say, "Oh, Damn it, cut the finger off." Morgan noted that the Army of the Potomac seldom had the opportunity to do this, as Lee's men so often held the field after a battle. "Luckily for the Confederate dead," he later wrote, "their clothing offered no temptation for our men."[16]

Some of the hardened veterans in the Second Corps were just as callous to their own people. Hundreds of civilians from the Gettysburg area flocked to the battlefield out of curiosity or a desire to scavenge leather, stray horses, and anything else of value that the army might leave behind. The soldiers naturally felt little sympathy for these civilians who only came to "gaze with ludicrous horror at the black and mutilated dead who are strewn everywhere." But one man in the 8th Ohio went too far. He played a cruel joke on a middle-aged citizen by giving him an unexploded artillery shell as a souvenir. The civilian placed it in a satchel around his shoulder and began to walk away, but a more sympathetic soldier saw what had happened and explained the danger to the civilian. The elderly man "laid it upon the ground as delicately as though it were a child," recalled Thomas Francis Galwey.[17]

After spending most of the day burying the dead, collecting equipment, and snidely commenting on the civilian tourists, the men of Hancock's Second Corps prepared to move out. They left the scene of their triumph over Pickett, Pettigrew, and Trimble about five o'clock that afternoon and marched a few miles away, beginning a long and cautious series of movements toward Lee's escaping army. The Confederate wagon train bearing the wounded reached the Potomac first, but it was harassed all the way by aggressive Union cavalry. Many times the Yankees managed to slip in between Imboden's accompanying horsemen and capture a few wagons. Pvt. William H. Adams of the 8th Virginia was caught in the cross fire of one such raid. He crouched as low in the wagon as possible and survived the hail of bullets that tore the canvas covering.[18]

Even when they reached the river, the wounded were nearly taken by the Federal horsemen. Imboden was forced to organize a defense on July 6 when two Union cavalry divisions approached his position on the east bank of the Potomac opposite a town called Falling Waters, just south of Williamsport. Imboden called on the slightly wounded for help, and Col. William R. Aylett, who had been injured during the bombardment, came forward to command a group of wagon drivers in defending the train.[19]

The rest of Lee's army came to the river in stages during the following days; it dug a heavy line of earthworks to defend the Rebel bridgehead on the east bank of the river because the heavy rains of the past few days had swollen the Potomac. Meade refused to attack these strong fortifications, giving Lee time to wait until the river crested and began to recede. He crossed on the night of July 13, leaving Heth's division, now led by Heth himself, to cover the crossing. It should have been an easy assignment, but the covering cavalry force that was supposed to screen Heth's front mistakenly retreated across the river. When the Federal cavalry came forward to discover what was happening, it launched an impromptu attack on Heth's men that came close to cutting them off from Virginia. Helped by some units of Pender's division, including Lowrance's brigade, they managed to fight their way to the pontoon bridge that had been constructed at Falling Waters. It was a confusing fight, but Pettigrew's old brigade did well, even though Pettigrew was seriously wounded and died on July 17. Brockenbrough's brigade lost several flags. The whole division suffered few killed or wounded, but hundreds of prisoners were taken in the desperate retreat across the river. It was the last fight of the Gettysburg campaign.[20]

When Cyril H. Tyler of the 7th Michigan saw some of Heth's men who had been captured at Falling Waters, he was impressed. "They was all tough smart looking chaps. They are such chaps as I dont like to run after to get a shot at they are men that can use a gun as good as we can and I never saw men fight better than they did at Gettysburg. They done all they could do to drive us from our works."[21]

· · · · · · ·

PRISONERS

When it left Gettysburg, the Confederate army left thousands of men behind, survivors of Pickett's, Pettigrew's, and Trimble's ill-fated attack who were languishing in Union field hospitals or dreading a future in Northern prison pens. Charles H. Merrick was a musician and overworked hospital attendant with the 8th Ohio. He had fifteen helpers but still felt overwhelmed. "Loads of rebel wounded still come in," he wrote on July 6, "and they say the field is Just covered with dead." While there were 1,200 wounded in his hospital before, that number had been reduced to 800 by July 7, and 300 of them were Confederates. Merrick recorded that at least 40 of those injured men "need constant care"; the rest were more lightly wounded and needed only to have their bandages changed now and then. By July 12 there were only 20 serious cases left; the rest had either died or been shipped to better hospitals to the north.[22]

Surg. Nathan Hayward of the 20th Massachusetts had a load of problems to deal with as he tried to care for a surfeit of Union and Confederate wounded. He had a plentiful supply of fresh water but lacked nearly everything else. His most pressing need was for blankets, for many men assigned to bury the dead from the hospitals used them to wrap the bodies. Hayward had to disobey orders to leave the available blankets in the Second Corps supply train for the soldiers on the front line in order to get some for wounded men who had no covering of any kind. He even had to steal blankets from other doctors. Hayward noted that there were far too few surgeons available for the job. "So short-handed are we that, operating almost constantly we are unable to supervise the conduct of attendants and nurses, who are overworked, many of them, and others lazy and ignorant." Despite these obstacles, the dedicated Hayward and others like him slowly brought order out of the chaos pervading the field hospitals for several days after the battle.[23]

Surviving in an overcrowded field hospital was not easy for the patients either. John Dooley of the 1st Virginia endured many trials in Union hands. The only water brought to him came from a muddy stream, and it had a strange taste as if polluted by blood and decomposing bodies. Dooley finally decided to refuse it, adding thirst to his list of complaints. Yet he was better off than many of his prisoner colleagues in the hospital. One man with a large hole in his head made by shell fragments walked mindlessly around, "wandering anywhere his cracked brain directs him. . . . He walks about as if nothing was the matter with him, and pays no attention to any advice given him." A lieutenant of the 24th Virginia had his leg amputated, but the attendants did a sloppy job of dressing the stump, for part of his flesh was exposed and stained with the mud that seemed to pervade the hospital area. He suffered much more from the chill, wet nights than from the amputation, and Dooley finally gave him his oilcloth. Rather than use it as shelter, the lieutenant doubled it up and used it to elevate his stump out of the mud. He was happy, and Dooley was pleased; "now we were both equal in regard to exposure to the weather, for neither of us had any covering except our clothes."[24]

Lewis A. Armistead did not win his battle for life. He tried valiantly to survive and even put on shows of bravado for the Yankees surrounding him. Drawing out some kernels of corn from his pants pocket, he told a surgeon, "Men who can subsist on raw corn, can never be whipped." Armistead seemed to have an "intense, all-consuming desire for the Confederates to win the battle," and he expressed his intention of dying "like a soldier." This he did at 9:00 A.M. on July 5.

His death perplexed Dr. Daniel G. Brinton, one of the attending Union physicians. In a postwar letter Brinton recalled only two wounds, one in the flesh of Armistead's right arm and the other in his left leg, neither of which were life threatening. Armistead had told Brinton that he was weak from too much exertion, lack of sleep, and "mental anxiety" for several days before Gettysburg, and the doctor could only assume that he expired as a result of "secondary fever & prostration." But Brinton apparently overlooked, or failed to remember, a third wound. The accounts of Armistead's wounding consistently indicate the general grabbed his abdomen or was doubled over with pain, neither of which seem to have been caused by the two flesh wounds in his limbs. There is little doubt that a third bullet caused a much more serious injury that directly led to his death. Brinton admitted in his postwar letter that he made no notes of the hundreds of cases he treated at Gettysburg, and thus he probably forgot Armistead's true condition. The Rebel general was buried at the field hospital, but his body was exhumed four weeks later, embalmed, and sent to Baltimore for permanent burial by his family.[25]

One wounded prisoner, Thomas L. Norwood of the 37th North Carolina, managed to escape his captors and make his way to Virginia. Norwood had been wounded in the shoulder and taken prisoner on the field. He praised the treatment accorded him by the Yankees but still burned with a desire to rejoin his friends. He was held at the seminary and recovered quickly enough to steal a student's blouse and walked by all the Federals westward along Chambersburg Pike. He encountered a civilian near the top of South Mountain who asked him if he was a Confederate. Norwood hesitated at first but then admitted the truth. It was a lucky break, for the citizen was a Southern sympathizer who took him home, fed him, and supplied the escaped prisoner with civilian clothes. Norwood continued south the next day, posing as a farm laborer looking for work. He often walked with columns of Federal soldiers, chatting freely with them, until his progress was halted by Meade's army near Hagerstown. But luck again smiled on Norwood, for another civilian came along who wanted him to work in his fields on the other side of the Federal army. He secured a pass for Norwood, but the Rebel gave him the slip after the pair made it through the Union picket lines. From there it was relatively easy for Norwood to make his way to Lee's army and freedom. He had walked forty miles, by his own estimation.[26]

The prisoners taken on July 3 had a long, unpleasant ordeal ahead of them — an ordeal that Norwood had conveniently avoided. Most of them were marched on July 4 and 5 nearly thirty miles to Westminster, Maryland, the nearest point at which to connect with the rail system. James Wentworth of the 8th Florida recalled that the prisoners were fed only hardtack during those two days and were exhausted by the time they boarded the trains. They reached Baltimore on July 5 to be greeted by crowds on the streets. Many civilians jeered at them with "groans and hisses and the words 'you're played out.' " The Rebels retorted with three cheers for Jefferson Davis and three groans for Lincoln. Some women in this divided city quietly slipped money to the prisoners as they marched through the streets toward Fort McHenry. Three days later they were moved on to Fort Delaware, which everyone agreed was a miserable place. Wentworth was disgusted by the green scum that covered the only available water. The island that Fort Delaware sat on was lower than the highest level of the river, and only a levee protected the inmates from inundation.

Wentworth called the place a "hog pen" with a perpetual layer of "soft black mud" on the ground.

Fortunately the Gettysburg prisoners were shipped to Johnson's Island in Lake Erie, near Sandusky, Ohio, by July 21. Conditions were far better there, although the Ohio Home Guards who watched over them had never seen combat and consequently were "pretty rough in their treatment of us," according to George W. Finley. Even when other prisoners disagreed with Finley and claimed to have received good treatment, they were weighed down with anxiety about their condition. John Dudley Whitehead quickly recovered from the slight injury to his knee caused by a shell fragment in the attack, but he desperately wanted to see his comrades in the 3rd Virginia and his family at home. This produced a dull ache in his mind that never went away. "I would give anything in the world if I was free again," lamented Joseph E. Purvis of the 19th Virginia, echoing the feelings of all prisoners. Many Rebel captives could only fall back on religion to soothe their minds. William Patterson Carey Thomas received a Bible from the chaplain of the 2nd New Hampshire while being held at Point Lookout Prison, on the southern tip of Maryland. Thomas had joined the 18th Virginia less than two months before Gettysburg. His Bible was well thumbed, and the passages "referring to imprisonment and condemnation of enemies" were particularly marked and worn, especially in the Book of Job. Thomas was allowed to write a one-page letter during the fourteen months of his imprisonment. He died in September 1864.

Albert Stacey Caison of the 26th North Carolina had been shot in the hand and hip when he was thirty yards from the stone fence. He had tried to escape but was cut off and gave up. His stay at Fort Delaware was awful; unused to vermin, Caison was horrified to find lice swarming the quarters in this low-lying mud hole. There was no clean water for bathing. Point Lookout was a haven compared with this place, even though the prisoners had to live seventeen to a tent and the rations were no better, for the disgusted captives at least had clean water. Clothing was in short supply, and ladies often visited the camp and yelled loudly to the officer in charge, so the Rebels could hear, "Major, how are Jeff Davis's cattle getting on?" Caison endured twenty months in prison, three and a half of which he spent at Fort Delaware, and emerged weighing barely ninety pounds. He "was almost a skeleton, and so weak I could hardly walk. But I was free, and going home, and that was the best tonic I could have."[27]

Benjamin Lyons Farinholt was one of the very few who managed to find a way out of their imprisonment. Farinholt was very active in the many social clubs at Johnson's Island, singing in the glee club, acting in theatrical productions, and reading a great deal. Several of his comrades had tried to escape from the island by swimming, but few were successful. Farinholt was determined to try. He concocted a simple plan and told virtually no one of it, except those who were instrumental in making it happen. He somehow altered a suit of clothes so that they roughly resembled a Federal uniform and waited until the lake was frozen the next winter. On Washington's birthday, 100 prisoners were allowed to go out and cut ice for the prison. Farinholt had previously arranged for two friends to start a fight to distract the guards; while their attention was diverted, he threw off the heavy shawl from his shoulders to reveal the suit of clothes that miraculously passed for a Union uniform. Farinholt began to walk three miles toward shore, barely making it past the guards. In Sandusky he discarded the fake uniform, having worn a suit of civilian clothes underneath, and bought tickets to travel by rail to Philadelphia and Baltimore with the small amount of cash he had managed to collect over the preceding several months. Farinholt crossed the Potomac River by booking passage on a civilian steamer. He borrowed a skiff from the boat's captain, claiming he wanted to visit friends on the Maryland shore, but rowed to Virginia instead when no one was looking. Farinholt reached his home on the Peninsula by March 22, 1864. He never returned to his regiment in Pickett's division but was shunted off to departmental duties elsewhere and commanded a small force of home guards in defending the Staunton River railroad bridge against Union cavalry in late June 1864.[28]

· · · · · · ·

AFTERMATH

Everyone — the armies, the prisoners, and even the wounded — eventually left Gettysburg, but they all took a bit of the battle with them. The Federals rejoiced over their repulse of the Rebel attack on July 3 and saw in Gettysburg proof that their cause was blessed. "I begin to have hopes of seeing the end of this rebellion," exclaimed Constant C. Hanks of the 80th New York; "the events of the past month has contributed a great deal to encourage the hearts of the Loyal & true hearted. . . . the history of the month gives us proof that God is still with & for us."[29]

While the Yankees brought renewed faith from the battlefield, the

Rebels took gloom and depression back home with them. The enormity of the fight impressed every survivor, and the strength of the Union position and its "fortifications" were emphasized in their letters home. Rumors of a return campaign into the North began to circulate as early as July 13, even before Lee's army had reached Virginia, but William H. Jones of the 19th Virginia wanted no part of another invasion. He had lost twenty pounds during the campaign and desperately wanted to go home. Robert Taylor Scott, a staff officer with Pickett, was convinced the defeat would prolong the war. It "was not God's will to give us rest and peace," he thought. "I have never been so completely worn out by the war, so sick and tired of it, my heart yearns for home and for you," he informed his wife. Others agreed that the war would drag on indefinitely now, but they were willing to endure it until peace on Southern terms could be obtained.[30]

It took a lot of emotional adjustment for the men of Pickett's command to come to terms with the heavy loss of friends and comrades. As soon as Henry T. Owen's 18th Virginia reached its old campground near Culpeper Court House on July 24, the enormity of the losses hit home with a vengeance. Little more than a month before, "the woods was white with tents and filled with men laughing and talking, sometimes so merry as to be boisterous — alas what a change!" he informed his wife. "I came to the familiar spot where my tent stood when we were here in June and how sad and lonely it made me feel to look around and miss so many friendly, familiar faces. Six staid in my tent then, now I only am left to visit the scene of our resting place." One of Owen's men also felt the emotional weight of what had happened. He sat down, held his head between his hands, and "presented the most disconsolate picture of distress I ever beheld." The survivors apparently decided to place their tents exactly where they had them in June, clearly demonstrating the loss of manpower. "Some squads are all gone," reported Owen, "and wide gaps are left between the tents."[31]

In the weeks following Gettysburg there were, at most, guarded comments about the need to buck up and endure the sadness caused by the defeat and the death of comrades. Only long after the war ended could one read assertions of anything more from the pens of Pickett's survivors. Chaplain John C. Granbery of the 11th Virginia admitted the defeat was "a sore disappointment," but it "did not break their spirit, nor impair their enthusiasm and faith in ultimate victory." The good chaplain wanted to remember the best of the war as he wrote in 1905, but he did not reflect the tenor of his comrades' feelings as they felt the bitterness of defeat in 1863.[32]

Pickett's men felt even worse when Lee entrusted several thousand prisoners to their keeping on the retreat to Virginia. The men "but little relished" this assignment, "most of them considering it as almost a disgrace." There was so much grumbling that Pickett was forced to complain to Lee. The army commander soothed his hurt pride by praising the division and its gallant attack. He meant no disparagement of their worth by making them prison guards; circumstances made it convenient that the Virginia division be assigned the task. Lee assured Pickett that he hoped to recruit the ranks and that his faith in the division was undiminished.[33]

The division commander could not restrain his bitterness when he drafted a report of the Gettysburg campaign. Pickett severely criticized the failure to bring up supports for his division, although exactly whom he targeted for blame is not known, for the report has not survived. Lee was so stunned by it that he gently counseled Pickett to destroy it. "You and your men have crowned yourselves with glory," he assured the division leader, "but we have the enemy to fight, and must carefully, at this critical moment, guard against dissensions which the reflections in your report will create." Pickett felt compelled to tear up the report, but he refused to comply with Lee's suggestion that he submit one limited only to a recitation of losses in his three brigades. The distraught division commander was not only angry at whomever he blamed for failing to bring up support; he was just as angry with Lee.[34]

Pickett himself began to come out of his depression by the time the division reached Virginia and got rid of its prisoners. He was rejoined by Corse's Virginia brigade, which brought much needed strength to the depleted command, and of course Pickett had a pending marriage to La Salle Corbell. It took some complicated planning to bring "Sally" to Petersburg, for she still lived in a part of Virginia that was more or less controlled by the Federals, but the two were married on September 15, 1863. Pickett continued to brood about July 3 for the rest of his life, often blaming the lack of supports for his disaster. He lived in a dream world. Pickett was convinced that if someone had come up to help him at the right time, his division could have smashed the Federal center and Lee would have wound up capturing Washington, D.C. Even if he was right, to a degree, about the lack of supports, his vision of what would have happened if he had broken through was very unrealistic.[35]

GLORY ENOUGH

Gradually Pickett's men recovered their spirit, but they remained wary, ever mindful of that fatal attack on July 3. The division was shipped to North Carolina that fall to guard rail lines and take advantage of any opportunity to attack Union garrisons. When rumors that the division would rejoin Lee for another raid north began to circulate in March 1864, Edward Cook Barnes noted that many men were not enthusiastic. "Gettysburg being ever vivid in our memory, we felt disposed, should it be left to us, rather to remain in the old North State, leaving all the glory to those already present with the A.N. Va."[36]

Members of Pettigrew's and Trimble's commands echoed much the same sentiments as Pickett's men. They reported the strength of the Union position — "I wondered at our Genls making any attempt to storm" it, wrote Lt. James M. Simpson of the 13th Alabama — and some of them severely criticized the whole affair. Chaplain Francis Milton Kennedy of the 28th North Carolina called Pickett's Charge *the mistake* of the campaign and it will be well for us if our repulse does not grow into our disaster." A survivor of Lowrance's brigade passed this judgment on the campaign after he returned to Virginia on July 14: "I hope we never will cross the Potomac again for I dont believe we ever made anything by crossing it yet."[37]

When Surgeon Wilson saw his 42nd Mississippi on dress parade for the first time after its return to Virginia, he was struck with sorrow. "The regiment was in command of a Captain. The Colonel, dead, the Lieutenant-Colonel, a hopeless cripple and the major severely wounded. Our gallant Adjutant escaped. Many of the company officers gone and in the ranks, great gaps, great gaps."[38]

Before his mortal wounding at Falling Waters, Pettigrew himself echoed Pickett's anguish about the lack of support during the attack. He told John Thomas Jones that Marshall's brigade would have entered and held the Union position "had not ——'s brigade given way. Oh! had they known the consequences that hung upon their action at that moment, they would have pressed on." Jones, in reporting this conversation, refused to name the faltering command, but it undoubtedly was Davis's brigade. Pettigrew also spread the unrealistic view that a successful attack on July 3 would have ended the war. He told several subordinate officers on July 4, "had we succeeded the evening before, no doubt our army would have been on the road to Washington and perhaps negotiations for peace would then be on foot."[39]

The losses in Lang's Florida brigade were so heavy that commissary officer Thomas Claybrook Elder sarcastically commented about how much easier it would be to feed the unit. "So many officers have been killed in our brigade," he continued, "that I shall have no difficulty in hiring a servant now." Bitterness pervaded the thoughts of many survivors of the Florida brigade. Council A. Bryan came from Pennsylvania blasting everything — the conduct of the campaign, the residents of Pennsylvania, and the loss of his brave men. "The wear & tear of this Campaign has made us reckless" of human life, he thought, and he feared that "their will Soon be none left." Isaac Sidney Barineau funneled his frustration into a proposal to fight more bitterly, to "raise the black flag and fight until one side or the other is killed out," as he put it. A month after expressing this extreme view, however, Barineau retracted it, acknowledging that many of his comrades refused to kill unarmed prisoners if they were presented with the opportunity to do so.[40]

Some men, especially officers, tended to downplay the effect of the defeat. Artilleryman James Dearing merely noted that the Rebels were "disappointed in the fruits of our Campaign." Cadmus Wilcox reported to his brother that the army simply "failed to accomplish what we intended." This was particularly amazing considering Wilcox's heavy loss and his emotional reaction to the repulse on the afternoon of July 3. Enlisted men tended to be much more blunt and honest. "I don't think our trip to Pennsylvania — everything considered — has paid at all," admitted a gunner in the Richmond Howitzers. Louisiana artilleryman W. Greene Raoul commented about how dark "our prospect seems to be now. Only a few weeks [ago we] were all in the highest spirits."[41]

It was therefore natural that at least some of the survivors of Pickett's Charge would blame Lee personally for the bloody failure, despite their great admiration for him. Tar Heel Sion H. Oxford of Lowrance's brigade admitted thinking such thoughts of the great man. He "has worsted our Army considerably by Marching them into the enemies countrie." Floridian J. B. Johnson reported an example of quiet, muted protest while passing a stalled cannon, stuck in the mud, on the retreat to Virginia. Lee had stopped to personally help the gunners out of their predicament and called on the passing infantrymen for aid. Johnson wrote, "Of course they responded, but for the first time they were silent in passing him, not a cheer for Lee. Every soldier in our army felt that some great blunder had been made at Gettysburg and they were sore over it."[42]

Yet Johnson admitted that the men could not blame Lee for long. As they pondered the problem over the next several weeks, they convinced themselves that it could not have been Lee's fault. The army leader had accumulated such a huge account of goodwill among his soldiers during the preceding year of unexampled battlefield victories that he was able to weather the brief and muted criticism with ease. They were convinced that Lee's assumption of responsibility for the failed attack was proof that he was shielding whoever was truly responsible for it. Those who were critical at first quickly came back to their old allegiance. W. B. Robertson of the 14th Virginia admitted to a woman named Mattie that he was "broke down" by the campaign, but he was "always up when Old Mars Bob Lee wants me to fight for him: but I tell you Mat that he puts me in some tight places sometimes."[43]

Lee underwent a period of anguish following Gettysburg. He tried to deflect blame from the soldiers who failed to break through Meade's line on July 3 and accepted responsibility for the outcome, but he also defended his judgment: "But with the knowledge I then had, & in the circumstances I was then placed, I do not know what better course I could have pursued." If the idea that Pickett's Charge might fail had entered his mind on the morning of July 3, he "should certainly have tried some other course. What the ultimate result would have been is not so clear to me." The failure of the attack sobered Lee and modified the inflated opinion he had harbored since Chancellorsville about the ability of his soldiers to accomplish great things. He finally admitted that more "may have been required of them than they were able to perform, but my admiration of their noble qualities and confidence in their ability to cope successfully with the enemy has suffered no abatement."[44]

Lee then turned his attention to rebuilding the army. He temporarily consolidated Fry's and Brockenbrough's depleted brigades and tried unsuccessfully to have more Mississippi regiments transferred from Posey's brigade to Davis's command to beef up its numbers. Lee fully admitted the heavy loss of manpower to the Richmond authorities, but he tried to argue that he had done as much damage to the enemy. He encouraged reform in the conscript system so that more men could be funneled to the troops in the field. In a move that astonished and pained the president, Lee even offered to give up his command of the army in early August, citing public criticism of his campaign. Davis quickly and graciously put an end to such thoughts, and the work of rebuilding continued.[45]

Putting the brigades and divisions back together, refilling the ranks, and resupplying their needs was a difficult and time-consuming job. One of the earliest steps toward rebuilding affected the emotions of the men.

In August a wave of religious revivalism swept through the ranks of Pickett's division. Services were held in the woods next to the division camp near the Rapidan River. "It was a remarkable and solemn sight to see thousands of roughly dressed hard fighting soldiers gathered together singing hymns and listening to what sometimes were exceedingly eloquent sermons," commented engineer officer William Alexander Gordon. Infantryman William H. Jones of the 19th Virginia was not surprised at the revival, for he expected some kind of major emotional change in his comrades after they had lost so many friends on July 3. The revival lasted more than a week in Armistead's battered brigade; eighteen men were baptized in a mill pond on August 30. Survivors of Garnett's brigade commented about the volume and intensity of preaching among their chaplains, leading one of them to hope that the revival would continue until "all the noble army are true soldiers of the cross as well as their country."[46]

Pickett's division languished for some time as the officers tried to rebuild its strength. Walter Harrison was sent to Richmond to round up all exchanged prisoners and convalescent men on sick leave, but he found few who were able to rejoin the ranks. In September the division was sent to the Richmond area, where it was dispersed and assigned to garrison duties. William R. Terry held command of Kemper's brigade while Eppa Hunton, barely recovered from his wound, took control of Garnett's old command. The two brigades were sent to Chaffin's farm below Richmond. Pickett tried to have William R. Aylett named to the command of Armistead's brigade in mid-August, recommending him very highly, but both Longstreet and Lee refused to authorize it because neither could credit the report of Armistead's death. Aylett resigned his commission the next month, and Brig. Gen. Seth M. Barton took command of the brigade. A stranger to the division, Barton had recently been exchanged after the fall of Vicksburg, where he held another brigade command. Barton's men were sent to Petersburg. Dispersed as it was, Pickett's command never again acted as a division until Terry's, Barton's, and Corse's brigades were brought together for the Bermuda Hundred campaign of May 1864.[47]

Throughout this time officers on all levels of command tried to bring the division back to life. "I found the brigade in a very bad fix," reported Eppa Hunton to his wife; "nearly all the field officers were either Killed or taken prisoners, the men a good deal disorganized by that fact & others and I have had to work hard to bring them up to something like discipline & drill." Lt. Christian S. Prillaman of the 57th Virginia had forty men in his Company B by mid-October, after Barton's brigade had been transferred to Kinston, North Carolina, but only three or four of them had gone through Pickett's Charge with him. Prillaman hoped that more slightly wounded men from the July 3 assault would return to duty, "for I shall respect them to the last hour of my life."[48]

Finding new men and trying to recall the old ones occupied the attention of regimental and company officers for months following Gettysburg. Henry T. Owen even went so far as to send a notice to the newspapers calling for public help in locating three deserters. "These boys were not hurt" in the assault "and while we were fighting just straggled off and are trying to make their way home." Apparently no one came to Owen's aid with information. Trying to fill the many vacancies left among regimental and company officers was just as difficult, for in every unit the chain of command was ravaged by losses. The lieutenant colonel of the 14th Virginia was promoted to colonel, leaving his position and the majority open. Of the three senior captains, one was a prisoner, another was disabled by wounds, and the third had "questionable" qualifications.[49]

Results of the rebuilding effort became evident by November 1863. Kemper's old brigade, now under Terry, had a paper strength of 1,200 men. Only one soldier in the brigade was barefoot, which Walter Harrison hailed in his inspection report as a vast improvement over the past. The equipment of the brigade was up to par in every category except ambulances, which were too few in number. But Harrison failed to note that the mood of the men might take much longer to repair than the loss of equipment. The replacements that filled the ranks after Gettysburg were not of the highest caliber. James F. Knick joined Garnett's old brigade in January 1864, and he had little heart for the war. Knick worried about his family's welfare, for there was as yet no one on his Virginia farm who could put in a spring crop. Everyone in the brigade seemed to think "that the old Surthen Confedert is A Bout to play out," Knick concluded. The men were tired of short rations that winter, and they threatened to "take thear furlow on thear shoulder & walk home" if more food did not become available.[50]

Further evidence that morale was much more difficult to repair than material support was seen in a raging controversy that erupted in the weeks after Gettysburg. Beginning with initial reports in a few Richmond newspapers and then spreading by word of mouth and through personal correspondence, survivors of Pickett's division complained loudly about the lack of support from Pettigrew's division. The trauma of the failed attack seemed to demand a scapegoat, and the Virginians naturally targeted their erstwhile colleagues to the left. Everyone would have done well to have heeded Lee's advice to Pickett when he suggested suppressing the division leader's scurrilous report, for Lee wanted to heal the emotional wounds of the campaign quickly and prepare everyone for further fighting. But the Virginians would not let this issue die. The public picked it up, and rumors about the cowardice of Pettigrew's division persisted. It was very unfair. As we have seen, two of the four brigades performed very well; one of the others did its best under difficult circumstances, and the fourth deserved censure for its role in the attack. Ironically, that brigade, Brockenbrough's, was a Virginia unit. No one in Pickett's division or in the general public paid any attention to these details. They tended to assume, confusing Pettigrew's brigade and Pettigrew's division, that the Tar Heels were primarily to blame for the failure of the attack because they supposedly ran away long before Pickett's men retreated. As Manes Marshall Collier of the 9th Virginia put it, "The day was ours and was only lost by the cowardice of those N.C. troops."[51]

The North Carolinians were not slow to respond, but they had an uphill struggle. Even though the *Richmond Daily Dispatch* admitted that Pettigrew's men did as well as Pickett's in the attack, the Virginians had the home state advantage. W. C. Garner of the 55th North Carolina wrote a letter to a female acquaintance with whom he hoped to open a friendly correspondence. He had no one else to socialize with, as "virginians in this country have no Sypathy for a north carolina soldier and as a general thing north carolina Soldiers have just as little sympathy for them." Armistead's old brigade under Barton got a taste of this when it was transferred to North Carolina that fall. The men were given the cold shoulder by civilians, who criticized Virginians for mistreating their Tar Heel comrades.[52]

The controversy intensified when a political firestorm broke out in North Carolina. William Holden, editor of the *North Carolina Standard*, published reports of meetings that were held in August in several Tar Heel counties that passed resolutions critical of the war. These people called for a cessation of the draft and for a negotiated settlement of the war. Holden became the spokesman for their views. Coupled with a marked increase in the desertion rate among North Carolina units, these events soured the Virginians even more on their Tar Heel colleagues. Twenty-one men deserted from Pettigrew's brigade, now led by John

Thomas Jones, in July, and sixty-three deserted in August. The increase in desertion probably was affected by the Holden controversy, but morale among Tar Heel soldiers was at a low ebb anyway in August. They were "getting very tired of fighting," thought Lt. Burwell Thomas Cotton of Lowrance's brigade. "The first thing a greater portion thinks about when there is a fight on hand is running." Lowrance felt "pained" to report the loss of men through desertion and advised that "every effort should be made to overhaul them, and every one should be shot."[53]

Loyal Tar Heels in Lee's army responded bitterly to Holden and were afraid the desertion problem was getting out of hand. A convention representing all North Carolina regiments met at Orange Court House on August 12 and passed resolutions deploring the peace meetings at home. They renounced the call for a negotiated settlement of the war and condemned Holden's action. Survivors of Pettigrew's brigade responded vigorously. John Thomas Jones admitted that Holden "certainly had a bad effect on some of our troops," but he went on to assert that the morale of most of the Carolina men was good and their confidence in Lee was unimpaired. "If we ever are subdued it will be the fault of the people at home and not the armies," Jones proclaimed. Commissary officer Benjamin Wesley Justice of the 47th North Carolina called the peace advocates "craven hearted" and told his wife, "We feel justly ashamed of our state."[54]

Lee was alarmed at the jump in desertions during August. He was afraid it would jeopardize his army's ability to fight and admitted that North Carolinians were the chief problem. "Great dissatisfaction is reported among the good men of the army at the apparent impunity of deserters," he warned President Davis. Lee's plan to combat these effects was to increase furloughs and to authorize the execution of deserters. "All has been done which forbearance and mercy call for," Lee concluded; the rest had to rely on "the rigid enforcement of the death penalty." Most of his Tar Heel officers and men, who remained loyal, agreed with Lee.[55]

The desertion problem was a blip in the post-Gettysburg history of the North Carolina units. It receded by late August as the first flush of despair over the battle evaporated and the men had had time to rest in camp and gather their nerves. "The soldiers are getting lively and desertion is not so common as it was a few weeks ago," commented Burwell Thomas Cotton by the end of the month. Food and other necessities were more plentiful, and Cotton was sure that desertion would be a thing of the past if Holden and his people would stop agitating for an end to the war. Yet Cotton was ready for the conflict to end on Southern terms. "I hope they will try and make peace," he admitted. "I never want to go in another fight. I can not escape always."[56]

The work of rebuilding the shattered brigades of Pettigrew's and Trimble's commands continued, in some ways, until the opening of the spring campaign of 1864. Bounties of $30 were offered to anyone who returned deserters to their regiments, and a few draftees were rounded up. Many companies of Pettigrew's brigade replenished their supplies of clothing, tents, and shoes that fall. Lt. Col. John R. Lane, who had been terribly wounded in the neck and head on July 1, came back to take charge of the 26th North Carolina in mid-November. He was shocked at the state of the regiment and threw himself into the task of equipping the survivors and recruiting new men. By late April 1864 the regiment had 760 members, compared with a strength of more than 800 on the morning of July 1 and only 70 right after the repulse two days later.[57]

Fry's brigade was so drained of manpower at Gettysburg that it never really recovered its former strength. It often was joined to other brigades in Heth's division because of its small size. Davis's Mississippi brigade remained intact throughout the remainder of the war, although at a much smaller size than before Gettysburg. Only Pettigrew's North Carolina brigade truly recovered from the Pennsylvania raid. With the addition of Brig. Gen. John R. Cooke's large North Carolina brigade in September, Heth once again had a powerful division that would continue to perform magnificently in the 1864–65 campaigns in Virginia.

The weakest link in Heth's division always remained Brockenbrough's Virginia brigade. At best it was like an appendage to the division rather than an integral part of it, barely contributing to the division's operations. At worst it completely failed to do its duty. The brigade fled when confronted by a small force of Union cavalry on the morning of June 3, 1864, at Cold Harbor, thus endangering Heth's left flank. The men refused to advance during an attack against entrenched Federals on September 30 during fighting to prevent a Union thrust to cut off the Boydton Plank Road, one of Lee's supply lines into Petersburg. The 22nd Virginia Battalion was by far the worst offender in the brigade. "This Battalion on every battle field, from Gettysburg up to the present time, has behaved in a most disgraceful manner," Heth informed Adj. Gen. Samuel Cooper. Lee finally issued an order to disband the battalion and redistribute its men, but for some unexplained reason the order was never executed. The battalion remained intact and on duty to the bitter end, losing most of its men in the disaster at Sailor's Creek during the Appomattox campaign.[58]

Trimble's two brigades also had a tough time rebuilding their strength. When Alfred Moore Scales recovered sufficiently from his July 1 wound to resume command of his brigade, he found his work cut out for him. Two regiments were commanded by lieutenants, and the brigade had a total of only three field officers rather than its normal complement of fifteen. Scales attributed nearly all the ills of the brigade to the fact that most of the experienced officers were killed, wounded, or in Northern prisons. The few enlisted men who remained were without proper direction, did not trust their temporary commanders, and were suffering from low morale. The brigade received a heavy influx of conscripts the following winter, but most of them seemed to be between forty and forty-five years of age, according to a member of the 34th North Carolina. They "made poor soldiers, and fell far short of filling the places of those who had been killed or disabled. Candor compels the admission that this grand old regiment toward the close of the war was not what it had been from the beginning."[59]

By the time the period of rebuilding was over and the major campaigns of 1864 started in Virginia, the argument between the Virginians and the North Carolinians over who was responsible for the failure of Pickett's Charge had died down. It resurfaced after the war when the Tar Heels mounted their strongest attack on the Virginians and the legend they created about Pickett's Charge. The appearance of many letters, written by Tar Heel survivors of the assault and published in North Carolina newspapers in the 1870s, brought the issue to a head. Editors led the charge. The *Raleigh News and Observer* poignantly asserted that the Tar Heels had "followed General Lee with unquestioned faith when living, and we revere his memory when dead, but we are not willing that even in solving the Gettysburg mystery or any other mystery of the war that undeserved censure should be cast upon North Carolina troops." The editor warned that Pickett's Virginians should not be allowed to "monopolize" all the "fatal honors of Gettysburg."[60]

Famous men took up the Carolinian cause. Isaac Trimble argued that it could as easily be said that Pickett's men failed Pettigrew as to assert the reverse. James H. Lane, although a Virginian by birth, stood up for his Tar Heel command in private correspondence and in published articles. James Longstreet, who had become persona non grata among Lee admirers, now fully understood the debilitating effect that the losses of July 1 had on Pettigrew's division. If Pickett's men had been through the maelstrom that day, as Pettigrew's men had, they would not have "felt the same zest for fighting that they did coming up fresh and feeling disparaged that the army had won new laurels in their absence." Longstreet admitted that Pettigrew's command had done as well as anyone in their condition. "They certainly made sufficient sacrifice," he rather sarcastically wrote, inserting another criticism of Lee, "and that was all we had left to do on that day."[61]

The Virginia veterans responded to these Tar Heel attacks as the controversy continued well into the twentieth century. When a pamphlet was published asserting that North Carolina troops had been first at Bethel, farthest at Gettysburg, and last at Appomattox, Robert A. Bright thought it should be slightly revised. "The 1st North Carolina Regt was at Bethel — Some of Her Troops were Farthest to the Rear at Gettysburg, But they Lasted until Appomattox." Even a member of Brockenbrough's brigade, P. C. Waring, had the temerity to side with his fellow Virginians in this controversy. He thought both sides, however, should pour oil on the troubled waters and heal their emotional scars. "There was 'Glory enough in that service for all,' " Waring asserted.[62]

· · · · · · ·

AFTER GETTYSBURG: THE FEDERALS

George Meade had weathered his first great storm after assuming command of the Army of the Potomac. He had acted as a true manager on July 3. Meade had established a good and smart defense, prepared a fallback option, provided plenty of reserves, and hovered around the scene of action to keep himself informed of developments. His style of leadership was oddly similar to Lee's in these regards, except, of course, that Meade was an exceptionally cautious commander who could never have duplicated the stunning offensive successes that Lee produced. Meade would continue to lead the Army of the Potomac like this for the remainder of the war; only the arrival of Ulysses S. Grant to direct its operations in the spring of 1864 enabled that army to bring Lee to Appomattox.[63]

Winfield Hancock was forever changed by his severe wound on July 3. His spirit never diminished, but his physical ability to campaign in the field was severely hampered by the bullet that smashed into his thigh at the height of Pickett's Charge. After spending a month in Philadelphia,

Hancock was moved to his father's home at Norristown because of the excessive heat in the city, but his wound refused to heal properly. Surgeon Daugherty had already removed a nail from the hole, but it now was evident that a bullet was still embedded in it. The nail itself had become an item of curiosity. Saddlers claimed that nails of that size were never used in their work, so curious acquaintances of Hancock gave up the theory that the bullet had smashed into his saddle first before driving the nail into his groin. The only other explanation, in their view, was that the Rebel musket that fired the bullet already had the nail in its barrel.[64]

While Hancock was trying to recover, Alexander Hays visited him at Norristown. During the course of the conversation the corps leader off-handedly asked Hays about Eliakim Sherrill, whom he had ordered under arrest for withdrawing his brigade without authorization on the evening of July 2. "I guess I ought to apologize to him," he said. Hays did not mince words. He had intervened to bring Sherrill out of arrest that night, in time for him to resume command of his brigade and help repel Pettigrew and Trimble. "That's just like all your d——d apologies, Hancock," snorted Hays. "They come too late. He's dead." Sherrill had been buried at his hometown, Geneva, New York, on July 12. Clinton MacDougall, his successor in command of the brigade, remained on leave during most of the fall and winter to recuperate from his wound before returning to duty in the spring of 1864. He led the brigade throughout the remainder of the war.[65]

Hancock had not even remembered Sherrill's name during the conversation with Hays, absorbed as he was by his own problems. The wound simply was not improving, and late in August another surgeon attended him. Dr. Louis W. Read, a resident of Norristown and medical director for the Pennsylvania Reserves, also was in charge of the McKim U.S. Military Hospital in Baltimore. He was all Hancock needed. Read was immediately convinced that a bullet was still in the wound, and he surmised that previous surgeons could not find it because they probed the hole while the general lay in bed. Read set up a chair on the dining table and asked Hancock to sit on it to duplicate his posture while sitting on his horse. This was the key to Read's success. He obtained a special probe and found the bullet on August 21; he removed it the next day. It was eight inches up the channel of the injury. Hancock quickly began to improve. He was moving about on crutches within a week and soon began making public appearances.[66]

Hancock traveled to his wife's family home near St. Louis to recuperate. There he spent six weeks trimming trees and waiting for his wound to heal completely, but he was disappointed in the latter. Even though no foreign objects remained in the hole, it refused to heal properly. The hip bones had been damaged, and Hancock was unable to ride a horse for many months. He reported for duty in December 1863 but had to ride in an ambulance most of the time. During the spring campaign he mounted a horse only when fighting was imminent and then quickly returned to his ambulance. A surgeon attended him daily, and the wound discharged pieces of bone throughout the summer of 1864.[67]

The Second Corps entered the spring campaign feeling the pride of having repulsed Lee's greatest assault at Gettysburg, but its fate was to take it on a very different road for the remainder of the war. The corps performed well at the Wilderness and fought its heart out on May 12 at Spotsylvania, when it conducted a massed assault on the Mule Shoe Salient, a fortified bulge in Lee's long line. It captured a portion of the Rebel line, along with more than 3,000 prisoners, but could not exploit its advantage. During the course of that terrible day the Second Corps fought a dogged battle with defending Rebels who were lodged on the opposite side of the parapet; the two sides clawed at each other in short-range fighting that exhausted the morale of the corps. That night the Rebels retreated to a new line of works built at the base of the bulge. From that day on the Second Corps experienced a long downhill slide. Its combat efficiency deteriorated during the continuous campaigning that Grant demanded of the Army of the Potomac. The nadir of this magnificent corps was reached at Petersburg. Some units of Hancock's command refused orders to attack heavily fortified Confederate positions during the assaults of June 18, and the corps was soundly defeated at the battle of Reams Station on August 25. Here Pettigrew's old North Carolina brigade, now led by Brig. Gen. William MacRae, cracked open Hancock's fortified line after the Federals had made a lodgement on the Weldon Railroad, Lee's lifeline from the south. The Tar Heels opened the way for other Confederate brigades to exploit their success, and the result was that the proud Second Corps, its ranks filled with draftees to replace those men lost since the Wilderness, collapsed and ran. Hancock was humiliated. After two more offensives he finally resigned his command in October 1864, his wound still not healed. It was an inglorious end for a remarkable commander. His corps went on to play a supporting role in the final drama that ended the Petersburg campaign, helping to chase Lee and corner him at Appomattox. Hancock ran unsuccessfully for president on the Democratic ticket in 1880 but lost to another former Union general, James A. Garfield.[68]

John Gibbon fared better than Hancock, for his wound was not as serious. He was taken to Westminster, where his wife's aunt took care of him, even though one of her sons was serving in the Confederate army. Then Gibbon was transported to Baltimore on July 5 to find that his family had been informed that he was dead. He had little trouble convincing them otherwise. The ambulance carrying him and several other officers wounded on July 3 threaded its way through a column of Rebel prisoners recently arrived from the scene of Pickett's Charge. Civilians crammed the sidewalks to see the spectacle.

Gibbon's recovery proceeded apace. He also had the opportunity to help Birkett D. Fry, who was being held at Fort McHenry. Rumors circulated that Fry had been the murderer of Brig. Gen. Robert L. McCook, who had been shot unarmed by Rebel cavalrymen while riding in an ambulance the previous August in Tennessee. Gibbon was certain Fry could not be the man. The two had been friends at West Point, and Gibbon knew his character. A note from the Federal general eased the suspicions of the authorities at Fort McHenry. Later, when he was better, Gibbon traveled to the fort to visit Fry, whom he had not seen in twenty years. The two warmly greeted each other and reminisced about their war experiences. Fry had also been wounded in front of Gibbon's command at Antietam.

Gibbon and his aide Frank Haskell attended the dedication of the soldiers' cemetery at Gettysburg on November 19, 1863, for the general was motivated by a strong desire to "look once more upon the scene of the battle." He and Haskell were not much impressed by the official ceremonies; they listened to part of Edward Everett's two-hour oration and then became bored. They walked over to the angle in the stone fence and regaled a few listeners with stories of the great assault, then returned to Cemetery Hill in time to catch Lincoln's famous ten-minute address. Haskell had the impractical idea that the dead should remain in the hastily dug graves where they already lay, rather than to be disinterred and removed to a central location.

Gibbon recovered in time to lead his division in the spring campaigns. He fought with Hancock about reorganizing the shattered Second Corps after Reams Station and eventually was promoted to command of the Twenty-fourth Corps, which he led in the final attacks that broke Lee's line at Petersburg on April 2, 1865. Gibbon continued in the postwar army and was wounded for the third time in his life in a battle against the Nez Percé at Big Hole Pass, Montana, in 1877.[69]

Frank Haskell had a brief war career after Gettysburg. His Dartmouth Latin professor had characterized him as a good scholar but "ambitious as Lucifer." Haskell had served obscurely as a staff officer for some time before Gettysburg, and July 3 had been his most memorable day. He experienced "the sacred rage of battle as never before," he later wrote, and longed for another "great hour" like the one he experienced while repelling Pickett's Charge. The fact that he had ridden through the maelstrom with several near-misses — a bullet hit his saddle, went through his pants and underwear, "but stopped at the skin above my right knee, and gave me but a *bruise*" — added a sense of inevitable glory to his future. He criticized those officers who shamelessly pushed their careers forward but in the same breath outlined his own plans to inveigle himself into a regimental command. He had a clear goal: to achieve a brigadier generalship before the end of the war. Haskell enlisted the recommendations of Meade, Hancock, and Gibbon to that end.

His opportunity came in February 1864 when his brother pulled strings with a friend who was the private secretary of the Wisconsin governor. The result was a promotion to colonel and command of the newly raised 36th Wisconsin. Haskell raced to Madison to take charge of the green recruits, telling a friend that he was certain he would die in battle as he would need to be in front of his men to urge them on to their work. His regiment saw its first combat on May 31 in the Cold Harbor campaign. Three days later Haskell was killed while leading the regiment forward during Grant's ill-fated June 3 attack at this place. Haskell was twenty yards in front of his men, urging them forward through the foggy dawn light, when he was hit in the head. He died three hours later, much to the grief of Gibbon, who had every intention of offering him a promotion to brigade command in the near future.[70]

While Haskell's promising career was cut short by battle, Alexander Webb's equally promising career also came to an untimely end on the battlefield. He was fully aware of what he had done on July 3. "No Genl. ever had more to depend upon his individual exertions than I had. Had Pickett broken through my lines this army would have been routed. My men did not know me. It was necessary to establish myself. They were to be made to feel that I ordered no man to go where I would not go myself." He later received a Congressional Medal of Honor for his work that day, and Webb was convinced he had become the object of envy among his fellow officers. He had few friends and some enemies in the army. Harrow apparently was quite jealous of Webb and lost command of Gibbon's division to the young brigadier. Harrow eventually was transferred to a brigade command in the Army of the Tennessee and performed well in the Atlanta campaign. He was killed in a train accident in Indiana after the war.

Webb shone again at the battle of Bristoe Station, where his division repelled an impromptu attack by two Rebel brigades. Covering the withdrawal of Meade's army to Manassas Junction, the Second Corps quickly took position along the tracks of the Orange and Alexandria Railroad on October 14, 1863, just in time to meet Pettigrew's old brigade of Tar Heels, now under Brig. Gen. William W. Kirkland, and John R. Cooke's North Carolina brigade of Heth's division. It was an unwise assault, set in motion by A. P. Hill, and was bluntly repulsed with heavy loss. Webb exulted in it. He wrote his wife that he had "just come out of another little Gettysburg fight." The men had every confidence in him, Webb thought, and he resolved to rise in the chain of command. "Once show these men that you are a fighting man & cool, & let them feel that in a fight you are near & directing all things, and you have the best fighting men in the world. But they are too intelligent to fight under fools." Webb had come to believe that he could handle men better than any other commander. "I believe I would put my sword through a skulker in a moment," he bragged, and then he added the highly improbable assertion, "I did at Gettysburg."[71]

Bristoe Station brought some of the combatants of July 3 together again. When wounded members of Kirkland's brigade saw the distinctive corps badge of their captors, they asked "if there was nothing but the 2d corps in this army?" James Mallon, commander of the 42nd New York on July 3, led Hall's brigade, and Francis Heath of the 19th Maine led Harrow's brigade. Mallon and Henry L. Abbott of the 20th Massachusetts had gotten to know and admire each other since Gettysburg. The two were concerned about each other's safety at the height of the fighting at Bristoe. As Mallon was walking over to tell Abbott not to expose himself, he was hit in the abdomen. Surg. John Perry dragged the unconscious colonel to nearby Broad Run, where he died just as the battle ended. Mallon, who was a newlywed, barely had time to bid a silent farewell to his friends. Abbot managed to spend a little time with him; "his eyes were glazing & he could no longer see me, he told me of his friendship." Abbott himself was killed a few months later in the fierce campaigns of 1864.[72]

Webb's career was cut short at Spotsylvania, where he was severely wounded in the head on May 12. A ball clipped the corner of his right eye, tearing the flesh off his temple bone, and he was incapacitated for eight months. He returned to duty in January 1865 as Meade's chief of staff. After the war he was a professor at West Point and president of the College of the City of New York. He held the latter position for thirty-three years before he died in 1911 at age seventy-six.[73]

Norman Hall should have risen after Gettysburg because of his solid performance on July 3, but fate dictated otherwise. Gettysburg was to be his last battle. He resigned his commission in 1864 due to poor health and died at age thirty in 1867. George Stannard and Theodore Gates also did very well on July 3 with no directions from superior officers and even less cooperation from the Second Corps troops to their right. Stannard went on to lead a brigade and a division of the Eighteenth Corps of the Army of the James and was lightly wounded at Cold Harbor, at Petersburg in July 1864, and in the attack on Fort Harrison in September. He lost an arm in the latter engagement. Stannard was then assigned departmental duties in the North, worked with the Freedman's Bureau after the war, and served as doorkeeper of the U,S. House of Representatives until his death in 1886. Gates went on to serve out the remainder of the war on provost duty with the Army of the Potomac and was never really engaged in another battle after Gettysburg.[74]

Alexander Hays also saw his promising career ended by a bullet. Reduced to brigade command after Gettysburg because of the consolidation of the Second and Third Corps, he was killed on May 5, 1864, the first day of fighting at the Wilderness. His old friend Ulysses S. Grant had by now been promoted to general-in-chief of the Union armies and was directing the Army of the Potomac in this confrontation with Lee. Thomas Smyth recovered quickly from his July 3 injury and continued to lead different brigades at the Wilderness, Spotsylvania, and Cold Harbor. He was promoted to brigadier general in October 1864 and was active during the Petersburg campaign. Smyth had the distinction of becoming the last Union general to die in the war. He was shot on April 7, 1865, during the final stages of the Appomattox campaign; the bullet shattered a cervical vertebra. Paralyzed, he asked the surgeons to tell him the truth about his condition. "Don't hesitate, Doctor, but speak candidly, for I am no coward and not afraid to die!" The injury took his life at 4:00 A.M. on April 9, 1865; later that day Lee surrendered to Grant.[75]

Henry Hunt strained his career in the Army of the Potomac over his disagreement with Hancock about control of the artillery fire on July 3. He requested to be relieved of responsibility as chief of artillery on July 26 over the issue, claiming that Meade's refusal firmly to establish the authority of the artillery chief as superior to that of corps commanders in matters concerning the guns would prevent him from doing his job efficiently. Meade stalled, desperate to retain Hunt's expertise but unwilling to ignore his own views that higher-ranking officers in any branch of the service should be obeyed without question on the battlefield. Meade's new chief of staff, Andrew Humphreys (who had taken over from the slightly injured Daniel Butterfield), acted as an intermediary, and eventually Hunt calmed down and withdrew his request. He continued to serve as artillery chief until Grant placed him in charge of siege operations at Petersburg in June 1864. Hunt became colonel of the 5th U.S. Artillery after the war and was governor of the Soldier's Home in Washington, D.C., until his death in 1889.[76]

. . . .

AFTER GETTYSBURG: THE CONFEDERATES

Robert E. Lee went through a brief period of doubt after the battle, but he quickly recovered. He spoke in ambivalent terms about the engagement at first, admitting that "our success at Gettysburg was not as great as reported." Lee never moved so far beyond that guarded statement to claim that a Confederate victory had been won, but he soon came to accept the failure stoically. His son noticed no change in his outward manner when he met his father soon after the campaign. "He was calm and dignified with all, at times bright and cheerful, and always had a playful smile and a pleasant word for those about him."[77]

His strategic thinking did not alter after Gettysburg, but his tactics did change. Gettysburg climaxed a yearlong period of command that saw the heady offensive triumphs of the Seven Days and Second Manassas. The invasion of Maryland was cruelly blunted with the slaughter at Antietam, to be followed by a defensive mode of operations that lasted for nine months and produced the stunning victories at Fredericksburg and Chancellorsville. The Pennsylvania raid was a reversal of that defensive mode, but its brutal failure led to another long period of acting on the defensive that lasted until the end of the war. The Army of Northern Virginia fought as hard as ever during the grueling Overland campaign from the Wilderness to Cold Harbor, and it lasted longer than one could have reasonably expected during the Petersburg campaign. But Lee burned to be on the tactical offensive during most of this time. He knew that a long, drawn-out defensive play around Richmond would inevitably result in a Union victory — not just a tactical victory, but the end of the war. The disparity of numbers did not prevent him from taking the offensive. He had been just as badly outnumbered in 1862, but Grant's offensive strategy and aggressive tactics kept him from striking. Perhaps the lesson of July 3 also played a role in this, for Lee would never repeat an attack like that one.

Lee refused to refight the battle of Gettysburg after the war, but his partisans were not so squeamish. "Somebody blundered at Gettysburg, but not Lee," asserted Rawley W. Martin. "He was too great a master of the art of war to have hurled a handful of men against an army." Other supporters argued that a movement around Meade's left, as Longstreet suggested, would never have succeeded due to Union vigilance and the ease with which the Federals could have maneuvered to counter it. William Allan asserted that success on July 3 was a more difficult prospect than it had been the preceding day, but it was not impossible. "Longstreet is to blame for poor coordination," Allan believed, which doomed Pickett's Charge.[78]

When Lee did venture to make a public statement about Gettysburg, he admitted his thinking on July 3 was too much influenced by his "great confidence felt in the splendid fighting qualities of his people." Those fighting men, who simply wanted "to be turned loose," had to be used to the fullest of their ability and enthusiasm in a supreme effort. Lee also felt that most of his subordinate commanders expressed confidence that the Union center could be breached that afternoon. He continued to believe that if the attack had been better coordinated with the help of all available resources, it might have succeeded.[79]

James Longstreet inevitably attracted all the blame for the failure, and he expended a lot of energy for the rest of his life trying to explain and deflect as much of it as possible. It is ironic that the men who conducted the attack seldom blamed Longstreet; Lee's partisans were the ones who refused to let him off easily. Longstreet's post-Gettysburg career continued the ups and downs that had already begun to characterize this good but venal soldier's life. He took a good part of his corps to the Army of Tennessee in September and played a leading role in achieving that army's only tactical victory at Chickamauga, an offensive triumph. But Longstreet argued viciously with its commander, Gen. Braxton Bragg, about the strategic follow-up. Sent off to Knoxville, Tennessee, Longstreet dallied with ineffectual plans to enter the heavily fortified city, which came to naught. He performed magnificently on the second day at the Wilderness by launching a counterstrike to save Lee's right wing and then turned in reliable performances on the defensive for the remainder of the war. Despite the misunderstandings and mismanagement of July 3, Longstreet and Lee worked well as a team. They prolonged the life of the Confederacy far more than lesser generals could have hoped during the long months of the Petersburg siege.[80]

Longstreet took several different tacks to explain July 3 during the postwar years. One of the most consistent was to remind everyone that the attack was Lee's idea, that he strenuously pointed out the weaknesses of the plan, but that the commander insisted he conduct it anyway. Longstreet argued that it should have been tried with at least twice as many men in the main assaulting column. He also tried to argue that Lee came to regret ordering it and even criticized Longstreet privately for going through with it. Longstreet pointed out to his commander that he had no discretion in the matter. He even tried to argue that Lee regretted not allowing him to move around Meade's left flank. His staff officer Thomas J. Goree took dispatches from eastern Tennessee to Lee's headquarters in Virginia during the winter of 1864 and talked privately with the commander about other matters. From reading Northern newspapers Lee, according to Goree, had come to believe that the Federals had stripped their left flank to strengthen the center by the morning of July 3, and therefore a flanking maneuver might have worked. It is difficult to know how much credence to place in these assertions. It is quite possible that there is a germ of truth in the notion that Lee went through a period of analysis and concluded, too late, that a flanking movement might have been worth trying. But Longstreet and his staff members were by no means unbiased; the general especially was guilty of attempts to manage the historical record. Lee's noble reluctance to talk too freely about touchy matters like this elicits admiration but also leads the historian to frustration.[81]

James Johnston Pettigrew did not live long enough to contribute to the controversy surrounding the attack, but Henry Heth refused to remain silent after the war. Although he did not lead his division in the assault, he firmly believed the attack had been a mistake. Heth sided with Longstreet, arguing that a flank movement would have been preferable. Yet Heth also was on friendly terms with Lee, having known his family before the war. He understood that Lee's overpowering confidence in the rank and file led him to order the assault. He reported conversing with the commander before the opening of the spring campaign of 1864 and hearing Lee admit that he had made a mistake in ordering the July 3 assault. Referring to rumors about his failure, Lee told Heth, "After it is all over, as stupid a fellow as I am can see the mistakes that were made." Lee added, "I notice, however, my mistakes are never told me until it is too late, and you, and all my officers know that I am always ready and anxious to have their suggestions."[82]

Longstreet used the reduced state of readiness of Heth's division as another excuse to explain the failure of the attack. He erroneously told Colonel Fremantle the day after the assault that Pettigrew's men were "young soldiers, who had never been under fire before." After the war Longstreet assured Heth that his division should never have been used that day. "That your division, with bloody noses, after its severe fight of the 1st, was put in to do a great part in the assault of the 3d was a grevious error."[83]

Edward Porter Alexander quietly supported Longstreet in the raging controversy over responsibility for the failure of the attack. He believed his former commander's judgment was essentially sound on that question but admitted that Longstreet gravely erred in his postwar politics. By openly espousing Republican policies during Reconstruction, Longstreet earned the hatred of most Southerners and soured any reservoir of goodwill toward his handling of the attack. Even Alexander could not forgive him for making snide comments about Lee, as Longstreet was wont to do in order to make his points. Alexander thought he had gone too far when he stated that Lee "was off his balance 'until enough blood was shed to appease him.' Many an old soldier will *never forgive* Longstreet such a sentiment." Longstreet outlived most of his detractors. He died in 1904 at age eighty-two.[84]

George Pickett never fully recovered from the trauma of July 3. He was shunted off to departmental command in eastern North Carolina and conducted an unsuccessful attack on New Bern. After capturing twenty-one Tar Heels who had deserted from the Confederate Home Guard to serve in Union regiments, Pickett impulsively hanged them. The Federal government tried to indict Pickett as a war criminal after Appomattox, but nothing came of it. Pickett was demoted to district command near Petersburg the following April and nearly suffered a nervous collapse when a vastly superior but poorly led Federal force, the Army of the James, threatened his command the next month. The situation was stabilized when Gen. Pierre G. T. Beauregard took charge and conducted a counterattack on May 16 that drove the Federals back to Bermuda Hundred, thus saving Petersburg and Richmond from capture. Even though Pickett was the senior major general in this district, neither Lee or Beauregard fully trusted his judgment. What followed for Pickett and his old division were many months of dreary trench duty with virtually no action to enliven the troops. Discipline became a problem, and nearly 10 percent of the division deserted in one week in early March 1865.

Pickett had an opportunity to redeem himself later that month when the last series of Union drives to outflank Lee at Petersburg led the commander to put him in charge of his right flank. Exactly why Lee chose Pickett remains a mystery. Given five brigades and a battery, he completely failed to hold the flank when an overwhelming force of Union cavalry and infantry attacked his position at Five Forks on April 1, 1865. The Confederates probably would not have been able to hold no matter who was in charge, but Pickett made things worse for himself by being absent from his command when the Yankees struck. He was attending a shad bake behind the lines with several other officers. No cowardice was involved; Pickett simply misjudged the situation by assuming that no attack was imminent, yet it left a bad taste in everyone's mouth. The Rebel defeat here was the turning point of the Petersburg campaign. It opened Lee's last important supply line, the South Side Railroad, to Union control and prompted Grant to order massive assaults along the Petersburg line on April 2. Lee relieved Pickett of his command during the retreat to Appomattox, but the forlorn Virginian tagged along with the army anyway, having nowhere else to go. Lee delivered one of the truly stinging comments of his life when he happened to see Pickett near the end of the campaign and remarked, "Is that man still with this army?"[85]

Pickett and his family fled to Canada after the war to avoid his pending indictment for the North Carolina hangings. When that threat evaporated, he returned to the United States to live out the remainder of his life. Pickett forever resented Lee for what happened on July 3, but he mostly remained silent about the war. The two met only once when Pickett happened to be in Richmond as Lee was visiting the city in March

1870. Pickett felt it his duty to pay his respects to the chief, but he did not want to be alone with him. He asked John Singleton Mosby to come along. The meeting in Lee's room of the Ballard Hotel was icy and lasted only two or three minutes. Later Pickett told Mosby that Lee "had his Division '*massacred*' at Gettysburg." Lee died soon after that brief visit, and Pickett passed away five years later at age fifty.[86]

Throughout the postwar years talk had freely circulated about Pickett's personal role in the attack. Many people, including some of his veterans, criticized the general for not taking a more active part in leading the charge instead of directing it from the rear. James Kemper was among these people. "Garnett, Armistead and myself managed our respective brigades, during this advance, without orders from anyone," he asserted. "I never saw Pickett who I understood remained with Longstreet." Kemper was not only wrong but ungenerous, yet his sentiments were bitterly echoed by other survivors of the assault. Lt. Col. Norbonne Berkeley of the 8th Virginia, who was severely wounded in the attack, did not believe Pickett played a large role in conducting it even though he recognized that the division leader probably needed to be in the rear. When he met Eppa Hunton, his old regimental and brigade commander, the two talked about it. Hunton asked him, "Do you believe that Pickett and his staff were in the charge at Gettysburg?" Berkeley replied no; "neither do I," retorted Hunton.[87]

Pickett's staff members rose to his defense, for they were also defending their own actions in the process. They held a meeting in Richmond in December 1894 to discuss their commander's role in the assault and concluded, not surprisingly, that Pickett had done no wrong in hanging back behind the command. They asserted that Pickett was "moving forward with his division, actively directing its movements, and in every respect participating in its dangers." The Pickett Camp of Confederate Veterans in Richmond felt compelled to issue a report to the same effect nine years later, yet these efforts did not stop the charges and questions about his conduct on July 3 from resurfacing throughout the next several decades.[88]

James Kemper outlived Pickett despite his disabling wound. His recovery was slow and uncertain, and his left leg was still paralyzed as of late September 1863. He improved enough to accept promotion to major general and the command of reserve troops in Virginia, but he never saw action again. Kemper practiced law after the war and served as governor of Virginia from 1874 to 1877. He quickly declined in health after that and was too infirm to deliver the dedicatory address at the unveiling of a monument to Pickett's division in Richmond in 1887. "My health is broken," he wrote, "and my tenure of life is extremely precarious. For months I have lived in my room. My increasing paralysis is such that even with the help of crutches I move with difficulty, pain and anguish." Yet he lived until 1895.[89]

Edward P. Alexander continued to serve the artillery arm of Lee's army in exemplary fashion. He accompanied Longstreet to Georgia and Tennessee and returned to the Army of Northern Virginia to participate in the Overland campaign. He was severely wounded in July 1864 in front of Petersburg and recovered early enough to take part in the Appomattox campaign. Alexander was a teacher, engineer, and railroad president after the war. He died in 1910 at age seventy-five. James Dearing, his colleague in the artillery, did not survive the war. He was promoted to a cavalry command with Pickett in North Carolina during the winter of 1863–64. Promotion to brigadier general came in April at age twenty-four. Dearing effectively led a mounted brigade throughout the rest of the war and was mortally wounded during the Appomattox campaign at a fight for possession of High Bridge near Farmville. According to some participants he was accidentally hit by fire from his own men. Dearing died on April 23, 1865, the last Confederate general to die of battle-related causes.[90]

Birkett Fry was exchanged in time to accept promotion to brigadier general in May 1864 and serve during the Petersburg campaign. He later commanded a district in South Carolina and emigrated to Cuba after the war. Fry returned to the United States in 1868 and entered business in Florida and Alabama. He was president of a cotton mill in Richmond when he died in 1891. His colleague Joseph R. Davis continued to lead his Mississippi brigade during the Overland campaign and the Petersburg campaign and until the end of the war. He practiced law in Biloxi, and he died in 1896.

Isaac Trimble lost his leg at Gettysburg but was exchanged in February 1865. He never served in the field again. Trimble wrote several articles and long letters regaling readers and private correspondents with his exploits during the war, particularly at Gettysburg. He died in 1888 at age eighty-six. James H. Lane continued his long war career after Gettysburg, leading his North Carolina brigade in numerous campaigns. On April 2, 1865, the Union Sixth Corps achieved the most decisive breakthrough of Lee's Petersburg line on his sector of the fortifications. No blame could be attached to either his leadership or the valor of his troops. Lane taught in several private schools in North Carolina and Virginia after the war and became a professor at Virginia Polytechnic Institute, the Missouri School of Mines, and the Alabama Polytechnic Institute. He died at Auburn, Alabama, in 1907 at age eighty.

Cadmus Wilcox rose to new heights after Gettysburg. He was promoted to major general and given command of Pender's division for the remainder of the war. Heavily involved in all the remaining campaigns of the Army of Northern Virginia, Wilcox was one of the up-and-coming officers who rose to prominence in 1864. He lived in Washington, D.C., after the war and was employed by the U.S. government in the Land Office during the Democratic administration of Grover Cleveland. He died in 1890. His colleague at Gettysburg, David Lang, ended the war in obscurity and lived a quiet life in peacetime. The same can be said for the remaining brigade leaders in the assaulting column. William L. J. Lowrance slipped back to regimental command when Alfred M. Scales returned to lead his brigade soon after the battle, and John M. Brockenbrough disappeared from his brigade after Gettysburg to be replaced by Brig. Gen. Henry Harrison Walker.[91]

For decades a curious infamy surrounded Pickett's Charge because it was widely believed that one of the members of John Wilkes Booth's conspiracy to assassinate Lincoln had participated in the assault. Lewis Thornton Powell, alias Lewis Payne, had served in Company I, 2nd Florida, in Lang's brigade. He had fought through the Peninsula campaign, the Seven Days, Second Manassas, and Antietam. He always claimed to have taken part in the July 3 attack and to have been wounded in the wrist and captured. Powell remained in Union territory and eventually wound up with Booth. His assignment was to assassinate Secretary of State William H. Seward, a task he attempted with vicious cruelty, wounding the secretary and nearly killing his son before fleeing. Powell was one of four people hung by a military tribunal for Lincoln's murder in July 1865. Such infamy would chill the heart of a Southern partisan who wanted only to believe that virtuous men swept across the valley between Seminary Ridge and the stone fence, but recent research has proved that Powell was lying about his participation in Pickett's Charge. He did serve in Lang's brigade at Gettysburg but was wounded on July 2, not the next day. He was picked up on July 3 and treated at the Twelfth Corps field hospital.[92]

FINAL RITES

Gettysburg lived with the men who survived it, and the families of those who did not, for the rest of their lives. There were a number of loose ends to be tied up: reburying the dead, erecting monuments, awarding honors, and returning personal effects taken as souvenirs during the first few hours following the repulse of the attack. These final rites were played out for as long as there were veterans left alive.

Reburying the dead was the first priority. The shallow graves scattered around the countryside interfered with the resumption of farming and often posed a health hazard as well. The Federals began the process by dedicating a national cemetery in November 1863, but Southerners had to wait until the war was over before they could begin similar efforts. They were motivated by the agony felt by all Victorians at not having the mortal remains of their loved ones buried in a pleasant spot near their homes. William McCulloch of the 14th Tennessee had been killed beside Sgt. June Kimble on the final approach to the rail fence that extended northward from the angle. Kimble later recalled that after the war McCulloch's father tried to find his son's body. He traveled to Gettysburg from Tennessee with money and the determination to succeed but had to go home empty handed. McCulloch had been buried in a mass grave, and his remains simply could not be picked out from the rest. There had to be some other way for people like the senior McCulloch to ease their loss.[93]

If individual remains could not be identified, then Southerners believed that all of their lost sons should be brought home as a group and treated as if every one of them were a hero. The Memorial Association of Virginia was created to "raise means for the purpose of removing the Confederate dead at Gettysburg to the soil of Virginia," in the words of Henry Moode, one of its agents. It was no easy task to find spare cash from among the economically strapped population of the South, but the effort had Robert E. Lee's full endorsement. He was keenly interested in the project, "since learning of the neglect of their remains on the battlefield." The fund-raising effort paid off, and Dr. Rufus B. Weaver of Gettysburg was put in charge of the exhumation of the Rebel dead. He sent several shipments of remains in 1872 and 1873 amounting to at least 2,935 men. There is every reason to believe that Richard B. Garnett's remains were among those exhumed from the battlefield of Pickett's

Charge. The dead were reinterred in Richmond's Hollywood Cemetery with great ceremony. Pickett, still bitter and near the end of his life, was the chief marshal of a column of more than 1,000 Confederate veterans, including James H. Lane. Most of the remains went to Virginia, but a set of 103 were sent to North Carolina. A visitor may walk through this section of Hollywood Cemetery today and gaze upon the headstones of many individuals who survived Pickett's Charge, died after the war, and were buried near their unidentified comrades.[94]

The next effort involved raising funds for a monument to Pickett's division. Pushed through in the following decade, the memorial was meant to honor the entire war history of the unit, not just its famous assault on July 3. Funds were also raised to transport the survivors of the division to the dedication, which took place on October 5, 1888. James L. Kemper was too infirm to deliver the dedicatory address, and William R. Aylett was not invited to do so even though he was willing; the veterans, for some unexplained reason, were critical of his war record. Eppa Hunton refused for his own reasons, and the officials of the Pickett's Division Association finally engaged R. Taylor Scott, one of Pickett's staff members, to give the speech. A contingent of veterans from the Union's Philadelphia Brigade attended the dedication as well. The monument cost $1,800, an enormous sum in the post–Civil War South. Placed in the same section of Hollywood Cemetery as the Gettysburg dead, it is probably the only monument to a Civil War division except those placed on battlefields.[95]

The field at Gettysburg is dotted with Union monuments, but the most controversial one was erected by the 72nd Pennsylvania veterans. They wanted to place it twenty feet from the west wall to honor their slow advance toward that fence near the close of the fighting on July 3, but the Gettysburg Battlefield Memorial Association wanted it placed at the regiment's position near the northeast angle. When the regimental committee began to dig the foundation for the monument near the fence, the chairman was arrested and held for bail according to a court injunction initiated primarily by veterans of the 69th Pennsylvania, who claimed that the 72nd had "never fought in the angle." The result was a massive court case between erstwhile comrades, the hiring of lawyers, the accumulation of reams of evidence, and a victory for the Battlefield Association in the Court of Common Pleas of Adams County in 1889. The 72nd veterans won an appeal to the Pennsylvania Supreme Court in 1890, and the monument was dedicated on July 4, 1891. It depicts a member of the 72nd, dressed in Zouave uniform, swinging his musket like a club, and it

Monument to the 72nd Pennsylvania inside the angle, erected after much argument with the veterans of the 69th Pennsylvania and a case that was resolved by the Pennsylvania Supreme Court. It is one of the most evocative monuments on any Civil War battlefield. (author's collection)

is one of the most impressive monuments on any Civil War battlefield. But it is a bit misleading. While the 72nd did fight its way down to the west wall and engaged in hand-to-hand combat inside the angle against some scattered Rebels, it does not deserve such a solitary and evocative memorial. The 69th Pennsylvania conducted much more intense hand-to-hand combat against great odds during a crucial phase of the fight. It is a shame that the monument does not honor their heroic stand instead of the cautious advance of the 72nd.[96]

While the Federal government issued twenty-four Congressional Medals of Honor to Union soldiers for repelling the attack, the Confederates barely managed to lay the groundwork for creating a similar award for their soldiers. The Rebel congress had already voted in October 1862 to create a Confederate Medal of Honor and a Roll of Honor, the former to be given for conspicuous courage in battle and the latter to contain the names of one private or noncommissioned officer of each company who participated in a significant victory for Confederate arms. Neither award really got off the ground even though a number of names were submitted for them before the end of the war. The Sons of Confederate Veterans decided to resurrect both awards in 1968. Two Rebels, Richard B. Garnett and Lt. William Alexander McQueen of Garden's Battery, were given the Medal of Honor for their role in the attack.[97]

Time healed many emotional wounds left from the war on both sides of the conflict. John James Warren of the 14th Virginia had been wounded in the leg during the retreat from high tide, and he often told his young son stories of the event. "His picture of the wounded, the maimed and the mangled was a night mare to my boyish mind," recalled C. D. Warren, but his father stopped recounting these tales after several years had passed. The same sort of reconciliation with feelings took place on a large scale at the many battlefield reunions held at Gettysburg. Survivors of Pickett's division often reenacted the charge with veterans of the Philadelphia Brigade, at times allowing their excitement to overcome their sense of time and trying to strike each other with their walking sticks. But the fiftieth anniversary reunion in 1913 saw only 120 of Pickett's men and 180 of Webb's command in attendance. Instead of cane play, the two sides shook hands as the elderly Rebels ambled up to the stone fence in a pitiful re-creation of their famous charge a half-century before.[98]

Many Federals had picked up personal items belonging to fallen Rebels on the battlefield to keep as souvenirs, but the passage of several decades and the growing reconciliation of the opposing sections led several of them to return the items. Armistead's sword had been taken by Sgt. Michael Specht of Company K, 72nd Pennsylvania. Specht kept it until 1906, when he gave it to the adjutant of the Philadelphia Brigade Association. It was eventually transferred to Sally Pickett, who in turn gave it to the Museum of the Confederacy. Contrary to legend, Armistead did not give his prayer book to Longstreet or to Henry Bingham to be passed on to Almira Hancock. He had already given it directly to Almira during the 1861 party at the Hancock house in Los Angeles.[99]

Col. James Hodges of the 14th Virginia had been killed in front of Gates's demibrigade late in the fight on July 3. His sword had been damaged by ordnance, but an enlisted man took his sword belt and gave it to Capt. John D. S. Cook of the 80th New York as a souvenir. Cook finally contacted Senator John W. Daniel of Virginia in 1903 about sending it back to Hodges's family. Daniel in turn contacted James F. Crocker, who got in touch with Hodges's widow, who gratefully received the belt. Gates picked up Hodges's diary on the battlefield, but what he eventually did with it remains a mystery.[100]

Even though Garnett's body was never identified, his sword was found in a pawnshop in Baltimore many years after the war by George H. Steuart, former commander of a Maryland brigade in the Second Corps of Lee's army at Gettysburg. Steuart bought it and passed it on to his nephew on his death in 1903. It went to Garnett's descendants through the intervention of one of Garnett's soldiers, Winfield Peters. Another item of personal equipment belonging to the general, his field glass, was returned to the family and eventually wound up in the Museum of the Confederacy.[101]

John A. Fite of the 7th Tennessee had given up his sword to Capt. S. A. Moore of the 14th Connecticut on July 3, and Moore kept it for nearly thirty years before he returned it to the Tennesseean. He contacted a Memphis newspaper for help and soon was in touch with Fite. Moore had the blade polished like new and soon put it into Fite's hands. The two became fast friends. Even Andrew Cowan, the New York artillerist, returned a sword he had picked up on the battlefield to its owner. He gave it to Pickett's veterans at the 1887 reunion, the first at which opponents on both sides of the stone fence gathered together at Gettysburg, and the sword eventually was returned to the brother of Lt. P. Fletcher Ford of the 57th Virginia, the original owner.[102]

The exchange of relics was decidedly one-sided; the victors picked up the spoils, and many years later, through guilt or a desire to heal the emotional divisions of the conflict, gave them back to their true owners. Edmund Berkeley had a different experience. He had carefully deposited his favorite pack of playing cards in a little hole with a stone on top during the bombardment, acting on a peculiarly Victorian conceit that such an item was an improper thing to have among his personal effects if he was killed. Fifteen years later Berkeley visited Gettysburg and asked a relic collector if anyone had ever discovered an old deck of cards on the battlefield. To his surprise the answer was yes. A local boy had found it and sold the pack to the collector for five cents. He took it to a fair and sold it for $10, even though the cards had deformed into "a mass of pulp."[103]

Everyone who felt the urge to return a sword or revisit the field tied up a loose end of their experience at Gettysburg on July 3. These men were the lucky ones, achieving some sense of closure. Many more had no opportunity to come to grips with their experience and remained silent sufferers of a wound, an emotional scar, or a bitter resentment at their defeat. Reconciliation on both a personal level and a public level often went hand-in-hand, as evidenced by the many reunions of Union and Confederate veterans that took place at Gettysburg well into the twentieth century. When the reunions died out, so did the legacy of Gettysburg for the men who faced one another across the valley on that hot July day in Pennsylvania.

EPILOGUE
MAKING SENSE OF
PICKETT'S CHARGE

· · · · · · · · · · ·

"The 3d of July is distinguished," wrote Frank Haskell two weeks after the battle. "Then occurred the 'great cannonade' — so we call it, — and so it would be called in any war, and in almost any battle. And besides this, the main operations, that followed, have few parallels in history, none in this war, of the magnitude and magnificence of the assault, single, and simultaneous, the disparity of the numbers engaged, and the brilliancy, completeness, and overwhelming character of the result, in favor of the side, numerically the weakest."[1]

Haskell was not just spouting his usual hyperbole but pinpointing some of the unique and impressive characteristics of Pickett's Charge. As a tactical operation it was unprecedented in the Civil War, even though some later operations, such as the Second Corps attack at Spotsylvania on May 12, would rival it. Yet the assault has become encrusted with a patina of legend that tends to obscure much of its reality and detail. A close evaluation of the charge will help us make sense of it. There are a number of issues to address. Another look at the preparation for the attack is in order, for only by maximizing all their resources could the Confederates have hoped to break through the Second Corps line. Second, bringing those resources to bear in a coordinated fashion was the next step toward success. We need also to examine the direction of advance as part of any effort to make sense of the charge. The role of supporting artillery, the influence of the terrain and fortifications, and the importance of the common soldier need to be illuminated. Finally, two significant questions must be addressed. Was Pickett's Charge the high-water mark of the Confederacy, the turning point of the war? And, a related question, could the attack have succeeded?

385

• • • • • • •
PREPARING THE CHARGE

"It seems to me there was some lack of judgment in the preparations," remarked Abner Doubleday in his history of the battles of Chancellorsville and Gettysburg. Thomas W. Hyde was an officer on the staff of Maj. Gen. John Sedgewick of the Sixth Corps. He witnessed the assault, visited the battlefield in the 1890s, and concluded that "it was badly managed as a military movement. It should have won. More men should have been put into it, at least one division from Ewell, more. Longstreet should have gone with it." While these two Federals believed that the assaulting column should have been enlarged, Isaac Trimble suggested in his diary that no matter how large, the column should have been advanced into the valley between the opposing lines under cover of darkness and then rushed headlong onto the Federal line at dawn.[2]

But Armistead L. Long pinpointed the key to the failure of the assault when he wrote that there was improper support on either flank of the column. Longstreet did his worst when he failed to arrange this vital aspect of the attack properly. He was motivated largely by a desire to reduce casualties in what he assumed would be a hopeless cause, thereby helping to ensure it would remain hopeless. It would be wrong to assume that the attack would have succeeded with adequate flank support, for the Federals were strong and well prepared and quite likely would have held anyway. But Pickett, Pettigrew, and Trimble had only the most narrow chance for success and needed every small advantage they could get.[3]

The question of a second wave has been broached by a modern historian, but there is no reason to believe that such a formation could have improved the chances of success. Lee did not have the manpower to array a substantial second line of battle behind the first, and it probably would have foundered on the wreckage of the first line atop Cemetery Ridge anyway. The experience of Trimble's two brigades clearly demonstrates this, for his men could not push the remnants of Pettigrew's division forward, nor could they go farther. Lane manfully replaced Davis's brigade to reconstitute a part of Pettigrew's left wing, to be sure, but both of Trimble's brigades could have better shored up Pettigrew's left if they had been arrayed to the left of Brockenbrough rather than behind Pettigrew's right.[4]

Longstreet does not deserve all of the blame for the failure to coordinate the attack properly, for Hill completely failed to contribute to its chances of success. He allowed his corps to operate on automatic pilot, with the result that Anderson's powerful division, which occupied key positions to the left and right of the assaulting column, was allowed to dissipate its strength in the useless attack by Wilcox and Lang. The other brigades of Anderson, to Pettigrew's left, remained tragically idle while Brockenbrough and Davis crumbled. Anderson had conducted the attack of the previous day with an equal lack of attention to detail. That assault on July 2 was even less well planned than the one on July 3, for only Wilcox, Lang, and Wright pressed forward with spirit. All three of them smashed into opposing Federal units and captured cannon, and at least Wright came close to achieving a breakthrough. Only through scrambling and tough fighting did the Federals hold these three brigades and save their line on July 2.

The Yankees were far better prepared for the attack of July 3, and even though Longstreet prepared far better for Pickett's Charge than Anderson had done for the assault of July 2, it still was not enough to overcome the Federals. Anderson again failed to make his division fully available to Lee and Longstreet; two of the worsted brigades that had attacked on July 2 attacked again to Pickett's right, while Wright, Posey, and Mahone remained uncommitted. Anderson and Hill share culpability for the failure to use all available manpower in the vicinity of the assault.

One can point to Hill's lack of experience as a corps commander and his personal feud with Longstreet to explain his failings on July 2 and 3. Much the same has been said of Anderson — that he was unused to Hill's style of command and failed to form a tight working relationship with the Virginian. But Edward Porter Alexander thought that lack of coordination on July 3 was due at least in part to "the fact that our staff organizations were never sufficiently extensive and perfect to enable the Commanding-General to be practically present every where and to thoroughly handle a large force on an extended field." Alexander pinpointed a real problem. A larger staff might well have investigated the readiness of the brigades involved in the assault and offered Lee a more thorough evaluation of how best to use the available manpower in the Confederate center. All of this information was gathered by Lee himself on a cursory inspection, while Longstreet seems to have given no thought whatever to these points.[5]

Another curious issue relates to the target of the attack. There is no creditable evidence that anyone pointed to the angle in the stone fence or the copse of trees before the assault and told someone to head there.

Pettigrew's instructions apparently were to advance directly forward, and his right flank naturally ended near the angle and the copse. Pickett's instructions apparently were to advance and move to the left to join Pettigrew, to make up for the 400-yard gap between their divisions, inadvertently created when Pickett was allowed to select a position for his men that morning without being told that he would have to join with Pettigrew. From the standpoint of the officers in Hays's division, it thus appeared that Zeigler's Grove, not the copse, was the true target of the Rebel attack. Selecting a prominent feature of the landscape — a tree, a church steeple, or a hill — to guide an infantry advance was common throughout Western military history, but it does not appear as if anyone deliberately told any subordinate to do so on this occasion.[6]

Would it have been better for Pickett to attack straight ahead, against Stannard's protruding position, than to have left-obliqued toward Pettigrew? Walter Harrison of Pickett's staff believed so, even though he wrongfully assumed Stannard's was a weak section of the line because his men were green. Two historians have recently argued that a straightforward attack against Stannard would have been a mistake, that the Vermont brigade had a lot of support nearby, and that the angle of the stone fence was lightly held and therefore a better point of contact. But the attack on the angle was a bloody failure, despite the comparatively few Federals who were there, and it was a failure at least in part because Pickett's division had to conduct the left oblique. If he had advanced straight ahead toward Stannard, he could have avoided the time and effort wasted in the oblique, reduced the enfilade fire delivered on his right flank, and brought his strong, fresh division to bear with crushing force on a large but inexperienced brigade. Stannard's men formed a protruding bastion in the Union line and thus were vulnerable to a smashing attack that could have wrapped around the Vermont regiments and forced them back. There were considerable reserves near Stannard, and therefore a complete breakthrough might have been impossible; but there is also good reason to expect that Pickett's men might have crushed the first line of defense in the upper reaches of Plum Run Valley.[7]

A straightforward advance by Pickett similar to Pettigrew's, however, was not possible unless Armistead moved up to close the gap between the two. Failing to close that gap would have allowed Gibbon's division to direct its fire onto the flank of both Pickett and Pettigrew. Again, failure to prepare the assaulting column carefully played a key role in the outcome.

All of this speculation begs one question: should the attack have taken place at all? Would it have been better to move around Meade's left flank, as Longstreet suggested? First, there is no doubt that Lee had to do something. He could not have broken off the engagement and retreated on the morning of July 3, not after the limited success of the day before and the stunning victory of July 1. A large strike at the Federals or a turning movement were the only options, for a general attack all along the line was out of the question due to the exhaustion of most of Lee's divisions. It is clear, with hindsight, that Longstreet's projected turning movement was impractical. Meade had guessed this might happen, and he thoroughly prepared for it by scouting the roads to his rear. Several Sixth Corps units placed near Little Round Top the evening before could have detected the flank movement soon after it started and delayed Longstreet while more help arrived. Even the day before, when Longstreet tried to move Hood and McLaws up to assault the Round Tops and the Sherfy peach orchard, he delayed the movement because he feared the Federals were able to see it from the heights. Moreover, Meade had a strong position already laid out along Pipe Creek and was well prepared to move to it if he was forced away from his strong position at Gettysburg. Longstreet's partisans tend to assume that since Pickett's Charge was a failure, then its alternative would have succeeded, but that is a false assumption. There is no guarantee that the turning movement would have forced Meade to give up his position at Gettysburg, and even if it had, there was another, even stronger position at Pipe Creek.[8]

If the choice was between attack and maneuver, Lee was probably right to assume that the attack option gave him the better chance of success, especially when one considers his overweening faith in the fighting ability of his men. There was nothing illogical about Lee's decision to attack the Federal center, given the history of his army during the past year and the tantalizing though limited success of July 2. The most that Longstreet's plan could offer the army was a prolongation of the campaign on another field of battle, with little guarantee that Lee could find a better tactical situation than what already existed at Gettysburg. Given the temporary nature of Lee's incursion onto Pennsylvania soil, the lack of a secure supply line with the South, and the losses already suffered at Gettysburg, Lee felt he needed a quicker decision. The odds against Confederate success were much longer on July 3 than on any other day of the battle, but they were not impossible, and the preparations for Pickett's Charge were more extensive than any other thus far in the army's history.

ARTILLERY, TERRAIN, FORTIFICATIONS,
AND THE COMMON SOLDIER

The guns were a large feature of the attack, particularly because of the massive barrage that preceded it. Many Federals believed their artillery played a role equally important to the infantry's in repelling the attack, while some Confederates thought their artillery's failure to dominate the field was significant in the outcome. One of Pickett's survivors later believed that the attack failed in part because the guns could not advance with the infantry to blast a path through the defending Unionists, but he attributed this to the exhaustion of their ammunition. Actually this sort of close support for an infantry advance was impracticable in the Civil War, for the infantry had to move much more swiftly than the gunners could move their pieces, set them up, find the range, and fire long enough to have an effect on the target. The closer they got to the enemy the more the gunners would be pelted with accurate small arms fire, not to mention the fire of Union artillery at point-blank range.[9]

The concentration of guns was probably bigger than for any other engagement during the Civil War. Similar but smaller concentrations had been accomplished by the Federals on the last day at Pea Ridge, at Malvern Hill, at Stones River, and for the attack through the Petersburg Crater. The Confederates concentrated significant numbers of guns at Shiloh for the attack on the Hornet's Nest. The Civil War was a transition phase in the sweep of Western military history in the area of artillery use. Theories about the effectiveness of creating grand "batteries" abounded even before 1861, but they were never really tried. The French gathered a large battery at the battle of Castiglione in 1796, during the wars of the French Revolution, but that amounted to only nineteen guns. The French once again concentrated their guns at the battle of Solferino in 1859 to soften the Austrian center and then attack it frontally. But the tendency for everyone in pre–Civil War armies was to disperse the artillery so it could support individual infantry units. Thus it was robbed of much potential for delivering an intense fire on a single point. Not until World War I would the theories be employed on a comprehensive and consistent basis. Part of the problem was technology, for the twentieth century ushered in revolutionary breakthroughs that produced heavier, more accurate, and much longer-ranged guns; the projectiles used in World War I were far heavier, more reliable, and more destructive as well.

The guns that roared on both sides of the valley on July 3 took these developments a little farther toward a twentieth-century battlefield where artillery was dominant.[10]

The relative ineffectiveness of the Confederate barrage was apparent to those infantrymen who had to attack through a hail of Union artillery fire that afternoon, but other men came to realize it later. Longstreet read Northern press reports of Pickett's Charge while waiting at Williamsport for the Potomac to recede and gently chided Alexander. "The Yankee papers say that our fire on the 3rd was very inaccurate passing far over the enemy. Caution your officers to take great pains in future."[11]

The failure of the Rebel artillery to pave the way decisively for the infantry assault was the result of several factors. Overshooting was one part of it, whether it was due to defective fuses that burned too long or failed to explode, or to the shallow target presented by the Union formation on Cemetery Ridge. The thin line of Federal infantry allowed only a narrow margin of error for Rebel gunners as they aimed straight toward it across the smoke-shrouded valley. Also, Lee's artillery chief Pendleton completely failed to coordinate the army's guns, and there was a fatal lack of cooperation between the artillery chiefs of the three corps. This was not much of a problem between the First and Third Corps, but the failure of Second Corps guns to coordinate their fire with that of Alexander and Walker was devastating. Only one of the Second Corp's five battalions fired at Cemetery Hill, perhaps loosing fifty rounds at Osborn's guns. These rounds did good execution; but for reasons not fully explained, the Confederate fire was not maintained, and Osborn's gunners could turn their attention on Pettigrew's hapless infantry a few minutes later. Pendleton also interfered by sending away Richardson's guns, which Alexander had planned to use in close infantry support, and by ordering Longstreet's reserve artillery train farther to the rear for its own protection. Both actions were meant well, but Pendleton failed to inform anyone he had done them, making it impossible for Alexander to use Richardson or to resupply his guns near the end of the bombardment and continue to soften the Federals for Pickett.[12]

The controversy between Hunt and Hancock over who should control the guns mirrored the trend toward concentration. Hunt held a modern attitude, that the artillery should be fully under the control of a chief artillery officer so that someone who understood the technical aspects of that arm could more effectively mass its firepower on selected targets. The argument between the two continued on paper many years after the war when Congress debated the best way to reorganize the army's artillery and engineering branches. Hancock recommended in public hearings the old-fashioned practice of allowing infantry brigade and division commanders to direct the artillery assigned to them, and Hunt conducted a writing campaign to high-level army officers refuting his arguments.[13]

It is no surprise that veteran artillerists supported Hunt's position. John C. Tidball, who had commanded a battery at Gettysburg, praised the brigading of the Union guns in the Army of the Potomac just before the battle and attributed much of the Federal success there to it. He also praised Lee's similar brigading scheme. Tidball also was convinced that the heavy damage done to Pickett while his men crossed the valley would not have been possible if control of the guns had been retained by infantry commanders. Artillery officers such as Tidball tended to argue that the guns played the decisive role in repelling the attack. Few men came to Hancock's defense. His former staff officer Francis A. Walker took up his chief's cause in a postwar article. Walker argued that neither Hunt nor any other artillery officer could understand the needs of the infantry sufficiently to appreciate Hancock's contention that they needed friendly artillery fire to bolster their morale. It was a weak argument, to be sure, for it ignored the tremendous advantages of concentration and short-changed the morale of the foot soldiers.[14]

The guns devastated the attacking columns partly because of the open nature of the landscape, which offered no obstruction to the view of the Union gunners. Walter Taylor was convinced that the terrain was a major factor in accounting for the attack's failure. Pickett's division "was not half so formidable or effective as it would have been had trees or hills prevented the enemy from so correctly estimating the strength of the attacking column, and our own troops from experiencing that sense of weakness which the known absence of support necessarily produced." It was an interesting argument, supported by James H. Lane, that emphasized the importance of using rough terrain and vegetation not only to shield the attack from the defenders but to keep accurate information about friendly support from the Rebel troops. For their part, the Federals often agreed. Even though they were awed by the sight of massed formations surging toward them across the open ground, which made some individuals nervous, many Unionists were delighted to be able to gauge quickly how strong and exposed the Rebels were as they crossed the valley. Color Sgt. John M. Dunn of the 1st Delaware put it well long after the war: "When we saw the Confederates advancing we felt if we could only have them cross the Emmettsburg Pike we would have them in a position to our own liking, where they had us frequently before. This would be their Fredericksburg, and it required no effort on our part to hold our fire until they crossed the pike." That Fredericksburg analogy was fully recognized by the Rebels themselves. In a letter to Governor Zebulon Vance written right after the battle, Capt. Joseph J. Young, the quartermaster of the 26th North Carolina, invoked the image of that terrible battle the previous December when he described the repulse: "It was a second Fredericksburg affair, only the wrong way."[15]

While the Confederates had a stone retaining wall at the foot of Marye's Heights to help them at Fredericksburg, the Federals had their low stone fence at Cemetery Ridge. The Rebels consistently magnified the size and importance of this feature until many of them were convinced they had attacked massive fortifications. Andrew Cowan was both amused and irritated by this kind of talk. He attended the reunion of blue and gray survivors at Gettysburg in 1887 and overheard a Confederate veteran tell his comrades that his men captured two lines of breastworks and entered a fort before he was taken prisoner. Cowan had to disabuse this man of his far-fetched notion later that day when he met him. It took some arguing and a minute examination of the angle to demonstrate to this man that not only was there no evidence of forts but that the rocky ground would never permit their construction.[16]

The fortifications that were used played a significant role. The stone fence marked the boundary between Union territory and Confederate ground by serving as a convenient line along which to establish the opposing formations. Without it Pickett's men undoubtedly would have continued moving eastward up the slope of Cemetery Ridge; when bullets are flying and the enemy is near, most soldiers find it difficult to pass any shelter. Hall's and Harrow's men extended this line southward by scratching out a crude earthwork that served the same purpose as the fence. One officer of the 20th Massachusetts later praised this little earthwork not only for saving lives but for bringing the Rebel advance to a halt. Interestingly, one of Pickett's survivors later thought the stone fence helped his people more than it hurt them. It provided a protective place for them to snuggle close to the enemy for many minutes. Vincent A. Tapscott believed his comrades could have held there indefinitely if Pettigrew's and Trimble's men had had a similar fence to hide behind that aligned with the west wall. If the entire attacking line had held there long enough, he thought, perhaps the Federals might have lost their nerve and retreated.[17]

Everyone agreed that the fences, especially those stout ones along Emmitsburg Road, were key features in determining the outcome of the assault. One of Lowrance's officers was convinced that the Rebels would have taken the Union position if these fences had not disrupted their formations. Color Sergeant Dunn expressed a typical Union feeling about them: "We saw the fences and knew their alignment would be broken. Once the touch of the elbow was gone the confidence of the charge was destroyed. For us to falter would be destruction, to be victorious was to stand and receive the shock, and we stood."[18]

But as Dunn suggested, the fences alone would not have broken up the attack. Stubborn resistance on the part of the Federals was even more important. The volume of musketry they poured into the open space between the fence and Emmitsburg Road was astonishing. It ripped into bodies and fence rails alike, devastating the formations and the features of the landscape. An observer found a board in the section of fence crossed by Fry and Lowrance that was riddled. It was sixteen feet long, fourteen inches wide, and one and a quarter inches thick, but it had 836 bullet holes.[19]

The role of the common soldier on both sides of the battlefield was paramount in Pickett's Charge. Despite the extensive planning and preparation on the Confederate side, and despite the inspirational leadership of Federal commanders, when the nub of the issue arrived, the ordinary soldier decided the fate of the nation. "Gettysburg was not won by strategy, tactics, or any display of superior generalship," opined James A. Wright of the 1st Minnesota. "It was won by the magnificent, persistent fighting of the men with the muskets — and their more immediate commanders." Like most Civil War engagements, brigade, regimental, and even company commanders tended to count more in determining the victor than did division, corps, or army leaders.[20]

On the Confederate side, no fault can be laid at Pickett's feet, for he appears to have done all that was possible to bring his division up to the Union position. His brigade leaders performed magnificently, as did his regimental officers, and the rank and file exceeded expectations. Pettigrew failed to handle Davis and Brockenbrough effectively, but his other two brigades were well managed. It is difficult to blame Pettigrew too much, new as he was to division leadership and with an exhausted and depleted command. It is even difficult to blame those members of Fry's and Marshall's brigades who remained, unwounded, in the comparative safety of Emmitsburg Road rather than join their comrades in attempting to advance into the face of that withering musketry coming from the Union line. If the fences and the slightly sunken roadbed had not been there, they would undoubtedly have continued with their comrades. Even more men of Davis's brigade appear to have stopped at the pike, and Brockenbrough's unfortunate men had every strike against them, including Brockenbrough's grossly inadequate leadership, the hail of artillery fire from Cemetery Ridge, and the stout resistance of the 8th Ohio in their front. Trimble's two brigades performed very well despite their depletion of numbers and loss of officers.

On the Union side the members of the 69th Pennsylvania played a huge role in stopping Pickett. The 72nd Pennsylvania performed well in a secondary role, but the 71st Pennsylvania performed poorly. It ran to save itself even though the 69th Pennsylvania, under much more pressure, did not run. The 19th Massachusetts, the 42nd New York, and the two companies of the 106th Pennsylvania anchored the shoulder of a ring of bluecoated troops that contained Armistead's attempted breakthrough. Hall's and Harrow's men reinforced and strengthened that shoulder; they could do relatively little more than that due to the obstacles, the copse and the 69th Pennsylvania, in their front. Gates's demibrigade supported that shoulder by re-forming the line along the stone fence and the earthwork to keep the Rebels from taking advantage of the shifting of Hall and Harrow to the copse.

Because of its flanking maneuver, Stannard's Vermont brigade has garnered the lion's share of the credit for breaking Pickett's Charge, but this has been overblown. The Vermonters hurt Pickett a lot, but there is no evidence that the flank fire was decisive. Pickett's men were stopped in their front, at the angle and along the fence-earthwork. The attack would have failed even if Stannard had not assumed a forward position. It is interesting to note that Pickett's men outflanked themselves, in a manner of speaking. Stannard did not have to move forward to get on their flank; he simply readjusted the position of two of his regiments to fire into the Rebels as they brought their right flank into his new line of fire. Also, the Wilcox-Lang attack was mostly stopped by the artillery, with the 16th Vermont delivering the coup de grâce.

Hays's men did stout service on the Union right; outnumbered greatly by Pettigrew and Trimble, they refused to yield. The 8th Ohio played a much more decisive role in annoying and dispersing Pettigrew's left flank than Stannard's men did on Pickett's right. It stopped Brockenbrough's disjointed advance and then forced Davis to retreat.

Hancock and Gibbon played no decisive role in repelling the Confederates. Both encouraged and inspired their men, but neither was responsible for initiating the flanking maneuver of Stannard. Also, Hancock had been wrong to interfere with Hunt's carefully considered plan to control the artillery fire during the bombardment. Hays also was a very effective inspirational leader; he encouraged his men to stockpile weapons so they could compensate for their sparse number with added firepower, a key element in the repulse of Pettigrew and Trimble. Despite Hays's competitiveness, eccentricities, and tasteless displays, he was an excellent division commander. His brigade leaders played little role in the repulse in contrast to Gibbon's brigade commanders and Stannard and Gates, who were instrumental in it.

. . . .

HIGH TIDES, TURNING POINTS, AND MIGHT-HAVE-BEENS

A short time after the end of the war, John B. Bachelder met Walter Harrison at Gettysburg. Bachelder, who had become the unofficial historian of the battle, and Harrison, a former member of Pickett's staff, spent quite a bit of time near the copse discussing the engagement. Harrison pointed out to the Yankee how the clump of trees had served to delineate the junction of the two Confederate wings. Bachelder was so taken by this that he improvised a catchy phrase for it. "Why, Colonel, as the battle of Gettysburg was the crowning event of this campaign, this copse of trees must have been the high water mark of the rebellion." Harrison readily agreed with this assessment, and from then on Bachelder religiously embellished the importance of the copse and of the attack. He claimed to have later prevented the owner of the land from chopping down the trees and eventually convinced the Gettysburg Battlefield Memorial Association to erect an iron fence around them in 1887. He also was the moving force behind the effort to create a bronze tablet at the clump, further solidifying its fame as the high-water mark of the Confederacy. The legend would grow with each passing generation.

Bachelder was a rather odd person. A civilian often called colonel because he had been offered that rank in the Pennsylvania militia before the war, Bachelder had accompanied the Army of the Potomac in the early phase of the Civil War, hoping to map and collect detailed information on the "decisive" engagement of the conflict. His effort to do the same historical work for the battle of Bunker Hill in the American Revolution seems to have primed him for this task. Gettysburg captured his imagination and seemed to him to be the truly decisive battle of the rebellion. He began studying the field and gathering information from participants right after Lee retreated from Pennsylvania, and he continued to do so for the rest of his long life. Bachelder, more than anyone else, was responsible for creating the myth that Gettysburg was the turning point of the Civil War and Pickett's Charge was the high-water mark of the Southern war effort.[21]

Many veterans of the attack, captivated by Bachelder's enthusiasm and devotion, agreed with him. "Without a doubt the third days fight at Gettysburg was the climax battle of the war," wrote Robert S. Henshaw of the 7th Virginia. Longstreet even admitted to this viewpoint nearly thirty years after the event by writing that the "Pickett charge was the crowning point of Gettysburg and Gettysburg of the war." Benjamin Lyons Farinholt of the 53rd Virginia waxed eloquent on this subject. "And when the sun went down on the shattered and broken columns of Pickett's Division in the final charge on Cemetery Hill at Gettysburg on the 3rd of July '63, the Southern Cross and all we fought for was as decisively lost as was the Crown of Napoleon when the Imperial Guards bearing the Eagles of France went down in the magnificent charge of Ney at Waterloo." Ironically, no one among the survivors of Pettigrew's, Trimble's, or Wilcox's and Lang's commands ever made such statements. They only recalled the terror, the killing, and their miraculous escape without investing the attack with anything more than what it was from a purely tactical viewpoint. The only time these veterans discussed Pickett's Charge as a high-water mark of the Confederacy was when they tried to counter the Virginians' unfair accusations about Pettigrew's men letting them down.[22]

Of course the ultimate expression of Pickett's Charge as a turning point of the war was penned by William Faulkner in his novel *Intruder in the Dust*.

For every Southern boy fourteen years old, not once but whenever he wants it, there is the instant when it's still not yet two oclock on that July afternoon in 1863, the brigades are in position behind the rail fence, the guns are laid and ready in the woods and the furled flags are already loosened to break out and Pickett himself with his long oiled ringlets and his hat in one hand probably and his sword in the other looking up the hill waiting for Longstreet to give the word and it's all in the balance, it hasn't happened yet, it hasn't even begun yet, it not only hasn't begun yet but there is still time for it not to begin against that position and those circumstances which made more men than Garnett and Kemper and Armistead and Wilcox look grave yet it's going to begin, we all know that, we have come too far with too much at stake and that moment doesn't need even a fourteen-year-old boy to think *This time. Maybe this time* with all this much to lose and all this much to gain: Pennsylvania, Maryland, the world, the golden dome of Washington itself to crown with desperate and unbelievable victory the desperate gamble, the cast made two years ago.[23]

Faulkner's breathless, almost juvenile wonder at the enormous weight of history that pivoted on the attack has resonated for decades in American culture. But is this importance justified? Was the assault truly the ending of something that might have led to Confederate independence? To answer yes to these questions is to assume that the tactical success of Pickett's Charge would have been translated into strategic success. In other words, the assumption is that Pickett, Pettigrew, and Trimble could have broken up Meade's position and forced the Army of the Potomac to retreat in a manner that would likely have resulted in some strategic gain for Lee. The true question, then, is how likely was it, and what would have been the probable result if the Confederates had broken through?

Pickett and his associates had a marginal chance, at best, of achieving a breakthrough. They had a better prospect of doing so at the angle because of the decimation of the Federal guns there during the bombardment, but even with their slim advantage they failed to crush Webb's embattled brigade. If the Rebel guns had been able to reduce McGilvery's and Osborn's concentrations of artillery during the barrage, the infantry might have had a better chance to accomplish something. Still, it is difficult to imagine a decisive breakthrough taking place anywhere along the line, least likely along Pettigrew's front. This is based mostly on our knowledge of what actually happened and how it took place; no one could have known for certain before the attack that there was no chance of a breakthrough, despite Longstreet's gut-level estimate.

Even if the Rebels could have broken through the Second Corps line, Meade had ample reserve troops in position to deal effectively with the result. The Sixth Corps was in easy supporting distance, and several brigades from other units were nearby as well. Lt. William B. Taylor of the 11th North Carolina guessed this fact a few weeks after the battle when he wrote to his mother that "even if our division had have gone over the walls there were enough of the enemy to have eaten us up and then not had half rations." If a breakthrough of the first line was marginally possible, then a follow-up to that success was unthinkable; Pickett's, Pettigrew's, and Trimble's bloodied commands could not have taken on all the Union reserves. Meade would have stayed on Cemetery Ridge in any case.[24]

One can take this scenario even further and ponder what would have happened if the unthinkable had taken place, if the Confederates had broken through the reserve troops as well. If Meade had been forced to evacuate his strong position at Gettysburg, he could easily have implemented his plan to retire to the even stronger Pipe Creek line in Maryland. The breakthrough would have affected a small portion of his large army, for the Confederate right and left had no plans to attack immediately after Pickett, Pettigrew, and Trimble surged across Cemetery Ridge. Most of Meade's army probably would have been able to retire in an orderly fashion along prearranged routes to a prepared defensive position. The road to Washington would have been blocked even more effectively than it had been at Gettysburg, and Lee's army would have been more exhausted and short of supplies. It was a fact of life in the Civil War that a defeated army had all the advantages in escaping the battlefield intact — it happened many times — while the victorious army had great difficulty discerning its enemy's escape route and organizing a sizable pursuit in time to catch it. In short, it is extremely difficult to foresee a strategic success in the Pennsylvania raid even if the ultimate tactical victory had taken place on July 3. Lee needed a quick battlefield decision in Pennsylvania; he could not afford to prolong this campaign indefinitely because he had no base of supplies and his army was dangerously extended.

Not only is it nearly impossible to believe that a tactical success on July 3 would have resulted in a strategic success in the campaign, but it is also extremely difficult to believe that there ever was a possibility of any kind that Lee's raid into Pennsylvania would have resulted in a decisive blow for Confederate independence. Lee himself never seemed to have believed that this one campaign was likely to bring the war to a close. He and Jackson had discussed the possibility of invading Pennsylvania as early as January 1863, right after the battle of Fredericksburg. The Army of Northern Virginia had been holding the line of the Rappahannock River, about sixty miles north of Richmond and some forty miles south of Washington, ever since the previous November. Lee chafed at remaining on the defensive for too long. The potential disaster he narrowly averted at Chancellorsville, when the Army of the Potomac outmaneuvered him while a good portion of his men under Longstreet were away, deeply worried the Rebel commander. He had achieved his greatest tactical victory there; but this success hid the fact that he easily could have seen his army destroyed if not for some lucky circumstances, and the losses he suffered were enormous. Lee realized he could not remain on the defensive along the Rappahannock line indefinitely and quickly decided to implement the long-contemplated northward thrust when Longstreet rejoined him.

Lee wanted to get away from the Rappahannock and draw his enemy out of Virginia to ground where he could be fought and defeated, in either Maryland or Pennsylvania. Lee also wanted to gather supplies in Northern territory, to compensate for the growing logistical difficulties his army faced while operating in depleted Virginia. He also hoped to encourage the growth of Copperhead sentiment in the Northern states by demonstrating that the war was not going well for Union arms. He knew that a short stab into southern Pennsylvania would disarrange any Union plans for an offensive toward Richmond. Lee also worried about the growing disparity of numbers between the opposing sides. That differential had not worried him too much in the heady days of 1862, but Chancellorsville had demonstrated that the North could conceivably hurl army after army against him, suffering defeats all the time, yet still win the war in the end. This latter reason for the campaign echoed a rather desperate tone that had crept into his strategic thinking.

All of these sound reasons for initiating the campaign, expressed by Lee in stages throughout June, never amounted to a decisive turning point in the war. Lee spoke of the campaign as if it were just one more step along the road toward a possible and distant victory. He fully understood that one campaign could not make or break a huge, complex war effort, and he was fully aware of the persistent lack of victory in each successive campaign fought by his Western colleagues in Tennessee and Mississippi, where the Rebels suffered a series of dismal defeats and consequent loss of territory. No quick strategic victory in Pennsylvania, no matter how spectacular, could offset the loss of Tennessee, Mississippi, and the Mississippi River.

Lee meant to keep all of his available troops in hand rather than allow the Richmond authorities to divert Pickett's division or any other troops to Bragg or Pemberton. He succeeded in convincing Davis that taking those troops on a northward drive would be the best way to use them, an idea seconded by modern-day historians who point out that these troops likely would have been wasted by the strategic bungling of the two main Western generals. Lee did not intend to occupy any Northern town or even hold any chunk of free territory permanently. His campaign was a raid, not an invasion, and Davis heartily endorsed such a move. But the president refused to be drawn into an all-or-nothing campaign. He insisted on retaining six brigades in the Richmond area that Lee sorely wanted in Pennsylvania, including Pickett's remaining brigades.

Following the defeat at Gettysburg and the retreat to Virginia, Lee pondered the unpleasant prospect of resuming his old position along the Rappahannock River. It was good only for repelling a frontal advance by the Yankees, he thought, for the Chancellorsville campaign had demonstrated to him how easily it could be turned. The truth was that with an intelligent commander in charge of the Army of the Potomac, that river line could not be held by Lee. He told Henry Heth a few months after Gettysburg that he was convinced that he had had no choice but to abandon the Rappahannock line after Chancellorsville. The general "considered the problem in every possible phase," as Heth remembered Lee's conversation, and "it resolved itself into the choice of one of two things — either to retire on Richmond and stand a siege, which must ultimately have ended in surrender, or to invade Pennsylvania. I chose the latter." That was why Lee persisted in believing that the Pennsylvania raid was the correct strategy for him to follow, and he told Heth that he continued to believe it was so even as he prepared to meet Grant in the spring of 1864. But there was no possibility of it ever happening again.

The Gettysburg battle resulted from a campaign that was inspired by Lee's almost desperate need to get away from an increasingly untenable position on the Rappahannock River. He further justified the raid to the authorities in Richmond by citing the need to forage off the enemy's countryside, encouraging antiwar dissent in the free states and spoiling any plans for a Union offensive in Virginia. He never looked on the Pennsylvania campaign as the one and only stroke to win Confederate independence.

Modern students have argued that a smashing Rebel victory on Northern soil, no matter what the purely military results, would have depressed Northern morale and led to some sort of collapse of willpower among the

Northern people. But they have forgotten that Union armies had been winning such smashing victories on Southern soil ever since Fort Donelson, yet the Confederate people continued to fight hard. Northern defeats on Southern soil, such as those suffered in the Seven Days, Second Manassas, and Chancellorsville, depressed Northern spirits but often led to renewed energy and war enthusiasm. After all, the Northern response to the Seven Days was to create a whole new set of war policies, including new calls for troops, confiscation of Southern property, and emancipation of the slaves, which were key elements in the eventual Union victory. In those cases military defeat led to a political renewal of the North's will to fight. An invading army on Pennsylvania soil energized the Northern war effort, and a victory by that army might well have intensified rather than decreased Northern measures to fight.[25]

Several historians have for some time questioned the commonly held assumption that the Pennsylvania raid was the Confederacy's best chance to win the war. They argue that the Western campaigns, especially those that drove along the rail line linking Louisville, Nashville, Chattanooga, and Atlanta, were much more decisive in determining the outcome of the war. Just as the Rebel defeat at Gettysburg did not destroy Confederate chances for winning the war, Meade's victory there did not ensure Northern victory. One historian has recently written that "Gettysburg did not change the eastern equilibrium. At most, Gettysburg restored a balance in the East that was threatening to tilt toward the Rebels after their great victories at Fredericksburg and Chancellorsville."[26]

If Lee did not believe his Pennsylvania raid would likely be a decisive blow for Confederate independence, then why did he persist in such aggressive tactics over the objections of his chief subordinate and in the face of heavy losses and limited success on July 1 and 2? Perhaps the answer lies in the strategic situation of his army. He was facing extreme logistical difficulties in this campaign, even though his penetration of Northern territory was slight. The army had no fully functioning supply line connecting it to the South, and Lee was unlikely to secure a base of operations in some Pennsylvania city. Thus it had to be content with what supplies of ammunition, medicine, and quartermaster stores it took with it. A Federal officer named George B. Davis compared the logistical and strategic situation of Lee's army with a spouting column of water "forced into the air by a powerful pump; it encountered constantly increasing resistance, the demands of gravity became steadily more urgent, while its velocity steadily diminished, and it received no increase of force as it ascended." In short, the Confederacy did not have the logistical capacity for sustaining a deep penetration of enemy territory or an extended stay during a limited penetration of it. This led some observers and armchair strategists to conclude that Lee would have been much better off fighting a major battle in Maryland.[27]

This helps to explain why he so stubbornly insisted on Pickett's Charge. Despite clear signs that the tactical offensive was paying diminishing returns from one day to the next at Gettysburg, he ignored reasonable arguments and pushed the plan through, with disastrous results. Lee found himself in enemy territory with a limited amount of supplies and the enemy fighting harder than ever before. He desperately wanted to pull off a miracle as had happened at Chancellorsville. But the Army of the Potomac was not demoralized or led by a man who had lost his nerve. While Lee and Pickett were about the only men who seemed to have thought the assault was a good idea, many others would later use phrases such as "heroic but foolish" to describe it.[28]

There was one way in which Pickett's Charge was a high-water mark, but it had nothing to do with the strategy of the war. It was the best day of fighting by Pickett's division, and despite their immense losses and the controversies about their role in it, the most famous day for the rest of the Confederate attacking column as well. "Never had the brigade been better handled, and never has it done better service in the field of battle," commented Maj. Charles S. Peyton when he wrote the report for Garnett's brigade after the battle. Similar judgments were touted by commanders for many units after every battle in the war, but no one could dispute the accuracy of Peyton's words.[29]

Symbolically Pickett's Charge was the high-water mark of Lee's army as a whole. That famous field force had many brilliant days of battle during the war, but none shone brighter in the public mind than July 3. Win or lose, those Rebels who tried to break the Second Corps line came to be admired by people on both sides of the valley that symbolically separated North and South for a few hours in July 1863.

ORDER OF BATTLE

. . . .

Army of the Potomac: Maj. Gen. George G. Meade

First Corps: Maj. Gen. John Newton

First Division: Brig. Gen. Abner Doubleday

First Brigade: Col. Chapman Biddle
80th New York: Col. Theodore B. Gates
151st Pennsylvania: Capt. Walter L. Owens (rest of brigade not engaged)

Third Brigade: Brig. Gen. George J. Stannard
13th Vermont: Col. Francis V. Randall
14th Vermont: Col. William T. Nichols
16th Vermont: Col. Wheelock G. Veazey (rest of brigade not engaged)

Second Corps: Maj. Gen. Winfield S. Hancock

Second Division: Brig. Gen. John Gibbon

First Brigade: Brig. Gen. William Harrow
19th Maine: Col. Francis E. Heath
15th Massachusetts: Lt. Col. George C. Joslin
1st Minnesota: Capt. Nathan S. Messick
82nd New York: Capt. John Darrow

Second Brigade: Brig. Gen. Alexander S. Webb
69th Pennsylvania: Col. Dennis O'Kane
71st Pennsylvania: Col. Richard Penn Smith
72nd Pennsylvania: Lt. Col. Theodore Hesser
106th Pennsylvania: Lt. Col. William L. Curry (Companies A and B, Capt.
John J. Sperry; rest of regiment not engaged)

Third Brigade: Col. Norman J. Hall
19th Massachusetts: Col. Arthur F. Devereux
20th Massachusetts: Col. Paul J. Revere

405

7th Michigan: Lt. Col. Amos E. Steele Jr.
42nd New York: Col. James E. Mallon
59th New York: Capt. William McFadden

Unattached
1st Company Massachusetts Sharpshooters: Capt. William Plumer

Third Division: Brig. Gen. Alexander Hays

First Brigade: Col. Samuel S. Carroll
8th Ohio: Lt. Col. Franklin Sawyer (rest of brigade not engaged)

Second Brigade: Col. Thomas A. Smyth
14th Connecticut: Maj. Theodore G. Ellis
1st Delaware: Lt. Col. Edward P. Harris
12th New Jersey: Maj. John T. Hill
10th New York Battalion: Maj. George F. Hopper
108th New York: Lt. Col. Francis E. Pierce

Third Brigade: Col. Eliakim Sherrill
39th New York (four companies): Maj. Hugo Hildebrandt
111th New York: Col. Clinton D. MacDougall
125th New York: Lt. Col. Levi Crandell
126th New York: Lt. Col. James M. Bull

Artillery Brigade, Second Corps: Capt. John G. Hazard
Battery B, 1st New York: Capt. James McKay Rorty
Battery A, 1st Rhode Island: Capt. William A. Arnold
Battery B, 1st Rhode Island: Lt. T. Fred Brown
Battery I, 1st U.S.: Lt. George A. Woodruff
Battery A, 4th U.S.: Lt. Alonzo H. Cushing

Army of Northern Virginia: Gen. Robert E. Lee

First Corps: Lt. Gen. James Longstreet

Pickett's Division: Maj. Gen. George E. Pickett

Kemper's Brigade: Brig. Gen. James L. Kemper
1st Virginia: Col. Lewis B. Williams
3rd Virginia: Col. Joseph Mayo Jr.
7th Virginia: Col. Waller Tazewell Patton
11th Virginia: Maj. Kirkwood Otey
24th Virginia: Col. William R. Terry

Garnett's Brigade: Brig. Gen. Richard B. Garnett
8th Virginia: Col. Eppa Hunton
18th Virginia: Lt. Col. Henry A. Carrington
19th Virginia: Col. Henry Gantt

28th Virginia: Col. Robert C. Allen
56th Virginia: Col. William D. Stuart

Armistead's Brigade: Brig. Gen. Lewis A. Armistead
  9th Virginia: Maj. John C. Owens
  14th Virginia: Col. James G. Hodges
  38th Virginia: Col. Edward C. Edmonds
  53rd Virginia: Col. William R. Aylett
  57th Virginia: Col. John Bowie Magruder

Artillery Battalion: Maj. James Dearing
  Blount's Virginia Battery: Capt. Joseph G. Blount
  Fauquier Virginia Artillery: Capt. Robert M. Stribling
  Hampden Virginia Artillery: Capt. William H. Caskie
  Richmond Fayette Artillery: Capt. Miles C. Macon

Third Corps: Lt. Gen. A. P. Hill

Anderson's Division: Maj. Gen. Richard H. Anderson

Wilcox's Brigade: Brig. Gen. Cadmus M. Wilcox
  8th Alabama: Lt. Col. Hilary A. Herbert
  9th Alabama: Capt. J. H. King
  10th Alabama: Lt. Col. James E. Shelley
  11th Alabama: Lt. Col. George E. Tayloe
  14th Alabama: Lt. Col. James A. Broome

Perry's Brigade: Col. David Lang
  2nd Florida: Capt. C. Seton Fleming
  5th Florida: Capt. R. N. Gardner
  8th Florida: Col. David Lang

Heth's Division: Brig. Gen. James J. Pettigrew

Archer's Brigade: Col. Birkett D. Fry
  5th Alabama Battalion: Maj. A. S. Van de Graaff
  13th Alabama: Lt. Col. William H. Betts
  1st Tennessee (Provisional Army): Col. Newton J. George
  7th Tennessee: Lt. Col. Samuel G. Shepard
  14th Tennessee: Capt. Bruce L. Phillips

Pettigrew's Brigade: Col. James K. Marshall
  11th North Carolina: Capt. Mark D. Armfield
  26th North Carolina: Maj. John T. Jones
  47th North Carolina: Col. George H. Faribault
  52nd North Carolina: Lt. Col. Marcus A. Parks

Davis's Brigade: Brig. Gen. Joseph R. Davis
  2nd Mississippi: Col. John M. Stone
  11th Mississippi: Col. Francis M. Greene

42nd Mississippi: Col. Hugh R. Miller
55th North Carolina: Capt. George A. Gilreath

Brockenbrough's Brigade: Col. John M. Brockenbrough
22nd Virginia Battalion: Maj. John S. Bowles
40th Virginia: Capt. T. E. Betts
47th Virginia: Col. Robert M. Mayo
55th Virginia: Col. William S. Christian

Artillery Battalion: Lt. Col. John J. Garnett
Donaldsonville Louisiana Battery: Capt. Victor Maurin
Huger Virginia Battery: Capt. Joseph D. Moore
Lewis's Virginia Battery: Capt. John W. Lewis
Norfolk Blues Virginia Light Artillery: Capt. Charles R. Grandy

Pender's Division: Maj. Gen. Isaac R. Trimble

Scales's Brigade: Col. William Lee J. Lowrance
13th North Carolina: Lt. Col. Henry A. Rogers
16th North Carolina: Capt. L. W. Stowe
22nd North Carolina: Col. James Conner
34th North Carolina: Lt. Col. George T. Gordon
38th North Carolina: Lt. Col. John Ashford

Lane's Brigade: Brig. Gen. James H. Lane
7th North Carolina: Capt. J. McLeod Turner
18th North Carolina: Col. John D. Barry
28th North Carolina: Col. Samuel D. Lowe
33rd North Carolina: Col. Clark M. Avery
37th North Carolina: Col. William M. Barbour

Artillery Battalion: Maj. William T. Poague
Albemarle Virginia Battery: Capt. James W. Wyatt
Brooke's Virginia Battery: Capt. Addison W. Utterback
Charlotte North Carolina Battery: Capt. Joseph Graham
Madison Mississippi Light Battery: Capt. George Ward

NOTES

. . . .

ABBREVIATIONS

AU	Auburn University, Auburn, Alabama
BPL	Boston Public Library, Boston, Massachusetts
BU	Boston University, Boston, Massachusetts
CHS	Connecticut Historical Society, Hartford
CWLM	Civil War Library and Museum, Philadelphia, Pennsylvania
CWM	College of William and Mary, Williamsburg, Virginia
ECU	East Carolina University, Greenville, North Carolina
EU	Emory University, Atlanta, Georgia
FB	Fredericksburg Battlefield, Fredericksburg, Virginia
FSA	Florida State Archives, Tallahassee
GHS	Georgia Historical Society, Savannah
GNMP	Gettysburg National Military Park, Gettysburg, Pennsylvania
HSP	Historical Society of Pennsylvania, Philadelphia
HU	Harvard University, Cambridge, Massachusetts
LC	Library of Congress, Washington, D.C.
LSU	Louisiana State University, Baton Rouge
MaryHS	Maryland Historical Society, Baltimore
MassHS	Massachusetts Historical Society, Boston
MC	Museum of the Confederacy, Richmond, Virginia
MDAH	Mississippi Department of Archives and History, Jackson
MHS	Minnesota Historical Society, Minneapolis
NCDAH	North Carolina Department of Archives and History, Raleigh
N-YHS	New-York Historical Society, New York
NYPL	New York Public Library, New York
NYSL	New York State Library, Albany
OHS	Ohio Historical Society, Columbus
OR	*The War of the Rebellion: A Compilation of the Official Records of the Union and Confederate Armies.* 70 vols. in 128. Washington, D.C.: Government Printing Office, 1880–1901. All citations refer to series 1 unless indicated otherwise.

PHMC	Pennsylvania Historical and Museum Commission, Harrisburg
PNB	Petersburg National Battlefield, Petersburg, Virginia
QU	Queen's University, Kingston, Ontario
RIHS	Rhode Island Historical Society, Providence
RU	Rutgers University, New Brunswick, New Jersey
SAHS	St. Augustine Historical Society, St. Augustine, Florida
SCL-DU	Special Collections Library, Duke University, Durham, North Carolina
SHC-UNC	Southern Historical Collection, University of North Carolina, Chapel Hill
SHSI	State Historical Society of Iowa, Des Moines
TSLA	Tennessee State Library and Archives, Nashville
USAMHI	United States Army Military History Institute, Carlisle Barracks, Pennsylvania
USMA	United States Army Military Academy, West Point, New York
UV	University of Vermont, Montpelier
UVA	University of Virginia, Charlottesville
VerHS	Vermont Historical Society, Montpelier
VHS	Virginia Historical Society, Richmond
VMI	Virginia Military Institute, Lexington
VSLA	Virginia State Library and Archives, Richmond
WI	Wistar Institute, Philadelphia, Pennsylvania
WLU	Washington and Lee University, Lexington, Virginia
WRHS	Western Reserve Historical Society, Cleveland, Ohio
YU	Yale University, New Haven, Connecticut

CHAPTER ONE

1. Byrne and Weaver, *Haskell of Gettysburg*, 136–45; Elmore, "Meteorological and Astronomical Chronology," 14, 19.

2. Elmore, "Meteorological and Astronomical Chronology," 14, 19; Buck diary, July 3, 1863, RU.

3. Thomas F. Galwey, "An Episode of the Battle of Gettysburg," in Ladd and Ladd, *Bachelder Papers*, 2:871.

4. Gallagher, *Fighting for the Confederacy*, 244–45; Edward P. Alexander to Longstreet, February 5, 1878, *Supplement to the Official Records*, 5:363 (unless otherwise noted, all references are to pt. 1).

5. Longstreet, *From Manassas to Appomattox*, 385–87; Longstreet to McLaws, July 25, 1873, McLaws Papers, SHC-UNC; Rollins, "Second Wave," 110; Robert E. Lee to Samuel Cooper, January 1864, *OR* 27(2):321; Longstreet to R. H. Chilton, July 27, 1863, *OR* 27(2):359; Longstreet, "General Longstreet's Account"; Wert, *General James Longstreet*, 282; Piston, "Cross Purposes," 31, 35, 38–40, 42–47; Coddington, *Gettysburg Campaign*, 454–64.

6. Wert, *General James Longstreet*, 19, 44–45, 47, 61, 67, 91, 96–97, 105, 117, 166–77, 197–201, 216–23, 234–38.

7. Longstreet, *From Manassas to Appomattox*, 388; Lee to John B. Hood, May 21, 1863, in Dowdey and Manarin, *Wartime Papers of Robert E. Lee*, 490; Piston, "Cross Purposes," 46.

8. Longstreet to R. H. Chilton, July 27, 1863, *OR* 27(2):359; Longstreet, *From Manassas to Appomattox*, 390; Longstreet, "Lee's Right Wing at Gettysburg," 343; Louis G. Young to W. J. Baker, February 10, 1864, *Richmond Daily Enquirer*, March 18, 1864; Joseph R. Davis to William H. Palmer, August 22, 1863, *OR* 27(2):651.

9. Rollins, "Second Wave."

10. Walter H. Taylor letter, 132–33; A. L. Long, *Memoirs of Robert E. Lee*, 288, 294; Piston, "Cross Purposes," 50–51.

11. Gallagher, *Fighting for the Confederacy*, 252; Lee to Samuel Cooper, January 1864, *OR* 27(2):320; Longstreet to R. H. Chilton, July 27, 1863, *OR* 27(2):359; Longstreet, *From Manassas to Appomattox*, 385–95; McLaws, "Gettysburg"; Rollins, "Second Wave," 108.

12. Walter H. Taylor letter, 133; "Another Witness," 461.

13. Robertson, *General A. P. Hill*, 95–97, 193, 219–22.

14. Wert, *General James Longstreet*, 285.

15. Talcott, "Third Day at Gettysburg," 40; Lee to Samuel Cooper, January 1864, *OR* 27(2):320; Birkett D. Fry to Bachelder, December 27, 1877, in Ladd and Ladd, *Bachelder Papers*, 1:517.

16. Ambrose P. Hill to R. H. Chilton, November 1863, *OR* 27(2):608.

17. Morris to W. Saunders, October 1, 1877, Morris Papers, SHC-UNC; Harris, *Historical Sketches*, 35.

18. Moore, "Battle of Gettysburg," 248–49.

19. Fry, "Pettigrew's Charge at Gettysburg," 92.

20. J. R. Hutter account, Daniel Papers, UVA.

21. W. Gart Johnson, "Reminiscences."

22. Rollins, "Second Wave," 110.

23. Lee to Samuel Cooper, January 1864, *OR* 27(2):320.

24. Gallagher, *Fighting for the Confederacy*, 244–50, 253–55; Edward P. Alexander to Bachelder, May 3, 1876, in Ladd and Ladd, *Bachelder Papers*, 1:484–88; Priest, *Into the Fight*, 24; Alexander letter, 106; Jennings Cropper Wise, *Long Arm of Lee*, 2:673; Longstreet, "General Longstreet's Account," 69–72; Alexander to Longstreet, August 10, 1863, *Supplement to the Official Records*, 5:358–60; Longstreet, *From Manassas to Appomattox*, 391. The notes exchanged between Longstreet and Alexander are in the Alexander Papers, LC. Alexander noted two different times for receipt of the first note, 11:45 and 12:00. The Alexander Papers at SHC-UNC contain typed copies of the notes.

25. William Miller Owen, "Recollections of the Third Day at Gettysburg," 148–49; Priest, *Into the Fight*, 188.

26. Joseph L. Thompson reminiscences, and Robert M. Stribling to Daniel, March 7, 1904, Daniel Papers, UVA.

27. Cockrell, *Gunner with Stonewall*, 74.

28. For the Seven Days campaign, see Sears, *To the Gates of Richmond*, 189–209, 308–36. For the assault on Fort Stedman, see Trudeau, *Last Citadel*, 329–54.

29. Piston, *Lee's Tarnished Lieutenant*, 60–61.

30. Walter Harrison, *Pickett's Men*, 183, convincingly suggests that no exact aiming point for the attack was identified before it began, and I uncovered no reliable source that disproves his contention.

31. Meade, *Life and Letters*, 2:96–97, 105–6; John Gibbon to George Meade, August 24, 1884, Meade Collection, HSP; Klein, "Meade's Pipe Creek Line," 133, 135, 143–47; Church, "Pipe Creek Line," 6, GNMP.

32. Gallagher, *Fighting for the Confederacy*, 246.

33. Hancock to Seth Williams, 1863, *OR* 27(1):372; Elmore, "Meteorological and Astronomical Chronology," 14.

CHAPTER TWO

1. Harrison and Busey, *Nothing but Glory*, 1, 4–6.

2. Gordon, *General George E. Pickett*, 12–14, 22–29, 35, 51–54, 75, 77–78, 82, 85–94, 98–100.

3. Stewart, *Pickett's Charge*, 172–73; Harrison and Busey, *Nothing but Glory*, 5–6, 170, 172; Busey and Martin, *Regimental Strengths and Losses*, 283; James Longstreet to Johnston, November 7, 1877, Johnston Papers, CWM; Charles Pickett to Owen, February 23, 1878, Owen Papers, VSLA.

4. Motts, *"Trust in God and Fear Nothing,"* 17–19, 24–26, 38–41; Poindexter, "Gen. Lewis Addison Armistead," 502.

5. Motts, *"Trust in God and Fear Nothing,"* 37; William Henry Cocke to parents, July 14, 1862, Cocke Family Papers, VHS; Robert K. Krick, "Armistead and Garnett," 117.

6. Motts, *"Trust in God and Fear Nothing,"* 17–19.

7. Burton, "River of Blood and the Valley of Death," 44–49, 54–62, 69–70; Garnett to Robert M. T. Hunter, April 1862; Samuel Cooper to Lee, May 6, 1862; and Garnett to Samuel Cooper, July 12, 1862, all in Garnett Papers, MC.

8. "An Epitome of the Blueridge Rifles," Simmons Papers, VSLA; C. F. James account, *Confederate Veteran* Papers, SCL-DU. See a series of articles regarding the role of Hood's Texas brigade at Gaines's Mill, in *Confederate Veteran* 6 (1898): 565–70.

9. Warner, *Generals in Gray*, 169; Woodward, *Major General James Lawson Kemper*, 1, 6–15, 20–22, 24–28, 42–46, 59–71, 75–78; G. W. Sidebottom account, December 17, 1910, *Confederate Veteran* Papers, SCL-DU.

10. Gordon, *General George E. Pickett*, 101; Lee to James A. Seddon, May 10, 1863, *OR* 25(2):790; Woodworth, *Davis and Lee at War*, 230–40; Harrison and Busey, *Nothing but Glory*, 1–2.

11. Harrison and Busey, *Nothing but Glory*, 4–6; Henry T. Owen, "Pickett's Division," Owen Papers, and John Bowie Magruder to Henry, May 23, 1863, Magruder Family Papers, VSLA.

12. Henry M. Talley to mother, June 11, 1863, Brown Papers, NCDAH; Owen to wife, June 13, 1863, Owen Papers, VSLA; Robert Taylor Scott to wife, June 12, 1863,

Keith Family Papers, VHS. Of these three correspondents, Talley was wounded and captured on July 3 and later exchanged.

13. Short to Balie, June 26, 1863, Short Letters, MC; Miller, "Wartime Letters," GNMP; Reeve to wife, June 22, 1863, Reeve Papers, SHC-UNC. Of these three correspondents, Short was captured on July 3 and died in prison; Reeve was wounded on July 3 but survived.

14. Burton, "River of Blood and the Valley of Death," 74; Harrison and Busey, *Nothing but Glory*, 2; Pierce, "Civil War Career of Richard Brooke Garnett," 95n, 98; Richard B. Garnett to Mrs. Dandridge, June 21, 25, 1863, Bedinger-Dandridge Family Papers, SCL-DU.

15. Harrison and Busey, *Nothing but Glory*, 3–4, 10–11; Lippitt diary, July 2, 1863, Lippitt Papers, SHC-UNC; Robert Anderson Bright to Owen, July 20, 1887, and Edward R. Baird to Owen, August 18, 1878, Owen Papers, VHS.

16. Lippitt diary, July 3, 1863, Lippitt Papers, SHC-UNC; Harrison and Busey, *Nothing but Glory*, 13–14; Woodward, *Major General James Lawson Kemper*, 87; Charles S. Peyton to Charles Pickett, July 9, 1863, *OR* 27(2):385.

17. Longstreet to R. H. Chilton, July 27, 1863, *OR* 27(2):359; Kemper to W. H. Swallow, February 4, 1886, Kemper Papers, VHS; Harrison and Busey, *Nothing but Glory*, 15–16; Joseph Mayo to Charles Pickett, July 25, 1863, Pickett Papers, SCL-DU.

18. Harrison and Busey, *Nothing but Glory*, 18–20.

19. J. B. Dameron reminiscences, and B. L. Farinholt to Daniel, April 15, 1905, Daniel Papers, UVA; Harrison and Busey, *Nothing but Glory*, 15, 18–19; Joseph Mayo to Charles Pickett, July 25, 1863, Pickett Papers, SCL-DU; Motts, *"Trust in God and Fear Nothing,"* 42; Charles S. Peyton to Charles Pickett, July 9, 1863, *OR* 27(2):385.

20. Walter Harrison, *Pickett's Men*, 91–92.

21. Burton, "River of Blood and the Valley of Death," 77.

22. Harrison and Busey, *Nothing but Glory*, 139; William H. Taylor, "Some Experiences of a Confederate Assistant Surgeon," 117.

23. Pfanz, *Gettysburg: Culp's Hill and Cemetery Hill*, 290–92, 310, 351–52.

24. Longacre, *Pickett*, 119–23.

25. Berkeley account, GNMP.

26. Mayo, "Pickett's Charge at Gettysburg," 328; Durkin, *John Dooley*, 102; Wiley, *Reminiscences of Big I*, 44; John Holmes Smith reminiscences, February 4–5, 1904, Daniel Papers, UVA; James H. Walker, "Survivor of Pickett's Division."

27. William H. Taylor, "Some Experiences of a Confederate Assistant Surgeon," 119; Loehr, " 'Old First' Virginia," 40; Crocker, "Gettysburg," 117–18, 126–27.

28. W. H. H. Winston reminiscences, June 10, 1905, and J. C. Granbery to Daniel, March 25, 1905, Daniel Papers, UVA; McCulloch, " 'High Tide at Gettysburg,' " 474; James H. Walker, "Survivor of Pickett's Division," 27.

29. Edmund Berkeley to Daniel, September 26, n.d., and Eppa Hunton questionnaire, February 15, 1904, Daniel Papers, SCL-DU; Hamilton, *Papers of Randolph Abbott Shotwell*, 2:4; Rawley W. Martin to Sylvester Chamberlain, August 11, 1897, Daniel Papers, UVA; James H. Walker, "Survivor of Pickett's Division," 27.

30. H. T. Owen, "Pickett at Gettysburg."

31. Powell, *Dictionary of North Carolina Biography*, 5:77–79; Wilson, *Carolina Cavalier*, 1–5, 8, 18–19, 38–63, 115–33.

32. Stewart, *Pickett's Charge*, 172–73; A. L. P. Vairin diary, July 1, 1863, MDAH; Martin, *Gettysburg*, 70–71, 80–81, 86, 119, 121, 138, 162, 344–67, 368–71.

33. Winschel, "Heavy Was Their Loss," pt. 2, 79; Swallow, "Third Day at Gettysburg," 565.

34. Longstreet to R. H. Chilton, July 27, 1863, *OR* 27(2):359; Stewart, *Pickett's Charge*, 87. Andrew Cross, a Christian Commission worker with the Rebel prisoners at Gettysburg, recalled a conversation he had with Capt. Benjamin F. Little of the 52nd North Carolina in Pettigrew's brigade. Little told him the division deployed with its "whole line two deep." It is unclear if Little or, for that matter, Cross meant there were two two-rank battle lines or just one line with two ranks of troops. Or it is possible Trimble's two brigades were counted as the second line. At any rate there is no clear evidence that Pettigrew deployed his division in two lines. See Cross, *The War*, 26–27.

35. *Tennesseeans in the Civil War*, pt. 1, 171; Warner, *Generals in Gray*, 11; Storch and Storch, " 'What a Deadly Trap We Were In,' " 13–14, 26.

36. Warner, *Generals in Gray*, 95; Storch and Storch, " 'What a Deadly Trap We Were In,' " 14; Welsh, *Medical Histories of Confederate Generals*, 74.

37. Ben W. Coleman to parents, April 26, 1863, Coleman Papers, TSLA.

38. Rooker, "Chronological Outline," TSLA; Wiley Woods, "The 1st Tennessee Flag at Gettysburg," *Confederate Veteran* Papers, SCL-DU.

39. Michael W. Taylor, "Col. James Keith Marshall," 78–80; Charles D. Walker, *Memorial*, 369–72, VMI.

40. W. B. Taylor to mother, GNMP.

41. Young, "Pettigrew's Brigade at Gettysburg, 1–3 July, 1863," 120; R. M. Tuttle to Daniel, June 3, 1903, Daniel Papers, UVA.

42. Gaston Broughton to editors, October 15, 1877, Grimes Papers, and Thomas J. Cureton to Lane, June 22, 1890, Lane Papers, SHC-UNC.

43. Winschel, "Heavy Was Their Loss," pt. 1, 6, 8; William Love, "Mississippi at Gettysburg," 44; Steven R. Davis, " '. . . Like Leaves in an Autumn Wind,' " 292, 295.

44. Warner, *Generals in Gray*, 68; Winschel, "Heavy Was Their Loss," pt. 1, 5, 11, 14.

45. Peel diary, 24, MDAH; Cockrell and Ballard, *Mississippi Rebel*, 197; Winschel, "Heavy Was Their Loss," pt. 2, 79.

46. Patterson, "In a Most Disgraceful Manner," 47; Jesse R. Bowles to sister, March 8, 1863, Bowles Family Papers, CWM; William J. Hatchett to parents, May [1863], Hatchett Letters, MC; Priest, *Into the Fight*, 87.

47. Kimble, "Tennesseeans at Gettysburg," 460.

48. Isaac Trimble, "Civil War Diary," 1, 5, 7–10, 12; Isaac R. Trimble to J. B. Bachelder, February 9, 1883, in Ladd and Ladd, *Bachelder Papers*, 2:926–27, 930–31; James H. Lane to Joseph A. Engelhard, August 13, 1863, and Engelhard to

William H. Palmer, November 4, 1863, *OR* 27(2):666; "Letter from General Trimble," 33.

49. Rawley, "Pender-Scales Brigade," 551–53; Lane, "Branch-Lane Brigade," 465, 467; Warner, *Generals in Gray*, 31, 172–73.

50. Scales to wife, April 19, June 20, 25, 1863, Scales Papers, NCDAH; Morris to family, June 24, 1863, Morris Papers, SHC-UNC.

51. Martin, *Gettysburg*, 188–89, 394, 396, 402–4, 426–27, 431–32.

52. Weymouth T. Jordan, *North Carolina Troops*, 9:285; William L. J. Lowrance to Joseph A. Engelhard, August 12, 1863, *OR* 27(2):671; N. S. Smith, "Additional Sketch," 698–99; Phillips, "James Henry Lane," 150–52.

53. Stewart, *Pickett's Charge*, 172–73; Trinque, "Arnold's Battery and the 26th North Carolina," 64; Talcott, "Third Day at Gettysburg," 44; McDaid, " 'Four Years of Arduous Service,' " 216.

54. Martin, *Gettysburg*, 394–96; Warner, *Generals in Gray*, 233–34.

55. E. M. Hays to John B. Bachelder, October 15, 1890, in Ladd and Ladd, *Bachelder Papers*, 3:1776–77.

56. Warner, *Generals in Gray*, 235–36; Elmore, "Florida Brigade at Gettysburg," 45, 47.

57. Pfanz, *Gettysburg: The Second Day*, 113, 364, 366, 372, 374, 410–14; Wilcox letter, 116.

58. Wilcox to Thomas S. Mills, July 17, 1863, *OR* 27(2):619; Wilcox, "General C. M. Wilcox on the Battle of Gettysburg," 119; Wilcox letter, 116.

59. David Lang to Thomas S. Mills, July 29, 1863, *OR* 27(2):632; Wentworth diary, GNMP; Reid to Hal, September 4, 1863, Reid Papers, SAHS; Groene, "Civil War Letters of Colonel David Lang," 355.

60. Lang to John B. Bachelder, October 16, 1893, Lang Letterbook, 1893–1909, FSA.

61. Clark, *Glance Backward*, 38–39.

62. Pfanz, *Gettysburg: The Second Day*, 380, 384, 387, 414.

63. Watts, "Something More about Gettysburg"; Lewis to mother, July 21, 1863, Lewis Papers, SHC-UNC.

64. Coddington, *Gettysburg Campaign*, 12–13.

65. Priest, *Into the Fight*, 10–11, 15, 26, 32–33, 37, 44, 183, 186, 189. See 181–98 for a detailed description of the artillery placement.

66. Cockrell, *Gunner with Stonewall*, 73–74.

67. Raoul to father, July 17, 1863, Raoul Letters, LSU.

68. Winters, *Battling the Elements*, 127–28; Shultz and Rollins, "Measuring Pickett's Charge," 117; L. L. Lomax to Daniel, April 24, n.d., Daniel Papers, SCL-DU; Hicks and Schultz, *Battlefields of the Civil War*, 134; Moore, "Battle of Gettysburg," 249; "Testimony about Battle of Gettysburg"; field visits to Gettysburg, March 25, 1997, and May 27, 1998.

69. Field visits to Gettysburg, March 25, 1997, and May 27, 1998; Christ, *Struggle for the Bliss Farm*, 4–5, 7, 34–77; Louis G. Young to W. J. Baker, February 10, 1864, *Richmond Daily Enquirer*, March 18, 1864.

CHAPTER THREE

1. Byrne and Weaver, *Haskell of Gettysburg*, 85.

2. Stewart, *Pickett's Charge*, 173–74.

3. Warner, *Generals in Blue*, 202–3; David M. Jordan, *Winfield Scott Hancock*, 33–34; Hancock, *Reminiscences of Winfield Scott Hancock*, 95; Pfanz, *Gettysburg: The Second Day*, 376.

4. Warner, *Generals in Blue*, 171; Bruce, *Twentieth Regiment of Massachusetts*, 288–89; Byrne and Weaver, *Haskell of Gettysburg*, 147; Gibbon, *Personal Recollections*, 146; Welsh, *Medical Histories of Union Generals*, 129.

5. Lash, "Philadelphia Brigade," 97–98; Kennedy, *Civil War Battlefield Guide*, 18.

6. John Gibbon to Francis A. Walker, n.d., 1887, Hancock Papers, USAMHI; Warner, *Generals in Blue*, 544–45; Gibbon to wife, June 30, 1863, Gibbon Papers, HSP; Lash, "Philadelphia Brigade," 98–99; Gambone, *Hancock at Gettysburg*, 7; Sword, "Facing the Gray Wave," 19–20; *In Memoriam*, 88–89.

7. Pfanz, *Gettysburg: The Second Day*, 387–89, 405, 419–20.

8. Alexander S. Webb to A. H. Embler, July 12, 1863, *OR* 27(1):427; *In Memoriam*, 83.

9. Pfanz, *Gettysburg: The Second Day*, 207, 220–21; Charles P. Horton to Bachelder, January 23, 1867, in Ladd and Ladd, *Bachelder Papers*, 1:294–95; R. Penn Smith to Isaac Wistar, July 29, 1863, Wistar Papers, WI; Alexander S. Webb to A. H. Embler, July 12, 1863, *OR* 27(1):427; R. Penn Smith to C. H. Banes, July 12, 1863, *OR* 27(1):432.

10. Lash, "Philadelphia Brigade," 100, 102; Bachelder to Fitzhugh Lee, December 1892, and Charles H. Banes testimony, April 24, 1890, in Ladd and Ladd, *Bachelder Papers*, 3:1701, 1900 (both Bachelder and Banes erred in believing that two or three companies of the 71st Pennsylvania were positioned in the angle before the artillery bombardment began); testimony of Alexander S. Webb, Anthony W. McDermott, Robert McBride, and James C. Lynch, *Supreme Court of Pennsylvania*, 126, 159, 219, 303; Samuel Roberts to H. W. Newton, February 13, 1890, Federal Soldiers' Letters, SHC-UNC; McDermott, *Brief History of the Sixty-Ninth Regiment*, 85.

11. Pfanz, *Gettysburg: The Second Day*, 70–71, 376, 378–80, 387–89, 405, 417; H. L. Abbott letter, n.d., *Reports, Letters & Papers*, 1:89, BPL; H. L. Abbott to Papa, July 6, 1863, in Robert Garth Scott, *Fallen Leaves*, 186; H. L. Abbott to Charles C. Paine, July 28, 1863, Paine Papers, MassHS. The existing remains of an earthwork on Hall's line are probably an accurate reproduction of the original.

12. Bruce, *Twentieth Regiment of Massachusetts*, 288; H. L. Abbott letter, n.d., *Reports, Letters & Papers*, 1:90, BPL; transcript of H. C. Mason diary, *Massachusetts Infantry, 20th Regiment, Diaries, 1863*, Military Historical Society of Massachusetts Collection, BU.

13. Waitt, *History of the Nineteenth*, 234–35; testimony of William A. Hill, *Supreme Court of Pennsylvania*, 208; extract of A. F. Devereux statement, January 14, 1887, Gettysburg Volume, Doubleday Papers, N-YHS; James E. Mallon to William R. Driver, July 16, 1863, *OR* 27(1):451; Priest, *Into the Fight*, 110; Stewart, *Pickett's Charge*, 51. Priest and Stewart place the 59th New York on Hall's right and the 20th

Massachusetts on his left, but that seems incorrect based on collateral evidence that I use in discussing the Confederate advance to the stone fence in Chapter 6.

14. Warner, *Generals in Blue*, 210–11; Welsh, *Medical Histories of Union Generals*, 154.

15. Pfanz, *Gettysburg: The Second Day*, 374, 384, 387–89; Coco, *From Ball's Bluff to Gettysburg*, 196–99, 201.

16. Pfanz, *Gettysburg: The Second Day*, 375, 377–79.

17. Ibid., 375, 410–14; Moe, *Last Full Measure*, 272, 275.

18. Moe, *Last Full Measure*, 281–82; Adams, "Nineteenth Maine at Gettysburg," 259; Hadden, "Granite Glory," 60; Stewart, *Pickett's Charge*, 51.

19. Warner, *Generals in Blue*, 344–45; John Newton to Seth Williams, September 30, 1863, *OR* 27(1):261–62.

20. Theodore B. Gates to Doubleday, January 30, 1864, *OR* 27(1):321; Dyer, *Compendium*, 3:1619; Martin, *Gettysburg*, 362–63.

21. Cook, "Personal Reminiscences of Gettysburg," 332; Theodore B. Gates to Rothermel, April 28, 1868, Rothermel Papers, PHMC; Theodore B. Gates to Doubleday, February 4, 1864, Gettysburg Volume, Doubleday Papers, N-YHS; Gates to Hardenburgh, GNMP; Stewart, *Pickett's Charge*, 173–74.

22. Theodore B. Gates to Doubleday, January 30, 1864, *OR* 27(1):321–22; Theodore B. Gates to Bachelder, January 30, 1864, and George G. Benedict to Bachelder, March 16, 1864, in Ladd and Ladd, *Bachelder Papers*, 1:84, 95–96; Theodore B. Gates to Doubleday, February 4, 1864, Gettysburg Volume, Doubleday Papers, N-YHS.

23. Coffin, *Nine Months to Gettysburg*, 4, 47, 117–23, 147–48; Jackson, *Time Exposure*, 41; Jackson diary, August 18, 1862, NYPL; Clarke, "Thirteenth Regiment," VerHS; Warner, *Generals in Blue*, 471.

24. Jackson to Mrs. Arabella R. Jackson, May 23, 28, 1863, Jackson Papers, SCL-DU.

25. Clarke, "Thirteenth Regiment," VerHS; extracts from George J. Stannard diary, June 25 to July 1, 1863, in Ladd and Ladd, *Bachelder Papers*, 1:51–53; Dickson, "Flying Brigade," 25; Palmer, *Second Brigade*, 203; Stewart, *Pickett's Charge*, 173–74.

26. George H. Scott, "Vermont at Gettysburg," 71; extract of Francis V. Randall to Hancock, November 16, 1863, MOLLUS-Massachusetts Commandery Collection, HU; Clarke, "Thirteenth Regiment," VerHS; Pfanz, *Gettysburg: The Second Day*, 415–16, 421.

27. Benedict, *Army Life in Virginia*, 174; Clarke, "Thirteenth Regiment," VerHS; George J. Stannard to C. Kingsbury, July 4, 1863, *OR* 27(1):349; Benedict, *Vermont at Gettysburgh*, 10; extract from George J. Stannard diary, July 3, 1863; Wheelock G. Veazey letter, n.d.; and George G. Benedict to Bachelder, March 16, 1864, all in Ladd and Ladd, *Bachelder Papers*, 1:55, 59, 96; Charles Cummings to wife, July 6, 1863, Cummings Papers, VerHS; field visit to Gettysburg, March 25, 1997.

28. Stewart, *Pickett's Charge*, 173–74; Warner, *Generals in Blue*, 223–24; Welsh, *Medical Histories of Union Generals*, 164; Winfield Scott, "Pickett's Charge," 902–3.

29. Warner, *Generals in Blue*, 465.

30. Archer, "Remembering the 14th Connecticut," 61, 65; Cowtan recollections, 1, Cowtan Papers, NYPL.

31. Pfanz, *Gettysburg: The Second Day*, 376–77; Stevens, *Souvenir of Excursion*, 16.

32. John M. Dunn address, *Report of Joint Committee*, 10; Theodore G. Ellis to Bachelder, January 21, 1864, and Henry S. Stevens to William H. Corbin, June 5, 1890, in Ladd and Ladd, *Bachelder Papers*, 1:79, 3:1731; Page, *History of the Fourteenth*, 151; Hamblen, *Connecticut Yankees*, 105; George Thornton Fleming, *Life and Letters of General Alexander Hays*, 453.

33. Haskin, *History of the First Regiment of Artillery*, 170.

34. Kennedy, *Civil War Battlefield Guide*, 113–15.

35. Bacarella, *Lincoln's Foreign Legion*, 117–18, 231–96; Murray, *Redemption of the "Harper's Ferry Cowards,"* 54–55, 58.

36. Bacarella, *Lincoln's Foreign Legion*, 117–18, 134; Murray, *Redemption of the "Harper's Ferry Cowards,"* 75–77; Samuel C. Armstrong to Bachelder, February 6, 1884, in Ladd and Ladd, *Bachelder Papers*, 2:1000.

37. Pfanz, *Gettysburg: The Second Day*, 376, 404–8; Campbell, " 'Remember Harper's Ferry!,' " pt. 1, 74–75; Benjamin W. Thompson, " 'This Hell of Destruction,' " 19; Murray, *Redemption of the "Harper's Ferry Cowards,"* 118.

38. Campbell, " 'Remember Harper's Ferry!,' " pt. 1, 71; Murray, *Redemption of the "Harper's Ferry Cowards,"* 61.

39. George Thornton Fleming, *Life and Letters of General Alexander Hays*, 453; Henry S. Stevens to William H. Corbin, June 5, 1890, and Isaac M. Lusk to Clinton D. MacDougall, June 25, 1890, in Ladd and Ladd, *Bachelder Papers*, 3:1731, 1737; Benjamin W. Thompson, " 'This Hell of Destruction,' " 20.

40. Sebastian D. Holmes to Clinton D. MacDougall, July 10, 1890, in Ladd and Ladd, *Bachelder Papers*, 3:1752.

41. William D. Taylor to Bachelder, September 22, 1891, ibid., 3:1822; Talbot, *Samuel Chapman Armstrong*, 91.

42. Emerson L. Bicknell to Bachelder, August 6, 1883, and William Plumer to Bachelder, March 20, 1885, in Ladd and Ladd, *Bachelder Papers*, 2:964, 1097.

43. Franklin Sawyer to J. G. Reid, July 5, 1863, *OR* 27(1):461; Christ, *Struggle for the Bliss Farm*, 3–6, 33; Franklin Sawyer to Bachelder, June 8, 1878, and May 11, 1880; Thomas F. Galwey to Bachelder, May 19, 1882; Sawyer to Bachelder, October 20, 1885; and Horace Judson to Bachelder, October 17, 1887, all in Ladd and Ladd, *Bachelder Papers*, 1:625, 663, 2:868–70, 1132, 3:1515.

44. Galwey, *Valiant Hours*, 109–11; Thomas F. Galwey, "An Episode of the Battle of Gettysburg," in Ladd and Ladd, *Bachelder Papers*, 2:871–74.

45. Franklin Sawyer to Bachelder, May 11, 1880, and October 20, 1885, in Ladd and Ladd, *Bachelder Papers*, 1:663, 2:1132; Sawyer to J. G. Reid, *OR* 27(1):461.

46. Warner, *Generals in Blue*, 242.

47. Shultz, *"Double Canister at Ten Yards,"* 3–8, 13–14; *History of the Fifth Massachusetts Battery*, 652, 654; Freeman McGilvery to Robert O. Tyler, n.d., 1863, *OR* 27(1):882; Charles A. Phillips to McGilvery, July 6, 1863, *OR* 27(1):885; Patrick Hart to C. H. Whittelsey, August 2, 1863, *OR* 27(1):888; Henry J. Hunt to Bach-

elder, August 22, 1874, in Ladd and Ladd, *Bachelder Papers*, 1:441; Priest, *Into the Fight*, 10.

48. Shultz, *"Double Canister at Ten Yards,"* 3–4, 9–12, 20, 25; testimony of Frederick Fuger, *Supreme Court of Pennsylvania*, 128; John H. Rhodes, *Gettysburg Gun*, 16, 28.

49. Shultz, *"Double Canister at Ten Yards,"* 3–4, 7–8.

50. Frederick Fuger, "Battle of Gettysburg and Personal Recollections of That Battle," 21–22, Webb Papers, YU; Aldrich, *History of Battery A*, 210–11.

51. William A. Arnold account, 2, Records of the Soldiers and Sailors Historical Society of Rhode Island, RIHS; Crumb, *Eleventh Corps Artillery*, 31; Henry J. Hunt to Seth Williams, September 27, 1863, *OR* 27(1):238.

52. Crumb, *Eleventh Corps Artillery*, 69–70.

53. Tidball, "Artillery Service in the War of the Rebellion," 688; Shultz, *"Double Canister at Ten Yards,"* 3–4. Stewart, *Pickett's Charge*, 114, quotes numbers of Union and Confederate artillery slightly different from mine.

54. Stewart, *Pickett's Charge*, 70.

55. George Thornton Fleming, *Life and Letters of General Alexander Hays*, 453; Stevens account, June 10, 1905, Stevens Papers, NCDAH; Stewart, *Pickett's Charge*, 70.

56. John M. Dunn address, *Report of Joint Committee*, 12.

57. Shultz, *"Double Canister at Ten Yards,"* 19; Andrew Cowan account, Webb Papers, YU.

58. Stewart, *Pickett's Charge*, 70; field visit to Gettysburg, June 1, 1998.

59. Theodore B. Gates to Abner Doubleday, January 30, 1864, *OR* 27(1):321; Winfield S. Hancock to Bachelder, December 17, 1885, in Ladd and Ladd, *Bachelder Papers*, 2:1162–64.

60. Samuel Roberts to Alexander S. Webb, August 18, 1883, in Ladd and Ladd, *Bachelder Papers*, 2:967.

61. Christ, *Struggle for the Bliss Farm*, 3–6, 18–24, 30–31, 33–34, 36, 38–44, 56, 58, 67, 69, 81; William A. Arnold account, 1, Records of the Soldiers and Sailors Historical Society of Rhode Island, RIHS.

62. Alexander Hays to C. H. Morgan, *OR* 27(1):454.

CHAPTER FOUR

1. William Miller Owen, "Recollections of the Third Day at Gettysburg," 149; Jennings Cropper Wise, *Long Arm of Lee*, 2:677; Alexander to Longstreet, February 5, 1878, Alexander Papers, SHC-UNC; Benjamin F. Eshleman to James B. Walton, August 11, 1863, *OR* 27(2):434.

2. Stewart, *Pickett's Charge*, 127; Gallagher, *Fighting for the Confederacy*, 257; Longstreet, *From Manassas to Appomattox*, 390–91; Charles S. Venable to Joseph J. Davis, August 12, 1889, *Raleigh News and Observer*, July 5, 1903; Walter Harrison, *Pickett's Men*, 95–96.

3. Henry J. Hunt to Seth Williams, September 27, 1863, *OR* 27(1):238–39;

Hunt to John B. Bachelder, January 6, 1866, and August 22, 1874, in Ladd and Ladd, *Bachelder Papers*, 1:228–29, 441.

4. James A. Wright, "Story of Co. F," 608, MHS; Ward, *History of the One Hundred and Sixth*, 164; Pfanz, *Gettysburg: The Second Day*, 359; Devereux, "Some Account of Pickett's Charge," 14; Waitt, *History of the Nineteenth*, 234–37; Christopher Smith account.

5. John M. Dunn address, *Report of Joint Committee*, 11; Richard S. Thompson, "Scrap of Gettysburg," 101; Bruce, *Twentieth Regiment of Massachusetts*, 290; Charles H. Morgan account, in Ladd and Ladd, *Bachelder Papers*, 3:1360; Murphey, *Four Years in the War*, 121.

6. James A. Wright, "Story of Co. F," 608, MHS; Oesterle memoir, USAMHI.

7. Van Rensselear diary, GNMP; Stevens, *Souvenir of Excursion*, 25; Devereux, "Some Account of Pickett's Charge," 14; Carpenter letter, MHS; Stevens, *Address Delivered at the Dedication*, 20; Crumb, *Eleventh Corps Artillery*, 34.

8. Haines, *History of the Men of Co. F*, 41; Benedict, *Army Life in Virginia*, 185.

9. Stevens, *Address Delivered at the Dedication*, 20; John M. Dunn address, *Report of Joint Committee*, 10; Richard S. Thompson, "Scrap of Gettysburg," 101; Page, *History of the Fourteenth*, 149.

10. Sears, *Mr. Dunn Browne's Experiences in the Army*, 115; Benedict, *Vermont at Gettysburgh*, 13; Benedict, *Army Life in Virginia*, 185; Crumb, *Eleventh Corps Artillery*, 32.

11. Washburn, *Complete Military History*, 52.

12. Stevens, *Address Delivered at the Dedication*, 21, 21n; Carpenter letter, MHS.

13. Tyler to father, July 7, 1863, Tyler Papers, SCL-DU; Sylvanus W. Curtis to Lorenzo Thomas, August 6, 1863, *OR* 27(1):445; Henry L. Abbott to Lieut. Driver, July 16, 1863, *OR* 27(1):449; Emmell, " 'Now is the Time for Buck & Ball,' " GNMP.

14. Francis V. Randall to John Newton, July 10, 1863, *OR* 27(1):352; George H. Scott, "Vermont at Gettysburg," 75; Sturtivant, *Pictorial History*, 295.

15. Samuel B. McIntyre to Clinton D. MacDougall, June 27, 1890, and David Shields to MacDougall, August 26, 1890, in Ladd and Ladd, *Bachelder Papers*, 3:1743, 1759; Benjamin W. Thompson, " 'This Hell of Destruction,' " 20–21.

16. Benjamin W. Thompson, " 'This Hell of Destruction,' " 20–21.

17. Isaac M. Lusk to MacDougall, June 25, 1890; Samuel B. McIntyre to Mac-Dougall, June 27, 1890; Thomas Geer to MacDougall, July 28, 1890; David Shields to MacDougall, August 26, 1890; and MacDougall to Gettysburg Memorial Association, August 27, 1890, all in Ladd and Ladd, *Bachelder Papers*, 3:1737–38, 1743, 1754, 1759, 1761.

18. Samuel B. McIntyre to MacDougall, June 27, 1890; Sebastian D. Holmes to MacDougall, July 10, 1890; and Thomas Geer to MacDougall, July 28, 1890, all in ibid., 1744, 1752, 1754.

19. Benjamin W. Thompson, " 'This Hell of Destruction,' " 20–21.

20. Eldred, "Only a Boy," 29–30, GNMP.

21. Theodore G. Ellis to William P. Seville, July 6, 1863, *OR* 27(1):467; Stevens, *Address Delivered at the Dedication*, 14; Waitt, *History of the Nineteenth*, 237.

22. Meade, *Life and Letters*, 2:107.

23. John Haley to Bachelder, February 21, 1882, in Ladd and Ladd, *Bachelder Papers*, 2:837, 839; Robert Hunt Rhodes, *All For the Union*, 116.

24. George G. Meade to John B. Bachelder, December 4, 1869, and Charles H. Morgan account, in Ladd and Ladd, *Bachelder Papers*, 1:379, 3:1360–61.

25. George G. Meade to John B. Bachelder, December 4, 1869, ibid., 1:379; Meade, *Life and Letters*, 2:107–8; Paul A. Oliver to George Meade, May 16, 1882; George Meade to W. S. Smith, March 21, 1891; and Emlen W. Carpenter to George Meade, September 27, 1880, all in Meade Collection, HSP.

26. Hunt, "Third Day at Gettysburg," 373–74.

27. Sword, "Capt. George F. Tait," 83–84; Stewart, *Pickett's Charge*, 146; Pfanz, *Gettysburg: Culp's Hill and Cemetery Hill*, 355, 360.

28. Byrne and Weaver, *Haskell of Gettysburg*, 148–49, 151–53; Gibbon, *Personal Recollections*, 147–50; Moe, *Last Full Measure*, 184–85.

29. Chauncey L. Harris to father, July 4, 1863, in Washburn, *Complete Military History*, 52; David Shields statement, Grimes Papers, SHC-UNC.

30. George Thornton Fleming, *Life and Letters of General Alexander Hays*, 451–52; Sword, "Facing the Gray Wave," 21.

31. David Shields to John B. Bachelder, August 27, 1884, in Ladd and Ladd, *Bachelder Papers*, 2:1068–69.

32. Bruce, *Twentieth Regiment of Massachusetts*, 296; Cook, "Personal Reminiscences of Gettysburg," 333; Hunt, "Third Day at Gettysburg," 374; Jacob B. Hardenburgh to Gates, October 9, 1878, Gates Papers, N-YHS; John Lonergan, "Lieut. John T. Sinnott," Benedict Family Papers, UV.

33. Benedict, *Army Life in Virginia*, 176; Richard S. Thompson, "Scrap of Gettysburg," 102; Benedict, *Vermont at Gettysburgh*, 14.

34. Waitt, *History of the Nineteenth*, 235–36; Priest, *Into the Fight*, 75–76; A. F. Devereux to William R. Driver, July 7, 1863, *OR* 27(1):443; Shultz, *"Double Canister at Ten Yards,"* 24.

35. John Deleven to Adelia A. Gardner, March 25, 1906, and Albert Straight to Mrs. Gardner, July 16, 1863, Gardner Papers, RIHS; John H. Rhodes, *Gettysburg Gun*, 18–19, 29; John H. Rhodes, *History of Battery B*, 210–11.

36. Christopher Smith account; Kent Masterson Brown, *Cushing of Gettysburg*, 222, 235.

37. Christopher Smith account; R. Penn Smith to Charles H. Banes, July 12, 1863, *OR* 27(1):432; Kent Masterson Brown, *Cushing of Gettysburg*, 238.

38. Stevens, *Souvenir of Excursion*, 35; testimony of Alexander S. Webb, *Supreme Court of Pennsylvania*, 159; Kent Masterson Brown, *Cushing of Gettysburg*, 242–43; Christopher Smith account.

39. Haskin, *History of the First Regiment of Artillery*, 169–70; Wafer diary, July 3, 1863, QU.

40. Charles Cowan, "Pickett's Charge," 26–28; Andrew Cowan to John B. Bachelder, August 26, 1866, and Charles H. Banes testimony, April 24, 1890, in Ladd and Ladd, *Bachelder Papers*, 1:281, 3:1702.

41. Shultz, *"Double Canister at Ten Yards,"* 32–34; John H. Rhodes, *Gettysburg Gun*, 21, 23–27.

42. Hunt, "Third Day at Gettysburg," 374; Shultz, *"Double Canister at Ten Yards,"* 31–34.

43. Parsons letter, GNMP.

44. Freeman McGilvery to Robert O. Tyler, 1863, *OR* 27(1):883–84; *History of the Fifth Massachusetts Battery*, 652.

45. David M. Jordan, *Winfield Scott Hancock*, 97; Gambone, *Hancock at Gettysburg*, 120.

46. Henry J. Hunt account, January 20, 1873; Hunt to William T. Sherman, February, 1882; and Patrick Hart to John B. Bachelder, February 23, 1891, all in Ladd and Ladd, *Bachelder Papers*, 1:425–26, 432–33, 2:826–27; 3:1798; Priest, *Into the Fight*, 203n; Freeman McGilvery to Robert O. Tyler, 1863, *OR* 27(1):884; Charles A. Phillips to McGilvery, July 6, 1863, *OR* 27(1):885; Patrick Hart to C. H. Whittelsey, August 2, 1863, *OR* 27(1):888.

47. Hunt to Bachelder, January 6, 1866, and May 8, 1875, in Ladd and Ladd, *Bachelder Papers*, 1:229, 443–44.

48. Charles H. Morgan account, ibid., 3:1361; Gallagher, *Fighting for the Confederacy*, 260.

49. Priest, *Into the Fight*, 63–64; Crumb, *Eleventh Corps Artillery*, 34–36, 72, 74.

50. Crumb, *Eleventh Corps Artillery*, 39–40; Hunt, "Third Day at Gettysburg," 374; and Longacre, *Man behind the Guns*, 173–74, support Hunt's claim to the idea of ordering an artillery cease-fire, but Priest, *Into the Fight*, 78, and Stewart, *Pickett's Charge*, 155, credit Osborn.

51. Meade, *Life and Letters*, 2:108; Henry H. Bingham to Hancock, January 5, 1869, and Hunt account, January 20, 1873, in Ladd and Ladd, *Bachelder Papers*, 1:353–54, 430.

52. Hunt to Bachelder, January 6, 1866, and Hunt account, January 20, 1873, in Ladd and Ladd, *Bachelder Papers*, 1:229, 432, 434; Shultz, *"Double Canister at Ten Yards,"* 35.

53. Crumb, *Eleventh Corps Artillery*, 40.

54. Simons, *Regimental History*, 136; Talbot, *Samuel Chapman Armstrong*, 92; Sawyer, *Military History*, 130; Galwey, *Valiant Hours*, 112–13.

55. Hawley to father, July 4, 1863, Hawley Collection, SHSI; Clifford to father, USAMHI.

56. James letter.

57. Peel diary, 27, MDAH; Edward Cook Barnes letter (before July 12, 1863), Barnes Family Manuscripts, UVA; Irvine, "Brig. Gen. Richard B. Garnett"; Joseph Mayo to Charles Pickett, July 25, 1863, and William W. Bentley to W. T. Fry, July 9, 1863, Pickett Papers, SCL-DU; Loehr, " 'Old First' Virginia," 33; Wiley, *Reminiscences of Big I*, 44.

58. J. B. Johnson, "Limited Review," FB; Clark, *Glance Backward*, 39; Hilary A. Herbert to Edward P. Alexander, August 8, 1869, McLaws Papers, SHC-UNC.

59. Isaac Trimble to Daniel, November 24, 1875, and Erasmus Williams reminiscences, Daniel Papers, UVA; Walthall reminiscences, GNMP.

60. Lightsey, *Veteran's Story*, 35–36; Cockrell and Ballard, *Mississippi Rebel*, 196–97.

61. Mayo, "Pickett's Charge at Gettysburg," 329–30.

62. Ibid., 331; Johnston, *Story of a Confederate Boy*, 216–18.

63. James L. Kemper to Edward P. Alexander, September 20, 1869, Dearborn Collection, HU; W. H. H. Winston reminiscences, June 10, 1905, Daniel Papers, UVA; Johnston, *Story of a Confederate Boy*, 206–7.

64. Johnston, *Story of a Confederate Boy*, 207; James L. Kemper to Edward P. Alexander, September 20, 1869, Dearborn Collection, HU.

65. Henry T. Owen, "Pickett's Division," 16, Owen Papers, VSLA; Wiley, *Reminiscences of Big I*, 44; Edmund Berkeley to Daniel, September 26, n.d., Daniel Papers, UVA; W. H. Adams reminiscences, 7, Adams Papers, EU.

66. Hamilton, *Papers of Randolph Abbott Shotwell*, 2:8.

67. Edmund Berkeley to Daniel, September 26, n.d., Daniel Papers, UVA.

68. Farinholt, "Battle of Gettysburg," 468; Timberlake to editors, VHS.

69. Fry, "Pettigrew's Charge at Gettysburg," 92; Simpson to mother, July 8, 1863, Allen-Simpson Papers, SHC-UNC.

70. Peel diary, 27, MDAH; Steven R. Davis, " '. . . Like Leaves in an Autumn Wind,' " 294; Maud Morrow Brown, *University Greys*, 37–43. See also material on Jeremiah S. Gage in the 11th Mississippi Regimental Folder, GNMP.

71. Thomas R. Friend to Charles Pickett, December 10, 1894, Pickett Papers, VHS; Irvine, "Brig. Gen. Richard B. Garnett"; Robert Tyler Jones, "Gen. L. A. Armistead' and R. Tyler Jones."

72. Clayton G. Coleman to Daniel, July 1, 1904, Daniel Papers, UVA.

73. Draft of memoir, 2, Farinholt Papers, VHS; Farinholt to Daniel, April 15, 1905, Daniel Papers, UVA.

74. Galloway, "Gettysburg," 388.

75. Joseph L. Thompson reminiscences, Daniel Papers, UVA; James Peter Williams to Pa, July 7, 1863, Williams Letters, VSLA.

76. Cockrell, *Gunner with Stonewall*, 76.

77. "Captain John Holmes Smith's Account," 190; John Holmes Smith reminiscences, February 4–5, 1904, Daniel Papers, UVA; Finley account.

78. Edward P. Alexander to John B. Bachelder, May 3, 1876, in Ladd and Ladd, *Bachelder Papers*, 1:489; Alexander letter, 107–8; Alexander notes to Pickett, 1:25 P.M. and 1:40 P.M., July 3, 1863, Alexander Papers, LC (typed transcripts of these notes are in Alexander Papers, SHC-UNC); Gallagher, *Fighting for the Confederacy*, 258–59; Thomas R. Friend to Charles Pickett, December 10, 1894, Pickett Papers, VHS; Stewart, *Pickett's Charge*, 158; Priest, *Into the Fight*, 77.

79. Longstreet, "General Longstreet's Account," 77; Edward P. Alexander to John B. Bachelder, May 3, 1876, in Ladd and Ladd, *Bachelder Papers*, 1:489; Pickett, *Pickett and His Men*, 300–301; *Gettysburg Compiler*, September 23, 1902.

80. Edward P. Alexander to G. Moxley Sorrel, August 10, 1863, *Supplement to the Official Records*, 5:361; John C. Haskell to Daniel, May 12, 1906, Daniel Papers, SCL-DU; Govan and Livingood, *Haskell Memoirs*, 50; Gallagher, *Fighting for the Confederacy*, 260–61; Edward P. Alexander to John B. Bachelder, May 3, 1876, in Ladd and Ladd, *Bachelder Papers*, 1:490; Longstreet, "General Longstreet's Account," 77;

Longstreet, *From Manassas to Appomattox*, 392; Longstreet to R. H. Chilton, July 27, 1863, *OR* 27(2):360.

81. Raoul to father, July 17, 1863, Raoul Letters, LSU; O'Farrell diary, July 4, 1863, MC; extract of report by Robert M. Stribling, n.d., Alexander Papers, SHC-UNC; James Dearing to J. B. Walton, August 16, 1863, *OR* 27(2):388–89.

82. Priest, *Into the Fight*, 189–98; Stewart, *Pickett's Charge*, 159; Frederick Fuger to George Meade, November 28, 1883, Meade Collection, HSP.

83. Stewart, *Pickett's Charge*, 160.

84. Alexander S. Webb to wife, July 6, 1863, and Wheelock G. Veazey letter, n.d., in Ladd and Ladd, *Bachelder Papers*, 1:18, 59; Gottfried, *Stopping Pickett*, 168; testimony of Samuel Roberts, *Supreme Court of Pennsylvania*, 152; Bruce, *Twentieth Regiment of Massachusetts*, 291; Sylvanus W. Curtis to William R. Driver, July 16, 1863, *OR* 27(1):448; Hawley to father, July 4, 1863, Hawley Collection, SHSI; Sawyer, *Military History*, 130.

85. Johnston, *Story of a Confederate Boy*, 207; Stewart, *Pickett's Charge*, 140, 161; "Captain John Holmes Smith's Account," 190; Eppa Hunton questionnaire, February 15, 1904, Daniel Papers, SCL-DU; Bell, *11th Virginia Infantry*, 39; John Holmes Smith reminiscences, February 4–5, 1904, Daniel Papers, UVA; Durkin, *John Dooley*, 103; Charles S. Peyton to Charles Pickett, July 9, 1863, *OR* 27(2):385; Cadmus M. Wilcox to Thomas S. Mills, July 17, 1863, *OR* 27(2):620; Joseph R. Davis to William H. Palmer, August 22, 1863, *OR* 27(2):650; Divine, *Eighth Virginia Infantry*, 22.

CHAPTER FIVE

1. McCulloch, " 'High Tide at Gettysburg,' " 474.

2. Shotwell, "Virginia and North Carolina in the Battle of Gettysburg," 90; Hamilton, *Papers of Randolph Abbott Shotwell*, 2:9; Johnston, *Story of a Confederate Boy*, 207–8; Benjamin L. Farinholt to Daniel, April 15, 1905, Daniel Papers, UVA; Berkeley, "Rode with Pickett," 175.

3. Benjamin L. Farinholt to Daniel, April 15, 1905, Daniel Papers, UVA; Thomas R. Friend to Charles Pickett, December 10, 1894, Pickett Papers, VHS.

4. Johnston, *Story of a Confederate Boy*, 208; William Miller Owen, "Recollections of the Third Day at Gettysburg," 150.

5. John Holmes Smith reminiscences, February 4–5, 1904, Daniel Papers, UVA; Johnston, *Story of a Confederate Boy*, 204–5.

6. Durkin, *John Dooley*, 104–5; Robertson, *Eighteenth Virginia Infantry*, 21.

7. Raoul to father, July 17, 1863, Raoul Letters, LSU; Easley, "With Armistead When He Was Killed."

8. Durkin, *John Dooley*, 105; Elmore, "Meteorological and Astronomical Chronology," 14; Wiley, *Reminiscences of Big I*, 45; J. R. Hutter account, Daniel Papers, UVA.

9. Carter, "Flag of the Fifty-Third Va."; Robert Tyler Jones, "Gen. L. A. Armistead and R. Tyler Jones"; Lewis, *Recollections*, 83.

10. Robertson, *Eighteenth Virginia Infantry*, 21.

11. Kemper to W. H. Swallow, February 4, 1886, Kemper Papers, VHS.

12. Finley account; John Holmes Smith reminiscences, February 4–5, 1904, and W. H. H. Winston reminiscences, June 10, 1905, Daniel Papers, UVA; William W. Bentley to W. T. Fry, July 9, 1863, Pickett Papers, SCL-DU; Reeve reminiscences, Reeve Papers, SHC-UNC; McCulloch, " 'High Tide at Gettysburg,' " 474; James H. Walker, "Charge of Pickett's Division," 6, Walker Papers, VSLA.

13. Longstreet, "Lee's Right Wing at Gettysburg," 345.

14. Harrison and Busey, *Nothing but Glory*, 137; "Equine Heroes," 482, GNMP; Robert A. Bright to Owen, July 20, 1887, Owen Papers, VHS; Bright to Charles Pickett, October 15, 1892, Pickett Papers, VHS; Eppa Hunton questionnaire, February 15, 1904, Daniel Papers, SCL-DU; Berkeley account, GNMP.

15. Compton, *Reminiscences*, 13; Lang to Bachelder, October 16, 1893, David Lang Letterbook, 1893–1909, FSA; Wilcox, "General C. M. Wilcox on the Battle of Gettysburg," 6; J. B. Johnson, "Limited Review," FB.

16. Easley, "With Armistead When He Was Killed"; Reeve reminiscences, Reeve Papers, SHC-UNC.

17. Irvine, "Brig. Gen. Richard B. Garnett"; Harrison and Busey, *Nothing but Glory*, 83.

18. F. M. Bailey to Daniel, December 22, 1904; W. P. Jesse reminiscences, March 1905; and J. B. Dameron reminiscences, all in Daniel Papers, UVA.

19. Hamilton, *Papers of Randolph Abbott Shotwell*, 2:12; Joseph R. Cabell to Arthur S. Segar, July 11, 1863, Letter Book of Armistead, Barton, and Steuart Brigades, MC; Shultz and Rollins, "Measuring Pickett's Charge," 117; Hunt, "Third Day at Gettysburg," 374.

20. Erasmus Williams reminiscences; H. C. Michie to Daniel, January 27, 1904; and J. B. Dameron reminiscences, all in Daniel Papers, UVA; Finley account; Hamilton, *Papers of Randolph Abbott Shotwell*, 2:12; Edward Cook Barnes letter (before July 12, 1863), Barnes Family Manuscripts, UVA.

21. Draft of memoir, Farinholt Papers, VHS; W. B. Robertson to Mattie, July 28, 1863, Daniel Papers, UVA.

22. "Captain John Holmes Smith's Account," 191.

23. Loehr, " 'Old First' Virginia," 40; Loehr, *War History*, 36; Shotwell, "Virginia and North Carolina in the Battle of Gettysburg," 91; Hamilton, *Papers of Randolph Abbott Shotwell*, 2:10; Adams, "Nineteenth Maine at Gettysburg," 260; John Holmes Smith reminiscences, February 4–5, 1904, Daniel Papers, UVA.

24. Charles Cummings to wife, July 6, 1863, Cummings Papers, VerHS; Durkin, *John Dooley*, 108; Mayo, "Pickett's Charge at Gettysburg," 333; Thomas H. Oakes account, *War Recollections of the Confederate Veterans of Pittsylvania County*, 51–52.

25. Bright, "Pickett's Charge at Gettysburg," 264; field visit to Gettysburg, May 27, 1998. The existing Codori barn is larger than the one-story log structure with siding that existed on the same site in 1863, but I assume it would have been possible to have seen the top of it from the Confederate artillery line even then. See Harrison and Busey, *Nothing but Glory*, 130. Priest, *Into the Fight*, 231n, argues that Garnett initially aimed his brigade at Cemetery Hill, considerably to the north, but its alignment was skewed by the fences along Emmitsburg Road, which he struck at

a severe diagonal. Priest believes this tended to deflect the line of advance more toward the southeast, toward Cemetery Ridge. There is no evidence of any kind to support this contention.

26. Bright, "Pickett's Charge at Gettysburg," 264; Edmund Berkeley letter, September 26, n.d., Daniel Papers, UVA; Harrison and Busey, *Nothing but Glory*, 68–69; Kemper to W. H. Swallow, February 4, 1886, Kemper Papers, VHS.

27. Walter Harrison, *Pickett's Men*, 183.

28. Edmund Berkeley letter, September 26, n.d., Daniel Papers, UVA.

29. George Thornton Fleming, *Life and Letters of General Alexander Hays*, 456.

30. John Holmes Smith reminiscences, February 4–5, 1904, Daniel Papers, UVA; Finley account; Owen to H. A. Carrington, January 27, 1878, Owen Papers, VSLA.

31. Bright, "Pickett's Charge at Gettysburg," 264.

32. J. R. Hutter account, Daniel Papers, UVA; Durkin, *John Dooley*, 106; Harrison and Busey, *Nothing but Glory*, 185.

33. Reeve reminiscences, Reeve Papers, SHC-UNC.

34. Field visit to Gettysburg, May 27, 1998.

35. William S. Symington to Charles Pickett, October 17, 1892, and Thomas R. Friend to Pickett, December 10, 1894, Pickett Papers, VHS; Bright, "Pickett's Charge at Gettysburg," 264; Longacre, *Pickett*, 123–25.

36. Thomas R. Friend to Charles Pickett, December 10, 1894, Pickett Papers, VHS; Bright, "Pickett's Charge at Gettysburg," 264; J. F. Crocker to Daniel, September 15, 1903, Daniel Papers, UVA.

37. Bright, "Pickett's Charge at Gettysburg," 264; William S. Symington to Charles Pickett, October 17, 1892, Pickett Papers, VHS. Priest, *Into the Fight*, 228n, claims that Symington tried to stem the flow of stragglers from Marshall's brigade at this stage of the attack but that he seized the flag of the 47th North Carolina instead of the 11th North Carolina. There is no evidence to support this contention.

38. Bright, "Pickett's Charge at Gettysburg," 264–65; Bright to Charles Pickett, October 15, 1892, Pickett Papers, VHS; Longstreet, "Lee's Right Wing at Gettysburg," 346–47; Stewart, *Pickett's Charge*, 195; Longstreet, *From Manassas to Appomattox*, 394; Fremantle, *Three Months in the Southern States*, 264–66.

39. Longstreet, *From Manassas to Appomattox*, 393; Sorrel, *Recollections of a Confederate Staff Officer*, 164.

40. Bright, "Pickett's Charge at Gettysburg," 265; Charles Pickett to editor of *Richmond Times*, November 11, 1894, Pickett Papers, VHS.

41. Eppa Hunton questionnaire, February 15, 1904, Daniel Papers, SCL-DU.

42. Gallagher, *Fighting for the Confederacy*, 260–62; Alexander letter, 108; Alexander to Bachelder, May 3, 1876, in Ladd and Ladd, *Bachelder Papers*, 1:490; Alexander to G. Moxley Sorrel, August 10, 1863, *Supplement to the Official Records*, 5:361.

43. Gallagher, *Fighting for the Confederacy*, 262–63.

44. Priest, *Into the Fight*, 114–15; Clemmer, *Valor in Gray*, 305, 307–9, 313; *History of the Fifth Massachusetts Battery*, 653. Shultz, "Double Canister at Ten Yards," 64, estimates that McQueen's gun received fire from at least eight Union batteries, or about forty-eight cannon.

45. Govan and Livingood, *Haskell Memoirs*, 50–51.

46. Fry, "Pettigrew's Charge at Gettysburg," 92; Peel diary, 28, MDAH; William B. Taylor to mother, July 29, 1863, in Mast, "Six Lieutenants," 13.

47. Underwood, "Twenty-Sixth Regiment," 365; Thomas J. Cureton to Lane, June 22, 1890, Lane Papers, SHC-UNC; John T. Jones, "Pettigrew's Brigade at Gettysburg," 133; Moore, "Battle of Gettysburg," 250; Harris, *Historical Sketches*, 36.

48. Max R. Williams, " 'Awful Affair,' " 48; Thomas J. Cureton to Lane, June 22, 1890, Lane Papers, SHC-UNC.

49. Young, *Battle of Gettysburg*, 5.

50. Hamilton, *Papers of Randolph Abbott Shotwell*, 2:17; "Letter from General Trimble," 31.

51. Shotwell, "Virginia and North Carolina in the Battle of Gettysburg," 92; Walter H. Taylor letter, 134.

52. "Letter from General Trimble," 33–34; James H. Lane to Joseph A. Engelhard, August 13, 1863, *OR* 27(2):666.

53. Harris, *Historical Sketches*, 36; "Another Witness," 463; Isaac Trimble to Daniel, November 24, 1875, Daniel Papers, SCL-DU.

54. Peel diary, 29, MDAH; William Love, "Mississippi at Gettysburg," 44; Underwood, "Twenty-Sixth Regiment," 366.

55. Wiley Woods, "The 1st Tennessee Flag at Gettysburg," *Confederate Veteran* Papers, SCL-DU; James M. Simpson to wife, July 16, 1863, Allen-Simpson Papers, SHC-UNC.

56. Speer, *Voices From Cemetery Hill*, 107; Moore, "Battle of Gettysburg," 251; Rogers, "Additional Sketch," 108.

57. Rogers, "Additional Sketch," 108.

58. Christ, *Struggle for the Bliss Farm*, 79; A. S. Haynes to editors, October 8, 1877, Grimes Papers, SHC-UNC; Young, *Battle of Gettysburg*, 6; Isaac R. Trimble to W. H. Swallow, February 8, 1886, in Ladd and Ladd, *Bachelder Papers*, 2:1199.

59. Cockrell and Ballard, *Mississippi Rebel*, 198; Young, *Battle of Gettysburg*, 6; Joseph R. Davis to William H. Palmer, August 22, 1863, *OR* 27(2):651; "Another Witness," 461; Peel diary, 29, MDAH.

60. Dunaway, *Reminiscences of a Rebel*, 91; Robert E. L. Krick, *Fortieth Virginia Infantry*, 20; William S. Christian to Daniel, October 24, 1904, Daniel Papers, UVA; Robert M. Mayo to H. H. Walker, August 13, 1863, Heth Papers, MC; Patterson, " 'In a Most Disgraceful Manner,' " 47.

61. Robert E. L. Krick, *Fortieth Virginia Infantry*, 29; Christ, *Struggle for the Bliss Farm*, 79; Watts, "Something More about Gettysburg"; Michael W. Taylor, *To Drive the Enemy from Southern Soil*, 413.

62. Michael W. Taylor, *To Drive the Enemy from Southern Soil*, 412–413.

63. Robert M. Mayo to H. H. Walker, August 13, 1863, Heth Papers, MC; Priest, *Into the Fight*, 103–4; Stewart, *Pickett's Charge*, 193; Potter, "Battle of Gettysburg."

64. George Thornton Fleming, *Life and Letters of General Alexander Hays*, 456; Sawyer, *Military History*, 131; Thomas F. Galwey to Bachelder, May 19, 1882, in Ladd and Ladd, *Bachelder Papers*, 2:870; Sawyer to J. G. Reid, July 5, 1863, *OR*

27(1):462; Galwey, *Valiant Hours*, 114–16; James H. Lane to editors, September 7, 1877, Grimes Papers, SHC-UNC.

65. Robert M. Mayo to H. H. Walker, August 13, 1863, Heth Papers, MC; William S. Christian to Daniel, October 24, 1904, Daniel Papers, UVA.

66. McDaid, " 'Four Years of Arduous Service,' " 218; William L. J. Lowrance to Joseph A. Engelhard, August 12, 1863, *OR* 27(2):671; J. McLeod Turner to editors, October 10, 1877, and W. B. Shepard to editors, September 18, 1877, Grimes Papers, SHC-UNC; Charles S. Venable to Joseph J. Davis, August 12, 1889, *Raleigh News and Observer*, July 5, 1903. Priest, *Into the Fight*, 97–98, 228n, discounts J. McLeod Turner's claim that the men of Brockenbrough's brigade fled through Trimble's formation. He believes it must have been stragglers from Marshall's and Fry's brigades, but there is no evidence to support this contention.

67. Robert M. Mayo to H. H. Walker, August 13, 1863, Heth Papers, MC; Dunaway, *Reminiscences of a Rebel*, 92–93; Richard Rouzie to sister, July 9, 1863, Rouzie Papers, CWM; unsigned letter to editor, July 29, 1863, *Richmond Daily Enquirer*, August 4, 1863.

68. J. McLeod Turner to editors, October 10, 1877, Grimes Papers, SHC-UNC; Joseph A. Engelhard to William H. Palmer, November 4, 1863, *OR* 27(2):659; Harris, *Historical Sketches*, 36.

69. Birkett D. Fry to Bachelder, January 26, 1878, in Ladd and Ladd, *Bachelder Papers*, 1:523; Christ, *Struggle for the Bliss Farm*, 79.

70. Fry, "Pettigrew's Charge at Gettysburg," 93; Turney, "First Tennessee at Gettysburg," 536.

71. Stevens, *Souvenir of Excursion*, 29. Col. Samuel G. Shepard of the 7th Tennessee claimed that the joining of Fry and Garnett took place a little more than halfway to the Union line. See Shepard to William H. Palmer, August 10, 1863, *OR* 27(2):647. One of Pickett's men, George W. Finley of the 56th Virginia in Garnett's brigade, believed it took place just as the two commands reached the stone fence, but most observers argued that the junction was made just as the two commands reached Emmitsburg Road. See Finley account.

72. Edmund Rice to Doubleday, April 19, 1887, Gettysburg Volume, Doubleday Papers, N-YHS; Byrne and Weaver, *Haskell of Gettysburg*, 157.

73. Norman J. Hall to A. H. Embler, July 17, 1863, *OR* 27(1):439; Carpenter letter, MHS; James A. Wright, "Story of Co. F," 610, MHS; Willey, "Story of My Experiences," LC.

74. Byrne and Weaver, *Haskell of Gettysburg*, 158.

75. Jacob B. Hardenburgh to Gates, October 9, 1878, Gates Papers, N-YHS; James A. Wright, "Story of Co. F," 610, MHS; Bond recollections, MHS.

76. Ford, *Story of the Fifteenth Regiment*, 276.

77. McDermott, *Brief History of the Sixty-Ninth Regiment*, 31; testimony of McKeever, *Supreme Court of Pennsylvania*, 259; McDermott to Bachelder, June 2, 1886, in Ladd and Ladd, *Bachelder Papers*, 3:1410–11.

78. Testimony of Samuel Roberts, *Supreme Court of Pennsylvania*, 312.

79. Gibbon, *Personal Recollections*, 150–51; Byrne and Weaver, *Haskell of Gettysburg*, 159; Stevens, *Address Delivered at the Dedication*, 22.

80. Byrne and Weaver, *Haskell of Gettysburg*, 160–61; Meade, *Life and Letters*, 2:108.

81. Testimony of James Lynch, *Supreme Court of Pennsylvania*, 303; Ward, *History of the One Hundred and Sixth*, 165–66; Clifford to father, USAMHI.

82. Shultz, *"Double Canister at Ten Yards,"* 41–46; Longacre, *Man behind the Guns*, 176; *History of the Fifth Massachusetts Battery*, 652–53, 655; Henry J. Hunt to Seth Williams, September 27, 1863, *OR* 27(1):239; Freeman McGilvery to Robert O. Tyler, n.d., 1863, *OR* 27(1):884; Patrick Hart to C. H. Whittelsey, August 2, 1863, *OR* 27(1):888; Patrick Hart to Bachelder, February 23, 1891, in Ladd and Ladd, *Bachelder Papers*, 3:1798; Robert Garth Scott, *Fallen Leaves*, 188.

83. Henry J. Hunt account, January 20, 1873, in Ladd and Ladd, *Bachelder Papers*, 1:430–31; John G. Hazard to C. H. Morgan, August 1, 1863, *OR* 27(1):480; Alexander S. Webb to A. H. Embler, July 12, 1863, *OR* 27(1):428; Shultz, *"Double Canister at Ten Yards,"* 37.

84. Testimony of Frederick Fuger and William S. Stockton, *Supreme Court of Pennsylvania*, 128–29, 243; Alexander S. Webb to A. H. Embler, July 12, 1863, *OR* 27(1):428; McDermott, *Brief History of the Sixty-Ninth Regiment*, 31; Richard Penn Smith interview, *Gettysburg Compiler*, June 7, 1887; Lash, "Philadelphia Brigade," 104; Penn Smith to Rothermel, November 25, 1867, Rothermel Papers, PHMC; Penn Smith to Isaac Wistar, July 29, 1863, Wistar Papers, WI.

85. Burns diary, July 3, 1863, USAMHI; testimony of William S. Stockton, *Supreme Court of Pennsylvania*, 243; Richard Penn Smith interview, *Gettysburg Compiler*, June 7, 1887.

86. William A. Arnold account, 2, Records of the Soldiers and Sailors Historical Society of Rhode Island, RIHS; Buell, *Cannoneer*, 95–96.

87. George A. Bowen, "Diary of Captain George D. Bowen," 135; Richard S. Thompson, "Scrap of Gettysburg," 102.

88. Stevens, *Souvenir of Excursion*, 29; Hawley to father, July 4, 1863, Hawley Collection, SHSI; George Thornton Fleming, *Life and Letters of General Alexander Hays*, 457.

89. Haines, *History of the Men of Co. F*, 41; Emmell, " 'Now is the Time for Buck & Ball,' " GNMP; Bee, *Boys from Rockville*, 150.

90. Bacarella, *Lincoln's Foreign Legion*, 139; Chauncey L. Harris to father, July 4, 1863, in Washburn, *Complete Military History*, 52; Belknap diary, July 3, 1863, USAMHI; Haskin, *History of the First Regiment of Artillery*, 170.

91. Alexander Hays to C. H. Morgan, July 8, 1863, *OR* 27(1):454; Theodore G. Ellis to William P. Seville, July 6, 1863, *OR* 27(1):467; Goodrich to friends, July 17, 1863, Goodrich Papers, CHS; Mead to wife, USAMHI; Hawley to father, July 4, 1863, Hawley Collection, SHSI; Chauncey L. Harris to father, July 4, 1863, in Washburn, *Complete Military History*, 52; Winfield Scott, "Pickett's Charge," 906–7; L. A. B. letter, July 6, 1863, *Rochester Daily Democrat and American*, July 14, 1863; Calvin A. Haynes to wife, July 19, 1863, Haynes Letters, NYSL.

92. Clinton D. MacDougall to Gettysburg Memorial Association, August 27, 1890, in Ladd and Ladd, *Bachelder Papers*, 3:1763; Hawley to father, July 4, 1863, Hawley Collection, SHSI; Christopher Mead to wife, July 6, 1863, USAMHI.

93. Crumb, *Eleventh Corps Artillery*, 42–43; Shultz, *"Double Canister at Ten Yards,"* 37–40.

CHAPTER SIX

1. Isaac R. Trimble to W. H. Swallow, February 8, 1886, in Ladd and Ladd, *Bachelder Papers*, 2:1199; Samuel G. Shepard to William Brown, August 10, 1863, *OR* 27(2):647; Moore, "Battle of Gettysburg," 250; Turney, "First Tennessee at Gettysburg," 536.

2. Moore, "Battle of Gettysburg," 250; Swallow, "Third Day at Gettysburg," 568; Kimble, "Tennesseeans at Gettysburg," 460–61.

3. Rogers, "Additional Sketch," 108–9.

4. Michael W. Taylor, "Col. James Keith Marshall," 87, 87n; Underwood, "Twenty-Sixth Regiment," 365; Gragg, *Covered with Glory*, 192; Marshall to uncle, VMI. Other sources, such as Robinson, "Fifty-Second Regiment," 238, claim that Marshall was shot in the body near the stone fence, but they present evidence less reliable than that in Taylor's article.

5. "Letter from General Trimble," 33.

6. Shotwell, "Virginia and North Carolina in the Battle of Gettysburg," 94; Mrs. N. G. Robertson account, n.d., *Confederate Veteran* Papers, SCL-DU; Moore, "Battle of Gettysburg," 249; John H. Moore to Bachelder, in Ladd and Ladd, *Bachelder Papers*, 2:914.

7. J. McLeod Turner to editors, October 10, 1877, Grimes Papers, SHC-UNC.

8. Turney, "First Tennessee at Gettysburg," 536; Fite memoir, 87, TSLA; Fulton, *Family Record and War Reminiscences*, 103; McComb, "Historical Sketch," 43–44, MC.

9. Kimble, "W. H. McCulloch," MC.

10. Swallow, "Third Day at Gettysburg," 568; Moore, "Battle of Gettysburg," 250; Fite memoir, 87, TSLA; Wiley Woods, "The 1st Tennessee Flag at Gettysburg," *Confederate Veteran* Papers, SCL-DU.

11. Hawley to father, July 4, 1863, Hawley Collection, SHSI; Bee, *Boys from Rockville*, 150; McComb, "Historical Sketch," 43–44, MC.

12. David Shields statement, n.d., Grimes Papers, and Thomas J. Cureton to Lane, June 22, 1890, Lane Papers, SHC-UNC.

13. James H. Lane to editors, September 7, 1877, Grimes Papers, SHC-UNC; Baker, "Tribute to Capt. Magruder and Wife."

14. Baker, "Tribute to Capt. Magruder and Wife"; Peel diary, 30–31, MDAH; Thomas Geer to Clinton D. MacDougall, July 28, 1890, in Ladd and Ladd, *Bachelder Papers*, 3:1754.

15. Heflin, *Blind Man*, 24–25; Young, *Battle of Gettysburg*, 6.

16. Young, *Battle of Gettysburg*, 6.

17. David Shields to Bachelder, August 27, 1884, and John L. Brady to Bachelder, May 24, 1886, in Ladd and Ladd, *Bachelder Papers*, 2:1068, 3:1398; Seville, *History of the First Regiment*, 81–82.

18. Goodrich to friends, July 17, 1863, Goodrich Papers, CHS; Stevens, *Souvenir*

of Excursion, 27; Stevens account, June 10, 1905, Stevens Papers, NCDAH; Stevens, *Address Delivered at the Dedication*, 23; Theodore G. Ellis to Bachelder, November 3, 1870, in Ladd and Ladd, *Bachelder Papers*, 1:408; Page, *History of the Fourteenth*, 152.

19. Richard S. Thompson, "Scrap of Gettysburg," 105–6; Toombs, *New Jersey Troops*, 194.

20. John M. Dunn address, *Report of Joint Committee*, 14–15; William A. Arnold account, 2, Records of the Soldiers and Sailors Historical Society of Rhode Island, RIHS; George Thornton Fleming, *Life and Letters of General Alexander Hays*, 406; Toombs, *New Jersey Troops*, 298.

21. Samuel B. McIntyre to Clinton D. MacDougall, June 27, 1890, in Ladd and Ladd, *Bachelder Papers*, 3:1747.

22. George A. Bowen, "Diary of Captain George D. Bowen," 133–34.

23. Samuel B. McIntyre to Clinton D. MacDougall, June 27, 1890, and David Shields to MacDougall, August 26, 1890, in Ladd and Ladd, *Bachelder Papers*, 3:1744, 1759.

24. David Shields statement, n.d., Grimes Papers, SHC-UNC; John L. Brady to Bachelder, May 24, 1886, and Clinton D. MacDougall to Gettysburg Memorial Association, August 27, 1890, in Ladd and Ladd, *Bachelder Papers*, 3:1398–99, 1762.

25. Belknap diary, July 3, 1863, USAMHI.

26. Murray, *Redemption of the "Harper's Ferry Cowards,"* 147; Samuel B. McIntyre to Clinton D. MacDougall, June 17, 1890, and MacDougall to Gettysburg Memorial Association, August 27, 1890, in Ladd and Ladd, *Bachelder Papers*, 3:1744–45, 1762; Gambone, *Hancock at Gettysburg*, 179.

27. Murray, *Redemption of the "Harper's Ferry Cowards,"* 60–61; David Shields to Bachelder, August 27, 1884, and Clinton D. MacDougall to Gettysburg Memorial Association, August 27, 1890, in Ladd and Ladd, *Bachelder Papers*, 2:1068, 3:1762.

28. Seville, *History of the First Regiment*, 82, 86; Maull, *Life and Military Services*, 14–15.

29. Haskin, *History of the First Regiment of Artillery*, 169–70; Crary, *Dear Belle*, 209.

30. Haskin, *History of the First Regiment of Artillery*, 169–70, 545; Shultz, *"Double Canister at Ten Yards,"* 51, 54.

31. Samuel Roberts to Alexander S. Webb, August 18, 1883, in Ladd and Ladd, *Bachelder Papers*, 2:967; John M. Dunn address, *Report of Joint Committee*, 13–14.

32. David Shields statement, n.d., Grimes Papers, SHC-UNC; Horace Judson to Bachelder, October 17, 1887, in Ladd and Ladd, *Bachelder Papers*, 3:1514–15; Potter, "Battle of Gettysburg."

33. Thomas F. Galwey to Bachelder, May 19, 1882, in Ladd and Ladd, *Bachelder Papers*, 2:870; Franklin Sawyer letter, July 4, 1863, in Daggett, "Those Whom You Left behind You," 360–61; Galwey, *Valiant Hours*, 117.

34. Franklin Swayer to J. G. Reid, July 5, 1863, *OR* 27(1):462; Sawyer, *Military History*, 131; Horace Judson to Bachelder, October 17, 1887, in Ladd and Ladd, *Bachelder Papers*, 3:1516.

35. Talbot, *Samuel Chapman Armstrong*, 92, 93n; Simons, *Regimental History*, 137–38; Potter, "Battle of Gettysburg"; Campbell, "'Remember Harper's Ferry!,'" pt. 2, 106; Samuel C. Armstrong to Bachelder, February 6, 1884, and William D.

Taylor to Bachelder, September 22, 1891, in Ladd and Ladd, *Bachelder Papers*, 2:1001, 3:1822.

36. Charles A. Richardson to Bachelder, May 8, 1868, and John I. Brinkerhoff to Clinton D. MacDougall, July 9, 1890, in Ladd and Ladd, *Bachelder Papers*, 1:341, 3:1750.

37. Samuel C. Armstrong to Bachelder, February 6, 1884, ibid., 2:1001.

38. Murray, *Redemption of the "Harper's Ferry Cowards,"* 139; Campbell, " 'Remember Harper's Ferry!,' " pt. 2, 107; Emerson Bicknell to Bachelder, August 6, 1883, in Ladd and Ladd, *Bachelder Papers*, 2:964.

39. Samuel C. Armstrong to Bachelder, February 13, 1884, in Ladd and Ladd, *Bachelder Papers*, 2:1019; George Thornton Fleming, *Life and Letters of General Alexander Hays*, 438–39; Busey and Martin, *Regimental Strengths and Losses*, 244.

40. Owen to H. A. Carrington, January 27, 1878, Owen Papers, VSLA; H. T. Owen, "Pickett at Gettysburg"; McCulloch, " 'High Tide at Gettysburg,' " 474.

41. William W. Bentley to W. T. Fry, July 9, 1863, Pickett Papers, SCL-DU.

42. Field visits to Gettysburg, March 25, 1997, and May 27, 1998.

43. Mayo, "Pickett's Charge at Gettysburg," 332; Carter, "Flag of the Fifty-Third Va."; Poindexter, "Armistead at the Battle of Gettysburg," 186; Crocker, "Gettysburg," 132; Rawley W. Martin to Daniel, August 11, 1887, Daniel Papers, UVA.

44. J. R. Hutter account, n.d., Daniel Papers, UVA; Harrison and Busey, *Nothing but Glory*, 43.

45. Compton, *Reminiscences*, 17; Bachelder to Fitzhugh Lee, December 1892, in Ladd and Ladd, *Bachelder Papers*, 3:1899–1900; Berkeley account, GNMP.

46. James A. Wright, "Story of Co. F," 610, MHS; James letter; Harrison and Busey, *Nothing but Glory*, 67; David Shields statement, Grimes Papers, SHC-UNC.

47. James W. Clay account, in Peters, "Lost Sword of Gen. Richard B. Garnett," 29; Edmund Rice to Doubleday, April 19, 1997, Gettysburg Volume, Doubleday Papers, N-YHS.

48. Wiley, *Reminiscences of Big I*, 46; Samuel Roberts to Alexander S. Webb, August 18, 1883, in Ladd and Ladd, *Bachelder Papers*, 2:967; Hamilton, *Papers of Randolph Abbott Shotwell*, 2:13; Swallow, "Third Day at Gettysburg," 566–67; J. B. Dameron reminiscences, Daniel Papers, UVA; Finley account; W. P. Jesse reminiscences, March 1905, Daniel Papers, UVA.

49. John C. Timberlake to editors, September 24, 1877, Grimes Papers, SHC-UNC; Sale, "Reminiscences"; Lewis, *Recollections*, 84.

50. Rawley W. Martin to Daniel, August 11, 1887, Daniel Papers, UVA; Timberlake to editors, VHS; Sale, "Reminiscences."

51. Owen to H. A. Carrington, January 27, 1878, Owen Papers, VSLA; H. T. Owen, "Pickett at Gettysburg."

52. Charles S. Peyton to Charles Pickett, July 9, 1863, *OR* 27(2):386.

53. Harrison and Busey, *Nothing but Glory*, 70–71; Joseph Mayo to Charles Pickett, July 25, 1863, Pickett Papers, SCL-DU; Reeve reminiscences, Reeve Papers, SHC-UNC.

54. Priest, *Into the Fight*, 235n; Owen to H. A. Carrington, January 27, 1878, Owen Papers, VSLA.

55. H. T. Owen, "Pickett at Gettysburg"; Edward Cook Barnes letter (before July 12, 1863), Barnes Family Manuscripts, UVA; Lochren, "First Minnesota at Gettysburg," 53.

56. Harrison and Busey, *Nothing but Glory*, 70.

57. Robert A. Bright to Charles Pickett, October 15, 1892, Pickett Papers, VHS; Bright, "Pickett's Charge at Gettysburg," 265.

58. Harrison and Busey, *Nothing but Glory*, 83; Charles S. Peyton to Charles Pickett, July 9, 1863, *OR* 27(2):386; Hamilton, *Papers of Randolph Abbott Shotwell*, 2:13.

59. W. P. Jesse reminiscences, March 1905, Daniel Papers, UVA; Holland, "With Armistead at Gettysburg"; Hunton, *Autobiography*, 100.

60. Finley account; Lewis, *Recollections*, 84–85; Wiley, *Reminiscences of Big I*, 46.

61. H. T. Owen, "Pickett at Gettysburg"; Charles S. Peyton to Charles Pickett, July 9, 1863, *OR* 27(2):386.

62. Finley account.

63. Ibid.; Bachelder to Fitzhugh Lee, December 1892, in Ladd and Ladd, *Bachelder Papers*, 3:1900; Robert W. Douthat questionnaire (January 1905), Daniel Papers, UVA.

64. Mayo, "Pickett's Charge at Gettysburg," 333; Joseph Mayo to Charles Pickett, July 25, 1863, Pickett Papers, SCL-DU; Loehr, " 'Old First' Virginia," 36; J. R. Hutter account, Daniel Papers, UVA.

65. John Holmes Smith reminiscences, February 4–5, 1904, Daniel Papers, UVA; "Captain John Holmes Smith's Account," 191.

66. John Holmes Smith reminiscences, February 4–5, 1904, Daniel Papers, UVA; *Richmond Daily Dispatch*, July 13, 1863.

67. Carter, "Flag of the Fifty-Third Va.," 263; Robert Tyler Jones, "Gen. L. A. Armistead and R. Tyler Jones," 271.

68. Clement, *History of Pittsylvania County*, 249; Priest, *Into the Fight*, 237n; Timberlake to editors, VHS; E. M. Magruder to sister, August 1863, Magruder Papers, SCL-DU.

69. Easley, "With Armistead When He Was Killed."

70. Charles S. Peyton to Charles Pickett, July 9, 1863, *OR* 27(2):386; Harrison and Busey, *Nothing but Glory*, 87.

71. Shultz, *"Double Canister at Ten Yards,"* 67; Charles S. Peyton to Charles Pickett, July 9, 1863, *OR* 27(2):386; H. T. Owen, "Pickett's Attack"; Robert W. Douthat account, January 1905, and Douthat to Daniel, January 14, 1905, Daniel Papers, UVA.

72. Porter, "Confederate Soldier," 460.

73. Adams, "Nineteenth Maine at Gettysburg," 260–61.

74. George J. Stannard to C. Kingsbury, July 4, 1863, *OR* 27(1):350; Stannard diary, July 3, 1863; Wheelock G. Veazey letter, n.d.; and George G. Benedict to Bachelder, March 16, 1864, all in Ladd and Ladd, *Bachelder Papers*, 1:55, 60, 96; William T. Nichols to George G. Benedict, March 18, 1864, Benedict Family Papers, UV; Benedict, *Army Life in Virginia*, 177.

75. Benedict, *Vermont at Gettysburgh*, 16; Wheelock G. Veazey letter, n.d., in Ladd

and Ladd, *Bachelder Papers*, 1:60; George J. Stannard to C. Kingsbury, July 4, 1863, *OR* 27(1):349.

76. William T. Nichols to George G. Benedict, March 18, 1864, Benedict Family Papers, UV; Clarke, "Thirteenth Regiment," VerHS; George H. Scott, "Vermont at Gettysburg," 77; Francis V. Randall to John Newton, July 10, 1863, *OR* 27(1):353.

77. John Newton to Seth Williams, September 30, 1863, *OR* 27(1):262; Theodore B. Gates to Thomas A. Rowley, July 4, 1863, *OR* 27(1):318; Gates to Abner Doubleday, January 30, 1864, *OR* 27(1):322; Gates to Bachelder, January 30, 1864, in Ladd and Ladd, *Bachelder Papers*, 1:85; Jacob B. Hardenburgh to Gates, October 9, 1878, Gates Papers, N-YHS; Gates to Rothermel, April 28, 1868, Rothermel Papers, PHMC; Osborne, *Civil War Diaries of Col. Theodore B. Gates*, 93.

78. Bond recollections, MHS; James A. Wright, "Story of Co. F," 611, MHS; Clifford to father, USAMHI.

79. Norman J. Hall to A. H. Embler, July 17, 1863, *OR* 27(1):439; Sylvanus W. Curtis to William R. Driver, July 16, 1863, *OR* 27(1):448; *Reports, Letters & Papers*, 2:61, BPL.

80. George J. Stannard diary, July 3, 1863, in Ladd and Ladd, *Bachelder Papers*, 1:56; Stannard to C. Kingsbury, July 4, 1863, *OR* 27(1):350.

81. William E. Barrow to Norman J. Hall, August 12, 1866, and Hall to Barrow, August 18, 1866, in Ladd and Ladd, *Bachelder Papers*, 1:274–75, 279.

82. Winfield S. Hancock to Seth Williams, n.d., 1863, *OR* 27(1):374; George J. Stannard to Doubleday, September 3, 1865, Gettysburg Volume, Doubleday Papers, N-YHS; Clarke, "Hancock and the Vermont Brigade," 225–26. After the war Hancock cautioned people not to give undue credit to the Vermont brigade for repelling Pickett's Charge. Gibbon also believed they received too much praise, arguing that Pickett's momentum had already stopped by the time Stannard's flanking fire was brought to bear. See Winfield S. Hancock to Francis Walker, April 16, 1884, and John Gibbon to Francis Walker, March 14, 1886, Sessler Collection, CWLM.

83. George H. Scott to Doubleday, March 12, 1869, and Doubleday to Scott, April 6, 1869, Gettysburg Volume, Doubleday Papers, N-YHS; Sturtivant, *Pictorial History*, 305; Francis V. Randall to John Newton, July 10, 1863, *OR* 27(1):353; George H. Scott, "Vermont at Gettysburg," 77–78; Benedict, *Vermont at Gettysburgh*, 17.

84. Clarke, "Thirteenth Regiment," VerHS; Clarke, "Hancock and the Vermont Brigade," 225; Benedict, *Vermont at Gettysburgh*, 17.

85. Francis V. Randall to John Newton, July 10, 1863, *OR* 27(1):353; Benedict, *Vermont at Gettysburgh*, 18; George H. Scott, "Vermont at Gettysburg," 78.

86. Sturtivant, *Pictorial History*, 309, 313; Wheelock G. Veazey to G. G. Benedict, July 11, 1864, Benedict Family Papers, UV; Veazey letter, n.d., and Bachelder to Fitzhugh Lee, December 1892, in Ladd and Ladd, *Bachelder Papers*, 1:60–61, 3:1902.

87. Wheelock G. Veazey to G. G. Benedict, July 11, 1864, Benedict Family Papers, UV; Benedict, *Vermont at Gettysburgh*, 18.

88. Benedict, *Vermont at Gettysburgh*, 16; Andrew Cowan address, *In Memoriam*,

66; Charles Cowan, "Pickett's Charge," 28; Andrew Cowan to C. H. Tompkins, August 15, 1863, *OR* 27(1):690.

89. Charles Cowan, "Pickett's Charge," 29; Andrew Cowan to Bachelder, December 2, 1885, in Ladd and Ladd, *Bachelder Papers*, 2:1156; Longacre, *Man behind the Guns*, 176–77, 179; Hunt to Mary, July 4, 1863, Hunt Papers, LC.

90. Andrew Cowan to C. H. Tompkins, August 15, 1863, *OR* 27(1):690; Priest, *Into the Fight*, 141; Stewart, *Pickett's Charge*, 223, 228; William McFadden to Horace P. Rugg, July 16, 1863, *OR* 27(1):452–53; Henry N. Hamilton to Bachelder, April 22, 1864, in Ladd and Ladd, *Bachelder Papers*, 1:179.

91. Andrew Cowan to Bachelder, August 26, 1866, and December 2, 1885, in Ladd and Ladd, *Bachelder Papers*, 1:282, 2:1156–57; Andrew Cowan, "Cowan's New York Battery"; Andrew Cowan to C. H. Tompkins, August 15, 1863, *OR* 27(1):690; Charles Cowan, "Pickett's Charge," 29; Andrew Cowan account, Webb Papers, YU; J. W. C. to editors, July 4, 1863, *Auburn Daily Advertiser and Union*, July 11, 1863.

92. Shultz, *"Double Canister at Ten Yards,"* 48–50, 57–58; Wheeler, *Letters of William Wheeler*, 413.

93. James A. Wright, "Story of Co. F," 611, MHS; Heath to Connor, GNMP.

94. Norman J. Hall to A. H. Embler, July 17, 1863, *OR* 27(1):439; Edmund Rice to Doubleday, April 19, 1887, Gettysburg Volume, Doubleday Papers, N-YHS.

95. Tyler to father, July 29, 1863, Tyler Papers, SCL-DU; Oesterle memoir, USAMHI; Henry L. Abbott to William Driver, July 16, 1863, *OR* 27(1):445; Abbott to Papa, July 6, 1863, and to Oliver Wendell Holmes Jr., July 18, 1863, in Robert Garth Scott, *Fallen Leaves*, 188, 194; Abbott letter, n.d., *Reports, Letters & Papers*, 1:90–91, BPL; Daniel McAdams, "A Short History of the Service of Daniel McAdams in Company I, 20 Regiment Mass Vol 30 years after the War, Wrote from Memory," MOLLUS-Massachusetts Commandery Collection, HU.

96. *Reports, Letters & Papers*, 2:61, BPL; Anthony W. McDermott to Bachelder, June 2, 1886, in Ladd and Ladd, *Bachelder Papers*, 3:1410; McDermott letter, GNMP; testimony of John Buckley, *Supreme Court of Pennsylvania*, 135.

97. Anthony W. McDermott to Bachelder, June 2, 1886, in Ladd and Ladd, *Bachelder Papers*, 3:1410; Frederick Fuger, "Battle of Gettysburg and Personal Recollections of That Battle," 23–24, Webb Papers, YU; Kent Masterson Brown, *Cushing of Gettysburg*, 251; testimony of Frederick Fuger, *Supreme Court of Pennsylvania*, 129–30; Fuger letter, n.d., in Stevens, *Souvenir of Excursion*, 35.

98. Lash, "Philadelphia Brigade," 106; Ashe, "Pettigrew-Pickett Charge," 151; Richard Penn Smith to Charles H. Banes, July 12, 1863, *OR* 27(1):432; Alexander S. Webb to A. H. Embler, July 12, 1863, *OR* 27(1):428; Winfield S. Hancock to Seth Williams, n.d., 1863, *OR* 27(1):374; Penn Smith to Wistar, July 29, 1863, Wistar Papers, WI; Penn Smith to Rothermel, n.d., Rothermel Papers, PHMC; Richard Penn Smith interview, *Gettysburg Compiler*, June 7, 1887.

99. Lash, "Philadelphia Brigade," 106; testimony of William S. Stockton, *Supreme Court of Pennsylvania*, 243; Byrne and Weaver, *Haskell of Gettysburg*, 162, 164.

100. Christopher Smith account.

101. William Davis to Charles H. Banes, July 12, 1863, *OR* 27(1):431; McDermott, *Brief History of the Sixty-Ninth Regiment*, 31; testimony of Robert Whittick,

Supreme Court of Pennsylvania, 79–81; John Buckley to Bachelder, n.d., and Anthony W. McDermott to Bachelder, June 2, 1886, in Ladd and Ladd, *Bachelder Papers*, 3:1403, 1411; Gottfried, *Stopping Pickett*, 170.

102. Nevins, *Diary of Battle*, 252.

CHAPTER SEVEN

1. Morris to W. Saunders, October 1, 1877, Morris Papers, SHC-UNC.

2. E. B. Withers to editors, October 8, 1877; J. McLeod Turner to editors, October 10, 1877; Thomas L. Norwood to editors, October 6, 1877; and Thomas P. Molloy to editors, September 29, 1877, all in Grimes Papers, SHC-UNC; Harris, *Historical Sketches*, 37.

3. Henry Moore to editors, November 6, 1877, Grimes Papers, SHC-UNC.

4. Van Swaringen reminiscences, GNMP.

5. Wiley Woods, "The 1st Tennessee Flag at Gettysburg," *Confederate Veteran* Papers, SCL-DU.

6. Underwood, "Twenty-Sixth Regiment," 366; Benjamin F. Little to editors, September 20, 1877, and A. S. Haynes to editors, October 8, 1877, Grimes Papers, SHC-UNC; Caison, "Southern Soldiers in Northern Prisons," 160.

7. David Shields statement, Grimes Papers, SHC-UNC; Richard S. Thompson, "Scrap of Gettysburg," 106; Toombs, *New Jersey Troops*, 300; Swallow, "Third Day at Gettysburg," 568; John M. Dunn address, *Report of Joint Committee*, 15.

8. Aldrich, *History of Battery A*, 217.

9. John T. Jones, "Pettigrew's Brigade at Gettysburg," 134.

10. Louis G. Young to W. J. Baker, February 10, 1864, *Richmond Daily Enquirer*, March 18, 1864; Joseph J. Davis to editors, September 20, 1877, Grimes Papers, SHC-UNC.

11. Aldrich, *History of Battery A*, 216; Weymouth T. Jordan, *North Carolina Troops*, 7:467; Henry W. Newton to Noble, August 8, 1913, Noble Papers, SHC-UNC; Gragg, *Covered with Glory*, 199. Recent historians have discounted this episode of Pettigrew's attack. Priest, *Into the Fight*, 222n, does not believe it happened at all. Trinque, "Arnold's Battery and the 26th North Carolina," 61–67, believes it happened but not to the 26th. Trinque argues that the blast affected the 16th North Carolina of Lowrance's brigade, based on his assumption that the 26th was too far north to have been hit by the fire. Since Fry's brigade did not advance beyond the rail fence, it is safe to assume that the gun was aimed diagonally to the right front to fire at those groups of Marshall's brigade that did advance beyond the fence. Trinque argues that no source coming from Marshall's brigade supports the claim in Aldrich's book, but he did not know of Samuel Wagg's death, the circumstances of which are in his service record.

12. Baker, "Tribute to Capt. Magruder and Wife," 507; Reid, "Peril by Rock Fence at Gettysburg"; Cooke, "Fifty-Fifth Regiment," 301; William Love, "Mississippi at Gettysburg," 46–47; Winschel, "Heavy Was Their Loss," pt. 2, 82–83; Steven R. Davis, " '. . . Like Leaves in an Autumn Wind,' " 296.

13. William L. J. Lowrance to Joseph A. Engelhard, August 12, 1863, *OR*

27(2):671–72; Joseph A. Engelhard to editors, September 27, 1877, Grimes Papers, SHC-UNC.

14. Henry C. Moore to editors, November 6, 1877, Grimes Papers, SHC-UNC.

15. J. G. Harris to editors, November 28, 1877; Thomas P. Molloy to editors, September 29, 1877; J. McLeod Turner to editors, October 10, 1877; P. C. Carlton to editors, September 26, 1877; and Thomas L. Norwood to editors, October 6, 1877, all in Grimes Papers, SHC-UNC; Harris, *Historical Sketches*, 37.

16. D. M. McIntire to editors, October 1, 1877; E. B. Withers to editors, October 8, 1877; and Thomas P. Molloy to editors, September 29, 1877, Grimes Papers, SHC-UNC; Mills, *History of the Sixteenth North Carolina*, 38; Louis G. Young to W. J. Baker, February 10, 1864, *Richmond Daily Enquirer*, March 18, 1864; Moore, "Battle of Gettysburg," 251.

17. Longstreet, "Lee's Right Wing at Gettysburg," 346; Michael W. Taylor, "Unmerited Censure of Two Maryland Staff Officers," 82–83; James H. Lane to editors, September 7, 1877, Grimes Papers, SHC-UNC.

18. Thorp, "Forty-Seventh Regiment," 91; James H. Lane to editors, September 7, 1877, Grimes Papers, SHC-UNC; Lane to Joseph A. Engelhard, August 13, 1863, *OR* 27(2):666.

19. Joseph H. Saunders to editors, September 22, 1877, Grimes Papers, and W. L. Saunders telegram to Kate Baylan, July 14, 1863, Saunders Papers, SHC-UNC.

20. Lane to Joseph A. Engelhard, August 13, 1863, Lane Papers, AU.

21. Fry, "Pettigrew's Charge at Gettysburg," 93; Underwood, "Twenty-Sixth Regiment," 374; Thomas J. Cureton to Lane, June 22, 1890, Lane Papers, SHC-UNC.

22. J. McLeod Turner to editors, October 10, 1877, Grimes Papers, SHC-UNC; Isaac Trimble to Bachelder, February 8, 1883, in Ladd and Ladd, *Bachelder Papers*, 2:933–34; Isaac Trimble, "Civil War Diary," 12; John M. Dunn address, *Report of Joint Committee*, 13; Trimble to Daniel, November 24, 1875, Daniel Papers, SCL-DU; "Letter from General Trimble," 35; "Another Witness," 463.

23. Dula memoir, 9, SCL-DU; Simons, *Regimental History*, 138; Morris to W. Saunders, October 1, 1877, Morris Papers, and Daniel F. Kenney to editors, October 23, 1877, Grimes Papers, SHC-UNC.

24. Robert M. Mayo to H. H. Walker, August 13, 1863, Heth Papers, MC; William S. Christian to Daniel, October 24, 1904, Daniel Papers, UVA.

25. Franklin Sawyer to Doctor, July 17, 1863, newspaper clipping in Sexton Papers, OHS; Sawyer to J. G. Reid, July 5, 1863, *OR* 27(1):462.

26. William E. Potter to George Meade, December 23, 1886, Meade Collection, HSP; Simons, *Regimental History*, 139; Aaron P. Seeley to Clinton MacDougall, June 25, 1890, in Ladd and Ladd, *Bachelder Papers*, 3:1739.

27. Seville, *History of the First Regiment*, 83; William P. Seville to John T. Dent, n.d., 1863, *OR* 27(1):469; E. F. Rickards to James Scott, August 2, 1863, *Delaware Republican*, August 24, 1863.

28. Page, *History of the Fourteenth*, 153, 156; Richard S. Thompson, "Scrap of Gettysburg," 106; Stevens, *Souvenir of Excursion*, 31.

29. Gulian V. Weir to C. H. Whittelsey, September 30, 1863, *OR* 27(1):880; Weir, "Recollections," GNMP; Shultz, *"Double Canister at Ten Yards,"* 56, 66; Shultz, "Gulian V. Weir's 5th U.S. Artillery," 94; Baldwin to father, GNMP; Stevens, *Souvenir of Excursion*, 33.

30. Weir, "Recollections," GNMP.

31. Carter, "Flag of the Fifty-Third Va."; Swallow, "Third Day at Gettysburg," 569; H. C. Michie to V. A. Tapscott, February 21, 1904, Daniel Papers, UVA; Sale, "Reminiscences"; draft of memoir, Farinholt Papers, VHS.

32. John C. Timberlake to editors, September 24, 1877, Grimes Papers, SHC-UNC; Timberlake to editors, VHS.

33. Alexander S. Webb to A. H. Embler, July 12, 1863, *OR* 27(1):428. Webb, in a letter to his father dated July 17, 1863 (Webb Papers, YU), estimated the strength of Armistead's contingent at 150 men. Benjamin Lyons Farinholt later estimated it to be 300 men in a letter to Daniel, April 15, 1905 (Daniel Papers, UVA). The 16 men named in various sources as having followed Armistead were Pvt. Erasmus Williams, Company H, 14th Virginia; Maj. John C. Timberlake, 53rd Virginia; Pvt. Robert B. Damron, Company D, 56th Virginia; Capt. Benjamin Lyons Farinholt, Company E, 53rd Virginia; Lt. George W. Finley, Company K, 56th Virginia; Lt. J. Irving Sale, Company H, 53rd Virginia; Lt. Col. Rawley W. Martin, 53rd Virginia; Lt. Hutchings L. Carter, Company I, 53rd Virginia; Lt. William H. Bray, Company E, 53rd Virginia; Lt. James W. Whitehead Jr., Company I, 53rd Virginia; Sgt. Thomas B. Tredway, Company I, 53rd Virginia; Pvt. James C. Coleman, Company I, 53rd Virginia; Pvt. Milton Harding, Company G, 9th Virginia; Pvt. Marcus A. Cogbill, Company D, 14th Virginia; Sgt. Drewry B. Easley, Company H, 14th Virginia; and Lt. Thomas C. Holland, Company G, 28th Virginia. Of the 17 men, including Armistead, 2 were killed, 1 was wounded and made it back to Confederate lines, 7 were wounded and captured (2 of this number later died in Northern hands), 6 were captured, and 1 survived unscathed. The rosters in Harrison and Busey, *Nothing but Glory*, provide information on the fate of these men.

34. Testimony of Anthony W. McDermott, *Supreme Court of Pennsylvania*, 234; McDermott to Bachelder, June 2, 1886, in Ladd and Ladd, *Bachelder Papers*, 3:1411.

35. Benjamin L. Farinholt to Daniel, April 15, 1905, Daniel Papers, UVA; draft of memoir, Farinholt Papers, VHS; testimony of James Wilson, *Supreme Court of Pennsylvania*, 137.

36. Draft of memoir, Farinholt Papers, VHS; Easley, "With Armistead When He Was Killed"; Anthony W. McDermott to Bachelder, June 2, 1886, in Ladd and Ladd, *Bachelder Papers*, 3:1412–13; testimony of McDermott and Frederick Fuger, *Supreme Court of Pennsylvania*, 221, 229, 130–31; Thomas M. Aldrich to Bryan Grimes, July 17, 1913, Grimes Papers, SHC-UNC; Devereux to S. O'Donnell, May 24, 1889, Devereux Papers, WRHS.

37. Milton Harding, "Where General Armistead Fell," 371; H. C. Michie to V. A. Tapscott, February 21, 1904, Daniel Papers, UVA; Easley, "With Armistead When He Was Killed"; Easley to Townsend, USAMHI.

38. Holland, "With Armistead at Gettysburg," 62.

39. Benjamin L. Farinholt to Daniel, April 15, 1905, and Erasmus Williams

reminiscences, Daniel Papers, UVA; John C. Timberlake to editors, September 24, 1877, Grimes Papers, SHC-UNC; Timberlake to editors, VHS.

40. Easley to Townsend, USAMHI.

41. Benjamin L. Farinholt to Daniel, April 15, 1905, and J. P. Jones to Daniel, February 24, 1904, Daniel Papers, UVA; Alexander S. Webb to A. H. Embler, July 12, 1863, *OR* 27(1):428; Webb to father, July 17, 1863, Webb Papers, YU.

42. Irvine, "Brig. Gen. Richard B. Garnett"; Clay, "About the Death of General Garnett"; Finley account; Stephen Davis, "Death and Burials of General Richard Brooke Garnett," 115; Harrison and Busey, *Nothing but Glory*, 78; Elliott Johnston to Elizabeth Taylor Bliss Dandridge, July 18, 1863, Chisholm Papers, VHS.

43. Berkeley account, GNMP; Eppa Hunton questionnaire, February 15, 1904, Daniel Papers, SCL-DU.

44. Kemper to W. H. Swallow, February 4, 1886, and to John Holmes Bocock, October 6, 1863, Kemper Papers, VHS; *Richmond Daily Dispatch*, July 13, 1863. Several sources, including Harrison and Busey, *Nothing but Glory*, 65–66, indicate Kemper was wounded near the stone fence, but the evidence supporting his injury on the Codori farm is very convincing.

45. Mayo, "Pickett's Charge at Gettysburg," 333; Harrison and Busey, *Nothing but Glory*, 74; Loehr, "'Old First' Virginia," 35; J. J. Hurt to [Daniel], October 28, 1904, Daniel Papers, UVA; Crocker, "Gettysburg," 132; Woodworth to Gates, GNMP.

46. Divine, *Eighth Virginia Infantry*, 24; W. H. Adams reminiscences, Adams Papers, EU; Morgan, *Personal Reminiscences*, 167.

47. W. P. Jesse reminiscences, March 1905, Daniel Papers, UVA; Reeve reminiscences, Reeve Papers, SHC-UNC.

48. Joseph Mayo to Charles Pickett, July 25, 1863, Pickett Papers, SCL-DU; Marcus A. Cogbill to E. Scott Gibbs, September 28, 1894, Pickett Papers, VHS; John Holmes Smith reminiscences, February 4–5, 1904, Daniel Papers, UVA.

49. John Holmes Smith reminiscences, February 4–5, 1904, Daniel Papers, UVA.

50. Edmund Berkeley to Daniel, September 26, n.d., Daniel Papers, UVA; John C. Timberlake to editors, September 24, 1877, Grimes Papers, SHC-UNC.

51. H. C. Michie to V. A. Tapscott, February 21, 1904, Daniel Papers, UVA; A. N. Jones to W. T. Fry, July 5, 1863, Pickett Papers, SCL-DU.

52. Kemper to W. H. Swallow, February 4, 1886, Kemper Papers, VHS.

53. Joseph R. Cabell to Arthur S. Segar, July 11, 1863, Letter Book of Armistead, Barton, and Steuart Brigades, MC; Sawyer, *Military History*, 132.

54. Raoul to father, July 17, 1863, Raoul Letters, LSU.

55. Testimony of McKeever and Anthony W. McDermott, *Supreme Court of Pennsylvania*, 260, 220, 228; McDermott, *Brief History of the Sixty-Ninth Regiment*, 31–32; William Davis to Charles H. Banes, July 12, 1863, *OR* 27(1):431; McDermott to Bachelder, October 21, 1889, in Ladd and Ladd, *Bachelder Papers*, 3:1656.

56. Testimony of Robert Whittick and McKeever, *Supreme Court of Pennsylvania*, 79–81, 257–58; Anthony W. McDermott to Bachelder, October 21, 1889, in Ladd and Ladd, *Bachelder Papers*, 3:1656.

57. Kathleen Georg Harrison, " 'Ridges of Grim War,' " 39; testimony of William S. Stockton, *Supreme Court of Pennsylvania*, 244.

58. Testimony of Alexander S. Webb and William H. Good, *Supreme Court of Pennsylvania*, 160, 35; Charles H. Banes testimony, April 24, 1890, in Ladd and Ladd, *Bachelder Papers*, 3:1705, 1708–9.

59. Samuel Roberts to H. W. Newton, February 13, 1890, Federal Soldiers' Letters, SHC-UNC; testimony of Samuel Roberts and James Wilson, *Supreme Court of Pennsylvania*, 149–50, 137, 140–41; Roberts to Alexander S. Webb, August 18, 1883, in Ladd and Ladd, *Bachelder Papers*, 2:966; Lash, "Philadelphia Brigade," 108.

60. Testimony of William H. Good, James Wilson, Samuel Roberts, and Henry Russell, *Supreme Court of Pennsylvania*, 35, 137, 149, 97–102; Samuel Roberts to Alexander S. Webb, August 18, 1883, in Ladd and Ladd, *Bachelder Papers*, 2:966.

61. Testimony of James Lynch, *Supreme Court of Pennsylvania*, 304.

62. James E. Mallon to William R. Driver, July 16, 1863, *OR* 27(1):451.

63. Winfield S. Hancock to Rothermel, December 31, 1868, Rothermel Papers, PHMC; Arthur F. Devereux to Bachelder, July 22, 1889, in Ladd and Ladd, *Bachelder Papers*, 3:1609–10; testimony of Arthur F. Devereux, *Supreme Court of Pennsylvania*, 184; Devereux to E. D. Townsend, n.d., 1878, in Waitt, *History of the Nineteenth*, 253; Devereux, "Some Account of Pickett's Charge," 16–17; Edmund Rice to Doubleday, April 19, 1887, Gettysburg Volume, Doubleday Papers, N-YHS.

64. Edmund Rice to Doubleday, April 19, 1887, Gettysburg Volume, Doubleday Papers, N-YHS; testimony of Arthur Devereux, William A. Hill, and James A. Lynch, *Supreme Court of Pennsylvania*, 184–86, 209, 308; Devereux to William R. Driver, July 7, 1863, *OR* 27(1):443–44; Waitt, *History of the Nineteenth*, 242.

65. Alexander S. Webb to wife, July 6, 1863, in Ladd and Ladd, *Bachelder Papers*, 1:19; Devereux, "Some Account of Pickett's Charge," 19.

66. Winfield S. Hancock to Rothermel, December 31, 1868, and January 21, 1869, Rothermel Papers, PHMC; extract from W. G. Mitchell, "General Hancock at the Battle of Gettysburg," Benedict Family Papers, UV. Hancock claimed that before he reached Stannard's brigade, he came across "a small detachment which he supposed was a decimated battalion of the Second Corps." It was firing into the Rebel flank all alone. Hancock ordered it to return to the breastwork occupied by Stannard's men, assuring the commander he would advance more troops to its support so a greater number of men could fire into the Rebels. This contingent, also described as "the little squad of men," was never identified. Hancock later contended it contained no more than fifteen or twenty files, and he thought it was too small to do much good. It is entirely unclear which unit Hancock referred to, or even if the incident actually happened. See the sources already cited in this note for information on this subject.

67. Edward Moale to John Gibbon, June 25, 1866, and Gibbon to Francis A. Walker, March 14, 1884, in Ladd and Ladd, *Bachelder Papers*, 1:263, 2:1030–31; Gibbon, *Personal Recollections*, 151–52; Gibbon to Francis Walker, March 14, 1884, Sessler Collection, CWLM.

68. John Gibbon to Edward Moale, June 17, 1866; Gibbon note, July 18, 1866;

Gibbon to Francis Wessels, August 6, 1866; and Gibbon to Bachelder, August 25, 1866, all in Ladd and Ladd, *Bachelder Papers*, 1:260–61, 264, 272, 278; Gibbon, *Personal Recollections*, 152–53, 168; Francis Wessels to Joseph H. Collins, August 13, 1863, Meade Collection, HSP.

69. Byrne and Weaver, *Haskell of Gettysburg*, 165–66, 166n; Alexander S. Webb to Rothermel, January, n.d., Rothermel Papers, PHMC.

70. Norman J. Hall to A. H. Embler, July 17, 1863, *OR* 27(1):439.

71. George N. Macy to Bachelder, May 12, 1866, in Ladd and Ladd, *Bachelder Papers*, 1:252–53.

72. Henry L. Abbott letter, n.d., *Reports, Letters & Papers*, 1:91, BPL; Abbott to George N. Macy, July 27, 1863, MOLLUS-Massachusetts Commandery Collection, HU; Abbott to William R. Driver, July 16, 1863, *OR* 27(1):445–46; H. C. Mason diary, *Massachusetts Infantry, 20th Regiment, Diaries, 1863*, Military Historical Society of Massachusetts Collection, BU; Robert Garth Scott, *Fallen Leaves*, 188; George N. Macy to Bachelder, May 12, 1886, in Ladd and Ladd, *Bachelder Papers*, 1:253; *Reports, Letters & Papers*, 2:61, BPL; Abbott to Charles C. Paine, July 28, 1863, Paine Papers, MassHS.

73. George N. Macy to Bachelder, May 12, 1866, in Ladd and Ladd, *Bachelder Papers*, 1:253; Macy to Charles C. Paine, July 23, 1863, Paine Papers, MassHS.

74. Sylvanus W. Curtis to Lorenzo Thomas, August 6, 1863, *OR* 27(1):450.

75. Anthony W. McDermott to Bachelder, October 10, 1889, in Ladd and Ladd, *Bachelder Papers*, 3:1647–48; Edmund Rice to Doubleday, April 19, 1887, Gettysburg Volume, Doubleday Papers, N-YHS.

76. Byrne and Weaver, *Haskell of Gettysburg*, 167; Adams, "Nineteenth Maine at Gettysburg," 262.

77. Bond recollections, and James A. Wright, "Story of Co. F," 611, MHS; Edmund Rice to Doubleday, April 19, 1887, Gettysburg Volume, Doubleday Papers, N-YHS.

78. A. C. Plaisted to Bachelder, June 11, 1870, and Anthony W. McDermott to Bachelder, September 17, October 10, 1889, in Ladd and Ladd, *Bachelder Papers*, 1:393, 3:1628, 1648; Priest, *Into the Fight*, 142, 144; extract from W. G. Mitchell, "General Hancock at the Battle of Gettysburg," Benedict Family Papers, UV; Stewart, *Pickett's Charge*, 173.

79. Theodore B. Gates to Thomas A. Rowley, July 4, 1863, *OR* 27(1):319; Gates to Rothermel, April 28, 1868, Rothermel Papers, PHMC; Van Rensselear diary, and Gates to Hardenburgh, GNMP; Gates, "Movements and Service of the 'Ulster Guard,'" xxviii; Gates to Doubleday, February 4, 1864, Gettysburg Volume, Doubleday Papers, N-YHS; Cook, "Personal Reminiscences of Gettysburg," 334; Jacob B. Hardenburgh to Gates, October 9, 1878, Gates Papers, N-YHS; Dreese, *151st Pennsylvania*, 77.

80. George J. Stannard diary, July 3, 1863, in Ladd and Ladd, *Bachelder Papers*, 1:56; Benedict, *Army Life in Virginia*, 182–83.

81. Benedict, *Army Life in Virginia*, 183–84; George J. Stannard diary, July 3, 1863, in Ladd and Ladd, *Bachelder Papers*, 1:56.

82. Benedict, *Army Life in Virginia*, 184; Francis A. Walker, *General Hancock*, 144–

45; Bingham, "Anecdotes," WRHS; George J. Stannard diary, July 3, 1863, and Charles H. Morgan account, n.d., in Ladd and Ladd, *Bachelder Papers*, 1:56, 3:1363.

83. Field visit to Gettysburg, March 25, 1997; Winfield Hancock to Francis Walker, December 12, 1885, Sessler Collection, CWLM; Gambone, *Hancock at Gettysburg*, 141.

84. Alexander S. Webb to father, July 17, 1863, Webb Papers, YU; Webb to A. H. Embler, July 12, 1863, *OR* 27(1):428; Webb to Rothermel, January, n.d., Rothermel Papers, PHMC; Arthur F. Devereux to E. D. Townsend, n.d., 1878, in Waitt, *History of the Nineteenth*, 254.

85. Testimony of Alexander S. Webb, *Supreme Court of Pennsylvania*, 160–61; Webb to Rothermel, January, n.d., Rothermel Papers, PHMC.

86. Webb to wife, July 5, 1863, Webb Papers, YU; Webb to wife, July 6, 1863, and Charles H. Banes testimony, in Ladd and Ladd, *Bachelder Papers*, 1:19, 3:1711; Richard Penn Smith to Wistar, July 29, 1863, Wistar Papers, WI.

87. Anthony W. McDermott to Bachelder, September 17, 1889, in Ladd and Ladd, *Bachelder Papers*, 3:1627–28; William Davis to Charles H. Banes, July 12, 1863, *OR* 27(1):431; Webb to father, July 17, 1863, Webb Papers, YU.

88. Anthony W. McDermott to Bachelder, June 2, 1886, in Ladd and Ladd, *Bachelder Papers*, 3:1414; William Davis to Charles Banes, July 12, 1863, *OR* 27(1): 431; Gottfried, *Stopping Pickett*, 174.

89. McDermott, *Brief History of the Sixty-Ninth Regiment*, 32; McDermott to Bachelder, June 2, 1886, in Ladd and Ladd, *Bachelder Papers*, 3:1411–12.

90. Anthony W. McDermott to Bachelder, June 2, 1886, in Ladd and Ladd, *Bachelder Papers*, 3:1413; Edmund Rice to Doubleday, April 19, 1887, Gettysburg Volume, Doubleday Papers, N-YHS.

91. Norman J. Hall to A. H. Embler, July 17, 1863, *OR* 27(1):439; Hancock to Seth Williams, n.d., 1863, *OR* 27(1):374; Edmund Rice to Doubleday, April 19, 1887, Gettysburg Volume, Doubleday Papers, N-YHS.

92. Norman J. Hall to A. H. Embler, July 17, 1863, *OR* 27(1):440; Sylvanus W. Curtis to Lorenzo Thomas, August 6, 1863, *OR* 27(1):450; George W. LaPointe to Bachelder, May 24, 1882, in Ladd and Ladd, *Bachelder Papers*, 2:880; Henry A. Abbott letter, n.d., *Reports, Letters & Papers*, 1:95, BPL; Devereux, "Some Account of Pickett's Charge," 18.

93. Waitt, *History of the Nineteenth*, 240; Edmund Rice to Doubleday, April 19, 1887, Gettysburg Volume, Doubleday Papers, N-YHS; Bruce, *Twentieth Regiment of Massachusetts*, 294; Norman J. Hall to A. H. Embler, July 17, 1863, *OR* 27(1):439.

94. Edmund Rice to Doubleday, April 19, 1887, Gettysburg Volume, Doubleday Papers, N-YHS.

95. A. C. Plaisted to Bachelder, June 11, 1870, in Ladd and Ladd, *Bachelder Papers*, 1:393; Lochren, "First Minnesota at Gettysburg," 53; John Day Smith, *History of the Nineteenth Regiment*, 82.

96. Plummer, "John W. Plummer's Account," 180; Moe, *Last Full Measure*, 293; Lancaster memoir, GNMP; John Day Smith, *History of the Nineteenth Regiment*, 82.

97. John Day Smith, *History of the Nineteenth Regiment*, 82; Moe, *Last Full Measure*,

290; Henry D. O'Brien to Bachelder, March 23, 1883, in Ladd and Ladd, *Bachelder Papers*, 2:936; James A. Wright, "Story of Co. F," 618, MHS.

98. Theodore B. Gates to Thomas A. Rowley, July 4, 1863, *OR* 27(1):319; Gates to Bachelder, January 30, 1864, in Ladd and Ladd, *Bachelder Papers*, 1:85; Dreese, *151st Pennsylvania*, 77; Jacob B. Hardenburgh to Gates, October 9, 1878, Gates Papers, N-YHS.

99. Cook, "Personal Reminiscences of Gettysburg," 334–35; Dreese, *151st Pennsylvania*, 75.

100. Haskell wrote a dramatic but wholly unreliable account, which showered undeserved criticism on Major Roberts, of how he cajoled, shamed, and prodded the 72nd Pennsylvania into advancing. See Byrne and Weaver, *Haskell of Gettysburg*, 169–70.

101. Anthony W. McDermott to Bachelder, September 17, 1889, in Ladd and Ladd, *Bachelder Papers*, 3:1628; Ward, *History of the One Hundred and Sixth*, 166; testimony of Henry Russell, James Wilson, and Samuel Roberts, *Supreme Court of Pennsylvania*, 97–102, 137, 150.

102. Testimony of Robert McBride, Samuel Roberts, and James Lynch, *Supreme Court of Pennsylvania*, 125, 151, 306, 312; Roberts to Alexander S. Webb, August 18, 1883, and Charles H. Banes testimony, in Ladd and Ladd, *Bachelder Papers*, 2:966, 3:1709.

103. Samuel Roberts to Alexander S. Webb, August 18, 1883, in Ladd and Ladd, *Bachelder Papers*, 2:966; testimony of William H. Good, Thomas Read, and Samuel Roberts, *Supreme Court of Pennsylvania*, 36, 57, 156; Gottfried, *Stopping Pickett*, 173.

104. Testimony of William S. Stockton, *Supreme Court of Pennsylvania*, 244; Richard Penn Smith to Rothermel, Rothermel Papers, PHMC.

105. Arthur F. Devereux to Bachelder, July 22, 1889, and Anthony W. McDermott to Bachelder, October 21, 1889, in Ladd and Ladd, *Bachelder Papers*, 3:1610, 1655; Lash, "Philadelphia Brigade," 108; testimony of James Wilson, *Supreme Court of Pennsylvania*, 141.

106. Devereux, "Some Account of Pickett's Charge," 18; Norman J. Hall to A. H. Embler, July 17, 1863, *OR* 27(1):440; Waitt, *History of the Nineteenth*, 243; Edmund Rice to Doubleday, April 19, 1887, Gettysburg Volume, Doubleday Papers, N-YHS.

107. Lash, "Philadelphia Brigade," 110; Edmund Rice to Doubleday, April 19, 1887, Gettysburg Volume, Doubleday Papers, N-YHS; Waitt, *History of the Nineteenth*, 244.

108. Draft of biographical sketch of Paine; Henry L. Abbott to Charles C. Paine, July 13, 28, 1863; and L. E. Hibbard to Charles C. Paine, July 17, 1863, all in Paine Papers, MassHS.

109. Lochren, "First Minnesota at Gettysburg," 53–54; Adams, "Nineteenth Maine at Gettysburg," 262; James A. Wright, "Story of Co. F," 612, MHS.

110. James A. Wright, "Story of Co. F," 199, 615–16, MHS.

111. Bond recollections, MHS.

112. A. C. Plaisted to Bachelder, June 11, 1870, in Ladd and Ladd, *Bachelder Papers*, 1:393; James A. Wright, "Story of Co. F," 612, MHS.

113. Walter P. Owens to George F. McFarland, August 6, 1866, in Ladd and Ladd, *Bachelder Papers*, 1:269–70; Theodore B. Gates to Thomas A. Rowley, July 4, 1863, *OR* 27(1):319; Gates to Doubleday, August 13, 1863, Gettysburg Volume, Doubleday Papers, N-YHS; Van Rensselear diary, July 3, 1863, GNMP; Gates to Rothermel, April 28, 1868, Rothermel Papers, PHMC.

114. Benedict, *Vermont at Gettysburgh*, 18; Benedict, *Army Life in Virginia*, 178; Clarke, "Thirteenth Regiment," VerHS; Wheelock G. Veazey to George G. Benedict, July 11, 1864, Benedict Family Papers, UV.

CHAPTER EIGHT

1. Fortin, "Colonel Hilary A. Herbert's History," 126; J. B. Johnson, "Limited Review," FB.

2. Wilcox, "General C. M. Wilcox on the Battle of Gettysburg," 120; Cadmus M. Wilcox to Thomas S. Mills, July 17, 1863, *OR* 27(2):620; Swallow, "Third Day at Gettysburg," 569; Harrison and Busey, *Nothing but Glory*, 169.

3. Fortin, "Colonel Hilary A. Herbert's History," 125–26; Clark, *Glance Backward*, 40; David Lang to Thomas S. Mills, July 29, 1863, *OR* 27(2):633; Pigman diary, July 3, 1863, Pigman Papers, GHS; Hilary A. Herbert to Alexander, August 18, 1903, Alexander Papers, SHC-UNC; Gallagher, *Fighting for the Confederacy*, 265.

4. Wilcox letter, 117; Lang to Bachelder, October 16, 1893, Lang Letterbook, 1893–1909, FSA.

5. Lang to Bachelder, October 16, 1893, Lang Letterbook, 1893–1909, FSA; Francis P. Fleming, *Memoir of Capt. C. Seton Fleming*, 82; Wentworth diary, GNMP.

6. Cadmus M. Wilcox to Thomas S. Mills, July 17, 1863, *OR* 27(2):620; Harrison and Busey, *Nothing but Glory*, 69; Loehr, *War History of the Old First Virginia*, 36; Lang to Bachelder, October 16, 1893, Lang Letterbook, 1893–1909, FSA.

7. Clark, *Glance Backward*, 40; Dunham diary, SAHS; Wentworth diary, GNMP.

8. Lang to Bachelder, October 16, 1893, Lang Letterbook, 1893–1909, FSA; Coles and Waters, "Forgotten Sacrifice," 45.

9. Lang to Bachelder, October 16, 1893, Lang Letterbook, 1893–1909, FSA.

10. Henry J. Hunt to Seth Williams, September 27, 1863, *OR* 27(1):240; Patrick Hart to C. H. Whittelsey, August 2, 1863, *OR* 27(1):888; Andrew R. McMahon to C. H. Whittelsey, July 17, 1863, *OR* 27(1):889; Hunt, "Third Day at Gettysburg," 375; Elmore, "Florida Brigade at Gettysburg," 54; Shultz, *"Double Canister at Ten Yards,"* 59–60.

11. George J. Stannard diary, July 3, 1863, and Wheelock G. Veazey letter, n.d., in Ladd and Ladd, *Bachelder Papers*, 1:56, 62; Veazey to Benedict, VerHS; Benedict, *Vermont at Gettysburgh*, 19.

12. Francis V. Randall to John Newton, July 10, 1863, *OR* 27(1):353.

13. Wilcox letter, 117; Clark, *Glance Backward*, 40–41; Cadmus M. Wilcox to Thomas S. Mills, July 17, 1863, *OR* 27(2):620; Wilcox autobiography, 6, Wilcox Papers, LC; Fortin, "Colonel Hilary A. Herbert's History," 125.

14. David Lang to Thomas S. Mills, July 29, 1863, *OR* 27(2):632; *History of the*

Fifth Massachusetts Battery, 653; Lang to Bachelder, October 16, 1893, Lang Letterbook, 1893–1909, FSA.

15. George J. Stannard to C. Kingsbury, July 4, 1863, *OR* 27(1):350; Wheelock G. Veazey letter, n.d., in Ladd and Ladd, *Bachelder Papers*, 1:62; Veazey to Benedict, VerHS; Charles Cummings to wife, July 6, 1863, Cummings Papers, VerHS; Coffin, *Full Duty*, 196.

16. Wheelock G. Veazey letter, n.d., in Ladd and Ladd, *Bachelder Papers*, 1:62–63; Veazey to Benedict, VerHS; Benedict, *Vermont at Gettysburgh*, 19–20; David Lang to Thomas S. Mills, July 29, 1863, *OR* 27(2):632. Wilcox claimed in his report that his brigade had only a few minutes' contact with the Union infantry and did not inflict much damage on them, but there appears to be no reason to believe that his command had any contact at all with the advancing Vermonters. See Cadmus M. Wilcox to Thomas S. Mills, July 17, 1863, *OR* 27(2):620. The third flag that reportedly was claimed by Veazey's men remains a mystery. It could not have been that of the 5th Florida, for those colors were taken off the field by their owners. Benedict claimed that the third flag was lost when it was thrown away by a sergeant; see Benedict, *Army Life in Virginia*, 179.

17. George J. Stannard diary, July 3, 1863, in Ladd and Ladd, *Bachelder Papers*, 1:56; Benedict, *Army Life in Virginia*, 180–81.

18. Francis P. Fleming, *Memoir of Capt. C. Seton Fleming*, 82; Pogue to Fleming, FSA; Coles and Waters, "Forgotten Sacrifice," 44; Coffin, *Full Duty*, 196.

19. Wentworth diary, GNMP.

20. Cadmus M. Wilcox to Thomas S. Mills, July 17, 1863, *OR* 27(2):620; David Lang to Thomas S. Mills, July 29, 1863, *OR* 27(2):633; Lang to Bachelder, October 16, 1893, Lang Letterbook, 1893–1909, FSA; Francis P. Fleming, *Memoir of Capt. C. Seton Fleming*, 79–80.

21. Lang to Bachelder, October 16, 1893, Lang Letterbook, 1893–1909, FSA.

22. Benedict, *Army Life in Virginia*, 186, 188; George J. Stannard diary, July 3, 1863, in Ladd and Ladd, *Bachelder Papers*, 1:57.

23. Henry J. Hunt to Bachelder, January 6, 1866, in Ladd and Ladd, *Bachelder Papers*, 1:230; Hunt to Seth Williams, September 27, 1863, *OR* 27(1):240; Hamilton, *Papers of Randolph Abbott Shotwell*, 2:15.

24. Walter H. Taylor letter, 136; McLaws, "Gettysburg," 87; Longstreet, "General Longstreet's Account," 84; Longstreet, *From Manassas to Appomattox*, 396–97.

25. Longstreet to R. H. Chilton, July 27, 1863, *OR* 27(2):360; Richard H. Anderson to William H. Palmer, August 7, 1863, *OR* 27(2):614–15; Ambrose R. Wright to Thomas S. Mills, September 28, 1863, *OR* 27(2):625; Talcott, "Third Day at Gettysburg," 43, 45; Aldrich, *History of Battery A*, 216–17; Samuel E. Baker to Stanhope Posey, July 30, 1863, *Supplement to the Official Records*, 5:407; Kirkpatrick diary, July 3, 1863, FB; Lewis to mother, July 21, 1863, Lewis Papers, SHC-UNC; Watts, "Something More about Gettysburg," 67.

26. Byrne and Weaver, *Haskell of Gettysburg*, 176; Dreese, *151st Pennsylvania*, 78; Andrew Cowan, "Cowan's New York Battery"; Shultz, *"Double Canister at Ten Yards,"* 61; George Thornton Fleming, *Life and Letters of General Alexander Hays*, 462; John

Newton to Seth Williams, September 30, 1863, *OR* 27(1):262; Pfanz, *Gettysburg: Culp's Hill and Cemetery Hill*, 355.

27. Wiley, *Reminiscences of Big I*, 46–47.

28. "Captain John Holmes Smith's Account," 193; John Holmes Smith reminiscences, February 4–5, 1904, Daniel Papers, UVA.

29. Shotwell, "Virginia and North Carolina in the Battle of Gettysburg," 94–95; Hamilton, *Papers of Randolph Abbott Shotwell*, 2:23–24, 26–27.

30. Gordon memoirs, 140, WLU; Harrison and Busey, *Nothing but Glory*, 121.

31. Owen to Henry A. Carrington and to Charles Marshall, January 27, 1878, Owen Papers, VSLA; Harrison and Busey, *Nothing but Glory*, 121–22; H. T. Owen, "Pickett at Gettysburg"; Jedediah Hotchkiss journal, *Supplement to the Official Records*, 5:381.

32. William W. Wood to James D. Darden, July 9, 1863, Letter Book of Armistead, Barton, and Steuart Brigades, MC.

33. Harrison and Busey, *Nothing but Glory*, 122; Woodward, *Major General James Lawson Kemper*, 101.

34. Peters, "Lost Sword of Gen. Richard B. Garnett," 30.

35. Moore, "Battle of Gettysburg," 251; Van de Graaff to wife, GNMP.

36. June Kimble, "An Incident at Gettysburg," Tennessee Regiments Collection, MC; Kimble, "Tennesseeans at Gettysburg," 461.

37. F. S. Harris Letter, *Lebanon Democrat*, August 10, 1899.

38. Benjamin F. Little to editors, September 20, 1877, and W. B. Shepard to editors, September 18, 1877, Grimes Papers, and Thomas J. Cureton to Lane, June 22, 1890, Lane Papers, all in SHC-UNC.

39. William L. J. Lowrance to Joseph A. Engelhard, August 12, 1863, *OR* 27(2):672; Floyd memoir, 8–9, VHS.

40. Timberlake to editors, VHS.

41. J. R. Hutter account, Daniel Papers, UVA.

42. Fite memoir, 87–88, TSLA.

43. R. S. Williams, "Thirteenth Regiment," 672; Weymouth T. Jordan, *North Carolina Troops*, 5:366.

44. Finley account; J. McLeod Turner to editors, October 10, 1877, Grimes Papers, SHC-UNC.

45. Stephen F. Brown, "The Hatchet Incident," and Brown to H. A. Huse, November 27, 1901, Brown Papers, VerHS; Sturtivant, *Pictorial History*, 309.

46. "Testimony about Battle of Gettysburg," 524; Cook, "Personal Reminiscences of Gettysburg," 335; Theodore B. Gates to Abner Doubleday, January 30, 1864, *OR* 27(1):322; F. S. Harris Letter, *Lebanon Democrat*, August 10, 1899.

47. Irby, *Historical Sketch of the Nottoway Grays*, 28.

48. Heflin, *Blind Man*, 25.

49. Bush reminiscences, 3–4, NCDAH.

50. Devereux, "Some Account of Pickett's Charge," 18–19; Moe, *Last Full Measure*, 290; Stevens, *Address Delivered at the Dedication*, 24–25; Samuel B. McIntyre to Clinton MacDougall, June 27, 1890, in Ladd and Ladd, *Bachelder Papers*, 3:1744–45.

51. Fry, "Pettigrew's Charge at Gettysburg," 93.

52. Finley account; Peel diary, 32–33, MDAH; Cowtan, *Services of the Tenth New York*, 210–11; Sword, "Capt. George F. Tait," 84–85; George F. Hopper to William P. Seville, July 16, 1863, *OR* 27(1):471.

53. Franklin Sawyer letter, July 4, 1863, in Daggett, "Those Whom You Left behind You," 361–62; Sawyer to J. G. Reid, July 5, 1863, *OR* 27(1):462.

54. Hawley to father, July 4, 1863, Hawley Collection, SHSI; Stevens account, June 10, 1905, Stevens Papers, NCDAH; John M. Dunn address, *Report of Joint Committee*, 16; Alexander S. Webb to A. H. Embler, July 12, 1863, *OR* 27(1):428; Alexander Hays to Charles H. Morgan, July 8, 1863, *OR* 27(1):454; Thomas A. Smyth to George P. Corts, July 17, 1863, *OR* 27(1):465; John T. Hill to Col. Morris, July 16, 1863, *OR* 27(1):470; Aaron P. Seeley to Lieut. Sheldon, n.d., 1863, *OR* 27(1):476; Stewart, *Pickett's Charge*, 263.

55. Kennedy, *Civil War Battlefield Guide*, 285, 423; Calkins, *Appomattox Campaign*, 114.

56. Rollins, *"Damned Red Flags,"* 219–20, 226–27, 229; List of Men in the Army of the Potomac Who Captured Rebel Flags since July 1, 1863, *OR*, ser. 3, 4:815–16; "Medal of Honor at Gettysburg."

57. Carter, "Flag of the Fifty-Third Va."; testimony of Anthony W. McDermott, *Supreme Court of Pennsylvania*, 235; McDermott to Bachelder, October 21, 1889, in Ladd and Ladd, *Bachelder Papers*, 3:1655–56; Alexander S. Webb to A. H. Embler, July 12, 1863, *OR* 27(1):428; Waitt, *History of the Nineteenth*, 246, 254.

58. George Thornton Fleming, *Life and Letters of General Alexander Hays*, 461, 463, 467–69; Thomas A. Smyth to George P. Corts, July 17, 1863, *OR* 27(1):465; Stevens account, June 10, 1905, Stevens Papers, NCDAH; Hawley to father, July 4, 1863, Hawley Collection, SHSI; Page, *History of the Fourteenth*, 154; Wiley Woods, "The 1st Tennessee Flag at Gettysburg," *Confederate Veteran* Papers, SCL-DU; Stevens, *Souvenir of Excursion*, 32.

59. John T. Dent to William P. Seville, n.d., 1863, *OR* 27(1):469; John M. Dunn address, *Report of Joint Committee*, 16; John L. Brady to Bachelder, May 24, 1886, and Franklin Sawyer to Bachelder, May 11, 1880, in Ladd and Ladd, *Bachelder Papers*, 3:1399–1400, 1:663; Sawyer, *Military History*, 132.

60. John M. Dunn address, *Report of Joint Committee*, 16; George Thornton Fleming, *Life and Letters of General Alexander Hays*, 464–65; Goodrich to friends, July 17, 1863, Goodrich Papers, CHS.

61. George Thornton Fleming, *Life and Letters of General Alexander Hays*, 463.

62. Norman J. Hall to A. H. Embler, July 17, 1863, *OR* 27(1):440; Sylvanus W. Curtis to Lorenzo Thomas, August 6, 1863, *OR* 27(1):450; Patrick Hart to Bachelder, February 23, 1891, in Ladd and Ladd, *Bachelder Papers*, 3:1798.

63. Gates to Hardenburgh, GNMP; Cook, "Personal Reminiscences of Gettysburg," 340.

64. Richard Penn Smith interview, *Gettysburg Compiler*, June 7, 1887; George Thornton Fleming, *Life and Letters of General Alexander Hays*, 433, 461; Webb to wife, August 8, 1863, Alexander S. Webb Papers, YU.

65. James A. Wright, "Story of Co. F," 613, MHS; Oesterle memoir, USAMHI; Andrew Cowan, "Cowan's New York Battery."

66. Andrew Cowan, "Cowan's New York Battery"; Frederick Fuger, "Battle of Gettysburg and Personal Recollections of That Battle," 13–14, Webb Papers, YU.

67. Testimony of Arthur Devereux, *Supreme Court of Pennsylvania*, 187; Devereux to Bachelder, July 22, 1889, in Ladd and Ladd, *Bachelder Papers*, 3:1610; Henry L. Abbott to Lieut. Driver, July 16, 1863, *OR* 27(1):446.

68. Testimony of Arthur Devereux, *Supreme Court of Pennsylvania*, 187; Devereux to Bachelder, July 22, 1889, and Charles H. Banes testimony, in Ladd and Ladd, *Bachelder Papers*, 3:1610, 1706; Alexander S. Webb to A. H. Embler, July 12, 1863, *OR* 27(1):428.

69. Winfield S. Hancock to Rothermel, December 31, 1868, and Alexander N. Dougherty to William G. Mitchell, January 2, 1869, Rothermel Papers, PHMC; David M. Jordan, *Winfield Scott Hancock*, 99; Hancock to Meade, July 3, 1863, *OR* 27(1):366; Hancock, *Reminiscences of Winfield Scott Hancock*, 97.

70. W. E. B., "John Gibbon," 106, Gibbon Papers, USMA; Gibbon, *Personal Recollections*, 170; Byrne and Weaver, *Haskell of Gettysburg*, 188–93.

71. George Thornton Fleming, *Life and Letters of General Alexander Hays*, 410, 462.

72. William G. Mitchell to Winfield S. Hancock, January 10, 1866; James Mead to Mitchell, January 24, 1868; George G. Meade to Bachelder, December 4, 1869; John Egan to George Meade Jr., February 8, 1870; and George Meade Jr. to Bachelder, May 6, 1882, all in Ladd and Ladd, *Bachelder Papers*, 1:231, 321, 380, 389–90, 2:854–56; William G. Mitchell to Rothermel, December 19, 1870, Rothermel Papers, PHMC; Byrne and Weaver, *Haskell of Gettysburg*, 174–75.

73. Meade, *Life and Letters*, 2:110; Henry L. Abbott to John Codman Ropes, August 1, 1863, MOLLUS-Massachusetts Commandery Collection, HU; Hunt, "Third Day at Gettysburg," 376; James A. Hall to George Meade, July 11, 1887, Meade Collection, HSP; Greene, "From Gettysburg to Falling Waters," 183–84; Sauers, " 'Rarely Has More Skill, Vigor, or Wisdom Been Shown,' " 243–44.

74. Cook, "Personal Reminiscences of Gettysburg," 337.

75. Longstreet, "Lee's Right Wing at Gettysburg," 347; Longstreet, "General Longstreet's Account," 84; Longstreet to Owen, March 24, 1878, Owen Papers, VHS; Longstreet, *From Manassas to Appomattox*, 395; Dunaway, *Reminiscences of a Rebel*, 93.

76. Pickett to editor of *Richmond Times*, November 11, 1894, Pickett Papers, VHS; Longacre, *Pickett*, 127; Gordon, *General George E. Pickett*, 114–18; Loehr, " 'Old First' Virginia," 37; Loehr, *War History*, 38.

77. Bright, "Pickett's Charge at Gettysburg," 266.

78. Gordon memoirs, 140, WLU.

79. Bright, "Pickett's Charge at Gettysburg," 266; Edward Cook Barnes letter, n.d., Barnes Family Manuscripts, UVA.

80. George L. Christian reminiscences, July 4, 1898, Daniel Papers, UVA.

81. Joseph J. Davis to Venable, July 30, 1889, Venable Papers, VHS; Charles S. Venable to Joseph J. Davis, August 12, 1889, *Raleigh News and Observer*, July 5, 1903; Moore, "Battle of Gettysburg," 251.

82. Charles Marshall to Owen, January 28, 1878, Owen Papers, VSLA; Moore, "Battle of Gettysburg," 251; *Florida Sentinel*, September 15, 1863; Charles S. Venable to Joseph J. Davis, August 12, 1889, *Raleigh News and Observer*, July 5, 1903.

83. Cockrell, *Gunner With Stonewall*, 76; Gallagher, *Fighting for the Confederacy*, 265–66; Alexander letter, 109–10.

84. Fremantle, *Three Months in the Southern States*, 268–71.

85. J. B. Johnson, "Limited Review," FB; Fremantle, *Three Months in the Southern States*, 269. It is interesting that Wilcox remembered a different version of his meeting with Lee after the repulse. Rather than crying about his losses, he insisted that he calmly, even politely, warned Lee that the artillery was in danger if the Federals advanced, as the batteries were out of ammunition. See Wilcox autobiography, 6, Wilcox Papers, LC.

86. Clifford to father, August 15, 1863, USAMHI; George Thornton Fleming, *Life and Letters of General Alexander Hays*, 463; Doubleday, *Chancellorsville and Gettysburg*, 196; Abner Doubleday to Bachelder, November 24, 1885, in Ladd and Ladd, *Bachelder Papers*, 2:1149–51; Waitt, *History of the Nineteenth*, 245.

87. Galwey, *Valiant Hours*, 119.

88. Lippitt diary, July 3, 1863, Lippitt Papers, SHC-UNC; Frey, *Longstreet's Assault*, 159–89; George Phifer Erwin to father, Wills Papers, and Reeve reminiscences, Reeve Papers, SHC-UNC.

89. Peel diary, 35–36, MDAH.

90. Timberlake to editors, VHS.

91. Wentworth diary, GNMP.

92. Fite memoir, 88–89, TSLA.

93. Henry H. Bingham to Winfield S. Hancock, January 5, 1869, and testimony of Charles H. Banes, in Ladd and Ladd, *Bachelder Papers*, 1:351–52, 3:1704–5, 1705n, 1713; Francis Wessels to Joseph H. Collins, August 13, 1863, Meade Collection, HSP; Doubleday, *Chancellorsville and Gettysburg*, 195.

94. Bachelder to Fitzhugh Lee, December 1892, in Ladd and Ladd, *Bachelder Papers*, 3:1901; Motts, *"Trust in God and Fear Nothing,"* 46; Holland, "With Armistead at Gettysburg."

95. Durkin, *John Dooley*, 109–11.

96. Samuel C. Armstrong to Bachelder, February 6, 1884, and Andrew Cowan to Bachelder, December 2, 1885, in Ladd and Ladd, *Bachelder Papers*, 2:1002, 1157; Nevins, *Diary of Battle*, 252; Nesbit, "Recollections of Pickett's Charge"; Albert Stokes Emmell to aunt, July 17, 1863, in Emmell, "Now is the Time for Buck & Ball," GNMP; Winfield Scott, "Pickett's Charge," 911; R. Penn Smith to Wistar, July 29, 1863, Wistar Papers, WI; Eldred, "Only a Boy," 32, GNMP; Horatio Rogers Jr., letter, July 17, 1863, *Providence Evening Bulletin*, July 23, 1863.

97. William A. Tuttle to W. A. Setser, July 18, 1863, in Mast, "Setser Letters," 14.

98. Harrison and Busey, *Nothing but Glory*, 169; Busey and Martin, *Regimental Strength and Losses*, 283–84.

99. Charles S. Peyton to Charles Pickett, July 9, 1863, OR 27(2):387; Loving account, 11–12, 40, VSLA; Edmund R. Cocke to Owen, September 17, 1880,

Owen Papers, VSLA; Henry A. Carrington account, December 28, 1867, Carring-ton Family Papers, VHS; William F. Fox to Daniel, November 18, 1904, and casualty statements, Daniel Papers, UVA.

100. Stewart, *Pickett's Charge*, 263; Busey and Martin, *Regimental Strengths and Losses*, 290–91; Weymouth T. Jordan, *North Carolina Troops*, 5:6–105, 7:463–601, 11:244–363, 12:415–521.

101. Steven R. Davis, " '. . . Like Leaves in an Autumn Wind,' " 297; D. C. Love, *Prairie Guards*, 13; Cockrell and Ballard, *Mississippi Rebel*, 198.

102. McCall, "What the Tennesseans Did at Gettysburg," GNMP.

103. John T. Jones to father, July 17, 1863, Jones Papers, SHC-UNC; Under-wood, "Twenty-Sixth Regiment," 366; Tuttle, "Addenda, Unparalleled Loss," 3; Martin and Outlaw, "Eleventh Regiment," 590; Thorp, "Forty-Seventh Regiment," 92.

104. Stewart, *Pickett's Charge*, 263; Busey and Martin, *Regimental Strengths and Losses*, 292; Flowers, "Thirty-Eighth Regiment," 692; Speer, *Voices from Cemetery Hill*, 107.

105. Wilcox letter, 117; Busey and Martin, *Regimental Strengths and Losses*, 294.

106. Mann, *They Were Heard From*, 9, VMI.

107. Busey and Martin, *Regimental Strengths and Losses*, 240–41.

108. Ibid., 243; Sylvanus W. Curtis to Lorenzo Thomas, August 6, 1863, *OR* 27(1):450; Webb to father, July 17, 1863, Webb Papers, YU; Gottfried, *Stopping Pickett*, 178–79.

109. Kent Masterson Brown, *Cushing of Gettysburg*, 258; William A. Arnold ac-count, 1–3, Records of the Soldiers and Sailors Historical Society of Rhode Island, RIHS; Aldrich, *History of Battery A*, 219; Busey and Martin, *Regimental Strengths and Losses*, 244.

110. Busey and Martin, *Regimental Strengths and Losses*, 243–244; Byrne and Weaver, *Haskell of Gettysburg*, 199.

111. Stewart, *Pickett's Charge*, 173–74, 266; Loehr, " 'Old First' Virginia," 34.

112. Elmore, "Meteorological and Astronomical Chronology," 14, 19.

113. Sylvanus W. Curtis to Lorenzo Thomas, August 6, 1863, *OR* 27(1):450; John M. Dunn address, *Report of Joint Committee*, 16–17; J. B. Johnson, "Limited Review," FB.

114. Benjamin W. Thompson, " 'This Hell of Destruction,' " 22–23.

115. Ibid.; Lancaster memoir, GNMP; Goodrich to friends, July 17, 1863, Good-rich Papers, CHS.

116. Waitt, *History of the Nineteenth*, 245.

117. Galloway, "Gettysburg," 389.

118. Johnston, *Story of a Confederate Boy*, 218–19.

119. George A. Bowen, "Diary of Captain George D. Bowen," 134.

120. Charles H. Morgan account, n.d., in Ladd and Ladd, *Bachelder Papers*, 3:1366; Welsh, *Medical Histories of Confederate Generals*, 74.

121. George Thornton Fleming, *Life and Letters of General Alexander Hays*, 421; Hays to Charles H. Morgan, July 8, 1863, *OR* 27(1):454.

CHAPTER NINE

1. Elmore, "Meteorological and Astronomical Chronology," 15–16.

2. Talbot, *Samuel Chapman Armstrong*, 94.

3. Weymouth T. Jordan, *North Carolina Troops*, 4:477; Small, *Road to Richmond*, 107–8.

4. Clay account, in Peters, "Lost Sword of Gen. Richard B. Garnett," 30.

5. Thomas W. Setser to W. A. Setser, July 29, 1863, in Mast, "Setser Letters," 14.

6. Jedediah Hotchkiss journal, July 3, 1863, *Supplement to the Official Records*, 5:381; Robert E. Lee to Samuel Cooper, July 31, 1863, *OR* 27(2):309; Imboden, "Confederate Retreat from Gettysburg," 422–24.

7. Diary and Medical Record Book, July 4, 1863, Lippitt Papers, SHC-UNC; Johnston, *Story of a Confederate Boy*, 219; Winschel, "Heavy Was Their Loss," pt. 2, 85.

8. Isaac Trimble, "Civil War Diary," 12–13; Welsh, *Medical Histories of Confederate Generals*, 217; Woodward, *Major General James Lawson Kemper*, 101–4; Harrison and Busey, *Nothing but Glory*, 122; Edward Cook Barnes letter, n.d., Barnes Family Manuscripts, UVA.

9. E. W. Rowe to I. W. Goss, December 16, 1863, Goss Papers, MC.

10. Elmore, "Meteorological and Astronomical Chronology," 16.

11. Goodrich to friends, July 17, 1863, Goodrich Papers, CHS; Lancaster memoir, GNMP.

12. Galwey, *Valiant Hours*, 121; Oesterle memoir, USAMHI; John Day Smith, *History of the Nineteenth Regiment*, 93.

13. George A. Bowen, "Diary of Captain George D. Bowen," 135–36.

14. Aldrich, *History of Battery A*, 221; Ford, *Story of the Fifteenth Regiment*, 286; Charles H. Morgan account, n.d., in Ladd and Ladd, *Bachelder Papers*, 3:1366–67; Alexander S. Webb to A. H. Embler, July 12, 1863, *OR* 27(1):428; Alexander Hays to Charles H. Morgan, July 8, 1863, *OR* 27(1):454.

15. Morning Report, MC; Page, *History of the Fourteenth*, 160–62.

16. Charles H. Morgan account, n.d., in Ladd and Ladd, *Bachelder Papers*, 3:1367.

17. Galwey, *Valiant Hours*, 121–22.

18. John Day Smith, *History of the Nineteenth Regiment*, 93; Goodrich to friends, July 17, 1863, Goodrich Papers, CHS; W. H. Adams reminiscences, Adams Papers, EU.

19. Imboden, "Confederate Retreat from Gettysburg," 426–27.

20. Kennedy, *Civil War Battlefield Guide*, 213.

21. Tyler to father, July 29, 1863, Tyler Papers, SCL-DU.

22. Merrick to Min, July 6, 1863, Merrick Papers, WRHS.

23. Hayward to father, July 8, 1863, Hayward Letters, MassHS.

24. Durkin, *John Dooley*, 112–13.

25. Motts, *"Trust in God and Fear Nothing,"* 46–48; Daniel G. Brinton to Henry H. Bingham, March 22, 1869, in Ladd and Ladd, *Bachelder Papers*, 1:358–59; Holland, "With Armistead at Gettysburg," 62.

26. Thomas L. Norwood to father, July 16, 1863, Norwood Papers, SHC-UNC.

27. Wentworth diary, GNMP; Finley, *My Experiences As a Prisoner of War*, 1–2; Whitehead to sister, July 22, August 5, 1863, and to friend, August 8, 1863, Whitehead Papers, VHS; Purvis diary, USAMHI; George Harwell Bond to the Secretary of the Virginia Historical Society, November 4, 1937, Thomas Papers, VHS; Caison, "Southern Soldiers in Northern Prisons," 160–63.

28. Farinholt, "Battle of Gettysburg," 470; Farinholt, "Escape from Johnson's Island," 514–15, 517; Farinholt, "Perils in Escaping from Prison," 547, 549.

29. Hanks to mother, August 5, 1863, Hanks Papers, SCL-DU.

30. William R. Aylett to wife, July 19, 1863, Aylett Family Papers, VHS; J. S. D. Cullen to sister, July 8, 1863, Daniel Papers, UVA; Jones to wife, July 13, 1863, Jones Papers, SCL-DU; Robert Taylor Scott to wife, July 16, 1863, Keith Family Papers, VHS; Funsten to Buck, July 29, 1863, Funsten Papers, SHC-UNC.

31. Owen to Harriet, July 24, 1863, Owen Papers, VSLA.

32. J. C. Granbery to Daniel, March 25, 1905, Daniel Papers, UVA.

33. Loehr, " 'Old First' Virginia," 38; Robert E. Lee to George E. Pickett, July 9, 1863, *OR* 27(3):986–87.

34. A. L. Long, *Memoirs of Robert E. Lee*, 294–95; Pickett, *Pickett and His Men*, 313; Gordon, *General George E. Pickett*, 118–19; Longacre, *Pickett*, 128–29.

35. Longacre, *Pickett*, 130–33.

36. Edward Cook Barnes to mother, August 21, 1863, and March 8, 1864, Barnes Family Manuscripts, UVA.

37. James M. Simpson to mother, July 8, 1863, Allen-Simpson Papers, and Kennedy diary, July 4, 1863, SHC-UNC; Thompson to mother, July 20, 1863, Thompson Papers, N-YHS.

38. Winschel, "Heavy Was Their Loss," pt. 2, 84–85.

39. Thorp, "Forty-Seventh Regiment," 92; John T. Jones, "Pettigrew's Brigade at Gettysburg," 134.

40. Elder to wife, July 4, 1863, Elder Papers, VHS; Bryan to wife, July 22, 1863, Bryan Papers, FSA; Isaac Sidney Barineau to sister, July 10, August 6, 1863, Barineau Collection, USAMHI.

41. Dearing to mother, July 26, 1863, Dearing Papers, UVA; Wilcox to John Wilcox, July 17, 1863, Wilcox Papers, LC; Williams to Pa, July 7, 1863, Williams Letters, VSLA; Raoul to father, July 17, 1863, Raoul Letters, LSU.

42. Sion H. Oxford to Rebecca, July 17, 1863, McCall Papers, SCL-DU; J. B. Johnson, "Limited Review," FB.

43. J. B. Johnson, "Limited Review," FB; E. M. Hays to Bachelder, October 15, 1890, in Ladd and Ladd, *Bachelder Papers*, 3:1775–76; J. J. Renfroe to Brother Henderson, n.d., *South Western Baptist*, August 13, 1863; W. B. Robertson to Mattie, July 28, 1863, Daniel Papers, UVA; Gallagher, "Lee's Army Has Not Lost Any of Its Prestige," 4, 9.

44. Lee to Jefferson Davis, July 31, 1863, in Dowdey and Manarin, *Wartime Papers of Robert E. Lee*, 565; Lee to Samuel Cooper, July 31, 1863, *OR* 27(2):309; Gallagher, "Lee's Army Has Not Lost Any of Its Prestige," 16–22.

45. Robert E. Lee to Jefferson Davis, July 27, 29, 1863, *OR* 27(3):1040–41, 1048–49; Lee to Davis, August 8, 1863, in Horn, *Robert E. Lee Reader*, 337–38.

46. Gordon memoirs, 119–20, WLU; Jones to wife, August 20, 1863, Jones Papers, SCL-DU; Eppa Hunton to wife, August 31, 1863, Hunton Family Papers, VHS.

47. Walter Harrison, *Pickett's Men*, 108–9; Pickett to Cooper, GNMP.

48. Eppa Hunton to wife, August 31, 1863, Hunton Family Papers, VHS; Christian S. Prillaman to Sallie, October 11, 1863, Prillaman Letters, FB.

49. Owen to Harriet, July 18, 1863, Owen Papers, VSLA; William R. Aylett to Charles Pickett, October 2, 1863, Letter Book of Armistead, Barton, and Steuart Brigades, MC.

50. Harrison Inspection Book, 8–9, SHC-UNC; Knick to wife and children, February 21, 1864, Knick Letter, VSLA.

51. Reardon, *Pickett's Charge in History and Memory*, 32–34, 51–57; Collier to mother, August 24, 1863, Collier Papers, EU.

52. *Richmond Daily Dispatch*, July 13, 1863; W. C. Gardner to Miss Liddy, September 16, 1863, Roach Family Papers, ECU; "B" letter, October 21, 1863, Cocke Family Papers, VHS.

53. *Richmond Daily Enquirer*, August 15, 1863; Burwell Thomas Cotton to brother, August 8, 1863, in Michael W. Taylor, *Cry Is War, War, War*, 151.

54. *Richmond Daily Enquirer*, August 15, 1863; John Thomas Jones to father, August 17, 1863, Jones Papers, SHC-UNC; Justice to wife, August 9, 1863, Justice Papers, EU; William L. J. Lowrance to Joseph A. Engelhard, July 30, 1863, *OR* 27(3):1052.

55. Robert E. Lee to Jefferson Davis, August 17, 1863, *OR* 29(2):649–50; Emory A. Thomas, *Robert E. Lee*, 308–9; Scales to wife, October 1, 1863, Scales Papers, NCDAH; Burwell Thomas Cotton to sister, September 23, October 3, 1863, in Michael W. Taylor, *Cry Is War, War, War*, 155, 157.

56. Burwell Thomas Cotton to sister, August 29, 1863, in Michael W. Taylor, *Cry Is War, War, War*, 154.

57. Underwood, "Twenty-Sixth Regiment," 380–81, 400, 414.

58. Patterson, "In a Most Disgraceful Manner," 46–47; William E. Cameron to Daniel, December 27, 1906, Daniel Papers, SCL-DU.

59. Scales to wife, August 10, 1863, Scales Papers, NCDAH; Lattimore, "Thirty-Fourth Regiment," 587.

60. *Raleigh News and Observer*, August 30, 1877; Reardon, *Pickett's Charge in History and Memory*, 131–54.

61. "Letter from General Trimble," 32; James H. Lane to McCorkle, March 20, 1896, McCorkle Papers, WLU; Longstreet, "Lee's Right Wing at Gettysburg," 353.

62. Robert W. Douthat to Daniel, January 10, 1905; Robert A. Bright to Daniel, November 19, 1903; and P. C. Waring to Daniel, February 1, 1904, all in Daniel Papers, UVA.

63. Cleaves, *Meade of Gettysburg*, 170–333.

64. Hancock, *Reminiscences of Winfield S. Hancock*, 97–98; Benedict, *Army Life in*

Virginia, 184n; Charles H. Morgan account, n.d., in Ladd and Ladd, *Bachelder Papers*, 3:1363–64.

65. Mahood, *"Written in Blood,"* 160; Calkins, *Appomattox Campaign*, 214.

66. Gambone, *Hancock at Gettysburg*, 168–70.

67. Hancock, *Reminiscences of Winfield S. Hancock*, 101, 103; Bingham, "Anecdotes," 1874, WRHS.

68. Francis A. Walker, *History of the Second Army Corps*, 350–672; Welsh, *Medical Histories of Union Generals*, 150–51.

69. Gibbon, *Personal Recollections*, 170–73, 184; Byrne and Weaver, *Haskell of Gettysburg*, 232–34; Warner, *Generals in Blue*, 297; Welsh, *Medical Histories of Union Generals*, 129–30.

70. Byrne and Weaver, *Haskell of Gettysburg*, 1, 88, 204, 207, 237–45; George Raymer to H. M. Haskell, June 26, 1882, Haskell Family Collection, PHMC; Gibbon to Mama, June 4, 1864, Gibbon Papers, MaryHS.

71. Webb to Annie, July 27, October 22, 1863; Webb to wife, August 2, 1863; and Webb to father, October 16, 1863, all in Webb Papers, YU; Welsh, *Medical Histories of Union Generals*, 154.

72. Franklin Sawyer to Sexton, October 22, 1863, Sexton Papers, OHS; Henry L. Abbott to father, October 17, 1863, in Robert Garth Scott, *Fallen Leaves*, 223–24.

73. Sword, "Facing the Gray Wave," 24; Warner, *Generals in Blue*, 544–45; Welsh, *Medical Histories of Union Generals*, 361.

74. Pfanz, *Gettysburg: The Second Day*, 71; Warner, *Generals in Blue*, 471–72; Welsh, *Medical Histories of Union Generals*, 318–19.

75. Warner, *Generals in Blue*, 224, 466; Calkins, *Appomattox Campaign*, 140–41; Welsh, *Medical Histories of Union Generals*, 314–15.

76. Hunt to Andrew A. Humphreys, July 26, 27, 1863; Humphreys to Hunt, July 19, 27, 1863, all in Hunt Papers, LC; Warner, *Generals in Blue*, 242–43; Kross, " 'I Do Not Believe That Pickett's Division Would Have Reached Our Line,' " 304–5.

77. Emory A. Thomas, *Robert E. Lee*, 306–7; Lee, *Recollections and Letters*, 103.

78. Rawley W. Martin to Daniel, August 11, 1887, Daniel Papers, UVA; Allan, "Reply to General Longstreet," 355; "Letter from General Fitz. Lee," 73.

79. "Letter from General Fitz. Lee," 73; Lee, *Recollections and Letters*, 102.

80. Wert, *General James Longstreet*, 298–406; Reardon, "James Longstreet's Virginia Defenders," 245–69.

81. Fremantle, *Three Months in the Southern States*, 274–75; Longstreet, "General Longstreet's Account," 83; Longstreet, "Lee's Right Wing at Gettysburg," 345, 349; Thomas J. Goree to Longstreet, May 17, 1875, Longstreet Papers, SHC-UNC.

82. "Letter from Major-General Henry Heth," 151–52, 159–60.

83. Fremantle, *Three Months in the Southern States*, 274; James Longstreet to Heth, February 14, 1897, Heth Papers, MC.

84. Edward Porter Alexander to Mr. Bancroft, October 30, 1904, Longstreet Papers, SCL-DU; Wert, *General James Longstreet*, 407–27.

85. Gordon, *General George E. Pickett*, 123–24, 128–34, 136, 139, 143, 145–52, 154.

86. Ibid., 157, 161–63, 167; Mosby to Eppa Hunton, March 28, 1911, Mosby Papers, VHS; Longacre, *Pickett*, 179.

87. James L. Kemper to Edward P. Alexander, September 20, 1869, Dearborn Collection, HU; Berkeley account, GNMP.

88. Edward R. Baird to Owen, September 22, 1908, Owen Papers, VSLA; clipping of *Richmond Times*, December 19, 1894, Pickett Papers, VHS; report of committee by Pickett Camp, Confederate Veterans, November 14, 1913, Gregory Family Papers, VHS; Reardon, *Pickett's Charge in History and Memory*, 154–65.

89. Edward Cook Barnes to mother, September 25, 1863, Barnes Family Manuscripts, UVA; Kemper to Richard L. Maury, April 7, 1887, Kemper Papers, VHS; Warner, *Generals in Gray*, 170; Woodward, *Major General James Lawson Kemper*, 117–94.

90. Warner, *Generals in Gray*, 4; Calkins, *Appomattox Campaign*, 141–43.

91. Warner, *Generals in Gray*, 69, 96, 173, 311, 337–38.

92. Prior, "Lewis Payne," 1, 3–5; Ownsby, *Alias "Paine,"* 15.

93. Kimble, "W. H. McCulloch," MC.

94. Henry Moode to Sam Tate, April 29, 1870, Tennessee Historical Society Correspondence, TSLA; Lee to Mrs. George W. Randolph, March 8, 1870, Lee Letterbook, 1866–1870, VHS; Richter, "Removal of the Confederate Dead from Gettysburg," 115; Stephen Davis, "Death and Burials of General Richard Brooke Garnett," 116; Reardon, *Pickett's Charge in History and Memory*, 79–80; visit to Hollywood Cemetery, March 20, 1996.

95. Broadside, ca. October 1888, Reeve Papers, SHC-UNC; Reardon, *Pickett's Charge in History and Memory*, 103–6.

96. John Reed address, *Pennsylvania at Gettysburg*, 412–13; Gottfried, *Stopping Pickett*, 177.

97. Clemmer, *Valor in Gray*, xv, xix–xxi, 259, 313, 447.

98. C. D. Warner sketch, United Daughters of the Confederacy, Virginia Division, Boydton, Mecklenburg Co. Chapter No. 157, Scrapbook, 1913–1957, VHS; Gottfried, *Stopping Pickett*, 176–77.

99. Motts, *"Trust in God and Fear Nothing,"* 49.

100. "Story of a Sword," GNMP; Theodore B. Gates to Rothermel, April 28, 1868, Rothermel Papers, PHMC.

101. Peters, "Lost Sword of Gen. Richard B. Garnett," 26–27.

102. Page, *History of the Fourteenth*, 158; Reardon, *Pickett's Charge in History and Memory*, 105–6.

103. Edmund Berkeley to Daniel, September 26, n.d., Daniel Papers, UVA.

EPILOGUE

1. Byrne and Weaver, *Haskell of Gettysburg*, 186.

2. Doubleday, *Chancellorsville and Gettysburg*, 188; Hyde, "Recollections of the Battle of Gettysburg," 204; Isaac Trimble, "Civil War Diary," 12.

3. A. L. Long, *Memoirs of Robert E. Lee*, 290.

4. Rollins, "Second Wave," 96.

5. Wert, *General James Longstreet*, 285; Robertson, *General A. P. Hill*, 219–22; Alexander letter, 110.

6. George Thornton Fleming, *Life and Letters of General Alexander Hays*, 432, 451, 459–60; Nosworthy, *Anatomy of Victory*, 309–10.

7. Harrison and Busey, *Nothing but Glory*, 68.

8. Coddington, *Gettysburg Campaign*, 456–57.

9. Charles G. Treat to Fred I. H. Orcutt, December 30, 1891, Howard Papers, WRHS; Hazelwood, "Gettysburg Charge," 236.

10. Rothenburg, *Art of Warfare in the Age of Napoleon*, 117, 129; Stewart, *Pickett's Charge*, 83.

11. James Longstreet to Edward Porter Alexander, July 12, 1863, Cameron Scrapbook, PNB.

12. Carmichael, " 'Every Map of the Field Cries Out About It,' " 273–75, 280–81.

13. Henry J. Hunt to William T. Sherman, February 1882, in Ladd and Ladd, *Bachelder Papers*, 2:790–828.

14. Tidball, "Artillery Service in the War of the Rebellion," 687, 692, 698–99; Crary, *Dear Belle*, 209, 211; Francis A. Walker, "General Hancock and the Artillery at Gettysburg," 386.

15. Walter H. Taylor letter, 135; James H. Lane to editors, September 7, 1877, Grimes Papers, SHC-UNC; John M. Dunn address, *Report of Joint Committee*, 16; J. J. Young to Zebulon Vance, July 4, 1863, *OR* 27(2):645.

16. Andrew Cowan address, *In Memoriam*, 64.

17. H. L. Abbott letter, n.d., *Reports, Letters & Papers*, 1:95, BPL; V. A. Tapscott to Daniel, February 29, 1904, Daniel Papers, UVA.

18. Henry C. Moore to editors, November 6, 1877, Grimes Papers, SHC-UNC; John M. Dunn address, *Report of Joint Committee*, 16.

19. Swallow, "Third Day at Gettysburg," 572.

20. James A. Wright, "Story of Co. F," 628, MHS.

21. John B. Bachelder to C. H. Buehler, February 1, 1894, in Ladd and Ladd, *Bachelder Papers*, 3:1854–58; Sauers, "John B. Bachelder," 115–27.

22. Robert S. Henshaw, "A Virginia 'Reb,' " *Confederate Veteran* Papers, SCL-DU; Blackford, *Annals of the Lynchburg Home Guard*, 103–4; James Longstreet to Maj. Nash, September 3, 1892, Pickett Papers, VHS; B. L. Farinholt to Daniel, April 15, 1905, Daniel Papers, UVA.

23. Faulkner, *Intruder in the Dust*, 194–95.

24. William B. Taylor to mother, July 29, 1863, in Mast, "Six Lieutenants," 13.

25. Rollins, " 'Ruling Ideas' of the Pennsylvania Campaign," 14–15; Longstreet, "Lee's Invasion of Pennsylvania," 244–51; Coddington, *Gettysburg Campaign*, 7–11; Woodworth, *Davis and Lee at War*, 226–29, 236, 238–41; Harsh, *Confederate Tide Rising*, 67; McMurry, "Pennsylvania Gambit and the Gettysburg Splash," 197–99; "Letter from General Fitz. Lee," 70–71; "Letter from Major-General Henry Heth," 153–57; Robert E. Lee to James A. Seddon, June 8, 13, 1863, *OR* 27(3):868–69,

886; Lee to Jefferson Davis, June 10, 23, 25, July 29, 1863, *OR* 27(3):881, 925, 931–32, 1048–49; Lee to Samuel Cooper, January 1864, *OR* 27(2):313.

26. McMurry, "Pennsylvania Gambit and the Gettysburg Splash," 201.

27. George B. Davis, "Strategy of the Gettysburg Campaign," 377; "Letter from General Fitz. Lee," 70.

28. "Letter from the Count of Paris"; Woodworth, *Davis and Lee at War*, 244–45; Longstreet, "Lee's Right Wing at Gettysburg," 341–43.

29. Charles S. Peyton to Charles Pickett, July 9, 1863, *OR* 27(2):387.

BIBLIOGRAPHY

* * * * * * * * * * *

ARCHIVAL SOURCES

Auburn University, Auburn, Alabama
    James H. Lane Papers
Boston Public Library, Boston, Massachusetts
    Reports, Letters & Papers Appertaining to the 20th Mass. Vol. Inf. Vols. 1 and 2
Boston University, Special Collections, Boston, Massachusetts
    Military Historical Society of Massachusetts Collection
    John Codman Ropes Papers
Civil War Library and Museum, Philadelphia, Pennsylvania
    Sessler Collection
College of William and Mary, Special Collections, Williamsburg, Virginia
    Barker-Cooke Papers
    Bowles Family Papers
    Joseph E. Johnston Papers
    Rouzie Papers
Connecticut Historical Society, Hartford
    Loren Goodrich Papers
Duke University, Special Collections Library, Durham, North Carolina
    Bedinger-Dandridge Family Papers
    Confederate Veteran Papers
    John Warwick Daniel Papers
    A. J. Dula Memoir
    Constant C. Hanks Papers
    Josephus Jackson Papers
    William H. Jones Papers
    James Longstreet Papers
    Rebecca Mariah McCall Papers
    John Bowie Magruder Papers
    Munford-Ellis Family Papers
    George Edward Pickett Papers
    Cyril H. Tyler Papers

East Carolina University, Special Collections, Greenville, North Carolina
  Davis Family Papers
  Roach Family Papers
Emory University, Special Collections, Atlanta, Georgia
  W. H. Adams Papers
  James Marshall Collier Papers
  Benjamin Wesley Justice Papers
  James A. Patton Papers
Florida State Archives, Tallahassee
  Council A. Bryan Papers
  David Lang Letterbooks, 1886–89, 1893–1909
  D. M. Pogue to C. Seton Fleming, April 9, 1906, United Daughters of the
    Confederacy, Anna Jackson Chapter No. 224, Records, 1862–65, 1898–
    1900
Fredericksburg Battlefield, Fredericksburg, Virginia
  E. P. Alexander Letter
  J. B. Johnson, "A Limited Review of What One Man Saw of the Battle of
    Gettysburg"
  James J. Kirkpatrick Diary
  Prillaman Letters
Georgia Historical Society, Savannah
  William Penn Pigman Papers
Gettysburg National Military Park, Gettysburg, Pennsylvania
  Homer Baldwin to father, July 7, 1863, Battery C, 5th U.S. Artillery Folder
  Norbonne Berkeley Account, 8th Virginia Regimental Folder
  Henry H. Bingham Letters, Participants Accounts, Hancock Folder
  Ronald A. Church, "The Pipe Creek Line: An Overview," Pipe Creek Line
    Folder
  N. Eldred, "Only a Boy: A First-Hand Account of the Civil War," 111th New
    York Regimental Folder
  Albert Stokes Emmell, " 'Now is the Time for Buck & Ball': The Life & Civil
    War Experience of Albert Stokes Emmell," 12th New Jersey Regimental
    Folder
  "Equine Heroes of Pickett's Charge," July 3 Folder
  Augustus Evander Floyd Reminiscences, 18th North Carolina Regimental
    Folder
  Jeremiah S. Gage Letter, 11th Mississippi Regimental Folder
  Theodore B. Gates to Jacob B. Hardenburgh, December 18, 1876, 80th New
    York Regimental Folder
  Francis E. Heath to Selden Connor, n.d., 19th Maine Regimental Folder
  John P. Lancaster Memoir, 19th Maine Regimental Folder
  John T. McCall, "What the Tennesseans Did at Gettysburg," 7th Tennessee
    Regimental Folder
  Anthony McDermott Letter, June 4, 1887, unidentified newspaper clipping,
    69th Pennsylvania Regimental Folder

William A. Miller, "Wartime Letters of William A. Miller," 18th Virginia
    Regimental Folder
Augustin N. Parsons Letter, June 2, 1889
George E. Pickett to Samuel Cooper, August 11, 1863, with Longstreet's and
    Lee's endorsements, 53rd Virginia Regimental Folder
Raymond Jenkins Reid Letter, 2nd Florida Regimental Folder
Edmund Rice Letter, 19th Massachusetts Regimental Folder
T. Jefferson Rush Letter, 71st Pennsylvania Regimental Folder
"Story of a Sword," 80th New York Regimental Folder
W. B. Taylor to mother, June 22, 1863, 11th North Carolina Regimental Folder
A. S. Van de Graaff to wife, July 8, 1863, 5th Alabama Battalion Folder
Walter A. Van Rensselear Diary, 80th New York Regimental Folder
Wilbur F. Van Swaringen Reminiscences, 28th North Carolina Regimental
    Folder
Harold Malcolm Walthall Reminiscences, 1st Virginia Regimental Folder
Gulian V. Weir, "Recollections of the 3d day at Gettysburg with Battery 'C' "
James Wentworth Diary, newspaper clipping, 8th Florida Regimental Folder
T. D. Witherspoon Letter, 42nd Mississippi Regimental Folder
M. J. C. Woodworth to Theodore B. Gates, October 3, 1888, 80th New York
    Regimental Folder
Harvard University, Houghton Library, Cambridge, Massachusetts
    Dearborn Collection
    MOLLUS-Massachusetts Commandery Collection
Historical Society of Pennsylvania, Philadelphia
    John Gibbon Papers
    George Gordon Meade Collection
Library of Congress, Manuscripts Division, Washington, D.C.
    Edward Porter Alexander Papers
    Thomas Francis Galwey Papers
    Henry Jackson Hunt Papers
    Cadmus Marcellus Wilcox Papers
    Henry Stevens Willey, "The Story of My Experiences during the Civil War,
        1862–1863"
Louisiana State University, Special Collections, Baton Rouge
    W. Greene Raoul Letters
Maryland Historical Society, Baltimore
    John Gibbon Papers
Massachusetts Historical Society, Boston
    Nathan Hayward Letters
    Sumner Paine Papers
    Paul J. Revere Papers
Minnesota Historical Society, Minneapolis
    Daniel Bond Recollections
    Alfred P. Carpenter Letter, July 30, 1863
    James A. Wright, "The Story of Co. F, 1st Regiment Minn. Infantry"

Mississippi Department of Archives and History, Jackson
   William Peel Diary
   A. L. P. Vairin Diary
   J. J. Wilson Papers
Museum of the Confederacy, Richmond, Virginia
   Richard B. Garnett Papers
   William W. Goss Papers
   George K. Griggs Diary
   Robert G. Haile Diary
   William J. Hatchett Letters
   Henry Heth Papers
   June Kimble, "An Incident at Gettysburg"
   ———, "W. H. McCulloch," Tennessee Regiments Collection
   Letter Book of Armistead, Barton, and Steuart Brigades, Feb. 14, 1863–Nov.
      19, 1864
   William M. McComb, "Historical Sketch of the 14th Tenn Regt of Infantry,
      CSA 1861–1865," Tennessee Regiments Collection
   Morning Report of Co. E, 14th Virginia
   John O'Farrell Diary
   "Records of Capt. B. F. Howard's Company 'I' 1st Va Infantry Regt."
   William B. Short Letters
New-York Historical Society, New York
   Abner Doubleday Papers
   Theodore Burr Gates Papers
   W. G. Thompson Papers
New York Public Library, New York
   Charles W. Cowtan Papers
   William Henry Jackson Diary
   Letter Book, Light Division
New York State Library, Manuscripts and Special Collections, Albany
   Calvin A. Haynes Letters
   Aaron Meyers Letters
North Carolina Department of Archives and History, Raleigh
   Henry C. Brown Papers
   J. A. Bush Sr. Reminiscences, Lowry Shuford Collection
   John B. Neathery Papers
   Alfred Moore Scales Papers
   H. S. Stevens Papers
Ohio Historical Society, Columbus
   Samuel Sexton Papers
Pennsylvania Historical and Museum Commission, Harrisburg
   Haskell Family Collection
   Peter F. Rothermel Papers
Petersburg National Battlefield, Petersburg, Virginia
   Cameron Scrapbook

Queen's University, Kingston, Ontario
    Francis Moses Wafer Diary
Rhode Island Historical Society, Providence
    Adelia A. Gardner Papers
    Records of the Soldiers and Sailors Historical Society of Rhode Island
Rutgers University Library, New Brunswick, New Jersey
    Alfred M. Buck Diary
    E. M. Woodward Collection
St. Augustine Historical Society, St. Augustine, Florida
    David L. Dunham Diary, Dunham Biographical File
    Raymond Jenkins Reid Papers
State Historical Society of Iowa, Des Moines
    William Hawley Collection
Tennessee State Library and Archives, Nashville
    Ben. W. Coleman Papers
    John A. Fite Memoir
    Thomas Herndon Papers
    Edgar Quarles Rooker, "A Chronological Outline of the Military Career of
        Asaph Hill with Particular Emphasis on the Seventh Tennessee Infantry
        Regiment and the Tennessee (Archer's) Brigade"
    Tennessee Historical Society Correspondence
United States Army Military History Institute, Carlisle Barracks, Pennsylvania
    Ann Barineau Collection, Civil War Miscellaneous Collection
    Charles W. Belknap Diary, Robert L. Brake Collection
    William J. Burns Diary, Pennsylvania "Save the Flag" Collection
    Wilbur M. Clifford to father, August 15, 1863, Robert L. Brake Collection
    Drewry B. Easley to Howard Townsend, July 24, 1913, Robert L. Brake
        Collection
    Winfield Scott Hancock Papers, MOLLUS Collection
    William J. Hatchett Papers, *Civil War Times Illustrated* Collection
    Christoper Mead to wife, July 6, 1863, Robert L. Brake Collection
    Frederick Oesterle Memoir, *Civil War Times Illustrated* Collection
    Joseph E. Purvis Diary, *Civil War Times Illustrated* Collection
United States Military Academy Library, West Point, New York
    John Gibbon Papers
University of Chicago Library, Chicago, Illinois
    Herbert C. Hason Diary, Lincoln Collection
University of North Carolina, Southern Historical Collection, Chapel Hill
    Edward Porter Alexander Papers
    Allen-Simpson Papers
    Federal Soldiers' Letters
    David Funsten Papers
    Bryan Grimes Papers
    Walter Harrison Inspection Book
    Edmund Walter Jones Papers

Francis Milton Kennedy Diary
John Randolph Lane Papers
Harry Lewis Papers
Charles Edward Lippitt Papers
James Longstreet Papers
Lafayette McLaws Papers
Rawley W. Martin Papers
William Groves Morris Papers
Marcus Cicero Stephens Noble Papers
Joseph Caldwell Norwood Papers
William Nelson Pendleton Papers
Edward Payson Reeve Papers
Joseph H. Saunders Papers
George Phifer Wills Papers
University of Vermont, Bailey-Howe Library, Burlington
Benedict Family Papers
University of Virginia, Special Collections, Charlottesville
Barnes Family Manuscripts
John Warwick Daniel Papers
James Dearing Papers
Vermont Historical Society, Montpelier
Stephen F. Brown Papers
Albert Clarke, "The Thirteenth Regiment"
Charles Cummings Papers
Wheelock Veazey to George G. Benedict, July 11, 1864
Virginia Historical Society, Richmond
Aylett Family Papers
Carrington Family Papers
William Garnett Chisholm Papers
Cocke Family Papers
Robert William Douthat Papers
Thomas Claybrook Elder Papers
Benjamin Lyons Farinholt Papers
Augustus Evander Floyd Memoir
Gregory Family Papers
Hunton Family Papers
Keith Family Papers
James Lawson Kemper Papers
Robert Edward Lee Letterbook
John Singleton Mosby Papers
Henry Theveatt Owen Papers
Charles Pickett Papers
George Edward Pickett Papers
David Washington Pipes Memoir
William Patterson Carey Thomas Papers

John C. Timberlake to editors of *Richmond Dispatch*, October 29, 1887
United Daughters of the Confederacy, Virginia Division, Boydton,
    Mecklenburg County Chapter No. 157
Charles Scott Venable Papers
John Dudley Whitehead Papers
Virginia Military Institute Archives, Lexington
    B. David Mann, *They Were Heard From: VMI Alumni in the Civil War*
    F. Lewis Marshall to uncle, October 6, 1863
    Charles D. Walker, *Memorial, Virginia Military Institute*, 1875
Virginia State Library and Archives, Richmond
    Moses Barker Papers
    Sue B. Christian Collection
    James F. Knick Letter
    Edward Baker Loving Account
    Magruder Family Papers
    L. M. Moore Letter
    Thomas T. Munford Letter
    Newton Brothers Papers
    Henry T. Owen Papers
    J. K. Simmons Papers
    James H. Walker Papers
    James Peter Williams Letters
Washington and Lee University, Special Collections, Lexington, Virginia
    William Alexander Gordon Memoirs
    Charles E. McCorkle Papers
Western Reserve Historical Society, Cleveland, Ohio
    Henry H. Bingham, "Anecdotes Concerning Gen. Hancock and Other
        Officers at Gettysburg and Elsewhere"
    Arthur F. Devereux Papers
    Oliver Otis Howard Papers
    Charles H. Merrick Papers
Wistar Institute, Philadelphia, Pennsylvania
    Isaac Wistar Papers
Yale University Library, New Haven, Connecticut
    Alexander Stewart Webb Papers

NEWSPAPERS

Atlanta Journal
Auburn Daily Advertiser and Union
Delaware Republican (Wilmington)
Florida Sentinel (Tallahassee)
Gettysburg Compiler
Lebanon Democrat
Providence Evening Bulletin

Raleigh News and Observer
Richmond Daily Dispatch
Richmond Daily Enquirer
Rochester Daily Democrat and American
Savannah Daily News
South Western Baptist
Springfield Daily Republican

BOOKS, ARTICLES, DISSERTATIONS, AND THESES

Adams, Silas. "The Nineteenth Maine at Gettysburg." In *War Papers Read before the Commandery of the State of Maine, Military Order of the Loyal Legion of the United States*, 4:250–63. Portland, Maine: Lefavor-Tower, 1915.

Aldrich, Thomas M. *The History of Battery A, First Rhode Island Light Artillery, in the War to Preserve the Union, 1861–1865.* Providence: Snow and Farnham, 1904.

Alexander, E. P. "The Great Charge and Artillery Fighting at Gettysburg." In *Battles and Leaders of the Civil War*, edited by Robert Underwood Johnson and Clarence Clough Buel, 3:357–68. New York: Thomas Yoseloff, 1956.

———. Letter. *Southern Historical Society Papers* 4 (1877): 97–111.

Allan, William. "Letter from Colonel William Allan of Ewell's Staff." *Southern Historical Society Papers* 4 (1877): 79–80.

———. "A Reply to General Longstreet." In *Battles and Leaders of the Civil War*, edited by Robert Underwood Johnson and Clarence Clough Buel, 3:355–56. New York: Yoseloff, 1956.

Andrus, Michael J. *The Brooke, Fauquier, Loudon and Alexandria Artillery.* Lynchburg: H. E. Howard, 1990.

"Another Witness: Gettysburg." *Our Living and Our Dead* 3 (1875): 457–63.

Archer, John M. "Remembering the 14th Connecticut Volunteers." *Gettysburg Magazine*, no. 9 (1993): 61–79.

Ashe, S. A. *The Charge at Gettysburg.* Raleigh: Capitol, 1902.

———. "The Pettigrew-Pickett Charge, Gettysburg, 3 July, 1863." In *Histories of the Several Regiments and Battalions from North Carolina in the Great War, 1861–'65*, edited by Walter Clark, 5:137–59. Goldsboro, N.C.: Nash Brothers, 1901.

Bacarella, Michael. *Lincoln's Foreign Legion: The 39th New York Infantry, the Garibaldi Guard.* Shippensburg, Pa.: White Mane, 1996.

Baker, Andrew J. "Tribute to Capt. Magruder and Wife." *Confederate Veteran* 6 (1898): 507.

Bartlett, Napier. *A Soldier's Story of the War: Including the Marches and Battles of the Washington Artillery, and of Other Louisiana Troops.* New Orleans: Clark and Hofeline, 1874.

Bee, Robert L. "Fredericksburg on the Other Leg: Sergeant Ben Hirst's Narrative of Important Events, Gettysburg, July 3, 1863." In *The Third Day at Gettysburg and Beyond*, edited by Gary W. Gallagher, 132–60. Chapel Hill: University of North Carolina Press, 1994.

———, ed. *The Boys from Rockville: Civil War Narrative of Sgt. Benjamin Hirst, Company D, 14th Connecticut Volunteers.* Knoxville: University of Tennessee Press, 1998.

Bell, Robert T. *11th Virginia Infantry.* Lynchburg: H. E. Howard, 1985.

Benedict, G. G. *Army Life in Virginia.* Burlington, Vt.: Free Press, 1895.

———. *Vermont at Gettysburgh.* Burlington, Vt.: Free Press, 1870.

———. "Vermont at Gettysburgh." In *Gettysburg Sources,* compiled by James L. McLean Jr. and Judy W. McLean, 1:84–115. Baltimore: Butternut and Blue, 1986.

Berkeley, Edmund. "Rode with Pickett." *Confederate Veteran* 38 (1930): 175.

Blackford, Charles M., Jr. *Annals of the Lynchburg Home Guard.* Lynchburg: John W. Rohr, 1891.

Bond, W. R. *Pickett or Pettigrew? An Historical Essay.* Weldon, N.C.: Hall and Sledge, 1888.

Bowen, George A., ed. "The Diary of Captain George D. Bowen, 12th New Jersey Volunteers." *Valley Forge Journal* 2 (1984): 116–45.

Bowen, Roland E. " 'Nothing But Cowards Run.' " *Civil War,* no. 50 (1995): 42–49.

Bright, Robert A. "Pickett's Charge at Gettysburg." *Confederate Veteran* 38 (1930): 263–66.

Brown, Kent Masterson. *Cushing of Gettysburg: The Story of a Union Artillery Commander.* Lexington: University Press of Kentucky, 1993.

Brown, Maud Morrow. *The University Greys, Company A, Eleventh Mississippi Regiment, Army of Northern Virginia, 1861–1865.* Richmond: Garrett and Massie, 1940.

Bruce, George A. *The Twentieth Regiment of Massachusetts Volunteer Infantry, 1861–1865.* Boston: Houghton Mifflin, 1906.

Buell, Augustus. *The Cannoneer: Recollections of Service in the Army of the Potomac.* Washington, D.C.: National Tribune, 1890.

Burton, Matthew Wade. "The River of Blood and the Valley of Death: The Lives of Two Cousins for the Cause, Robert Selden Garnett and Richard Brooke Garnett, C.S.A." Master's thesis, Bowling Green State University, 1996.

Busey, John W., and David G. Martin. *Regimental Strengths and Losses at Gettysburg.* Hightstown, N.J.: Longstreet House, 1986.

Byrne, Frank L., and Andrew T. Weaver, eds. *Haskell of Gettysburg: His Life and Civil War Papers.* Kent, Ohio: Kent State University Press, 1989.

Caison, Albert Stacey. "Southern Soldiers in Northern Prisons." *Southern Historical Society Papers* 23 (1895): 158–65.

Calkins, Chris M. *The Appomattox Campaign, March 29–April 9, 1865.* Conshohocken, Pa.: Combined Books, 1997.

Campbell, Eric A. " 'Remember Harper's Ferry!': The Degradation, Humiliation, and Redemption of Col. George L. Willard's Brigade." Pts. 1 and 2. *Gettysburg Magazine,* no. 7 (1992): 62–77; no. 8 (1993): 95–110.

"Captain John Holmes Smith's Account." *Southern Historical Society Papers* 32 (1904): 189–95.

Carmichael, Peter S. " 'Every Map of the Field Cries Out About It': The Failure of Confederate Artillery at Pickett's Charge." In *Three Days at Gettysburg: Essays on Confederate and Union Leadership*, edited by Gary W. Gallagher, 270–83. Kent, Ohio: Kent State University Press, 1999.

Carter, James T. "Flag of the Fifty-Third Va. Regiment." *Confederate Veteran* 10 (1902): 263.

Chapman, Craig S. *More Terrible Than Victory: North Carolina's Bloody Bethel Regiment, 1861–1865*. Washington, D.C.: Brassey's, 1998.

Christ, Elwood W. *The Struggle for the Bliss Farm at Gettysburg, July 2nd and 3rd, 1863*. Baltimore: Butternut and Blue, 1994.

Clark, George. *A Glance Backward*. Houston: Rein and Sons, 1914.

Clarke, Albert. "Hancock and the Vermont Brigade." *Journal of the Military Service Institution of the United States* 48 (1911): 224–29.

Clay, James W. "About the Death of General Garnett." *Confederate Veteran* 14 (1906): 81.

Cleaves, Freeman. *Meade of Gettysburg*. Norman: University of Oklahoma Press, 1960.

Clement, Maud Carter. *The History of Pittsylvania County, Virginia*. Lynchburg: J. P. Bell, 1929.

Clemmer, Gregg S. *Valor in Gray: The Recipients of the Confederate Medal of Honor*. Staunton, Va.: Hearthside, 1996.

Cockrell, Monroe F., ed. *Gunner with Stonewall: Reminiscences of William Thomas Poague*. Jackson, Tenn.: McCowat-Mercer, 1957.

Cockrell, Thomas D., and Michael B. Ballard, eds. *A Mississippi Rebel in the Army of Northern Virginia: The Civil War Memoirs of Private David Holt*. Baton Rouge: Louisiana State University Press, 1995.

Coco, Gregory A., ed. *From Ball's Bluff to Gettysburg . . . and Beyond: The Civil War Letters of Private Roland E. Bowen, 15th Massachusetts Infantry, 1861–1864*. Gettysburg: Thomas, 1994.

Coddington, Edwin B. *The Gettysburg Campaign: A Study in Command*. New York: Charles Scribner's Son, 1968.

———. "Rothermel's Paintings of the Battle of Gettysburg." *Pennsylvania History* 27 (1960): 1–27.

Coffin, Howard. *Full Duty: Vermonters in the Civil War*. Woodstock, Vt.: Countryman Press, 1993.

———. *Nine Months to Gettysburg: Stannard's Vermonters and the Repulse of Pickett's Charge*. Woodstock, Vt.: Countryman Press, 1997.

Coles, David J., and Zack C. Waters. "Forgotten Sacrifice: The Florida Brigade at the Battle of Gettysburg." *Apalachee* 11 (1991–96): 36–49.

Compton, E. H. *Reminiscences of Edward Howard Compton: A Survivor of Second Battle of Manassas and the Battle of Gettysburg*. Front Royal, Va.: n.p., n.d.

Cook, John D. S. "Personal Reminiscences of Gettysburg." *War Talks in Kansas: A Series of Papers Read before the Kansas Commandery of the Military Order of the Loyal Legion of the United States*, 321–41. Kansas City, Mo.: Franklin Hudson, 1906.

Cooke, Charles M. "Fifty-Fifth Regiment." In *Histories of the Several Regiments and*

Battalions from North Carolina in the Great War, 1861–'65, edited by Walter Clark, 3:287–312. Goldsboro, N.C.: Nash Brothers, 1901.

Cowan, Andrew. "Cowan's New York Battery." *National Tribune*, November 12, 1908.

Cowan, Charles. "Pickett's Charge." *Civil War Times Illustrated* 3 (1964): 26–29.

Cowtan, Charles W. *Services of the Tenth New York Volunteers (National Zouaves,) in the War of the Rebellion*. New York: Charles H. Ludwig, 1882.

Crary, Catherine S. *Dear Belle: Letters from a Cadet and Officer to His Sweetheart, 1858–1865*. Middletown, Conn.: Wesleyan University Press, 1965.

Crocker, James F. "Gettysburg: Pickett's Charge." *Southern Historical Society Papers* 33 (1905): 111–34.

———. *Gettysburg: Pickett's Charge and Other War Addresses*. Portsmouth, Va.: W. A. Fiske, 1915.

Cross, Andrew. *The War: Battle of Gettysburg and the Christian Commission*. N.p., 1865.

Crumb, Herb S., ed. *The Eleventh Corps Artillery at Gettysburg: The Papers of Major Thomas Ward Osborn, Chief of Artillery*. Hamilton, N.Y.: Edmonston, 1991.

Dabney, T. G. Letter. *Confederate Veteran* 6 (1898): 570.

Daggett. "Those Whom You Left behind You." In *Glimpses of the Nation's Struggle, Fifth Series: Papers Read before the Minnesota Commandery of the Military Order of the Loyal Legion of the United States, 1897–1902*, 332–64. St. Paul: Review Publishing, 1903.

Davis, George B. "The Strategy of the Gettysburg Campaign." In *Campaigns in Virginia, Maryland and Pennsylvania, 1862–1863: Papers of the Military Historical Society of Massachusetts*, 3:376–414. Boston: Griffith-Stillings, 1903.

Davis, Stephen. "The Death and Burials of General Richard Brooke Garnett." *Gettysburg Magazine*, no. 5 (1991): 107–16.

Davis, Steven R. "'. . . Like Leaves in an Autumn Wind': The 11th Mississippi Infantry in the Army of Northern Virginia." *Civil War Regiments* 2 (1992): 269–312.

Devereux, Arthur F. "Some Account of Pickett's Charge at Gettysburg." *Magazine of American History* 18 (July–December 1887): 13–19.

Dickson, Christopher C. "The Flying Brigade: Brig. Gen. George Stannard and the Road to Gettysburg." *Gettysburg Magazine*, no. 16 (1997): 6–26.

Divine, John E. *Eighth Virginia Infantry*. Lynchburg: H. E. Howard, 1983.

Doubleday, Abner. *Chancellorsville and Gettysburg*. New York: Blue and Gray, 1959.

Dowdey, Clifford, and Louis H. Manarin, eds. *The Wartime Papers of Robert E. Lee*. New York; Da Capo, 1961.

Dreese, Michael A. *The 151st Pennsylvania Volunteers at Gettysburg: Like Ripe Apples in a Storm*. Jefferson, N.C.: McFarland, 2000.

Dunaway, Wayland Fuller. *Reminiscences of a Rebel*. New York: Neale, 1913.

Durkin, Joseph T., ed. *John Dooley, Confederate Soldier: His War Journal*. Washington, D.C.: Georgetown University Press, 1945.

Dyer, Frederick H. *A Compendium of the War of the Rebellion*. 3 vols. New York: Yoseloff, 1959.

Easley, D. B. "With Armistead When He Was Killed." *Confederate Veteran* 20 (1912): 379.

Elmore, Thomas L. "The Florida Brigade at Gettysburg." *Gettysburg Magazine*, no. 15 (1996): 45–59.

———. "A Meteorological and Astronomical Chronology of the Gettysburg Campaign." *Gettysburg Magazine*, no. 13 (1995): 7–21.

Farinholt, B. L. "Battle of Gettysburg: Johnson's Island." *Confederate Veteran* 5 (1897): 467–70.

———. "Escape from Johnson's Island." *Confederate Veteran* 5 (1897): 514–17.

———. "Perils in Escaping from Prison." *Confederate Veteran* 5 (1897): 547–50.

Faulkner, William. *Intruder in the Dust*. New York: Random House, 1948.

Felton, Silas. "Pursuing the Elusive 'Cannoneer.' " *Gettysburg Magazine*, no. 9 (1993): 33–39.

Fields, Frank E., Jr. *28th Virginia Infantry*. Lynchburg: H. E. Howard, 1985.

Finley, G. W. Account. *Buffalo Evening News*, May 29, 1894.

———. *My Experiences As a Prisoner of War*. N.p., n.d.

Fleming, Francis P. *Memoir of Capt. C. Seton Fleming, of the Second Florida Infantry, C.S.A.* Jacksonville, Fla.: Times-Union, 1884.

Fleming, George Thornton, ed. *Life and Letters of General Alexander Hays*. Pittsburgh: Gilbert, Adams, Hays, 1919.

Flowers, George W. "Thirty-Eighth Regiment." In *Histories of the Several Regiments and Battalions from North Carolina in the Great War, 1861–'65*, edited by Walter Clark, 2:675–97. Goldsboro, N.C.: Nash Brothers, 1901.

Ford, Andrew E. *The Story of the Fifteenth Regiment Massachusetts Volunteer Infantry in the Civil War, 1861–1864*. Clinton, Mass.: W. J. Coulter, 1898.

Fortin, Maurice S., ed. "Colonel Hilary A. Herbert's History of the Eighth Alabama Volunteer Regiment, C.S.A." *Alabama Historical Quarterly* 39 (1977): 5–321.

Freeman, Douglas Southall. *Lee's Lieutenants: A Study in Command*. 3 vols. New York: Charles Scribner's Sons, 1942.

———. *R. E. Lee: A Biography*. 4 vols. New York: Charles Scribner's Sons, 1934.

Fremantle, Arthur James Lyon. *Three Months in the Southern States: April–June, 1863*. Lincoln: University of Nebraska Press, 1991.

Frey, Donald J. *Longstreet's Assault — Pickett's Charge: The Lost Record of Pickett's Wounded*. Shippensburg, Pa.: Burd Street Press, 2000.

Fry, B. D. "Pettigrew's Charge at Gettysburg." *Southern Historical Society Papers* 7 (1879): 91–93.

Fulton, William Frierson. *Family Record and War Reminiscences*. N.p., n.d.

Gallagher, Gary W. "Lee's Army Has Not Lost Any of Its Prestige: The Impact of Gettysburg on the Army of Northern Virginia and the Confederate Home Front." In *The Third Day at Gettysburg and Beyond*, edited by Gary W. Gallagher, 1–30. Chapel Hill: University of North Carolina Press, 1994.

———, ed. *Fighting for the Confederacy: The Personal Recollections of General Edward Porter Alexander*. Chapel Hill: University of North Carolina Press, 1987.

Galloway, Felix Richard. "Gettysburg: The Battle and the Retreat." *Confederate Veteran* 21 (1913): 388–89.

Galwey, Thomas Francis. *The Valiant Hours*. Harrisburg: Stackpole, 1961.

Gambone, A. M. *Hancock at Gettysburg . . . and Beyond*. Baltimore: Butternut and Blue, 1997.

Gates, Theodore B. "Movements and Service of the 'Ulster Guard,' Twentieth Regiment New York State Militia For the Year Ending December 31, 1863." *Address Delivered Wednesday, 28th November, 1866*. N.p., n.d.

Gibbon, John. *Personal Recollections of the Civil War*. New York: G. P. Putnam's Sons, 1928.

Gordon, Lesley J. *General George E. Pickett in Life and Legend*. Chapel Hill: University of North Carolina Press, 1998.

Gottfried, Bradley M. *Stopping Pickett: The History of the Philadelphia Brigade*. Shippensburg, Pa.: White Mane, 1999.

Govan, Gilbert, and James Livingood, eds. *The Haskell Memoirs: John Cheves Haskell*. New York: G. P. Putnam's Sons, 1960.

Gragg, Rod. *Covered with Glory: The 26th North Carolina Infantry at Gettysburg*. New York: Harper Collins, 2000.

Greenberg, Henry J. "Pickett's Charge: The Reason Why." *Gettysburg Magazine*, no. 5 (1991): 103–6.

Greene, A. Wilson. "From Gettysburg to Falling Waters: Meade's Pursuit of Lee." In *The Third Day at Gettysburg and Beyond*, edited by Gary W. Gallagher, 161–201. Chapel Hill: University of North Carolina Press, 1994.

Groene, Bertram H., ed. "Civil War Letters of Colonel David Lang." *Florida Historical Quarterly* 54 (1976): 340–66.

Hadden, R. Lee. "The Granite Glory: The 19th Maine at Gettysburg." *Gettysburg Magazine*, no. 13 (1995): 50–63.

Haines, William P. *History of the Men of Co. F, with Description of the Marches and Battles of the 12th New Jersey Vols*. Mickelton, N.J.: n.p., 1897.

Hamblen, Charles P. *Connecticut Yankees at Gettysburg*. Kent, Ohio: Kent State University Press, 1993.

Hamilton, J. G. DeRoulhac, ed. *The Papers of Randolph Abbott Shotwell*. 2 vols. Raleigh: North Carolina Historical Commission, 1931.

Hancock, Almyra. *Reminiscences of Winfield Scott Hancock by His Wife*. New York: Charles L. Webster, 1887.

Harding, Milton. "Where General Armistead Fell." *Confederate Veteran* 19 (1911): 371.

Harris, James. *Historical Sketches, Seventh Regiment North Carolina Troops*. Mooresville, N.C.: n.p., n.d.

Harrison, Kathleen Georg. " 'Ridges of Grim War.' " *Blue and Gray Magazine* 9 (1988): 10–52.

Harrison, Kathy Georg, and John W. Busey. *Nothing but Glory: Pickett's Division at Gettysburg*. Gettysburg: Thomas Publications, 1987.

Harrison, Walter. *Pickett's Men: A Fragment of War History*. New York: Van Nostrand, 1870.

Harsh, Joseph L. *Confederate Tide Rising: Robert E. Lee and the Making of Southern Strategy, 1861–1862*. Kent, Ohio: Kent State University Press, 1998.

Hartwig, D. Scott. "It Struck Horror to Us All." *Gettysburg Magazine*, no. 4 (1991): 89–100.

Haskin, William L., comp. *The History of the First Regiment of Artillery from Its Organization in 1821, to January 1st, 1876*. Portland, Maine: Thurston, 1879.

Hazelwood, Martin W. "Gettysburg Charge, Paper As To Pickett's Men." *Southern Historical Society Papers* 23 (1895): 229–37.

Heflin, W. P. *Blind Man "On the Warpath."* N.p., n.d.

Heth, Henry. Letter. *Southern Historical Society Papers* 4 (1877): 151–60.

Hicks, Robert W., and Frances E. Schultz. *Battlefields of the Civil War*. Topsfield, Mass.: Salem House, 1989.

History of the Fifth Massachusetts Battery. Boston: Luther E. Cowles, 1902.

Hogan, N. B. Letter. *Confederate Veteran* 6 (1898): 567–68.

Holland, T. C. "With Armistead at Gettysburg." *Confederate Veteran* 29 (1921): 62.

Horn, Stanley F., ed. *The Robert E. Lee Reader*. Indianapolis: Bobbs-Merrill, 1961.

Hunt, Henry J. "The Third Day at Gettysburg." In *Battles and Leaders of the Civil War*, edited by Robert Underwood Johnson and Clarence Clough Buel, 3:369–85. New York: Yoseloff, 1956.

Hunton, Eppa. *Autobiography of Eppa Hunton*. Richmond: William Byrd, 1933.

Hyde, Thomas W. "Recollections of the Battle of Gettysburg." *War Papers Read before the Commandery of the State of Maine, Military Order of the Loyal Legion of the United States*, 1:199–206. Portland, Maine: Thurston, 1898.

Imboden, John D. "The Confederate Retreat from Gettysburg." In *Battles and Leaders of the Civil War*, edited by Robert Underwood Johnson and Clarence Clough Buel, 3:420–29. New York: Yoseloff, 1956.

Inman, Arthur Crew, ed. *Soldier of the South: General Pickett's War Letters to His Wife*. Boston: Houghton Mifflin, 1928.

In Memoriam: Alexander Stewart Webb, 1835–1911. Albany, N.Y.: J. B. Lyon, 1916.

"In the Field and on the Town with the Washington Artillery: Selections from Documents in the Museum of the Confederacy Collections." *Civil War Regiments* 5 (1995): 92–154.

Irby, Richard. *Historical Sketch of the Nottoway Grays*. Richmond: J. W. Fergusson, 1878.

Irvine, R. H. "Brig. Gen. Richard B. Garnett." *Confederate Veteran* 23 (1915): 391.

Jackson, William Henry. *Time Exposure: The Autobiography of William Henry Jackson*. New York: G. P. Putnam's Sons, 1940.

James, John T. Letter. July 9, 1863. *Philadelphia Weekly Times*, October 21, 1882.

Johnson, W. Gart. "Reminiscences of Lee and Gettysburg." *Confederate Veteran* 1 (1893): 246.

Johnston, David E. *The Story of a Confederate Boy in the Civil War*. Radford, Va.: Commonwealth Press, 1980.

Jones, John T. "Pettigrew's Brigade at Gettysburg." In *Histories of the Several Regiments and Battalions from North Carolina in the Great War, 1861–'65*, edited by Walter Clark, 5:133–35. Goldsboro, N.C.: Nash Brothers, 1901.

Jones, Robert Tyler. "Gen. L. A. Armistead and R. Tyler Jones." *Confederate Veteran* 2 (1894): 271.

Jordan, David M. *Winfield Scott Hancock: A Soldier's Life*. Bloomington: Indiana University Press, 1988.

Jordan, Ervin L., Jr., and Herbert A. Thomas Jr. *Nineteenth Virginia Infantry*. Lynchburg: H. E. Howard, 1987.

Jordan, Weymouth T., comp. *North Carolina Troops, 1861–1865, a Roster*. 14 vols. Raleigh: North Carolina Department of Archives and History, 1966–97.

Kennedy, Frances H., ed. *The Civil War Battlefield Guide*. 2nd ed. Boston: Houghton Mifflin, 1998.

Kimble, June. "Tennesseeans at Gettysburg: The Retreat." *Confederate Veteran* 18 (1910): 460–61.

Klein, Frederic Shriver. "Meade's Pipe Creek Line." *Maryland Historical Magazine* 57 (1962): 133–49.

Krick, Robert E. L. *Fortieth Virginia Infantry*. Lynchburg: H. E. Howard, 1985.

Krick, Robert K. "Armistead and Garnett: The Parallel Lives of Two Virginia Soldiers." In *The Third Day at Gettysburg and Beyond*, edited by Gary W. Gallagher, 93–131. Chapel Hill: University of North Carolina Press, 1994.

Kross, Gary M. " 'I Do Not Believe That Pickett's Division Would Have Reached Our Line': Henry J. Hunt and the Union Artillery on July 3, 1863." In *Three Days at Gettysburg: Essays on Confederate and Union Leadership*, edited by Gary W. Gallagher, 284–305. Kent, Ohio: Kent State University Press, 1999.

Ladd, David L., and Audrey J. Ladd, eds. *The Bachelder Papers: Gettysburg in Their Own Words*. 3 vols. Dayton, Ohio: Morningside, 1994–95.

Lane, James H. "The Branch-Lane Brigade." In *Histories of the Several Regiments and Battalions from North Carolina in the Great War, 1861–'65*, edited by Walter Clark, 4:465–79. Goldsboro, N.C.: Nash Brothers, 1901.

Lash, Gary G. "The Philadelphia Brigade at Gettysburg." *Gettysburg Magazine*, no. 7 (1992): 97–113.

Lattimore, T. D. "Thirty-Fourth Regiment." In *Histories of the Several Regiments and Battalions from North Carolina in the Great War, 1861–'65*, edited by Walter Clark, 2:581–90. Goldsboro, N.C.: Nash Brothers, 1901.

Lee, Robert E. *Recollections and Letters of General Robert E. Lee, by His Son*. New York: Doubleday, Page, 1904.

"Letter from General Fitz. Lee." *Southern Historical Society Papers* 4 (1877): 69–74.

"Letter from General Trimble." *Southern Historical Society Papers* 9 (1881): 29–35.

"Letter from Major-General Henry Heth of A. P. Hill's Corps, A.N.V." *Southern Historical Society Papers* 4 (1877): 151–60.

"Letter from the Count of Paris." *Southern Historical Society Papers* 5 (1878): 88–89.

Lewis, John H. *Recollections from 1860 to 1865*. Washington, D.C.: Peake, 1895.

Lightsey, Ada Christine. *The Veteran's Story*. Meridian, Miss.: Mindian News, 1899.

Lochren, William. "The First Minnesota at Gettysburg." *Glimpses of the Nation's Struggle: A Series of Papers Read before the Minnesota Commandery of the Military Order of the Loyal Legion of the United States*, 3rd ser., 42–56. St. Paul: D. D. Merrill, 1893.

Loehr, Charles T. "The 'Old First' Virginia at Gettysburg." *Southern Historical Society Papers* 32 (1904): 33–40.

——. *War History of the Old First Virginia Infantry Regiment*. Richmond: William Ellis Jones, 1884.

Long, A. L. *Memoirs of Robert E. Lee*. New York: J. M. Stoddart, 1886.

Long, Roger. "The Confederate Prisoners of Gettysburg." *Gettysburg Magazine*, no. 2 (1990): 91–112.

——. "Dr. Billy's Battles." *Gettysburg Magazine*, no. 16 (1997): 86–94.

——. "Gen. Isaac R. Trimble in Captivity." *Gettysburg Magazine*, no. 1 (1989): 125–28.

——. "Maj. Joseph H. Saunders, 33rd North Carolina, C.S.A." *Gettysburg Magazine*, no. 10 (1994): 102–6.

——. "Over the Wall." *Gettysburg Magazine*, no. 13 (1995): 64–74.

Longacre, Edward G. *The Man behind the Guns: A Biography of General Henry Jackson Hunt*. New York: A. S. Barnes, 1977.

——. *Pickett, Leader of the Charge: A Biography of General George E. Pickett, C.S.A.* Shippensburg, Pa.: White Mane, 1995.

Longstreet, James. *From Manassas to Appomattox*. Bloomington: Indiana University Press, 1960.

——. "General Longstreet's Account of the Campaign and Battle." *Southern Historical Society Papers* 5 (1878): 54–86.

——. "Lee's Invasion of Pennsylvania." In *Battles and Leaders of the Civil War*, edited by Robert Underwood Johnson and Clarence Clough Buel, 3:244–51. New York: Yoseloff, 1956.

——. "Lee's Right Wing at Gettysburg." In *Battles and Leaders of the Civil War*, edited by Robert Underwood Johnson and Clarence Clough Buel, 3:339–54. New York: Yoseloff, 1956.

Love, D. C. *The Prairie Guards*. Columbus, Miss.: n.p., 1890.

Love, William. "Mississippi at Gettysburg." *Publications of the Mississippi Historical Society* 9 (1906): 25–51.

McCulloch, Robert. "The 'High Tide at Gettysburg.' " *Confederate Veteran* 21 (1913): 473–76.

McDaid, William Kelsey. " 'Four Years of Arduous Service': The History of the Branch-Lane Brigade in the Civil War." Ph.D. diss., Michigan State University, 1987.

McDermott, Anthony W. *A Brief History of the Sixty-Ninth Regiment Pennsylvania Veteran Volunteers*. Philadelphia: D. J. Gallagher, n.d.

McLaws, Lafayette. "Gettysburg." *Southern Historical Society Papers* 7 (1879): 79–89.

McMurry, Richard M. "The Pennsylvania Gambit and the Gettysburg Splash." In *The Gettysburg Nobody Knows*, edited by Gabor S. Boritt, 175–202. New York: Oxford University Press, 1997.

Mahood, Wayne. *"Written in Blood": A History of the 126th New York Infantry in the Civil War*. Hightstown, N.J.: Longstreet House, 1997.

Marshall, Jeffrey D., ed. *A War of the People: Vermont Civil War Letters*. Hanover, N.H.: University Press of New England, 1999.

Martin, David G. *Gettysburg, July 1*. Conshohocken, Pa.: Combined Books, 1995.

Martin, W. J., and E. R. Outlaw. "Eleventh Regiment." In *Histories of the Several*

Regiments and Battalions from North Carolina in the Great War, 1861–'65, edited by
    Walter Clark, 1:583–604. Raleigh: E. M. Uzzell, 1901.

Mast, Greg. "Six Lieutenants: Vignettes of Tar Heels at Gettysburg." *Military
    Images* 13 (1991): 6–13.

———, ed. "The Setser Letters." Pt. 3. *Company Front* (1989): 9–15.

Maull, D. W. *The Life and Military Services of the Late Brigadier General Thomas A.
    Smyth.* Wilmington, Del.: H. & E. F. James, 1870.

Mayo, Joseph. "Pickett's Charge at Gettysburg." *Southern Historical Society Papers* 34
    (1906): 327–35.

Meade, George. *The Life and Letters of George Gordon Meade.* 2 vols. New York:
    Charles Scribner's Sons, 1913.

"The Medal of Honor at Gettysburg." *Blue and Gray Magazine* 9 (1988): 29.

Meinhard, Robert W. "The First Minnesota at Gettysburg." *Gettysburg Magazine*,
    no. 5 (1991): 79–88.

Metts, James I. *Longstreet's Charge at Gettysburg, Pa.* N.p., n.d.

Mills, George H. *History of the Sixteenth North Carolina (Originally Sixth N.C.)
    Regiment in the Civil War.* Rutherfordton, N.C.: n.p., 1901.

Moe, Richard. *The Last Full Measure: The Life and Death of the First Minnesota
    Volunteers.* New York: Avon, 1993.

Moore, J. H. "The Battle of Gettysburg." In *The Military Annals of Tennessee,
    Confederate*, 1st ser., edited by John Berrien Lindsley, 244–53. Nashville: J. M.
    Lindsley, 1886.

Morgan, W. H. *Personal Reminiscences of the War of 1861–5.* Lynchburg: J. P. Bell,
    1911.

Motts, Wayne E. *"Trust in God and Fear Nothing": Gen. Lewis A. Armistead, CSA.*
    Gettysburg: Farnsworth House, 1994.

Murphey, Thomas G. *Fours Years in the War: The History of the First Regiment of
    Delaware Veteran Volunteers.* Philadelphia: James S. Claxton, 1866.

Murray, R. L. *The Redemption of the "Harper's Ferry Cowards": The Story of the 111th
    and 126th New York State Volunteer Regiments at Gettysburg.* N.p., 1994.

Nesbit, J. W. "Recollections of Pickett's Charge." *National Tribune*, November 16,
    1916.

Nevins, Allan, ed. *A Diary of Battle: The Personal Journals of Colonel Charles S.
    Wainwright, 1861–1865.* New York: Harcourt, Brace and World, 1962.

Nosworthy, Brent. *The Anatomy of Victory: Battle Tactics, 1689–1763.* New York:
    Hippocrene Books, 1992.

Osborne, Seward R., ed. *The Civil War Diaries of Col. Theodore B. Gates, 20th New York
    State Militia.* Hightstown, N.J.: Longstreet House, 1991.

Owen, H. T. "Pickett at Gettysburg." *Philadelphia Weekly Times*, March 26, 1881.

Owen, William Miller. "Recollections of the Third Day at Gettysburg." *United
    Service, a Monthly Magazine* 13 (1885): 148–51.

Ownsby, Betty O. *Alias "Paine": Lewis Thornton Powell, the Mystery Man of the Lincoln
    Conspiracy.* Jefferson, N.C.: McFarland, 1993.

Page, Charles D. *History of the Fourteenth Regiment, Connecticut Vol. Infantry.*
    Meriden, Conn.: Horton, 1906.

Palmer, Edwin Franklin. *The Second Brigade; or, Camp Life*. Montpelier, Vt.: E. P. Walton, 1864.

Parker, William L. *General James Dearing, CSA*. Lynchburg: H. E. Howard, 1990.

Patch, Charles A. "Pickett's Division at Gettysburg." *Confederate Veteran* 6 (1898): 569–70.

Patterson, Gerard A. "In a Most Disgraceful Manner." *Civil War Times Illustrated* 29 (1990): 46–47.

Pennsylvania at Gettysburg: Ceremonies at the Dedication of the Monuments. Vol. 1. Harrisburg: William Stanley Ray, 1904.

Peters, Winfield. "About the Death of General Garnett." *Confederate Veteran* 14 (1906): 81.

———. "The Lost Sword of Gen. Richard B. Garnett, Who Fell at Gettysburg." *Southern Historical Society Papers* 33 (1903): 26–31.

Pfanz, Harry W. *Gettysburg: Culp's Hill and Cemetery Hill*. Chapel Hill: University of North Carolina Press, 1993.

———. *Gettysburg: The Second Day*. Chapel Hill: University of North Carolina Press, 1987.

Phillips, Kenneth Edward. "James Henry Lane and the War for Southern Independence." Ph.D. diss., Auburn University, 1982.

Pickett, LaSalle Corbell. *Pickett and His Men*. Atlanta: Foote and Davies, 1899.

Pierce, John E. "The Civil War Career of Richard Brooke Garnett: A Quest for Vindication." Master's thesis, Virginia Polytechnic Institute, 1969.

Piston, William Garrett. "Cross Purposes: Longstreet, Lee, and Confederate Attack Plans for July 3 at Gettysburg." In *The Third Day at Gettysburg and Beyond*, edited by Gary W. Gallagher, 31–55. Chapel Hill: University of North Carolina Press, 1994.

———. *Lee's Tarnished Lieutenant: James Longstreet and His Place in Southern History*. Athens: University of Georgia Press, 1987.

Plummer, John W. "John W. Plummer's Account." In *Rebellion Record*, edited by Frank Moore, 10:178–81. New York: D. Van Nostrand, 1867.

Poindexter, James E. "Armistead at the Battle of Gettysburg." *Southern Historical Society Papers* 39 (1914): 186–87.

———. "General Armistead's Portrait Presented." *Southern Historical Society Papers* 37 (1909): 144–51.

———. "Gen. Lewis Addison Armistead." *Confederate Veteran* 22 (1914): 502–4.

Porter, John W. H. "The Confederate Soldier." *Confederate Veteran* 24 (1916): 460–61.

Potter, T. S. "The Battle of Gettysburg." *National Tribune*, August 5, 1882.

Powell, William S., ed. *Dictionary of North Carolina Biography*. 5 vols. Chapel Hill: University of North Carolina Press, 1979–94.

Priest, John Michael. *Into the Fight: Pickett's Charge at Gettysburg*. Shippensburg, Pa.: White Mane, 1998.

Priors, Leon O. "Lewis Payne, Pawn of John Wilkes Booth." *Florida Historical Quarterly* 43 (1964): 1–20.

Rawley, T. L. "The Pender-Scales Brigade." In *Histories of the Several Regiments and*

Battalions from North Carolina in the Great War, 1861–'65, edited by Walter Clark, 4:551–54. Goldsboro, N.C.: Nash Brothers, 1901.

Ray, Frederic. "Pickett's Charge: Story Behind Painting." *Civil War Times Illustrated* 5 (1966): 25–27.

Reardon, Carol. " 'I Think the Union Army Had Something to Do with It': The Pickett's Charge Nobody Knows." In *The Gettysburg Nobody Knows*, edited by Gabor S. Boritt, 122–43. New York: Oxford University Press, 1997.

———. "James Longstreet's Virginia Defenders." In *Three Days at Gettysburg: Essays on Confederate and Union Leadership*, edited by Gary W. Gallagher, 245–69. Kent, Ohio: Kent State University Press, 1999.

———. *Pickett's Charge in History and Memory*. Chapel Hill: University of North Carolina Press, 1997.

———. "Pickett's Charge: The Convergence of History and Myth in the Southern Past." In *The Third Day at Gettysburg and Beyond*, edited by Gary W. Gallagher, 56–92. Chapel Hill: University of North Carolina Press, 1994.

Reid, W. D. Letter. *Confederate Veteran* 6 (1898): 570.

———. "Peril by Rock Fence at Gettysburg." *Confederate Veteran* 19 (1911): 66.

Report of Joint Committee to Mark the Positions Occupied by the 1st and 2d Delaware Regiments at the Battle of Gettysburg, July 2d and 3d, 1863. Dover: Delawarean Office, 1887.

Rhodes, John H. *The Gettysburg Gun*. Providence: Soldiers and Sailors Society of Rhode Island, 1892.

———. *The History of Battery B, First Regiment Rhode Island Light Artillery in the War to Preserve the Union, 1861–1865*. Providence: Snow and Farnham, 1894.

Rhodes, Robert Hunt, ed. *All for the Union: The Civil War Diary and Letters of Elisha Hunt Rhodes*. New York: Orion, 1985.

Richter, Edward G. J. "The Removal of the Confederate Dead from Gettysburg." *Gettysburg Magazine*, no. 2 (1990): 113–22.

Riggs, David F. *7th Virginia Infantry*. Lynchburg: H. E. Howard, 1982.

Robertson, James I. *Eighteenth Virginia Infantry*. Lynchburg: H. E. Howard, 1984.

———. *General A. P. Hill: The Story of a Confederate Warrior*. New York: Random House, 1987.

Robinson, John H. "Fifty-Second Regiment." In *Histories of the Several Regiments and Battalions from North Carolina in the Great War, 1861–'65*, edited by Walter Clark, 3:223–53. Goldsboro, N.C.: Nash Brothers, 1901.

Rogers, J. Rowan. "Additional Sketch: Forty-Seventh Regiment." In *Histories of the Several Regiments and Battalions from North Carolina in the Great War, 1861–'65*, edited by Walter Clark, 3:103–12. Goldsboro, N.C.: Nash Brothers, 1901.

Rollins, Richard. *"The Damned Red Flags of the Rebellion": The Confederate Battle Flag at Gettysburg*. Redondo Beach, Calif.: Rank and File, 1997.

———. " 'The Ruling Ideas' of the Pennsylvania Campaign: James Longstreet's 1873 Letter to Lafayette McLaws." *Gettysburg Magazine*, no. 17 (1997): 7–16.

———. "The Second Wave of Pickett's Charge." *Gettysburg Magazine*, no. 18 (1998): 96–113.

———, ed. *Pickett's Charge! Eyewitness Accounts*. Redondo Beach, Calif.: Rank and File, 1994.

Rothenburg, Gunther E. *The Art of Warfare in the Age of Napoleon*. Bloomington: Indiana University Press, 1978.

Sale, J. Irving. "Reminiscences." *Philadelphia Press*, July 4, 1887.

Sauers, Richard Allen. "John B. Bachelder: Government Historian of the Battle of Gettysburg." *Gettysburg Magazine*, no. 3 (1990): 115–27.

———. " 'Rarely Has More Skill, Vigor, or Wisdom Been Shown': George G. Meade on July 3 at Gettysburg." In *Three Days at Gettysburg: Essays on Confederate and Union Leadership*, edited by Gary W. Gallagher, 231–44. Kent, Ohio: Kent State University Press, 1999.

Sawyer, Franklin. *A Military History of the 8th Regiment Ohio Vol. Inf'y*. Cleveland: Fairbanks, 1881.

Scott, George H. "Vermont at Gettysburg." In *Gettysburg Sources*, compiled by James L. McLean Jr. and Judy W. McLean, 1:58–80. Baltimore: Butternut and Blue, 1986.

Scott, Robert Garth, ed. *Fallen Leaves: The Civil War Letters of Major Henry Livermore Abbott*. Kent, Ohio: Kent State University Press, 1991.

Scott, Winfield. "Pickett's Charge as Seen from the Front Line." In *The Gettysburg Papers*, compiled by Ken Bandy and Florence Freeland, 2:897–911. Dayton, Ohio: Morningside, 1978.

Sears, Stephen W., ed. *Mr. Dunn Browne's Experiences in the Army: The Civil War Letters of Samuel W. Fiske*. New York: Fordham University Press, 1998.

———. *To the Gates of Richmond: The Peninsula Campaign*. New York: Ticknor and Fields, 1992.

Seville, William P. *History of the First Regiment, Delaware Volunteers*. Gettysburg: Longstreet House, 1986.

Shotwell, Randolph Abbott. "Virginia and North Carolina in the Battle of Gettysburg." *Our Living and Our Dead* 4 (1876): 80–97.

Shultz, David. *"Double Canister at Ten Yards": The Federal Artillery and the Repulse of Pickett's Charge*. Redondo Beach, Calif.: Rank and File, 1995.

———. "Gulian V. Weir's 5th U.S. Artillery, Battery C." *Gettysburg Magazine*, no. 18 (1998): 77–95.

Shultz, David, and Richard Rollins. "Measuring Pickett's Charge." *Gettysburg Magazine*, no. 17 (1997): 108–17.

Simons, Ezra D. *A Regimental History: The One Hundred and Twenty-Fifth New York State Volunteers*. New York: Ezra D. Simons, 1888.

Small, Harold Adams, ed. *The Road to Richmond: The Civil War Memoirs of Major Abner R. Small of the Sixteenth Maine Volunteers*. Berkeley: University of California Press, 1939.

Smith, Christopher. Account. *Buffalo Evening News*, May 29, 1894.

Smith, John Day. *The History of the Nineteenth Regiment of Maine Volunteer Infantry, 1861–1865*. Minneapolis: Great Western, 1909.

Smith, N. S. "Additional Sketch: Thirteenth Regiment." In *Histories of the Several*

Regiments and Battalions from North Carolina in the Great War, 1861–'65, edited by
Walter Clark, 1:689–99. Goldsboro, N.C.: Nash Brothers, 1901.

Sorrel, G. Moxley. *Recollections of a Confederate Staff Officer.* Jackson, Tenn.:
McCowat-Mercer, 1958.

Speer, Allen Paul, ed. *Voices from Cemetery Hill: The Civil War Diary, Reports, and
Letters of Colonel William Henry Asbury Speer, 1861–1864.* Johnson City, Tenn.:
Overmountain Press, 1997.

Stevens, H. S. *Address Delivered at the Dedication, Monument of the 14th Conn. Vols.*
Middletown, Conn.: Pelton and King, 1884.

——. *Souvenir of Excursion to Battlefields by the Society of the Fourteenth Connecticut
Regiment.* Washington, D.C.: Gibson Brothers, 1893.

Stewart, George R. *Pickett's Charge: A Microhistory of the Final Attack at Gettysburg, July
3, 1863.* Boston: Houghton Mifflin, 1959.

Storch, Marc, and Beth Storch. " 'What a Deadly Trap We Were In': Archer's
Brigade on July 1, 1863." *Gettysburg Magazine*, no. 6 (1992): 13–27.

Sturtivant, Ralph Orson. *Pictorial History, Thirteenth Regiment Vermont Volunteers, War
of 1861–1865.* N.p., 1910.

Supplement to the Official Records of the Union and Confederate Armies. 100 vols.
Wilmington, N.C.: Broadfoot: 1993–2000.

Supreme Court of Pennsylvania, Middle District, May Term, 1891. N.p., n.d.

Swallow, W. H. "The Third Day at Gettysburg." *Southern Bivouac* 1 (1886): 562–
72.

Sword, Wiley. "Alexander Webb and His Colt Navy Revolver: In the 'Pinch of the
Fight' during 'Pickett's Charge' at Gettysburg." *Gettysburg Magazine*, no. 15
(1996): 91–100.

——. "Capt. George F. Tait and the 10th New York Zouaves Encounter 'Pickett's
Charge.' " *Gettysburg Magazine*, no. 16 (1997): 81–85.

——. "Facing the Gray Wave: Alexander Webb at Gettysburg." *Civil War Times
Illustrated* 19 (1981): 18–25.

Talbot, Edith Armstrong. *Samuel Chapman Armstrong: A Biographical Study.* New
York: Doubleday, Page, 1904.

Talcott, T. M. R. "The Third Day at Gettysburg." *Southern Historical Society Papers* 41
(1916): 37–48.

Taylor, Michael W. "Col. James Keith Marshall: One of Three Brigade
Commanders Killed in the Pickett-Pettigrew-Trimble Charge." *Gettysburg
Magazine*, no. 15 (1996): 78–90.

——. "North Carolina in the Pickett-Pettigrew-Trimble Charge at Gettysburg."
Gettysburg Magazine, no. 8 (1993): 67–93.

——. "The Unmerited Censure of Two Maryland Staff Officers, Maj. Osmun
Latrobe and First Lt. W. Stuart Symington." *Gettysburg Magazine*, no. 13 (1995):
75–88.

——, ed. *The Cry Is War, War, War: The Civil War Correspondence of Lts. Burwell
Thomas Cotton and George Job Huntley, 34th Regiment North Carolina Troops.*
Dayton, Ohio: Morningside, 1994.

———. *To Drive the Enemy from Southern Soil: The Letters of Col. Francis Marion Parker and the History of the 30th Regiment North Carolina Troops*. Dayton, Ohio: Morningside, 1998.

Taylor, Walter H. Letter. *Southern Historical Society Papers* 4 (1877): 124–39.

———. "Memorandum by Colonel Walter H. Taylor of General Lee's Staff." *Southern Historical Society Papers* 4 (1877): 84–85.

Taylor, William H. "Some Experiences of a Confederate Assistant Surgeon." *Transactions of the College of Physicians of Philadelphia* 28 (1906): 91–121.

Tennesseans in the Civil War. 2 pts. Nashville: Civil War Centennial Commission, 1964.

"Testimony about Battle of Gettysburg." *Confederate Veteran* 18 (1910): 524–25.

Thomas, Emory A. *Robert E. Lee*. New York: Norton, 1995.

Thomas, Herbert A., Jr. "The 19th Virginia Regiment, 1861–1865." *Magazine of Albemarle County History* 25 (1966–67): 5–35.

Thompson, Benjamin W. " 'This Hell of Destruction': The Benjamin W. Thompson Memoirs." *Civil War Times Illustrated* 12 (1973): 12–23.

Thompson, Richard S. "A Scrap of Gettysburg." In *Military Essays and Recollections: Papers Read before the Commandery of the State of Illinois, Military Order of the Loyal Legion of the United States*, 3:97–109. Chicago: Dial, 1899.

Thorp, John H. "Forty-Seventh Regiment." In *Histories of the Several Regiments and Battalions from North Carolina in the Great War, 1861–'65*, edited by Walter Clark, 3:83–101. Goldsboro, N.C.: Nash Brothers, 1901.

Tidball, J. C. "Artillery Service in the War of the Rebellion." *Journal of the Military Service Institution of the United States* 13 (1892): 677–704.

Todd, George T. "Gaines's Mill: Pickett and Hood." *Confederate Veteran* 6 (1898): 565–67.

Toombs, Samuel. *New Jersey Troops in the Gettysburg Campaign from June 5 to July 31, 1863*. Orange, N.J.: Evening Mail, 1888.

Trimble, Isaac. "The Civil War Diary of General Isaac Ridgeway Trimble." *Maryland Historical Magazine* 17 (1922): 1–20.

———. "North Carolinians at Gettysburg." *Southern Historical Monthly* 1 (1876): 56–63.

Trimble, Tony L. "Paper Collars: Stannard's Brigade at Gettysburg." *Gettysburg Magazine*, no. 2 (1990): 75–79.

Trinque, Bruce A. "Arnold's Battery and the 26th North Carolina." *Gettysburg Magazine*, no. 12 (1995): 61–67.

Trudeau, Noah Andre. *The Last Citadel: Petersburg, Virginia, June 1864–April 1865*. Baton Rouge: Louisiana State University Press, 1991.

Tucker, Glenn. "What Became of Pickett's Report on his Assault at Gettysburg?" *Civil War Times Illustrated* 6 (1967): 37–39.

Turney, J. B. "The First Tennessee at Gettysburg." *Confederate Veteran* 8 (1900): 535–37.

Tuttle, R. M. "Addenda: Unparalleled Loss." In *History of the Twenty-Sixth Regiment of the North Carolina Troops in the Great War, 1861–'65*, edited by George C. Underwood, 1–6. Goldsboro, N.C.: Nash Brothers, 1901.

Underwood, George C. "Twenty-Sixth Regiment." In *Histories of the Several Regiments and Battalions from North Carolina in the Great War, 1861–'65*, edited by Walter Clark, 2:303–423. Goldsboro, N.C.: Nash Brothers, 1901.

Waitt, Ernest Linden, comp. *History of the Nineteenth Regiment Massachusetts Volunteer Infantry, 1861–1865*. Salem, Mass.: Salem Press, 1906.

Walker, Francis A. *General Hancock*. New York: Appleton, 1894.

———. "General Hancock and the Artillery at Gettysburg." In *Battles and Leaders of the Civil War*, edited by Robert Underwood Johnson and Clarence Clough Buel, 3:385–86. New York: Yoseloff, 1956.

———. *History of the Second Army Corps in the Army of the Potomac*. New York: Charles Scribner's Sons, 1887.

Walker, James H. "The Charge of Pickett's Division." *Blue and Gray* 1 (1893): 221–23.

———. "A Survivor of Pickett's Division." *Blue and Gray* 2 (1893): 27.

Wallace, Lee A., Jr. *1st Virginia Infantry*. Lynchburg: H. E. Howard, 1991.

Ward, Joseph R. C. *History of the One Hundred and Sixth Regiment Pennsylvania Volunteers*. Philadelphia: Grant, Faires and Rodgers, 1883.

Warner, Ezra J. *Generals in Blue: Lives of the Union Commanders*. Baton Rouge: Louisiana State University Press, 1964.

———. *Generals in Gray: Lives of the Confederate Commanders*. Baton Rouge: Louisiana State University Press, 1959.

The War of the Rebellion: A Compilation of the Official Records of the Union and Confederate Armies. 70 vols. in 128. Washington, D.C.: U.S. Government Printing Office, 1880–1901.

War Recollections of the Confederate Veterans of Pittsylvania County, Virginia, 1861–1865. N.p., 1961.

Washburn, George H. *A Complete Military History and Record of the 108th Regiment N.Y. Vols. from 1862 to 1864*. Rochester, N.Y.: E. R. Andrews, 1894.

Watts, A. T. "Something More about Gettysburg." *Confederate Veteran* 6 (1898): 67.

Welsh, Jack D. *Medical Histories of Confederate Generals*. Kent, Ohio: Kent State University Press, 1995.

———. *Medical Histories of Union Generals*. Kent, Ohio: Kent State University Press, 1996.

Wert, Jeffry D. *General James Longstreet, the Confederacy's Most Controversial Soldier: A Biography*. New York: Simon and Schuster, 1993.

Wheeler, William. *Letters of William Wheeler of the Class of 1855, Y.C.* N.p., 1875.

White, William S. *Contributions to a History of the Richmond Howitzer Battalion*. Richmond: Carlton McCarthy, 1883.

Wilcox, C. M. "General C. M. Wilcox on the Battle of Gettysburg." *Southern Historical Society Papers* 6 (1878): 117–21.

———. Letter. *Southern Historical Society Papers* 4 (1877): 111–17.

Wiley, Bell Irvin, ed. *Reminiscences of Big I*. Jackson, Tenn.: McCowat-Mercer, 1956.

Williams, Max R., ed. "An Awful Affair." *Civil War Times Illustrated* 23 (1984): 46–49.

Williams, Max R., and J. G. deRoulhac Hamilton, eds. *The Papers of William*

Alexander Graham. Vol. 5. Raleigh: North Carolina Office of Archives and History, 1973.

Williams, R. S. "Thirteenth Regiment." In *Histories of the Several Regiments and Battalions from North Carolina in the Great War, 1861–'65,* edited by Walter Clark, 1:653–87. Goldsboro, N.C.: Nash Brothers, 1901.

Williamson, Edward C., ed. "Francis P. Fleming in the War for Southern Independence." Pt. 3. *Florida Historical Quarterly* 28 (1949–50): 143–55.

Wilson, Clyde N. *Carolina Cavalier: The Life and Mind of James Johnston Pettigrew.* Athens: University of Georgia Press, 1990.

Winschel, Terrence J. "The Gettysburg Diary of Lieutenant William Peel." *Gettysburg Magazine,* no. 9 (1993): 98–107.

———. "The Gettysburg Experience of James J. Kirkpatrick." *Gettysburg Magazine,* no. 8 (1993): 111–19.

———. "Heavy Was Their Loss: Joe Davis's Brigade at Gettysburg." Pt. 1. *Gettysburg Magazine,* no. 2 (1990): 5–14.

———. "Heavy Was Their Loss: Joe Davis's Brigade at Gettysburg." Pt. 2. *Gettysburg Magazine,* no. 3 (1990): 77–85.

Winters, Harold A. *Battling the Elements: Weather and Terrain in the Conduct of War.* Baltimore: Johns Hopkins University Press, 1998.

Wise, George. Letter. *Confederate Veteran* 6 (1898): 568–69.

Wise, Jennings Cropper. *The Long Arm of Lee.* 2 vols. Lynchburg: J. P. Bell, 1915.

Woodward, Harold R., Jr. *Major General James Lawson Kemper, C.S.A.: The Confederacy's Forgotten Son.* Natural Bridge Station, Va.: Rockbridge, 1993.

Woodworth, Steven E. *Davis and Lee at War.* Lawrence: University Press of Kansas, 1995.

Wright, Steven J. " 'Don't Let Me Bleed to Death': The Wounding of Maj. Gen. Winfield Scott Hancock." *Gettysburg Magazine,* no. 6 (1992): 87–92.

Wright, Steven J., and Blake A. Magner. "John Gibbon: The Man and the Monument." *Gettysburg Magazine,* no. 13 (1995): 119–27.

Young, Louis G. *The Battle of Gettysburg.* Savannah: n.p., 1900.

———. "Pettigrew's Brigade at Gettysburg." *Our Living and Our Dead* 1 (1875): 552–58.

———. "Pettigrew's Brigade at Gettysburg, 1–3 July, 1863." In *Histories of the Several Regiments and Battalions from North Carolina in the Great War, 1861–'65,* edited by Walter Clark, 5:113–32. Goldsboro, N.C.: Nash Brothers, 1901.

Young, William A., Jr., and Patricia C. Young. *56th Virginia Infantry.* Lynchburg: H. E. Howard, 1990.

INDEX

· · · · · · · · · · ·

219–21, 266–67, 425 (n. 25), 439 (n. 44)

Cogbill, Pvt. Marcus A., 438 (n. 33)

Coleman, Ben W., 60

Coleman, Clayton G., 157

Coleman, Pvt. James C., 438 (n. 33)

Collier, Manes Marshall, 360

Colston, Lt. Frederick M., 328

Colvill, Col. William, Jr., 95

Congressional Medal of Honor, 381

Connecticut units
—artillery
  1st Battery, 114
—infantry
  14th, 104–5, 118, 123, 128–29, 133, 145, 152, 195, 198–99, 201–2, 205, 210, 259, 312, 316–18, 338, 344, 346, 383, 406

Conner, Col. James, 408

Cook, Capt. John D. S., 98, 289, 314, 320, 324, 382

Cook, Cpl. Nathan, 289

Cooke, Brig. Gen. John R., 362, 369

Cooper, Adj. Gen. Samuel, 42, 362

Copse, 90, 173–74, 388, 396

Corbell, LaSalle, 37–38, 51, 354, 382

Corse, Brig. Gen. Montgomery D., 38, 44–45, 354, 358

Cort, Capt. George P., 319

Cotton, Lt. Burwell Thomas, 361

Couch, Maj. Gen. Darius N., 34, 83

Cowan, Andrew, 144, 241–43, 307, 321, 383, 393

Crandell, Lt. Col. Levi, 140, 406

Crocker, Lt. James F., 53, 178, 382

Cross, Andrew, 414 (n. 34)

Culp's Hill, 7, 35

Cummings, Lt. Col. Charles, 303

Cunningham, Pvt. George H., 293

Cureton, Capt. Thomas J., 183, 205, 256, 311

Currens, John, 50

Curry, Lt. Col. William L., 405

Curtis, Maj. Sylvanus W., 336

Cushing, Lt. Alonzo, 89, 116, 121,

196, 228, 243–45, 336; during bombardment, 138, 141–44, 150, 406

Dalton, Sgt. Francis W., 224

Damron, Pvt. Robert B., 438 (n. 33)

Daniel, Sen. John W, 382

Darrow, Capt. John, 405

Davis, George B., 402

Davis, Jefferson, 45, 62

Davis, Capt. Joseph J., 252

Davis, Brig. Gen. Joseph R., 15, 57, 62–63, 69, 156, 164, 334, 355, 357, 362, 377, 386, 407; during advance, 178, 182–83, 186–90, 205, 208–9, 216–17, 248, 252

Davis, Capt. William, 246, 284–85

Dawson, Lt. Charles G., 155

DeCastro, Cpl. Joseph H., 286

Dearing, Maj. James, 30–31, 37, 48–49, 52, 75, 154, 180, 226, 356, 377, 407

Dehn, Cpl. John, 288

Delaware units
—infantry
  1st, 102, 104, 107, 109, 119, 121, 122, 128, 133, 199, 205, 210–12, 216, 251, 257, 259, 318, 337, 392, 406

Deleven, John, 142

Deming, Pvt. William, 319

Dent, Lt. John T., 259

Devereux, Col. Arthur F., 91, 93, 141, 275–76, 279, 283, 286, 292, 315, 321–22, 405

Dewey, Capt. George A., 258

Donnelly, Pvt. Thomas, 285

Dooley, Lt. John E., 167, 173, 176, 332, 349

Doubleday, Brig. Gen. Abner, 97, 99, 239, 332, 405

Dougherty, Dr. Alexander, 282, 322

Douglas, Henry Kyd, 42

Douthat, Capt. Robert W., 232, 308

Dow, Capt. Edwin B., 114, 196

McFadden, Capt. William, 406

McFarland, Lt. Col. George M., 97

McGilvery, Maj. Freeman, 114, 119, 141, 145–47, 163, 171, 185, 196, 299–300, 320

McGuire, Dr. Hunter, 343

McLaws, Maj. Gen. Lafayette, 5–6, 7–8, 16–18, 179

Macon, Capt. Miles C., 407

McQueen, Lt. William Alexander, 181, 382, 426 (n. 44)

MacRae, Brig. Gen. William, 366

Macy, Lt. Col. George N., 278

Magruder, Col. John Bowie, 45, 407

Mahone, Brig. Gen. William, 19, 74

Maine units
—artillery
  6th Battery, 114
—infantry
  16th, 341
  19th, 94–96, 100, 145, 152, 173, 196, 233–34, 236, 243, 276–77, 279, 288, 329, 344, 369, 405

Mallon, Col. James E., 93, 275–76, 322, 369, 406

Malvern Hill, battle of, 11, 31, 40, 53, 61, 113, 196

Manassas, battle of Second, 11

Marshall, Maj. Charles, 309, 328

Marshall, Col. James K., 61, 178, 182, 84, 186, 190, 201–3, 209, 245, 250, 334–35, 407, 426 (n. 37), 428 (n. 66), 430 (n. 4), 436 (n. 11)

Marshall, Lt. William C., 227

Martin, Lt. Col. Rawley W., 156, 224, 261, 264, 372, 438 (n. 33)

Massachusetts units
—artillery
  5th Battery, 114
  9th Battery, 115
—infantry
  1st Company Sharpshooters, 110, 215, 406
  15th, 74, 93–93, 96, 145, 194, 243, 280, 288, 293–94, 336, 405

19th, 91–93, 126–27, 133, 141, 275–80, 286, 292, 318, 321, 338–39, 395, 405

20th, 93, 140, 164, 196, 236, 244, 278–79, 292, 322, 348, 369, 405, 416 (n. 13)

Maurin, Capt. Victor, 408

Mayo, Col. Joseph, Jr., 52, 153–54, 176, 269, 406

Mayo, Col. Robert M., 64, 187–88, 191, 408

Meade, George, 323

Meade, Maj. Gen. George G., 6, 33–34, 85, 108, 195, 323–24, 364, 370–71, 389, 405; during bombardment, 133–36, 147

Merrick, Charles H., 348

Messick, Capt. Nathan S., 288, 405

Michie, Lt. Henry Clay, 261

Michigan units
—infantry
  7th, 91, 93, 127, 130, 143, 164, 236, 242, 244, 279, 320, 336–37, 348, 406
  24th, 58,

Miles, Col. Dixon S., 105

Miller, Col. Hugh R., 408

Miller, Capt. Merrit B., 125

Miller, Lt. William A., 46

Milton, Gov. John, 303

Milton, Lt. Richard, 115

Minnesota units
—infantry
  1st, 71–72, 95–96, 100, 108, 126, 130, 133, 193–94, 226, 235, 243, 279, 288–89, 293, 321, 394, 405

Mississippi units
—artillery
  Madison Light Battery, 408
—infantry
  2nd, 62–63, 343, 407
  11th, 62–63, 156, 185, 205–6, 208, 211–12, 252, 314, 344, 407
  16th, 75, 122, 306, 334
  18th, 22

INDEX

174, 181, 219, 224–26, 229, 234,
236, 266, 281, 319, 370, 388, 395,
440 (n. 66); and flanking move-
ment, 237–40; and repulse of
Wilcox-Lang attack, 298, 300, 302–
3, 305
Steele, Lt. Col. Amos E., Jr., 279, 406
Steuart, Brig. Gen. George H., 89, 383
Stevens, Chap. Henry S., 104, 118
Stewart, George, 336
Stockton, Sgt. Maj. William S., 245,
273, 291
Stone, Brig. Gen. Charles P., 86
Stone, Col. John M., 407
Stone Fence, 118, 247
Stoughton, Brig. Gen. Edwin, 99
Stowe, Capt. L. W., 408
Straight, Sgt. Albert, 142
Stewart, Lt. James, 198
Stribling, Capt. Robert M., 30, 407
Stuart, John T., 37
Stuart, Col. William D., 407
Sturtivant, Ralph Orison, 130
Suffolk, siege of, 12
Symington, Stuart, 178–79, 297, 426
(n. 37)

Talley, Henry M., 46, 413 (n. 12)
Tapscott, Vincent A., 393
Tayloe, Lt. Col. George E., 407
Taylor, Capt. Junius, 304
Taylor, Col. Walter H., 16, 184, 392
Taylor, Lt. William B., 61, 399
Taylor, Asst. Surg. William H., 50
Tennessee units
—infantry
   1st, 60, 185, 192–93, 204–5, 250,
      253–54, 312, 318, 334, 407
   7th, 21, 59–60, 201, 203–4, 310,
      311–12, 314, 334, 383, 407
   14th, 60, 64, 204–5, 310, 318, 334,
      379, 407
Terry, Col. William R., 225, 358–59,
   406
Thomas, Pvt. Daniel, 256

Thomas, Brig. Gen. Edward L., 19, 74,
   186
Thomas, William Patterson Carey, 351
Thompson, Capt. Benjamin W., 108,
   131–33, 338
Thompson, Capt. George, 262
Thompson, Capt. James, 114
Thompson, Lt. Joseph L., 30, 158
Thompson, Capt. Richard S., 198,
   251
Thorp, Capt. John H., 254
Tidball, John C., 392
Timberlake, Maj. John C., 223, 231,
   261, 264, 269, 312, 330, 438
   (n. 33)
Tredway, Sgt. Thomas B., 438 (n. 33)
Trimble, Maj. Gen. Isaac R., 18, 26,
   32, 69, 153, 164, 182, 184–86,
   190–91, 202, 209, 248, 253–54,
   271, 335, 362–63, 377, 386, 408,
   414 (n. 34), 428 (n. 66); back-
   ground of, 64–67; wounding of,
   256–57, 343
Troutman, Lt. Charles E., 215
Tschudy, Lt. Col. Martin, 285
Turnbull, Lt. John G., 115
Turner, Capt. J. McLeod, 190, 249,
   253, 313, 408, 428 (n. 66)
Turney, Capt. Jacob B., 193, 250
Tuttle, Lt. William A., 333
Tyler, Cyril H., 130, 244, 348
Tyler, Pres. John, 157
Tyson, John, 339

United States units
—artillery
   Battery I, 1st Artillery, 105, 115
   Battery F, 3rd Artillery, 115
   Battery K, 3rd Artillery, 115
   Battery A, 4th Artillery, 89, 114,
      116, 406
   Battery B, 4th Artillery, 198
   Battery C, 5th Artillery, 94, 259
   Battery D, 5th Artillery, 113
Utterback, Capt. Addison W., 408